Brian Gayle

http://support.sas.com/ CRSOLATA /279

SAS® Programming 3: Advanced Techniques and Efficiencies

var1 = put(Q3, FMT)

Q3='Oct, Nov, Dec'

MNTH = SCAN(VAR1, 1, ',') ;

OUTPUT

MNTH = SCAN(VAR1, 2, ',') ;

OUTPUT.

Course Notes

SAS® Programming 3: Advanced Techniques and Efficiencies Course Notes was developed by Linda Jolley and Jane Stroupe. Additional contributions were made by Kay Alden, Alistair Horn, Marjorie Lampton, Robert Ligtenberg, Linda Mitterling, Georg Morsing, Kent Reeve, and Jane Whitten. Editing and production support was provided by the Curriculum Development and Support Department.

SAS® Programming 3: Advanced Techniques and Efficiencies Course Notes

---

Book code E1517, course code LWPRG3, prepared date 29Jun2009. LWPRG3_002

ISBN 978-1-60764-240-4

Table of Contents

Course Description

- This course is for SAS programmers who prepare data for analysis. The comparisons of manipulation techniques and resource cost benefits are designed to help programmers choose the most appropriate technique for their data situation.You will learn how to compare various SAS programming techniques that enable you to
- control memory, I/O, and CPU resources
- create and use indexes
- combine data horizontally and vertically
- use hash and hiter DATA step component objects, arrays, and formats as lookup tables
- compress SAS data sets
- sample your SAS data sets.

To learn more…

For information on other courses in the curriculum, contact the SAS Education Division at 1-800-333-7660, or send e-mail to training@sas.com. You can also find this information on the Web at support.sas.com/training/ as well as in the Training Course Catalog.

For a list of other SAS books that relate to the topics covered in this Course Notes, USA customers can contact our SAS Publishing Department at 1-800-727-3228 or send e-mail to sasbook@sas.com. Customers outside the USA, please contact your local SAS office.

Also, see the Publications Catalog on the Web at support.sas.com/pubs for a complete list of books and a convenient order form.

Prerequisites

This course is **not** appropriate for beginning SAS software users. Before attending this course, you should have at least nine months of SAS programming experience and should have completed the SAS® Programming 2: Data Manipulation Techniques course. Specifically, you should be able to do the following:

- understand your operating system file structures and perform basic operating system tasks
- understand programming logic concepts
- understand the compilation and execution process of the DATA step
- use different varieties of input to create SAS data sets from external files
- use SAS software to access SAS libraries
- create and use SAS date values
- read, concatenate, merge, match-merge, and interleave SAS data sets
- use the DROP=, KEEP=, and RENAME= data set options
- create multiple output data sets
- use array processing and DO loops to process data iteratively
- use SAS functions to perform data manipulation and transformations

Chapter 1 Introduction

1.1 Course Logistics

Objectives

- List the tasks in the SAS Programming 3 course.
- Explain the naming convention that is used for the course files.
- Compare the three levels of exercises that are used in the course.
- Describe, at a high level, how data is used and stored at Orion Star Sports & Outdoors.
- Navigate to the Help facility.

3

Tasks in the SAS Programming 3 Course

The course topics include techniques for the following data management tasks:

- compressing SAS data sets
- creating indexes for a quick retrieval of subsets
- performing table lookups using arrays, hash objects, or formats
- combining data by merging, using the SQL procedure, or using multiple SET statements
- combining summary and detail data
- sorting and grouping data
- developing a program quickly

4

Resource Utilization

As programmers, you want to perform these tasks as efficiently as possible and optimize the use of the following resources:

- programmer time
- I/O
- CPU
- memory
- data storage space
- network bandwidth

5

Business Scenarios

The business scenarios are opportunities to compare multiple techniques for performing the tasks.

For example:

Task: Table Lookups

Possible Techniques:

- DATA step MERGE statement
- PROC SQL joins
- Formats in PUT functions or in FORMAT statements
- DATA step arrays
- DATA step hash objects

6

1.01 Multiple Answer Poll

What type(s) of SAS programs do you write?

a. Data manipulation with the DATA step
b. Data analysis with procedures
c. Report writing
d. A combination of the above
e. SAS training only; no programs written
f. Other

8

Filename Conventions

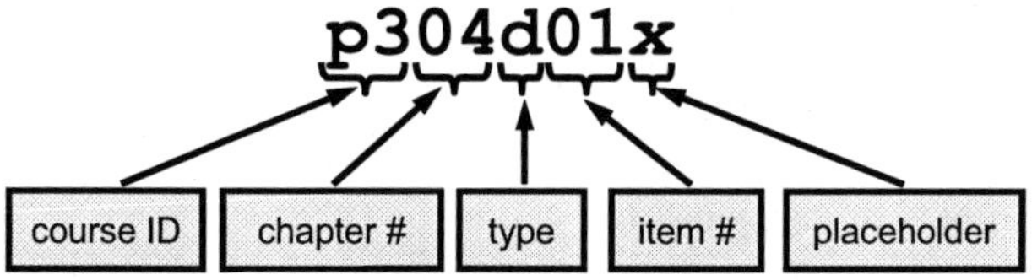

Code	Type
a	Activity
d	Demo
e	Exercise
s	Solution

- p304a01
- p304a02
- p304a02s
- p304d01
- p304d02
- p304e01
- p304e02
- p304s01
- p304s02

Example:
The SAS Programming 3 course ID is p3, so p304d01 = SAS Programming 3, Chapter 4, Demo 1.

9

Three Levels of Exercises

Level 1	The exercise mimics an example presented in the section.
Level 2	Less information and guidance are provided in the exercise instructions.
Level 3	Only the task you are to perform or the results to be obtained are provided. Typically, you will need to use the Help facility.

✎ You are not expected to complete all of the exercises in the time allotted. Choose the exercise or exercises that are at the level with which you are most comfortable.

10

Orion Star Sports & Outdoors

Orion Star Sports & Outdoors is a fictitious global sports and outdoors retailer with traditional stores, an online store, and a large catalog business.

The corporate headquarters is located in the United States with offices and stores in many countries throughout the world.

Orion Star has about 1,000 employees and 90,000 customers, processes approximately 150,000 orders annually, and purchases products from 64 suppliers.

11

Orion Star Data

As is the case with most organizations, Orion Star has a large amount of data about its customers, suppliers, products, and employees. Much of this information is stored in transactional systems in various formats.

Using applications and processes such as SAS Data Integration Studio, this transactional information was extracted, transformed, and loaded into a data warehouse.

Data marts were created to meet the needs of specific departments such as Marketing.

12

The SAS Help Facility

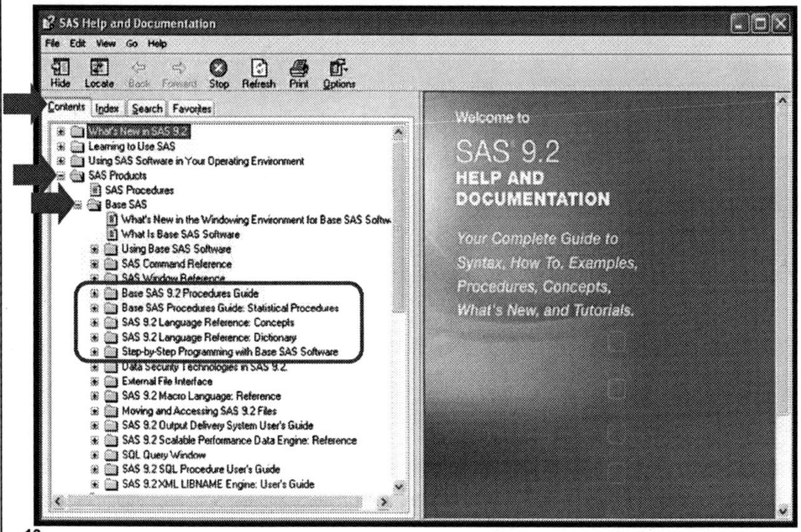

13

1.02 Quiz

- Start your SAS session.
- Open the Help facility.
- Determine the path to use to obtain information about the SAS component objects.

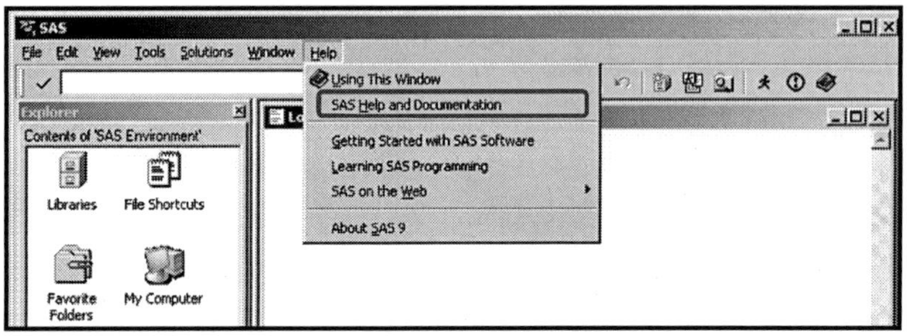

15

SAS OnlineDoc

You can also obtain information from SAS OnlineDoc.

Information relevant to this course can be found by following these paths in SAS OnlineDoc:

Contents tab

→ Products Documentation A-Z
→ Base SAS
→ SAS 9.2 Language Reference Dictionary
→ Dictionary of Component Object Language Elements

17

1.2 Measuring Efficiencies

Objectives

- Identify the resources used by a SAS program.
- Report computer resource usage using SAS system options.
- Interpret resource usage statistics in your operating environment.
- Benchmark resource usage.

20

Running a SAS Program

What resources are required to run a SAS program?

The **programmer** must perform the following tasks:

- determine program specifications
- write the program
- test the program
- execute the program
- maintain the program

21

Running a SAS Program

The **computer** must perform the following actions:

- load the required SAS software into memory
- compile the program
- read the data
- execute the compiled program
- store output data files
- store output reports

22

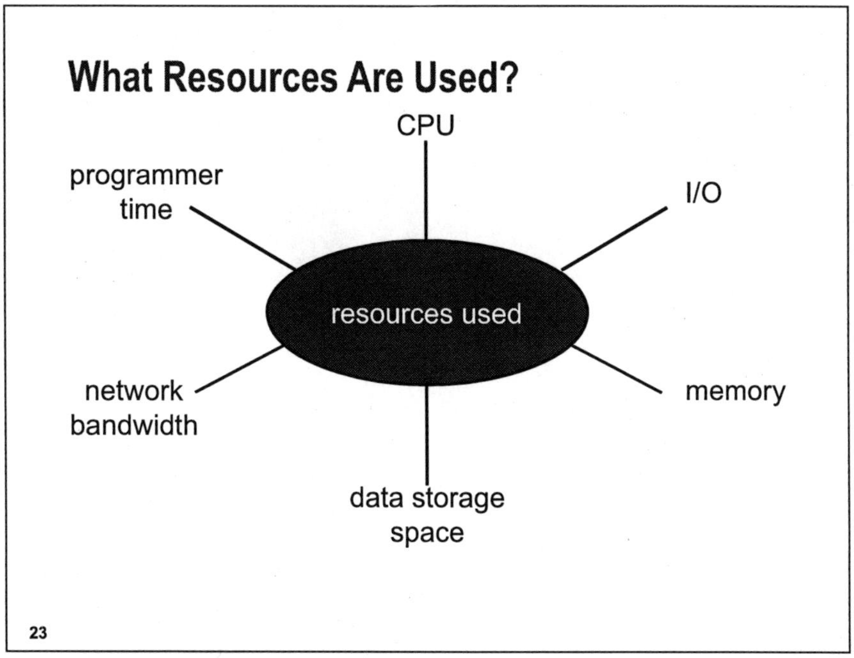

CPU	is a measurement of the amount of time that the central processing unit uses to perform requested tasks such as calculations, reading and writing data, conditional and iterative logic, and so on.
I/O	is a measurement of the read-and-write operations performed when data and programs are moved from a storage device to memory (input) or from memory to a storage or display device (output).
Memory	is the size of the work area required to hold executable program modules, data, and buffers.
Data storage space	is the amount of space on a disk or tape required to store data.
Programmer time	is the amount of time required for the programmer to write and maintain the program. This can be decreased through well-documented, best programming practices.
Network bandwidth	is the amount of data that can pass through a network interface over time. This time can be minimized by performing as much of the subsetting and summarizing as possible on the data host before transferring the results to the local computer. The network bandwidth is heavily dependent on network loads.

1.03 Multiple Answer Poll

Which of the following resources do you need to conserve?

a. CPU
b. I/O
c. Memory
d. Data storage space
e. Network bandwidth
f. Your time

25

Understanding Efficiency Trade-offs

When you decrease the use of one resource, the use of other resources might increase.

Resource usage is dependent on your data. A specific technique might be more efficient with one data set and less efficient with another.

26

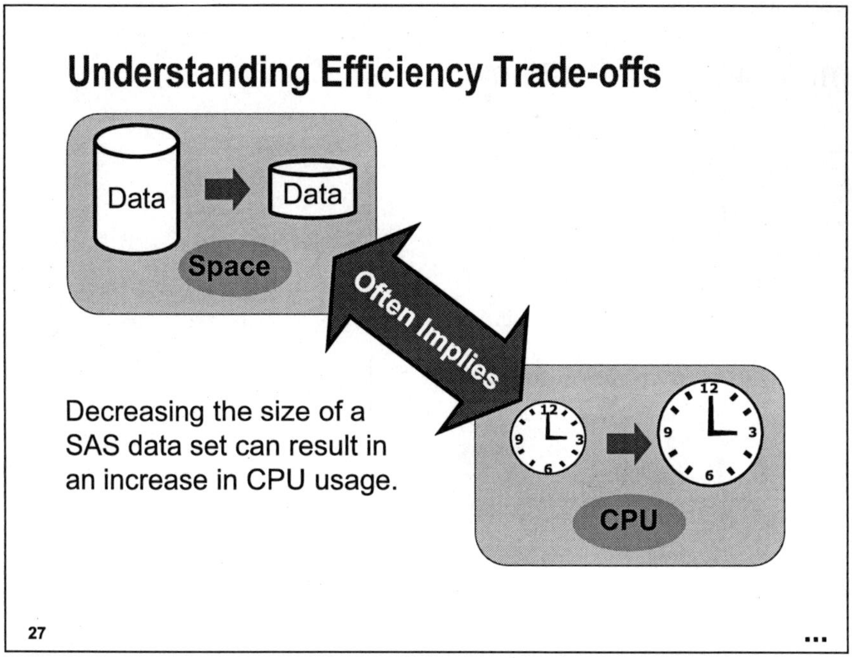

For example, data file compression might decrease storage use but increase processing time when SAS is reading the compressed data.

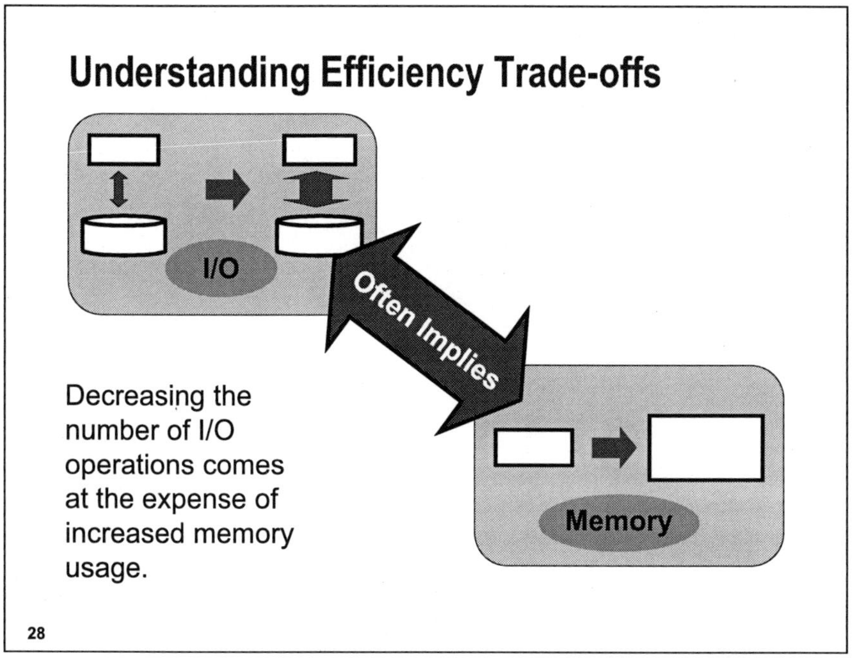

I/O can be decreased by increasing buffering space and memory usage.

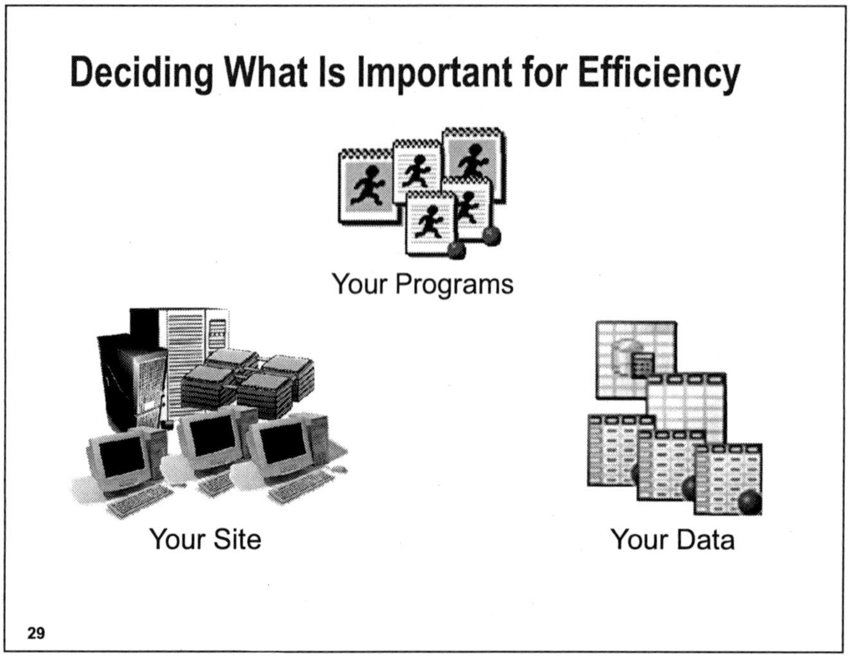

You must decide which factors are the most important for improving resource usage at your site. To make this decision, you must know the following:

- which resources are scarce or costly at your site
- how and when your programs will be used
- the type and volume of data that your programs will process

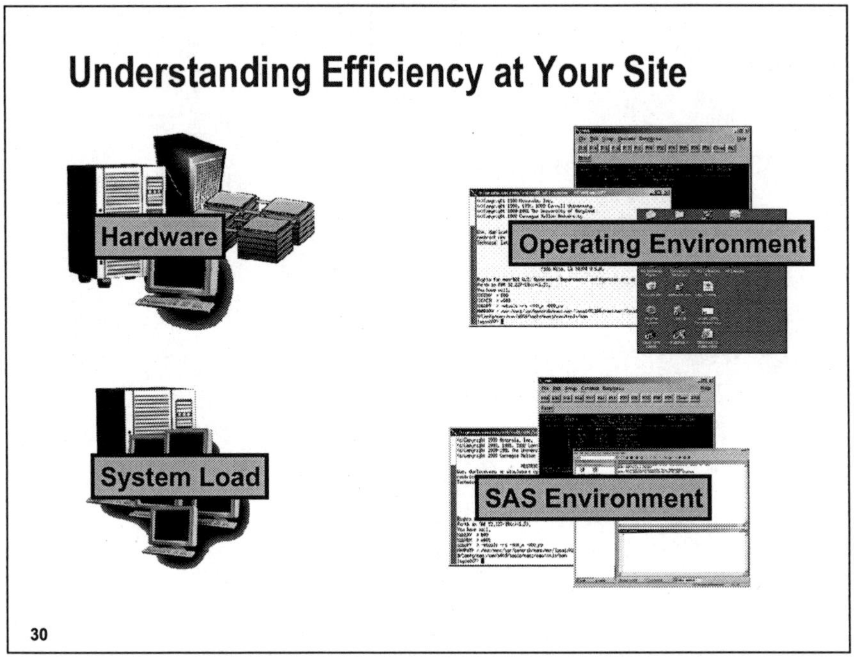

Environmental factors that affect the efficiency of SAS programs include the following:

Hardware	number of CPUs, amount of available memory, number of I/O controllers for data access, network infrastructure
Operating environment	resource allocation, scheduling algorithms, and I/O methods
System load	the number of users or jobs sharing system resources, including network bandwidth and network traffic
SAS environment	which SAS software products are installed, how they were installed, and which methods are available to run SAS programs at your site

Often, one or two resources constitute the limiting factor or bottleneck within an organizational computing environment. Tuning can be used to shift dependence away from a constrained resource. By tuning your SAS programs to use the more available resources, you might improve the performance.

1.04 Multiple Choice Poll

This class uses SAS 9.2.

What is the latest version of SAS that are you running?

a. SAS 8.2
b. SAS 9.1
c. SAS 9.2
d. Other

32

Knowing How Your Program Will Be Used

The importance of efficiency increases with the following:

- the complexity of the program and/or the size of the files being processed
- the number of times that the program will be executed

33

Knowing Your Data

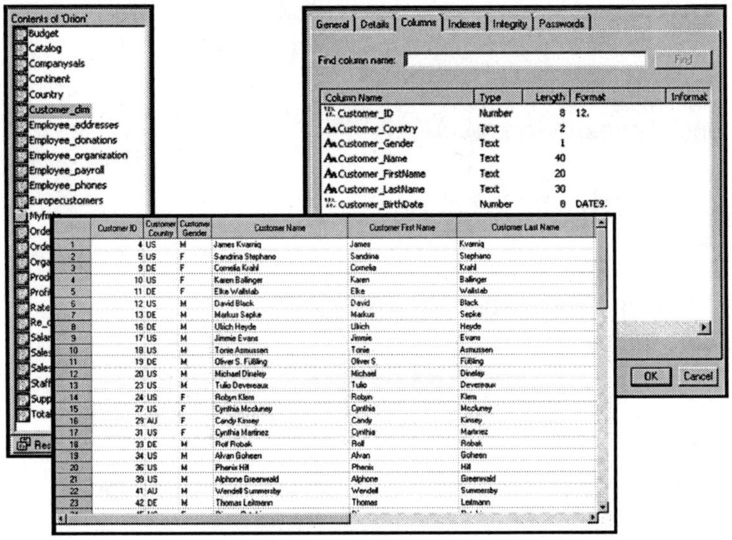

34

When you know the characteristics of your data, you can select the techniques that best suit those characteristics.

1.05 Multiple Answer Poll

What type(s) of data do you use?

a. SAS data sets
b. External files
c. Data from a relational database – for example, Oracle, Teradata, or SQL Server
d. Excel spreadsheets
e. OLAP cubes
f. Information maps
g. Other

36

Considering Trade-Offs

In this class, many tasks are performed using one or more techniques.

To decide which technique is most efficient for a given task, *benchmark*, or measure and compare, the resource usage of each technique.

You should benchmark with the actual data to determine which technique is the most efficient.

⚠ The effectiveness of any efficiency technique depends greatly on the data with which you use the technique.

37

Running Benchmarks: Guidelines

To benchmark your programming techniques, do the following:

- Turn on the appropriate options to report resource usage.
- Test each technique in a separate SAS session.
- Test only one technique or change at a time, with as little additional code as possible.
- Run your tests under the conditions that your final program will use (for example, batch execution, large data sets, and so on).

38

continued...

Running Benchmarks: Guidelines

- Run each program several times and base your conclusions on averages, not on a single execution. (This is more critical when you benchmark elapsed time.)
- Exclude outliers from the analysis because that data might lead you to tune your program to run less efficiently than it should.
- Turn off the options that report resource usage after testing is finished, because they consume resources.

⚠ In a multi-user environment, other computer activities might affect the running of your program.

39

1.06 Multiple Choice Poll

Which of the following SAS programs should be benchmarked?

a. A report that shows all the customers in the United Kingdom in March 2006
b. A report that calculates trends in sales at the end of every day for every department
c. A report showing the projected total cost of a 5% cost-of-living increase in employee salaries for a Human Resources project conducted on January 1, 2007
d. A yearly report that calculates the average sales of a line of apparel for the clothing manager

41

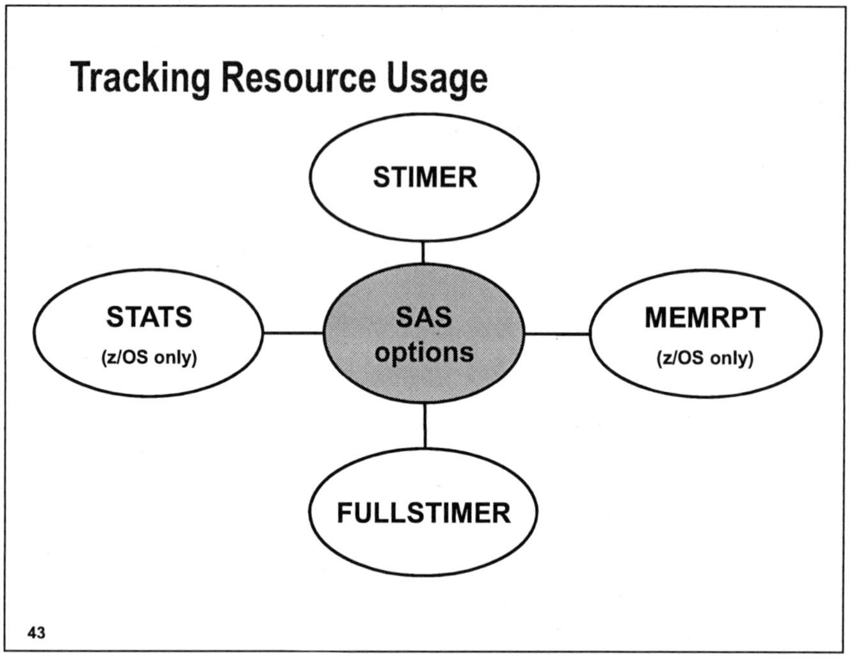

There are four SAS system options that you can use to track and report on resource utilization:

STIMER	tracks the CPU time used to perform a task (DATA or PROC step).	
MEMRPT	tracks memory used to perform a task.	z/OS only
FULLSTIMER	tracks usage of additional resources and divides CPU into system CPU time and user CPU time. This option is ignored unless STIMER or MEMRPT is in effect.	
STATS	writes information tracked by the above options to the SAS log.	z/OS only

The availability, usage, and aliases of these options are specific to the operating environment.

Tracking Resources with SAS Options

Windows, UNIX

```
OPTIONS STIMER | NOSTIMER;
```

```
OPTIONS NOFULLSTIMER | FULLSTIMER;
```

z/OS

```
STIMER | NOSTIMER
```

Invocation option only

```
OPTIONS STATS | NOSTATS;
```

```
OPTIONS MEMRPT | NOMEMRPT;
```

```
OPTIONS NOFULLSTIMER | FULLSTIMER;
```

44

	z/OS	Windows	UNIX
FULLSTIMER	B	B	B
STIMER	I D	B D	B D
STATS	B D	N/A	N/A
MEMRPT	B D	N/A	N/A

I Invocation option only

B Can be set at invocation or by using an OPTIONS statement

N/A Not available (The functionality is part of the STIMER option under UNIX and Windows.)

D Default

You can find more information about operating environment dependencies in the SAS documentation for your operating environment.

Use the OPTIONS procedure with the HOST option to determine the default settings of these options at your site.

```
proc options host;
run;
```

Business Scenario

You should benchmark to determine the most efficient technique for creating a new variable based on a condition.

The following methods can be used:

- IF-THEN with an assignment statement
- IF-THEN/ELSE with an assignment statement
- SELECT/WHEN with an assignment statement

45

1.07 Quiz

1. Open and submit **p301a01a**.
   Record the User CPU ____________
   Exit the SAS System.
2. Start SAS.
   Open and submit **p301a01b**.
   Record the User CPU ____________
   Exit the SAS System.
3. Start SAS.
   Open and submit **p301a01c.**
   Record the User CPU ____________
4. Which technique is most efficient?

In z/OS, record the CPU.

47

p301a01a

```
options fullstimer;
data test1;
   length var $ 30;
   retain var2-var50 0 var51-var100 'ABC';
   do var1=1 to 1000000;
      if var1<1000 then var='Less than 1,000';
      if 1000<=var1<10000 then var='Between 1,000 and 10,000';
      if 10000<=var1<100000 then var='Between 10,000 and 100,000';
      if 100000<=var1<500000 then var='Between 100,000 and 500,000';
      if 500000<=var1<1000000 then var=
                         'Between 500,000 and 1,000,000';
      output;
   end;
run;
```

(Continued on the next page.)

p301a01b

```
options fullstimer;
data test1;
   length var $ 30;
   retain var2-var50 0 var51-var100 'ABC';
   do var1=1 to 1000000;
      if var1<1000 then var='Less than 1,000';
      else if 1000<=var1<10000 then var='Between 1,000 and 10,000';
      else if 10000<=var1<100000 then var=
                   var='Between 10,000 and 100,000';
      else if 100000<=var1<500000 then
                   var='Between 100,000 and 500,000';
      else if 500000<=var1<1000000 then
                    var='Between 500,000 and 1,000,000';
      else var='Over 1,000,000';
      output;
   end;
run;
```

p301a01c

```
options fullstimer;
data test1;
   length var $ 30;
   retain var2-var50 0 var51-var100 'ABC';
   do var1=1 to 1000000;
      select;
         when (var1<1000) var='Less than 1,000';
         when (1000<=var1<10000) var='Between 1,000 and 10,000';
         when (10000<=var1<100000) var='Between 10,000 and 100,000';
         when (100000<=var1<500000) var='Between 100,000 and 500,000';
         when (500000<=var1<1000000)
                                 var='Between 500,000 and 1,000,000';
         otherwise var='Over 1,000,000';
      end;
      output;
   end;
run;
```

Windows Log

Partial SAS Log

```
options fullstimer;

data test1;
   length var $ 30;
   retain var2-var50 0 var51-var100 'ABC';
   do var1=1 to 1000000;
      if var1<1000 then var='Less than 1,000';
      if 1000<=var1<10000 then var='Between 1,000 and 10,000';
      if 10000<=var1<100000 then var='Between 10,000 and 100,000';
      if 100000<=var1<500000 then var='Between 100,000 and 500,000';
      if 500000<=var1<1000000 then var='Between 500,000 and 1,000,000';
      output;
   end;
run;

NOTE: The data set WORK.TEST1 has 1000000 observations and 101 variables.
NOTE: DATA statement used (Total process time):
      real time           44.79 seconds
      user cpu time       0.42 seconds
      system cpu time     5.18 seconds
      Memory                             301k
      OS Memory                          7024k
      Timestamp            3/4/2009  5:28:01 PM
```

48

p301a01a

Description of FULLSTIMER statistics in the Windows operating environment:

Real Time	the amount of time spent to process the SAS job. Real time is also referred to as *elapsed time*
User CPU Time	the CPU time spent to execute the SAS code as written by the user
System CPU Time	the CPU time spent to perform operating system tasks (system overhead tasks) that support the execution of SAS code
Memory	the amount of memory required to run a step
OS Memory	the largest amount of memory that SAS requested from the operating system during the step
Timestamp	the date and time that the statistics were produced

UNIX Log

Partial SAS Log

```
options fullstimer;

data test1;
   length var $ 30;
   retain var2-var50 0 var51-var100 'ABC';
   do var1=1 to 1000000;
      if var1<1000 then var='Less than 1,000';
      if 1000<=var1<10000 then var='Between 1,000 and 10,000';
      if 10000<=var1<100000 then var='Between 10,000 and 100,000';
      if 100000<=var1<500000 then var='Between 100,000 and 500,000';
      if 500000<=var1<1000000 then var='Between 500,000 and 1,000,000';
      output;
   end;
run;

NOTE: The data set WORK.TEST1 has 1000000 observations and 101 variables.
NOTE: DATA statement used (Total process time):
      real time           24.23 seconds
      user cpu time       1.49 seconds
      system cpu time     3.47 seconds
      Memory                             266k
      Page Faults                        0
      Page Reclaims                      246
      Page Swaps                         0
      Voluntary Context Switches         1360
      Involuntary Context Switches       130
      Block Input Operations             7
      Block Output Operations            75124
```

49 p301a01a

SAS uses the **getrusage()** and **times()** UNIX system calls for your operating environment to obtain the statistics presented with FULLSTIMER.

Different "flavors" of UNIX show different statistics. This log was obtained on a Solaris system.

Description of FULLSTIMER statistics in the UNIX operating environment:

Real Time	the amount of time spent to process the SAS job. Real time is also referred to as *elapsed time*
User CPU Time	the CPU time spent to execute the SAS code as written by the user
System CPU Time	the CPU time spent to perform operating system tasks (system overhead tasks) that support the execution of SAS code
Memory	the amount of memory required to run a step
OS Memory	the largest amount of memory that SAS requested from the operating system during the step
Timestamp	the date and time that the statistics were produced
Page Faults	the number of pages that SAS tried to access but were not in the main memory and required I/O activity
Page Reclaims	the number of pages that were accessed without I/O activity

(Continued on the next page.)

Page Swaps	the number of times that a SAS process was swapped out of main memory
Voluntary Context Switches	the number of times that the SAS process had to pause because of a resource constraint such as a disk drive
Involuntary Context Switches	the number of times that the operating system forced the SAS session to pause processing to enable other processes to run
Block Input Operations	the number of I/O operations that were performed to read the data into memory
Block Output Operations	the number of I/O operations that were performed to write the data to a file

z/OS Log

Partial SAS Log

```
7     options fullstimer;
8
9     data test1;
10       length var $ 30;
11       retain var2-var50 0 var51-var100 'ABC';
12       do var1=1 to 1000000;
13          if var1<1000 then var='Less than 1,000';
14          if 1000<=var1<10000 then var='Between 1,000 and 10,000';
15          if 10000<=var1<100000 then var='Between 10,000 and 100,000';
16          if 100000<=var1<500000 then var='Between 100,000 and 500,000';
17          if 500000<=var1<1000000 then var='Between 500,000 and 1,000,000';
18          output;
19       end;
20    run;

NOTE: The data set WORK.TEST1 has 1000000 observations and 101 variables.
NOTE: The DATA statement used the following resources:
      CPU     time -          00:00:03.00
      Elapsed time -          00:00:19.33
      EXCP count   - 4067
      Task  memory - 6994K (131K data, 6863K program)
      Total memory - 14433K (3488K data, 10945K program)
```

50

p301a01a

Description of FULLSTIMER statistics in the z/OS operating environment:

CPU Time	The actual time spent on the task. This number should be constant (within .02 seconds) across repetitions of the same job.
Elapsed Time	The wall-clock time required to complete the task. Because elapsed time varies greatly for several runs of the same job due to differences in waiting time caused by other tasks being performed by the CPU, it is not normally used to benchmark programs.
EXCP Count	The number of I/O operations required to transfer external data to and from memory. EXCP is the acronym for **EX**ecute **C**hannel **P**rogram.
Task Memory	The actual memory required for a task in kilobytes with breakdowns for data and program storage. This number is stable for a given task.
Total Memory	The memory required for all tasks in kilobytes. This session total is useful for deciding the minimum region size required for the job to execute successfully.

1.3 SAS DATA Step Processing

Objectives

- List the attributes of a data set page and define how it relates to the structure of SAS data sets.
- Describe how SAS reads and writes data.

53

SAS Data Set Pages

A SAS *data set page* has the following attributes:

- It is the unit of data transfer between the operating system buffers and SAS buffers in memory.
- It includes the number of bytes used by the descriptor portion, the data values, and any operating system overhead.
- It is fixed in size when the data set is created, either to a default value or to a value specified by the programmer.

54

By default, SAS uses the minimum optimal page size for the operating environment.

Using PROC CONTENTS to Report Page Size

```
proc contents data=orion.sales_history;
run;
```

Partial PROC CONTENTS Output

16,384*18=
294,912 bytes

```
                 Engine/Host Dependent Information

Data Set Page Size            16384
Number of Data Set Pages      18
First Data Page               1
Max Obs per Page              92
Obs in First Data Page        72
Number of Data Set Repairs    0
File Name                     S:\workshop\sales_history.sas7bdat
Release Created               9.0201M0
Host Created                  XP_PRO
```

55

The total number of bytes occupied by **orion.sales_history** can be calculated as shown below:

(16,384 * 18)=294,912 bytes

1.08 Quiz

Use one of the following to determine the page size of the **orion.customer_dim** SAS data set:

- the CONTENTS procedure
- the DATASETS procedure
- the SAS Explorer window

What is the page size of the SAS data set **orion.customer_dim**?

57 p301a02

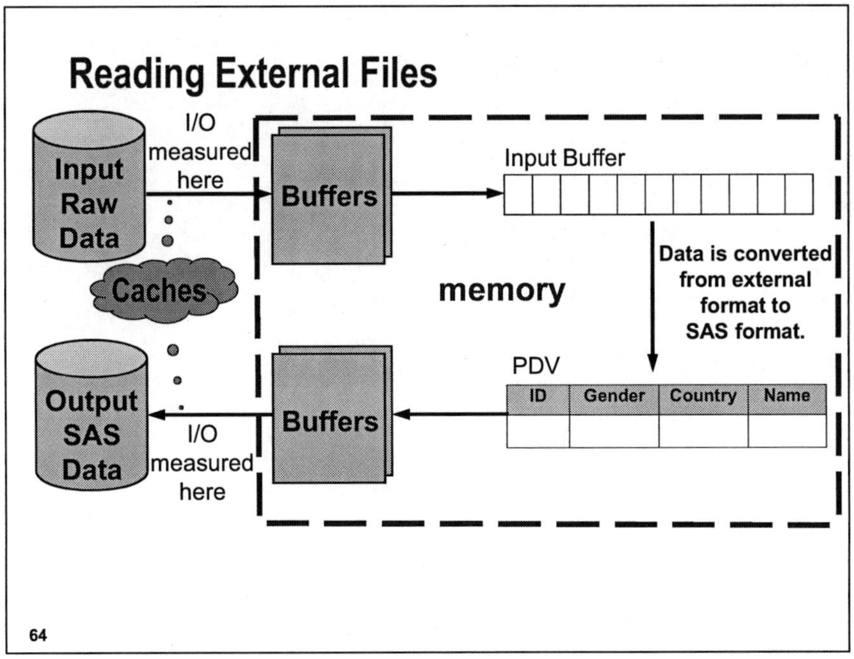

When a raw data file is read with INFILE and INPUT statements, the following occur:

- A block of data is read into a buffer in memory. The size of each buffer is the block size of the input raw data file. In Windows and UNIX, the data might be cached so that the data is copied from disk to an area of memory managed by the operating environment before it is copied into the buffer managed by SAS.
- Each record of the raw data file is copied into an input buffer.
- The data is converted from an external format to the SAS format using the instructions provided in the INPUT statement and is stored in an area of SAS memory called the *program data vector* (*PDV*). Any subsequent processing specified in the DATA step is performed on the values in the PDV.
- At the end of an iteration for the DATA step, the contents of the PDV are copied to an output buffer in memory.
- After the buffer (or multiple buffers) is full, the data in the buffer is written to the output SAS data set in one output operation.
- Sequential processing continues until the pointer reaches the end-of-file marker in the raw data file.

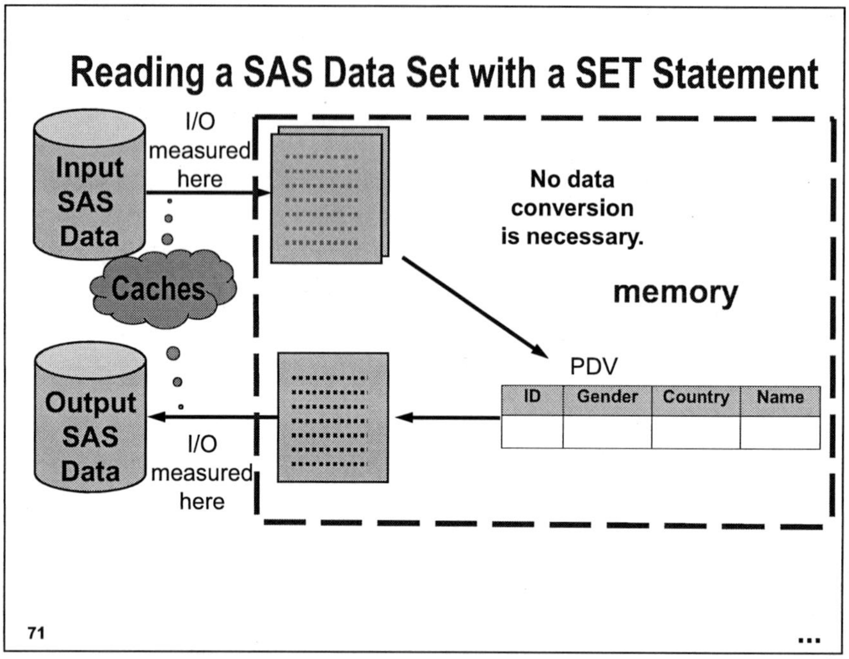

When a SAS data set is read with a SET or MERGE statement, the following occur:

- A page (or multiple pages) is read into a buffer (or multiple buffers) in memory. The size of each buffer is the page size of the input SAS data set. In Windows and UNIX, the data might be cached so that the data is copied from disk to an area of memory managed by the operating environment before it is copied into the buffer managed by SAS.
- The data in the buffer is read sequentially and copied into the program data vector (PDV) one observation at a time.
- Each observation of the new SAS data set is copied into a buffer (or multiple buffers). An observation must fit entirely into the buffer or the observation is written to another buffer.
- After the buffer (or multiple buffers) is full, the data in the buffer is written to the output SAS data set in one output operation.
- Sequential processing continues until the pointer reaches the end-of-file marker in the input SAS data set.

Exercises

Level 1

1. Benchmarking

Open the program **p301e01.sas** (Windows or UNIX) or **'.prg3.sascode(p301e01)'** (z/OS).

Use best practices to benchmark the program, change it according to step **1.d**, and determine which resource(s) were conserved.

```
data order_fact;
   infile 'order_fact.dat' pad; ①
   input @37 Order_Date date9. @; ②
   input  @1 Customer_ID 12.
         @13 Employee_ID 12.
         @25 Street_ID 12.
         @46 Delivery_Date date9.
         @55 Order_ID 12.
         @67 Order_Type 2.
         @69 Product_ID 12.
         @81 Quantity 4.
         @90 Total_Retail_Price 13.
        @105 CostPrice_Per_Unit 10.
        @115 Discount 5.;
   if year(Order_Date)=2006;
   format Customer_ID Employee_ID Street_ID Order_ID
          Product_ID 12. Order_Date Delivery_Date date9.
          Order_Type 2. Quantity 4. Total_Retail_Price dollar13.2
          CostPrice_Per_Unit dollar10.2 Discount Percent.;
run;
```

Notes about the syntax:

①	*PAD*	controls whether SAS pads the records that are read from an external file with blanks to the length that is specified in the LRECL= option. The LRECL= option specifies the logical record length; it is dependent on the operating environment.
②	*@*	holds an input record for the execution of the next INPUT statement within the same iteration of the DATA step. This line-hold specifier is called a *trailing @*.

a. Turn on the appropriate options for reporting the resource statistics in the log.

b. Submit the program.

c. Record the following resource utilizations:

1) User CPU Time: ,01 ____________________

2) I/O: ____________________
(not applicable on Windows)

3) User Memory: 319k ____________________

d. Move the subsetting IF closer to the top of the DATA step. Make sure that you move the subsetting IF to the appropriate location in the program.

e. Submit the revised program and record the following resource utilizations:

1) User CPU Time: .01 ____________________

2) I/O: ____________________
(not applicable on Windows)

3) User Memory: 217 ____________________

f. Were any resource(s) conserved when you moved the IF statement?

yes - user memory ____________________

Level 2

2. Investigating the WORK System Option

a. In either the SAS Help facility (available from the Help menu or the Help icon in your SAS session) or SAS OnlineDoc (available via a Web browser at support.sas.com/documentation/index.html), find information about the WORK SAS system option. The menu tree for finding the information in the SAS Help facility is shown below:

Using SAS Software in Your Operating Environment ⇨ ***<your operating system here>*** ⇨ **Features of the SAS Language** ⇨ **System Options under *<your operating system here>*** ⇨ **WORK**

The menu tree for finding the information in the SAS OnlineDoc is shown below:

Base SAS ⇨ **SAS 9.2 Companion for *<your operating system here>* HTML** ⇨ **Features of the SAS Language for *<your operating system here>*** (menu tree on left side) ⇨ **System Options under *<your operating system here>*** ⇨ **WORK System Option**

b. Answer the following questions:

1) Can you submit the WORK system option in an OPTIONS statement? (YES or NO) ________

2) Explain why or why not.

____

____

____

Level 3

3. Investigating the UTILLOC SAS System Option

In either the SAS Help facility (available from the Help menu or the Help icon in your SAS session) or SAS OnlineDoc (available via a Web browser at support.sas.com/documentation/index.html), find information about the UTILLOC SAS system option.

Answer the following questions:

a. What is the advantage of using the UTILLOC SAS system option?

____

____

____

b. Can both the WORK and UTILLOC SAS system options be specified in the same OPTIONS statement? (YES or NO) ____________________

c. Explain your answer to part **b**.

____

____

____

____

1.4 Chapter Review

Chapter Review

1. What are the six resources consumed by SAS programs?

2. What is the correct way to benchmark SAS programs?

3. What is a SAS data set page size?

75

1.5 Solutions

Solutions to Exercises

1. Benchmarking

a. Turn on the appropriate options for reporting the resource statistics in the log.

```
options fullstimer;

data order_fact;
     <additional SAS code>
run;
```

b. Submit the program.

c. Record the following resource utilizations:

1) User CPU Time: ____________________

2) I/O: ____________________
   (not applicable on Windows)

3) User Memory: ____________________

The answers are specific to your operating environment.

d. Move the subsetting IF closer to the top of the DATA step. Make sure that you move the subsetting IF to the appropriate location in the program.

```
data order_fact;
   infile 'order_fact.dat' pad;
   input @37 Order_Date date9. @;
   if year(Order_Date)=2006;
   input  @1 Customer_ID 12.
         @13 Employee_ID 12.
         @25 Street_ID 12.
         @46 Delivery_Date date9.
         @55 Order_ID 12.
         @67 Order_Type 2.
         @69 Product_ID 12.
         @81 Quantity 4.
         @90 Total_Retail_Price 13.
        @105 CostPrice_Per_Unit 10.
        @115 Discount 5.;
   format Customer_ID Employee_ID Street_ID Order_ID Product_ID 12.
          Order_Date Delivery_Date date9.
          Order_Type 2. Quantity 4. Total_Retail_Price dollar13.2
          CostPrice_Per_Unit dollar10.2 Discount Percent.;
run;

proc print data=order_fact;
   title 'Year 2006 Orders';
run;
```

e. Submit the revised program and record the following resource utilizations:

1) User CPU Time: ______________________

2) I/O: ______________________
(not applicable on Windows)

3) User Memory: ______________________

The answers are specific to your operating environment.

f. Were any resource(s) conserved when you moved the IF statement?

You should see less CPU utilization when you move the IF statement closer to the top of the program because, for observations not involved in the subset, numeric values are not converted. As the subset becomes smaller relative to the number of records in the raw data file, more CPU is conserved.

2. **Investigating the WORK System Option**

   a. In either the SAS Help facility or SAS OnlineDoc, find information about the WORK SAS system option.

   b. Answer the following questions:

      1) Can you submit the WORK system option in an OPTIONS statement? (YES or NO) NO

      2) Explain why or why not.

         All file locations for SAS utilities must be set at SAS invocation, rather than in an OPTIONS statement.

3. **Investigating the UTILLOC SAS System Option**

   In either the SAS Help facility or SAS OnlineDoc, find information about the UTILLOC SAS system option.

   Answer the following questions:

   a. What is the advantage of using the UTILLOC SAS system option?

      You can avoid storing the utility swap files in the Work library, which frees space for temporary SAS files. You can send the utility swap files to an under-utilized file system.

   b. Can both the WORK and UTILLOC SAS system options be specified in the same OPTIONS statement?(YES or NO) YES

   c. Explain your answer to part **b**.

      The WORK SAS system option points to the storage location for temporary SAS files. The UTILLOC SAS system option specifies where utility swap files from SAS steps are stored. The WORK SAS files are available to your entire SAS session unless they are specifically deleted. The UTILLOC swap files are erased when the SAS step successfully completes.

Solutions to Student Activities (Polls/Quizzes)

1.02 Quiz – Correct Answer

Determine the path to use to obtain information about the SAS component objects.

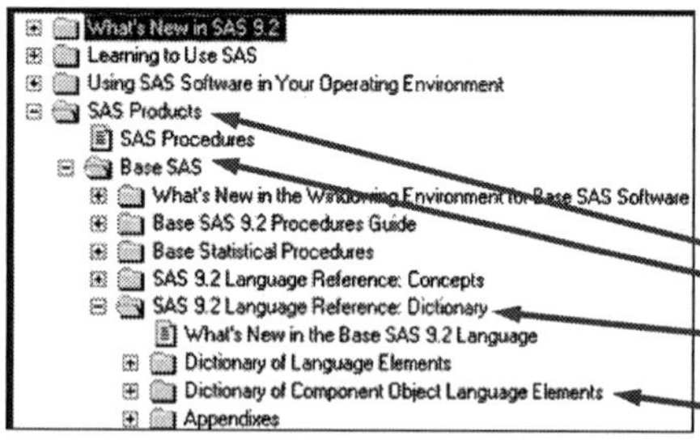

Information relevant to this course can be found by following these paths in the SAS Help facility:

Contents tab
→ SAS Products
→ Base SAS
→ SAS 9.2 Language Reference Dictionary
→ Dictionary of Component Object Language Elements

16

1.06 Multiple Choice Poll – Correct Answer

Which of the following SAS programs should be benchmarked?

a. A report that shows all the customers in the United Kingdom in March 2006
b. A report that calculates trends in sales at the end of every day for every department
c. A report showing the projected total cost of a 5% cost-of-living increase in employee salaries for a Human Resources project conducted on January 1, 2007
d. A yearly report that calculates the average sales of a line of apparel for the clothing manager

42

1.08 Quiz – Correct Answer

Use one of the following to determine the page size of the `orion.customer_dim` SAS data set:

- the CONTENTS procedure
- the DATASETS procedure
- the SAS Explorer window

What is the page size of the SAS data set `orion.customer_dim`?

16,384 bytes in Windows
24,576 bytes in UNIX
18,432 bytes in z/OS

58 p301a02

Solutions to Chapter Review

Chapter Review Answers

1. What are the six resources consumed by SAS programs?
   - **programmer time**
   - **network bandwidth**
   - **CPU**
   - **Memory**
   - **I/O**
   - **disk storage space**

76

continued...

Chapter Review Answers

2. What is the correct way to benchmark SAS programs?
   a. **Turn on the system options to report resource usage.**
   b. **Test each technique in a separate SAS session.**
   c. **Test only one technique or change at a time.**
   d. **Run the test under final conditions.**
   e. **Run each program three to five times and average the results.**
   f. **Exclude outliers**
   g. **Turn off the resource usage reporting options.**

77

continued...

Chapter Review Answers

3. What is a SAS data set page size?

   The size of the SAS data set page is the unit of data transfer between the system buffers and the SAS buffers in memory. The default transfer is one data set page at a time.

   The page size determines the amount of memory that is used when data is read and written. The number of pages effects the I/O.

78

Chapter 2 Controlling I/O Processing and Memory

2.1 Controlling I/O

Objectives

- Describe the importance of conserving I/O.
- List techniques for reducing I/O.

3

I/O (Review)

SAS programs typically perform the following tasks:

- reading data sets sequentially
- performing analysis and data manipulation
- writing data sets sequentially or writing reports

I/O is one of the most important factors for optimizing performance.

4

Where Is I/O Measured? (Review)

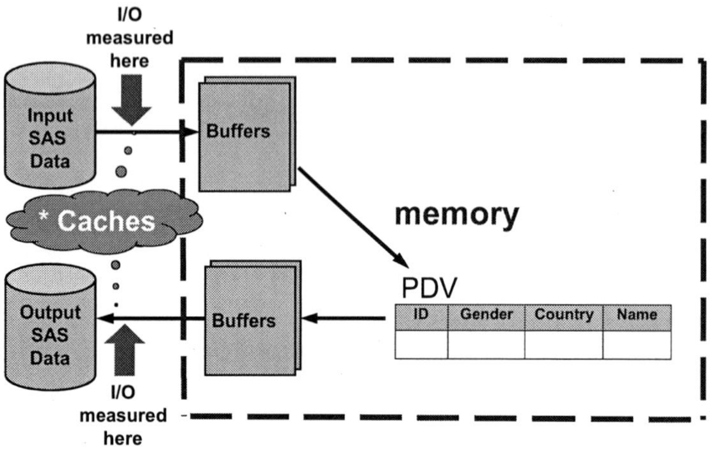

* Windows and UNIX Only

5

Using the Operating Environment Cache in Windows and UNIX

Windows and UNIX use a file-caching mechanism in the background.

- A file *cache* is an area in memory that holds recently accessed data.
- By default, SAS reads and writes data through the operating environment file cache, not by direct I/O.
- File caching is beneficial if the same data is used more than once.
- File caching adds overhead to sequential I/O.

6

Techniques for Reducing I/O Operations

1. Minimize the number of variables and observations.
2. Reduce the number of times that the data is processed.
3. Create a SAS data file when processing the same raw data file repeatedly.
4. Use the SASFILE statement to process a small SAS data set repeatedly. → loads it into memory
5. Minimize the size of the SAS data set.
6. Use appropriate BUFSIZE= and/or BUFNO= options for random or sequential access.

7

continued...

Techniques for Reducing I/O Operations

7. Bypass system file caching in Windows and UNIX.
8. Create views in programs that require intermediate temporary SAS data files.
9. Create indexes on variables used for WHERE processing.

8

Technique 1: Process Only the Necessary Variables and Observations

Simple techniques can conserve I/O. The amount of I/O saved depends on the size of the subset being processed.

- Reduce the number of variables
  - DROP or KEEP statements
  - DROP= or KEEP= data set options
- Reduce the number of observations
  - WHERE statement
  - WHERE= data set option
  - OBS= and FIRSTOBS= data set options

9

Subsetting Data

Program 1: Subsetting in the Procedure

One way to create a subset is to use the WHERE statement in a procedure.

```
data bonus;
   set orion.staff;
   YrEndBonus=Salary*0.05;
run;
proc means data=bonus mean sum;
   where Job_Title contains 'Manager';
   class Manager_ID;
   var YrEndBonus;
run;
```

✎ The data set **bonus** contains 11 variables and 424 observations.

10 p302d01

Subsetting Data

Program 2: Subsetting in the DATA Step

A more efficient way to subset would be in the DATA step.

```
data bonus(keep=Manager_ID YrEndBonus);
   set orion.staff(keep=Job_Title Salary Manager_ID);
   where Job_Title contains 'Manager';
   YrEndBonus=Salary*0.05;
run;
proc means data=bonus mean sum;
   class Manager_ID;
   var YrEndBonus;
run;
```

I/O savings result from reducing the number of variables and observations in the input and output data sets.

The data set **bonus** contains 2 variables and 41 observations..

p302d01

11

Because of the way that SAS reads data, the savings in the DATA step are when the data set **bonus** is output. Fewer variables and observations are written, so more can go on a single data set page.

Using the KEEP=/DROP= Options

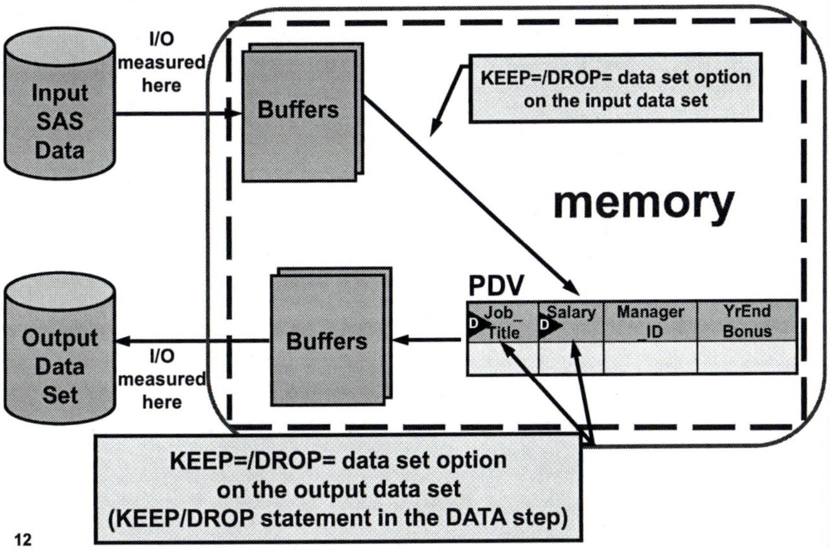

12

Setup for the Poll

p302d01 Program 1

```
data bonus;
   set orion.staff;
   YrEndBonus=Salary*0.05;
run;
proc means data=bonus mean sum;
   where Job_Title contains 'Manager'
   class Manager_ID;
   var YrEndBonus;
run;
```

I/O savings results from reducing the number of variables and observations in the input and output data sets.

p302d01 Program 2

```
data bonus(keep=Manager_ID YrEndBonus
   set orion.staff(keep=Job_Title Salary Manager_ID);
   where Job_Title contains 'Manager';
   YrEndBonus=Salary*0.05;
run;
proc means data=bonus mean sum;
   class Manager_ID;
   var YrEndBonus;
run;
```

14

2.01 Multiple Choice Poll

In addition to the I/O decrease when the DATA step creates **bonus**, where does Program 2 have additional decrease of I/O?

a. Fewer variables are read into the program data vector from **orion.staff** in Program 2 because of the KEEP= data set option.

b. The PROC MEANS in Program 2 loads a smaller version of **bonus**.

c. There is no additional decrease in I/O; all of the decrease in I/O occurs when the data set **bonus** is created by the DATA step.

15

Technique 2: Reducing the Number of Times that Data Is Processed

The following techniques reduce the number of times that data is processed:

- Subset data within a procedure step if possible.
- Create SAS data files. SAS can process SAS data files more efficiently than raw data files.
- Use engines efficiently.
- Use indexes.
- Access data through SAS views.

17

Subsetting Data within a Procedure Step

Program 1: Subset in the DATA Step

You can subset in the DATA step first, and then execute the procedure on a smaller data set.

```
data big_salaries;
   set orion.staff;
   where Salary > 50000;
run;

proc means data=big_salaries mean sum;
   class Manager_ID;
   var Salary;
run;
```

18 p302d02

Subsetting Data within a Procedure Step

Program 2: Subset in the Procedure

A better way is to execute only one step and subset in that step.

```
proc means data=orion.staff mean sum;
   class Manager_ID;
   var Salary;
   where Salary > 50000;
run;
```

I/O savings results from avoiding an extra step for subsetting.

19 p302d02

Technique 3: Creating a SAS Data File

Program 1: Write two programs. Each program should create a temporary SAS data set to read in the same raw data file and create a report.

```
data prices;
   infile 'prices.dat' dlm='*';
   input Product_ID : 12. Start_Date : date9. End_Date : date9.
         Unit_Cost_Price:dollar7.2 Unit_Sales_Price:dollar7.2;
run;
proc print data=prices(obs=5);
  title1 "Prices Data Set";
run;
```

```
data prices;
   infile 'prices.dat' dlm='*';
   input Product_ID : 12. Start_Date : date9. End_Date : date9.
         Unit_Cost_Price:dollar7.2 Unit_Sales_Price:dollar7.2;
run;
proc means data=prices(keep=Unit_Cost_Price Unit_Sales_Price);
  var Unit_Cost_Price Unit_Sales_Price;
run;
```

20 p302d03

Creating a SAS Data File

Program 2: Create a permanent SAS data set by reading in the raw data file one time. Write two programs using the SAS data set to create a report.

```
data orion.prices;
   infile 'prices.dat' dlm='*';
   input Product_ID : 12. Start_Date : date9.
         End_Date : date9.
         Unit_Cost_Price : dollar7.2
         Unit_Sales_Price : dollar7.2;
run;
proc print data=orion.prices(obs=5);
  title1 "Prices Data Set";
run;
```

I/O savings from reading the raw data once

```
proc means data=orion.prices
      (keep=Unit_Cost_Price Unit_Sales_Price);
  var Unit_Cost_Price Unit_Sales_Price;
run;
```

21 p302d03

Technique 4: SASFILE Global Statement

If your program uses the same data set multiple times, the SASFILE statement can reduce I/O resources.

- The SASFILE statement loads the SAS data set into memory in its entirety, instead of a few pages at a time.
- After it is loaded, the data set is held in memory for subsequent DATA and PROC step processing.
- A second SASFILE statement closes the file and frees the SAS buffers.
- It is useful for data sets that fit entirely into memory.
- The SASFILE statement should not be used if the data set is larger than available physical memory.

⚠ The reduction in I/O resources comes at the cost of increased memory usage.

22

✎ The SASFILE statement can also reduce execution (CPU) time.

Business Scenario

Create reports using the PRINT, TABULATE, MEANS, and FREQUENCY procedures against a single SAS data set.

```
sasfile orion.customer_dim load;

proc freq data=orion.customer_dim;
   tables Customer_Country Customer_Type
run;
proc print data=orion.customer_dim noobs
   where Customer_Type='Orion Club Gold
   var Customer_ID Customer_Name Custome
run;
proc means data=orion.customer_dim mean
   var Customer_Age;
   class Customer_Group;
run;
proc tabulate data=orion.customer_dim fo
   class Customer_Age_Group Customer_Typ
   table Customer_Type All=Total,
         Customer_Age_Group*n=' ' All=To
run;

sasfile orion.customer_dim close;
```

The **`orion.customer_dim`** data set is read into memory only once instead of four times. This results in one-fourth as many I/O operations, which can also reduce elapsed time. However, it comes at the expense of increased memory usage.

23

p302d04

SASFILE Global Statement

General form of the SASFILE statement:

SASFILE *<libref.>member-name*
<(password-data-set-option(s))>
OPEN | LOAD | CLOSE;

- When the SASFILE statement executes, SAS allocates the number of buffers based on the number of pages in the SAS data set and index file.
- If the file in memory increases in size during processing by editing or appending data, the number of buffers also increases.

24

OPEN	opens the file and allocates the buffers, but defers reading the data into memory until a procedure or a statement that references the file is executed.
LOAD	opens the file, allocates the buffers, and reads the data into memory.
CLOSE	frees the buffers and closes the file.

Exercises

Level 1

1. Using the SASFILE Statement

a. Open the program **p302e01** and submit it.

p302e01

```
proc print data=orion.organization_dim noobs;
   where Department='Administration';
   var Employee_ID Employee_Country Section Job_Title;
run;

proc means data=orion.organization_dim min mean max;
   var Salary;
   class Department;
run;

proc report data=orion.organization_dim headline headskip nowd;
   column Company Department Employee_Hire_Date
          Employee_BirthDate HiredAge;
   define Company/order;
   define Department/order;
   define HiredAge/computed format=12.2 'Age when Hired';
   compute HiredAge;
      HiredAge=yrdif(Employee_BirthDate.sum,
                     Employee_Hire_Date.sum,'Act/Act');
   endcomp;
run;

proc freq data=orion.organization_dim;
   table Department*Company/norow nocol;
run;

proc means data=orion.organization_dim min mean max maxdec=2;
   class Company;
   var Salary;
run;
```

b. Note the following resource utilizations:

1) User CPU Time: [illegible] 0 / [illegible] 0/0/0

2) I/O: ____________________
(not applicable on Windows)

3) User Memory: [illegible] 202 / 6646 / 6820 / 337 / 6830

c. Add the appropriate statement(s) to open and load the entire `orion.organization_dim` data set into memory. At the end of the program, close the data set.

d. Submit the revised program.

e. Note the following resource utilizations:

1) User CPU Time: ______________________________

2) I/O: ______________________________
(not applicable on Windows)

3) User Memory: 103/6540/ 6714 /237/6731

f. Which resources were conserved?

____

Level 2

2. Using Multiple SASFILE Statements

a. Open the program **p302e02** and submit it.

p302e02

```
options fullstimer;
proc means data=orion.employee_donations sum mean median;
   class Recipients;
   var Qtr1-Qtr4;
run;

proc freq data=orion.employee_donations;
   tables Recipients;
run;

proc report data=orion.employee_addresses  headline headskip nowd;
   columns Employee_ID Employee_Name City State;
   define State/width=5;
   where Country='US';
run;

proc freq data=orion.employee_addresses;
   tables Country;
run;

proc sql;
   select Employee_Name,
          sum(Qtr1, Qtr2, Qtr3, Qtr4) as Total_Contribution,
          Recipients
      from orion.employee_addresses  as a,
           orion.employee_donations as d
         where a.Employee_ID=d.Employee_ID;
quit;
options nofullstimer;
```

b. Add the appropriate statement(s) to open and load both the `orion.employee_addresses` and `orion.employee_donations` data sets into memory. At the end of the program, close the data sets.

c. Submit the revised program.

Level 3

3. Using the APPEND Procedure with the SASFILE Statement

a. Open the program **p302e03** that contains a PROC COPY step to copy the data sets `orion.sales` and `orion.nonsales` to your Work library so that you can maintain the integrity for those original data sets. Submit the program.

b. Add the appropriate statement(s) to open and load the entire `work.sales` data set into memory, a PROC APPEND step to append the temporary `work.nonsales` data set to the temporary `work.sales` data set, and a PROC PRINT step to print the `work.sales` data set. At the end of the program, close the data set.

c. Submit the revised program.

2.2 Controlling Data Set Size

Objectives

- List techniques to reduce data storage.
- Describe how SAS stores numeric values.
- Describe how to safely reduce the space required to store numeric values in SAS data sets.

28

Techniques for Reducing Data Set Size

1. Store integers as reduced-length numerics.
2. Compress the data set.

✎ Reducing the size of a SAS data set reduces the I/O required to process it.

29

Characteristics of Numeric Variables

Numeric variables have the following characteristics:

- are stored as floating-point numbers in real-binary representation
  - store multiple digits per byte
  - use a minimum of one byte to store the sign and exponent of the value (depending on the operating environment) and use the remaining bytes to store the mantissa of the value
- take 8 bytes of storage per variable, by default, but can be reduced in size
- always have a length of 8 bytes in the PDV

30

Default Length of Numeric Variables

The number 35,298 can be written as follows:

SAS stores numeric variables in floating-point form:

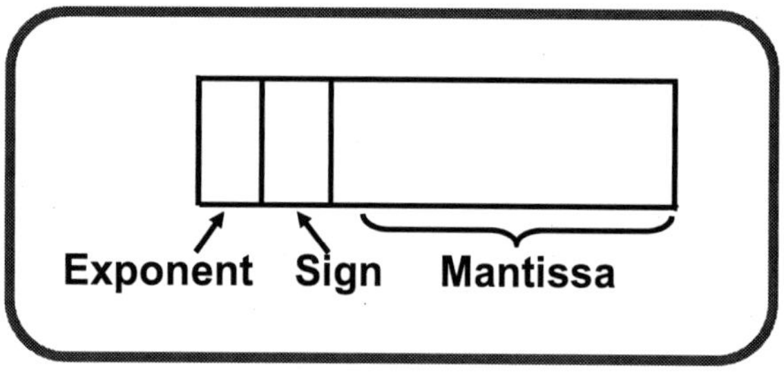

31

SAS stores numeric values in native floating-point representation.

Summary of Floating-Point Numbers Stored in 8 Bytes

Representation	Base	Exponent Bits	Maximum Mantissa Bits
IBM mainframe	16	7	56
IEEE (UNIX, Windows, Open VMS Alpha)	2	11	52

Assigning the Length of Numeric Variables

You can use a LENGTH statement to assign a length from 2 to 8 bytes to numeric variables.

```
data emps_short;
   length Street_ID Employee_ID Manager_ID
          Street_Number Employee_Hire_Date
          Employee_Term_Date Birth_Date 4
          Dependents 3;
   merge employee_addresses
         employee_organization
         employee_payroll
         employee_phones;
   by Employee_ID;
run;
```

If the variable is character, the length applies to the program data vector and the output data set. If the variable is numeric, the length applies only to the output data set; therefore, for numeric data, the LENGTH statement does not need to be before the READ statement.

32 p302d05

To decrease the length of all numeric variables, you can use the DEFAULT= option in the LENGTH statement:

```
data emps_short;
   length default=4;
   <additional SAS code>
run;
```

Comparing Results

To determine whether the data sets **emps_short** and **emps** are equivalent, you can use the COMPARE procedure.

```
proc compare data=emps compare=emps_short;
run;
```

33 p302d06

General form of PROC COMPARE:

```
PROC COMPARE <option(s)>;
     BY <DESCENDING> variable-1 ...
        <DESCENDING> variable-n>
        <NOTSORTED>;
     ID <DESCENDING> variable-1
        <...<DESCENDING> variable-n>
        <NOTSORTED>;
     VAR variable(s);
     WITH variable(s);
RUN;
```

Task	Statement
Compare the contents of SAS data sets, or compare two variables.	PROC COMPARE
Produce a separate comparison for each BY group.	BY
Identify variables to use to match observations.	ID
Restrict the comparison to values of specific variables.	VAR
Compare variables of different names.	WITH and VAR
Compare two variables in the same data set.	WITH and VAR

Comparing Data Sets

Partial PROC COMPARE Output

```
                    The COMPARE Procedure
         Comparison of WORK.EMPS with WORK.EMPS_SHORT
                        (Method=EXACT)

                     Observation Summary

Observation       Base  Compare

First Obs            1        1
Last  Obs          923      923

Number of Observations in Common: 923.
Total Number of Observations Read from WORK.EMPS: 923.
Total Number of Observations Read from WORK.EMPS_SHORT: 923.

Number of Observations with Some Compared Variables Unequal: 0.
Number of Observations with All Compared Variables Equal: 923.

NOTE: No unequal values were found. All values compared are exactly equal.
```

34 p302d06

The COMPARE procedure is part of Base SAS.

Possible Storage Lengths for Integer Values

Windows and UNIX

Length (bytes)	Largest Integer Represented Exactly
3	8,192
4	2,097,152
5	536,870,912
6	137,438,953,472
7	35,184,372,088,832
8	9,007,199,254,740,992

35

The numbers are consecutive. For example, you can store numbers from -8192 to 8192 consecutively in 3 bytes on ASCII systems.

Possible Storage Lengths for Integer Values

z/OS

Length (bytes)	Largest Integer Represented Exactly
2	256
3	65,536
4	16,777,216
5	4,294,967,296
6	1,099,511,627,776
7	281,474,946,710,656
8	72,057,594,037,927,936

36

The numbers are consecutive. For example, you can store numbers from –256 continuously to 256 in 2 bytes on EBCDIC systems.

Assigning the Length of Numeric Variables

The use of a numeric length less than 8 bytes does the following:

- causes the number to be truncated to the specified length when the value is written to the SAS data set

⚠ This reduces the number of bytes available for the mantissa, which reduces the precision of the number that can be accurately stored.

- causes the number to be expanded to 8 bytes in the PDV when the data set is read by padding the mantissa with binary zeros

✎ Numbers are always 8 bytes in length in the PDV.

37

✎ SAS procedures also expand numbers to 8 bytes in memory.

Dangers of Reduced-Length Numeric Variables

It is **not** recommended that you change the length of non-integer numeric variables.

```
data test;
   length x 4;
   X=1/10;
   Y=1/10;
run;

data _null_;
   set test;
   put X=;
   put Y=;
run;
```

38 p302a01

In the same way that a decimal number system cannot store the fraction 1/3 exactly in a finite number of digits, a binary number system (or multiple thereof, such as octal or hexadecimal) cannot store the fraction 1/10 exactly in any finite number of digits.

2.02 Poll

Open the program **p302a01** and submit it.

Look at the log.

Are the values of X and Y equal?

- ❍ Yes
- ❍ No

40

Numeric Precision

Partial SAS Log (Windows)

```
data test;
   length x 4;
   X=1/10;
   Y=1/10;
run;

NOTE: The data set WORK.TEST has 1 observations and 2 variables.
NOTE: DATA statement used (Total process time):
      real time           0.00 seconds
      cpu time            0.00 seconds


data _null_;
   set test;
   put X=;
   put Y=;
run;

x=0.0999999642
y=0.1
NOTE: There were 1 observations read from the data set WORK.TEST.
NOTE: DATA statement used (Total process time):
      real time           0.03 seconds
      cpu time            0.00 seconds
```

42

Dangers of Reduced-Length Numeric Variables

It is **not** recommended that you reduce the length of integer numeric variables inappropriately or that you reduce the length of variables that hold large integer numeric values. This example illustrates the effect of inappropriately reducing integer values.

```
data test;
   length X 3;
   X=8193;
run;

data _null_;
   set test;
   put X=;
run;
```

p202d07

43

This example illustrates the dangers of inappropriately reducing integer values.

Numeric Precision

Partial SAS Log (Windows)

```
120  data test;
121     length X 3;
122     X=8193;
123  run;

NOTE: The data set WORK.TEST has 1 observations and 1
variables.
NOTE: DATA statement used (Total process time):
      real time           0.00 seconds
      cpu time            0.00 seconds

124
125  data _null_;
126     set test;
127     put X=;
128  run;

X=8192
NOTE: There were 1 observations read from the data set
WORK.TEST.
NOTE: DATA statement used (Total process time):
      real time           0.00 seconds
      cpu time            0.00 seconds
```

44

Advantages and Disadvantages of Reduced-Length Numeric Variables

Advantages	Disadvantages
Conserves data storage space	Uses additional CPU to read
Requires less I/O to read	Can alter high-precision values such as non-integer and large integer values

45

Exercises

Level 1

4. Creating Reduced Length Numerics

The data set **orion.internet** contains the orders placed over the Internet. The data set **orion.retail** contains the items purchased in a store. The data set **orion.catalog** contains the items purchased from the catalog.

a. Use PROC CONTENTS to determine the names and types of the variables in each of those data sets.

b. Open the program **p302e04**. Edit the DATA step to concatenate the three data sets to create a data set named **all_customers**. Appropriately reduce the length of the numeric variables using an adequate length for the values of the variables.

p302e04

```
data all_customers;

   set orion.catalog orion.internet orion.retail;
run;
```

c. Use PROC CONTENTS to check the length of the numeric variables.

Level 2

5. Creating Reduced Length Numerics and Precision

Open the program **p302e05** and submit it. At what point in the sequence of numbers does the length of the variable **Num5** lose precision? ______________________________

p302e05

```
data five;
   length Num5 5 Num8 8;
   do Num8=1e10 to 1e13 by 1e11;
      Num5=Num8;
      output;
   end;
run;

proc print data=five;
title 'Reducing the length of numeric data to 5';
format Num5 Num8 20.;
run;
```

Level 3

6. Determining the Minimum Number of Bytes for Reduced Length Numerics

The following program from the Help facility finds the minimum length of bytes (MINLEN) needed for numbers stored in a native SAS data set named **numbers**. The **numbers** data set contains the variable **Value**. The variable **Value** contains a range of numbers. In this example, the range is 8191 to 8194 for Windows and UNIX and from 269 to 272 for z/OS.

p302e06

```
/*  Windows and UNIX DATA step */
data numbers;
   input Value;
   datalines;
8191
8192
8193
8194
;

/*  z/OS DATA step */
/*
data numbers;
   input Value;
   datalines;
269
270
271
272
;
*/
data temp;
   set numbers;
   X=Value;
   do L=8 to 1 by -1;
      if X NE trunc(X,L) then
      do;
         MinLen=L+1;
         output;
         return;
      end;
   end;
run;

title;
proc print noobs;
   var Value MinLen;
run;
```

a. Run the program that is stored in **p302e06** and examine the output.

b. Investigate the Help facility to determine why the minimum length for the number 8194 is less than that of the number 8193 (Windows and UNIX) or why 272 is less than that of the number 271 (z/OS). The information can be found by following this path:

SAS Products ⇨ **Base SAS** ⇨ **SAS Language References: Concepts** ⇨ **SAS System Concepts** ⇨ **SAS Variables** ⇨ **Numeric Precision in SAS Software**

2.3 Compressing SAS Data Sets

Objectives

- Define the structure of a compressed SAS data file.
- Create a compressed SAS data file.
- List the advantages and disadvantages of compression.

49

2.03 Poll

By default, the observations in a SAS data file have varying lengths.

❍ Yes

❍ No

51

Simplified Uncompressed Data File Structure

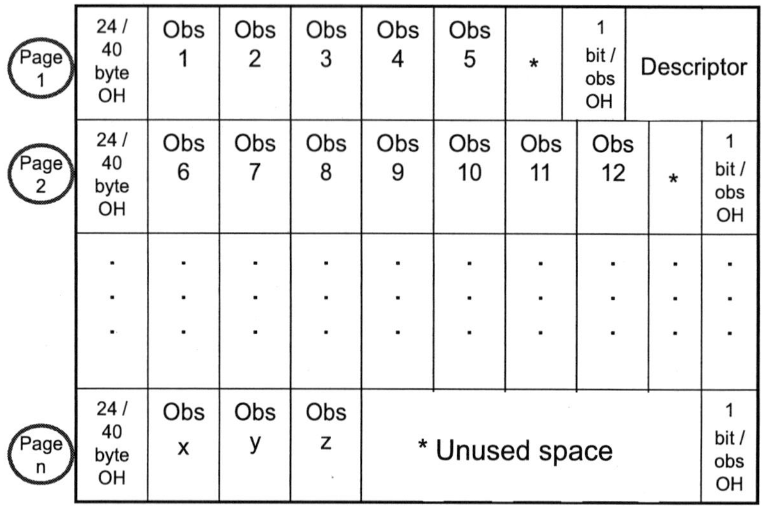

53

This is a visualization tool to help you understand how SAS data files are structured. SAS data files are not actually stored in exactly this manner.

Uncompressed SAS Data File

The following are features of uncompressed SAS data files:

- All observations use the same number of bytes.
- Each variable occupies the same number of bytes in every observation.
- Character values are padded with blanks.
- Numeric values are padded with binary zeros.
- The descriptor portion of the data set uses part of the first data set page.

54

continued...

Uncompressed SAS Data File

- There is a 24-byte overhead at the beginning of each page on 32-bit systems.
- There is a 40-byte overhead at the beginning of each page on 64-bit systems.
- There is a 1-bit per observation overhead, rounded up to the nearest byte.
- New observations are added at the end of the file. If a new page is needed for a new observation, a whole data set page is added.
- Deleted observation space is never reused, unless the entire data file is rebuilt.

55

In an uncompressed SAS data file, each observation is a fixed-length record.

Simplified Structure of a Compressed Data Set

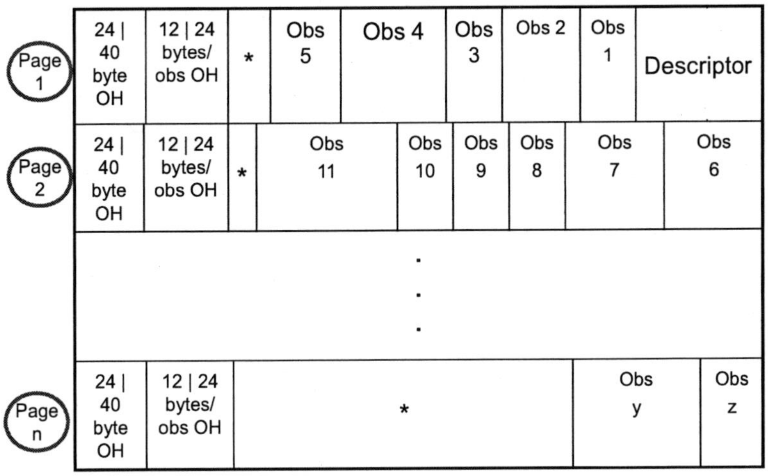

* Unused space

56

This is a visual depiction of the storage used for a compressed SAS data file.

Compressed SAS Data File

Features of compressed SAS data files:

- Each observation is a single string of bytes. Variable types and boundaries are ignored.
- Each observation can have a different length.
- Consecutive repeating characters and numbers are collapsed into fewer bytes.
- If an updated observation is larger than its original size, it is stored on either the same data set page or on a different page with a pointer to the original page.
- The descriptor portion of the data set is stored at the end of the first data set page.

57

continued...

SAS data files, but not views, can be stored in compressed form.

Compressed SAS Data File

- There is a 24-byte overhead at the beginning of each page on 32-bit systems.
- There is a 40-byte overhead at the beginning of each page on 64-bit systems.
- There is a 12-byte-per-observation overhead on 32-bit systems.
- There is a 24-byte-per-observation overhead on 64-bit systems.
- Deleted observation space can be reused if the REUSE=YES data set or system option was turned on when the SAS data file was compressed.

58

Compressing a file reduces the number of bytes required to represent each observation. In a compressed file, each observation is a variable-length record.

Compressing SAS Files

There are two different algorithms that can be used to compress files:

- the RLE (run length encoding) compression algorithm (compress=YES | CHAR)
- the RDC (Ross Data Compression) algorithm (COMPRESS=BINARY)

⚠ The optimal algorithm depends on the characteristics of your data.

59

Creating a Compressed Data File

To create a compressed data file, use the COMPRESS= output data set option or system option.

General forms of the COMPRESS= options:

```
SAS-data-set(COMPRESS=NO | YES | CHAR | BINARY)

OPTIONS COMPRESS=NO | YES | CHAR | BINARY;
```

60

COMPRESS= Value	Action
NO	does not compress the data file (default).
CHAR | YES	uses the run-length encoding (RLE) compression algorithm, which compresses repeating consecutive bytes, such as trailing blanks or repeated zeros.
BINARY	uses Ross Data Compression (RDC), which combines run-length encoding and sliding window compression.

The COMPRESS= data set option overrides the COMPRESS= system option.

The COMPRESS= options interact with two other system or data set options, POINTOBS= and REUSE=. See "COMPRESS= Data Set Option" in the dictionary of SAS language elements in *SAS® Language Reference: Dictionary* in the Base SAS documentation or use the online Help facility for additional information about these interactions.

Comparing Compression Methods

COMPRESS=YES | CHAR

- is effective with character data that contains repeated characters (such as blanks).

COMPRESS=BINARY

- takes significantly more CPU time to uncompress than COMPRESS=YES | CHAR
- is more efficient with observations greater than a 1000 bytes in length
- can be very effective with numeric data
- can be effective with character data that contains patterns, rather than simple repetitions.

61

2.04 Quiz

Open the program **p302a02**.

1. Change the data set name to **`empchar`**. Add the COMPRESS=CHAR data set option to the DATA step and submit the program.
   By what percentage was the data set reduced or increased?
2. Change the data set name to **`empbin`**. Add the COMPRESS=BINARY data set option to the DATA step and submit the program.
   By what percentage was the data set reduced or increased?

63

Using the COMPRESS=CHAR Option

Partial SAS Log (Windows)

```
data empchar(compress=char);
   merge employee_addresses employee_organization
         employee_payroll employee_phones;
   by Employee_ID;
run;

NOTE: There were 424 observations read from the data set WORK.EMPLOYEE_ADDRESSES.
NOTE: There were 424 observations read from the data set WORK.EMPLOYEE_ORGANIZATION.
NOTE: There were 424 observations read from the data set WORK.EMPLOYEE_PAYROLL.
NOTE: There were 923 observations read from the data set WORK.EMPLOYEE_PHONES.
NOTE: The data set WORK.EMPCHAR has 923 observations and 21 variables.
NOTE: Compressing data set WORK.EMPCHAR decreased size by 60.71 percent.
      Compressed is 11 pages; un-compressed would require 28 pages.
NOTE: DATA statement used (Total process time):
      real time           0.04 seconds
      cpu time            0.01 seconds
```

65

Using the COMPRESS=BINARY Option

Partial SAS Log (Windows)

```
data empbin(compress=binary);
   merge employee_addresses employee_organization
         employee_payroll employee_phones;
   by Employee_ID;
run;

NOTE: There were 424 observations read from the data set WORK.EMPLOYEE_ADDRESSES.
NOTE: There were 424 observations read from the data set WORK.EMPLOYEE_ORGANIZATION.
NOTE: There were 424 observations read from the data set WORK.EMPLOYEE_PAYROLL.
NOTE: There were 923 observations read from the data set WORK.EMPLOYEE_PHONES.
NOTE: The data set WORK.EMPBIN has 923 observations and 21 variables.
NOTE: Compressing data set WORK.EMPBIN decreased size by 57.14 percent.
      Compressed is 12 pages; un-compressed would require 28 pages.
NOTE: DATA statement used (Total process time):
      real time           0.03 seconds
      cpu time            0.03 seconds
```

67

Summary of Compression Results

Data Set	Option Used	Algorithm Used	Number of Bytes	Decreased Size
employees	None	None	458,752	0%
empchar	YES | CHAR	RLE	180,224	60.71%
empbin	BINARY	RDC	196,608	57.14%

✎ Your results might differ, depending on SAS option settings and the operating system.

68

The above comparison is for SAS 9.2 running on a Windows platform.

How SAS Compresses Data

A SAS data file has these variables:

Name	Type	Length
LastName	Character	20
FirstName	Character	15

In uncompressed form, all observations use 35 bytes for these two variables.

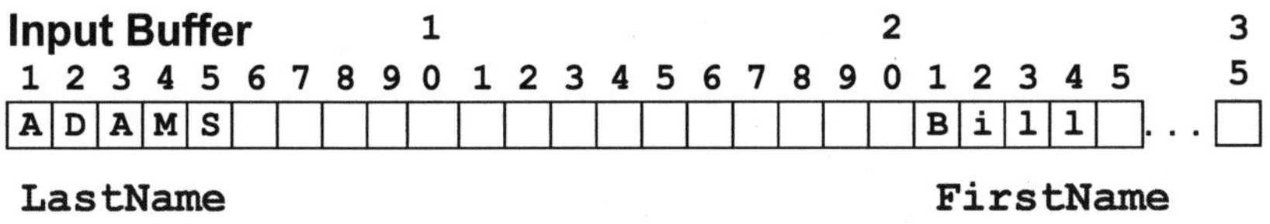

69

Using COMPRESS=CHAR | YES

In run-length encoding compressed form, the **LastName** and **FirstName** values for this observation use only 13 bytes.

1	2	3	4	5	6	7	8	9	10	11	12	13
@	A	D	A	M	S	#	@	B	I	L	L	#

LastName FirstName

- The @ is a symbol that indicates how many uncompressed characters follow.
- The # is a symbol that indicates the number of blanks repeated at this point in the observation.

70

Using COMPRESS=BINARY

Ross Data Compression uses both run-length encoding and sliding window compression.

A SAS data set has these variables:

Name	Type	Length
Answer1	Numeric	8
...		
Answer200	Numeric	8

In uncompressed form, the SAS data file resembles this:

Answer1	Answer2	Answer2	Answer4	Answer5	Answer6	...	Answer200
1	2	1	2	1	2	...	2
1	1	1	1	1	1	...	1
2	2	2	2	2	2	...	2

71

Each uncompressed observation occupies 1600 bytes of storage.

Using COMPRESS=BINARY

In Ross Data Compression form, the first observation in the data file resembles this:

1	2	3	4	5	6	7	8	9
@	+ 1	1	#	@	+ 1	2	#	%

- The @ is a symbol that indicates how many uncompressed characters follow.
- The # is a symbol that indicates the number of binary zeros repeated at this point in the observation.
- The % is a symbol that indicates how many times these values are repeated.

72

+/1 indicates the sign and exponent.

SAS data compression is always an experiment.

Compression Dependencies

Some data sets do not compress well or at all.

Because there is higher overhead for each observation, a data file can occupy more space in compressed form than in uncompressed form if the file has the following characteristics:

- few repeated characters
- small physical size
- few missing values
- short text strings

73

Compression Dependencies

SAS Log (Windows)

```
1    data orders(compress=yes);
2       set orion.orders;
3    run;

NOTE: There were 490 observations read from the data set ORION.ORDERS.
NOTE: The data set WORK.ORDERS has 490 observations and 6 variables.
NOTE: Compressing data set WORK.ORDERS decreased size by 0.00 percent.
      Compressed is 7 pages; un-compressed would require 7 pages.
NOTE: DATA statement used (Total process time):
      real time           1.04 seconds
      cpu time            0.12 seconds
```

```
55   data orders(compress=binary);
56      set orion.orders;
57   run;

NOTE: There were 490 observations read from the data set ORION.ORDERS.
NOTE: The data set WORK.ORDERS has 490 observations and 6 variables.
NOTE: Compressing data set WORK.ORDERS increased size by 28.57 percent.
      Compressed is 9 pages; un-compressed would require 7 pages.
NOTE: DATA statement used (Total process time):
      real time           0.09 seconds
      cpu time            0.09 seconds
```

p302d08

74

Compression Dependencies

When you use the COMPRESS= data set option or the COMPRESS= system option, SAS knows the following:

- the size of the overhead introduced by compression
- the maximum size of an observation

If the maximum size of the observation is less than the 12-byte (32-bit systems) or 24-byte (64-bit system) overhead introduced by compression, SAS does the following:

- disables compression
- creates an uncompressed data set
- issues a note stating that the file was not compressed

75

Compression Dependencies

SAS Log (Windows)

```
18   data test(compress=yes);
19      x=1;
20   run;

NOTE: Compression was disabled for data set WORK.TEST because
      compression overhead would increase the size of the data set.
NOTE: The data set WORK.TEST has 1 observations and 1 variables.
NOTE: DATA statement used (Total process time):
      real time           0.00 seconds
      cpu time            0.00 seconds
```

76

p302d09

Compression Trade-Offs

Uncompressed	Compressed
Usually requires more disk storage	Usually requires less disk storage
Requires less CPU time to prepare an observation for I/O	Requires more CPU time to prepare an observation for I/O
Uses more I/O operations	Uses fewer I/O operations

The savings in I/O operations greatly outweigh the increase in CPU time.

77

continued...

Compression Trade-Offs

Uncompressed	Compressed
An updated observation fits in its original location.	An updated observation might be moved from its original location.
Deleted observation space is never reused.	Deleted observation space can be reused.
New observations are always inserted at the end of the data file.	When REUSE=YES, new observations might not be inserted at the end of the data file.

78

Exercises

Level 1

7. Effects of Reading Compressed SAS Data Files

a. Submit the program **p302e07**.

b. Compare the user CPU time for reading **employees**, **emps_short**, **empchar**, and **empbin**.

employees: ______________________

emps_short: ______________________

empchar: ______________________

empbin: ______________________

Level 2

8. Compressing SAS Data Files

The following is the list of variables in the data set **orion.product_list**:

```
                    Alphabetic List of Variables and Attributes

       #    Variable          Type    Len    Format    Label

       1    Product_ID        Num       8    12.       Product ID
       4    Product_Level     Num       8    12.       Product Level
       2    Product_Name      Char     45              Product Name
       5    Product_Ref_ID    Num       8    12.       Product Reference ID
       3    Supplier_ID       Num       8    12.       Supplier ID
```

The following is the list of variables in the data set **orion.supplier**:

```
                    Alphabetic List of Variables and Attributes

     #    Variable              Type    Len    Format    Label

     6    Country               Char      2              Country
     3    Street_ID             Num       8    12.       Street ID
     5    Sup_Street_Number     Char      8              Supplier Street Number
     4    Supplier_Address      Char     45              Supplier Address
     1    Supplier_ID           Num       8    12.       Supplier ID
     2    Supplier_Name         Char     30              Supplier Name
```

a. You need to merge the two data sets together by **Supplier_ID** and create a compressed SAS data set named **supplier_names**.

Which method of compression do you think would be the most appropriate?

____

b. Merge **orion.product_list** and **orion.supplier** to create a data set **supplier_names**. Compress it using the method that you predicted in part **a**.

c. Merge **orion.product_list** and **orion.supplier** to create a data set **supplier_names**. Compress it using the alternative method.

d. Which method was better? ______________________________

e. Why was that method better? ______________________________

Your results might vary from the suggested solutions depending on the operating platform and method used to create the data on that platform.

Level 3

9. Compressing a Library

a. Write a LIBNAME statement to assign the libref **orcomp** to the path as listed below. Use the LIBNAME statement option COMPRESS=YES to compress the data sets that will be written to that data library.

Operating Environment	Library Location
Windows	C:\temp
UNIX	~/temp
z/OS	.prg3.tempdata

b. Write a PROC COPY step to copy data sets from the **orion** library to the **orcomp** library. The PROC COPY step should copy only those data sets that begin with the letter "**c**". In addition, ensure that you do not compress any of the data sets created in exercises after this one.

Hint: If you do not see compression messages the first time that you submit your code, look in the Help facility or SAS OnlineDoc at the options for the PROC COPY statement.

c. Did any of them get larger? Yes or No

d. Why or why not? ______________________________

____

____

e. Write a PROC DATASETS step with a DELETE statement to delete the library **orcomp**.

2.4 Controlling Memory (Self-Study)

Objectives

- Investigate techniques for controlling memory.
- Use system options to specify the amount of memory available.

82

Comparing Memory, I/O, and CPU Resources

The techniques that reduce CPU and I/O can increase memory usage.

- Efficient use of the I/O subsystem uses larger buffers and/or multiple buffers.
- These buffers share memory space with the other memory demands of your SAS session.

⚠ Benchmark carefully to balance the need to conserve memory with the need to reduce CPU and I/O.

83

Memory is a bigger issue on shared SAS systems (Windows servers, UNIX, z/OS) than on stand-alone SAS systems (Windows PCs). Most individual SAS users will not encounter memory problems unless their SAS programs use procedures with many distinct categorical values, perform sorts of large SAS data sets, or use large in-memory lookup tables. In the first two cases, the swapping of utility files to disk when physical memory is fully used can also increase the use of CPU and I/O resources.

Reducing Memory Usage

- Use small data set page sizes when you create data sets that will be accessed in a sparse, random pattern.
- Use a single read buffer when the data is accessed randomly instead of sequentially.
- Use BY-group processing instead of CLASS statements in those procedures that support both, especially where you have pre-sorted data or can use an existing index.

84

Using the BY Statement

Instead of using a CLASS statement to group data, you can use the BY statement to specify the variables whose values define the subgroup combinations for an analysis by a SAS procedure.

85

Using the BY Statement

What are the differences between using a BY statement and using a CLASS statement in a procedure?

BY Statement	CLASS Statement
The data set must be sorted or indexed on the BY variables.	The data set does not need to be sorted or indexed on the CLASS variables.
BY-group processing holds only one BY group in memory at a time.	The CLASS statement accumulates aggregates for all CLASS groups simultaneously in memory.
A percentage for the entire report cannot be calculated with procedures such as the REPORT or TABULATE procedures.	A percentage for the entire report can be calculated with procedures such as the REPORT or TABULATE procedures.

86

PROC MEANS with a BY Statement

```
proc means data=orion.order_fact mean median
           maxdec=2;
   format Order_Date year4.;
   by Order_Date;
   var Quantity -- CostPrice_Per_Unit;
run;
```

87 p302d10

PROC MEANS with a BY Statement

Partial PROC MEANS Output with a BY Statement

```
--------------------Date Order was placed by Customer=2003-------------------

                              The MEANS Procedure

Variable            Label                                 Mean          Median
-------------------------------------------------------------------------------
Quantity            Quantity Ordered                      1.82            2.00
Total_Retail_Price  Total Retail Price for This Product 177.59          105.95
CostPrice_Per_Unit  Cost Price Per Unit                  42.72           31.80
-------------------------------------------------------------------------------

-------------------- Date Order was placed by Customer=2004 --------------------

Variable            Label                                 Mean          Median
-------------------------------------------------------------------------------
Quantity            Quantity Ordered                      1.69            1.00
Total_Retail_Price  Total Retail Price for This Product 146.13           85.65
CostPrice_Per_Unit  Cost Price Per Unit                  37.10           25.68
-------------------------------------------------------------------------------
```

88

PROC MEANS with a CLASS Statement

```
proc means data=orion.order_fact mean median
           maxdec=2;
   format Order_Date year4.;
   class Order_Date;
   var Quantity -- CostPrice_Per_Unit;
run;
```

89

p302d10

PROC MEANS with a CLASS Statement

Partial PROC MEANS Output with a CLASS Statement

The MEANS Procedure

Date Order was placed by Customer	N Obs	Variable	Label	Mean	Median
2003	128	Quantity	Quantity Ordered	1.82	2.00
		Total_Retail_Price	Total Retail Price for This Product	177.59	105.95
		CostPrice_Per_Unit	Cost Price Per Unit	42.72	31.80
2004	108	Quantity	Quantity Ordered	1.69	1.00
		Total_Retail_Price	Total Retail Price for This Product	146.13	85.65
		CostPrice_Per_Unit	Cost Price Per Unit	37.10	25.68
2005	90	Quantity	Quantity Ordered	1.70	1.00
		Total_Retail_Price	Total Retail Price for This Product	187.20	77.00
		CostPrice_Per_Unit	Cost Price Per Unit	49.45	25.20
2006	143	Quantity	Quantity Ordered	1.57	1.00
		Total_Retail_Price	Total Retail Price for This Product	149.70	92.80
		CostPrice_Per_Unit	Cost Price Per Unit	44.25	29.95
2007	148	Quantity	Quantity Ordered	1.93	2.00
		Total_Retail_Price	Total Retail Price for This Product	157.49	80.95
		CostPrice_Per_Unit	Cost Price Per Unit	37.53	21.35

90

2.05 Quiz

Open and submit the program **p302a03**. Answer the following questions:

1. What is the advantage of technique 1?

2. What is the advantage of technique 2?

92

p302a03

```
options fullstimer;

/*  Set up for TABULATE demo */

data order_fact(index=(Order_Date));
   set orion.order_fact;
run;

/*  Technique 1 */

proc tabulate data=order_fact;
   format Order_Date year4.;
   class Order_Date;
   var Quantity -- CostPrice_Per_Unit;
   tables Order_Date*(Quantity Total_Retail_Price CostPrice_Per_Unit),
          n mean median pctsum;
run;

/*  Technique 2 */

proc tabulate data=order_fact;
   format Order_Date year4.;
   by Order_Date;
   var Quantity -- CostPrice_Per_Unit;
   tables Quantity Total_Retail_Price CostPrice_Per_Unit,
          n mean median pctsum;
run;

options nofullstimer;
```

Using Memory System Options

The operating environment will use disk-based virtual memory when physical memory is depleted. This adversely affects performance.

Use these SAS system options to limit the amount of memory used by SAS:

- REALMEMSIZE=
- MEMSIZE=

⚠ Set the REALMEMSIZE= and MEMSIZE= options to values below the amount of available physical memory to prevent page thrashing or memory swapping.

95

Consult the SAS OnlineDoc to see specifics for each operating environment.

Using System Options to Control Memory

The total amount of memory that a SAS job can consume is limited by the MEMSIZE= **invocation** system option.

```
-MEMSIZE=n | n K | n M | n G | hexX | MIN | MAX
```

96

Consult the SAS OnlineDoc for specifics for each operating environment.

Using the MEMSIZE= Option

The MEMSIZE= option places a limit on the total amount of memory that SAS dynamically allocates at any time. This memory is supported by a combination of real memory and space for utility files on disk.

Increase this option's value in small increments until you find your optimal value.

✎ SAS does not automatically reserve or allocate the amount of memory that you specify in the MEMSIZE= system option. SAS will use only as much memory as it needs to complete a process.

97

Using the REALMEMSIZE= System Option

Some SAS procedures use the REALMEMSIZE= **invocation** option to specify how much memory* the procedure can allocate and use without inducing excessive page swapping.

```
-REALMEMSIZE=n | nK | nM | nG | hexX | MIN | MAX
```

The REALMEMSIZE= option should never be set beyond the amount of real memory.

* In UNIX and z/OS, REALMEMSIZE= specifies real (physical) memory. In Windows, REALMEMSIZE= specifies virtual memory.

98

2.5 Controlling the Page Size and the Number of Available Buffers (Self-Study)

Objectives

- Control the page size of a SAS data set.
- Use system and data set options to control memory usage.
- Describe the effect of operating environment caching.

101

Data Set Page Size (Review)

The page size of a SAS data set is specified in bytes. The data set page is the unit of data transfer between the SAS storage device and main memory.

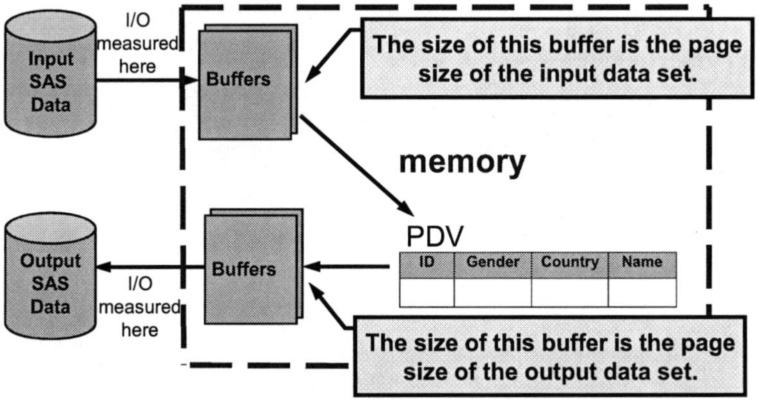

102

Controlling Page Size and Memory Usage

You can use the BUFSIZE= system option or data set option to control the page size of an **output** SAS data set.

```
BUFSIZE= n | nK | nM | nG | nT | hexX | MIN | MAX
```

You can use the BUFNO= system option or data set option to control the number of SAS buffers open simultaneously in memory.

```
BUFNO= n
```

103

BUFSIZE= can only be used on output SAS data sets. BUFSIZE= sets the page size of a SAS data file, which is a permanent attribute of the data set.

Increasing the BUFSIZE= option is sometimes useful for SAS data sets that are read sequentially (top to bottom). Using a small BUFSIZE= value and BUFNO=1 is useful for SAS data sets that are read using random access.

BUFSIZE= Value	Specifies
n | *n*K | *n*M | *n*G | *n*T	specifies the page size in multiples of 1 (bytes); 1,024 (kilobytes); 1,048,576 (megabytes); 1,073,741,824 (gigabytes); or 1,099,511,627,776 (terabytes). For example, a value of 8 specifies 8 bytes, and a value of 3M specifies 3,145,728 bytes. **The default is 0, which causes SAS to use the minimum optimal page size for the operating environment.**
*hex*X	specifies the page size as a hexadecimal value. You must specify the value beginning with a number (0-9), followed by an X. For example, the value 2dx sets the page size to 45 bytes.
MIN	sets the page size to the smallest possible number in your operating environment, down to the smallest four-byte, signed integer, which is $-2^{31}-1$, or approximately -2 billion bytes. This setting might cause unexpected results and should be avoided. Use BUFSIZE=0 in order to reset the buffer page size to the default value in your operating environment.
MAX	sets the page size to the maximum possible number in your operating environment, up to the largest four-byte, signed integer, which is $2^{31}-1$, or approximately 2 billion bytes.

The specific values for the BUFSIZE= option depend on your operating environment.

Controlling Page Size and Memory Usage

The product of BUFNO= and BUFSIZE= determines how much data can be transferred in a read operation.

BUFSIZE	BUFNO	Bytes transferred in one I/O
16384	2	32,768

Increasing either BUFSIZE= or BUFNO= increases the amount of data that can be transferred in a read operation.

In Windows and UNIX, using the default BUFSIZE and BUFNO is recommended.

104

Controlling Memory Usage

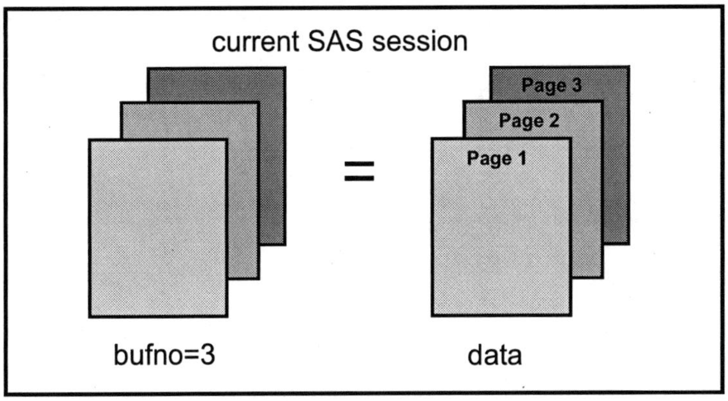

The buffer number is not a permanent attribute of the data set and is valid only for the current step or SAS session.

105

Using the Operating Environment Cache in Windows and UNIX (Review)

- A file cache is an area of memory that holds recently accessed data.
- By default, SAS reads and writes data through the operating environment file cache, not by direct I/O.
- The maximum I/O throughput rate depends on how fast the operating environment file cache can process the data.

106

For information about structuring RAID arrays and SAN arrays optimally for SAS, see this white paper: *Best Practices for Configuring your IO Subsystem for SAS® 9 Applications* (support.sas.com/rnd/papers/sgf07/sgf2007-iosubsystem.pdf).

Using the SGIO System Option in Windows

The SGIO invocation system option performs the following functions:

- activates the Scatter-Read/Gather-Write I/O feature, which disables file caching
- improves I/O performance for SAS I/O files that require a single sequential pass

General form of the SGIO system option:

```
NOSGIO | SGIO;
```

107

The default is NOSGIO.

✎ SGIO is available as a data set option in SAS 9.2.

Using the SGIO System Option in Windows

When SGIO is active, SAS does the following:

- uses the number of buffers that are specified by the BUFNO= system option to transfer data between disk and RAM
- bypasses Windows File Caching when reading or writing data
- reads ahead of the number of pages specified by the BUFNO= system option and places the data in memory before it is needed

When the data is needed, it is already in memory and there is, in effect, a direct memory access.

⚠ Try different values of the BUFNO= system option to tune each SAS job or DATA step.

108

Scatter-read/gather-write is active only for SAS I/O opened in INPUT or OUTPUT mode. If any SAS I/O files are opened in UPDATE or RANDOM mode, SGIO is inactive for that process. Compressed and encrypted files can also be read ahead using scatter-read/gather-write. I/O performance usually improves as the value for the BUFNO increases.

Using Direct File I/O in UNIX

The ENABLEDIRECTIO and USEDIRECTIO LIBNAME statement options, when used together, perform the following functions:

- activate direct I/O access
- bypass UNIX file caching
- improve I/O performance for SAS I/O files that require a single sequential pass

The LIBNAME statement option enables direct I/O to any file in the library. The data set option allows direct I/O to the data set for this SAS program step only.

109

Data sets in the library specified without the USEDIRECTIO data set option use UNIX caching.

Using Direct File I/O in UNIX

General form of the ENABLEDIRECTIO and USEDIRECTIO= LIBNAME statement options:

```
LIBNAME libref 'directory' USEDIRECTIO=NO|YES
                           ENABLEDIRECTIO;
```

The USEDIRECTIO option can also be a data set option.

General form of the USEDIRECTIO SAS data set option:

```
SAS-data-set-name (USEDIRECTIO=NO|YES)
```

110

For more information about using direct file I/O in UNIX, refer to the following:

support.sas.com/documentation/cdl/en/hostunx/61879/HTML/default/chloptfmain.htm

2.6 Chapter Review

Chapter Review

1. What is the purpose of the SASFILE statement?

2. Name the two techniques for reducing data set size.

3. What are the two types of SAS compression?

112

2.7 Solutions

Solutions to Exercises

1. **Using the SASFILE Statement**

   a. Open the program **p302e01** and submit it.

   b. Note the following resource utilizations:

   1) User CPU Time: ______________________________

   2) I/O: ______________________________
   (not applicable on Windows)

   3) User Memory: ______________________________

   The answers are specific to your operating environment.

   c. Add the appropriate statement(s) to open and load the entire data set **`orion.organization_dim`** into memory. At the end of the program, close the data set.

d. Submit the revised program.

p302s01

```
options fullstimer;
sasfile orion.organization_dim load;

proc print data=orion.organization_dim noobs;
   where Department='Administration';
   var Employee_ID Employee_Country Section Job_Title;
run;

proc means data=orion.organization_dim min mean max;
   var Salary;
   class Department;
run;

proc report data=orion.organization_dim headline headskip nowd;
   column Company Department Employee_Hire_Date
          Employee_BirthDate HiredAge;
   define Company/order;
   define Department/order;
   define HiredAge/computed format=12.2 'Age when Hired';
   compute HiredAge;
      HiredAge=yrdif(Employee_BirthDate.sum,
                     Employee_Hire_Date.sum,'Act/Act');
   endcomp;
run;

proc freq data=orion.organization_dim;
   table Department*Company/norow nocol;
run;

proc means data=orion.organization_dim min mean max maxdec=2;
   class Company;
   var Salary;
run;

sasfile orion.organization_dim close;
options nofullstimer;
```

e. Note the following resource utilizations:

1) User CPU Time: ______________________________

2) I/O: ______________________________
(not applicable on Windows)

3) User Memory: ______________________________

✎ The answers are specific to your operating environment.

f. Which resources were conserved?

User CPU time should decrease. If I/O is reported, there should be a significant drop in I/O.

2. Using Multiple SASFILE Statements

a. Open the program **p302e02** and submit it.

b. Add the appropriate statement(s) to open and load both the **orion.employee_addresses** and **orion.employee_donations** data sets into memory. At the end of the program, close the data sets.

c. Submit the revised program.

p302s02

```
options fullstimer;
sasfile orion.employee_addresses open;
sasfile orion.employee_donations open;

proc means data=orion.employee_donations sum mean median;
   class Recipients;
   var Qtr1-Qtr4;
run;

proc freq data=orion.employee_donations;
   tables Recipients;
run;

proc report data=orion.employee_addresses  headline headskip nowd;
   columns Employee_ID Employee_Name City State;
   where Country='US';
run;

proc freq data=orion.employee_addresses;
   tables Country;
run;

proc sql;
   select Employee_Name,
          sum(Qtr1, Qtr2, Qtr3, Qtr4) as Total_Contribution,
          Recipients
      from orion.employee_addresses  as a,
           orion.employee_donations as d
         where a.Employee_ID=d.Employee_ID;
quit;

sasfile orion.employee_addresses close;
sasfile orion.employee_donations close;
options nofullstimer;
```

3. Using the APPEND Procedure with the SASFILE Statement

a. Open the program **p302e03**.

b. Add the appropriate statement(s) to open and load the entire **work.sales** data set into memory, a PROC APPEND step to append the temporary **work.nonsales** data set to the temporary **sales** data set, and a PROC PRINT step to print the **work.sales** data set. At the end of the program, close the data set.

c. Submit the revised program.

p302s03

```
/**************************************/
/* The COPY procedure is creating a   */
/* temporary copy of the data sets    */
/* orion.sales and                    */
/* orion.nonsales                     */
/* so the integrity of the original   */
/* data can be maintained for other   */
/* demos and exercises.               */
/**************************************/

proc copy in=orion out=work;
   select sales nonsales;
run;

sasfile sales open;

proc append base=sales data=nonsales force;
run;

proc print data=sales;
run;

sasfile sales close;
```

4. Creating Reduced Length Numerics

a. Use PROC CONTENTS to determine the names and types of the variables in each of the data sets.

p302s04

```
proc contents data=orion.catalog;
run;

proc contents data=orion.internet;
run;

proc contents data=orion.retail;
run;
```

b. Open the program **p302e04**. Edit the DATA step to concatenate the three data sets to create a data set named **all_customers**. Appropriately reduce the length of the numeric variables using an adequate length for the values of the variables.

p302s04

```
/**************************************/
/*  Do not reduce the length of       */
/*  the variables Total_Retail_Price  */
/*  or CostPrice_Per_Unit because     */
/*  they are not integer values.      */
/**************************************/

data all_customers;
   length Customer_ID Employee_ID Street_ID
          Order_Date Delivery_Date
          Order_ID Product_ID 4 Quantity 3;
   set orion.catalog orion.internet orion.retail;
run;
```

c. Use PROC CONTENTS to check the length of the numeric variables.

p302s04

```
proc contents data=all_customers;
run;
```

5. Creating Reduced Length Numerics and Precision

Open the program **p302e05** and submit it. At what point in the sequence of numbers does the length of the variable **Num5** lose precision?

The variable **Num5** loses precision at the number 610000000000 on Windows and UNIX and at 1010000000000 on z/OS.

6. Determining the Minimum Number of Bytes for Reduced Length Numerics

a. Run the program that is stored in **p302e06** and examine the output.

b. Investigate the Help facility to determine why the minimum length for the number 8194 is less than that of the number 8193 (Windows and UNIX) or why 272 is less than that of the number 271 (z/OS).

The minimum length required for the value 271 (or 8193) is greater than the minimum required for the value 272 (or 8194). This fact illustrates that it is possible for the largest number in a range of numbers to require fewer bytes of storage than a smaller number. If precision is needed for all numbers in a range, you should use the minimum length for all the numbers, not only the largest one.

7. Effects of Reading Compressed SAS Data Files

a. Submit the program **p302e07**.

b. Compare the user CPU time for reading **employees**, **emps_short**, **empchar**, and **empbin**.

CPU times vary by platform and other factors not controllable by SAS.

8. Compressing SAS Data Files

a. Which method of compression do you think would be the most appropriate?

Because the data set **supplier_name** is heavily character data, CHAR is probably most appropriate.

b. Merge **orion.product_list** and **orion.supplier** to create a data set **supplier_names**. Compress it using the method you predicted in part **a**.

p302s08

```
proc sort data=orion.product_list out=product_list;
   by Supplier_ID;
run;

data sales(compress=char);
   merge orion.supplier product_list;
   by Supplier_ID;
run;
```

c. Merge **orion.product_list** and **orion.supplier** to create a data set **supplier_names**. Compress it using the alternative method.

p302s08

```
proc sort data=orion.product_list out=product_list;
   by Supplier_ID;
run;

data sales(compress=binary);
   merge orion.supplier product_list;
   by Supplier_ID;
run;
```

d. Which method was better?

CHAR

e. Why was that method better?

Heavily character data

9. Compressing a Library

a. Write a LIBNAME statement to assign the libref **orcomp** to the path as listed below. Use the LIBNAME statement option COMPRESS=YES to compress the data sets that will be written to that data library.

b. Write a PROC COPY step to copy data sets from the **orion** library to the **orcomp** library. The PROC COPY step should copy only those data sets that begin with the letter "**c**". In addition, ensure that you do not compress any of the data sets created in exercises after this one.

c. Did any of them get larger? **Yes** or No

d. Why or why not? Some of the data sets increased in size. They were not large data sets.

e. Write a PROC DATASETS step.

p302s09

```
libname orcomp 'C:\temp' compress=yes;                    /* Windows */
* libname orcomp '~/temp' compress=yes;                     /* UNIX    */
* libname orcomp '.workshop.tempdata' compress=yes; /* z/OS    */

proc copy in=orion out=orcomp noclone;
   select c: ;
run;
proc datasets lib=orcomp;
   delete c: ;
quit;
libname orcomp clear;
```

Solutions to Student Activities (Polls/Quizzes)

2.01 Multiple Choice Poll – Correct Answer

In addition to the I/O decrease when the DATA step creates **`bonus`**, where does Program 2 have additional decrease of I/O?

a. Fewer variables are read into the program data vector from **`orion.staff`** in Program 2 because of the KEEP= data set option.

b. The PROC MEANS in Program 2 loads a smaller version of **`bonus`**.

c. There is no additional decrease in I/O; all of the decrease in I/O occurs when the data set **`bonus`** is created by the DATA step.

16

2.02 Poll – Correct Answer

Open the program **p302a01** and submit it.

Look at the log.

Are the values of X and Y equal?

❍ Yes

❍ No

41

2.03 Poll – Correct Answer

By default, the observations in a SAS data file have varying lengths.

❍ Yes
❍ No

By default, SAS observations have a fixed length.

52

2.04 Quiz – Correct Answer

Open the program **p302a02**.

1. Change the data set name to **empchar**. Add the COMPRESS=CHAR data set option to the DATA step and submit the program.
   By what percentage was the data set reduced or increased?

```
data empchar(compress=char);
   merge employee_addresses
         employee_organization
         employee_payroll
         employee_phones;
   by Employee_ID;
run;
```

64

continued...

2.04 Quiz – Correct Answer

Open the program **p302a02**.

2. Change the data set name to **empbin**. Add the COMPRESS=BINARY data set option to the DATA step and submit the program.
   By what percentage was the data set reduced or increased?

```
data empbin(compress=binary);
   merge employee_addresses
         employee_organization
         employee_payroll
         employee_phones;
   by Employee_ID;
run;
```

66

continued...

2.05 Quiz – Correct Answer

Open and submit the program **p302a03**. Answer the following questions:

1. What is the advantage of technique 1?

   Technique 1 enables the correct use of the PCTSUM statistic.

2. What is the advantage of technique 2?

93

2.05 Quiz – Correct Answer

Open and submit the program **p302a03**. Answer the following questions:

1. What is the advantage of technique 1?

   Technique 1 enables the correct use of the PCTSUM statistic.

2. What is the advantage of technique 2?

   Technique 2 uses much less memory, but the results for the PCTSUM statistic are not what you want.

94

Solutions to Chapter Review

Chapter Review – Correct Answers

1. What is the purpose of the SASFILE statement?
   The SASFILE statement is used to load an entire SAS data set into memory and hold it there for subsequent DATA or PROC steps to process.
2. Name the two techniques for reducing data set size.
   Storing integer numbers as reduced length numerics and SAS data compression
3. What are the two types of SAS compression?
   CHAR and binary

113

Chapter 3 Accessing Observations

3.1 Creating an Index

Objectives

- Define indexes.
- List the uses of indexes.
- Use the DATA step to create indexes.
- Use PROC DATASETS to create and maintain indexes.
- Use PROC SQL to create and maintain indexes.

3

3.01 Multiple Answer Poll

Do any of the data files that you use have indexes?

a. Yes, my SAS data sets have indexes.
b. Yes, I use data from an RDBMS (such as Oracle, Teradata, Sybase, or DB2) that has indexes.
c. No, none of the data that I use has indexes.

5

Using Indexes

An *index* is an optional file that you can create for a SAS data file that does the following:

- points to observations based on the values of one or more key index variables
- provides direct access to specific observations

✎ An index locates an observation by value.

6

Simplified Index File

The index file consists of entries that are organized in a tree structure and connected by pointers.

Partial Listing of **orion.sales_history**

Customer_ID	Employee_ID	. . .
14958	121031	. . .
14844	121042	. . .
14864	99999999	. . .
14909	120436	. . .
14862	120481	. . .
14853	120454	. . .
14838	121039	. . .
14842	121051	. . .
14815	99999999	. . .
14797	120604	. . .
. . .	. . .	. . .

Simplified Index

Customer_ID Key Value	Record Identifier (RID) Page(obs, obs, ...)
4006	17(85)
4021	17(89)
4059	17(90)
4063	17(80, 86)
. . .	
14958	1(1, 24)
14972	1(14)
. . .	

✎ The index is stored with the key values in ascending sorted order.

The Purpose of Indexes

Indexes can provide direct access to observations in SAS data sets to accomplish the following:

- yield faster access to small subsets (WHERE)
- return observations in sorted order (BY)
- perform table lookup operations (SET with KEY=)
- join observations (PROC SQL)
- modify observations (MODIFY with KEY=)

8

Why Use an Index?

How is data processed if the input data is not indexed?

```
data customer14958;
   set orion.sales_history;
   where Customer_ID=14958;
run;
```

9

Reading SAS Data Sets without an Index

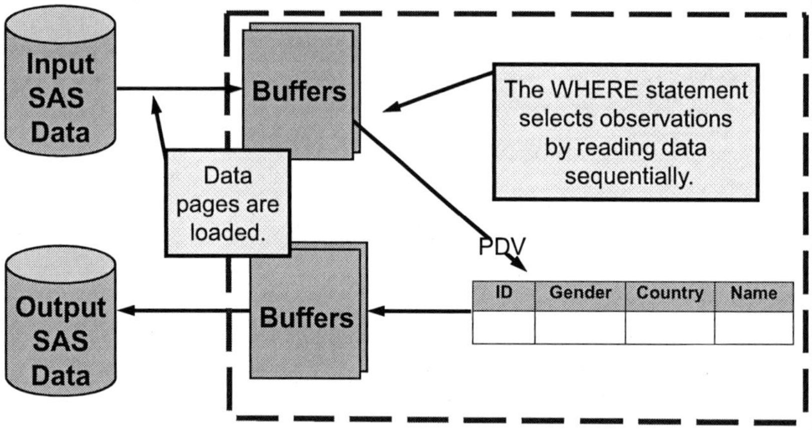

15

Why Use an Index?

How is data processed if the input data is indexed?

```
data customer14958;
   set orion.sales_history;
   where Customer_ID=14958;
run;
```

16

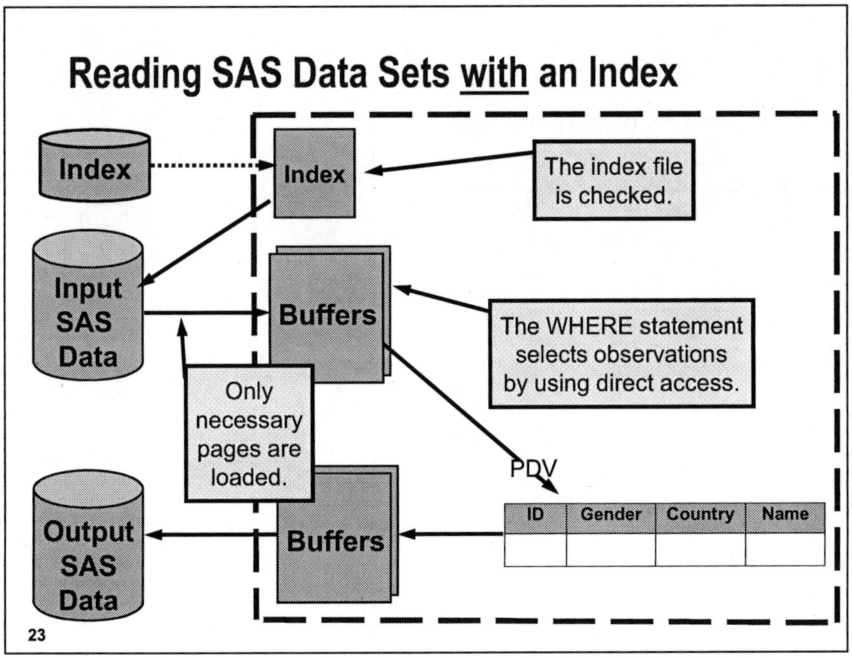

When SAS uses an index to process data, SAS does the following:

- performs a binary search on the index file
- positions the index to the first entry containing a qualified value
- transfers a page of data containing the first record identifier for the qualified value to a buffer
- directly accesses the value specified by the record identifier
- positions the index to the next entry containing a qualified value
- transfers the page of data, if it is not already in the buffer
- directly accesses the value specified by the record identifier
- continues to process the data until there is no more data that satisfies the WHERE expression

If the stored data values are sorted in ascending order by the indexed variables, fewer I/O operations are required. If the data is not sorted on the index key values, but observations with the same key values are near each other in the file, I/O will be minimized.

Number of Index Buffers (Self-Study)

The buffer size of a SAS index is the unit of data transfer between the SAS storage device and main memory.

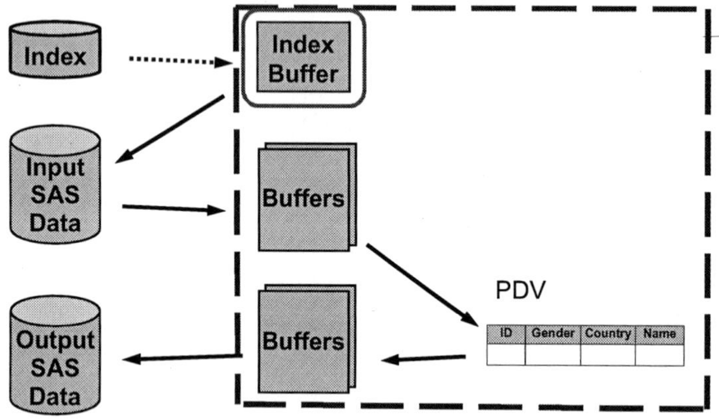

24

Controlling the Number of Index Buffers (Self-Study)

You can use the IBUFNO= system option to control the number of index buffers that are open simultaneously in memory.

```
IBUFNO=n | nK | nM | nG | nT
```

25

SAS automatically allocates a minimal number of buffers in order to navigate the index file. Typically, you do not need to specify extra buffers. However, using IBUFNO= to specify extra buffers can improve execution time by limiting the number of input/output operations that are required for a particular index file. However, the improvement in execution time comes at the expense of increased memory consumption.

Whereas too few buffers allocated to the index file decrease performance, over-allocation of index buffers creates performance problems as well. Experimentation is the best way to determine the optimal number of index buffers. For example, experiment with IBUFNO=3, then IBUFNO=4, and so on, until you find the least number of buffers that produces satisfactory performance results.

IBUFSIZE= Value	Specifies
n | *n*K | *n*M | *n*G | *n*T	specifies the number of extra index buffers to be allocated in multiples of 1 (bytes); 1,024 (kilobytes); 1,048,576 (megabytes); 1,073,741,824 (gigabytes); or 1,099,511,627,776 (terabytes). For example, a value of **8** specifies eight buffers, and a value of **3k** specifies 3,072 buffers. The maximum value is 10,000.
*hex*X	specifies the number of extra index buffers as a hexadecimal value. You must specify the value beginning with a number (0-9), followed by an X.
MIN	sets the number of extra index buffers to 0. This is the default.
MAX	sets the number of extra index buffers to 0. This is the default

How Is the Index File Checked?

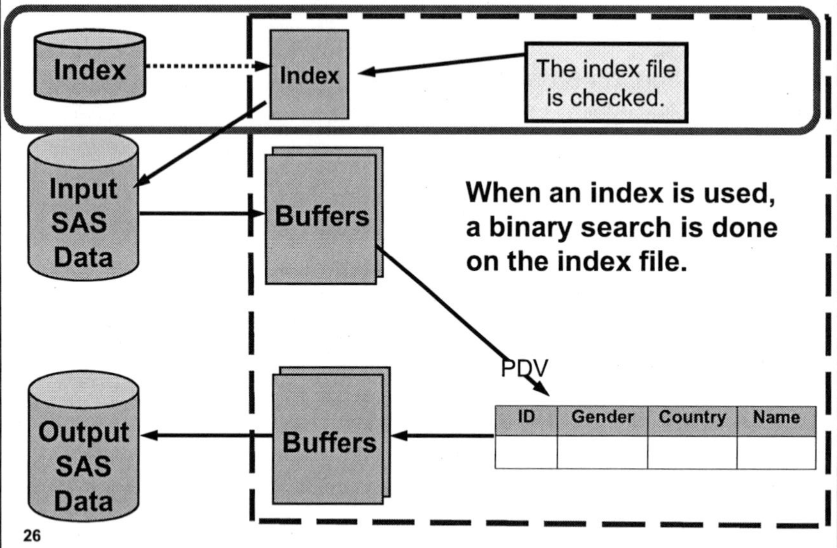

26

Using a Binary Search

Partial Listing of
`orion.sales_history`

RID	Customer_ ID	Employee_ ID	. . .
1	14958	121031	. . .
2	14844	121042	. . .
3	14864	99999999	. . .
4	14909	120436	. . .
.	.	.	
22	[illegible]	[illegible]	. . .
23	14844	121042	. . .
24	14958	121031	. . .
25	14821	120918	. . .
. . .	. . .	. . .	. . .

```
where Customer_ID=14958;
```

Simplified Index File

Customer_ ID Key Value	Record Identifier (RID) Page(obs, obs, ...)
4006	17(85)
4021	17(89)
4059	17(90)
4063	17(80, 86)
. . .	
14958	1(1, 24)
14972	1(14)
. . .	

27 ...

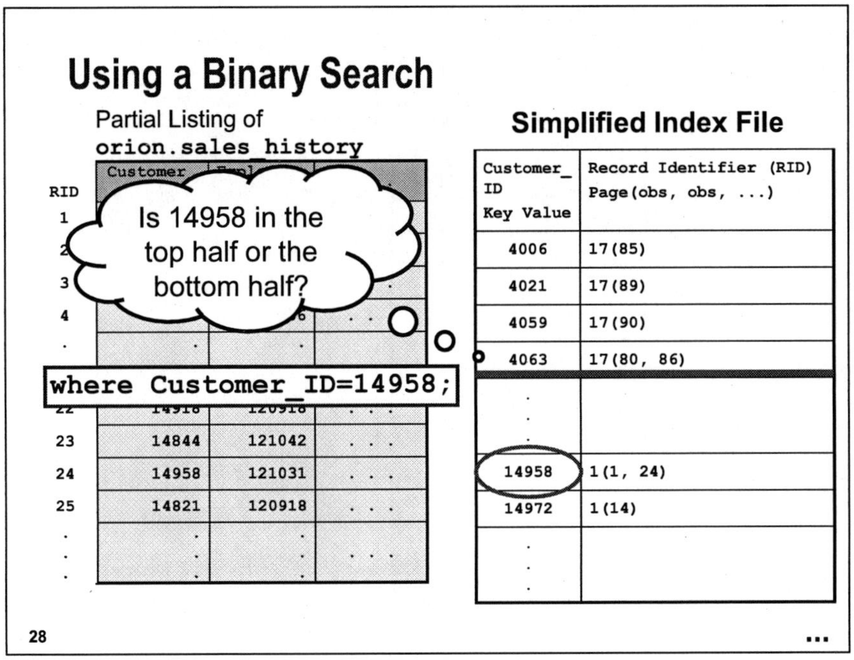

The binary search essentially divides the index file in half and asks, "Is the key value that I am searching for above or below the halfway point?" The binary search continues to divide the remaining portions of the index file in half until the key value is found.

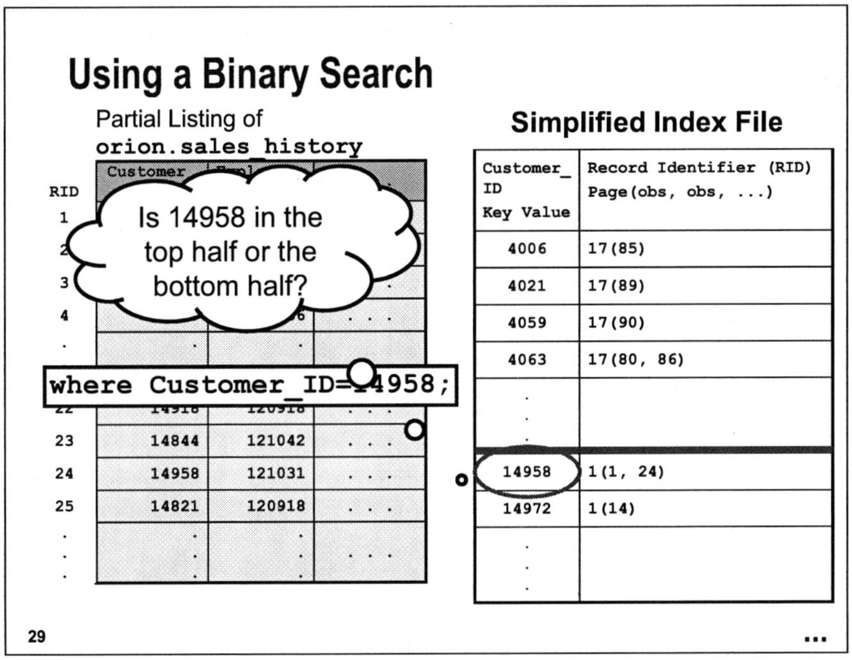

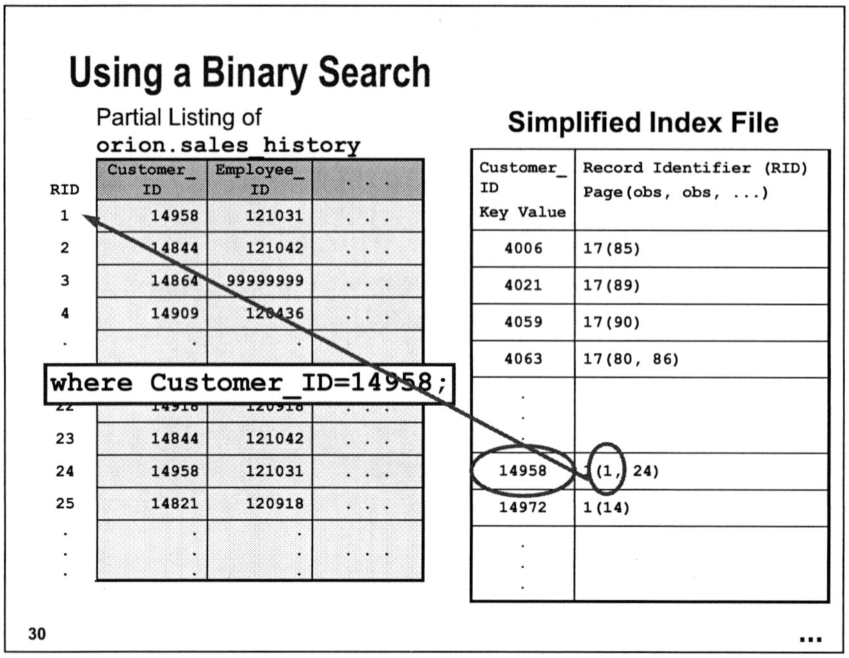
Using a Binary Search
Partial Listing of
orion.sales_history
RID
Customer_ ID
Employee_ ID
. . .
1 14958 121031 . . .
2 14844 121042 . . .
3 14864 99999999 . . .
4 14909 120436 . . .
where Customer_ID=14958;
23 14844 121042 . . .
24 14958 121031 . . .
25 14821 120918 . . .
Simplified Index File
Customer_ ID Key Value
Record Identifier (RID) Page(obs, obs, ...)
4006 17(85)
4021 17(89)
4059 17(90)
4063 17(80, 86)
14958 1(1, 24)
14972 1(14)
30
...

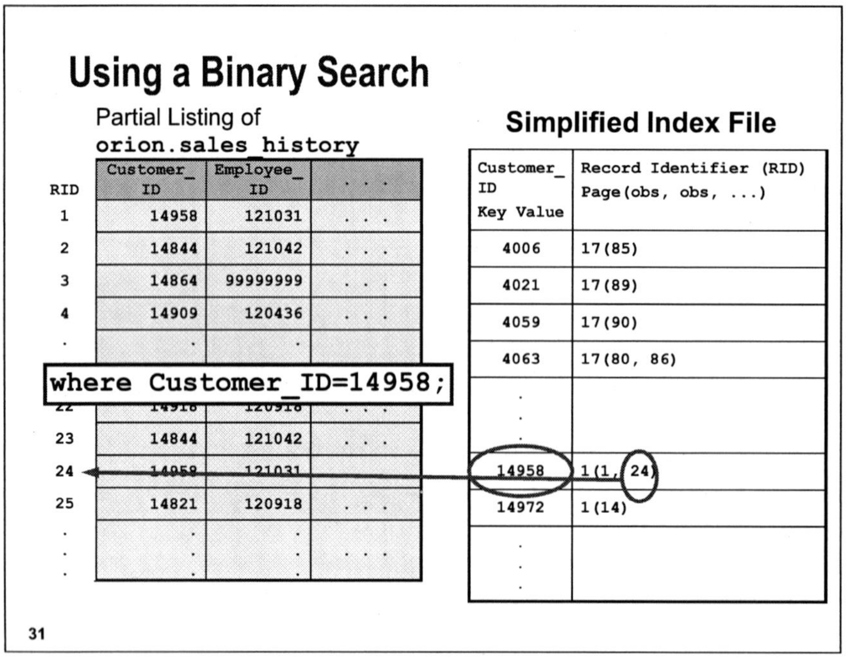
Using a Binary Search
Partial Listing of
orion.sales_history
RID
Customer_ ID
Employee_ ID
. . .
1 14958 121031 . . .
2 14844 121042 . . .
3 14864 99999999 . . .
4 14909 120436 . . .
where Customer_ID=14958;
23 14844 121042 . . .
24 14958 121031
25 14821 120918 . . .
Simplified Index File
Customer_ ID Key Value
Record Identifier (RID) Page(obs, obs, ...)
4006 17(85)
4021 17(89)
4059 17(90)
4063 17(80, 86)
14958 1(1, 24)
14972 1(14)
31

3.02 Multiple Choice Poll

If the WHERE statement retrieves a small subset of data, which of these resources is conserved?

a. I/O
b. Disk space
c. Memory
d. Programmer time

33

Business Scenario

The SAS data set **orion.sales_history** is often queried with a WHERE statement.

Partial Listing of **orion.sales_history**

Customer_ID	...	Order_ID	Order_Type	Product_ID	...	Product_Group	...
14958	...	1230016296	1	210200600078	...	N.D. Gear, Kids	...
14844	...	1230096476	1	220100100354	...	Eclipse Clothing	...
14864	...	1230028104	2	240600100115	...	Bathing Suits	...
14909	...	1230044374	1	240100200001	...	Darts	...
14862	...	1230021668	1	240500200056	...	Running Clothes	...
14853	...	1230021653	1	220200200085	...	Shoes	...
14838	...	1230140184	1	220100300042	...	Knitwear	...
14842	...	1230025285	1	240200100053	...	Golf	...
14815	...	1230109468	3	230100700004	...	Tents	...
14797	...	1230168587	1	220101000004	...	Shorts	...

35

Business Scenario

You need to create three indexes on the most frequently used subsetting columns.

Index Name	Index Variables
Customer_ID	Customer_ID
Product_Group	Product_Group
SaleID	Order_ID Product_ID

Partial Listing of **orion.sales_history**

Customer_ID	. . .	Order_ID	Order_Type	Product_ID	. . .	Product_Group	. . .
14958	. . .	1230016296	1	210200600078	. . .	N.D. Gear, Kids	. . .
14844	. . .	1230096476	1	220100100354	. . .	Eclipse Clothing	. . .

36

Creating an Index

Customer_ID
Order_ID
Product_ID
Product_Group

Key variables in **orion.sales_history**

Customer_ID
Product_Group
SaleID

Indexes in the index file for **orion.sales_history**

sales_history.sas7bdat   sales_history.sas7bndx

Directory-based Index File Naming Conventions

Index Name	Index Variables	Index Type
Customer_ID	Customer_ID	Simple
Product_Group	Product_Group	Simple
SaleID	Order_ID Product_ID	Composite

37

Index Terminology

There are two types of indexes.

Type	Based On	Name	Example
Simple	the value of only one variable	automatically given the same name as its key variable	`Customer_ID` `Product_Group`

Composite	the values of more than one variable concatenated to form a single value	must be given a name that is not the same as any variable or existing index	`SaleID=`
			`(Order_ID`
			`Product_ID)`

38

Index Terminology

Index options include the following:

UNIQUE	Values of the key variable(s) must be unique. This option prevents an observation with a duplicate value for the key variable(s) from being added to the data set.

Partial Listing of **`orion.sales_history`**

Customer_ID	Employee_ID	. . .	Order_ID	Order_Type	Product_ID	Quantity	. . .
14958	121031	. . .	1230016296	1	210200600078	1	. . .
14844	121042	. . .	1230098476	1	220100100354	1	. . .
14864	99999999	. . .	1230028104	2	240600100115	1	. . .
14909	120436	. . .	1230044374	1	240100200001	1	. . .
14862	120481	. . .	1230021668	1	240500200056	1	. . .
14853	120454	. . .	1230021653	1	220200200085	3	. . .
14838	121039	. . .	1230140184	1	220100300042	4	. . .

The concatenation of the values for **`Order_ID`** and **`Product_ID`** forms a unique identifier for a row of data.

39

In an existing data set, if the variable(s) on which you attempt to create a unique index has duplicate values, the index is not created and an error message is written to the SAS log.

Index Terminology

Index options include the following:

NOMISS	excludes all observations with missing values from the index. Observations with missing values can still be read from the data set, but not using the index.

- If there is a large number of missing values for the key variable(s), the NOMISS option can create a smaller index file.
- An index created with the NOMISS option is not used for the following processing:
  - a BY statement
  - a WHERE expression satisfied by missing values

⚠ NOMISS cannot be used when you create indexes using PROC SQL.

40

3.03 Multiple Answer Poll

On which of these indexed variables can you assign the UNIQUE option?

a. **`Customer_ID`** in an **`orders`** data set where a customer can place multiple orders

b. **`Order_Date`** in an **`orders`** data set

c. **`Employee_ID`** in a data set containing each individual employee and the family members' names stored in variables **`Dependent1`** – **`Dependent10`**

d. **`Product_ID`** in a data set containing the product identifier and the product description

42

Creating Indexes

To create indexes at the same time that you create a data set, use the INDEX= data set option on the output data set.

To create or delete indexes on existing data sets, use one of the following:

- DATASETS procedure
- SQL procedure

44

Creating Indexes

When you create the index, do the following:

- designate the key variable(s)
- specify the UNIQUE and/or the NOMISS index option if appropriate
- select a valid SAS name for the index (composite index only)

A data set can have these index features:

- multiple simple and composite indexes
- character and numeric key variables

45

Creating an Index with the INDEX= Data Set Option

```
options msglevel=i;
data orion.sales_history(index=
               (Customer_ID Product_Group
                SaleID=(Order_ID Product_ID)/unique));
   set orion.history;
   Value_Cost=CostPrice_Per_Unit*Quantity;
   Year_Month=mdy(Month_Num, 15, input(Year_ID,4.));
   format Value_Cost dollar12.
          Year_Month monyy7.;
   label Value_Cost="Value Cost"
         Year_Month="Month/Year";
run;
```

The following code would delete the indexes:

```
data orion.sales_history;
   set orion.sales_history;
run;
```

46 p303d01

Creating an Index with the INDEX= Data Set Option

General form of the INDEX= data set option:

SAS-data-file-name **(INDEX =**
(index-specification-1</option> </option>
...<index-specification-n</option> </option> **>));**

For increased efficiency, use the INDEX= option to create indexes when you initially create a SAS data set.

47

The following are conditions for an *index-specification*:

simple index	the name of the key variable
composite index	*index-name*=(list of key variables)

You can specify the UNIQUE and/or the NOMISS option with the INDEX= data set option. **Each** option is preceded by a slash (/).

The INDEX= data set option can also be used in procedures with OUT= options and with ODS OUTPUT statements.

Viewing Information about Indexes

To display information in the log concerning index creation or index usage, change the value of the MSGLEVEL= system option from its default value of N to I.

General form of the MSGLEVEL= system option:

OPTIONS MSGLEVEL=N | I;

```
options msglevel=i;
data orion.sales_history(index=
      (Customer_ID Product_Group
       SaleID=(Order_ID
               Product_ID)/unique));
set orion.sales_history;
run;

NOTE: There were 1500 observations read from the data set ORION.SALES_HISTORY.
NOTE: The data set ORION.SALES_HISTORY has 1500 observations and 22 variables.
NOTE: Composite index SaleID has been defined.
NOTE: Simple index Product_Group has been defined.
NOTE: Simple index Customer_ID has been defined.
```

48

N	prints notes, warnings, and error messages. This is the default.
I	prints informational or INFO notes that pertain to index creation and usage, merge processing, host sort utilities, and threading in addition to notes, warnings, and error messages.

Creating an Index with the INDEX= Data Set Option

Advantages	Disadvantages
You can create the data set and the index in one step.	To create an additional index, you must re-create the existing indexes.
SAS only reads the data once.	You need to know in advance that indexes are needed.

49

Managing Indexes with PROC DATASETS

```
options msglevel=n;
proc datasets library=orion nolist;
   modify sales_history;
      index create Customer_ID;
      index create Product_Group;
      index create SaleID=(Order_ID
                           Product_ID)/unique;
quit;
```

The following code would delete the indexes:

```
proc datasets library=orion nolist;
   modify sales_history;
      index delete Customer_ID
            Product_Group SaleID;
quit;
```

50

p303d02

The value for the MSGLEVEL= SAS system option is set to **n** because PROC DATASETS issues its own notes.

Managing Indexes with PROC DATASETS

You can use the DATASETS procedure on existing data sets to create or delete indexes.

General form of the PROC DATASETS step to delete or create indexes:

```
PROC DATASETS LIBRARY=libref NOLIST;
     MODIFY SAS-data-set-name;
          INDEX DELETE index-name;
          INDEX CREATE index-specification
                              < / options>;
QUIT;
```

51

The INDEX CREATE statement in PROC DATASETS cannot be used if the index to be created already exists.

If the index to be created already exists, you must do the following:

- delete the existing index of the same name
- create the new index

If you delete and create indexes in the same step, delete indexes first so that the newly created indexes can reuse the space of the deleted indexes.

You can specify the UNIQUE or NOMISS option in the INDEX CREATE statement.

3.04 Quiz

Open and submit the program **p303a01**.

What error messages are in the log?

p303a01

```
options msglevel=n;
proc datasets library=orion nolist;
   modify sales_history;
      index create Customer_ID;
      index create Product_Group;
      index create SaleID=(Order_ID
                   Product_ID)/unique;
quit;
```

53

Managing Indexes with PROC DATASETS

Advantages	Disadvantages
Additional indexes can be created without re-creating the original indexes.	You can only create indexes on existing SAS data sets and existing variables.
One or more indexes can be deleted without deleting all of the indexes on the data set.	PROC DATASETS cannot perform data manipulation.
	If an index exists, it must be deleted before it can be re-created.

55

Managing Indexes with PROC SQL

```
options msglevel=n;
proc sql;
   create index Customer_ID
      on orion.sales_history(Customer_ID);
   create index Product_Group
      on orion.sales_history(Product_Group);
   create unique index SaleID
      on orion.sales_history(Order_ID, Product_ID);
quit;
```

Name of Index

Variable Name

The following code would delete the indexes:

```
proc sql;
   drop index Customer_ID, Product_Group, SaleID
      from orion.sales_history;
quit;
```

56

p303d03

The value for the MSGLEVEL= SAS system option is set to **n** because PROC SQL issues its own notes.

Managing Indexes with PROC SQL

You can use PROC SQL on existing data sets to create or delete indexes.

General form of the PROC SQL step to create or delete indexes:

```
PROC SQL;
      DROP INDEX index-name
            FROM table-name;
      CREATE <option> INDEX  index-name
            ON table-name(column-name-1,...
                              column-name-n);
QUIT;
```

57

PROC SQL cannot be used if the index to be created already exists.

If the index to be created already exists, you must do the following:

- drop the existing index of the same name
- create the new index

The SQL procedure CREATE|DROP INDEX syntax is ANSI standard syntax. You can specify the UNIQUE option in the CREATE INDEX statement. You cannot use the NOMISS option with the SQL procedure.

Managing Indexes with PROC SQL

Advantages	Disadvantages
Additional indexes can be created without re-creating the original indexes.	You can only create indexes on existing SAS data sets and existing variables.
One or more indexes can be deleted without deleting all of the indexes on the data set.	The CREATE INDEX statement cannot perform data manipulation.
	If an index exists, it must be deleted before it can be re-created.

58

Comparing Techniques for Index Creation

INDEX= Data Set Option	PROC DATASETS	PROC SQL
You can create the SAS data set at the same time that the index is created.	You can only create indexes on existing SAS data sets and existing variables.	You can only create indexes on existing SAS data sets and existing variables.
To create an additional index, you must re-create the existing indexes.	Additional indexes can be created without re-creating the original indexes.	Additional indexes can be created without re-creating the original indexes.
The DATA step can perform data manipulation at the same time that the index is created.	PROC DATASETS cannot perform data manipulation.	The CREATE INDEX statement cannot perform data manipulation.
To delete one or more indexes, you must re-create the other required indexes.	One or more indexes can be deleted without deleting all of the indexes on the data set.	One or more indexes can be deleted without deleting all of the indexes on the data set.
An existing index can be re-created without first deleting it.	If an index exists, it must be deleted before it can be re-created.	If an index exists, it must be deleted before it can be re-created.

59

Documenting Indexes

The following can be used to document indexes:

- SAS Explorer
- PROC CONTENTS
- PROC DATASETS
- SAS Management Console

60

Properties Window in SAS Explorer

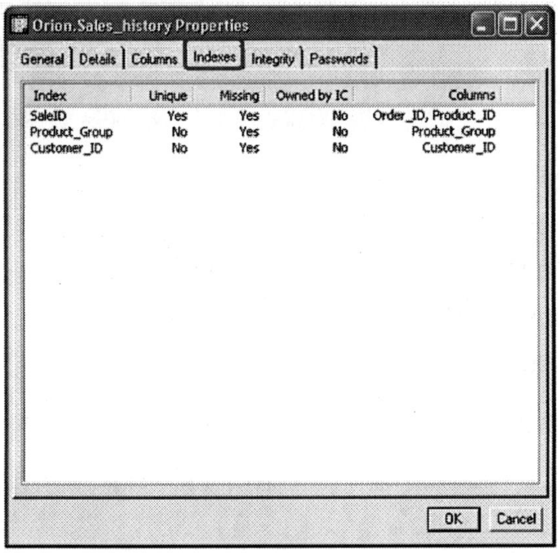

61

Index Documentation

```
proc contents data=orion.sales_history;
run;
```

```
proc datasets lib=orion nolist;
   contents data=sales_history;
quit;
```

These two steps produce identical output.

Partial PROC DATASETS Output

Alphabetic List of Indexes and Attributes

#	Index	Unique Option	# of Unique Values	Variables
1	Customer_ID		1046	
2	Product_Group		56	
3	SaleID	YES	1500	Order_ID Product_ID

62 p303d04

Exercises

Level 1

1. **Creating Indexes**

   a. Open the program **p303e01**, and add the INDEX= option to create two indexes:

   - a simple index **`Customer_ID`**, based on the variable **`Customer_ID`**
   - a unique index **`Order_ID`**, based on the variable **`Order_ID`**

   b. Use PROC SQL to delete the **`Order_ID`** index from the **`orders`** data set.

   c. Use PROC DATASETS to create a composite index named **`OrDate`** based on the **`Order_ID`** and **`Order_Date`** variables for the **`orders`** data set.

   d. Use PROC CONTENTS or PROC DATASETS to look at the index information.

Level 2

2. **Updating Indexes**

   a. Use the **`orion.price_list`** SAS data set to create a temporary data set named **`price_list`** that contains a new variable named **`Unit_Profit`** that is the difference between the variables **`Unit_Sales_Price`** and **`Unit_Cost_Price`**. Create a unique index on the **`Product_ID`** variable.

   b. Open the program **p303e02** and submit it.

   c. View the log, and determine whether the new observation was added.

   d. Why or why not?

Level 3

3. **Creating Indexes on New Variables**

   a. Create a temporary SAS data set named **`all_staff`** by concatenating the data sets **`orion.sales`** and **`orion.nonsales`**.

   b. Create a new variable named **`Age_Hired`** that is the number of years between the variables **`Hire_Date`** and **`Birth_Date`**.

   c. Index the **`all_staff`** data set on the variable **`Age_Hired`**.

3.2 Using an Index

Objectives

- Describe when an index is used for WHERE statement processing.
- Describe when an index is **not** used for WHERE statement processing.

66

Index Usage Possible

An index **might** be used when a WHERE expression references one of the following:

- a simple index key variable
- the primary key variable of a composite index

⚠ Although a WHERE expression can consist of multiple conditions specifying different variables, SAS uses only one index to process the WHERE expression.

67

Index Usage Possible

A WHERE condition might possibly use an index, provided the condition contains any one of the following:

- a comparison operator or the IN operator
- the NOT operator
- the special WHERE operators (CONTAINS, LIKE, IS NULL|IS MISSING, and BETWEEN...AND)
- the TRIM or SUBSTR functions (provided the second argument of the SUBSTR function is 1)

68

General form of the SUBSTR function:

SUBSTR(*variable*, *position*, *<length>*)**;**

Subtle improvements have been made to the circumstances under which SAS uses an index in SAS 9.2. Trailing blanks in the CONTAINS operator pattern to be searched for are ignored. Escape characters in the LIKE operator are permitted. Examples are provided in the table below:

Condition	Examples

Comparison operators and the IN operator	`where Customer_ID=14864;`
	`where Order_ID < 5000;`
	`where Customer_ID in (9313,14864);`

Comparison operators with NOT	`where Customer_ID ne 14864;` `where Customer_ID not in (9313,14864);`
Comparison operators with the colon modifier The colon modifier (=:) indicates a *starts with* condition. It cannot be used in the SQL procedure.	`where Product_Group =: 'S';`
CONTAINS operator	`where Product_Group contains 'Eclipse';` `where Product_Group contains 'Eclipse   ';`

Fully bounded range conditions specifying both an upper and a lower limit, which includes the BETWEEN-AND operator	`where 5000 < Order_ID < 10000;` `where Order_ID between 5000 and 10000;`

Pattern-matching operator LIKE	`where Product_Group like '%Shoes';`
	`where Product_Group like 'G___';`
	`where Product_Group like 'Girls\_Shoes';`

IS NULL or IS MISSING operator	`where Product_Group is null;` `where Product_Group is missing;`
TRIM function	`where trim(Product_Group)='Clothes';`
The SUBSTR function with the conditions that the starting position=1 and the length is less than or equal to the length of the string variable	`where substr(Product_Group,1,5)= 'Orion';`

✎ For more information about when index usage is possible, see **SAS 9.2 Language Reference: Concepts** ⇨ **SAS Files Concepts** ⇨ **SAS Data Files** ⇨ **Understanding SAS Indexes** in the Help facility.

Setup for the Poll

The following indexes were created on the **orion.sales_history** data set.

Partial PROC DATASETS Output

Alphabetic List of Indexes and Attributes

#	Index	Unique Option	# of Unique Values	Variables
1	Customer_ID		1046	
2	Product_Group		56	
3	SaleID	YES	1500	Order_ID Product_ID

70

3.05 Multiple Answer Poll

Which of the following WHERE conditions could possibly use an index?

a. `where Product_ID=220100300042;`

b. `where Customer_ID ne 3245;`

c. `where Customer_ID=15020 or Customer_ID=14853;`

d. `where Order_ID=1230036183;`

e. `where Customer_ID='3245';`

71

When Is an Index Not Used?

An index is **not** used in the following circumstances:

- with a subsetting IF statement in a DATA step
- with particular WHERE expressions
- if SAS determines that all observations will satisfy the WHERE expression
- if SAS determines that it is more efficient to read the data sequentially

73

3.06 Multiple Choice Poll

When does the subsetting IF statement select observations?

a. before the observation is copied into the PDV
b. after the observation is in the PDV

75

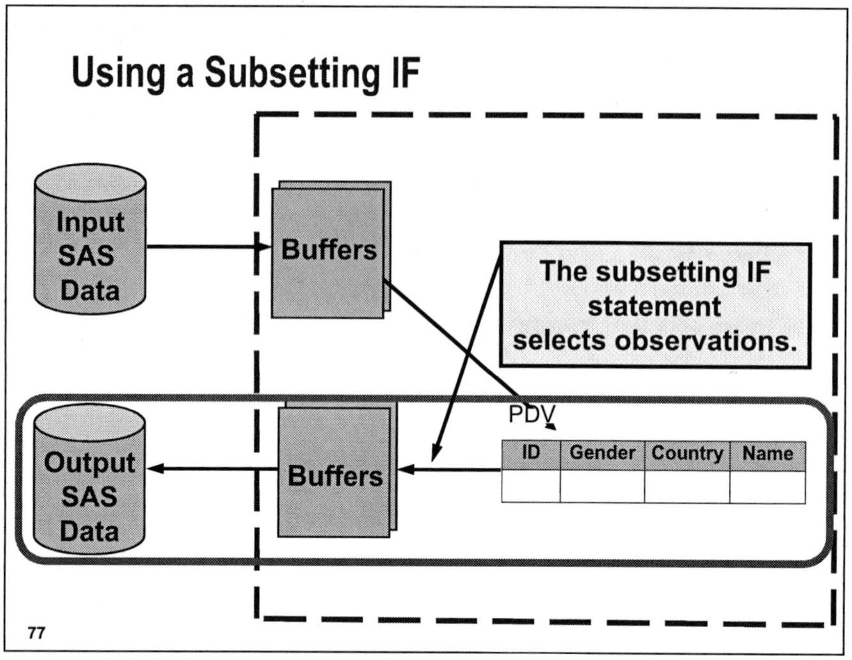
Using a Subsetting IF
Input SAS Data
Buffers
The subsetting IF statement selects observations.
PDV
ID
Gender
Country
Name
Output SAS Data
Buffers
77

No Index Usage

SAS does not use an index when a WHERE expression references an indexed variable if the following conditions exist:

- No single index can supply all required observations.
- Any function other than TRIM or SUBSTR appears in the WHERE expression.
- The SUBSTR function does not search a string beginning at the first position.
- The SOUNDS-LIKE operator (=*) is used.

78

Condition	Examples
No single index can supply all required observations.	`where Employee_ID=99999999 or Order_Type=1;`
Any function other than TRIM or SUBSTR appears in the WHERE expression.	`where scan(Product_Group,2,' ')='Shoes';`
The SUBSTR function does not search a string beginning at the first position.	`where substr(Product_Group,5,1)=' ';`
The SOUNDS-LIKE operator (=*) is used.	`where Product_Group=*'gulf';`

For more information about when an index is not used, see **SAS 9.2 Language Reference: Concepts** ⇨ **SAS Files Concepts** ⇨ **SAS Data Files** ⇨ **Understanding SAS Indexes** in the Help facility.

Compound Optimization

A WHERE expression that references multiple variables can take advantage of a composite index.

compound optimization	use of a composite index to optimize some WHERE expressions that involve multiple variables

```
where Order_ID=240200100038 and
      Product_ID=1230151326;
```

79

Compound Optimization

For compound optimization to occur, **all** of the following must be true:

- At least the first two key variables in the composite index must be used in the WHERE conditions.
- The conditions must be connected using the AND operator.
- At least one condition must use the EQ, equal sign (=), or IN operator.

80

3.07 Multiple Choice Poll

Which of the following WHERE statements can use the composite index **SaleID** for compound optimization?

a. `where Order_ID=240200100038 or Product_ID=1230151326;`

b. `where Order_ID=. and Product_ID=1230151326;`

c. `where int(Order_ID/1000000000)=240 and Product_ID=1230151326;`

d. `where Order_ID>240000000000 and Product_ID<1240000000;`

82

WHERE Expression Index Usage

SAS uses the following steps to decide whether to evaluate a WHERE expression using a sequential read or using an index:

- Determine whether the WHERE expression can be satisfied by an existing index.
- Select the best index, if several indexes are available.
- Estimate the number of observations that qualify.
- Compare the probable resource usage for both methods.

✎ SAS estimates the I/O operations for indexed access based on the subset size and sort order.

84

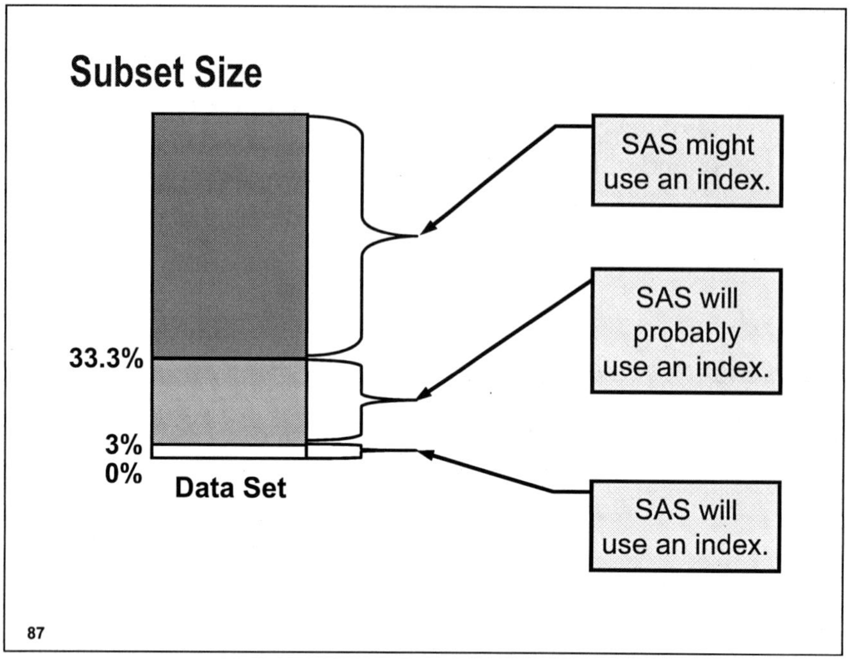

To determine whether it is more efficient to satisfy the WHERE expression by using the index or by reading the data sequentially, SAS uses these guidelines:

- If only a few observations are qualified, it is more efficient to use the index than to do a sequential search of the entire data file.
- If most or all of the observations qualify, then it is more efficient to read the data file sequentially.

If the subset is between small and large, other factors such as data order are important.

Subset Size

The SAS index includes cumulative percentiles or centiles. By default, SAS stores 21 centiles or every 5th percentile of the index. This information is used to estimate the size of a qualifying subset.

centiles	provide information about the distribution of values in an index.

88

For information about updating and viewing the centile information, see the UPDATE CENTILES information in the SAS documentation for the DATASETS procedure and the CENTILES option for the PROC CONTENTS statement.

3.08 Multiple Choice Poll

Which of the following is used to determine the I/O to read a SAS data set sequentially?

a. the page size of the input data set and the number of buffers available
b. the number of observations and the number of variables
c. the page size of the output data set and the number of output buffers available

90

Review of Factors Affecting I/O

The following factors affect I/O:

- size of the subset relative to the size of the data file
- order of data with regard to the chosen index
- page size of the data file
- number of buffers allocated
- cost to uncompress a compressed file for a sequential read

92

Data Order

For data that is sorted and indexed on the same variable(s), retrieval time through the index is much faster than either sorted or indexed data alone.

```
where Customer_ID in (14844, 14620, 13337, 13350);
```

Unsorted Data Set

Obs	Customer_ID
10	14844
11	14844
31	14620
35	14620
45	14620
51	14620
213	13337
222	13337
223	13337
235	13350
237	13350

Sorted Data Set

Obs	Customer_ID
1286	13337
1287	13337
1288	13337
1291	13350
1292	13350
1448	14620
1449	14620
1450	14620
1451	14620
1477	14844
1478	14844

93

All of the observations meeting a specific criteria (**Customer_ID = 14844**) are on the same or adjacent data set pages. Thus, fewer data set pages must be read to retrieve the same selected observations.

Controlling WHERE Processing Index Usage

You can control index usage for WHERE processing with these data set options:

IDXWHERE=YES	tells SAS to choose the best index to optimize a WHERE expression and to disregard the possibility that a sequential search of the data set might be more resource efficient.
IDXWHERE=NO	tells SAS to ignore all indexes and satisfy the conditions of a WHERE expression with a sequential search of the data set.
IDXNAME=*index-name*	directs SAS to use a specific index.

⚠ Use the IDXWHERE=NO option when you know an available index will not optimize WHERE clause processing.

94

Using the IDXWHERE= Option

To ensure that SAS uses an index when printing the data for **Customer_ID in (14844,4983,5862,10032) and Product_Group contains 'Shoes'**, use the following code:

```
options msglevel=i;
proc print data=orion.sales_history(idxwhere=yes);
   where Customer_ID in (14844,4983,5862,10032)
         and Product_Group contains 'Shoes';
   var Customer_ID Product_ID Product_Group ;
   title 'With an Index';
run;
```

95 p303d05

Using the IDXWHERE= Option

Partial SAS Log

```
1669  options msglevel=i;
1670  proc print data=orion.sales_history(idxwhere=yes);
1671     where Customer_ID in (14844,4983,5862,10032)
1672           and Product_Group contains 'Shoes';
INFO: Data set option (IDXWHERE=YES)forced an index to be used rather
      than a sequential pass for where-clause processing.
INFO: Index Customer_ID selected for WHERE clause optimization.
1673     var Customer_ID Product_ID Product_Group ;
1674     title 'With an Index';
1675  run;
```

96

p303d05

Using the IDXNAME= Option

Because using the index on **Customer_ID** returns a smaller subset than would the index on **Product_Group**, the IDXNAME= data set option can be used.

```
options msglevel=i;
proc print data=orion.sales_history(idxname=Customer_ID);
   where Customer_ID in (14844,4983,5862,10032)
         and Product_Group contains 'Shoes';
   var Customer_ID Product_ID Product_Group ;
   title 'With an Index';
run;
```

Use the IDXNAME= option when you know the better index so SAS does not need to do the evaluation.

97

p303d06

Using the IDXNAME= Option

Partial SAS Log

```
92   options msglevel=i;
193  proc print data=orion.sales_history(idxname=Customer_ID);
194     where Customer_ID in (14844,4983,5862,10032)
195           and Product_Group contains 'Shoes';
INFO: Index Customer_ID selected for WHERE clause optimization.
196     var Customer_ID Product_ID Product_Group ;
197     title 'With an Index';
198  run;

NOTE: There were 3 observations read from the data set
ORION.SALES_HISTORY.
      WHERE Customer_ID in (4983, 5862, 10032, 14844) and
            Product_Group contains 'Shoes';
NOTE: PROCEDURE PRINT used (Total process time):
      real time           0.15 seconds
      cpu time            0.01 seconds
```

98

Maintaining Indexes

Data Management Tasks	Index Action Taken
Copy the data set with the COPY procedure or the DATASETS procedure	Index file constructed for new data file
Move the data set with the MOVE option in the COPY procedure	Index file deleted from IN= library; rebuilt in OUT= library
Copy the data set with a drag-and-drop action in SAS Explorer	Index file constructed for new file

99

continued...

Maintaining Indexes

Data Management Tasks	Index Action Taken
Rename the data set	Index file renamed
Rename the variable	Variable renamed to new name in index file
Add observations	Value/Identifier pairs added
Delete observations	Value/Identifier pairs deleted; space recovered for re-use
Update observations	Value/Identifier pairs updated if values change

The APPEND procedure and the INSERT INTO statement in the SQL procedure update the index file after all the data is appended or inserted.

100

continued...

Indexes are maintained by updates in place, such as using the VIEWTABLE window to update, add, or delete observations, and the APPEND or SQL procedure to append data. Using the Explorer window or the DATASETS procedure also maintains indexes when data sets or variables are renamed. However, re-creating a data set with the SET, MERGE, or UPDATE statement does **not** automatically maintain indexes.

Maintaining Indexes

Data Management Tasks	Index Action Taken

Delete a data set.
`proc datasets lib=work;`
`   delete a;`
`run;`
	Index file deleted

Rebuild a data set with a DATA step.
`data a;`
`   set a;`
`run;`
	Index file deleted

Sort the data set in place with the FORCE option in the SORT procedure.
`proc sort data=a force;`
`   by var;`
`run;`
	Index file deleted

101

If you use the UPLOAD procedure or the DOWNLOAD procedure in SAS/CONNECT, the index is re-created by default when you upload or download a single data set and omit the OUT= option or when you upload or download a SAS data library. Use the INDEX=NO data set option to upload or download without re-creating the index.

Index re-created:

```
proc upload data=schedule;
run;
```

Index not re-created:

```
proc download data=Sales(index=no);
run;
```

If you are using the CPORT procedure to create transport files, you can use the INDEX=YES option in the PROC CPORT statement to transport the index file along with the data set. INDEX=YES is the default.

Guidelines for Indexing

Suggested guidelines for creating indexes:

- Create an index when you intend to retrieve a small subset of observations from a large data file.
- Do not create an index if the data file page count is less than three pages. It is faster to access the data sequentially.
- Create indexes on variables that are discriminating. These variables precisely identify observations that satisfy WHERE expressions.
- When you create a composite index, make the first key variable the most discriminating.
- Consider the cost of maintaining an index for a data file that is frequently changed.

102

continued...

A variable such as **`Gender`** is not discriminating. A *discriminating variable* is one that enables you to break the data into many small groups or subsets.

Guidelines for Indexing

- To minimize I/O for indexed access, sort the data by the key variable(s) before creating the index. Maintain the data file in sorted order by the key variable to improve performance.
- Minimize the number of indexes to reduce disk storage and update costs. Create indexes only on variables that are often used in queries or BY-group processing (when the data cannot be sorted).
- Consider how often your applications use an index. An index must be used often in order to compensate for the resources used in creating and maintaining it.
- When you create an index to process a WHERE expression, do not try to create one index that might be used to satisfy every conceivable query.

103

Index Trade-offs

Advantages	Disadvantages
fast access to a small subset of observations	extra CPU cycles and I/O operations to create and maintain an index
values returned in sorted order	increased CPU to read the data
can enforce uniqueness	extra disk space to store the index file
	extra memory to load the index pages and the compiled SAS C code to use the index

104

Exercises

Level 1

4. Using an Index

Open the program **p303e04**, and submit it. Consult the log and answer the questions following the program code shown here.

p303e04

```
options msglevel=I;

*** Example 1;

data rdu;
   set orion.sales_history;
   if Order_ID=1230166613;
run;

*** Example 2;

proc print data=orion.sales_history;
   where Order_ID=1230166613 or Product_ID=220200100100;
run;

*** Example 3;

proc print data=orion.sales_history;
   where Product_Group ne 'Shoes';
run;

*** Example 4;

proc print data=orion.sales_history;
   where Customer_ID=12727;
run;

**** Example 5;

proc print data=orion.sales_history;
   where Product_ID=220101400233;
run;

*****Example 6;

data saleshistorycopy;
   set orion.sales_history;
run;
```

Questions:

a. Does Example 1 use an index? Why or why not?

NO

Replace the IF statement with a WHERE statement, and resubmit the program. Does the example now use an index? Why or why not?

SALEID

b. Does Example 2 use an index? Why or why not?

NO AND

Replace the OR operator with the AND operator, and resubmit the program. Does the example now use an index? Why or why not?

YES SALEID

c. Does Example 3 use an index? Why or why not?

NO

Replace the NE operator with the EQ operator, and resubmit the program. Does the example now use an index? Why or why not?

NOT
NO - SORTED TO INDEX ORDER

d. Does Example 4 use an index? Why or why not?

CUST ID

Add the IDXWHERE=NO data set option and resubmit the program. Is the output from the PROC PRINT step with an index different from the output from the PROC PRINT step without an index? NO

What message do you see in the log?

Data set option forced sequential pass of the data rather than index

e. Does Example 5 use an index? Why or why not?

yes product grp

f. In Example 6, does the data set **saleshistorycopy** have an index?

NO

Level 2

5. Suppressing Index Usage

Create a detail report from the **orion.supplier** SAS data set that lists all of the variables and observations where **Supplier_ID** is greater than 1000. Ensure that the data is processed sequentially.

Level 3

6. Updating Centile Information for an Index

a. Submit program **p303e06**. Do **not** clear your SAS Output window or the Results window!

p303e06

```
data orders(index=(Order_ID/unique Customer_ID));
   set orion.orders;
run;

proc contents data=orders centiles;
run;
```

b. Using the DATASETS procedure, set the indicator for updating the centile information about the **Order_ID** index to 1% of the data.

c. Submit the program **p303e06c**, which adds new observations to the **orders** data set.

d. Submit a PROC CONTENTS step to view the contents of **orders**. Compare the centile information from step **6.a.** to the current centile information. Were the centiles updated or not?

e. Why or why not?

3.3 Creating a Sample Data Set (Self-Study)

Objectives

- Create a systematic sample.
- Create a random sample with replacement.
- Create a random sample without replacement.

108

Business Scenario

The Marketing Department wants to send customer satisfaction questionnaires to a sample of the customers in the `orion.order_fact` SAS data set.

Partial Listing of `orion.order_fact`

Customer_ID	Employee_ID	Street_ID	Order_Date	Delivery_Date	Order_ID	. . .
63	121039	9260125492	11JAN2003	11JAN2003	1230058123	...
5	99999999	9260114570	15JAN2003	19JAN2003	1230080101	...
45	99999999	9260104847	20JAN2003	22JAN2003	1230106883	...
41	120174	1600101527	28JAN2003	28JAN2003	1230147441	...
183	120134	1600100760	27FEB2003	27FEB2003	1230315085	...
.	.	.	.	.	.	

109

Business Scenario

Select a subset by reading every 50th observation from observation number 1 to the end of the SAS data set.

```
data subset;
③ do PickIt=1 to TotObs by 50; ②
      set orion.order_fact(keep=Customer_ID
            Employee_ID Street_ID Order_ID)
         point=PickIt
         nobs=TotObs; ①
      output; ④
   end;
   stop; ⑤
run;
```

110 p303d07

① The NOBS= option creates a temporary numeric variable that contains the total number of observations in the input data. This variable is populated at *compilation.*

② You can refer to the NOBS= variable in executable statements that appear before the SET statement.

③ The DO loop assigns a value to the variable **PickIt**. **PickIt** is used by the POINT= option in the SET statement to select an observation from the SAS data set. **PickIt** must have a value before the SET statement executes.

④ The OUTPUT statement writes the PDV values to the SAS data set.

⑤ The STOP statement stops the DATA step from continuing to execute after the five observations are selected. Without a STOP statement, the DATA step continues in an infinite loop.

3.09 Quiz

Are POINT= and NOBS= individual statements or part of the SET statement?

```
data subset;
   do PickIt=1 to TotObs by 50;
      set orion.order_fact(keep=Customer_ID
               Employee_ID Street_ID Order_ID)
            point=PickIt
            nobs=TotObs;
        output;
   end;
   stop;
run;
```

112 p303d07

Using the POINT= Option

To create a sample, use the POINT= option in the SET statement.

General form of the POINT= option:

SET *data-set-name* POINT=*point-variable*;

The *point-variable* has the following attributes:

- names a temporary numeric variable that contains the number of the observation to read
- must be given a value before the execution of the SET statement
- must be a variable (for example, X) and not a constant value (for example, 12)
- must be a valid observation number

114

The POINT= option value should be an integer greater than zero and less than or equal to the number of observations in the SAS data set.

- If the value is not integral, the SET statement effectively applies the FLOOR function to the value.
- If, during processing, the POINT= value does not match an observation number (is negative or is greater than NOBS), a data error results and no observation is read by the SET statement. The DATA step will output the current contents of the PDV and continue processing.

Using the Number of Observations

You can use the NOBS= option in the SET statement to determine how many observations there are in a SAS data set.

General form of the SET statement:

SET *SAS-data-set* NOBS=*variable*;

The NOBS= option creates a temporary variable whose value has the following characteristics:

- is the number of observations in the input data set(s)
- is assigned during compilation
- is retained
- should not be modified during execution

115

Using the STOP Statement

The POINT= option has the following features:

- uses direct-access read mode
- does not detect the end-of-file marker

To prevent the DATA step from looping continuously, use the STOP statement.

General form of the STOP statement:

STOP;

116

Compilation

```
data subset;
   do PickIt=1 to TotObs by 50;
      set orion.order_fact
          (keep=Customer_ID
                Employee_ID
                Street_ID
                Order_ID)
          point=PickIt
          nobs=TotObs;
      output;
   end;
   stop;
run;
```

PDV

PickIt	Tot Obs	Customer_ ID	Employee_ ID	Street_ ID	Order_ID	_N_
.	617	.	.	.	.	.

117 p303d07 ...

During compilation, the value for **TotObs** is retrieved from the descriptor portion of **orion.order_fact**.

Execution

Partial Listing of orion.order_fact

obs	Customer _ID	Employee _ID	. . .
1	63	121039	. . .
2	5	99999999	. . .
	.	.	. . .
50	17023	99999999	. . .
51	17023	99999999	. . .
	.	.	. . .

```
data subset;
   do PickIt=1 to TotObs by 50;
      set orion.order_fact
          (keep=Customer_ID
                Employee_ID
                Street_ID
                Order_ID)
          point=PickIt
          nobs=TotObs;
      output;
   end;
   stop;
run;
```

PDV

PickIt	Tot Obs	Customer_ ID	Employee_ ID	Street_ ID	Order_ID	_N_
1	617	63	121039	9260125492	1230058123	1

119 ...

The SET statement executes and reads the first observation. The first observation is read because the variable **PickIt** has a value of 1, not because SAS is reading sequentially.

Execution

Partial Listing of
orion.order_fact

obs	Customer_ID	Employee_ID	. . .
1	63	121039	. . .
2	5	99999999	. . .
	.	.	. . .
50	17023	99999999	. . .
51	17023	99999999	. . .
	.	.	. . .

```
data subset;
   do PickIt=1 to TotObs by 50;
      set orion.order_fact
          (keep=Customer_ID
                Employee_ID
                Street_ID
                Order_ID)
          point=PickIt
          nobs=TotObs;
      output;
   end;
   stop;
run;
```

Output current observation

PDV

PickIt	Tot Obs	Customer_ID	Employee_ID	Street_ID	Order_ID	_N_
1	617	63	121039	9260125492	1230058123	1

120 ...

Execution

Partial Listing of
orion.order_fact

obs	Customer_ID	Employee_ID	. . .
1	63	121039	. . .
2	5	99999999	. . .
	.	.	. . .
50	17023	99999999	. . .
51	17023	99999999	. . .
	.	.	. . .

```
data subset;
   do PickIt=1 to TotObs by 50;
      set orion.order_fact
          (keep=Customer_ID
                Employee_ID
                Street_ID
                Order_ID)
          point=PickIt
          nobs=TotObs;
      output;
   end;
   stop;
run;
```

PDV

PickIt	Tot Obs	Customer_ID	Employee_ID	Street_ID	Order_ID	_N_
51	617	17023	99999999	2600100021	1230931366	1

123 ...

This time when the SET statement executes, observation 51 is read from **orion.order_fact**.

Execution

Partial Listing of **orion.order_fact**

obs	Customer_ID	Employee_ID	...
1	63	121039	...
2	5	99999999	...
	.	.	...
50	17023	99999999	...
51	17023	99999999	...
	.	.	...

```
data subset;
   do PickIt=1 to TotObs by 50;
      set orion.order_fact
         (keep=Customer_ID
               Employee_ID
               Street_ID
               Order_ID)
         point=PickIt
         nobs=TotObs;
      output;
   end;
   stop;
run;
```

Output current observation

PDV

PickIt	TotObs	Customer_ID	Employee_ID	Street_ID	Order_ID	_N_
51	617	17023	99999999	2600100021	1230931366	1

124 ...

Execution

Partial Listing of **orion.order_fact**

obs	Customer_ID	Employee_ID	...
1	63	121039	...
2	5	99999999	...
	.	.	...
50	17023	99999999	...
51	17023	99999999	...
	.	.	...

PickIt > TotObs

```
data subset;
   do PickIt=1 to TotObs by 50;
      set orion.order_fact
         (keep=Customer_ID
               Employee_ID
               Street_ID
               Order_ID)
         point=PickIt
         nobs=TotObs;
      output;
   end;
   stop;
run;
```

PDV

PickIt	TotObs	Customer_ID	Employee_ID	Street_ID	Order_ID	_N_
651	617	215	120175	1600102721	1243963366	1

126 ...

When **PickIt** has a value of 651, its value is greater than the range (1-617) in the iterative DO loop.

Execution

Partial Listing of
orion.order_fact

obs	Customer_ID	Employee_ID	. . .
1	63	121039	. . .
2	5	99999999	. . .
	.	.	. . .
50	17023	99999999	. . .
51	17023	99999999	. . .
	.	.	. . .

```
data subset;
   do PickIt=1 to TotObs by 50;
      set orion.order_fact
         (keep=Customer_ID
               Employee_ID
               Street_ID
               Order_ID)
         point=PickIt
                       ;
   end;
   stop;
run;
```

Execution stops.

PDV

PickIt	TotObs	Customer_ID	Employee_ID	Street_ID	Order_ID	_N_
651	617	215	120175	1600102721	1243963366	1

127 ...

Control goes to the next executable statement after the end of the DO loop.

Resulting Data Set

Partial Listing of **subset**

Systematic Sample

Obs	Customer_ID	Employee_ID	Street_ID	Order_ID
1	63	121039	9260125492	1230058123
2	17023	99999999	2600100021	1230931366
3	17	121037	9260123306	1231757107
4	195	120160	1600101663	1232590052
5	41	120134	1600101527	1233545775
6	11171	99999999	2600100032	1235176942
7	10	121043	9260129395	1237327705
8	53	120121	1600103258	1238674844
9	90	121040	9260111614	1239543223
10	89	121061	9260116551	1240549230
11	27	99999999	9260105670	1241930625
12	41	120195	1600101527	1242838815
13	215	120175	1600102721	1243963366

128

Creating a Random Sample

Instead of creating a systematic sample, create a random sample where each observation has an equal chance of being selected.

There are two types of random samples:

- *with replacement*, where an observation might be selected more than one time
- *without replacement*, where an observation cannot be selected more than once

You can use the RANUNI function to generate random numbers from a uniform distribution.

General form of the RANUNI function:

RANUNI(*seed*)

129

The UNIFORM function is an alias for the RANUNI function.

The *seed* is an initial starting point that the RANUNI function uses to generate streams of random numbers. The seed must be an integer with a value less than 2^{31}-1 (2,147,483,647).

A 0 argument for the RANUNI function uses the system clock time, which results in a different stream of random numbers each time that the program is run.

Using the RANUNI Function

The RANUNI function returns a rational number between 0 and 1 (non-inclusive) generated from a uniform distribution.

ranuni(*seed*)

Examples:

Random number

.01253689

.95196500

130 ...

Using the RANUNI Function

If you want a **number** between 0 and 5 (non-inclusive), multiply the number returned from the RANUNI function by 5.

ranuni(*seed*) * 5

Examples:

Random number * 5

.01253689 ➔ 0.06268445

.95196500 ➔ 4.75982500

131 ...

Using the RANUNI and CEIL Functions

If you want an **integer** between 1 and 5 (inclusive), use the CEIL function on the number returned by multiplying the random number by 5.

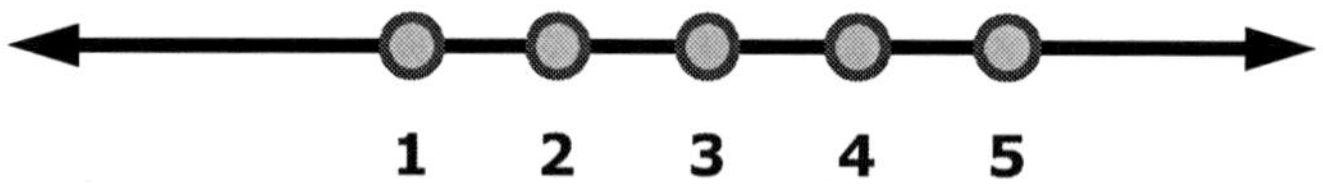

ceil(ranuni(*seed*) * 5)

Examples:

Random number * 5 CEIL( )

.01253689 ➔ 0.06268445 ➔ 1

.95196500 ➔ 4.75982500 ➔ 5

132

The CEIL function returns the smallest integer that is greater than or equal to the argument.

Setup for the Poll

Instead of the CEIL function, would the INT function return the same results?

```
ceil(ranuni(seed) * 5)
```

```
int(ranuni(seed) * 5)
```

134

3.10 Poll

Instead of the CEIL function, would the INT function return the same results?

- ❍ Yes
- ❍ No

135

Creating a Random Sample

p303d08

Create a random sample **with replacement**. A sample with replacement can contain duplicate observations because an observation can be selected more than one time.

p303d08

```
data subset(drop=i SampSize);
   SampSize=10;
   do i=1 to SampSize;
      PickIt=ceil(ranuni(0)*TotObs);
      ObsPicked=PickIt;
      set orion.order_fact point=PickIt nobs=TotObs;
      output;
    end;
    stop;
run;

proc print data=subset;
   title 'A Random Sample with Replacement';
   var ObsPicked Customer_ID Order_Date Delivery_Date Order_ID;
run;
```

PROC PRINT Output

A Random Sample with Replacement

Obs	Obs Picked	Customer_ID	Order_ Date	Delivery_ Date	Order_ID
1	17	20	01APR2003	01APR2003	1230498538
2	499	46966	07APR2007	08APR2007	1241909303
3	200	41	20AUG2004	20AUG2004	1233545775
4	416	12	03AUG2006	03AUG2006	1239836937
5	216	19873	27OCT2004	03NOV2004	1233998114
6	548	27	12JUL2007	17JUL2007	1242782701
7	290	70221	12AUG2005	14AUG2005	1236694462
8	46	75	03JUN2003	03JUN2003	1230841466
9	422	90	23AUG2006	23AUG2006	1239994933
10	129	53	13JAN2004	13JAN2004	1232087464

With a seed value of 0, you get different results each time that the program is executed, but it is possible that some of the same observations that were selected in previous executions will be selected.

p303d09

Create a random sample **without** replacement. A sample without replacement cannot contain duplicate observations because after an observation is output to **work.subset**, it cannot be selected again programmatically.

p303d09

```
data subset(drop=ObsLeft SampSize);
 ① SampSize=10;
 ② ObsLeft=TotObs;
   do while(SampSize>0 and ObsLeft>0);
    ③ PickIt+1;
      if ranuni(0)<SampSize/ObsLeft then
         do;
            ObsPicked=PickIt;
            set orion.order_fact point=PickIt
                             nobs=TotObs;
            output;
            SampSize=SampSize-1;
         end;
      ObsLeft=ObsLeft-1;
   end;
   stop;
run;

proc print data=subset;
   title 'A Random Sample without Replacement';
   var ObsPicked Customer_ID Order_Date Delivery_Date Order_ID;
run;
```

① **SampSize** is the number of observations wanted in the sample.

② **ObsLeft** is the number of observations that still need to be selected. The start value is equal to **TotObs**, the total number of observations in the data set being sampled.

③ **PickIt** is the number of the observation to be read in the sample data set. Because it is used in a SUM statement, its starting value is 0.

PROC PRINT Output

```
                       A Random Sample without Replacement

              Obs                     Order_     Delivery_
     Obs     Picked    Customer_ID      Date        Date              Order_ID

       1       48               56   11JUN2003   11JUN2003          1230885738
       2       50            17023   20JUN2003   25JUN2003          1230931366
       3       51            17023   20JUN2003   25JUN2003          1230931366
       4      128               45   31DEC2003   31DEC2003          1232007700
       5      153               89   31MAR2004   03APR2004          1232601472
       6      162               34   16APR2004   16APR2004          1232709115
       7      276               36   15JUN2005   18JUN2005          1236113431
       8      388               45   29MAY2006   29MAY2006          1239312711
       9      410               13   23JUL2006   28JUL2006          1239744161
      10      586              171   16OCT2007   16OCT2007          1243643970
```

With a seed value of 0, you get different results each time that the program is executed, but it is possible that some of the same observations will be selected as were selected in previous executions.

In each iteration of the DO loop, the following occur:

1. **`PickIt`** is incremented by 1.
2. The IF expression **`ranuni(0) < Sampsize/ObsLeft`** is evaluated.
   a. If true, these actions occur:
      1) The observation **`PickIt`** is selected in the sample.
      2) **`SampSize`** is decreased by 1.
   b. If false, the observation **`PickIt`** is skipped.
3. **`ObsLeft`** is decreased by 1.

The process ends when **`SampSize`** is 0; no additional observations are needed.

Be aware of the following:

- Each observation is considered for selection.
- An observation number is considered only once.
- The data set is read only when an observation number is selected.

This is an adaptation of a sampling routine that was used by statisticians for many years.

- The sample size is fixed.
- An observation can be selected only once.
- Each observation has an equal probability of being selected.
- The selection probability for an observation is independent of the selection of another observation.

Using the SURVEYSELECT Procedure

The SURVEYSELECT procedure has the following attributes:

- provides a variety of methods for selecting probability-based random samples
- can select a simple random sample or can sample according to a complex multistage sample design that includes stratification, clustering, and unequal probabilities of selection
- is part of SAS/STAT

138

Using the SURVEYSELECT Procedure

This program creates a SAS data set, **ordersample**, that contains 10 observations randomly selected, without replacement, from the **orion.order_fact** SAS data set.

```
proc surveyselect data=orion.order_fact
                 (keep=Customer_ID Employee_ID
                       Street_ID Order_ID)
                  out=ordersample
                  method=srs n=10;
run;
```

139 p303d10

Using the SURVEYSELECT Procedure

General form of the SURVEYSELECT procedure:

```
PROC SURVEYSELECT options;
     STRATA variables;
     CONTROL variables;
     SIZE variable;
     ID variables;
RUN;
```

140

STRATA	partitions the input data set into non-overlapping groups defined by the STRATA variables. PROC SURVEYSELECT then selects independent samples from these strata, according to the selection method and design parameters specified in the PROC SURVEYSELECT statement. PROC SURVEYSELECT expects the input data set to be sorted in the order of the STRATA variables.
CONTROL	names variables for sorting the input data set. The CONTROL variables can be character or numeric. PROC SURVEYSELECT sorts the input data set by the CONTROL variables before selecting the sample. If you also specify a STRATA statement, PROC SURVEYSELECT sorts by the CONTROL variables within the strata.
SIZE	names one and only one size measure variable, which contains the size measures to be used when sampling with probability proportional to size. The SIZE variable must be numeric. When the value of an observation's SIZE variable is missing or non-positive, that observation has no chance of being selected for the sample.
ID	names variables from the DATA= input data set to be included in the OUT= data set of selected units. If there is no ID statement, PROC SURVEYSELECT includes all variables from the DATA= data set in the OUT= data set. The ID variables can be character or numeric.

Using the SURVEYSELECT Procedure

The PROC SURVEYSELECT statement performs the following tasks:

- invokes the procedure
- optionally identifies input and output data sets
- specifies the sample selection method, the sample size, and other sample design parameters

The PROC SURVEYSELECT statement is the only statement required to create a simple random sample.

141

Options for the SURVEYSELECT Procedure

The following options can be specified in the PROC SURVEYSELECT statement:

To do this:	Use this option:
Specify the input data set	DATA=
Specify the output data set	OUT=
Suppress displayed output	NOPRINT
Specify selection method	METHOD=
Specify sample size	SAMPSIZE= N=
Specify random number seed	SEED=

142

Methods Used by the SURVEYSELECT Procedure

Selected values for the METHOD= option are as follows:

SYS	This method of systematic random sampling selects units at a fixed interval throughout the sampling frame or stratum after a random start.
URS	This method of unrestricted random sampling selects units with equal probability and with replacement. Because units are selected with replacement, a unit can be selected for the sample more than once.
SRS	This method of simple random sampling selects units with equal probability and without replacement. The selection probability for each individual unit equals n/N.

143

Using the SURVEYSELECT Procedure

This program creates a SAS data set, **ordersample**, that contains 10 observations randomly selected, without replacement, from the **orion.order_fact** SAS data set.

```
proc surveyselect data=orion.order_fact
                 (keep=Customer_ID Employee_ID
                       Street_ID Order_ID)
                  out=ordersample
                  method=srs n=10;
run;
```

144

p303d10

Using the SURVEYSELECT Procedure

In addition to creating the SAS data set, **`ordersample`**, PROC SURVEYSELECT provides the following information in the Output window:

```
          The SURVEYSELECT Procedure

Selection Method    Simple Random Sampling

    Input Data Set                ORDER_FACT
    Random Number Seed             525990001 ❶
    Sample Size                           10
    Selection Probability           0.016207 ❷
    Sampling Weight                     61.7 ❸
    Output Data Set              ORDERSAMPLE
```

145

① Because the SEED= option is not specified in the PROC SURVEYSELECT statement, the seed value is obtained using the datetime value from the computer's clock.

② The Selection Probability for each individual unit is calculated as 10/617 (sample size/number of observations in the input data set).

③ The Sampling Weight is the inverse of the selection probability, 617/10.

Comparison of the DATA Step and the SURVEYSELECT Procedure

DATA Step	PROC SURVEYSELECT
full power of DATA step processing	less coding
can create multiple output data sets	one output data set with additional statistics
part of Base SAS	part of SAS/STAT

146

Exercises

Level 1

7. Generating a Systematic Sample

Generate a systematic sample by selecting every tenth supplier starting with observation 10 from the data set **orion.shoe_vendors**. The sample should contain only the variables **Product_Line**, **Product_ID**, **Product_Name**, and **Supplier_Name**. Name the output data set **shoe_sample**.

Level 2

8. Generating a Random Sample with Replacement

Generate a random sample **with** replacement of 50 customers from **orion.customer_dim**. If the customer age is less than 40, place those customers in a data set named **underforty**. If the customer age is greater than or equal to 40, place the customers in a data set named **fortyplus**.

If you obtain zero observations in one of the data sets, run the program again. It is possible that the selected observations might all be 40 or older or all could be less than 40. If you used a constant seed in the RANUNI function, change the seed value and resubmit the program.

Level 3

9. Generating a Random Sample without Replacement

Generate a random sample without replacement of approximately 10% of the data in **orion.customer_dim**.

3.4 Chapter Review

Chapter Review

1. What is one purpose of an index?
2. What are the three ways to create an index?
3. What SAS system option is used to view information about index usage in the log?
4. How can you tell whether a SAS data set has an index?
5. Which functions can use an index?

149

continued...

Chapter Review

6. Does a subsetting IF use an index?
7. Which DATA set option forces SAS to use an index for WHERE clause processing?
8. Does sorting a data set before indexing help the index perform better?
9. Does a DATA step using a SET statement that reads and writes the same data set automatically maintain an index?

150

3.5 Solutions

Solutions to Exercises

1. **Creating Indexes**

   a. Open the program **p303e01**, and add the INDEX= option to create two indexes:
   - a simple index **Customer_ID**, based on the variable **Customer_ID**
   - a unique index **Order_ID**, based on the variable **Order_ID**

   p303s01

```
options msglevel=i;
data orders(index= Customer_ID Order_ID / unique));
   set orion.orders;
   Days_To_Delivery=Delivery_Date - Order_Date;
run;
options msglevel=n;
```

   b. Use PROC SQL to delete the **Order_ID** index from the **orders** data set.

```
proc sql;
   drop index Order_ID
      from orders;
quit;
```

   c. Use PROC DATASETS to create a composite index **OrDate** based on the **Order_ID** and **Order_Date** variables for the **orders** data set.

```
proc datasets library=work nolist;
   modify orders;
   index create OrDate=(Order_ID Order_Date);
quit;
```

   d. Use PROC CONTENTS or PROC DATASETS to look at the index information.

```
/*  CONTENTS solution */
proc contents data=orders;
run;
/*  DATASETS solution */
proc datasets library=work nolist;
   contents data=orders;
quit;
```

2. Updating Indexes

a. Use the **`orion.price_list`** SAS data set to create a temporary data set named **`price_list`** that contains a new variable named **`Unit_Profit`** that is the difference of the variables **`Unit_Sales_Price`** and **`Unit_Cost_Price`**. Create a unique index on the **`Product_ID`** variable.

p303s02

```
data price_list(index=(Product_ID / unique));
   set orion.price_list;
   Unit_Profit=Unit_Sales_Price - Unit_Cost_Price;
run;
```

b. Open the program **p303e02** and submit it.

c. View the log and determine whether the new observation was added.

Partial SAS Log

```
208  /*  Part b */
209  proc sql;
210     insert into price_list(Product_ID, Start_Date,
211                            End_Date, Unit_Cost_Price,
212                            Unit_Sales_Price, Factor,Unit_Profit)
213        values (210200100009, '15FEB2007'd, '31DEC9999'd, 15.50, 34.70, 1.00,
213!  19.20);
ERROR: Duplicate values not allowed on index Product_ID for file PRICE_LIST.
NOTE: This insert failed while attempting to add data from VALUES clause 1 to
      the data set.
NOTE: Deleting the successful inserts before error noted above to restore table
      to a consistent state.
214  quit;
NOTE: The SAS System stopped processing this step because of errors.
NOTE: PROCEDURE SQL used (Total process time):
      real time           0.31 seconds
      cpu time            0.04 seconds
```

d. Why or why not?

The new observation was not added because an observation with the value `210200100009` for **`Product_ID`** already exists in the data set **`price_list`**. The unique index prevents the second observation from being added.

3. Creating Indexes on New Variables

a. Create a temporary SAS data set named **`all_staff`** by concatenating the data sets **`orion.sales`** and **`orion.nonsales`**.

b. Create a new variable named **`Age_Hired`** that is the number of years between the variables **`Hire_Date`** and **`Birth_Date`**.

c. Index the **all_staff** data set on the variable **Age_Hired**.

p303s03

```
data all_staff(index=(Age_Hired));
   set orion.sales orion.nonsales;
   Age_Hired=int((Hire_Date - Birth_Date) / 365.25);
run;
```

4. Using an Index

Open the program **p303e04**, and submit it. Consult the log and answer the questions.

Questions:

a. Does Example 1 use an index? Why or why not?

No, the code uses an IF statement, not a WHERE statement.

Replace the IF statement with a WHERE statement, and resubmit the program. Does the example now use an index? Why or why not?

Yes, the WHERE statement uses the **SALEID** index.

b. Does Example 2 use an index? Why or why not?

No, the WHERE statement uses the OR operator, which prohibits index use.

Replace the OR operator with the AND operator, and resubmit the program. Does the example now use an index? Why or why not?

Yes, the WHERE statement uses both of the variables in the composite **SALEID** index with the AND operator.

c. Does Example 3 use an index? Why or why not?

No, too much of the data satisfied the WHERE statement criteria.

Replace the NE operator with the EQ operator, and resubmit the program. Does the example now use an index? Why or why not?

No, the data is too randomly distributed. The following INFO message is in the log:

```
INFO: Index Product_Group not used. Sorting into index order may help.
```

d. Does Example 4 use an index? Why or why not?

Yes, only a small subset of the data that satisfied the WHERE statement criteria was returned.

Add the IDXWHERE=NO data set option and resubmit the program. Is the output from the PROC PRINT step with an index different from the output from the PROC PRINT step without an index? No, the results are the same.

What message do you see in the log?

```
INFO: Data set option (IDXWHERE=NO) forced a sequential pass of the data rather than use
of an index for where-clause processing.
```

e. Does Example 5 use an index? Why or why not?

No, there is no index on the **Product_ID** variable in **orion.sales_history**. Even though **Product_ID** is part of the composite **Sale_ID** index, it cannot be used because it is not the primary key.

f. In Example 6, does the data set **SalesHistoryCopy** have an index?

No, the DATA step re-creates **orion.sales_history** as **work.saleshistorycopy**. The index is not copied when the data set is created in the DATA step.

5. Suppressing Index Usage

Create a detail report from the **orion.supplier** SAS data set that lists all of the variables and observations where **Supplier_ID** is greater than 1000. Ensure that the data is processed sequentially.

p303s05

```
options msglevel=i;
proc print data=orion.supplier(idxwhere=no);
   where Supplier_ID > 1000;
run;
```

6. Updating Centile Information for an Index

a. Submit the program **p303e06**. Do **not** clear your SAS Output window or the Results window!

Partial PROC CONTENTS Output

```
                    Alphabetic List of Indexes and Attributes

                                          Current     # of
                    Unique     Update     Update     Unique
#    Index          Option    Centiles    Percent    Values    Variables

... Lines Removed ...

2    Order_ID       YES              5          0       490
                                                               1230058123
                                                               1230699509
                                                               1231135703
                                                               1231544990
                                                               1231956902
                                                               1232601472
                                                               1233078086
                                                               1233920786
                                                               1234588648
                                                               1236055696
                                                               1237478988
                                                               1238353296
                                                               1238846184
                                                               1239408849
                                                               1240137702
                                                               1240692950
                                                               1241652707
                                                               1242265757
                                                               1242923327
                                                               1243568955
                                                               1244296274
```

b. Using the DATASETS procedure, set the indicator for updating the centile information about the **Order_ID** index to 1% of the data.

p303s06

```
proc datasets lib=work nolist;
   modify orders;
      index centiles Order_ID / updatecentiles=1;
quit;
```

c. Submit the program **p303e06c**, which adds new observations to the **work.orders** data set.

d. Submit a PROC CONTENTS step to view the contents of **orders**. Compare the centile information from step **6.a.** to the current centile information. Were the centiles updated or not?

Yes

```
proc contents data=orders centiles;
run;
```

Partial PROC CONTENTS Output

```
                    Alphabetic List of Indexes and Attributes

                                            Current    # of
                    Unique     Update       Update     Unique
#    Index          Option     Centiles     Percent    Values    Variables

... Lines Removed ...

2    Order_ID       YES               1           0       495
                                                                 1230058123
                                                                 1230699509
                                                                 1231169108
                                                                 1231544990
                                                                 1231976710
                                                                 1232618023
                                                                 1233131266
                                                                 1233920795
                                                                 1234665265
                                                                 1236113431
                                                                 1237664026
                                                                 1238370259
                                                                 1238872273
                                                                 1239418524
                                                                 1240283215
                                                                 1240870047
                                                                 1241789227
                                                                 1242477751
                                                                 1243039354
                                                                 1243670182
                                                                 1244554085
```

e. Why or why not?

More than 1% of the data was changed when adding five observations.

7. Generating a Systematic Sample

Generate a systematic sample by selecting every tenth supplier starting with observation 10 from the data set **orion.shoe_vendors**. The sample should contain only the variables **Product_Line**, **Product_ID**, **Product_Name**, and **Supplier_Name**. Name the output data set **shoe_sample**.

p303s07

```
data shoe_sample;
   do i=10 to TotObs by 10;
      set orion.shoe_vendors(keep=Product_Line Product_ID
                                  Product_Name Supplier_Name)
          nobs=TotObs
          point=i;
      output;
   end;
   stop;
run;

proc print data=shoe_sample;
  title "Systematic Sample  of Shoe Vendors";
run;
```

8. Generating a Random Sample with Replacement

Generate a random sample **with** replacement of 50 customers from **orion.customer_dim**. If the customer age is less than 40, place those customers in a data set named **underforty**. If the customer age is greater than or equal to 40, place them in a data set named **fortyplus**.

p303s08

```
data underforty fortyplus;
   drop i SampSize;
   SampSize=50;
   do i=1 to SampSize;
      PickIt=ceil(ranuni(0) * TotObs);
      set orion.customer_dim point=PickIt nobs=TotObs;
      if Customer_Age < 40 then output underforty;
         else output fortyplus;
    end;
    stop;
run;

proc print data=fortyplus;
   title 'Customers Forty or Older';
run;

proc print data=underforty;
   title 'Customers under Forty';
run;
```

9. Generating a Random Sample without Replacement

Generate a random sample **without** replacement of approximately 10% of the data in **orion.customer_dim**.

p303s09

```
data sample(drop=ObsLeft SampSize);
   SampSize=int(.10 * TotObs);
   ObsLeft=TotObs;
   do while(SampSize > 0 and ObsLeft > 0);
      PickIt + 1;
      if ranuni(0) < SampSize / ObsLeft then
         do;
            ObsPicked=PickIt;
            set orion.customer_dim point=PickIt
                                   nobs=TotObs;
            output;
            SampSize=SampSize - 1;
         end;
      ObsLeft=ObsLeft - 1;
   end;
   stop;
run;

/* to get an approximate 10% sample */
data sample;
   set orion.customer_dim;
   if ranuni(0) <= .10;
run;
```

Solutions to Student Activities (Polls/Quizzes)

3.02 Multiple Choice Poll – Correct Answer

If the WHERE statement retrieves a small subset of data, which of these resources is conserved?

a. I/O
b. Disk space
c. Memory
d. Programmer time

34

3.03 Multiple Answer Poll – Correct Answers

On which of these indexed variables can you assign the UNIQUE option?

a. **`Customer_ID`** in an **`orders`** data set where a customer can place multiple orders
b. **`Order_Date`** in an **`orders`** data set
c. **`Employee_ID`** in a data set containing each individual employee and the family members' names stored in variables **`Dependent1`** – **`Dependent10`**
d. **`Product_ID`** in a data set containing the product identifier and the product description

43

3.04 Quiz – Correct Answer

Open and submit the program **p303a01**.

What error messages are in the log?

```
1     options msglevel=n;
2     proc datasets library=orion nolist;
3        modify sales_history;
4           index create Customer_ID;
ERROR: An index named Customer_ID with the same definition already exists for
       file ORION.SALES_HISTORY.DATA.
5           index create Product_Group;
6           index create SaleID=(Order_ID
7                        Product_ID)/unique;
8     quit;

NOTE: Statements not processed because of errors noted above.
NOTE: The SAS System stopped processing this step because of errors.
NOTE: PROCEDURE DATASETS used (Total process time):
      real time           0.48 seconds
      cpu time            0.09 seconds
```

If an index exists, it must be deleted before it can be re-created.

54

3.05 Multiple Answer Poll – Correct Answers

Which of the following WHERE conditions could possibly use an index?

a. `where Product_ID=220100300042;`
(b.) `where Customer_ID ne 3245;`
(c.) `where Customer_ID=15020 or Customer_ID=14853;`
(d.) `where Order_ID=1230036183;`
e. `where Customer_ID='3245';`

72

a. No, there is no index on **Product_ID**.

b. Yes, although this would be a large subset, an index might be used.

c. Yes, SAS converts the WHERE statement to the following code:

```
where Customer_ID in (15020, 14853);
```

d. Yes, **Order_ID** is the primary key variable in the **SaleID** index, so that index could be used.

e. This statement would not execute because there is a syntax error. The WHERE statement requires a numeric constant (3245) because **Customer_ID** is a numeric variable.

3.06 Multiple Choice Poll – Correct Answer

When does the subsetting IF statement select observations?

a. before the observation is copied into the PDV

b. after the observation is in the PDV

76

3.07 Multiple Choice Poll – Correct Answer

Which of the following WHERE statements can use the composite index **SaleID** for compound optimization?

a. `where Order_ID=240200100038 or Product_ID=1230151326;`

b. `where Order_ID=. and Product_ID=1230151326;`

c. `where int(Order_ID/1000000000)=240 and Product_ID=1230151326;`

d. `where Order_ID>240000000000 and Product_ID<1240000000;`

83

a. No, the WHERE statement uses the OR comparison operator.

b. Yes, the WHERE statement can use **SALEID**. The conditions for compound optimization are met.

c. No, the WHERE statement uses a function on the variable **Order_ID** that is not the TRIM or SUBSTR function.

d. No, the WHERE statement does not use either the EQ or IN operator in one of the conditions.

3.08 Multiple Choice Poll – Correct Answer

Which of the following is used to determine the I/O to read a SAS data set sequentially?

a. the page size of the input data set and the number of buffers available
b. the number of observations and the number of variables
c. the page size of the output data set and the number of output buffers available

91

3.09 Quiz – Correct Answer

Are POINT= and NOBS= individual statements or part of the SET statement?

```
data subset;
   do PickIt=1 to TotObs by 50;
      set orion.order_fact(keep=Customer_ID
                Employee_ID Street_ID Order_ID)
          point=PickIt
          nobs=TotObs;
        output;
   end;
   stop;
run;
```

POINT= and NOBS= are part of the SET statement.

113 p303d07

3.10 Poll – Correct Answer

Instead of the CEIL function, would the INT function return the same results?

❍ Yes

❍ No (circled)

The INT function returns the integer portion of its argument, which could possibly be 0 and never be 5.

136

Solutions to Chapter Review

Chapter Review – Correct Answers

1. What is one purpose of an index?

   An index can be used to perform any of these tasks:

   - **yield faster access to small subsets (WHERE)**
   - **return observations in sorted order (BY)**
   - **perform table lookup operations (SET with KEY=)**
   - **join observations (PROC SQL)**
   - **modify observations (MODIFY with KEY=)**

2. What are the three ways to create an index?

   The INDEX= data set option, the DATASETS procedure, and the SQL procedure

151

continued...

Chapter Review – Correct Answers

3. What SAS system option is used to view information about index usage in the log?

   MSGLEVEL=I

4. How can you tell whether a SAS data set has an index?

   Use the CONTENTS or DATASETS procedure, the PROPERTIES window from the SAS Explorer, or SAS Management Console.

5. Which functions can use an index?

   TRIM and SUBSTR (under the condition that the second argument must be 1)

6. Does a subsetting IF use an index?

   No

152

continued...

Chapter Review – Correct Answers

7. Which DATA set option forces SAS to use an index for WHERE clause processing?

   IDXWHERE=YES or IDXNAME=*index-name*

8. Does sorting a data set before indexing help the index perform better?

   Yes

9. Does a DATA step using a SET statement that reads and writes the same data set automatically maintain an index?

   No

153

Chapter 4 Introduction to Lookup Techniques

4.1 Introduction to Lookup Techniques

Objectives

- Define table lookup.
- List table lookup techniques.

3

Table Lookups

Lookup *values* for a table lookup can be stored in the following:

- array
- hash object
- format
- data set

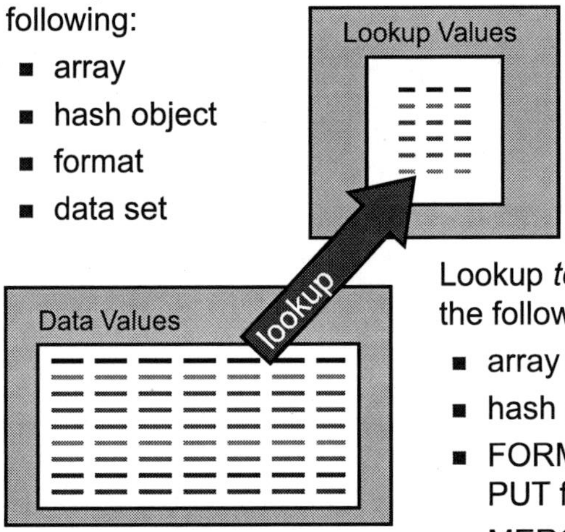

Lookup *techniques* include the following:

- array subscript value
- hash object key value
- FORMAT statement, PUT function
- MERGE, SET/SET, join

4

The hash object is new in SAS®9.

4.01 Multiple Choice Poll

Which of these is an example of a table lookup?

a. You have the data for January sales in one data set, February sales in a second data set, and March sales in a third. You need to create a report for the entire first quarter.

b. You want to send birthday cards to employees. The employees' names and addresses are in one data set and their birthdates are in another.

c. You need to calculate the amount each customer owes for his purchases. The price per item and the number of items purchased are stored in the same data set.

6

Overview of Table Lookup Techniques

- Arrays, hash objects, and formats provide an in-memory lookup table.
- The DATA step MERGE statement, multiple SET statements in the DATA step, and SQL procedure joins use lookup values that are stored on disk.

8

4.2 In-Memory Lookup Techniques

Objectives

- Describe arrays as a lookup technique.
- Describe hash objects as a lookup technique.
- Describe formats as a lookup technique.

10

4.02 Multiple Answer Poll

Which techniques do you currently use when you perform table lookups with a single data set?

a. Arrays
b. Hash object
c. Formats
d. None of the above

12

Overview of Arrays

An array is similar to a numbered row of buckets.

1 2 3 4

- SAS puts a value in a bucket based on the bucket number.
- A value is retrieved from a bucket based on the bucket number.

15

Overview of Arrays

General form of the ARRAY statement:

```
DATA data-set-name;
     ARRAY array-name { subscript } <$><length>
                 <array-elements> <(initial-value-list)>;
     < read statement (s)>
     new-variable=array-name{subscript-value};
RUN;
```

The ARRAY statement associates variables or initial values to be retrieved using the array name and a subscript value.

The assignment statement retrieves values from the array based on the value of the subscript.

✎ The read statement can be SET, MERGE or INFILE/INPUT statements.

16

Overview of Arrays

```
data country_info;
   array Cont_Name{91:96} $ 30 _temporary_
         ('North America',
          ' ',
          'Europe',
          'Africa',
          'Asia',
          'Australia/Pacific');
   set orion.country;
   Continent=Cont_Name{Continent_ID};
run;
```

The ARRAY statement associates variables or initial values to be retrieved using the array name and a subscript value.

The assignment statement retrieves values from the array based on the value of the subscript.

17 p304d01

Setup for the Poll

p304d01

```
data country_info;
   array Cont_Name{91:96} $ 30 _temporary_
         ('North America',
          ' ',
          'Europe',
          'Africa',
          'Asia',
          'Australia/Pacific');
   set orion.country;
   Continent=Cont_Name{Continent_ID};
run;
```

19

4.03 Multiple Choice Poll

In **p304d01**, how many elements are in the array `Cont_name`?

a. 0
b. 5
c. 6
d. unknown

20

Overview of a Hash Object

A hash object is similar to rows of buckets that are identified by the value of a key.

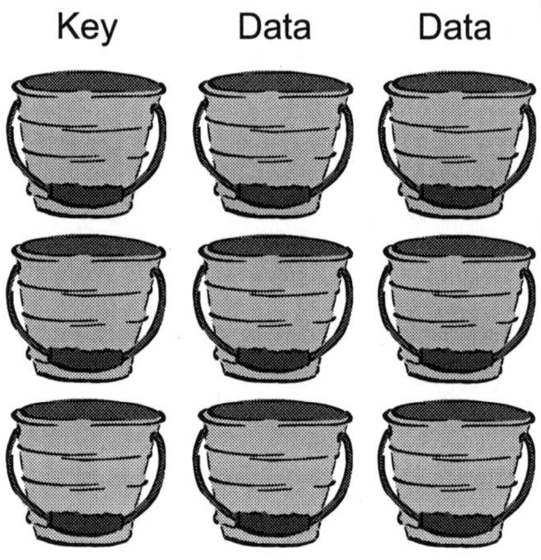

- SAS puts value(s) in the **data** bucket(s) based on the value(s) in the **key** bucket.
- Value(s) are retrieved from the **data** bucket(s) based on the value(s) in the **key** bucket.

24

Overview of Hash Objects

General form of the hash object:

DATA *data-set-name*;
< *read statement(s)* >
IF _N_=1 THEN DO;
DECLARE HASH *object-name(<attribute:value>)*;
object-name.**DEFINEKEY(**'*key-name*'**);**
object-name.**DEFINEDATA(**'*data-name*'**);**
object-name.**DEFINEDONE();**
END;
return-code=*object-name*.**FIND**(<key: *value*>);
RUN;

The syntax within the DO group defines and can populate the hash object.

The FIND method retrieves the data value based on the key value.

The read statement can be SET, MERGE, or INFILE/INPUT statements.

25

Overview of Hash Objects

```
data country_info;
   length Continent_Name $ 30;
   if _N_=1 then do;
      declare hash Cont_Name(dataset:'orion.continent');
      Cont_Name.definekey('Continent_ID');
      Cont_Name.definedata('Continent_Name');
      Cont_Name.definedone();
   end;
   set orion.country;
   rc=Cont_Name.find(key:Continent_ID);
   if rc=0;
run;
```

The syntax within the DO group defines and populates the hash object.

The FIND method retrieves the data value based on the key value.

p304d02

26

Setup for the Poll

p304d02

```
data country_info;
   length Continent_Name $ 30;
   if _N_=1 then do;
      declare hash Cont_Name(dataset:'orion.continent');
      Cont_Name.definekey('Continent_ID');
      Cont_Name.definedata('Continent_Name');
      Cont_Name.definedone();
   end;
   set orion.country;
   rc=Cont_Name.find(key:Continent_ID);
   if rc=0;
run;
```

28

4.04 Multiple Choice Poll

In **p304d02**, how many times do the statements in the DO group execute?

a. only once

b. once for every observation in the data set **`orion.country`**

c. once for every observation in the data set **`orion.continent`**

29

Overview of a Format

A *format* is similar to rows of buckets that are identified by the data value.

Data Value Label

- SAS puts data values and label values in the buckets when the format is used in a FORMAT statement, PUT function, or PUT statement.
- SAS uses a binary search on the **data value** bucket in order to return the value in the **label** bucket.

33

Overview of a Format

General form of the user-defined format:

```
PROC FORMAT;
   VALUE <$>fmtname range-1=label-1
                         . . .
                    range-n=label-n;
RUN;

DATA data-set-name;
     < read statement(s)>;
     new-variable=PUT(variable,fmtname.);
RUN;
```

The FORMAT step compiles the format and stores it on disk.

When the PUT function executes, the format is loaded into memory, and a binary search is used to retrieve the format value.

✎ The read statement can be SET, MERGE, or INFILE/INPUT statements.

34

Overview of a Format

```
proc format;
   value Cont_Name
               91='North America'
               93='Europe'
               94='Africa'
               95='Asia'
               96='Australia/Pacific';
run;

data country_info;
   set orion.country;
   Continent=put(Continent_ID,Cont_Name.);
run;
```

The FORMAT step compiles the format and stores it on disk.

When the PUT function executes, the format is loaded into memory, and a binary search is used to retrieve the format value.

35

p304d03

4.3 Disk Storage Techniques

Objectives

- List methods for combining data horizontally.
- Use multiple SET statements to combine data horizontally.
- Compare methods for combining SAS data sets.

37

Combining Data Horizontally

DATA step techniques for combining data horizontally include using the following:

- MERGE statement
- multiple SET statements
- UPDATE statement
- MODIFY statement

In addition, you can use the SQL procedure with an inner or outer join.

38

4.05 Multiple Answer Poll

Which techniques do you currently use when you perform table lookups with multiple data sets?

a. MERGE statement
b. Joins
c. Multiple SET statements
d. UDPATE statement
e. MODIFY statement
f. None of the above

40

Overview of Merges and Joins

The DATA step MERGE and the SQL join operators are similar to multiple stacks of buckets that are referred to by the value of one or more common variables.

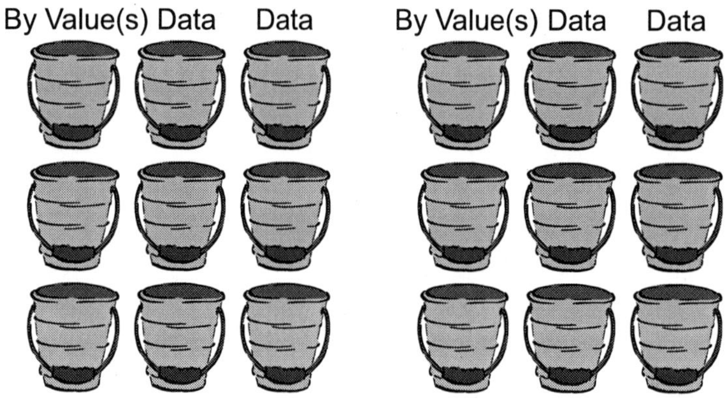

41

DATA Step MERGE Statement

General form of the DATA step merge:

DATA *data-set-name*;
  MERGE *SAS-data-sets*;
  BY *variables*;
RUN;

Matches on equal values for like-named variables:

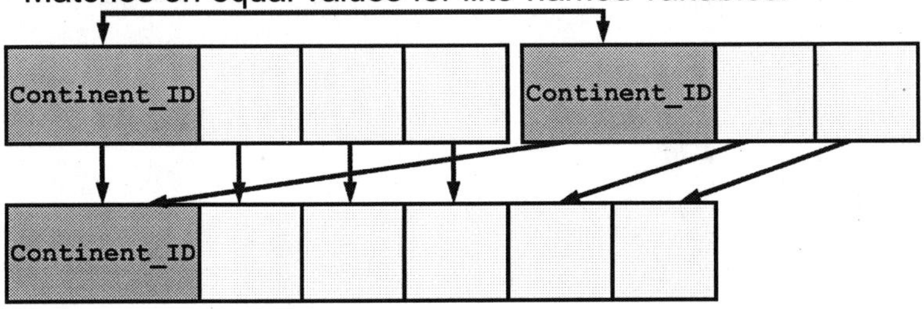

42

DATA Step MERGE Statement

```
proc sort data=orion.country out=country;
   by Continent_ID;
run;

data country_info;
   merge country orion.continent;
   by Continent_ID;
run;
```

Matches on equal values for like-named variables

43

p304d04

Setup for the Poll

p304d04

```
proc sort data=orion.country out=country;
   by Continent_ID;
run;

data country_info;
   merge country orion.continent;
   by Continent_ID;
run;
```

45

4.06 Multiple Choice Poll

In **p304d04**, if the data set **`country`** has seven observations and the data set **`orion.continent`** has five observations, what stops the execution of the DATA step?

a. end of file for the data set **`country`**

b. end of file for the data set **`orion.continent`**

46

The SQL Procedure

You can use an SQL procedure inner or outer join to create a SAS data set.

General form of the SQL procedure CREATE TABLE statement with an inner join:

PROC SQL;
    CREATE TABLE *SAS-data-set* **AS**
    SELECT *column-1, column-2,… ,column-n*
        FROM *table-1, table-2,…,table-n*
        WHERE *joining criteria*
        ORDER BY *sorting criteria*;
QUIT;

Performs an inner join based on the WHERE criteria

48

The SQL Procedure

```
proc sql;
   create table country_info as
   select country.*, Continent_Name
       from orion.country, orion.continent
       where country.Continent_ID=
             continent.Continent_ID;
   order by country.Continent_ID;
quit;
```

Performs an inner join where the `Continent_ID` values from both data sets are equal

p304d05

49

4.07 Multiple Choice Poll

Which of the following is true of the SQL inner join?

a. The resulting data set contains only the observations with matching key values.

b. The resulting data set contains both the observations with matching key values and those observations where the key values do not match.

51

Multiple SET Statements

The DATA step with multiple SET statements combines data sets by performing one-to-one reading.

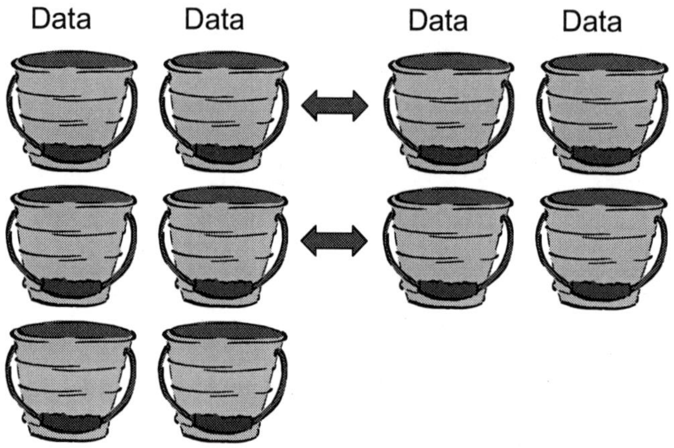

53

Multiple SET Statements

You can use multiple SET statements to combine observations from several SAS data sets.

When you use multiple SET statements, the following occurs:

- Processing stops when SAS encounters the end-of-file marker on either data set.
- The variables in the PDV are not reinitialized when a second SET statement is executed.

54

Multiple SET Statements

General form of the DATA step with multiple set statements:

```
DATA data-set-name;
    SET SAS-data-set;
    SET SAS-data-set;
RUN;
```

55

Multiple SET Statements

```
data country_info;
   set orion.country;
   set orion.continent;
run;
```

Listing of **country_info**

Obs	Country	Country_ Name	Population	Country_ ID	Continent_ ID	Country_Former Name	Continent_Name
1	AU	Australia	20,000,000	160	91		North America
2	CA	Canada	.	260	93		Europe
3	DE	Germany	80,000,000	394	94	East/West Germany	Africa
4	IL	Israel	5,000,000	475	95		Asia
5	TR	Turkey	70,000,000	905	96		Australia/Pacific

56 p304d06

Execution

one

X	Y
1	2
2	3
3	4

two

Z
A
B

```
data three;
   set one;
   set two;
   Total=X+Y;
run;
```

PDV

X	Y	Z	Total	_N_
1	2		.	1

57 ...

Execution

one

X	Y
1	2
2	3
3	4

two

Z
A
B

```
data three;
   set one;
   set two;
   Total=X+Y;
run;
```

PDV

X	Y	Z	Total	D	_N_
1	2	A	.		1

58 ...

Execution

one

X	Y
1	2
2	3
3	4

two

Z
A
B

```
data three;
   set one;
   set two;
   Total=X+Y;
run;
```

PDV

X	Y	Z	Total	D	_N_
1	2	A	3		1

59 ...

Execution

one

X	Y
1	2
2	3
3	4

two

Z
A
B

```
data three;
   set one;
   set two;
   Total=X+Y;
run;
```

Implicit OUTPUT;
Implicit RETURN;

PDV

X	Y	Z	Total	D _N_
1	2	A	3	1

60 ...

Execution

one

X	Y
1	2
2	3
3	4

two

Z
A
B

```
data three;
   set one;
   set two;
   Total=X+Y;
run;
```

Initialize PDV

PDV

X	Y	Z	Total	D _N_
1	2	A	.	2

61 ...

Execution

one

X	Y
1	2
2	3
3	4

two

Z
A
B

```
data three;
   set one;
   set two;
   Total=X+Y;
run;
```

PDV

X	Y	Z	Total	D _N_
2	3	A	.	2

62 ...

Execution

one

X	Y
1	2
2	3
3	4

two

Z
A
B

```
data three;
   set one;
   set two;
   Total=X+Y;
run;
```

PDV

X	Y	Z	Total	D _N_
2	3	B	.	2

63 ...

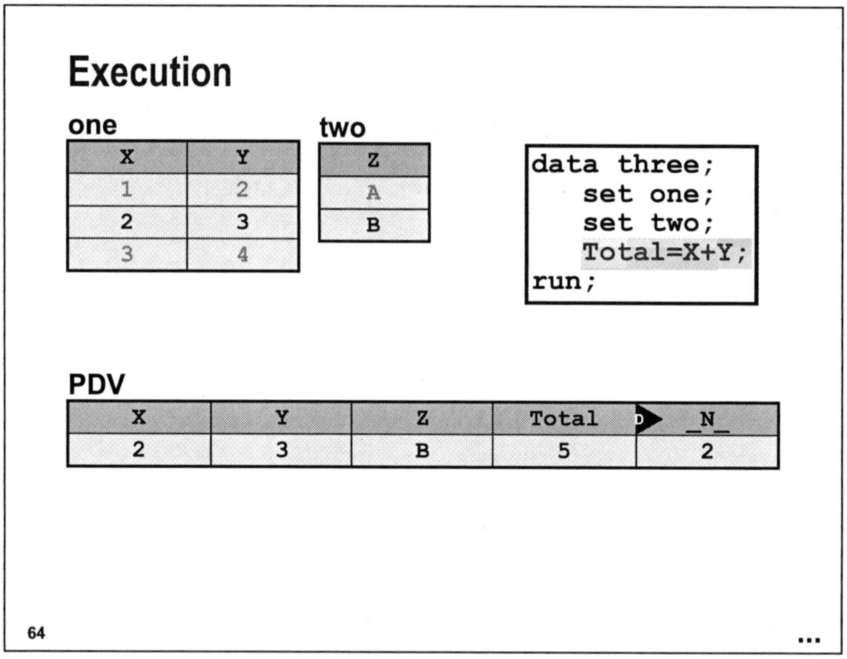
Execution
one
X Y
1 2
2 3
3 4
two
Z
A
B
data three;
set one;
set two;
Total=X+Y;
run;
PDV
X Y Z Total D _N_
2 3 B 5 2
64
...

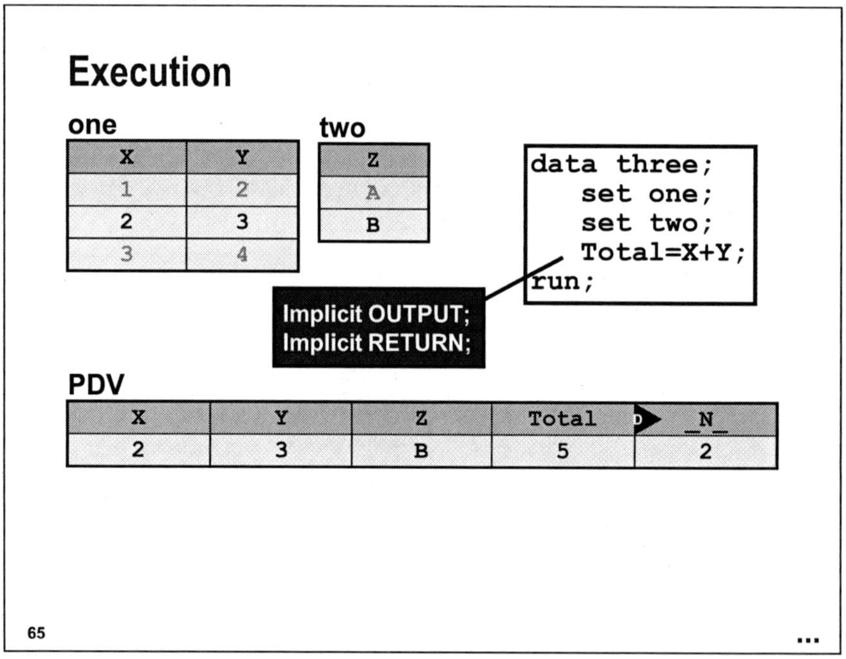
Execution
one
X Y
1 2
2 3
3 4
two
Z
A
B
data three;
set one;
set two;
Total=X+Y;
run;
Implicit OUTPUT;
Implicit RETURN;
PDV
X Y Z Total D _N_
2 3 B 5 2
65
...

Execution

one

X	Y
1	2
2	3
3	4

two

Z
A
B

```
data three;
   set one;
   set two;
   Total=X+Y;
run;
```

Initialize PDV

PDV

X	Y	Z	Total	D _N_
2	3	B	.	3

66 ...

Execution

one

X	Y
1	2
2	3
3	4

two

Z
A
B

```
data three;
   set one;
   set two;
   Total=X+Y;
run;
```

PDV

X	Y	Z	Total	D _N_
3	4	B	.	3

67 ...

Execution

one

X	Y
1	2
2	3
3	4

two

Z
A
B

EOF

```
data three;
   set one;
   set two;
   Total=X+Y;
run;
```

Processing stops

PDV

X	Y	Z	Total	D _N_
3	4	B	.	3

three

X	Y	Z	Total
1	2	A	3
2	3	B	5

68

Setup for the Poll

The previous example created a data set named **three** with two observations.

one

X	Y
1	2
2	3
3	4

two

Z
A
B

```
data three;
   set one;
   set two;
   Total=X+Y;
run;
```

Using the same **one** and **two** data sets, if the SET statements were reversed, how many observations would be in the data set **three**?

```
data three;
   set two;
   set one;
   Total=X+Y;
run;
```

70

4.08 Multiple Choice Poll

Using the same **one** and **two** data sets, if the SET statements were reversed, how many observations would be in the data set **three**?

a. 5
b. 2
c. 3
d. 6

71

DATA Step Methods for Reading SAS Data

Code	Which variables are reinitialized to missing at the top of the DATA step?	What stops the DATA step?
`data two; set one; New_Var=Value; run;`	variables created in the DATA step	end of the file for data set **one**
`data three; merge one two; by Var; New_Var=Value; run;`	▪ variables created in the DATA step ▪ all variables when the BY value changes	the last end of file that is encountered
`data three; set one two; New_Var=Value; run;`	▪ variables created in the DATA step ▪ all variables when SAS finishes reading data set **one** and starts reading data set **two**	end of the file for data set **two**
`data three; set one; set two; New_Var=Value; run;`	variables created in the DATA step	the first end of file that is encountered

73

4.4 Chapter Review

Chapter Review

1. What are the three types of in-memory table lookups?

2. What are three types of disk storage table lookups?

3. When multiple SET statements are executed, when does execution stop?

74

4.5 Solutions

Solutions to Student Activities (Polls/Quizzes)

4.01 Multiple Choice Poll – Correct Answer

Which of these is an example of a table lookup?

a. You have the data for January sales in one data set, February sales in a second data set, and March sales in a third. You need to create a report for the entire first quarter.

(b.) You want to send birthday cards to employees. The employees' names and addresses are in one data set and their birthdates are in another.

c. You need to calculate the amount each customer owes for his purchases. The price per item and the number of items purchased are stored in the same data set.

7

4.03 Multiple Choice Poll – Correct Answer

In **p304d01**, how many elements are in the array `Cont_name`?

a. 0

b. 5

(c.) 6

d. unknown

21

4.04 Multiple Choice Poll – Correct Answer

In **p304d02**, how many times do the statements in the DO group execute?

a. only once
b. once for every observation in the data set `orion.country`
c. once for every observation in the data set `orion.continent`

30

4.06 Multiple Choice Poll – Correct Answer

In **p304d04**, if the data set `country` has seven observations and the data set `orion.continent` has five observations, what stops the execution of the DATA step?

a. end of file for the data set `country`
b. end of file for the data set `orion.continent`

47

4.07 Multiple Choice Poll – Correct Answer

Which of the following is true of the SQL inner join?

a. The resulting data set contains only the observations with matching key values.
b. The resulting data set contains both the observations with matching key values and those observations where the key values do not match.

52

4.08 Multiple Choice Poll – Correct Answer

Using the same **one** and **two** data sets, if the SET statements were reversed, how many observations would be in the data set **three**?

a. 5
b. 2
c. 3
d. 6

72

Solutions to Chapter Review

Chapter Review – Correct Answers

1. What are the three types of in-memory table lookups?
   arrays, hash objects, and formats
2. What are three types of disk storage table lookups?
   PROC SQL, the DATA step with a MERGE statement, or the DATA step with multiple SET statements
3. When multiple SET statements are executed, when does execution stop?
   Execution stops when the first end of file is encountered.

75

Chapter 5 Using DATA Step Arrays

5.1 Using One-Dimensional Arrays

Objectives

- Define one-dimensional arrays.
- Use a one-dimensional array for a table lookup task.

3

Overview of Arrays (Review)

An array is similar to a row of numbered buckets.

- SAS puts a value in a bucket based on the bucket number.
- A value is retrieved from a bucket based on the bucket number.

4

Defining Arrays (Review)

An *array* is a temporary grouping of SAS variables that are arranged in a particular order and identified by an array name.

The following tasks can be accomplished using an array:

- performing repetitive calculations on a group of variables
- creating many variables with the same attributes
- restructuring data
- performing a table lookup with one or more numeric factors

✎ An array exists only for the duration of the current DATA step.

5

Using One-Dimensional Arrays (Review)

To use an array, declare the array by using an ARRAY statement.

General form of the one-dimensional ARRAY statement:

> **ARRAY** *array-name* {*number-of-elements*} <$> <*length*>
> <*list-of-variables*> <(*initial-values*)>;

6

array-name	is a SAS name that identifies the group of variables.
number-of- elements	is the number of variables in the group. You must enclose this value in parentheses, braces, or brackets.
$	indicates that the elements in the array are character elements.
length	specifies the length of elements in the array that were not previously assigned a length.
list-of-variables	is a list of the names of the variables in the group. All variables that are defined in a given array must be of the same type, either all character or all numeric.
initial-values	gives initial values for the corresponding positional elements in the array.
TEMPORARY	is a keyword that can be used instead of *list-of-variables* to define an array that is not associated with program data vector variables. Arrays of temporary elements are useful when the only purpose for creating an array is to perform a calculation. To preserve the result of the calculation, assign it to a variable. You can improve performance time by using temporary data elements.

Using One-Dimensional Arrays (Review)

Examples of an ARRAY statement follow.

```
array numarray{3} Num1 - Num3;
```

```
array char{4} $ 6;
```

Array Name

```
array num{5} _temporary_ (5, 6, 7, 8, 9);
```

```
array yr{2000:2002} Yr2000 Yr2001 Yr2002;
```

8

...

Using One-Dimensional Arrays (Review)

Examples of an ARRAY statement follow.

```
array numarray{3} Num1 - Num3;
```

```
array char{4} $ 6;
```

number of elements

```
array num{5} _temporary_ (5, 6, 7, 8, 9);
```

```
array yr{2000:2002} Yr2000 Yr2001 Yr2002;
```

9

...

Using One-Dimensional Arrays (Review)

Examples of an ARRAY statement follow.

```
array numarray{3} Num1 - Num3;
```

names three numeric variables

```
array char{4} $ 6;
```

creates four character variables, char1 – char4, each a length of 6

```
array num{5} _temporary_ (5, 6, 7, 8, 9);
```

creates temporary numeric elements, and stores the numeric values 5, 6, 7, 8, 9

```
array yr{2000:2002} Yr2000 Yr2001 Yr2002;
```

names three numeric variables

10

5.01 Multiple Choice Poll

How many elements are referenced by the following ARRAY statement?

```
array numarray{*} Num1 - Num12;
```

a. 0
b. 1
c. 12
d. Unknown

12

The DIM Function

You can use the DIM function to return the number of elements in an array. For example, use the DIM function to provide the end value for a DO loop.

```
array numarray{*} Num1 - Num12;
    <additional statements>
do i=1 to dim(numarray);
    <additional statements>
end;
```

Equivalent code:

```
array numarray{12} Num1 - Num12;
    <additional statements>
do i=1 to 12;
    <additional statements>
end;
```

14

The DIM function returns the number of elements in a one-dimensional array.

General form of the DIM function:

DIM(*array-name*)

array-name specifies the name of an array that was previously defined in the same DATA step.

Business Scenario

The data set **orion.employee_payroll** contains each employee's hired date and current salary.

Partial Listing of **orion.employee_payroll**

Employee_ID	Employee_Gender	Salary	Birth_Date	Employee_Hire_Date	Employee_Term_Date	Marital_Status	Dependents
120101	M	163040	18AUG1976	01JUL2003	.	S	0
120102	M	108255	11AUG1969	01JUN1989	.	O	2
120103	M	87975	22JAN1949	01JAN1974	.	M	1
120104	F	46230	11MAY1954	01JAN1981	.	M	1
120105	F	27110	21DEC1974	01MAY1999	.	S	0
...	...	...	...	...	...	...	...

15

Business Scenario

The data set **`orion.salary_stats`** contains statistics for all Orion Star employees for the years 1974 through 2007. For example, the average salary of the employees hired in 1974 is currently $39,243.61.

Partial Listing of **`orion.salary_stats`**

Statistic	Yr1974	Yr1975	Yr1976	. . .	Yr2006	Yr2007
Num_of_Emps	61	4	6	. . .	97	3
Median_Salary	30025	29442.5	30020	. . .	26970	27240
Std_Salary	28551.9	9918.35	22356.91	. . .	2579.67	2922.12
Sum_Salary	2393860	132150	235030	. . .	2704720	86585
Avg_Salary	39243.61	33037.5	39171.67	. . .	27883.71	28861.67

16

Business Scenario

The two data sets must be combined to calculate the difference between the average salary and the actual current salary for each employee based on the year of hire.

Partial Listing of **`compare`**

Using One Dimensional Arrays

Obs	Employee_ID	Year_ Hired	Salary	Average	Salary_Dif
1	120101	2003	$163,040.00	$35,082.50	$127,957.50
2	120102	1989	$108,255.00	$88,588.75	$19,666.25
3	120103	1974	$87,975.00	$39,243.61	$48,731.39
4	120104	1981	$46,230.00	$36,436.67	$9,793.33
5	120105	1999	$27,110.00	$36,533.75	$-9,423.75
6	120106	1974	$26,960.00	$39,243.61	$-12,283.61
7	120107	1974	$30,475.00	$39,243.61	$-8,768.61
8	120108	2006	$27,660.00	$27,883.71	$-223.71

17

Setup for the Poll

The two data sets that need to be combined are as follows:

Partial Listing of **orion.salary_stats**

Statistic	Yr1974	Yr1975	Yr1976	. . .	Yr2006	Yr2007
Avg_Salary	39243.61	33037.5	39171.67	. . .	27883.71	28861.67

Partial Listing of **orion.employee_payroll**

Employee _ID	Employee _Gender	Salary	Birth_ Date	Employee_ Hire_Date	. . .
120101	M	163040	18AUG1976	01JUL2003	. . .
120102	M	108255	11AUG1969	01JUN1989	. . .
120103	M	87975	22JAN1949	01JAN1974	. . .
120104	F	46230	11MAY1954	01JAN1981	. . .
120105	F	27110	21DEC1974	01MAY1999	. . .

19

5.02 Poll

Can the two data sets be merged with the DATA step MERGE statement or joined with the SQL procedure without pre-processing the data?

❍ Yes

❍ No

20

5.03 Poll

What do the two data sets have in common?

❍ They have the year in common.

❍ They have nothing in common.

22

Using a One-Dimensional Array

```
data compare;
   keep Employee_ID Year_Hired Salary Average
        Salary_Dif;
   format Salary Average Salary_Dif dollar12.2;
① array yr{1974:2007} Yr1974-Yr2007;
② if _N_=1 then set orion.salary_stats
         (where=(Statistic='Avg_Salary'));
   set orion.employee_payroll
       (keep=Employee_ID
             Employee_Hire_Date
             Salary);
   Year_Hired=year(Employee_Hire_Date);
③ Average=yr{Year_Hired};
   Salary_Dif=Salary-Average;
run;
```

24

p305d01

① The array **yr** is associated with the variables **Yr1974**, **Yr1975**, **Yr1976**, and so forth through **YR2007**.

② Read only the observation where the value of the variable **Statistic** is Avg_Salary.

③ The value of the element on the **yr** array is referenced positionally by the value of the variable **Year_Hired** and is assigned to the variable **Average**.

Execution

Partial Listing of `orion.salary_stats`

Statistic	Yr1974	Yr1975	Yr1976	. . .
Avg_Salary	39243.61	33037.5	39171.67	. . .

Partial Listing of `orion.employee_payroll`

Employee_ID	Employee_Hire_Date	Salary
120101	01JUL2003	163040
120102	01JUN1989	108255
120103	01JAN1974	87975
120104	01JAN1981	46230
120105	01MAY1999	27110

```
data compare;
   keep Employee_ID Year_Hired Salary Average
        Salary_Dif;
   format Salary Average Salary_Dif dollar12.2;
   array yr{1974:2007} Yr1974-Yr2007;
   if _N_=1 then set orion.salary_stats
         (where=(Statistic='Avg_Salary'));
   set orion.employee_payroll
      (keep=Employee_ID Employee_Hire_Date Salary);
   Year_Hired=year(Employee_Hire_Date);
   Average=yr{Year_Hired};
   Salary_Dif=Salary-Average;
run;
```

Partial PDV

Salary	Average	Salary_Dif	D Yr1974 yr{1974}	D Yr1975 yr{1975}	D Yr1976 yr{1976}	D Yr1977 yr{1977}	D Yr1978 yr{1978}	. . .
.	.	.	39243.61	33037.5	39171.67	34170	37506.25	

D Yr2003 yr{2003}	D Yr2004 yr{2004}	. . .	D Yr2007 yr{2007}	D Statistic	Employee_ID	D Employee_Hire_Date	Year_Hired	D _N_
35082.5	29904.44		28861.67	Avg_Salary	.	.	.	1

26 ...

Execution

Partial Listing of `orion.salary_stats`

Statistic	Yr1974	Yr1975	Yr1976	. . .
Avg_Salary	39243.61	33037.5	39171.67	. . .

Partial Listing of `orion.employee_payroll`

Employee_ID	Employee_Hire_Date	Salary
120101	01JUL2003	163040
120102	01JUN1989	108255
120103	01JAN1974	87975
120104	01JAN1981	46230
120105	01MAY1999	27110

```
data compare;
   keep Employee_ID Year_Hired Salary Average
        Salary_Dif;
   format Salary Average Salary_Dif dollar12.2;
   array yr{1974:2007} Yr1974-Yr2007;
   if _N_=1 then set orion.salary_stats
         (where=(Statistic='Avg_Salary'));
   set orion.employee_payroll
      (keep=Employee_ID Employee_Hire_Date Salary);
   Year_Hired=year(Employee_Hire_Date);
   Average=yr{Year_Hired};
   Salary_Dif=Salary-Average;
run;
```

Partial PDV

Salary	Average	Salary_Dif	D Yr1974 yr{1974}	D Yr1975 yr{1975}	D Yr1976 yr{1976}	D Yr1977 yr{1977}	D Yr1978 yr{1978}	. . .
163040	.	.	39243.61	33037.5	39171.67	34170	37506.25	

D Yr2003 yr{2003}	D Yr2004 yr{2004}	. . .	D Yr2007 yr{2007}	D Statistic	Employee_ID	D Employee_Hire_Date	Year_Hired	D _N_
35082.5	29904.44		28861.67	Avg_Salary	120101	01JUL2003	.	1

27 ...

Execution

Partial Listing of orion.employee_payroll

Employee_ID	Employee_Hire_Date	Salary
120101	01JUL2003	163040
120102	01JUN1989	108255
120103	01JAN1974	87975
120104	01JAN1981	46230
120105	01MAY1999	27110

Partial Listing of orion.salary_stats

Statistic	Yr1974	Yr1975	Yr1976	. . .
Avg_Salary	39243.61	33037.5	39171.67	. . .

```
data compare;
   keep Employee_ID Year_Hired Salary Average
        Salary_Dif;
   format Salary Average Salary_Dif dollar12.2;
   array yr{1974:2007} Yr1974-Yr2007;
   if _N_=1 then set orion.salary_stats
        (where=(Statistic='Avg_Salary'));
   set orion.employee_payroll
      (keep=Employee_ID Employee_Hire_Date Salary);
   Year_Hired=year(Employee_Hire_Date);
   Average=yr{Year_Hired};
   Salary_Dif=Salary-Average;
run;
```

Partial PDV

Salary	Average	Salary_Dif	D Yr1974 yr{1974}	D Yr1975 yr{1975}	D Yr1976 yr{1976}	D Yr1977 yr{1977}	D Yr1978 yr{1978}	. . .
163040	.	.	39243.61	33037.5	39171.67	34170	37506.25	

D Yr2003 yr{2003}	D Yr2004 yr{2004}	. . .	D Yr2007 yr{2007}	D Statistic	Employee_ID	D Employee_Hire_Date	Year_Hired	D _N_
35082.5	29904.44		28861.67	Avg_Salary	120101	01JUL2003	2003	1

28 ...

Execution

Partial Listing of orion.employee_payroll

Employee_ID	Employee_Hire_Date	Salary
120101	01JUL2003	163040
120102	01JUN1989	108255
120103	01JAN1974	87975
120104	01JAN1981	46230
120105	01MAY1999	27110

Partial Listing of orion.salary_stats

Statistic	Yr1974	Yr1975	Yr1976	. . .
Avg_Salary	39243.61	33037.5	39171.67	. . .

```
data compare;
   keep Employee_ID Year_Hired Salary Average
        Salary_Dif;
   format Salary Average Salary_Dif dollar12.2;
   array yr{1974:2007} Yr1974-Yr2007;
   if _N_=1 then set orion.salary_stats
        (where=(Statistic='Avg_Salary'));
   set orion.employee_payroll
      (keep=Employee_ID Employee_Hire_Date Salary);
   Year_Hired=year(Employee_Hire_Date);
   Average=yr{2003};
   Salary_Dif=Salary-Average;
run;
```

Partial PDV

Salary	Average	Salary_Dif	D Yr1974 yr{1974}	D Yr1975 yr{1975}	D Yr1976 yr{1976}	D Yr1977 yr{1977}	D Yr1978 yr{1978}	. . .
163040	35082.5	.	39243.61	33037.5	39171.67	34170	37506.25	

D Yr2003 yr{2003}	D Yr2004 yr{2004}	. . .	D Yr2007 yr{2007}	D Statistic	Employee_ID	D Employee_Hire_Date	Year_Hired	D _N_
35082.5	29904.44		28861.67	Avg_Salary	120101	01JUL2003	2003	1

30 ...

Execution

Partial Listing of **orion.salary_stats**

Statistic	Yr1974	Yr1975	Yr1976	. . .
Avg_Salary	39243.61	33037.5	39171.67	. . .

Partial Listing of **orion.employee_payroll**

Employee_ID	Employee_Hire_Date	Salary
120101	01JUL2003	163040
120102	01JUN1989	108255
120103	01JAN1974	87975
120104	01JAN1981	46230
120105	01MAY1999	27110

```
data compare;
   keep Employee_ID Year_Hired Salary Average
        Salary_Dif;
   format Salary Average Salary_Dif dollar12.2;
   array yr{1974:2007} Yr1974-Yr2007;
   if _N_=1 then set orion.salary_stats
          (where=(Statistic='Avg_Salary'));
   set orion.employee_payroll
       (keep=Employee_ID Employee_Hire_Date Salary);
   Year_Hired=year(Employee_Hire_Date);
   Average=yr{Year_Hired};
   Salary_Dif=Salary-Average;
run;
```

Partial PDV

Salary	Average	Salary_Dif	D Yr1974 yr{1974}	D Yr1975 yr{1975}	D Yr1976 yr{1976}	D Yr1977 yr{1977}	D Yr1978 yr{1978}	. . .
163040	35082.5	127957.5	39243.61	33037.5	39171.67	34170	37506.25	

D Yr2003 yr{2003}	D Yr2004 yr{2004}	. . .	D Yr2007 yr{2007}	D Statistic	Employee_ID	D Employee_Hire_Date	Year_Hired	D _N_
35082.5	29904.44		28861.67	Avg_Salary	120101	01JUL2003	2003	1

31 ...

Execution

Partial Listing of **orion.salary_stats**

Statistic	Yr1974	Yr1975	Yr1976	. . .
Avg_Salary	39243.61	33037.5	39171.67	. . .

Partial Listing of **orion.employee_payroll**

Employee_ID	Employee_Hire_Date	Salary
120101	01JUL2003	163040
120102	01JUN1989	108255
120103	01JAN1974	87975
120104	01JAN1981	46230
120105	01MAY1999	27110

```
data compare;
   keep Employee_ID Year_Hired Salary Average
        Salary_Dif;
   format Salary Average Salary_Dif dollar12.2;
   array yr{1974:2007} Yr1974-Yr2007;
   if _N_=1 then set orion.salary_stats
          (where=(Statistic='Avg_Salary'));
   set orion.employee_payroll
       (keep=Employee_ID Employee_Hire_Date Salary);
   Year_Hired=year(Employee_Hire_Date);
   Average=yr{Year_Hired};
   Salary_Dif=Salary-Average;
run;
```

Implicit OUTPUT;
Implicit RETURN;

Partial PDV

Salary	Average	Salary_Dif	D Yr1974 yr{1974}	D Yr1975 yr{1975}	D Yr1976 yr{1976}	D Yr1977 yr{1977}	D Yr1978 yr{1978}	. . .
163040	35082.5	127957.5	39243.61	33037.5	39171.67	34170	37506.25	

D Yr2003 yr{2003}	D Yr2004 yr{2004}	. . .	D Yr2007 yr{2007}	D Statistic	Employee_ID	D Employee_Hire_Date	Year_Hired	D _N_
35082.5	29904.44		28861.67	Avg_Salary	120101	01JUL2003	2003	1

32 ...

Execution

Partial Listing of **orion.employee_payroll**

Employee_ID	Employee_Hire_Date	Salary
120101	01JUL2003	163040
120102	01JUN1989	108255
120103	01JAN1974	87975
120104	01JAN1981	46230
120105	01MAY1999	27110

Partial Listing of **orion.salary_stats**

Statistic	Yr1974	Yr1975	Yr1976	. . .
Avg_Salary	39243.61	33037.5	39171.67	. . .

```
data compare;
   keep Employee_ID Year_Hired Salary Average
        Salary_Dif;
   format Salary Average Salary_Dif dollar12.2;
   array yr{1974:2007} Yr1974-Yr2007;
   if _N_=1 then set orion.salary_stats
         (where=(Statistic='Avg_Salary'));
   set orion.employee_payroll
      (keep=Employee_ID Employee_Hire_Date Salary);
   Year_Hired=year(Empl
   Average=yr{Year_Hire
   Salary_Dif=Salary-Av
run;
```

Continue until EOF

Partial PDV

Salary	Average	Salary_Dif	yr{1974} D Yr1974	yr{1975} D Yr1975	yr{1976} D Yr1976	yr{1977} D Yr1977	yr{1978} D Yr1978	. . .
163040	35082.5	127957.5	39243.61	33037.5	39171.67	34170	37506.25	

yr{2003} D Yr2003	yr{2004} D Yr2004	. . .	yr{2007} D Yr2007	D Statistic	Employee_ID	D Employee_Hire_Date	Year_Hired	D _N_
35082.5	29904.44		28861.67	Avg_Salary	120101	01JUL2003	2003	1

33

Resulting Data

```
proc print data=compare(obs=8);
   var Employee_ID Year_Hired Salary Average Salary_Dif;
   title 'Using One Dimensional Arrays';
run;
```

PROC PRINT Output

Using One Dimensional Arrays

Obs	Employee_ID	Year_Hired	Salary	Average	Salary_Dif
1	120101	2003	$163,040.00	$35,082.50	$127,957.50
2	120102	1989	$108,255.00	$88,588.75	$19,666.25
3	120103	1974	$87,975.00	$39,243.61	$48,731.39
4	120104	1981	$46,230.00	$36,436.67	$9,793.33
5	120105	1999	$27,110.00	$36,533.75	$-9,423.75
6	120106	1974	$26,960.00	$39,243.61	$-12,283.61
7	120107	1974	$30,475.00	$39,243.61	$-8,768.61
8	120108	2006	$27,660.00	$27,883.71	$-223.71

34

p305d01

5.04 Multiple Answer Poll

Which of the following ARRAY statements are similar to the statement

```
array yr{1974:2007} Yr1974-Yr2007;
```

and will compile without errors?

a. `array yr{34} Yr1974-Yr2007;`

b. `array yr{1974-2007} Yr1974-Yr2007;`

c. `array yr{74:07} Yr1974-Yr2007;`

d. `array yr{74-07} Yr1974-Yr2007;`

e. `array yr{*} Yr1974-Yr2007;`

36

Using either of the alternative ARRAY statements, you must change the array reference that creates the variable **Average**.

p305d01a

```
data compare;
   keep Employee_ID Year_Hired Salary Average Salary_Dif;
   format Salary Average Salary_Dif dollar12.2;
① array yr{34} Yr1974-Yr2007;
   if _N_=1 then
      set orion.salary_stats(where=(Statistic='Avg_Salary'));
   set orion.employee_payroll;
② Year_Hired=year(Employee_Hire_Date)-1973;
   Average=yr{Year_Hired};
   Salary_Dif=Salary-Average;
run;
```

① The array **yr** is associated with the variables **Yr1974**, **Yr1975**, **Yr1976**, and so forth through **YR2007**.

② Because the subscript values for the **yr** array are 1 to 34, adjust the **Year_Hired** variable so that **yr{1}** corresponds to 1974, **yr{2}** corresponds to 1975, and so forth. The value of the element of the **yr** array is referenced positionally by the value of the variable **Year_Hired** and is assigned to the variable **Average**.

Exercises

Level 1

1. Using a One-Dimensional Array to Combine Data

The data set **orion.retail** has information about retail sales.

Partial Listing of **orion.retail**

Partial orion.retail Data Set

Obs	Customer_ID	Employee_ID	Street_ID	Order_ Date	Delivery_ Date	Order_ID
1	63	121039	9260125492	11JAN2003	11JAN2003	1230058123
2	41	120174	1600101527	28JAN2003	28JAN2003	1230147441
3	183	120134	1600100760	27FEB2003	27FEB2003	1230315085
4	56	121059	9260111871	15MAR2003	15MAR2003	1230404278
5	183	120149	1600100760	22MAR2003	22MAR2003	1230440481

Obs	Product_ID	Quantity	Total_Retail_ Price	CostPrice_ Per_Unit	Discount
1	220101300017	1	$16.50	$7.45	.
2	240600100010	2	$32.00	$6.50	.
3	240200200039	3	$63.60	$8.80	.
4	220200300002	2	$75.00	$17.05	.
5	230100600005	1	$129.80	$63.20	.

The data set **orion.retail_information** has statistics about those retail sales.

Partial Listing of **orion.retail_information**

Partial orion.retail_information Data Set

Obs	Statistic	Month1	Month2	Month3
1	Sum_Retail_Price	$1,599.80	$1,160.80	$113.70
2	Mean_Retail_Price	$228.54	$193.47	$28.43
3	Median_Retail_Price	$258.20	$123.30	$27.65

Obs	Month4	Month5	Month6	Month7	Month8
1	$671.10	$520.70	$561.99	$288.29	$1,033.40
2	$83.89	$86.78	$70.25	$48.05	$103.34
3	$49.10	$68.30	$52.20	$44.90	$54.25

Obs	Month9	Month10	Month11	Month12
1	$425.70	$736.10	$2,399.30	$1,347.58
2	$70.95	$105.16	$218.12	$134.76
3	$65.35	$101.50	$69.40	$61.70

a. Combine the two data sets to create a data set named **`compare`**. The data set should contain the variables from **`orion.retail`** and variables named **`Month`** and **`Median_Retail_Price`**, where **`Month`** is the month of the date that the product was ordered. Format **`Median_Retail_Price`** with dollar signs and two digits to the right of the decimal point.

b. Print the first eight observations of the resulting data set.

PROC PRINT Output

Partial Compare Data Set

Obs	Customer_ID	Employee_ID	Street_ID	Order_ Date	Delivery_ Date	Order_ID
1	63	121039	9260125492	11JAN2003	11JAN2003	1230058123
2	41	120174	1600101527	28JAN2003	28JAN2003	1230147441
3	183	120134	1600100760	27FEB2003	27FEB2003	1230315085
4	56	121059	9260111871	15MAR2003	15MAR2003	1230404278
5	183	120149	1600100760	22MAR2003	22MAR2003	1230440481
6	183	120134	1600100760	25MAR2003	25MAR2003	1230455630
7	20	121066	9260118934	01APR2003	01APR2003	1230498538
8	79	121045	9260101874	18APR2003	18APR2003	1230591684

Obs	Product_ID	Quantity	Total_Retail_ Price	CostPrice_ Per_Unit	Discount	Month	Median_ Retail_ Price
1	220101300017	1	$16.50	$7.45	.	1	$258.20
2	240600100010	2	$32.00	$6.50	.	1	$258.20
3	240200200039	3	$63.60	$8.80	.	2	$123.30
4	220200300002	2	$75.00	$17.05	.	3	$27.65
5	230100600005	1	$129.80	$63.20	.	3	$27.65
6	240200100233	2	$91.80	$22.45	.	3	$27.65
7	230100300006	1	$68.50	$34.35	.	4	$49.10
8	240200100076	4	$1,796.00	$246.55	.	4	$49.10

Level 2

2. Using a One-Dimensional Array as a Lookup Table

The data set **`orion.shoe_stats`** contains statistics for the shoe product lines.

Listing of **`orion.shoe_stats`**

orion.shoe_stats Data Set

Obs	Stat	Product21	Product22	Product23	Product24
1	Frequency	66.000	277.000	.	18.000
2	Mfg_Suggested_Retail_Price_Mean	70.788	174.292	.	173.056
3	Mfg_Suggested_Retail_Price_Min	17.000	13.000	.	5.000
4	Mfg_Suggested_Retail_Price_Max	130.000	385.000	.	398.000
5	Mfg_Suggested_Retail_Price_Median	68.000	164.000	.	190.500
6	Mfg_Suggested_Retail_Price_StdDev	21.731	71.703	.	141.389

a. Use arrays to create a data set named **`trans`** that has 24 observations.

b. Print the **trans** data set.

PROC PRINT Output

The TRANS data set

Obs	Stat	Product_ Line	Value
1	Frequency	21	66.000
2	Frequency	22	277.000
3	Frequency	23	.
4	Frequency	24	18.000
5	Mfg_Suggested_Retail_Price_Mean	21	70.788
6	Mfg_Suggested_Retail_Price_Mean	22	174.292
7	Mfg_Suggested_Retail_Price_Mean	23	.
8	Mfg_Suggested_Retail_Price_Mean	24	173.056
9	Mfg_Suggested_Retail_Price_Min	21	17.000
10	Mfg_Suggested_Retail_Price_Min	22	13.000
11	Mfg_Suggested_Retail_Price_Min	23	.
12	Mfg_Suggested_Retail_Price_Min	24	5.000
13	Mfg_Suggested_Retail_Price_Max	21	130.000
14	Mfg_Suggested_Retail_Price_Max	22	385.000
15	Mfg_Suggested_Retail_Price_Max	23	.
16	Mfg_Suggested_Retail_Price_Max	24	398.000
17	Mfg_Suggested_Retail_Price_Median	21	68.000
18	Mfg_Suggested_Retail_Price_Median	22	164.000
19	Mfg_Suggested_Retail_Price_Median	23	.
20	Mfg_Suggested_Retail_Price_Median	24	190.500
21	Mfg_Suggested_Retail_Price_StdDev	21	21.731
22	Mfg_Suggested_Retail_Price_StdDev	22	71.703
23	Mfg_Suggested_Retail_Price_StdDev	23	.
24	Mfg_Suggested_Retail_Price_StdDev	24	141.389

Level 3

3. Using a One-Dimensional Array

a. Use the program **p305e03** to create a temporary data set named **order_fact** for the year 2007 and customer IDs 89 and 2550, sorted by **Order_Type**.

The PROC SQL step creates a report showing the number of observations for each value of the **Order_Type** variable for the **Customer_ID** values 89 and 2550.

Partial Listing of **order_fact**

order_fact

Obs	Customer_ID	Order_ Type	Order_ Date	Delivery_ Date	Quantity
1	89	1	03JAN2007	04JAN2007	6
2	89	1	01OCT2007	01OCT2007	1
3	89	1	01OCT2007	01OCT2007	1
4	89	1	15DEC2007	15DEC2007	4
5	89	2	17JUN2007	21JUN2007	2
6	2550	3	04MAY2007	09MAY2007	3
7	2550	3	04MAY2007	09MAY2007	1

b. Create the data set named **`all`** that has one observation for each **`Order_Type`** where there are a varying number of observations for each **`Order_Type`** in the original data set **`order_fact`**. Use the maximum number of observations for each order type as the array dimension to create three arrays that create variables to hold the order dates, the delivery dates, and the quantity.

c. Print the first three observations of **`all`**.

PROC PRINT Output

```
                              The Resulting Data Set

             Ordered_     Ordered_     Ordered_     Ordered_    Delivery_    Delivery_
Obs           Date1        Date2        Date3        Date4        Date1        Date2

  1        03JAN2007    01OCT2007    01OCT2007    15DEC2007    04JAN2007    01OCT2007
  2        17JUN2007            .            .            .    21JUN2007            .
  3        04MAY2007    04MAY2007            .            .    09MAY2007    09MAY2007

          Delivery_    Delivery_
Obs         Date3        Date4      Quantity1    Quantity2    Quantity3    Quantity4

  1        01OCT2007    15DEC2007        6            1            1            4
  2                .            .        2            .            .            .
  3                .            .        3            1            .            .

                                    Order_      Delivery_     Order_
Obs    n      Customer_ID            Date          Date         Type      Quantity

  1    4               89       15DEC2007     15DEC2007         1           4
  2    1               89       17JUN2007     21JUN2007         2           2
  3    2             2550       04MAY2007     09MAY2007         3           1
```

5.2 Using Multidimensional Arrays

Objectives

- Define a multidimensional array.
- Explain the differences between a one-dimensional array and a multidimensional array.
- Use a multidimensional array as a lookup table.

41

Business Scenario

The SAS data set **orion.profit** has information about every company for the years 2003 through 2007, separated by month.

Partial Listing of **orion.profit(where=(Sales ne .))**

Company	YYMM	Sales	Cost	Salaries	Profit
Logistics	03M01	$457,809	$210,914	$127,525	$119,370
Logistics	03M02	$325,138	$149,718	$127,525	$47,895
Logistics	03M03	$276,805	$127,827	$134,198	$14,780
Logistics	03M04	$558,806	$264,868	$134,198	$159,741
Logistics	03M05	$641,954	$303,324	$134,198	$204,432
Logistics	03M06	$827,976	$389,207	$134,198	$304,571
Logistics	03M07	$819,373	$389,020	$138,047	$292,306
Logistics	03M08	$794,750	$373,204	$140,206	$281,340

42

5.05 Quiz

What is the type of the variable **YYMM** in the data set `orion.profit`?

44

Business Scenario

This table contains the budgeted amounts for each of those months and years. Each row represents a month, and each column represents a year.

Yr2003	Yr2004	Yr2005	Yr2006	Yr2007
$1,590,000	$1,880,000	$2,300,000	$1,960,000	$1,970,000
$1,290,000	$1,550,000	$1,830,000	$1,480,000	$1,640,000
$1,160,000	$1,380,000	$1,640,000	$1,410,000	$1,440,000
$1,710,000	$2,100,000	$2,420,000	$2,130,000	$2,270,000
$1,990,000	$2,350,000	$2,840,000	$2,480,000	$2,670,000
$2,560,000	$3,020,000	$3,580,000	$3,070,000	$3,410,000
$2,590,000	$2,890,000	$3,550,000	$3,010,000	$3,490,000
$2,550,000	$2,840,000	$3,580,000	$3,030,000	$3,500,000
$1,070,000	$1,180,000	$1,550,000	$1,260,000	$1,520,000
$1,160,000	$1,270,000	$1,600,000	$1,360,000	$1,700,000
$1,260,000	$1,470,000	$1,780,000	$1,540,000	$1,950,000
$2,870,000	$3,120,000	$3,760,000	$3,210,000	$4,370,000

46

continued...

The budget values in the table are not stored in a SAS data set.

Business Scenario

You need to combine the budget amounts in the table with the actual amount in the SAS data set to create the following report:

Listing of **budget_amt**

Actual vs Budgeted Amounts (Two Observations)

Company	YYMM	Sales	Cost	Salaries	Profit	BudgetAmt
Logistics	03M01	$457,809	$210,914	$127,525	$119,370	$1,590,000
Logistics	03M02	$325,138	$149,718	$127,525	$47,895	$1,290,000

47

5.06 Quiz

What do the data set **orion.profit** and the lookup table have in common?

Partial Listing of **orion.profit (where=(Sales ne .))**

Company	YYMM	Sales	Cost	Salaries	Profit
Logistics	03M01	$457,809	$210,914	$127,525	$119,370
Logistics	03M02	$325,138	$149,718	$127,525	$47,895
Logistics	03M03	$276,805	$127,827	$134,198	$14,780
Logistics	03M04	$558,806	$264,868	$134,198	$159,741

Yr2003	Yr2004	Yr2005	Yr2006	Yr2007
$1,590,000	$1,880,000	$2,300,000	$1,960,000	$1,970,000
$1,290,000	$1,550,000	$1,830,000	$1,480,000	$1,640,000

49

Overview of Two-Dimensional Arrays

To combine the table of budgeted values with the data set containing the profit, use a two-dimensional array.

A two-dimensional array is similar to a row of buckets.

1,1 1,2 2,1 2,2

- SAS puts a value in a bucket based on multiple numbers.
- Values are retrieved from a bucket based on multiple numbers.

51

Using Multidimensional Arrays

General form for the multidimensional ARRAY statement:

ARRAY *array-name* {…,*rows, cols*} <$> <*length*>
<*elements*> <(*initial values*)>;

rows specifies the number of array elements in a row arrangement.

cols specifies the number of array elements in a column arrangement.

Example:

```
array B{2,5} B1-B10;
```

52

The keyword _TEMPORARY_ can be used instead of *elements* to avoid creating new variables in the program data vector.

Using Multidimensional Arrays

```
array B{2,5} B1-B10 (1590000, 1880000, 2300000, 1960000, 1970000,
                     1290000, 1550000, 1830000, 1480000, 1640000);
```

Yr2003	Yr2004	Yr2005	Yr2006	Yr2007
$1,590,000	$1,880,000	$2,300,000	$1,960,000	$1,970,000
$1,290,000	$1,550,000	$1,830,000	$1,480,000	$1,640,000
$1,160,000	$1,380,000	$1,640,000	$1,410,000	$1,440,000
$1,710,000	$2,100,000	$2,420,000	$2,130,000	$2,270,000
$1,990,000	$2,350,000	$2,840,000	$2,480,000	$2,670,000
$2,560,000	$3,020,000	$3,580,000	$3,070,000	$3,410,000
$2,590,000	$2,890,000	$3,550,000	$3,010,000	$3,490,000
$2,550,000	$2,840,000	$3,580,000	$3,030,000	$3,500,000
$1,070,000	$1,180,000	$1,550,000	$1,260,000	$1,520,000
$1,160,000	$1,270,000	$1,600,000	$1,360,000	$1,700,000
$1,260,000	$1,470,000	$1,780,000	$1,540,000	$1,950,000
$2,870,000	$3,120,000	$3,760,000	$3,210,000	$4,370,000

53

For this example, only the first two rows are included in the array.

The initial values fill all the columns in a row before moving on to the next row.

Using Multidimensional Arrays

```
array B{2,5} B1-B10 (1590000, 1880000, 2300000, 1960000, 1970000,
                     1290000, 1550000, 1830000, 1480000, 1640000);
```

PDV

B{1,1}	B{1,2}	B{1,3}	B{1,4}	B{1,5}	B{2,1}	B{2,2}	B{2,3}	B{2,4}	B{2,5}
B1	B2	B3	B4	B5	B6	B7	B8	B9	B10
1590000	1880000	2300000	1960000	1970000	1290000	1550000	1830000	1480000	1640000

54

When you use a multidimensional array, the following statements are true:

- You must supply a subscript value for each dimension to process a specific array element.
- You can use a DO loop to process elements in a given dimension.
- You can use nested DO loops to process elements in more than one dimension.

5.07 Multiple Answer Poll

Which of the following would be equivalent to the following ARRAY statement ?

```
array B{2,5} B1-B10 (1590000, 1880000, 2300000, 1960000, 1970000,
                     1290000, 1550000, 1830000, 1480000, 1640000);
```

a. `array B{*} B1-B10`
```
        (1590000, 1880000, 2300000, 1960000, 1970000,
         1290000, 1550000, 1830000, 1480000, 1640000);
```

b. `array B{2,2003:2007} B1-B10`
```
        (1590000, 1880000, 2300000, 1960000, 1970000,
         1290000, 1550000, 1830000, 1480000, 1640000);
```

c. `array B{2,5} (1590000, 1880000, 2300000, 1960000,`
```
                 1970000, 1290000, 1550000, 1830000,
                 1480000, 1640000);
```

d. `array B{2,5} _temporary_ (1590000, 1880000, 2300000,`
```
                            1960000, 1970000, 1290000,
                            1550000, 1830000, 1480000,
                            1640000);
```

56

Business Scenario

Find the budgeted amounts for each company, year, and month.

Partial Listing of `orion.profit (where=(Sales ne .))`

Company	YYMM	Sales	Cost	Salaries	Profit
Logistics	03M01	$457,809	$210,914	$127,525	$119,370
Logistics	03M02	$325,138	$149,718	$127,525	$47,895

+

Yr2003	Yr2004	Yr2005	Yr2006	Yr2007
$1,590,000	**$1,880,000**	**$2,300,000**	**$1,960,000**	**$1,970,000**
$1,290,000	**$1,550,000**	**$1,830,000**	**$1,480,000**	**$1,640,000**

=

Partial Listing of `budget_amt`

Company	YYMM	Sales	Cost	Salaries	Profit	BudgetAmt
Logistics	03M01	$457,809	$210,914	$127,525	$119,370	$1,590,000
Logistics	03M02	$325,138	$149,718	$127,525	$47,895	$1,290,000

58

Using Multidimensional Arrays

Find the budgeted amounts for each company, year, and month.

Yr2003	Yr2004	Yr2005	Yr2006	Yr2007
$1,590,000	$1,880,000	$2,300,000	$1,960,000	$1,970,000
$1,290,000	$1,550,000	$1,830,000	$1,480,000	$1,640,000

Company	YYMM
Logistics	03M01
Logistics	03M02

59

Using Multidimensional Arrays

```
data budget_amt;
   drop Y M;
 ① array B{2,2003:2007} _temporary_
          (1590000, 1880000, 2300000,
           1960000, 1970000, 1290000,
           1550000, 1830000, 1480000,
           1640000);
   set orion.profit(where=(Sales ne .)
                    obs=2);
 ② Y=year(YYMM);
 ③ M=month(YYMM);
 ④ BudgetAmt=B{M,Y};
run;
```

60 p305d02

① Ten hard-coded values initialize the array. The _TEMPORARY_ keyword creates an array that is not associated with variables in the program data vector.

② The variable **Y** (the column number) is calculated using the YEAR function on the date variable, **YYMM**.

③ The variable **M** (the row number) is created using the MONTH function on the date variable, **YYMM**.

④ The row and column numbers are used to look up the values of **Budget** in the array **B**.

Execution

Partial Listing of **orion.profit**

Company	YYMM	Sales	Cost	. . .
Logistics	03M01	457809	210914	. . .
Logistics	03M02	325138	149718	. . .

```
data budget_amt;
   drop Y M;
   array B{2,2003:2007} _temporary_
          (1590000, 1880000, 2300000,
           1960000, 1970000, 1290000,
           1550000, 1830000, 1480000,
           1640000);
   set orion.profit(where=(Sales ne .)
                    obs=2);
   Y=year(YYMM);
   M=month(YYMM);
   BudgetAmt=B{M,Y};
run;
```

B{1,2003}	B{1,2004}	B{1,2005}	B{1,2006}	B{1,2007}	B{2,2003}	B{2,2004}	B{2,2005}	B{2,2006}	B{2,2007}
1590000	1880000	2300000	1960000	1970000	1290000	1550000	1830000	1480000	1640000

PDV

Company	YYMM	Sales	Cost	Salaries	Profit	D Y	D M	BudgetAmt	D _N_
Logistics	03M01	457809	210914	127525	119370	.	.	.	1

62 ...

Execution

Partial Listing of **orion.profit**

Company	YYMM	Sales	Cost	. . .
Logistics	03M01	457809	210914	. . .
Logistics	03M02	325138	149718	. . .

```
data budget_amt;
   drop Y M;
   array B{2,2003:2007} _temporary_
          (1590000, 1880000, 2300000,
           1960000, 1970000, 1290000,
           1550000, 1830000, 1480000,
           1640000);
   set orion.profit(where=(Sales ne .)
                    obs=2);
   Y=year(YYMM);
```

```
BudgetAmt=B{1,2003};
```

B{1,2003}	B{1,2004}	B{1,2005}	B{1,2006}	B{1,2007}	B{2,2003}	B{2,2004}	B{2,2005}	B{2,2006}	B{2,2007}
1590000	1880000	2300000	1960000	1970000	1290000	1550000	1830000	1480000	1640000

PDV

Company	YYMM	Sales	Cost	Salaries	Profit	D Y	D M	BudgetAmt	D _N_
Logistics	03M01	457809	210914	127525	119370	2003	1	1590000	1

65 ...

Execution

Partial Listing of **orion.profit**

Company	YYMM	Sales	Cost	. . .
Logistics	03M01	457809	210914	. . .
Logistics	03M02	325138	149718	. . .

```
data budget_amt;
   drop Y M;
   array B{2,
           (1
           19
           15
           1640000);
   set orion.profit(where=(Sales ne .)
                    obs=2);
   Y=year(YYMM);
   M=month(YYMM);
   BudgetAmt=B{M,Y};
run;
```

Implicit OUTPUT;
Implicit RETURN;

B{1,2003}	B{1,2004}	B{1,2005}	B{1,2006}	B{1,2007}	B{2,2003}	B{2,2004}	B{2,2005}	B{2,2006}	B{2,2007}
1590000	1880000	2300000	1960000	1970000	1290000	1550000	1830000	1480000	1640000

PDV

Company	YYMM	Sales	Cost	Salaries	Profit	D Y	D M	BudgetAmt	D _N_
Logistics	03M01	457809	210914	127525	119370	2003	1	1590000	1

66 ...

Execution

Partial Listing of **orion.profit**

Company	YYMM	Sales	Cost	. . .
Logistics	03M01	457809	210914	. . .
Logistics	03M02	325138	149718	. . .

```
data budget_amt;
   drop Y M;
   array B{2,2003:2007} _temporary_
           (1590000, 1880000, 2300000,
            1960000, 1970000, 1290000,
            1550000, 1830000, 1480000,
            1640000);
   set orion.profit(where=(Sales ne .)
                    obs=2);
   Y=year(YYMM);
   M=month(YYMM);
   BudgetAmt=B{M,
run;
```

Reinitialize PDV

B{1,2003}	B{1,2004}	B{1,2005}	B{1,2006}	B{1,2007}	B{2,2003}	B{2,2004}	B{2,2005}	B{2,2006}	B{2,2007}
1590000	1880000	2300000	1960000	1970000	1290000	1550000	1830000	1480000	1640000

PDV

Company	YYMM	Sales	Cost	Salaries	Profit	D Y	D M	BudgetAmt	D _N_
Logistics	03M01	457809	210914	127525	119370	.	.	.	2

67 ...

Execution

Partial Listing of `orion.profit`

Company	YYMM	Sales	Cost	. . .
Logistics	03M01	457809	210914	. . .
Logistics	03M02	325138	149718	. . .

```
data budget_amt;
   drop Y M;
   array B{2,2003:2007} _temporary_
          (1590000, 1880000, 2300000,
           1960000, 1970000, 1290000,
           1550000, 1830000, 1480000,
           1640000);
   set orion.profit(where=(Sales ne .)
                    obs=2);
   Y=year(YYMM);
   M=month(YYMM);
   BudgetAmt=B{M,Y};
run;
```

B{1,2003}	B{1,2004}	B{1,2005}	B{1,2006}	B{1,2007}	B{2,2003}	B{2,2004}	B{2,2005}	B{2,2006}	B{2,2007}
1590000	1880000	2300000	1960000	1970000	1290000	1550000	1830000	1480000	1640000

PDV

Company	YYMM	Sales	Cost	Salaries	Profit	D Y	D M	BudgetAmt	D _N_
Logistics	03M02	325138	149718	127525	47895	2003	2	.	2

68 ...

Execution

Partial Listing of `orion.profit`

Company	YYMM	Sales	Cost	. . .
Logistics	03M01	457809	210914	. . .
Logistics	03M02	325138	149718	. . .

```
data budget_amt;
   drop Y M;
   array B{2,2003:2007} _temporary_
          (1590000, 1880000, 2300000,
           1960000, 1970000, 1290000,
           1550000, 1830000, 1480000,
           1640000);
   set orion.profit(where=(Sales ne .)
                    obs=2);
   Y=year(YYMM);
   M=month(YYMM);
```

```
BudgetAmt=B{2,2003};
```

B{1,2003}	B{1,2004}	B{1,2005}	B{1,2006}	B{1,2007}	B{2,2003}	B{2,2004}	B{2,2005}	B{2,2006}	B{2,2007}
1590000	1880000	2300000	1960000	1970000	1290000	1550000	1830000	1480000	1640000

PDV

Company	YYMM	Sales	Cost	Salaries	Profit	D Y	D M	BudgetAmt	D _N_
Logistics	03M02	325138	149718	127525	47895	2003	2	1290000	2

70 ...

Execution

Partial Listing of **orion.profit**

Company	YYMM	Sales	Cost	. . .
Logistics	03M01	457809	210914	. . .
Logistics	03M02	325138	149718	. . .

```
data budget_amt;
   drop Y M;
   array B{2
          (1
          19
          15
          1640000);
   set orion.profit(where=(Sales ne .)
                    obs=2);
   Y=year(YYMM);
   M=month(YYMM);
   BudgetAmt=B{M,Y};
run;
```

Implicit OUTPUT;
Implicit RETURN;

B{1,2003}	B{1,2004}	B{1,2005}	B{1,2006}	B{1,2007}	B{2,2003}	B{2,2004}	B{2,2005}	B{2,2006}	B{2,2007}
1590000	1880000	2300000	1960000	1970000	1290000	1550000	1830000	1480000	1640000

PDV

Company	YYMM	Sales	Cost	Salaries	Profit	D Y	D M	BudgetAmt	D _N_
Logistics	03M02	325138	149718	127525	47895	2003	2	1290000	2

71 ...

Execution

Partial Listing of **orion.profit**

Company	YYMM	Sales	Cost	. . .
Logistics	03M01	457809	210914	. . .
Logistics	03M02	325138	149718	. . .

```
data budget_amt;
   drop Y M;
   array B{2,2003:2007} _temporary_
          (1590000, 1880000, 2300000,
           1960000, 1970000, 1290000,
           1550000, 1830000, 1480000,
           1640000);
   set orion.profit(where=(Sales ne .)
                    obs=2);
   Y=year(YYMM);
   M=month(YYMM);
   etAmt=B{M,Y};
```

Execution stops.

B{1,2003}	B{1,2004}	B{1,2005}	B{1,2006}	B{1,2007}	B{2,2003}	B{2,2004}	B{2,2005}	B{2,2006}	B{2,2007}
1590000	1880000	2300000	1960000	1970000	1290000	1550000	1830000	1480000	1640000

PDV

Company	YYMM	Sales	Cost	Salaries	Profit	D Y	D M	BudgetAmt	D _N_
Logistics	03M02	325138	149718	127525	47895	2003	2	1290000	2

72 ...

Exercises

Level 1

4. Using a Two-Dimensional Array

Orion Star wants to send discount coupons to their customers. The amounts of the discounts are given in the following table:

Previous Quantity Ordered

OrderType	1	2	3	4	5	6
1	10	10	15	20	20	25
2	10	15	20	25	25	30
3	10	15	15	20	25	25

The data set **orion.order_fact** contains the variables **Customer_ID**, **Quantity**, and **Order_Type**.

Partial Listing of **orion.order_fact**

```
                          Order_
  Obs    Customer_ID       Type     Quantity

    1             63          1            1
    2              5          2            1
    3             45          2            1
    4             41          1            2
    5            183          1            3
    6             79          2            1
    7             23          2            1
    8             23          2            2
    9             45          2            2
   10             45          2            1
```

a. Use a two-dimensional array to combine the data set with the table of values to create a data set named **customer_coupons** with a variable named **Coupon_Value**.

b. Print the first five observations of the **customer_coupons** data set.

PROC PRINT Output

```
                              The Coupon Value

                                 Order_                 Coupon_
      Obs      Customer_ID        Type      Quantity     Value

       1                63          1           1          10
       2                 5          2           1          10
       3                45          2           1          10
       4                41          1           2          10
       5               183          1           3          15
```

Level 2

5. Using a Two-Dimensional Array

The following table shows the average manufacturer's suggested retail price for shoes, based on the product line and product category.

Product Category

Product Line	1	2
21	.	70.79
22	173.79	174.40
23	.	.
24	29.65	287.8

The data set **orion.shoe_sales** contains the **Product_ID**, the **Product_Name**, and the **Total_Retail_Price** for all of the shoes sold by Orion Star.

Partial Listing of **orion.shoe_sales**

```
                                                                Total_Retail_
  Product_ID     Product_Name                                        Price

220200200024     Pro Fit Gel Gt 2030 Women's Running Shoes          $178.50
220200100092     Big Guy Men's Air Terra Sebec Shoes                 $83.00
240200100043     Bretagne Performance Tg Men's Golf Shoes L.        $282.40
220100700024     Armadillo Road Dmx Women's Running Shoes            $99.70
220200300157     Hardcore Men's Street Shoes Large                  $220.20
240200100051     Bretagne Stabilites 2000 Goretex Shoes             $420.90
220200100035     Big Guy Men's Air Deschutz Viii Shoes              $125.20
220200100090     Big Guy Men's Air Terra Reach Shoes                $177.20
220200200018     Lulu Men's Street Shoes                            $132.80
240200100052     Bretagne Stabilities Tg Men's Golf Shoes            $99.70
```

a. Create a data set named **combine** using a two-dimensional array to combine the table of values with the product line and the product category ID. The product line is the first two digits of the **Product_ID** variable. The product category ID is the third and fourth digits of the **Product_ID** variable.

b. Print the first five observations of the **combine** data set.

PROC PRINT Output

```
                                                                          Total_Retail_
 Obs     Product_ID                  Product_Name                               Price

  1    220200200024    Pro Fit Gel Gt 2030 Women's Running Shoes               $178.50
  2    220200100092    Big Guy Men's Air Terra Sebec Shoes                      $83.00
  3    240200100043    Bretagne Performance Tg Men's Golf Shoes L.             $282.40
  4    220100700024    Armadillo Road Dmx Women's Running Shoes                 $99.70
  5    220200300157    Hardcore Men's Street Shoes Large                       $220.20

                                                 Manufacturer_
                         Product_    Product_      Suggested_
 Obs      Prod_ID          Line       Cat_ID         Price

  1    220200200024        22           2           174.40
  2    220200100092        22           2           174.40
  3    240200100043        24           2           287.80
  4    220100700024        22           1           173.79
  5    220200300157        22           2           174.40
```

Level 3

6. Using a Three-Dimensional Array

The warehouse location for the products in the **orion.product_list** data set is given in the following table:

Warehouse Locations

Product_Line	Product_Cat_ID	Product_Loc_ID	Warehouse
21	0	0	A2100
21	0	1	A2101
21	1	0	A2110
21	1	1	A2111
21	2	0	A2120
21	2	1	A2121
22	0	0	B2200
22	0	1	B2201
22	1	0	B2210
22	1	1	B2211
22	2	0	B2220
22	2	1	B2221

Open the program **p305e06** that retrieves the Level 1products from the **`orion.product_list`** data set.

p305e06

```
data few_warehouses;
   set orion.product_list(keep=Product_ID Product_Name
                                Product_Level
                          where=(Product_Level=1));
   Prod_ID=put(Product_ID,12.);
   Product_Line=input(substr(Prod_ID,1,2),2.);
   Product_Cat_ID=input(substr(Prod_ID,12,1),1.);
   if Product_Line in (21,22) and Product_Cat_ID<2;
run;
```

Modify **p305e06** to obtain the desired results.

a. Type the values of the **`Warehouse`** column into a three-dimensional array using the values of **`Product_Line`**, **`Product_Cat_ID`**, and **`Product_Loc_ID`** as the dimensions.

b. Create a data set named **`warehouses`**. Use the **`Product_ID`** variable to determine the values of **`Product_Line`**, **`Product_Cat_ID`**, and **`Product_Loc_ID`**.

- The product line is the first two digits of the **`Product_ID`** variable.
- The product category ID is the third and fourth digits of the **`Product_ID`** variable.
- The product location ID identifies the location within a warehouse of the product and is the last digit of the **`Product_ID`** variable.

c. Print the first five observations of the **`warehouses`** data set.

PROC PRINT Output

Obs	Product_ID	Product_Name	Product_ Line	Product_ Cat_ID	Product_ Loc_ID	Warehouse
1	210000000000	Children	21	0	0	A2100
2	210100000000	Children Outdoors	21	0	1	A2110
3	210100100000	Outdoor things, Kids	21	0	1	A2110
4	210200000000	Children Sports	21	0	2	A2120
5	210200100000	A-Team, Kids	21	0	2	A2120

5.3 Loading a Multidimensional Array from a SAS Data Set

Objectives

- Load a multidimensional array from a SAS data set.
- Identify the advantages of an array as a lookup table.
- Identify the disadvantages of an array as a lookup table.

76

Business Scenario

Budget values are stored in a SAS data set named `orion.budget` where the rows represent months and the columns represent years.

Load the array from the values in the SAS data set.

Listing of `orion.budget`

Month	Yr2003	Yr2004	Yr2005	Yr2006	Yr2007
1	$1,590,000	$1,880,000	$2,300,000	$1,960,000	$1,970,000
2	$1,290,000	$1,550,000	$1,830,000	$1,480,000	$1,640,000
3	$1,160,000	$1,380,000	$1,640,000	$1,410,000	$1,440,000
4	$1,710,000	$2,100,000	$2,420,000	$2,130,000	$2,270,000
5	$1,990,000	$2,350,000	$2,840,000	$2,480,000	$2,670,000
6	$2,560,000	$3,020,000	$3,580,000	$3,070,000	$3,410,000
7	$2,590,000	$2,890,000	$3,550,000	$3,010,000	$3,490,000
8	$2,550,000	$2,840,000	$3,580,000	$3,030,000	$3,500,000
9	$1,070,000	$1,180,000	$1,550,000	$1,260,000	$1,520,000
10	$1,160,000	$1,270,000	$1,600,000	$1,360,000	$1,700,000
11	$1,260,000	$1,470,000	$1,780,000	$1,540,000	$1,950,000
12	$2,870,000	$3,120,000	$3,760,000	$3,210,000	$4,370,000

77

Stored Array Values

Array values should be read from a SAS data set when the following conditions exist:

- There are too many values to initialize easily in the array.
- The values change frequently.
- The same values are used in many programs.

78

Using Multidimensional Arrays

```
data budget_amt;
   drop Yr2003-Yr2007 Month I J Y M;
   array B{12,2003:2007} _temporary_;
   if _N_=1 then do I=1 to 12; ①
      set orion.budget;
      array tmp{2003:2007} Yr2003-Yr2007;
    ② do J=2003 to 2007;
       ③ B{I,J}=tmp{J};
      end;
   end;
   set orion.profit(where=(Sales ne .));
   Y=year(YYMM);
   M=month(YYMM);
   BudgetAmt=B{M,Y};
run;
```

79 p305d03

The subscript variables **I** and **J** are used to process all the budget values in **orion.budget**.

① For each value of **I**, the SET statement reads an observation from the data set **orion.budget** and fills a row in the **tmp** array.

② For each value of **J**, the yearly budget value, referenced through **tmp{J}**, is assigned to the corresponding position **J** in the current row of the **B** array. The current row of the **B** array is referenced by the value of **I**.

③ The two-dimensional array **B** is loaded with the values of the **tmp** array.

5.08 Multiple Choice Poll

How many elements are in the array defined by the following ARRAY statement?

```
array B{12,2003:2007} _temporary_;
```

a. 0
b. 24
c. 48
d. 60

81

Execution

Partial Listing of **orion.budget**

Month	Yr2003	Yr2004	. . .
1	1590000	1880000	. . .
2	1290000	1550000	. . .
3	1160000	1380000	. . .
4	1710000	2100000	. . .
.	.	.	. . .

```
data budget_amt;
   drop Yr2003-Yr2007 Month I J Y M;
   array B{12,2003:2007} _temporary_;
   if _N_=1 then do I=1 to 12;
      set orion.budget;
      array tmp{2003:2007} Yr2003-Yr2007;
      do J=2003 to 2007;
         B{I,J}=tmp{J};
      end;
   end;
   set orion.profit(where=(Sales ne .));
   Y=year(YYMM);
   M=month(YYMM);
   BudgetAmt=B{M,Y};
run;
```

B{1,2003}	B{1,2004}	B{1,2005}	B{1,2006}	B{1,2007}	B{2,2003}	B{2,2004}		B{12,2006}	B{12,2007}
							. . .		

Partial PDV

		tmp{2003}	tmp{2004}	tmp{2005}	tmp{2006}	tmp{2007}		
D I	D Month	D Yr2003	D Yr2004	D Yr2005	D Yr2006	D Yr2007	D J	Company
1	1	1590000	1880000	2300000	1960000	1970000	.	

YYMM	Sales	Cost	Salaries	Profit	D Y	D M	Budget Amt	D _N_
.	.	.	.	.	.	.	.	1

85 ...

Execution

Partial Listing of **orion.budget**

Month	Yr2003	Yr2004	. . .
1	1590000	1880000	. . .
2	1290000	1550000	. . .
3	1160000	1380000	. . .
4	1710000	2100000	. . .
.	.	.	. . .

```
data budget_amt;
   drop Yr2003-Yr2007 Month I J Y M;
   array B{12,2003:2007} _temporary_;
   if _N_=1 then do I=1 to 12;
      set orion.budget;
      array tmp{2003:2007} Yr2003-Yr2007;
      do J=2003 to 2007;
         B{I,J}=tmp{J};
      end;
   end;
   set orion.profit(where=(Sales ne .));
   Y=year(YYMM);
   M=month(YYMM);
   BudgetAmt=B{M,Y};
run;
```

B{1,2003}	B{1,2004}	B{1,2005}	B{1,2006}	B{1,2007}	B{2,2003}	B{2,2004}		B{12,2006}	B{12,2007}
							. . .		

Partial PDV

		tmp{2003}	tmp{2004}	tmp{2005}	tmp{2006}	tmp{2007}		
D I	D Month	D Yr2003	D Yr2004	D Yr2005	D Yr2006	D Yr2007	D J	Company
1	1	1590000	1880000	2300000	1960000	1970000	2003	

YYMM	Sales	Cost	Salaries	Profit	D Y	D M	Budget Amt	D _N_
.	.	.	.	.	.	.	.	1

86 ...

Execution

Partial Listing of **orion.budget**

Month	Yr2003	Yr2004	. . .
1	1590000	1880000	. . .
2	1290000	1550000	. . .
3	1160000	1380000	. . .
4	1710000	2100000	. . .
.	.	.	. . .

```
data budget_amt;
   drop Yr2003-Yr2007 Month I J Y M;
   array B{12,2003:2007} _temporary_;
   if _N_=1 then do I=1 to 12;
      set orion.budget;
      array tmp{2003:2007} Yr2003-Yr2007;
        B{1,2003}=tmp{2003};
   end;
   set orion.profit(where=(Sales ne .));
   Y=year(YYMM);
   M=month(YYMM);
   BudgetAmt=B{M,Y};
run;
```

B{1,2003}	B{1,2004}	B{1,2005}	B{1,2006}	B{1,2007}	B{2,2003}	B{2,2004}		B{12,2006}	B{12,2007}
1590000							. . .		

Partial PDV

		tmp{2003}	tmp{2004}	tmp{2005}	tmp{2006}	tmp{2007}		
D I	D Month	D Yr2003	D Yr2004	D Yr2005	D Yr2006	D Yr2007	D J	Company
1	1	1590000	1880000	2300000	1960000	1970000	2003	

YYMM	Sales	Cost	Salaries	Profit	D Y	D M	Budget Amt	D _N_
.	.	.	.	.	.	.	.	1

88 ...

Execution

Partial Listing of **orion.budget**

Month	Yr2003	Yr2004	. . .
1	1590000	1880000	. . .
2	1290000	1550000	. . .
3	1160000	1380000	. . .
4	1710000	2100000	. . .
.	.	.	. . .

```
data budget_amt;
   drop Yr2003-Yr2007 Month I J Y M;
   array B{12,2003:2007} _temporary_;
   if _N_=1 then do I=1 to 12;
      set orion.budget;
      array tmp{2003:2007} Yr2003-Yr2007;
         B{1,2004}=tmp{2004};
   end;
   set orion.profit(where=(Sales ne .));
   Y=year(YYMM);
   M=month(YYMM);
   BudgetAmt=B{M,Y};
run;
```

B{1,2003}	B{1,2004}	B{1,2005}	B{1,2006}	B{1,2007}	B{2,2003}	B{2,2004}	. . .	B{12,2006}	B{12,2007}
1590000	1880000						. . .		

Partial PDV

D I	D Month	D Yr2003 tmp{2003}	D Yr2004 tmp{2004}	D Yr2005 tmp{2005}	D Yr2006 tmp{2006}	D Yr2007 tmp{2007}	D J	Company
1	1	1590000	1880000	2300000	1960000	1970000	2004	

YYMM	Sales	Cost	Salaries	Profit	D Y	D M	Budget Amt	D _N_
.	.	.	.	.	.	.	.	1

91 ...

Execution

Partial Listing of **orion.budget**

Month	Yr2003	Yr2004	. . .
1	1590000	1880000	. . .
2	1290000	1550000	. . .
3	1160000	1380000	. . .
4	1710000	2100000	. . .
.	.	.	. . .

```
data budget_amt;
   drop Yr2003-Yr2007 Month I J Y M;
   array B{12,2003:2007} _temporary_;
   if _N_=1 then do I=1 to 12;
      set orion.budget;
      array tmp{2003:2007} Yr2003-Yr2007;
      do J=2003 to 2007;
         B{I,J}=tmp{J};
      end;
   end;
   set orion.profit(where=(Sales ne .));
   Y=year(YYMM);
   M=month(YYMM);
   BudgetAmt=B{M,Y};
run;
```

B{1,2003}	B{1,2004}	B{1,2005}	B{1,2006}	B{1,2007}	B{2,2003}	B{2,2004}	. . .	B{12,2006}	B{12,2007}
1590000	1880000	2300000	1960000	1970000			. . .		

Partial PDV

D I	D Month	D Yr2003 tmp{2003}	D Yr2004 tmp{2004}	D Yr2005 tmp{2005}	D Yr2006 tmp{2006}	D Yr2007 tmp{2007}	D J	Company
2	1	1590000	1880000	2300000	1960000	1970000	2008	

YYMM	Sales	Cost	Salaries	Profit	D Y	D M	Budget Amt	D _N_
.	.	.	.	.	.	.	.	1

93 ...

Execution

Partial Listing of **orion.budget**

Month	Yr2003	Yr2004	. . .
1	1590000	1880000	. . .
2	1290000	1550000	. . .
3	1160000	1380000	. . .
4	1710000	2100000	. . .
.	.	.	. . .

```
data budget_amt;
   drop Yr2003-Yr2007 Month I J Y M;
   array B{12,2003:2007} _temporary_;
   if _N_=1 then do I=1 to 12;
      set orion.budget;
      array tmp{2003:2007} Yr2003-Yr2007;
      do J=2003 to 2007;
         B{I,J}=tmp{J};
      end;
   end;
   set orion.profit(where=(Sales ne .));
   Y=year(YYMM);
   M=month(YYMM);
   BudgetAmt=B{M,Y};
run;
```

B{1,2003}	B{1,2004}	B{1,2005}	B{1,2006}	B{1,2007}	B{2,2003}	B{2,2004}		B{12,2006}	B{12,2007}
1590000	1880000	2300000	1960000	1970000			. . .		

Partial PDV

D I	D Month	D Yr2003 (tmp{2003})	D Yr2004 (tmp{2004})	D Yr2005 (tmp{2005})	D Yr2006 (tmp{2006})	D Yr2007 (tmp{2007})	D J	Company
2	2	1290000	1550000	1830000	1480000	1640000	2008	

YYMM	Sales	Cost	Salaries	Profit	D Y	D M	Budget Amt	D _N_
.	.	.	.	.	.	.	.	1

94 ...

Execution

Partial Listing of **orion.budget**

Month	Yr2003	Yr2004	. . .
1	1590000	1880000	. . .
2	1290000	1550000	. . .
3	1160000	1380000	. . .
4	1710000	2100000	. . .
.	.	.	. . .

```
data budget_amt;
   drop Yr2003-Yr2007 Month I J Y M;
   array B{12,2003:2007} _temporary_;
   if _N_=1 then do I=1 to 12;
      set orion.budget;
      array tmp{2003:2007} Yr2003-Yr2007;
      do J=2003 to 2007;
         B{I,J}=tmp{J};
      end;
   end;
   set orion.profit(where=(Sales ne .));
   Y=year(YYMM);
   M=month(YYMM);
   BudgetAmt=B{M,Y};
run;
```

B{1,2003}	B{1,2004}	B{1,2005}	B{1,2006}	B{1,2007}	B{2,2003}	B{2,2004}		B{12,2006}	B{12,2007}
1590000	1880000	2300000	1960000	1970000			. . .		

Partial PDV

D I	D Month	D Yr2003 (tmp{2003})	D Yr2004 (tmp{2004})	D Yr2005 (tmp{2005})	D Yr2006 (tmp{2006})	D Yr2007 (tmp{2007})	D J	Company
2	2	1290000	1550000	1830000	1480000	1640000	2003	

YYMM	Sales	Cost	Salaries	Profit	D Y	D M	Budget Amt	D _N_
.	.	.	.	.	.	.	.	1

95 ...

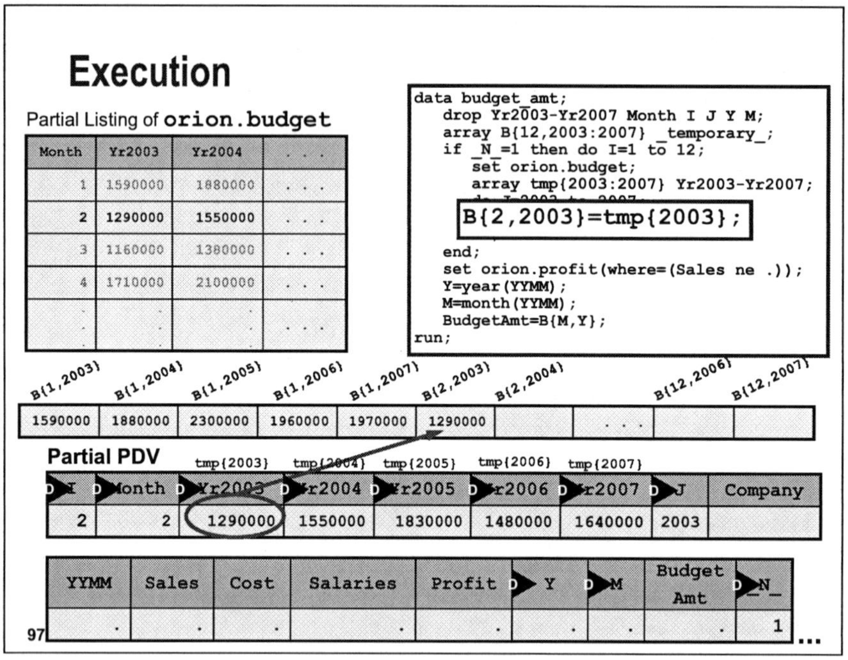
Execution
Partial Listing of orion.budget
Month | Yr2003 | Yr2004 | . . .
1 | 1590000 | 1880000 | . . .
2 | 1290000 | 1550000 | . . .
3 | 1160000 | 1380000 | . . .
4 | 1710000 | 2100000 | . . .
data budget_amt;
drop Yr2003-Yr2007 Month I J Y M;
array B{12,2003:2007} _temporary_;
if _N_=1 then do I=1 to 12;
set orion.budget;
array tmp{2003:2007} Yr2003-Yr2007;
B{2,2003}=tmp{2003};
end;
set orion.profit(where=(Sales ne .));
Y=year(YYMM);
M=month(YYMM);
BudgetAmt=B{M,Y};
run;
B{1,2003} B{1,2004} B{1,2005} B{1,2006} B{1,2007} B{2,2003} B{2,2004} B{12,2006} B{12,2007}
1590000 | 1880000 | 2300000 | 1960000 | 1970000 | 1290000 | | . . . | |
Partial PDV
tmp{2003} tmp{2004} tmp{2005} tmp{2006} tmp{2007}
I | Month | Yr2003 | Yr2004 | Yr2005 | Yr2006 | Yr2007 | J | Company
2 | 2 | 1290000 | 1550000 | 1830000 | 1480000 | 1640000 | 2003 |
YYMM | Sales | Cost | Salaries | Profit | Y | M | Budget Amt | _N_
. | . | . | . | . | . | . | . | 1
97
...

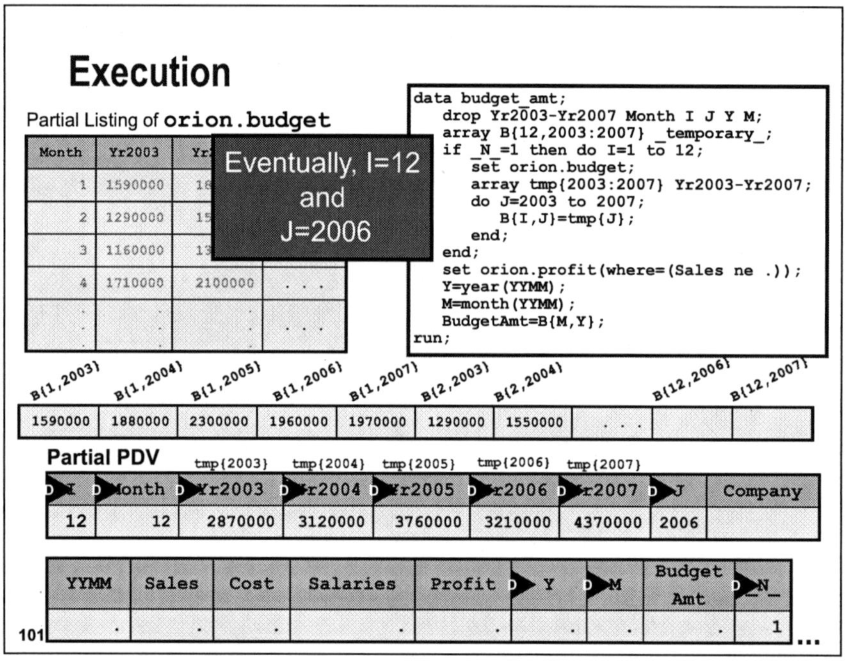
Execution
Partial Listing of orion.budget
Month | Yr2003
1 | 1590000
2 | 1290000
3 | 1160000
4 | 1710000 | 2100000 | . . .
Eventually, I=12 and J=2006
data budget_amt;
drop Yr2003-Yr2007 Month I J Y M;
array B{12,2003:2007} _temporary_;
if _N_=1 then do I=1 to 12;
set orion.budget;
array tmp{2003:2007} Yr2003-Yr2007;
do J=2003 to 2007;
B{I,J}=tmp{J};
end;
end;
set orion.profit(where=(Sales ne .));
Y=year(YYMM);
M=month(YYMM);
BudgetAmt=B{M,Y};
run;
B{1,2003} B{1,2004} B{1,2005} B{1,2006} B{1,2007} B{2,2003} B{2,2004} B{12,2006} B{12,2007}
1590000 | 1880000 | 2300000 | 1960000 | 1970000 | 1290000 | 1550000 | . . . | |
Partial PDV
tmp{2003} tmp{2004} tmp{2005} tmp{2006} tmp{2007}
I | Month | Yr2003 | Yr2004 | Yr2005 | Yr2006 | Yr2007 | J | Company
12 | 12 | 2870000 | 3120000 | 3760000 | 3210000 | 4370000 | 2006 |
YYMM | Sales | Cost | Salaries | Profit | Y | M | Budget Amt | _N_
. | . | . | . | . | . | . | . | 1
101
...

Execution

Partial Listing of **orion.budget**

Month	Yr2003	Yr2004	. . .
1	1590000	1880000	. . .
2	1290000	1550000	. . .
3	1160000	1380000	. . .
4	1710000	2100000	. . .
.	.	.	. . .

```
data budget_amt;
   drop Yr2003-Yr2007 Month I J Y M;
   array B{12,2003:2007} _temporary_;
   if _N_=1 then do I=1 to 12;
      set orion.budget;
      array tmp{2003:2007} Yr2003-Yr2007;
       B{12,2006}=tmp{2006};
   end;
   set orion.profit(where=(Sales ne .));
   Y=year(YYMM);
   M=month(YYMM);
   BudgetAmt=B{M,Y};
run;
```

B{1,2003}	B{1,2004}	B{1,2005}	B{1,2006}	B{1,2007}	B{2,2003}	B{2,2004}		B{12,2006}	B{12,2007}
1590000	1880000	2300000	1960000	1970000	1290000	1550000	. . .	3210000	

Partial PDV

		tmp{2003}	tmp{2004}	tmp{2005}	tmp{2006}	tmp{2007}		
D I	D Month	D Yr2003	D Yr2004	D Yr2005	D Yr2006	D Yr2007	D J	Company
12	12	2870000	3120000	3760000	3210000	4370000	2006	

YYMM	Sales	Cost	Salaries	Profit	D Y	D M	Budget Amt	D _N_
.	.	.	.	.	.	.	.	1

103 ...

Execution

Partial Listing of **orion.budget**

Month	Yr2003	Yr2004	. . .
1	1590000	1880000	. . .
2	1290000	1550000	. . .
3	1160000	1380000	. . .
4	1710000	2100000	. . .
.	.	.	. . .

```
data budget_amt;
   drop Yr2003-Yr2007 Month I J Y M;
   array B{12,2003:2007} _temporary_;
   if _N_=1 then do I=1 to 12;
      set orion.budget;
      array tmp{2003:2007} Yr2003-Yr2007;
       B{12,2007}=tmp{2007};
   end;
   set orion.profit(where=(Sales ne .));
   Y=year(YYMM);
   M=month(YYMM);
   BudgetAmt=B{M,Y};
run;
```

B{1,2003}	B{1,2004}	B{1,2005}	B{1,2006}	B{1,2007}	B{2,2003}	B{2,2004}		B{12,2006}	B{12,2007}
1590000	1880000	2300000	1960000	1970000	1290000	1550000	. . .	3210000	4370000

Partial PDV

		tmp{2003}	tmp{2004}	tmp{2005}	tmp{2006}	tmp{2007}		
D I	D Month	D Yr2003	D Yr2004	D Yr2005	D Yr2006	D Yr2007	D J	Company
12	12	2870000	3120000	3760000	3210000	4370000	2007	

YYMM	Sales	Cost	Salaries	Profit	D Y	D M	Budget Amt	D _N_
.	.	.	.	.	.	.	.	1

106 ...

Execution

Partial Listing of **orion.profit**

Company	YYMM	Sales	. . .
Logistics	03M01	457809	. . .
Logistics	03M02	325138	. . .
Logistics	03M03	276805	. . .
Logistics	03M04	558806	. . .
.	.	.	. . .

```
data budget_amt;
   drop Yr2003-Yr2007 Month I J Y M;
   array B{12,2003:2007} _temporary_;
   if _N_=1 then do I=1 to 12;
      set orion.budget;
      array tmp{2003:2007} Yr2003-Yr2007;
      do J=2003 to 2007;
         B{I,J}=tmp{J};
      end;
   end;
   set orion.profit(where=(Sales ne .));
   Y=year(YYMM);
   M=month(YYMM);
   BudgetAmt=B{M,Y};
run;
```

B{1,2003}	B{1,2004}	B{1,2005}	B{1,2006}	B{1,2007}	B{2,2003}	B{2,2004}	. . .	B{12,2006}	B{12,2007}
1590000	1880000	2300000	1960000	1970000	1290000	1550000	. . .	3210000	4370000

Partial PDV

D I	D Month	D Yr2003 (tmp{2003})	D Yr2004 (tmp{2004})	D Yr2005 (tmp{2005})	D Yr2006 (tmp{2006})	D Yr2007 (tmp{2007})	D J	Company
13	12	2870000	3120000	3760000	3210000	4370000	2008	Logistics

YYMM	Sales	Cost	Salaries	Profit	D Y	D M	Budget Amt	D _N_
03M01	457809	210914	127525	119370	.	.	.	1

110 ...

Execution

Partial Listing of **orion.profit**

Company	YYMM	Sales	. . .
Logistics	03M01	457809	. . .
Logistics	03M02	325138	. . .
Logistics	03M03	276805	. . .
Logistics	03M04	558806	. . .
.	.	.	. . .

```
data budget_amt;
   drop Yr2003-Yr2007 Month I J Y M;
   array B{12,2003:2007} _temporary_;
   if _N_=1 then do I=1 to 12;
      set orion.budget;
      array tmp{2003:2007} Yr2003-Yr2007;
      do J=2003 to 2007;
         B{I,J}=tmp{J};
      end;
   end;
   set orion.profit(where=(Sales ne .));
   Y=year(YYMM);
   M=month(YYMM);
   BudgetAmt=B{M,Y};
run;
```

B{1,2003}	B{1,2004}	B{1,2005}	B{1,2006}	B{1,2007}	B{2,2003}	B{2,2004}	. . .	B{12,2006}	B{12,2007}
1590000	1880000	2300000	1960000	1970000	1290000	1550000	. . .	3210000	4370000

Partial PDV

D I	D Month	D Yr2003 (tmp{2003})	D Yr2004 (tmp{2004})	D Yr2005 (tmp{2005})	D Yr2006 (tmp{2006})	D Yr2007 (tmp{2007})	D J	Company
13	12	2870000	3120000	3760000	3210000	4370000	2008	Logistics

YYMM	Sales	Cost	Salaries	Profit	D Y	D M	Budget Amt	D _N_
03M01	457809	210914	127525	119370	2003	1	.	1

111 ...

Execution

Partial Listing of **orion.profit**

Company	YYMM	Sales	. . .
Logistics	03M01	457809	. . .
Logistics	03M02	325138	. . .
Logistics	03M03	276805	. . .
Logistics	03M04	558806	. . .
.	.	.	. . .

```
data budget_amt;
   drop Yr2003-Yr2007 Month I J Y M;
   array B{12,2003:2007} _temporary_;
   if _N_=1 then do I=1 to 12;
      set orion.budget;
      array tmp{2003:2007} Yr2003-Yr2007;
      do J=2003 to 2007;
         B{I,J}=tmp{J};
      end;
   end;
   set orion.profit(where=(Sales ne .));
   Y=year(YYMM);
```

```
BudgetAmt=B{1,2003};
```

B{1,2003}	B{1,2004}	B{1,2005}	B{1,2006}	B{1,2007}	B{2,2003}	B{2,2004}		B{12,2006}	B{12,2007}
1590000	1880000	2300000	1960000	1970000	1290000	1550000	. . .	3210000	4370000

Partial PDV

		tmp{2003}	tmp{2004}	tmp{2005}	tmp{2006}	tmp{2007}		
I	Month	Yr2003	Yr2004	Yr2005	Yr2006	Yr2007	J	Company
13	12	2870000	3120000	3760000	3210000	4370000	2008	Logistics

YYMM	Sales	Cost	Salaries	Profit	Y	M	Budget Amt	_N_
03M01	457809	210914	127525	119370	2003	1	1590000	1

113 ...

Execution

Partial Listing of **orion.profit**

Company	YYMM	Sales	. . .
Logistics	03M01	457809	. . .
Logistics	03M02	325138	. . .
Logistics	03M03	276805	. . .
Logistics	03M04	558806	. . .
.	.	.	. . .

```
data budget_amt;
   drop Yr2003-Yr2007 Month I J Y M;
   array B{12,2003:2007} _temporary_;
   if _N_=1 then do I=1 to 12;
      set orion.budget;
      array tmp{2003:2007} Yr2003-Yr2007;
      do J=2003 to 2007;
         B{I,J}=tmp{J};
      end;
   end;
   set orion.profit(where=(Sales ne .));
   Y=year(YYMM);
   M=month(YYMM);
   BudgetAmt=B{M,Y};
run;
```

Implicit OUTPUT;
Implicit RETURN;

B{1,2003}	B{1,2004}	B{1,2005}	B{1,2006}	B{1,2007}	B{2,2003}	B{2,2004}		B{12,2006}	B{12,2007}
1590000	1880000	2300000	1960000	1970000	1290000	1550000	. . .	3210000	4370000

Partial PDV

		tmp{2003}	tmp{2004}	tmp{2005}	tmp{2006}	tmp{2007}		
I	Month	Yr2003	Yr2004	Yr2005	Yr2006	Yr2007	J	Company
13	12	2870000	3120000	3760000	3210000	4370000	2008	Logistics

YYMM	Sales	Cost	Salaries	Profit	Y	M	Budget Amt	_N_
03M01	457809	210914	127525	119370	2003	1	1590000	1

114 ...

Execution

Partial Listing of **orion.profit**

Company	YYMM	Sales	. . .
Logistics	03M01	457809	. . .
Logistics	03M02	325138	. . .
Logistics	03M03	276805	. . .
Logistics	03M04	558806	. . .
.	.	.	.

```
data budget_amt;
   drop Yr2003-Yr2007 Month I J Y M;
   array B{12,2003:2007} _temporary_;
   if _N_=1 then do I=1 to 12;
      set orion.budget;
      array tmp{2003:2007} Yr2003-Yr2007;
      do J=2003 to 2007;
         B{I,J}=tmp{J};
      end;
   end;
   set orion.profit(where=(Sales ne .));
   Y=year(YYMM);
   ...YMM);
   ...=B{M,Y};
```

Reinitialize PDV

B{1,2003}	B{1,2004}	B{1,2005}	B{1,2006}	B{1,2007}	B{2,2003}	B{2,2004}		B{12,2006}	B{12,2007}
1590000	1880000	2300000	1960000	1970000	1290000	1550000	. . .	3210000	4370000

Partial PDV

D I	D Month	D Yr2003	D Yr2004	D Yr2005	D Yr2006	D Yr2007	D J	Company
		tmp{2003}	tmp{2004}	tmp{2005}	tmp{2006}	tmp{2007}		
.	12	2870000	3120000	3760000	3210000	4370000	.	Logistics

YYMM	Sales	Cost	Salaries	Profit	D Y	D M	BudgetAmt	D _N_
03M01	457809	210914	127525	119370	.	.	.	2

115 ...

Execution

Partial Listing of **orion.profit**

Company	YYMM	Sales	. . .
Logistics	03M01	457809	. . .
Logistics	03M02	325138	. . .
Logistics	03M03	276805	. . .
Logistics	03M04	558806	. . .
.	.	.	. . .

```
data budget_amt;
   drop Yr2003-Yr2007 Month I J Y M;
   array B{12,2003:2007} _temporary_;
   if _N_=1 then do I=1 to 12;
      set orion.budget;
      array tmp{2003:2007} Yr2003-Yr2007;
      do J=2003 to 2007;
         B{I,J}=tmp{J};
      end;
   end;
   set orion.profit(where=(Sales ne .));
   Y=year(YYMM);
   M=month(YYMM);
   BudgetAmt=B{M,Y};
run;
```

B{1,2003}	B{1,2004}	B{1,2005}	B{1,2006}	B{1,2007}	B{2,2003}	B{2,2004}		B{12,2006}	B{12,2007}
1590000	1880000	2300000	1960000	1970000	1290000	1550000	. . .	3210000	4370000

Partial PDV

D I	D Month	D Yr2003	D Yr2004	D Yr2005	D Yr2006	D Yr2007	D J	Company
		tmp{2003}	tmp{2004}	tmp{2005}	tmp{2006}	tmp{2007}		
.	12	2870000	3120000	3760000	3210000	4370000	.	Logistics

YYMM	Sales	Cost	Salaries	Profit	D Y	D M	BudgetAmt	D _N_
03M02	325138	149718	127525	47895	.	.	.	2

117 ...

Execution

Partial Listing of **orion.profit**

Company	YYMM	Sales	. . .
Logistics	03M01	457809	. . .
Logistics	03M02	325138	. . .
Logistics	03M03	276805	. . .
Logistics	03M04	558806	. . .
.	.	.	. . .

```
data budget_amt;
   drop Yr2003-Yr2007 Month I J Y M;
   array B{12,2003:2007} _temporary_;
   if _N_=1 then do I=1 to 12;
      set orion.budget;
      array tmp{2003:2007} Yr2003-Yr2007;
      do J=2003 to 2007;
         B{I,J}=tmp{J};
      end;
   end;
   set orion.profit(where=(Sales ne .));
   Y=year(YYMM);
   M=month(YYMM);
   BudgetAmt=B{M,Y};
run;
```

B{1,2003}	B{1,2004}	B{1,2005}	B{1,2006}	B{1,2007}	B{2,2003}	B{2,2004}		B{12,2006}	B{12,2007}
1590000	1880000	2300000	1960000	1970000	1290000	1550000	. . .	3210000	4370000

Partial PDV

		tmp{2003}	tmp{2004}	tmp{2005}	tmp{2006}	tmp{2007}		
I	Month	Yr2003	Yr2004	Yr2005	Yr2006	Yr2007	J	Company
.	12	2870000	3120000	3760000	3210000	4370000	.	Logistics

YYMM	Sales	Cost	Salaries	Profit	Y	M	Budget Amt	_N_
03M02	325138	149718	127525	47895	2003	2	1290000	2

118 ...

Execution

Partial Listing of **orion.profit**

Company	YYMM	Sales	. . .
Logistics	03M01	457809	. . .
Logistics	03M02		
Logistics	03M03		
Logistics	03M04	558806	. . .
.	.	.	. . .

Continue until EOF

```
data budget_amt;
   drop Yr2003-Yr2007 Month I J Y M;
   array B{12,2003:2007} _temporary_;
   if _N_=1 then do I=1 to 12;
      set orion.budget;
      array tmp{2003:2007} Yr2003-Yr2007;
      o J=2003 to 2007;
         B{I,J}=tmp{J};
      nd;

   set orion.profit(where=(Sales ne .));
   Y=year(YYMM);
   M=month(YYMM);
   BudgetAmt=B{M,Y};
run;
```

B{1,2003}	B{1,2004}	B{1,2005}	B{1,2006}	B{1,2007}	B{2,2003}	B{2,2004}		B{12,2006}	B{12,2007}
1590000	1880000	2300000	1960000	1970000	1290000	1550000	. . .	3210000	4370000

Partial PDV

		tmp{2003}	tmp{2004}	tmp{2005}	tmp{2006}	tmp{2007}		
I	Month	Yr2003	Yr2004	Yr2005	Yr2006	Yr2007	J	Company
.	12	2870000	3120000	3760000	3210000	4370000	.	Logistics

YYMM	Sales	Cost	Salaries	Profit	Y	M	Budget Amt	_N_
03M02	325138	149718	127525	47895	2003	2	1290000	2

120 ...

Using an Array

Advantages of Using an Array	Disadvantages of Using an Array
faster than a hash object or format if you can use it	a contiguous chunk of memory requested at compile time
use of positional order	memory requirements to load the entire array
use of multiple values to determine the array element to be returned	requirement that you must have a numeric value as a pointer to the array elements
ability to use a non-sorted and non-indexed base data set	the return of only a single value from the lookup operation
use of numeric expressions to determine which element of the array is to be looked up; exact match not required	dimensions supplied at compile time by either hardcoding or macro variables

121

Review of Arrays

Array
An array uses less memory than other in-memory lookup techniques.
The size of the array is determined at compilation time.
The subscript value(s) must be numeric.
Subscript values must be consecutive integers.
One data value can be associated with the subscript value(s).
An array selects values by direct access based on the subscript value.
Arrays can only be used in the DATA step.

122

Exercises

Level 1

7. Using a Two-Dimensional Array

Orion Star wants to send discount coupons to the customers. The amounts of the discounts are given in the data set **orion.coupon_pct**.

Listing of **orion.coupon_pct**

orion.Coupon_Pct

Obs	OT	Quant	Value
1	1	1	10
2	1	2	10
3	1	3	15
4	1	4	20
5	1	5	20
6	1	6	25
7	2	1	10
8	2	2	15
9	2	3	20
10	2	4	25
11	2	5	25
12	2	6	30
13	3	1	10
14	3	2	15
15	3	3	15
16	3	4	20
17	3	5	25
18	3	6	25

The data set **orion.order_fact** contains variables **Customer_ID**, **Order_Type**, and **Quantity**.

Partial Listing of **orion.order_fact**

Obs	Customer_ID	Order_ Type	Quantity
1	63	1	1
2	5	2	1
3	45	2	1
4	41	1	2
5	183	1	3
6	79	2	1
7	23	2	1
8	23	2	2
9	45	2	2
10	45	2	1

a. Create a two-dimensional array with the values from **`orion.coupon_pct`**. Use values from **`orion.order_fact`** and the array to create a new variable named **`Coupon_Value`**. Name the new data set **`customer_coupons`**.

b. Print the first 10 observations of the **`customer_coupons`** data set.

PROC PRINT Output

The Coupon Value

Obs	Customer_ID	Order_ Type	Quantity	Coupon_ Value
1	63	1	1	10
2	5	2	1	10
3	45	2	1	10
4	41	1	2	10
5	183	1	3	15
6	79	2	1	10
7	23	2	1	10
8	23	2	2	15
9	45	2	2	15
10	45	2	1	10

Level 2

8. Using a Two-Dimensional Array

The data set **`orion.msp`** contains the average manufacturer's suggested retail price for shoes, based on the product line and the product category. The product group ID is the last two digits of **`Prod_Cat_ID`**.

Listing of **`orion.msp`**

orion.msp

Obs	Prod_ Line	Prod_ Cat_ID	Avg_Suggested_ Retail_Price
1	21	2101	.
2	21	2102	70.79
3	22	2201	173.79
4	22	2202	174.40
5	23	2301	.
6	23	2302	.
7	24	2401	29.63
8	24	2402	287.80

The data set **orion.shoe_sales** contains the **Product_ID**, the **Product_Name**, and the **Total_Retail_Price** for all of the shoes sold by Orion Star.

Partial Listing of **orion.shoe_sales**

Product_ID	Product_Name	Total_Retail_ Price
220200200024	Pro Fit Gel Gt 2030 Women's Running Shoes	$178.50
220200100092	Big Guy Men's Air Terra Sebec Shoes	$83.00
240200100043	Bretagne Performance Tg Men's Golf Shoes L.	$282.40
220100700024	Armadillo Road Dmx Women's Running Shoes	$99.70
220200300157	Hardcore Men's Street Shoes Large	$220.20
240200100051	Bretagne Stabilites 2000 Goretex Shoes	$420.90
220200100035	Big Guy Men's Air Deschutz Viii Shoes	$125.20
220200100090	Big Guy Men's Air Terra Reach Shoes	$177.20
220200200018	Lulu Men's Street Shoes	$132.80
240200100052	Bretagne Stabilities Tg Men's Golf Shoes	$99.70

a. Create a data set named **combine** using a two-dimensional array to combine the table of values from **orion.msp** with **orion.shoe_sales**. Create a new variable named **Manufacturer_Suggested_Price** based on the values of product line and product category. The product line is the first two digits of the **Product_ID** variable. The product category ID is the third and fourth digits of the **Product_ID** variable. Keep only the **Product_ID**, **Product_Name**, **Total_Retail_Price**, and **Manufacturer_Suggested_Price** variables. Format **Manufacturer_Suggested_Price** with dollar signs and two digits to the right of the decimal point.

b. Print the first five observations of the **combine** data set.

PROC PRINT Output

Obs	Manufacturer_ Suggested_ Price	Product_ID	Product_Name	Total_Retail_ Price
1	$174.40	220200200024	Pro Fit Gel Gt 2030 Women's Running Shoes	$178.50
2	$174.40	220200100092	Big Guy Men's Air Terra Sebec Shoes	$83.00
3	$287.80	240200100043	Bretagne Performance Tg Men's Golf Shoes L.	$282.40
4	$173.79	220100700024	Armadillo Road Dmx Women's Running Shoes	$99.70
5	$174.40	220200300157	Hardcore Men's Street Shoes Large	$220.20

Level 3

9. Using a Three-Dimensional Array

The data set **orion.warehouses** contains the warehouse location for all the products. The **Product_Line** variable has values from 21 to 24 inclusive, the **Product_Cat_ID** variable has values from 0 to 8 inclusive, and the variable **Product_Loc_ID** has values from 0 to 9 inclusive.

Partial Listing of **orion.warehouses**

orion.warehouses (Partial Data Set)

Obs	Product_ Line	Product_ Cat_ID	Product_ Loc_ID	Warehouse
1	21	0	0	A2100
2	21	0	1	A2101
3	21	1	0	A2110
4	21	1	1	A2111
5	21	2	0	A2120
6	21	2	2	A2122
7	21	2	3	A2123
8	21	2	4	A2124
9	21	2	5	A2125
10	21	2	6	A2126

a. Write a DATA step to create a data set named **warehouses**.

b. Load the values from **orion.warehouses** into a three-dimensional array.

c. Read only the variables **Product_ID**, **Product_Name**, and **Product_Level** and all of the observations from **orion.product_list** where **Product_Level** = 1. Use the **Product_ID** variable to determine the values of **Product_Line**, **Product_Cat_ID**, and **Product_Loc_ID**.

- The product line is the first two digits of the **Product_ID** variable.
- The product category ID is the third and fourth digits of the **Product_ID** variable.
- The product location ID identifies the location within a warehouse of the product and is the last digit of the **Product_ID** variable.

d. Use **Product_Line**, **Product_Cat_ID**, and **Product_Loc_ID** to retrieve the value from the array and create a variable named **Warehouse.**

e. Keep only the variables **Product_ID**, **Product_Name**, and **Warehouse**.

f. Print the first five observations of the **warehouses** data set.

PROC PRINT Output

warehouses

Obs	Warehouse	Product_ID	Product_Name
1	A2129	210200100009	Kids Sweat Round Neck,Large Logo
2	A2127	210200100017	Sweatshirt Children's O-Neck
3	A2122	210200200022	Sunfit Slow Swimming Trunks
4	A2123	210200200023	Sunfit Stockton Swimming Trunks Jr.
5	A2126	210200300006	Fleece Cuff Pant Kid'S

5.4 Chapter Review

Chapter Review

1. Define an array.

2. When is an array deleted from memory?

3. How can you visualize a two dimensional array?

125

Chapter Review

4. How many elements are created in the following ARRAY statement?

```
array myarray{5:9,7};
```

5. What are the names of the variables created by the ARRAY statement in question 4?

127

5.5 Solutions

Solutions to Exercises

1. Using a One-Dimensional Array to Combine Data

a. Combine the two data sets to create a data set named **compare**. The data set should contain the variables from **orion.retail** and variables named **Month** and **Median_Retail_Price** where **Month** is the month of the date that the product was ordered. Format **Median_Retail_Price** with dollar signs and two digits to the right of the decimal point.

a. Print the first eight observations of the resulting data set.

p305s01

```
data compare;
   drop Month1-Month12 Statistic;
   array mon{12} Month1-Month12;
   if _N_=1 then
      set orion.retail_information
                    (where=(Statistic='Median_Retail_Price'));
   set orion.retail;
   Month=month(Order_Date);
   Median_Retail_Price=mon(Month);
run;

proc print data=compare(obs=8);
  title 'Partial Compare Data Set';
run;
```

2. Using a One-Dimensional Array as a Lookup Table

a. Use arrays to create a data set named **trans** that has 24 observations.

b. Print the **trans** data set.

p305s02

```
data trans;
   drop Product21-Product24;
   array prod{21:24} Product21-Product24;
   set orion.shoe_stats;
   do Product_Line=21 to 24;
      Value=prod{Product_Line};
   output;
   end;
run;

proc print data=trans;
   title 'The TRANS data set';
run;
```

3. Using a One-Dimensional Array

a. Use the program **p305e03** to create a temporary data set **order_fact** for the year 2007 and customer IDs 89 and 2550, sorted by **Order_Type**.

b. Create the data set named **all** that has one observation for each **Order_Type** where there are a varying number of observations for each **Order_Type** in the original data set **order_fact**. Use the maximum number of observations for each order type as the array dimension to create three arrays that create variables to hold the order dates, the delivery dates, and the quantity.

c. Print the first three observations of **all**.

p305s03

```
/*************************************************************/
/* The SORT step limits the data to a few rows for practice */
/* and sorts the data to use with a BY statement in the     */
/* DATA step.                                               */
/*************************************************************/

proc sort data=orion.order_fact out=order_fact(keep=Customer_ID
                Order_Type Order_Date Delivery_Date Quantity);
   where Customer_ID in (89, 2550) and year(Order_Date)=2007;
   by Order_Type;
run;

/*************************************************************/
/* The SQL step counts the number of Order Types so that    */
/* you know the dimensions for the arrays that the program  */
/* needs.                                                   */
/*************************************************************/

proc sql;
   select Order_Type, count(*)
      from order_fact
         group by Order_Type;
quit;
```

(Continued on the next page.)

```
/****************************************************************/
/* The DATA step creates 4 variables for the order dates,      */
/* 4 for the delivery dates, and 4 for the quantities.         */
/* N is a counter of observations for each Order_Type.         */
/* N needs to initialized to 0 when the DATA step iterates.    */
/* The DATA step will execute a new time when the DO UNTIL     */
/* loop ends. This happens when the last observation           */
/* for an Order_Type has been processed.                       */
/* The three assignment statements in the DO loop              */
/* are creating the variables for each value of Order_Type.    */
/****************************************************************/

data all;
   array ordt{*} Ordered_Date1-Ordered_Date4;
   array deldt{*} Delivery_Date1-Delivery_Date4;
   array q{*} Quantity1 - Quantity4;
   format Ordered_Date1-Ordered_Date4
          Delivery_Date1-Delivery_Date4
          date9.;
   N=0;
   do until (last.Order_Type);
      set order_fact;
      by Order_Type;
      N+1;
      ordt{N}=Order_Date;
      deldt{N}=Delivery_Date;
      q{N}=Quantity;
   end;
run;

proc print data=all;
run;
```

(Continued on the next page.)

```
/*************************************************************/
/* to get a macro variable for the number of observations   */
/* in order_fact                                             */
/*                                                           */
/*  proc sql;                                                */
/*    create table temp as                                   */
/*       select count(*) as Num                              */
/*          from order_fact                                  */
/*             group by Customer_ID;                         */
/*        select max(num) into :NumObs                       */
/*            from temp;                                     */
/*                                                           */
/*  Then substitute &NumObs into the program instead of     */
/*  the 4                                                    */
/*************************************************************/

proc sort data=orion.order_fact out=order_fact(keep=Customer_ID
                Order_Type Order_Date Delivery_Date Quantity);
   where Customer_ID in (89, 2550) and year(Order_Date)=2007;
   by Order_Type;
run;

proc sql;
   create table temp as
      select count(*) as Num
         from order_fact
         group by Order_Type
   select max(num) into :NumObs
          from temp;
%let NumObs=&NumObs;
quit;

data all;
   array ordt{*} Ordered_Date1-Ordered_Date&NumObs;
   array deldt{*} Delivery_Date1-Delivery_Date&NumObs;
   array q{*} Quantity1 - Quantity&NumObs;
   format Ordered_Date1-Ordered_Date&NumObs
          Delivery_Date1-Delivery_Date&NumObs
          date9.;
   N=0;
   do until (last.Order_Type);
      set order_fact;
      by Order_Type;
      N+1;
      ordt{N}=Order_Date;
      deldt{N}=Delivery_Date;
      q{N}=Quantity;
   end;
run;
proc print data=all;
run;
```

4. Using a Two-Dimensional Array

a. Use a two-dimensional array to combine the data set with the table of values to create a data set named **customer_coupons** with a variable named **Coupon_Value**.

b. Print the first five observations of the **customer_coupons** data set.

p305s04

```
data customer_coupons;
   array pct{3,6} _temporary_ (10, 10, 15, 20, 20, 25,
                               10, 15, 20, 25, 25, 30,
                               10, 15, 15, 20, 25, 25);
   set orion.order_fact(keep=Customer_ID Order_Type Quantity);
   Coupon_Value=pct(Order_Type,Quantity);
run;

proc print data=customer_coupons(obs=5);
   title 'The Coupon Value';
run;
```

5. Using a Two-Dimensional Array

a. Create a data set named **combine** using a two-dimensional array to combine the table of values with the product line and the product category ID.

b. Print the first five observations of the **combine** data set.

p305s05

```
data combine;
   array msp{21:24,2} _temporary_
         (., 70.79, 173.79, 174.40, ., .,29.65, 287.8);
   set orion.shoe_sales;
   Prod_ID=put(Product_ID,12.);
   Product_Line=input(substr(Prod_ID,1,2),2.);
   Product_Cat_ID=input(substr(Prod_ID,3,2),2.);
   Manufacturer_Suggested_Price=msp{Product_Line,
                                    Product_Cat_ID};
run;

proc print data=combine(obs=5);
run;
```

6. Using a Three-Dimensional Array

Open the program **p305e06** that retrieves the Level 1products from the **orion.product_list** data set.

Modify **p305e06** to obtain the desired results.

a. Type the values of the **Warehouse** column into a three-dimensional array using the values of **Product_Line**, **Product_Grp_ID**, and **Product_Cat_ID** as the dimensions.

b. Create a data set named **warehouses**. Use the **Product_ID** variable to determine the values of **Product_Line**, **Product_Cat_ID**, and **Product_Loc_ID**.

- The product line is the first two digits of the **Product_ID** variable.
- The product category ID is the third and fourth digits of the **Product_ID** variable.
- The product location ID identifies the location within a warehouse of the product and is the last digit of the **Product_ID** variable.

b. Print the first five observations of the **warehouses** data set.

p305s06

```
data warehouses(drop=Prod_ID);
   array W{21:22,0:2,0:1} $ 5  _temporary_ ('A2100',
                                            'A2101',
                                            'A2110',
                                            'A2111',
                                            'A2120',
                                            'A2121',
                                            'B2200',
                                            'B2201',
                                            'B2210',
                                            'B2211',
                                            'B2220',
                                            'B2221');
   set orion.product_list(keep=Product_ID Product_Name
                                  Product_Level
                              where=(Product_Level=1));
   Prod_ID=put(Product_ID,12.);
   Product_Line=input(substr(Prod_ID,1,2),2.);
   Product_Cat_ID=input(substr(Prod_ID,12,1),1.);
   if Product_Line in (21,22) and Product_Cat_ID<2;
   Product_Loc_ID=input(substr(Prod_ID,12,1),1.);
   Warehouse=W(Product_Line, Product_Cat_ID, Product_Loc_ID);
run;

proc print data=warehouses(obs=5);
run;
```

7. Using a Two-Dimensional Array

a. Create a two-dimensional array with the values from **orion.coupon_pct**. Use values from **orion.order_fact** and the array to create a new variable named **Coupon_Value**. Name the new data set **customer_coupons**.

b. Print the first 10 observations of the **customer_coupons** data set.

p305s07

```
data customer_coupons;
   drop OT Quant Value i;
   array pct{3,6} _temporary_ ;
   if _N_=1 then do i=1 to All;
      set orion.coupon_pct nobs=All;
      pct{OT,Quant}=Value;
   end;
   set orion.order_fact(keep=Customer_ID Order_Type Quantity);
   Coupon_Value=pct(Order_Type,Quantity);
run;

proc print data=customer_coupons(obs=10);
   title 'The Coupon Value';
run;
```

8. Using a Two-Dimensional Array

a. Create a data set named **combine** using a two-dimensional array to combine the table of values from **orion.msp** with **orion.shoe_sales**. Create a new variable named **Manufacturer_Suggested_Price** based on the values of product line and product category. The product line is the first two digits of the **Product_ID** variable. The product category ID is the third and fourth digits of the **Product_ID** variable. Keep only the **Product_ID**, **Product_Name**, **Total_Retail_Price**, and **Manufacturer_Suggested_Price** variables. Format **Manufacturer_Suggested_Price** with dollar signs and two digits to the right of the decimal point.

b. Print the first five observations of the **combine** data set.

p305s08

```
data combine;
   array msp{21:24,2} _temporary_ ;
   keep Product_ID Product_Name Total_Retail_Price
        Manufacturer_Suggested_Price;
   format Manufacturer_Suggested_Price dollar8.2;
   if _N_= 1 then do i=1 to All;
      set orion.msp nobs=All;
      msp{Prod_Line,input(substr(put(Prod_Cat_ID,4.),3,2),2.)}
           =Avg_Suggested_Retail_Price;
   end;
   set orion.shoe_sales;
   Prod_ID=put(Product_ID,12.);
   Product_Line=input(substr(Prod_ID,1,2),2.);
   Product_Cat_ID=input(substr(Prod_ID,3,2),2.);
   Manufacturer_Suggested_Price=
                 msp{Product_Line, Product_Cat_ID};
run;

proc print data=combine(obs=5);
run;
```

9. Using a Three-Dimensional Array

a. Write a DATA step to create a data set named **warehouses**.

b. Load the values from **orion.warehouses** into a three-dimensional array.

c. Read only the variables **Product_ID**, **Product_Name**, and **Product_Level** and all of the observations from **orion.product_list** where **Product_Level** = 1. Use the **Product_ID** variable to determine the values of **Product_Line**, **Product_Cat_ID**, and **Product_Loc_ID**.

- The product line is the first two digits of the **Product_ID** variable.
- The product category ID is the third and fourth digits of the **Product_ID** variable.
- The product location ID identifies the location within a warehouse of the product and is the last digit of the **Product_ID** variable.

d. Use **Product_Line**, **Product_Cat_ID**, and **Product_Loc_ID** to retrieve the value from the array and create a variable named **Warehouse.**

e. Keep only the variables **Product_ID**, **Product_Name**, and **Warehouse**.

f. Print the first five observations of the **warehouses** data set.

p305s09

```
data warehouses;
   keep Product_ID Product_Name Warehouse;
   array w{21:24,0:8,0:9} $ 5  _temporary_ ;
   if _n_=1 then do i=1 to all;
      set orion.warehouses nobs=all;
      W{Product_Line, Product_Cat_ID, Product_Loc_ID}=Warehouse;
   end;
   set orion.product_list(keep=Product_ID Product_Name
                               Product_Level
                               where=(Product_Level=1));
   Prod_ID=put(Product_ID,12.);
   Product_Line=input(substr(Prod_ID,1,2),2.);
   Product_Cat_ID=input(substr(Prod_ID,3,2),2.);
   Product_Loc_ID=input(substr(Prod_ID,12,1),1.);
   Warehouse=w(Product_Line, Product_Cat_ID, Product_Loc_ID);
run;

proc print data=warehouses(obs=5);
   title 'warehouses';
run;
```

Solutions to Student Activities (Polls/Quizzes)

5.01 Multiple Choice Poll – Correct Answer

How many elements are referenced by the following ARRAY statement?

```
array numarray{*} Num1 - Num12;
```

a. 0
b. 1
c. 12 (circled)
d. Unknown

13

5.02 Poll – Correct Answer

Can the two data sets be merged with the DATA step MERGE statement or joined with the SQL procedure without pre-processing the data?

❍ Yes
❍ No (circled)

21

5.03 Poll – Correct Answer

What do the two data sets have in common?

- ❍ They have the year in common.
- ❍ They have nothing in common.

In the data set `orion.salary_stats`, the columns, except for the first, represent the year values.

In the data set `orion.employee_payroll`, the year values can be obtained from the `Employee_Hire_Date` variable.

23

5.04 Multiple Answer Poll – Correct Answers

Which of the following ARRAY statements are similar to the statement

```
array yr{1974:2007} Yr1974-Yr2007;
```

and will compile without errors?

a. `array yr{34} Yr1974-Yr2007;`
b. `array yr{1974-2007} Yr1974-Yr2007;`
c. `array yr{74:07} Yr1974-Yr2007;`
d. `array yr{74-07} Yr1974-Yr2007;`
e. `array yr{*} Yr1974-Yr2007;`

37

5.05 Quiz – Correct Answer

What is the type of the variable **YYMM** in the data set `orion.profit`?

Use PROC CONTENTS.

```
proc contents data=orion.profit;
run;
```

YYMM is a numeric variable. It represents a SAS date.

45

5.06 Quiz – Correct Answer

What do the data set `orion.profit` and the lookup table have in common?

They have the month and year in common. In the data set `orion.profit`, the month and year can be extracted from the variable YYMM. In the table, each row represents a month and each column represents a year.

50

5.07 Multiple Answer Poll – Correct Answers

Which of the following would be equivalent to the following ARRAY statement ?

```
array B{2,5} B1-B10 (1590000, 1880000, 2300000, 1960000, 1970000,
                     1290000, 1550000, 1830000, 1480000, 1640000);
```

a.
```
array B{*} B1-B10
      (1590000, 1880000, 2300000, 1960000, 1970000,
       1290000, 1550000, 1830000, 1480000, 1640000);
```

(b.)
```
array B{2,2003:2007} B1-B10
      (1590000, 1880000, 2300000, 1960000, 1970000,
       1290000, 1550000, 1830000, 1480000, 1640000);
```

(c.)
```
array B{2,5} (1590000, 1880000, 2300000, 1960000,
              1970000, 1290000, 1550000, 1830000,
              1480000, 1640000);
```

d.
```
array B{2,5} _temporary_ (1590000, 1880000, 2300000,
                          1960000, 1970000, 1290000,
                          1550000, 1830000, 1480000,
                          1640000);
```

57

5.08 Multiple Choice Poll – Correct Answer

How many elements are in the array defined by the following ARRAY statement?

```
array B{12,2003:2007} _temporary_;
```

a. 0
b. 24
c. 48
(d.) 60

82

Solutions to Chapter Review

Chapter Review – Correct Answers

1. Define an array.
   An *array* is a temporary grouping of SAS variables that are arranged in a particular order and identified by an array name.
2. When is an array deleted from memory?
   An array is deleted when the DATA step completes execution.
3. How can you visualize a two-dimensional array?
   As a table having a certain number of rows and a certain number of columns

126

Chapter Review – Correct Answers

4. How many elements are created in the following ARRAY statement?
   ```
   array myarray{5:9,7};
   ```
   35
5. What are the names of the variables created by the ARRAY statement in question 4?
   ```
   myarray1 - myarray35
   ```

128

Chapter 6 Using DATA Step Hash and Hiter Objects

6.1 Introduction

Objectives

- Define the DATA step hash object.

3

6.01 Poll

Have you used hash objects in SAS or other computer languages?

- ❍ Yes
- ❍ No

5

DATA Step Hash Objects

The DATA step *hash object* has the following attributes:

- provides in-memory data storage and retrieval
- has a data component and a key component
- uses the key for quick data retrieval
- can store multiple data items per key
- does not require the data to be sorted
- is sized dynamically

The hash object is a good choice for lookups using unordered data that can fit into memory.

6

Additional information about the hash object is available at the DATA Step Community Web site: support.sas.com/rnd/base/index-datastep.html

Overview of a Hash Object (Review)

A hash object is similar to rows of buckets that are identified by the value of a key.

Key Data Data

- SAS puts value(s) in the **data** bucket(s) based on the value(s) in the **key** bucket.
- Value(s) are retrieved from the **data** bucket(s) based on the value(s) in the **key** bucket.

7

DATA Step Hash Objects

The hash object resembles a table with rows and columns. The columns have the following characteristics:

- can be numeric or character
- can be loaded from hardcoded values
- can be loaded from a SAS data set
- exist for the duration of the DATA step
- can be output to a SAS data set

8

DATA Step Hash Objects

The key component has the following attributes:

- can consist of numeric and character values
- maps key values to data rows
- must be unique before SAS 9.2
- can be composite

The data component has the following attributes:

- can contain multiple data values per key value
- can consist of numeric and character values

⚠ Data components and key components are DATA step variables.

9

Using Hash Objects

The DATA step hash object has these characteristics:

- created with a DECLARE statement
- has attributes and methods
- manipulated with object dot syntax

An *attribute* is a property.

A *method* is a function.

10

6.2 Using Hash Object Methods

Objectives

- Investigate hash object syntax.
- Use hash object methods to load data into a hash object.
- Use a hash object method to match records.

12

Business Scenario

The SAS data set **orion.europe_customers** has variables that contain the customer type for the last year and for the current year.

Listing of **orion.europe_customers**

Customer_Name	Customer_Address	Country	LastYr Type	ThisYr Type
Cornelia Krahl	Kallstadterstr. 9	DE	20	20
Elke Wallstab	Carl-Zeiss-Str. 15	DE	10	20
Markus Sepke	Iese 1	DE	20	10
Ulrich Heyde	Oberstr. 61	DE	30	10
Oliver S. Füßling	Hechtsheimerstr. 18	DE	20	30
Rolf Robak	Münsterstraße 67	DE	10	30
Thomas Leitmann	Carl Von Linde Str. 13	DE	10	20
Gert-Gunter Mendler	Humboldtstr. 1	DE	20	30
Carsten Maestrini	Münzstr. 28	DE	20	30
Ines Deisser	Bahnweg 1	DE	10	20

13

Business Scenario

Customer descriptions must be assigned based on customer code values for member type. The values are shown in the table on the right but are not stored in a SAS data set.

Code	Member Type
10	Orion Club members
20	Orion Club Gold members
30	Internet/ Catalog customers

Listing of **orion.europe_customers**

Customer_Name	Customer_Address	Country	LastYr Type	ThisYr Type
Cornelia Krahl	Kallstadterstr. 9	DE	20	20
Elke Wallstab	Carl-Zeiss-Str. 15	DE	10	20
Markus Sepke	Iese 1	DE	20	10
Ulrich Heyde	Oberstr. 61	DE	30	10
Oliver S. Füßling	Hechtsheimerstr. 18	DE	20	30
Rolf Robak	Münsterstraße 67	DE	10	30
Thomas Leitmann	Carl Von Linde Str. 13	DE	10	20
Gert-Gunter Mendler	Humboldtstr. 1	DE	20	30
Carsten Maestrini	Münzstr. 28	DE	20	30
Ines Deisser	Bahnweg 1	DE	10	20

14

A set of lookup values can be stored in a hash object. Whereas an array uses a series of consecutive integers to address array elements, a hash object can use any combination of numeric and character values as addresses.

6.02 Multiple Answer Poll

Which of the following could be used to assign descriptions to each of the variables **ThisYrType** and **LastYrType**?

a. Merging
b. Formats
c. IF-THEN/ELSE
d. Arrays

16

Using Hash Objects

Load the code and member type into a hash object named **T**.

`Code` `MemberType`

HASH Object T

KEY	DATA
10	Orion Club members
20	Orion Club Gold members
30	Internet/Catalog Customers

18

Using Hash Objects

```
data mem_type;
   length Code $2 MemberType $40;
   if _N_=1 then do;
      declare hash T();
      T.definekey('Code');
      T.definedata('MemberType');
      T.definedone();
      T.add(key:'10', data:'Orion Club members');
      T.add(key:'20', data:'Orion Club Gold members');
      T.add(key:'30', data:'Internet/Catalog Customers');
   end;
   set orion.europe_customers;
   rc1=T.find(key:ThisYrType);
   if rc1=0 then ThisYrMember=MemberType;
   rc2=T.find(key:LastYrType);
   if rc2=0 then LastYrMember=MemberType;
run;
```

19 p306d01

Compilation

```
data mem_type;
   length Code $2 MemberType $40;
   if _N_=1 then do;
      declare hash T();
      T.definekey('Code');
      T.definedata('MemberType');
      T.definedone();
      T.add(key:'10',data:'Orion Club members');
      T.add(key:'20',data:'Orion Club Gold members');
      T.add(key:'30',data:'Internet/Catalog Customers');
   end;
   set orion.europe_customers;
   rc1=T.find(key:ThisYrType);
   if rc1=0 then ThisYrMember=MemberType;
   rc2=T.find(key:LastYrType);
   if rc2=0 then LastYrMember=MemberType;
run;
```

Partial PDV

Code	Member Type	Customer_ Name	...	LastYr Type	ThisYr Type	...

rc1	ThisYr Member	rc2	LastYr Member	D _N_
.		.		.

20 ...

Execution

Partial orion.europe_customers

Customer _Name	...	Last Yr Type	This Yr Type
Cornelia Krahl	..	20	20
Elke Wallstab	..	10	20
Markus Sepke	..	20	10
.	..	.	.

True

```
data mem_type;
   length Code $2 MemberType $40;
   if _N_=1 then do;
      declare hash T();
      T.definekey('Code');
      T.definedata('MemberType');
      T.definedone();
      T.add(key:'10',data:'Orion Club members');
      T.add(key:'20',data:'Orion Club Gold members');
      T.add(key:'30',data:'Internet/Catalog Customers');
   end;
   set orion.europe_customers;
   rc1=T.find(key:ThisYrType);
   if rc1=0 then ThisYrMember=MemberType;
   rc2=T.find(key:LastYrType);
   if rc2=0 then LastYrMember=MemberType;
run;
```

Partial PDV

Code	Member Type	Customer_ Name	...	LastYr Type	ThisYr Type	...

rc1	ThisYr Member	rc2	LastYr Member	D _N_
.		.		1

21 ...

Execution

Partial **orion.europe_customers**

Customer_Name	...	Last Yr Type	This Yr Type
Cornelia Krahl	...	20	20
Elke Wallstab	...	10	20

HASH Object T

```
data mem_type;
   length Code $2 MemberType $40;
   if _N_=1 then do;
      declare hash T();
      T.definekey('Code');
      T.definedata('MemberType');
      T.definedone();
      T.add(key:'10',data:'Orion Club members');
      T.add(key:'20',data:'Orion Club Gold members');
      T.add(key:'30',data:'Internet/Catalog Customers');
   end;
   set orion.europe_customers;
   rc1=T.find(key:ThisYrType);
   if rc1=0 then ThisYrMember=MemberType;
   rc2=T.find(key:LastYrType);
   if rc2=0 then LastYrMember=MemberType;
run;
```

Partial PDV

Code	Member Type	Customer_ Name	...	LastYr Type	ThisYr Type	...

rc1	ThisYr Member	rc2	LastYr Member	D _N_
.		.		1

22 ...

Execution

Partial **orion.europe_customers**

Customer_Name	...	Last Yr Type	This Yr Type
Cornelia Krahl	...	20	20
Elke Wallstab	...	10	20

HASH Object T

KEY: Code	DATA: MemberType

```
data mem_type;
   length Code $2 MemberType $40;
   if _N_=1 then do;
      declare hash T();
      T.definekey('Code');
      T.definedata('MemberType');
      T.definedone();
      T.add(key:'10',data:'Orion Club members');
      T.add(key:'20',data:'Orion Club Gold members');
      T.add(key:'30',data:'Internet/Catalog Customers');
   end;
   set orion.europe_customers;
   rc1=T.find(key:ThisYrType);
   if rc1=0 then ThisYrMember=MemberType;
   rc2=T.find(key:LastYrType);
   if rc2=0 then LastYrMember=MemberType;
run;
```

Partial PDV

Code	Member Type	Customer_ Name	...	LastYr Type	ThisYr Type	...

rc1	ThisYr Member	rc2	LastYr Member	D _N_
.		.		1

25 ...

Execution

Partial orion.europe_customers

Customer_Name	. .	Last Yr Type	This Yr Type
Cornelia Krahl	. .	20	20
Elke Wallstab	. .	10	20

HASH Object T

KEY: Code	DATA: MemberType
10	Orion Club members
20	Orion Club Gold members
30	Internet/Catalog Customers

```
data mem_type;
   length Code $2 MemberType $40;
   if _N_=1 then do;
      declare hash T();
      T.definekey('Code');
      T.definedata('MemberType');
      T.definedone();
      T.add(key:'10',data:'Orion Club members');
      T.add(key:'20',data:'Orion Club Gold members');
      T.add(key:'30',data:'Internet/Catalog Customers');
   end;
   set orion.europe_customers;
   rc1=T.find(key:ThisYrType);
   if rc1=0 then ThisYrMember=MemberType;
   rc2=T.find(key:LastYrType);
   if rc2=0 then LastYrMember=MemberType;
run;
```

Partial PDV

Code	Member Type	Customer_ Name	. . .	LastYr Type	ThisYr Type	. . .

rc1	ThisYr Member	rc2	LastYr Member	D _N_
.		.		1

29 ...

6.03 Multiple Answer Poll

When would you **not** use quotation marks around the value for an argument to a method?

a. The value is numeric.

b. The value is character.

c. The value of a PDV variable is wanted.

d. The value is character or numeric.

31

Declaring a Hash Object

```
declare hash T();
```

General form for the DECLARE statement:

DECLARE *object object-reference* (<*arg_tag-1*: *value-1* <,...*arg_tag-n*: *value-n*>>);

object	specifies the component object
object-reference	specifies the object-reference name for the component object
arg_tag	specifies the information that is used to create an instance of the component object
value	specifies the value for an argument tag

33

Valid values for *arg_tag* depend on the component object.

When a DATA step hash object is created, it is said to be *instantiated.*

Declaring a Hash Object

Valid values for *object* are as follows:

hash	indicates a hash object.
hiter	indicates a hash iterator object.

The *hiter* object retrieves data from the hash object in ascending or descending key order.

34

Hash Object Argument Tags

Argument_tag	Value Description
dataset: '*data-set_name*'	name of a SAS data set to load into the hash object
hashexp: *n*	hash object's table size, where the size of the hash table is 2^n (default n=8, max n=16)
ordered: 'NO' | 'ascending' | 'descending' | 'YES' | 'Y'	sort order for the OUTPUT method or the hash iterator object (default='NO')

35

Reference Information

HASHEXP

In order to maximize the efficiency of the hash object lookup routines, you should set the hash table size according to the amount of data in the hash object.

- The hash table is similar to an array of buckets. If the HASHEXP=4, the hash would have 16 buckets. This does not limit the hash table to 16 key values. Each bucket can hold an unlimited number of keys.
- When the DATA step adds data to the hash object or retrieves data values from the hash table, the key is passed to a hash function, which returns the number of the bucket in which to add data or from which to retrieve data.
- If the number of key and data combinations is larger than the number of buckets, performance might be reduced because more combinations will be stored per bucket in a binary tree structure.
- If the number of key and data combinations is smaller than the number of buckets, then some of the buckets will be empty, which wastes memory.

Try different HASHEXP values until you obtain the best result. For example, if the hash object contains a large number of items, a hash table size of 16 (**`hashexp=4`**) is not very efficient. A hash table size of 512 or 1024 (**`hashexp=9`** or **`10`**) results in better performance.

If there is not enough memory in which to load the hash object, the load fails.

Several techniques can be used to determine the amount of memory required by the hash object.

- The size of a hash record is approximately the sum of the sizes of values being placed into the record. For example, two million 64-byte records take approximately 128 MB. If the SAS system option MEMSIZE= is set larger than 128 MB and the machine can support executing SAS with at least 128 MB of memory free for loading the hash object, the hash object loads successfully.
- Use the FULLSTIMER SAS system option to determine how much memory the hash object uses with fewer records. For example, if you load approximately one-third of the records into the hash object, you can multiply the amount of memory reported by FULLSTIMER by three to determine the approximate amount of memory needed for the entire hash table. This is an estimate, because the reported memory usage includes the memory needed to execute the non-hash object portions of the DATA step.
- The maximum size of the hash object that you can load depends on the maximum amount of memory addressable per CPU on your particular operating system. For instance, a 4-CPU computer with 8 GB of memory might limit each CPU to 2 GB of memory. In this case, the maximum size of a hash object would be less than 2 GB.

Suggestions to avoid memory constraints include the following:

- Subset large data sets before loading the data into the hash object.
- Create a view of a large data set. The view should include syntax that limits the number of columns that need to be read from the large data set into the hash table.
- Make the length of the hash record as small as possible. For example, instead of the numeric values of 1 and 2, store the values as character '1' and '2'. Numeric data is always stored as 8 bytes in the hash record.

Declaring a Hash Object

Create a hash object named **T**.

```
declare hash T();
```

Create the **T** hash object and load it from **orion.members**.

```
declare hash T(dataset: 'orion.members');
```

Create the **T** hash object, assign a size, and specify a return order.

```
declare hash T(hashexp: 10,
               ordered: 'ascending');
```

⚠ The DECLARE statement is an executable statement.

36

In SAS 9.2, you can use data set options in the DECLARE statement when you load the hash object from a SAS data set.

Example:

```
declare hash T(dataset: 'orion.members(where=(Code=102)
                                    keep=Code Member_Type)';
```

Using Object Dot Syntax

```
T.definekey('Code');
T.definedata('MemberType');
T.definedone();
```

General form for object dot **method** syntax:

OBJECT.METHOD(<*arg_tag-1*: *value-1*
<,...*arg_tag-n*: *value-n*>>);

object	name of the object
method	method to invoke
arg_tag	name of an argument to be passed
value	value of the argument

37

Without the DEFINEDONE method, the log reports the following errors:

```
ERROR: Method defineDone must be called to complete initialization of hash object before line
       189 column 7.
ERROR: DATA STEP Component Object failure. Aborted during the EXECUTION phase.
NOTE: The SAS System stopped processing this step because of errors.
```

Selected hash object methods available in SAS 9.1 include the following:

DEFINEKEY	defines key variables for the hash object.
DEFINEDATA	defines data variables for the hash object.
DEFINEDONE	completes the initialization of the hash object.
ADD	adds key and data values to the hash object.
FIND	searches the hash object for a key value, and returns a zero if successful. If the key is in the hash object, then the FIND method also sets the data variable to the value of the data item so that it is available for use after the method call.
OUTPUT	outputs the hash object's data values to a SAS data set.
DELETE	deletes a hash object.
REPLACE	replaces the data for a key in the hash object.
REMOVE	removes a key and its associated data from the hash object.
CHECK	checks whether the specified key is stored in the hash object.
NUM_ITEMS	returns the number of items in the hash object.

Additional hash object methods available in SAS 9.2 include the following:

CLEAR	removes all items from the hash object without deleting the hash object instance.
EQUALS	determines whether two hash objects are equal.
FIND_NEXT	sets the current list item to the next item in the current key's multiple item list and sets the data for the corresponding data variables.
FIND_PREV	sets the current list item to the previous item in the current key's multiple item list and sets the data for the corresponding data variables.
HAS_NEXT	determines whether there is a next item in the current key's multiple data item list.
HAS_PREV	determines whether there is a previous item in the current key's multiple data item list.
REF	consolidates the FIND and ADD methods into a single method call.
REMOVEDUP	removes the data that is associated with the specified key's current data item from the hash object.
REPLACEDUP	replaces the data that is associated with the current key's current data item with new data.
SETCUR	specifies a starting key item for iteration.
SUM	retrieves the summary value for a given key from the hash table and stores the value in a DATA step variable.
SUMDUP	retrieves the summary value for the current data item of the current key and stores the value in a DATA step variable.

Loading Key and Data Values

Use the ADD method to load key and data values into the hash object.

```
T.add(key:'10',data:'Orion Club members');
T.add(key:'20',data:'Orion Club Gold members');
T.add(key:'30',data:'Internet/Catalog Customers');
```

38

6.04 Quiz

Why were the statements and methods that instantiate and load the hash object inside of an IF-THEN/DO group?

```
data mem_type;
   length Code $2 MemberType $40;
   if _N_=1 then do;
      declare hash T();
      T.definekey('Code');
      T.definedata('MemberType');
      T.definedone();
      T.add(key:'10',data:'Orion Club members');
      T.add(key:'20',data:'Orion Club Gold members');
      T.add(key:'30',data:'Internet/Catalog Customers');
   end;
   set orion.europe_customers;
   rc1=T.find(key:ThisYrType);
   if rc1=0 then ThisYrMember=MemberType;
   rc2=T.find(key:LastYrType);
   if rc2=0 then LastYrMember=MemberType;
run;
```

40

DEFINE ONCE.
SAVES MEMORY

Execution

Partial orion.europe_customers

Customer_Name	. .	Last Yr Type	This Yr Type
Cornelia Krahl	. .	20	20
Elke Wallstab	. .	10	20

HASH Object T

KEY: Code	DATA: MemberType
10	Orion Club members
20	Orion Club Gold members
30	Internet/Catalog Customers

```
data mem_type;
   length Code $2 MemberType $40;
   if _N_=1 then do;
      declare hash T();
      T.definekey('Code');
      T.definedata('MemberType');
      T.definedone();
      T.add(key:'10',data:'Orion Club members');
      T.add(key:'20',data:'Orion Club Gold members');
      T.add(key:'30',data:'Internet/Catalog Customers');
   end;
   set orion.europe_customers;
   rc1=T.find(key:ThisYrType);
   if rc1=0 then ThisYrMember=MemberType;
   rc2=T.find(key:LastYrType);
   if rc2=0 then LastYrMember=MemberType;
run;
```

Partial PDV

Code	Member Type	Customer_ Name	. . .	LastYr Type	ThisYr Type	. . .
		Cornelia Krahl		20	20	

rc1	ThisYr Member	rc2	LastYr Member	D _N_
.		.		1

43 ...

Execution

Partial orion.europe_customers

Customer_Name	. .	Last Yr Type	This Yr Type
Cornelia Krahl	. .	20	20
Elke Wallstab	. .	10	20

HASH Object T

KEY: Code	DATA: MemberType
10	Orion Club members
20	Orion Club Gold members
30	Internet/Catalog Customers

```
data mem_type;
   length Code $2 MemberType $40;
   if _N_=1 then do;
      declare hash T();
      T.definekey('Code');
      T.definedata('MemberType');
      T.definedone();
      T.add(key:'10',data:'Orion Club members');
      T.add(key:'20',data:'Orion Club Gold members');
      T.add(key:'30',data:'Internet/Catalog Customers');
   end;
   set orion.europe_customers;
   rc1=T.find(key:ThisYrType);
   if rc1=0 then ThisYrMember=MemberType;
   rc2=T.find(key:LastYrType);
   if rc2=0 then LastYrMember=MemberType;
run;
```

Partial PDV

Code	Member Type	Customer_ Name	. . .	LastYr Type	ThisYr Type	. . .
		Cornelia Krahl		20	20	

rc1	ThisYr Member	rc2	LastYr Member	D _N_
0		.		1

44 ...

Execution

Partial orion.europe_customers

Customer_Name	..	Last Yr Type	This Yr Type
Cornelia Krahl	..	20	20
Elke Wallstab	..	10	20

HASH Object T

KEY: Code	DATA: MemberType
10	Orion Club members
20	Orion Club Gold members
30	Internet/Catalog Customers

```
data mem_type;
   length Code $2 MemberType $40;
   if _N_=1 then do;
      declare hash T();
      T.definekey('Code');
      T.definedata('MemberType');
      T.definedone();
      T.add(key:'10',data:'Orion Club members');
      T.add(key:'20',data:'Orion Club Gold members');
      T.add(key:'30',data:'Internet/Catalog Customers');
   end;
   set orion.europe_customers;
   rc1=T.find(key:ThisYrType);
   if rc1=0 then ThisYrMember=MemberType;
   rc2=T.find(key:LastYrType);
   if rc2=0 then LastYrMember=MemberType;
run;
```

Partial PDV

Code	Member Type	Customer_ Name	...	LastYr Type	ThisYr Type	...
	Orion Club Gold members	Cornelia Krahl		20	20	

rc1	ThisYr Member	rc2	LastYr Member	D _N_
0		.		1

45 ...

Execution

Partial orion.europe_customers

Customer_Name	..	Last Yr Type	This Yr Type
Cornelia Krahl	..	20	20
Elke Wallstab	..	10	20

HASH Object T

KEY: Code	DATA: MemberType
10	Orion Club members
20	Orion Club Gold members
30	Internet/Catalog Customers

```
data mem_type;
   length Code $2 MemberType $40;
   if _N_=1 then do;
      declare hash T();
      T.definekey('Code');
      T.definedata('MemberType');
      T.definedone();
      T.add(key:'10',data:'Orion Club members');
      T.add(key:'20',data:'Orion Club Gold members');
      T.add(key:'30',data:'Internet/Catalog Customers');
   end;
   set orion.europe_customers;
   rc1=T.find(key:ThisYrType);
   if rc1=0 then ThisYrMember=MemberType;
   rc2=T.find(key:LastYrType);
   if rc2=0 then LastYrMember=MemberType;
run;
```

Partial PDV

Code	Member Type	Customer_ Name	...	LastYr Type	ThisYr Type	...
	Orion Club Gold members	Cornelia Krahl		20	20	

rc1	ThisYr Member	rc2	LastYr Member	D _N_
0	Orion Club Gold members	.		1

46 ...

Execution

Partial orion.europe_customers

Customer _Name	. .	Last Yr Type	This Yr Type
Cornelia Krahl	. .	20	20
Elke Wallstab	. .	10	20

HASH Object T

KEY: Code	DATA: MemberType
10	Orion Club members
20	Orion Club Gold members
30	Internet/Catalog Customers

```
data mem_type;
   length Code $2 MemberType $40;
   if _N_=1 then do;
      declare hash T();
      T.definekey('Code');
      T.definedata('MemberType');
      T.definedone();
      T.add(key:'10',data:'Orion Club members');
      T.add(key:'20',data:'Orion Club Gold members');
      T.add(key:'30',data:'Internet/Catalog Customers');
   end;
   set orion.europe_customers;
   rc1=T.find(key:ThisYrType);
   if rc1=0 then ThisYrMember=MemberType;
   rc2=T.find(key:LastYrType);
   if rc2=0 then LastYrMember=MemberType;
run;
```

Partial PDV

Code	Member Type	Customer_ Name	. . .	LastYr Type	ThisYr Type	. . .
	Orion Club Gold members	Cornelia Krahl		20	20	

rc1	ThisYr Member	rc2	LastYr Member	D _N_
0	Orion Club Gold members	0	Orion Club Gold members	1

50 ...

Execution

Partial orion.europe_customers

Customer _Name	. .	Last Yr Type	This Yr Type
Cornelia Krahl	. .	20	20
Elke Wallstab	. .	10	20

HASH Object T

KEY: Code	DATA: MemberType
10	Orion Club members
20	Orion Club Gold members
30	Internet/Catalog Customers

```
data mem_type;
   length Code $2 MemberType $40;
   if _N_=1 then do;
      declare hash T();
      T.definekey('Code');
      T.definedata('MemberType');
      T.definedone();
      T.add(key:'10',data:'Orion Club members');
      T.add(key:'20',data:'Orion Club Gold members');
      T.add(key:'30',data:'Internet/Catalog Customers');
   en
   se                   mers;
   rc                   ype);
   if                   mber=MemberType;
   rc2=T.find(key:LastYrType);
   if rc2=0 then LastYrMember=MemberType;
run;
```

Initialize PDV

Partial PDV

Code	Member Type	Customer_ Name	. . .	LastYr Type	ThisYr Type	. . .
		Cornelia Krahl		20	20	

rc1	ThisYr Member	rc2	LastYr Member	D _N_
.		.		2

52 ...

Execution

Partial orion.europe_customers

Customer_Name	. .	Last Yr Type	This Yr Type
Cornelia Krahl	. .	20	20
Elke Wallstab	. .	10	20

HASH Object T

KEY: Code	DATA: MemberType
10	Orion Club members
20	Orion Club Gold members
30	Internet/Catalog Customers

```
data mem_type;
   length Code $2 MemberType $40;
   if _N_=1 then do;
      declare hash T();
      T.definekey('Code');
      T.definedata('MemberType');
      T.definedone();
      T.add(key:'10',data:'Orion Club members');
      T.add(key:'20',data:'Orion Club Gold members');
      T.add(key:'30',data:'Internet/Catalog Customers');
   end;
   set orion.europe_customers;
   rc1=T.find(key:ThisYrType);
   if rc1=0 then ThisYrMember=MemberType;
   rc2=T.find(key:LastYrType);
   if rc2=0 then LastYrMember=MemberType;
run;
```

Partial PDV

Code	MemberType	Customer_Name	. . .	LastYrType	ThisYrType	. . .
	Orion Club members	Elke Wallstab		10	20	

rc1	ThisYrMember	rc2	LastYrMember	D _N_
0	Orion Club Gold members	0	Orion Club members	2

61 ...

Execution

Partial orion.europe_customers

Customer_Name	. .	Last Yr Type	This Yr Type
Cornelia Krahl	. .	20	20
Elke Wallstab	. .	10	20

HASH Object T

KEY: Code	DATA: MemberType
10	Orion Club members
20	Orion Club Gold members
30	Internet/Catalog Customers

```
data mem_type;
   length Code $2 MemberType $40;
   if _N_=1 then do;
      declare hash T();
      T.definekey('Code');
      T.definedata('MemberType');
      T.definedone();
      T.add(key:'10',data:'Orion Club members');
      T.add(key:'20',data:'Orion Club Gold members');
      T.add(key:'30',data:'Internet/Catalog Customers');
   end;
   set orion.europe_customers;
   rc1=T.find(key:ThisYrType);
   if rc1=0 then ThisYrMember=MemberType;
   rc2=T.find(key:LastYrType);
   if rc2=0 then LastYrMember=MemberType;
run;
```

Continue until EOF

Partial PDV

Code	MemberType	Customer_Name	. . .	LastYrType	ThisYrType	. . .
	Orion Club members	Ines Deisser		10	20	

rc1	ThisYrMember	rc2	LastYrMember	D _N_
0	Orion Club Gold members	0	Orion Club members	10

63 ...

Setup for the Poll

Partial **orion.europe_customers**

Customer _Name	. .	Last Yr Type	This Yr Type
Cornelia Krahl	. .	20	20
Elke Wallstab	. .	10	20

HASH Object T

KEY: Code	DATA: MemberType
10	Orion Club members
20	Orion Club Gold members
30	Internet/Catalog Customers

```
data mem_type;
   length Code $2 MemberType $40;
   if _N_=1 then do;
      declare hash T();
      T.definekey('Code');
      T.definedata('MemberType');
      T.definedone();
      T.add(key:'10',data:'Orion Club members');
      T.add(key:'20',data:'Orion Club Gold members');
      T.add(key:'30',data:'Internet/Catalog Customers');
   end;
   set orion.europe_customers;
   rc1=T.find(key:ThisYrType);
   if rc1=0 then ThisYrMember=MemberType;
   rc2=T.find(key:LastYrType);
   if rc2=0 then LastYrMember=MemberType;
run;
```

Partial PDV

Code	Member Type	Customer_ Name	. . .	LastYr Type	ThisYr Type	. . .
	Orion Club Gold members	Dane Heufmeister		40	20	

rc1	ThisYr Member	rc2	LastYr Member	D _N_
0	Orion Club Gold members	-2147450842		8

65

6.05 Multiple Choice Poll

What would be the value of **LastYrMember** if the value of **LastYrType** were not found in the hash object (**rc2 ne 0**)?

a. Missing
b. Orion Club members
c. Orion Club Gold members
d. Internet/Catalog

66

6.06 Quiz

Submit the program **p306a01** and examine the SAS log.
What are the notes about **`Code`** and **`MemberType`**?

Why do you get those notes?

69

6.07 Quiz

As the last statement in the DO group in the program **p306a01**, add the statement:

```
call missing(Code, MemberType);
```

Do the notes disappear?

72

CALL MISSING Routine

The CALL MISSING routine provides initial values to the variables.

CALL MISSING(*varname1*<, *varname2*, ...>);

Argument Type	Value Assigned	Length
Numeric	.	8
Character	Blank	Current length of character variable

74

If the current length of the character variable is any value up to the maximum length, the current length is not changed. Otherwise, if no length is set for the variable, the current length is set to 1.

The FIND Method

The FIND method locates the key value in the hash object and returns the data values.

General form of the FIND method:

rc=*object*.FIND(<KEY: *keyvalue-1*,..., KEY: *keyvalue-n*>);

The FIND method returns a numeric value that indicates whether the FIND method succeeded or failed.

The KEY: *keyvalue* is optional. If it is omitted, then the FIND method looks for the value of the PDV variable with the same name as the key in the hash object.

rc=*object*.FIND();

75

rc specifies whether the method succeeded or failed.

object specifies the name of the hash object.

KEY: *keyvalue* specifies the key value whose type must match the corresponding key variable that is specified in a DEFINEKEY method call. The number of KEY: *keyvalue* pairs depends on the number of key variables that you define by using the DEFINEKEY method.

Retrieving Matching Data

Use the FIND method to retrieve matching data from the hash object.

```
rc1=T.find(key:ThisYrType);
if rc1=0 then ThisYrMember=MemberType;
rc2=T.find(key:LastYrType);
if rc2=0 then LastYrMember=MemberType;
```

Values of the return code variable:

zero	success
nonzero	failure

If the program does not contain a return code variable for the method call and the method fails, then an appropriate error message is written to the log.

76

Exercises

Level 1

1. Using the ADD Method to Create a Hash Object with a Single Key

The following table shows the code that Orion Star uses for each type of order and the description of the order:

Order Code	Sale Type
1	Retail Sale
2	Catalog Sale
3	Internet Sale

The data set **orion.orders** contains the orders placed.

Partial Listing of **orion.orders**

Obs	Order_ID	Order_ Type	Employee_ID	Customer_ID	Order_ Date	Delivery_ Date
1	1232410925	3	99999999	4	02MAR2004	03MAR2004
2	1232455720	1	121100	4	09MAR2004	09MAR2004
3	1232530384	3	99999999	4	20MAR2004	21MAR2004
4	1232654929	3	99999999	4	08APR2004	09APR2004
5	1232709099	1	121041	4	16APR2004	16APR2004

a. Write a DATA step that creates a data set named **orders**.

b. Use the ADD method to create a hash table containing the values of the order type as the key values and the corresponding sale type as the data values. Use the FIND method to retrieve sale type based on the variable **Order_Type** in the data set **orion.orders**.

c. Keep only the variables **Order_ID**, **Order_Type**, and **Sale_Type**.

d. Print the first five observations from the **orders** data set.

Partial PROC PRINT Output

Obs	Sale_Type	Order_ID	Order_ Type
1	Retail Sale	1230058123	1
2	Catalog Sale	1230080101	2
3	Catalog Sale	1230106883	2
4	Retail Sale	1230147441	1
5	Retail Sale	1230315085	1

Level 2

2. Using the ADD Method with a Composite Key

The following table shows the state code, state name, country code, and country names of the states and countries for the Orion Star employees:

State	State Name	Country	Country Name
FL	Florida	US	United States
PA	Pennsylvania	US	United States
CA	California	US	United States
		AU	Australia

a. Write a DATA step to create a data set named **emps**.

b. Use the ADD method to add the composite key values for **State** and **Country** and the data values of **State_Name** and **Country_Name** from the table.

c. Read from the data set **orion.employee_addresses**.

d. Use the FIND method to perform the table lookup.

Hint: The resulting data set, **emps**, should have 424 observations. If you do not have 424 observations in the data set, determine why and fix the problem.

e. Print the first 10 observation of the data set **emps**.

Partial PROC PRINT Output

```
                      Partial Data Set emps
                                                  Employee_
     Obs    State_Name      Country_Name             ID          Country

       1    Florida         United States          121044          US
       2                    Australia              120145          AU
       3    Pennsylvania    United States          120761          US
       4    California      United States          120656          US
       5    Pennsylvania    United States          121107          US
       6    Florida         United States          121038          US
       7    Florida         United States          120273          US
       8    California      United States          120759          US
       9    Florida         United States          120798          US
      10    Florida         United States          121030          US
```

Level 3

3. Using the ADD Method and Creating a SAS Data Set from a Hash Object

The following table contains the continent ID, the location, and the name of the continent:

Continent ID	Continent Name	Location
91	North America	North
93	Europe	North
94	Africa	South
95	Asia	South
96	Australia/Pacific	South

a. Write a DATA step to create a hash object from the values in the table.

The hash object should be ordered in descending order.

b. After the hash object is created, use the OUTPUT method to create a SAS data set named **`continents`**.

Hint: Consult the SAS OnlineDoc to determine how to use the OUTPUT method.

c. Print the **`continents`** data set.

PROC PRINT Output

```
                              continents Data Set

                     Continent_
            Obs          ID          Continent_Name        Location

             1           96          Australia/Pacific       South
             2           95          Asia                    South
             3           94          Africa                  South
             4           93          Europe                  North
             5           91          North America           North
```

6.3 Loading a Hash Object with Data from a SAS Data Set

Objectives

- Load a hash object from a SAS data set.
- Use a hash object method to match records.

80

Business Scenario

The data set, **orion.supplier**, contains demographics about the suppliers for the products.

Partial Listing of **orion.supplier**

Supplier_ID	Supplier_Name	Street_ID	Supplier_Address	Sup_Street_Number	Country
50	Scandinavian Clothing A/S	6850100389	Kr. Augusts Gate 13	13	NO
109	Petterson AB	8500100286	Blasieholmstorg 1	1	SE
316	Prime Sports Ltd	9250103252	9 Carlisle Place	9	GB
755	Top Sports	3150108266	Jernbanegade 45	45	DK
772	AllSeasons Outdoor Clothing	9260115819	553 Cliffview Dr	553	US
. . .	. . .	. . .	. . .	. . .	. . .

81

Business Scenario

You need to combine **orion.supplier** with the data set, **orion.product_list**, which contains product information.

Partial Listing of **orion.product_list**

Product_ID	Product_Name	Supplier_ID	Product_Level	Product_Ref_ID
210000000000	Children	.	4	.
210100000000	Children Outdoors	.	3	210000000000
210100100000	Outdoor things, Kids	.	2	210100000000
210200000000	Children Sports	.	3	210000000000
210200100000	A-Team, Kids	.	2	210200000000
210200100009	Kids Sweat Round Neck,Large Logo	3298	1	210200100000
. . .	. . .	.	.	.

The first five values of Supplier_ID are missing.

82

Loading Data from a SAS Data Set

```
data supplier_info;
   drop rc;
   length Supplier_Name $ 40 Supplier_Address $ 45
          Country $ 2;
   if _N_=1 then do;
      declare hash S(dataset:'orion.supplier');
      S.definekey('Supplier_ID');
      S.definedata('Supplier_Name',
                   'Supplier_Address', 'Country');
      S.definedone();
      call missing(Supplier_Name,
                   Supplier_Address, Country);
   end;
   set orion.product_list;
   rc=S.find();
   if rc=0;
run;
```

83 p306d02

Execution

orion.product_list (obs=1)

Product_ID	Product_Name	Supplier_ID	Product_Level	Product_Ref_ID
210000000000	Children	.	4	.

Partial HASH Object S

KEY: Supplier_ID	DATA: Supplier_Name	DATA: Supplier_Address	DATA: Country
50	Scandinavian Clothing A/S	Kr. Augusts Gate 13	NO
109	Petterson AB	Blasieh-olmstorg 1	SE
316	Prime Sports Ltd	9 Carlisle Place	GB
.	.	.	.
3298	A Team Sports	2687 Julie Ann Ct	US

```
data supplier_info;
   drop rc;
   length Supplier_Name $ 40
          Supplier_Address $ 45
          Country $ 2;
   if _N_=1 then do;
      declare hash S(dataset:'orion.supplier');
      S.definekey('Supplier_ID');
      S.definedata('Supplier_Name',
                   'Supplier_Address',
                   'Country');
      S.definedone();
      call missing(Supplier_Name,
                   Supplier_Address,
                   Country);
   end;
   set orion.product_list;
   rc=S.find();
   if rc=0;
run;
```

Partial PDV

Supplier_Name	Supplier_Address	Country	Product_ID	Product_Name	Supplier_ID	...	D rc	D _N_
			.		.		.	1

84 ...

Execution

orion.product_list (obs=1)

Product_ID	Product_Name	Supplier_ID	Product_Level	Product_Ref_ID
210000000000	Children	.	4	.

Partial HASH Object S

KEY: Supplier_ID	DATA: Supplier_Name	DATA: Supplier_Address	DATA: Country
50	Scandinavian Clothing A/S	Kr. Augusts Gate 13	NO
109	Petterson AB	Blasieh-olmstorg 1	SE
316	Prime Sports Ltd	9 Carlisle Place	GB
.	.	.	.
3298	A Team Sports	2687 Julie Ann Ct	US

```
data supplier_info;
   drop rc;
   length Supplier_Name $ 40
          Supplier_Address $ 45
          Country $ 2;
   if _N_=1 then do;
      declare hash S(dataset:'orion.supplier');
      S.definekey('Supplier_ID');
      S.definedata('Supplier_Name',
                   'Supplier_Address',
                   'Country');
      S.definedone();
      call missing(Supplier_Name,
                   Supplier_Address,
                   Country);
   end;
   set orion.product_list;
   rc=S.find();
   if rc=0;
run;
```

Partial PDV

Supplier_Name	Supplier_Address	Country	Product_ID	Product_Name	Supplier_ID	...	D rc	D _N_
			210000000000	Children	.		.	1

85 ...

Execution

orion.product_list (obs=1)

Product_ID	Product_Name	Supplier_ID	Product_Level	Product_Ref_ID
210000000000	Children	.	4	.

Partial HASH Object S

KEY: Supplier_ID	DATA: Supplier_Name	DATA: Supplier_Address	DATA: Country
50	Scandinavian Clothing A/S	Kr. Augusts Gate 13	NO
109	Petterson AB	Blasieh-olmstorg 1	SE
316	Prime Sports Ltd	9 Carlisle Place	GB
.	.	.	.
3298	A Team Sports	2687 Julie Ann Ct	US

```
data supplier_info;
   drop rc;
   length Supplier_Name $ 40
          Supplier_Address $ 45
          Country $ 2;
   if _N_=1 then do;
      declare hash S(dataset:'orion.supplier');
      S.definekey('Supplier_ID');
      S.definedata('Supplier_Name',
                   'Supplier_Address',
                   'Country');
      S.definedone();
      call missing(Supplier_Name,
                   Supplier_Address,
                   Country);
   end;
   set orion.product_list;
   rc=S.find();
   if rc=0;
run;
```

2147450842

Partial PDV

Supplier_Name	Supplier_Address	Country	Product_ID	Product_Name	Supplier_ID	...	rc	_N_
			210000000000	Children	.		2147450842	1

86

...

Execution

orion.product_list (obs=1)

Product_ID	Product_Name	Supplier_ID	Product_Level	Product_Ref_ID
210000000000	Children	.	4	.

Partial HASH Object S

KEY: Supplier_ID	DATA: Supplier_Name	DATA: Supplier_Address	DATA: Country
50	Scandinavian Clothing A/S	Kr. Augusts Gate 13	NO
109	Petterson AB	Blasieh-olmstorg 1	SE
316	Prime Sports Ltd	9 Carlisle Place	GB
.	.	.	.
3298	A Team Sports	2687 Julie Ann Ct	US

```
data supplier_info;
   drop rc;
   length Supplier_Name $ 40
          Supplier_Address $ 45
          Country $ 2;
   if _N_=1 then do;
      declare hash S(dataset:'orion.supplier');
      S.definekey('Supplier_ID');
      S.definedata('Supplier_Name',
                   'Supplier_Address',
                   'Country');
      S.definedone();
      call missing(Supplier_Name,
                   Supplier_Address,
                   Country);
   end;
   set orion.product_list;
   rc=S.find();
   if rc=0;
run;
```

False

Partial PDV

Supplier_Name	Supplier_Address	Country	Product_ID	Product_Name	Supplier_ID	...	rc	_N_
			210000000000	Children	.		2147450842	1

87

...

Execution

orion.product_list (obs=6)

Product_ID	Product_Name	Supplier_ID	Product_Level	Product_Ref_ID
210200100009	Kids Sweat Round Neck,Large Logo	3298	1	210200100000

Partial HASH Object S

KEY: Supplier_ID	DATA: Supplier_Name	DATA: Supplier_Address	DATA: Country
50	Scandinavian Clothing A/S	Kr. Augusts Gate 13	NO
109	Petterson AB	Blasieh-olmstorg 1	SE
316	Prime Sports Ltd	9 Carlisle Place	GB
. . .	. . .	. . .	. . .
3298	A Team Sports	2687 Julie Ann Ct	US

```
data supplier_info;
   drop rc;
   length Supplier_Name $ 40
          Supplier_Address $ 45
          Country $ 2;
   if _N_=1 then do;
      declare hash S                         lier');
      S.definekey('S
      S.definedata('
                    '
                    '
      S.definedone()
      call missing(Supplier_Name,
                   Supplier_Address,
                   Country);
   end;
   set orion.product_list;
   rc=S.find();
   if rc=0;
run;
```

Continue until _N_=6

Partial PDV

Supplier_Name	Supplier_Address	Country	Product_ID	Product_Name	Supplier_ID	...	rc	_N_
			210200100009	Kids Sweat Round Neck,Large Logo	3298		.	6

88

...

Execution

orion.product_list (obs=6)

Product_ID	Product_Name	Supplier_ID	Product_Level	Product_Ref_ID
210200100009	Kids Sweat Round Neck,Large Logo	3298	1	210200100000

Partial HASH Object S

KEY: Supplier_ID	DATA: Supplier_Name	DATA: Supplier_Address	DATA: Country
50	Scandinavian Clothing A/S	Kr. Augusts Gate 13	NO
109	Petterson AB	Blasieh-olmstorg 1	SE
316	Prime Sports Ltd	9 Carlisle Place	GB
. . .	. . .	. . .	. . .
3298	A Team Sports	2687 Julie Ann Ct	US

```
data supplier_info;
   drop rc;
   length Supplier_Name $ 40
          Supplier_Address $ 45
          Country $ 2;
   if _N_=1 then do;
      declare hash S(dataset:'orion.supplier');
      S.definekey('Supplier_ID');
      S.definedata('Supplier_Name',
                   'Supplier_Address',
                   'Country');
      S.definedone();
      call missing(Supplier_Name,
                   Supplier_Address,
                   Country);
   end;
   set orion.product_list;
   rc=S.find();
   if rc=0;
run;
```

Partial PDV

Supplier_Name	Supplier_Address	Country	Product_ID	Product_Name	Supplier_ID	...	rc	_N_
			210200100009	Kids Sweat Round Neck,Large Logo	3298		0	6

89

...

Execution

orion.product_list (obs=6)

Product_ID	Product_Name	Supplier_ID	Product_Level	Product_Ref_ID
210200100009	Kids Sweat Round Neck,Large Logo	3298	1	210200100000

Partial HASH Object S

KEY: Supplier_ID	DATA: Supplier_Name	DATA: Supplier_Address	DATA: Country
50	Scandinavian Clothing A/S	Kr. Augusts Gate 13	NO
109	Petterson AB	Blasieh-olmstorg 1	SE
316	Prime Sports Ltd	9 Carlisle Place	GB
.	.	.	.
3298	A Team Sports	2687 Julie Ann Ct	US

```
data supplier_info;
   drop rc;
   length Supplier_Name $ 40
          Supplier_Address $ 45
          Country $ 2;
   if _N_=1 then do;
      declare hash S(dataset:'orion.supplier');
      S.definekey('Supplier_ID');
      S.definedata('Supplier_Name',
                   'Supplier_Address',
                   'Country');
      S.definedone();
      call missing(Supplier_Name,
                   Supplier_Address,
                   Country);
   end;
   set orion.product_list;
   rc=S.find();
   if rc=0;
run;
```

Partial PDV

Supplier_Name	Supplier_Address	Country	Product_ID	Product_Name	Supplier_ID	...	D rc	D _N_
A Team Sports	2687 Julie Ann Ct	US	210200100009	Kids Sweat Round Neck,Large Logo	3298		0	6

90

...

Execution

orion.product_list (obs=6)

Product_ID	Product_Name	Supplier_ID	Product_Level	Product_Ref_ID
210200100009	Kids Sweat Round Neck,Large Logo	3298	1	210200100000

Partial HASH Object S

KEY: Supplier_ID	DATA: Supplier_Name	DATA: Supplier_Address	DATA: Country
50	Scandinavian Clothing A/S	Kr. Augusts Gate 13	NO
109	Petterson AB	Blasieh-olmstorg 1	SE
316	Prime Sports Ltd	9 Carlisle Place	GB
.	.	.	.
3298	A Team Sports	2687 Julie Ann Ct	US

```
data supplier_info;
   drop rc;
   length Supplier_Name $ 40
          Supplier_Address $ 45
          Country $ 2;
   if _N_=1 then do;
      declare hash S(dataset:'orion.supplier');
      S.definekey('Supplier_ID');
      S.definedata('Supplier_Name',
                   'Supplier_Address',
                   'Country');
      S.definedone();
      call missing(Supplier_Name,
                   Supplier_Address,
                   Country);
   end;
   set orion.product_list;
   rc=S.find();
   if rc=0;
run;
```

True

Partial PDV

Supplier_Name	Supplier_Address	Country	Product_ID	Product_Name	Supplier_ID	...	D rc	D _N_
A Team Sports	2687 Julie Ann Ct	US	210200100009	Kids Sweat Round Neck,Large Logo	3298		0	6

91

...

Execution

orion.product_list (obs=6)

Product_ID	Product_Name	Supplier_ID	Product_Level	Product_Ref_ID
210200100009	Kids Sweat Round Neck,Large Logo	3298	1	210200100000

Partial HASH Object S

KEY: Supplier_ID	DATA: Supplier_Name	DATA: Supplier_Address	DATA: Country
50	Scandinavian Clothing A/S	Kr. Augusts Gate 13	NO
109	Petterson AB	Blasieh-olmstorg 1	SE
316	Prime Sports Ltd	9 Carlisle Place	GB
.	.	.	.
3298	A Team Sports	2687 Julie Ann Ct	US

```
data supplier_info;
   drop rc;
   length Supplier_Name $ 40
          Supplier_Address $ 45
          Country $ 2;
   if _N_=1 then do;
      declare hash S(d                          );
      S.definekey('Supp
      S.definedata('Sup
                  'Sup
                  'Country');
      S.definedone();
      call missing(Supplier_Name,
                   Supplier_Address,
                   Country);
   end;
   set orion.product_list;
   rc=S.find();
   if rc=0;
run;
```

Implicit OUTPUT;
Implicit RETURN;

Partial PDV

Supplier_Name	Supplier_Address	Country	Product_ID	Product_Name	Supplier_ID	...	D rc	D _N_
A Team Sports	2687 Julie Ann Ct	US	210200100009	Kids Sweat Round Neck,Large Logo	3298		0	6

92 ...

Execution

orion.product_list (obs=556)

Product_ID	Product_Name	Supplier_ID	Product_Level	Product_Ref_ID
240800200063	Top Equipe 99 Black	13198	1	210200100000

Partial HASH Object S

KEY: Supplier_ID	DATA: Supplier_Name	DATA: Supplier_Address	DATA: Country
50	Scandinavian Clothing A/S	Kr. Augusts Gate 13	NO
109	Petterson AB	Blasieh-olmstorg 1	SE
316	Prime Sports Ltd	9 Carlisle Place	GB
.	.	.	.
3298	A Team Sports	2687 Julie Ann Ct	US

```
data supplier_info;
   drop rc;
   length Supplier_Name $ 40
          Supplier_Address $ 45
          Country $ 2;
   if _N_=1 then do;
      declare hash S(dataset:'orion.supplier');
      S.definekey('Supplier_ID');
      S.definedata('Supplier_Name',
                   'Supplier_Address',

      S.definedone(
      call missing(

                   Country);
   end;
   set orion.product_list;
   rc=S.find();
   if rc=0;
run;
```

Continue until EOF

Partial PDV

Supplier_Name	Supplier_Address	Country	Product_ID	Product_Name	Supplier_ID	...	D rc	D _N_
Twain Inc	1648 Bloodworth St	US	240800200000	Top Equipe 99 Black	13198		0	556

93 ...

Results

```
proc print data=supplier_info(obs=10);
   var Product_ID Supplier_ID Supplier_Name
       Supplier_Address Country;
   title "Product Information";
run;
```

Partial PROC PRINT Output

Product Information

Obs	Product_ID	Supplier_ID	Supplier_Name	Supplier_Address	Country
1	210200100009	3298	A Team Sports	2687 Julie Ann Ct	US
2	210200100017	3298	A Team Sports	2687 Julie Ann Ct	US
3	210200200022	6153	Nautlius SportsWear Inc	56 Bagwell Ave	US
4	210200200023	6153	Nautlius SportsWear Inc	56 Bagwell Ave	US
5	210200300006	1303	Eclipse Inc	1218 Carriole Ct	US
6	210200300007	1303	Eclipse Inc	1218 Carriole Ct	US
7	210200300052	1303	Eclipse Inc	1218 Carriole Ct	US
8	210200400020	1303	Eclipse Inc	1218 Carriole Ct	US
9	210200400070	1303	Eclipse Inc	1218 Carriole Ct	US
10	210200500002	772	AllSeasons Outdoor Clothing	553 Cliffview Dr	US

94 p306d02

6.08 Multiple Choice Poll

The program **p306d02** created the variable `rc` and then dropped it. How can you avoid creating the variable so that you do not have to drop it?

a. Use a WHERE statement or a WHERE= data set option.

b. Use a KEEP= or DROP= data set option in `orion.product_list`.

c. Test the result of the FIND method in the subsetting IF statement.

d. Use a KEEP or DROP statement.

96

Not Creating rc

The program created the variable **rc** and then dropped it. How can you avoid creating the variable so that you do not have to drop it?

```
data supplier_info;
   length Supplier_Name $ 40 Supplier_Address $ 45
          Country $ 2;
   if _N_=1 then do;
      declare hash S(dataset:'orion.supplier');
      S.definekey('Supplier_ID');
      S.definedata('Supplier_Name',
                   'Supplier_Address', 'Country');
      S.definedone();
      call missing(Supplier_Name,
                   Supplier_Address,
                   Country);
   end;
   set orion.product_list;
   if S.find()=0;
run;
```

98

p306d02

6.09 Quiz

How do you know the lengths of the character variables **Supplier_Name**, **Supplier_Address**, and **Country**?

100

Defining PDV Variables

Instead of the LENGTH statement, you could use an IF-THEN statement.

```
data supplier_info;
   if _N_=1 then do;
      if 0 then set orion.supplier
                    (keep=Supplier_ID Supplier_Name
                          Supplier_Address Country);
      declare hash S(dataset:'orion.supplier');
      S.definekey('Supplier_ID');
      S.definedata('Supplier_Name',
                   'Supplier_Address','Country');
      S.definedone();
   end;
   set orion.product_list;
   if S.find()=0;
run;
```

⚠ Because the IF condition is false during execution, the SET statement is compiled, but not executed. The PDV includes all the kept variables from **orion.supplier**.

102 p306d02

Using DATA Set Options

In SAS 9.2, you can use SAS DATA set options to limit the amount of data loaded into a hash object.

```
data supplier_info;
   if _N_=1 then do;
      if 0 then set orion.supplier
                    (keep=Supplier_ID Supplier_Name
                          Supplier_Address Country);
      declare hash S(dataset:'orion.supplier(keep=
                          Supplier_ID Supplier_Name
                          Supplier_Address Country
                          where=(Country='US'))');
      S.definekey('Supplier_ID');
      S.definedata('Supplier_Name',
                   'Supplier_Address','Country');
      S.definedone();
   end;
   set orion.product_list;
   if S.find()=0;
run;
```

103 p306d03

Advantages and Disadvantages of Hash Objects

Advantages	Disadvantages
use of character and numeric keys	unique keys required before SAS 9.2
use of composite keys	DATA step only
faster lookup than formats or merges/joins	memory requirements
ability to be loaded from a SAS data set	
fine level of control (flexibility)	
ability to do chained lookups	

104

Comparing Arrays and Hash Objects

Array	Hash Object
The subscript value(s) must be numeric.	The keys can be character, numeric, or both.
One data value can be associated with the subscript value(s).	Multiple data items can be associated with the key value.
An array uses less memory than a hash object.	A hash object uses more memory than an array.
The size of the array is determined at compilation time.	The size of the hash object is determined at execution time.
Subscript values must be consecutive integers.	The keys do not have to be consecutive or sorted.
An array selects values by direct access based on the subscript value.	A hash object uses a hash function for the lookup process.
Arrays can only be used in the DATA step.	Hash objects can only be used in the DATA step.

105

Exercises

Level 1

4. Loading the Hash Object from a SAS Data Set

The data set **`orion.customer_type`** contains a variable **`Customer_Type_ID`** and a variable **`Customer_Type`** that is a description of the customer type.

Listing of **`orion.customer_type`**

orion.customer_type

Obs	Customer_ Type_ID	Customer_Type	Customer_ Group_ID	Customer_Group
1	1010	Orion Club members inactive	10	Orion Club members
2	1020	Orion Club members low activity	10	Orion Club members
3	1030	Orion Club members medium activity	10	Orion Club members
4	1040	Orion Club members high activity	10	Orion Club members
5	2010	Orion Club Gold members low activity	20	Orion Club Gold members
6	2020	Orion Club Gold members medium activity	20	Orion Club Gold members
7	2030	Orion Club Gold members high activity	20	Orion Club Gold members
8	3010	Internet/Catalog Customers	30	Internet/Catalog Customers

The data set **`orion.customer`** contains the **`Customer_ID`** variable and the **`Customer_Type_ID`** variable.

Partial Listing of **`orion.customer`**

Partial orion.customer

Obs	Customer_ID	Customer_ Type_ID
1	4	1020
2	5	2020
3	9	2020
4	10	1040
5	11	1040
6	12	1030
7	13	2010
8	16	3010
9	17	1030
10	18	1020

a. Write a DATA step to create a data set named **`customers`** that reads the variables **`Customer_ID`** and **`Customer_Type_ID`** from the data set **`orion.customer`**.

b. Create a hash object and load it with the data from **`orion.customer_type`**. The key should be the variable **`Customer_Type_ID`**, and the data item should be the variable **`Customer_Type`**.

c. Use the hash object to look up the **Customer_Type** description.

d. Print the first 10 observations of the **customers** data set.

Partial PROC PRINT Output

Partial customers Data Set

Obs	Customer_Type	Customer_ID	Customer_ Type_ID
1	Orion Club members low activity	4	1020
2	Orion Club Gold members medium activity	5	2020
3	Orion Club Gold members medium activity	9	2020
4	Orion Club members high activity	10	1040
5	Orion Club members high activity	11	1040
6	Orion Club members medium activity	12	1030
7	Orion Club Gold members low activity	13	2010
8	Internet/Catalog Customers	16	3010
9	Orion Club members medium activity	17	1030
10	Orion Club members low activity	18	1020

Level 2

5. Loading Multiple Hash Objects from SAS Data Sets

The data set **orion.product_list** contains the **Product_ID** and **Product_Name** for the products sold.

Partial Listing of **orion.product_list**

Partial orion.product_list

Obs	Product_ID	Product_Name
1	210000000000	Children
2	210100000000	Children Outdoors
3	210100100000	Outdoor things, Kids
4	210200000000	Children Sports
5	210200100000	A-Team, Kids

The data set **orion.customer_dim** contains the **Customer_ID**, **Customer_Country**, and **Customer_Name** for customers who made purchases.

Partial Listing of **orion.customer_dim**

Partial orion.customer_dim

Obs	Customer_ID	Customer_ Country	Customer_Name
1	4	US	James Kvarniq
2	5	US	Sandrina Stephano
3	9	DE	Cornelia Krahl
4	10	US	Karen Ballinger
5	11	DE	Elke Wallstab

The data set **orion.country** contains the **Country** and the **Country_Name**.

Partial Listing of **orion.country**

Partial orion.country

Obs	Country	Country_ Name
1	AU	Australia
2	CA	Canada
3	DE	Germany
4	IL	Israel
5	TR	Turkey

The data set **orion.order_fact** contains the **Customer_ID** and information about the orders.

Partial Listing of **orion.order_fact**

Partial orion.order_fact

Obs	Customer_ID	Order_ Date	Product_ID	Quantity	Total_Retail_ Price
1	63	11JAN2003	220101300017	1	$16.50
2	5	15JAN2003	230100500026	1	$247.50
3	45	20JAN2003	240600100080	1	$28.30
4	41	28JAN2003	240600100010	2	$32.00
5	183	27FEB2003	240200200039	3	$63.60

a. Create a data set named **billing** that reads **Customer_ID**, **Order_Date**, **Product_ID**, **Quantity**, and **Total_Retail_Price** from **orion.order_fact**.

b. Create a hash object from **orion.product_list** with the key **Product_ID** and the data **Product_Name**.

c. Create a hash object from **orion.customer_dim** with the key **Customer_ID** and the data **Customer_Country** and **Customer_Name**.

d. Create a hash object from **orion.country** with the key **Country** and the data **Country_Name**.

e. Use the three hash objects to look up the **Customer_Name**, **Country_Name**, and **Product_Name**.

f. Sort the **`billing`** data set by **`Customer_ID`** and **`Product_ID`** and print the first five observations.

Partial PROC PRINT Output

Billing Information
Using a HASH Data Step Object

Obs	Customer_ID	Customer_Name	Customer_ Country	Country_Name	Product_ID
1	4	James Kvarniq	US	United States	220101400145
2	4	James Kvarniq	US	United States	230100100053
3	4	James Kvarniq	US	United States	240500100017
4	4	James Kvarniq	US	United States	240500100029
5	4	James Kvarniq	US	United States	240500200083

Obs	Product_Name	Order_ Date	Quantity	Total_Retail_ Price
1	Essence.baseball Cap	16APR2004	1	$16.70
2	Monster Men's Pants with Zipper	18DEC2004	2	$92.60
3	A-team Sweat Round Neck, Small Logo	08APR2004	4	$214.00
4	Men's Sweatshirt w/Hood Big Logo	08APR2004	1	$58.90
5	Force Technical Jacket w/Coolmax	19AUG2004	3	$201.90

Level 3

6. Loading the Hash Object from a SAS Data Set and Retrieving Multiple Values

The data set **`orion.staff`** contains the employee ID and the manager ID for that employee.

Partial Listing of **`orion.staff`**

Partial orion.staff

Obs	Employee_ID	Start_ Date	End_Date	Job_Title	Salary
1	120101	01JUL2003	31DEC9999	Director	$163,040
2	120102	01JUN1989	31DEC9999	Sales Manager	$108,255
3	120103	01JAN1974	31DEC9999	Sales Manager	$87,975
4	120104	01JAN1981	31DEC9999	Administration Manager	$46,230
5	120105	01MAY1999	31DEC9999	Secretary I	$27,110

Obs	Gender	Birth_ Date	Emp_Hire_ Date	Emp_Term_ Date	Manager_ID
1	M	18AUG1976	01JUL2003	.	120261
2	M	11AUG1969	01JUN1989	.	120101
3	M	22JAN1949	01JAN1974	.	120101
4	F	11MAY1954	01JAN1981	.	120101
5	F	21DEC1974	01MAY1999	.	120101

The data set **orion.employee_addresses** contains the names of all employees.

Partial Listing of **orion.employee_addresses**

Partial orion.employee_addresses

Obs	Employee_ ID	Employee_Name	Street_ID	Street_ Number
1	121044	Abbott, Ray	9260116912	2267
2	120145	Aisbitt, Sandy	1600101803	30
3	120761	Akinfolarin, Tameaka	9260121030	5
4	120656	Amos, Salley	9260123736	3524
5	121107	Anger, Rose	9260120989	744

Obs	Street_Name	City	State	Postal_ Code	Country
1	Edwards Mill Rd	Miami-Dade	FL	33135	US
2	Bingera Street	Melbourne		2001	AU
3	Donnybrook Rd	Philadelphia	PA	19145	US
4	Calico Ct	San Diego	CA	92116	US
5	Chapwith Rd	Philadelphia	PA	19142	US

The data set **orion.employee_payroll** has **Employee_ID** and **Salary** for each employee.

Partial Listing of **orion.employee_payroll**

Partial orion.employee_payroll

Obs	Employee_ID	Employee_ Gender	Salary	Birth_ Date	Employee_ Hire_Date	Employee_ Term_Date	Marital_ Status	Dependents
1	120101	M	163040	6074	15887	.	S	0
2	120102	M	108255	3510	10744	.	O	2
3	120103	M	87975	-3996	5114	.	M	1
4	120104	F	46230	-2061	7671	.	M	1
5	120105	F	27110	5468	14365	.	S	0

a. Write a DATA step to create a data set named **manager** that reads the **Employee_ID** and **Salary** variables from **orion.employee_payroll**.

b. Create hash objects from the data sets **orion.employee_addresses** and **orion.staff**.

c. Use the hash object from **orion.staff** to return **Manager_ID** for each **Employee_ID** in **orion.employee_payroll**.

d. Use the hash object from **orion.employee_addresses** to retrieve the names for both employees and the manager for the employees.

e. Print the first five observations of the **manager** data set.

Partial PROC PRINT Output

Partial Manager Data Set

Obs	EmpName	ManagerName	Employee_ID	Salary	Manager_ ID
1	Lu, Patrick	Highpoint, Harry	120101	163040	120261
2	Zhou, Tom	Lu, Patrick	120102	108255	120101
3	Dawes, Wilson	Lu, Patrick	120103	87975	120101
4	Billington, Kareen	Lu, Patrick	120104	46230	120101
5	Povey, Liz	Lu, Patrick	120105	27110	120101

6.4 Using the DATA Step Hiter Object

Objectives

- Define a hiter object
- Investigate the methods for the hiter object
- Write a DATA step using the hiter object.

109

Defining the Hiter Object

The *hiter object* is a hash iterator object.

- Using the hiter object, you can access items in the hash table based on the location of the value of the key rather than the value of the key or you can use the hiter object to move forwards and/or backwards in the hash object.
- You cannot define a hiter object without first defining a hash object.

110

Using the DECLARE Statement for a Hiter Object

DECLARE HITER *iterator-name*('*hash-name*');

```
declare hash Customer(dataset:'orion.order_fact',
                      ordered:'descending');
customer.definekey('Total_Retail_Price', 'Customer_ID');
customer.definedata('Total_Retail_Price', 'Customer_ID'
                    'Product_ID');
customer.definedone();
declare hiter C('customer');
```

111

Selected Methods for the Hiter Object

FIRST()	returns the first data values in the underlying hash object based on the value of the key value(s).
LAST()	returns the last data values in the underlying hash object based on the value of the key value(s).
NEXT()	returns the data values for the next item in key order in the underlying hash object. A nonzero value is returned if the next item cannot be retrieved.
PREV()	returns the data values for the previous item in key order in the underlying hash object. A nonzero value is returned if the previous item cannot be retrieved.

112

Business Scenario

The data set **orion.order_fact** contains the total retail price of items that were ordered. You need to know the two customers who ordered the most expensive items and the two customers who ordered the least expensive items.

Partial Listing of **orion.order_fact**

Customer _ID	Employee _ID	Street_ID	. . .	Total_Retail _Price	CostPrice _Per_Unit	Discount
63	121039	9260125492	. . .	$16.50	$7.45	.
5	99999999	9260114570	. . .	$247.50	$109.55	.
45	99999999	9260104847	. . .	$28.30	$8.55	.
41	120174	1600101527	. . .	$32.00	$6.50	.
183	120134	1600100760	. . .	$63.60	$8.80	.
. . .	. . .	. . .	. . .	. . .	. . .	. . .

113

Hiter Object

```
data top bottom;
   drop i;
   if 0 then set orion.order_fact(keep=Customer_ID Product_ID
                                       Total_Retail_Price);
   if _N_=1 then do;
      declare hash Customer(dataset:'orion.order_fact',
                            ordered:'descending');
      customer.definekey('Total_Retail_Price', 'Customer_ID');
      customer.definedata('Total_Retail_Price', 'Customer_ID',
                          'Product_ID');
      customer.definedone();
      declare hiter C('customer');
   end;
   C.first();
   do i=1 to 2;
      output top;
      C.next();
   end;
   C.last();
   do i=1 to 2;
      output bottom;
      C.prev();
   end;
   stop;
run;
```

114 p306d04

Hiter Object

```
data top bottom;
   drop i;
   if 0 then set orion.order_fact(keep=Customer_ID Product_ID
                                        Total_Retail_Price);
   if _N_=1 then do;
      declare hash Customer(dataset:'orion.order_fact',
                            ordered:'descending');
      customer.definekey('Total_Retail_Price', 'Customer_ID');
      customer.definedata('Total_Retail_Price', 'Customer_ID',
                          'Product_ID');
      customer.definedone();
      declare hiter C('customer');
   end;
   C.first();
   do i=1 to 2;
      output top;
      C.next();
   end;
   C.last();
   do i=1 to 2;
      output bottom;
      C.prev();
   end;
   stop;
run;
```

115 p306d04

Execution

Partial Hash Object **customer**

KEY: Total_ Retail_ Price	KEY: Customer _ID	DATA: Total_ Retail_ Price	DATA: Customer _ID	DATA: Product_ ID
16.50	63	16.50	63	220101300017
247.50	5	247.50	5	230100500026
28.30	45	28.30	45	240600100080
32.00	41	32.00	41	240600100010
.	.	.	.	.
.	.	.	.	.
.	.	.	.	.
95.10	10	95.10	10	240500200016
48.20	10	[illegible]	[illegible]	40500200122
75.20	89	[illegible]	[illegible]	40700200018
33.80	5	[illegible]	[illegible]	20101400130

Notice the unordered hash object.

```
data top bottom;
   drop i;
   if 0 then set orion.order_fact
            (keep=Customer_ID Product_ID
                  Total_Retail_Price);
   if _N_=1 then do;
     declare hash
     customer(dataset:'orion.order_fact',
                 ordered:'descending');
     customer.definekey('Total_Retail_Price',
                          'Customer_ID');
     customer.definedata('Total_Retail_Price',
                          'Customer_ID',
                          'Product_ID');
    customer.definedone();
    declare hiter C('customer');
   end;
```

PDV

Customer_ID	Product_ ID	Total_ Retail_ Price	D i	D _N_
.	.	.	.	1

116 ...

Execution

Hiter C View of Partial Hash Object customer

KEY: Total_ Retail_ Price	KEY: Customer _ID	DATA: Total_ Retail_ Price	DATA: Customer _ID	DATA: Product_ ID
1937.20	70100	1937.20	70100	240200100173
1796.00	79	1796.00	79	240200100076
1687.50	16	1687.50	16	230100700009
1561.80	183	1561.80	183	240300300090
. . .	. . .	. . .		
3.20	69	3.20		004
3.00	5	3.00		433
2.70	11171	2.70		021
2.60	79	2.60		045

This is the hiter object's descending ordered view of the hash object.

```
data top bottom;
   drop i;
   if 0 then set orion.order_fact
              (keep=Customer_ID Product_ID
                    Total_Retail_Price);
   if _N_=1 then do;
      declare hash
      customer(dataset:'orion.order_fact',
                    ordered:'descending');
      customer.definekey('Total_Retail_Price',
                         'Customer_ID');
      customer.definedata('Total_Retail_Price',
                          'Customer_ID',
                          'Product_ID');
     customer.definedone();
     declare hiter C('customer');
   end;
```

PDV

Customer_ID	Product_ ID	Total_ Retail_ Price	D i	D _N_
.	.	.	.	1

117

Hiter Object

```
data top bottom;
   drop i;
   if 0 then set orion.order_fact(keep=Customer_ID Product_ID
                                        Total_Retail_Price);
   if _N_=1 then do;
      declare hash customer(dataset:'orion.order_fact',
                            ordered:'descending');
      customer.definekey('Total_Retail_Price', 'Customer_ID');
      customer.definedata('Total_Retail_Price', 'Customer_ID',
                          'Product_ID');
      customer.definedone();
      declare hiter C('customer');
   end;
   C.first();
   do i=1 to 2;
      output top;
      C.next();
   end;
   C.last();
   do i=1 to 2;
      output bottom;
      C.prev();
   end;
   stop;
run;
```

118

p306d04

Execution

Hiter C View of Partial Hash Object **customer**

KEY: Total_ Retail_ Price	KEY: Customer _ID	DATA: Total_ Retail_ Price	DATA: Customer _ID	DATA: Product_ ID
1937.20	70100	1937.20	70100	240200100173
1796.00	79	1796.00	79	240200100076
1687.50	16	1687.50	16	230100700009
1561.80	183	1561.80	183	240300300090
. . .	. . .	. . .	. . .	. . .
3.20	69	3.20	69	230100500004
3.00	5	3.00	5	240100100433
2.70	11171	2.70	11171	240200100021
2.60	79	2.60	79	230100500045

```
   C.first();
   do i=1 to 2;
      output top;
      C.next();
   end;
   C.last();
   do i=1 to 2;
      output bottom;
      C.prev();
   end;
   stop;
run;
```

PDV

Customer_ID	Product_ ID	Total_ Retail_ Price	D i	D _N_
70100	240200100173	1937.20	.	1

119 ...

Execution

Hiter C View of Partial Hash Object **customer**

KEY: Total_ Retail_ Price	KEY: Customer _ID	DATA: Total_ Retail_ Price	DATA: Customer _ID	DATA: Product_ ID
1937.20	70100	1937.20	70100	240200100173
1796.00	79	1796.00	79	240200100076
1687.50	16	1687.50	16	230100700009
1561.80	183	1561.80	183	240300300090
. . .	. . .	. . .	. . .	. . .
3.20	69	3.20	69	230100500004
3.00	5	3.00	5	240100100433
2.70	11171	2.70	11171	240200100021
2.60	79	2.60	79	230100500045

```
   C.first();
   do i=1 to 2;
      output top;
      C.next();
   end;
   C.last();
   do i=1 to 2;
      output bottom;
      C.prev();
   end;
   stop;
run;
```

PDV

Customer_ID	Product_ ID	Total_ Retail_ Price	D i	D _N_
70100	240200100173	1937.20	1	1

120 ...

Execution

Hiter C View of Partial Hash Object **customer**

KEY: Total_ Retail_ Price	KEY: Customer _ID	DATA: Total_ Retail_ Price	DATA: Customer _ID	DATA: Product_ ID
1937.20	70100	1937.20	70100	240200100173
1796.00	79	1796.00	79	240200100076
1687.50	16	1687.50	16	230100700009
1561.80	183	1561.80	183	240300300090
. . .	. . .	. . .		
3.20	69	3.20		
3.00	5	3.00	5	240100100433
2.70	11171	2.70	11171	240200100021
2.60	79	2.60	79	230100500045

```
   C.first();
   do i=1 to 2;
      output top;
      C.next();
   end;
   C.last();
   do i=1 to 2;
      output bottom;
      );
   stop;
run;
```

Output current observation

PDV

Customer_ID	Product_ ID	Total_ Retail_ Price	D i	D _N_
70100	240200100173	1937.20	1	1

121 ...

Execution

Hiter C View of Partial Hash Object **customer**

KEY: Total_ Retail_ Price	KEY: Customer _ID	DATA: Total_ Retail_ Price	DATA: Customer _ID	DATA: Product_ ID
1937.20	70100	1937.20	70100	240200100173
1796.00	79	1796.00	79	240200100076
1687.50	16	1687.50	16	230100700009
1561.80	183	1561.80	183	240300300090
. . .	. . .	. . .	. . .	. . .
3.20	69	3.20	69	230100500004
3.00	5	3.00	5	240100100433
2.70	11171	2.70	11171	240200100021
2.60	79	2.60	79	230100500045

```
   C.first();
   do i=1 to 2;
      output top;
      C.next();
   end;
   C.last();
   do i=1 to 2;
      output bottom;
      C.prev();
   end;
   stop;
run;
```

PDV

Customer_ID	Product_ ID	Total_ Retail_ Price	D i	D _N_
79	240200100076	1796.00	1	1

122 ...

Execution

Hiter C View of Partial Hash Object **customer**

KEY: Total_ Retail_ Price	KEY: Customer _ID	DATA: Total_ Retail_ Price	DATA: Customer _ID	DATA: Product_ ID
1937.20	70100	1937.20	70100	240200100173
1796.00	79	1796.00	79	240200100076
1687.50	16	1687.50	16	230100700009
1561.80	183	1561.80	183	240300300090
. . .	. . .	. . .	. . .	. . .
3.20	69	3.20	69	230100500004
3.00	5	3.00	5	240100100433
2.70	11171	2.70	11171	240200100021
2.60	79	2.60	79	230100500045

```
    C.first();
    do i=1 to 2;
       output top;
       C.next();
    end;
    C.last();
    do i=1 to 2;
       output bottom;
       C.prev();
    end;
    stop;
run;
```

PDV

Customer_ID	Product_ ID	Total_ Retail_ Price	D i	D _N_
79	240200100076	1796.00	2	1

123 ...

Execution

Hiter C View of Partial Hash Object **customer**

KEY: Total_ Retail_ Price	KEY: Customer _ID	DATA: Total_ Retail_ Price	DATA: Customer _ID	DATA: Product_ ID
1937.20	70100	1937.20	70100	240200100173
1796.00	79	1796.00	79	240200100076
1687.50	16	1687.50	16	230100700009
1561.80	183	1561.80	183	240300300090
. . .	. . .	. . .	. . .	. . .
3.20	69	3.20	69	230100500004
3.00	5	3.00	5	240100100433
2.70	11171	2.70	11171	240200100021
2.60	79	2.60	79	230100500045

```
    C.first();
    do i=1 to 2;
       output top;
       C.next();
    end;
    C.last();
    do i=1 to 2;
       output bottom;
       C.prev();
    end;
    stop;
run;
```

PDV

Customer_ID	Product_ ID	Total_ Retail_ Price	D i	D _N_
79	240200100076	1796.00	2	1

124 ...

Execution

Hiter C View of Partial Hash Object **customer**

KEY: Total_ Retail_ Price	KEY: Customer _ID	DATA: Total_ Retail_ Price	DATA: Customer _ID	DATA: Product_ ID
1937.20	70100	1937.20	70100	240200100173
1796.00	79	1796.00	79	240200100076
1687.50	16	1687.50	16	230100700009
1561.80	183	1561.80	183	240300300090
⋮	⋮	⋮	⋮	
3.20	69	3.20	69	
3.00	5	3.00	5	240100100433
2.70	11171	2.70	11171	240200100021
2.60	79	2.60	79	230100500045

```
   C.first();
   do i=1 to 2;
      output top;
      C.next();
   end;
   C.last();
   do i=1 to 2;
      output bottom;
   stop;
run;
```

Output current observation

PDV

Customer_ID	Product_ ID	Total_ Retail_ Price	D i	D _N_
79	240200100076	1796.00	2	1

125 ...

Execution

Hiter C View of Partial Hash Object **customer**

KEY: Total_ Retail_ Price	KEY: Customer _ID	DATA: Total_ Retail_ Price	DATA: Customer _ID	DATA: Product_ ID
1937.20	70100	1937.20	70100	240200100173
1796.00	79	1796.00	79	240200100076
1687.50	16	1687.50	16	230100700009
1561.80	183	1561.80	183	240300300090
⋮	⋮	⋮	⋮	⋮
3.20	69	3.20	69	230100500004
3.00	5	3.00	5	240100100433
2.70	11171	2.70	11171	240200100021
2.60	79	2.60	79	230100500045

```
   C.first();
   do i=1 to 2;
      output top;
      C.next();
   end;
   C.last();
   do i=1 to 2;
      output bottom;
      C.prev();
   end;
   stop;
run;
```

PDV

Customer_ID	Product_ ID	Total_ Retail_ Price	D i	D _N_
16	230100700009	1687.50	2	1

126 ...

Execution

Hiter C View of Partial Hash Object **customer**

KEY: Total_ Retail_ Price	KEY: Customer _ID	DATA: Total_ Retail_ Price	DATA: Customer _ID	DATA: Product_ ID
1937.20	70100	1937.20	70100	240200100173
1796.00	79	1796.00	79	240200100076
1687.50	16	1687.50	16	230100700009
1561.80	183	1561.80	183	240300300090
. . .	. . .	. . .	. . .	. . .
3.20	69	3.20	69	230100500004
3.00	5	3.00	5	240100100433
2.70	11171	2.70	11171	240200100021
2.60	79	2.60	79	230100500045

```
   C.first();
   do i=1 to 2;
      output top;
      C.next();
   end;
   C.last();
   do i=1 to 2;
      output bottom;
      C.prev();
   end;
   stop;
run;
```

PDV

Customer_ID	Product_ ID	Total_ Retail_ Price	D i	D _N_
16	230100700009	1687.50	3	1

127 ...

Execution

Hiter C View of Partial Hash Object **customer**

KEY: Total_ Retail_ Price	KEY: Customer _ID	DATA: Total_ Retail_ Price	DATA: Customer _ID	DATA: Product_ ID
1937.20	70100	1937.20	70100	240200100173
1796.00	79	1796.00	79	240200100076
1687.50	16	1687.50	16	230100700009
1561.80	183	1561.80	183	240300300090
. . .	. . .	. . .	. . .	. . .
3.20	69	3.20	69	230100500004
3.00	5	3.00	5	240100100433
2.70	11171	2.70	11171	240200100021
2.60	79	2.60	79	230100500045

```
   C.first();
   do i=1 to 2;
      output top;
      C.next();
   end;
   C.last();
   do i=1 to 2;
      output bottom;
      C.prev();
   end;
   stop;
run;
```

Exit the DO loop

PDV

Customer_ID	Product_ ID	Total_ Retail_ Price	D i	D _N_
16	230100700009	1687.50	3	1

128 ...

Execution

Hiter C View of Partial Hash Object **customer**

KEY: Total_ Retail_ Price	KEY: Customer _ID	DATA: Total_ Retail_ Price	DATA: Customer _ID	DATA: Product_ ID
1937.20	70100	1937.20	70100	240200100173
1796.00	79	1796.00	79	240200100076
1687.50	16	1687.50	16	230100700009
1561.80	183	1561.80	183	240300300090
. . .	. . .	. . .	. . .	. . .
3.20	69	3.20	69	230100500004
3.00	5	3.00	5	240100100433
2.70	11171	2.70	11171	240200100021
2.60	79	2.60	79	230100500045

```
    C.first();
    do i=1 to 2;
       output top;
       C.next();
    end;
    C.last();
    do i=1 to 2;
       output bottom;
       C.prev();
    end;
    stop;
run;
```

PDV

Customer_ID	Product_ ID	Total_ Retail_ Price	D i	D _N_
79	230100500045	2.60	3	1

129 ...

Execution

Hiter C View of Partial Hash Object **customer**

KEY: Total_ Retail_ Price	KEY: Customer _ID	DATA: Total_ Retail_ Price	DATA: Customer _ID	DATA: Product_ ID
1937.20	70100	1937.20	70100	240200100173
1796.00	79	1796.00	79	240200100076
1687.50	16	1687.50	16	230100700009
1561.80	183	1561.80	183	240300300090
. . .	. . .	. . .	. . .	. . .
3.20	69	3.20	69	230100500004
3.00	5	3.00	5	240100100433
2.70	11171	2.70	11171	240200100021
2.60	79	2.60	79	230100500045

```
    C.first();
    do i=1 to 2;
       output top;
       C.next();
    end;
    C.last();
    do i=1 to 2;
       output bottom;
       C.prev();
    end;
    stop;
run;
```

PDV

Customer_ID	Product_ ID	Total_ Retail_ Price	D i	D _N_
79	230100500045	2.60	1	1

130 ...

Execution

Hiter C View of Partial Hash Object **customer**

KEY: Total_ Retail_ Price	KEY: Customer _ID	DATA: Total_ Retail_ Price	DATA: Customer _ID	DATA: Product_ ID
1937.20	70100	1937.20	70100	240200100173
1796.00	79	1796.00	79	240200100076
1687.50	16	1687.50	16	230100700009
1561.80	183	1561.80	183	240300300090
.	.	.	.	.
3.20	69	3.20	69	2
3.00	5	3.00	5	2
2.70	11171	2.70	11171	2
2.60	79	2.60	79	230100500045

```
C.first();
do i=1 to 2;
   output top;
   C.next();
end;
C.last();
do i=1 to 2;
   output bottom;
   C.prev();
```

Output current observation

PDV

Customer_ID	Product_ ID	Total_ Retail_ Price	i	_N_
79	230100500045	2.60	1	1

131 ...

Execution

Hiter C View of Partial Hash Object **customer**

KEY: Total_ Retail_ Price	KEY: Customer _ID	DATA: Total_ Retail_ Price	DATA: Customer _ID	DATA: Product_ ID
1937.20	70100	1937.20	70100	240200100173
1796.00	79	1796.00	79	240200100076
1687.50	16	1687.50	16	230100700009
1561.80	183	1561.80	183	240300300090
.	.	.	.	.
3.20	69	3.20	69	230100500004
3.00	5	3.00	5	240100100433
2.70	11171	2.70	11171	240200100021
2.60	79	2.60	79	230100500045

```
   C.first();
   do i=1 to 2;
      output top;
      C.next();
   end;
   C.last();
   do i=1 to 2;
      output bottom;
      C.prev();
   end;
   stop;
run;
```

PDV

Customer_ID	Product_ ID	Total_ Retail_ Price	i	_N_
11171	240200100021	2.70	1	1

132 ...

Execution

Hiter C View of Partial Hash Object **customer**

KEY: Total_ Retail_ Price	KEY: Customer _ID	DATA: Total_ Retail_ Price	DATA: Customer _ID	DATA: Product_ ID
1937.20	70100	1937.20	70100	240200100173
1796.00	79	1796.00	79	240200100076
1687.50	16	1687.50	16	230100700009
1561.80	183	1561.80	183	240300300090
. . .	. . .	. . .	. . .	. . .
3.20	69	3.20	69	230100500004
3.00	5	3.00	5	240100100433
2.70	11171	2.70	11171	240200100021
2.60	79	2.60	79	230100500045

```
   C.first();
   do i=1 to 2;
      output top;
      C.next();
   end;
   C.last();
   do i=1 to 2;
      output bottom;
      C.prev();
   end;
   stop;
run;
```

PDV

Customer_ID	Product_ ID	Total_ Retail_ Price	D i	D _N_
11171	240200100021	2.70	2	1

133 ...

Execution

Hiter C View of Partial Hash Object **customer**

KEY: Total_ Retail_ Price	KEY: Customer _ID	DATA: Total_ Retail_ Price	DATA: Customer _ID	DATA: Product_ ID
1937.20	70100	1937.20	70100	240200100173
1796.00	79	1796.00	79	240200100076
1687.50	16	1687.50	16	230100700009
1561.80	183	1561.80	183	240300300090
. . .	. . .	. . .	. . .	. . .
3.20	69	3.20	69	230100500004
3.00	5	3.00	5	240100100433
2.70	11171	2.70	11171	240200100021
2.60	79	2.60	79	230100500045

```
   C.first();
   do i=1 to 2;
      output top;
      C.next();
   end;
   C.last();
   do i=1 to 2;
      output bottom;
      C.prev();
   end;
   stop;
run;
```

PDV

Customer_ID	Product_ ID	Total_ Retail_ Price	D i	D _N_
11171	240200100021	2.70	2	1

134 ...

Execution

Hiter C View of Partial Hash Object **customer**

KEY: Total_ Retail_ Price	KEY: Customer _ID	DATA: Total_ Retail_ Price	DATA: Customer _ID	DATA: Product_ ID
1937.20	70100	1937.20	70100	240200100173
1796.00	79	1796.00	79	240200100076
1687.50	16	1687.50	16	230100700009
1561.80	183	1561.80	183	240300300090
. . .	. . .	. . .	. . .	. . .
3.20	69	3.20		
3.00	5	3.00		
2.70	11171	2.70	11	
2.60	79	2.60	79	230100500045

```
C.first();
do i=1 to 2;
   output top;
   C.next();
end;
C.last();
do i=1 to 2;
   output bottom;
   C.prev();
```

Output current observation

PDV

Customer_ID	Product_ ID	Total_ Retail_ Price	D i	D _N_
11171	240200100021	2.70	2	1

135 ...

Execution

Hiter C View of Partial Hash Object **customer**

KEY: Total_ Retail_ Price	KEY: Customer _ID	DATA: Total_ Retail_ Price	DATA: Customer _ID	DATA: Product_ ID
1937.20	70100	1937.20	70100	240200100173
1796.00	79	1796.00	79	240200100076
1687.50	16	1687.50	16	230100700009
1561.80	183	1561.80	183	240300300090
. . .	. . .	. . .	. . .	. . .
3.20	69	3.20	69	230100500004
3.00	5	3.00	5	240100100433
2.70	11171	2.70	11171	240200100021
2.60	79	2.60	79	230100500045

```
C.first();
do i=1 to 2;
   output top;
   C.next();
end;
C.last();
do i=1 to 2;
   output bottom;
   C.prev();
end;
stop;
run;
```

PDV

Customer_ID	Product_ ID	Total_ Retail_ Price	D i	D _N_
5	240100100433	3.00	2	1

136 ...

Execution

Hiter C View of Partial Hash Object **customer**

KEY: Total_ Retail_ Price	KEY: Customer _ID	DATA: Total_ Retail_ Price	DATA: Customer _ID	DATA: Product_ ID
1937.20	70100	1937.20	70100	240200100173
1796.00	79	1796.00	79	240200100076
1687.50	16	1687.50	16	230100700009
1561.80	183	1561.80	183	240300300090
⋮	⋮	⋮	⋮	⋮
3.20	69	3.20	69	230100500004
3.00	5	3.00	5	240100100433
2.70	11171	2.70	11171	240200100021
2.60	79	2.60	79	230100500045

```
   C.first();
   do i=1 to 2;
      output top;
      C.next();
   end;
   C.last();
   do i=1 to 2;
      output bottom;
      C.prev();
   end;
   stop;
run;
```

PDV

Customer_ID	Product_ ID	Total_ Retail_ Price	D i	D _N_
5	240100100433	3.00	3	1

137 ...

Execution

Hiter C View of Partial Hash Object **customer**

KEY: Total_ Retail_ Price	KEY: Customer _ID	DATA: Total_ Retail_ Price	DATA: Customer _ID	DATA: Product_ ID
1937.20	70100	1937.20	70100	240200100173
1796.00	79	1796.00	79	240200100076
1687.50	16	1687.50	16	230100700009
1561.80	183	1561.80	183	240300300090
⋮	⋮	⋮	⋮	⋮
3.20	69	3.20	69	230100500004
3.00	5	3.00	5	240100100433
2.70	11171	2.70	11171	240200100021
2.60	79	2.60	79	230100500045

```
   C.first();
   do i=1 to 2;
      output top;
      C.next();
   end;
   C.last();
   do i=1 to 2;
      output bottom;
      C.prev();
   end;
   stop;
run;
```

Exit the DO loop

PDV

Customer_ID	Product_ ID	Total_ Retail_ Price	D i	D _N_
5	240100100433	3.00	3	1

138 ...

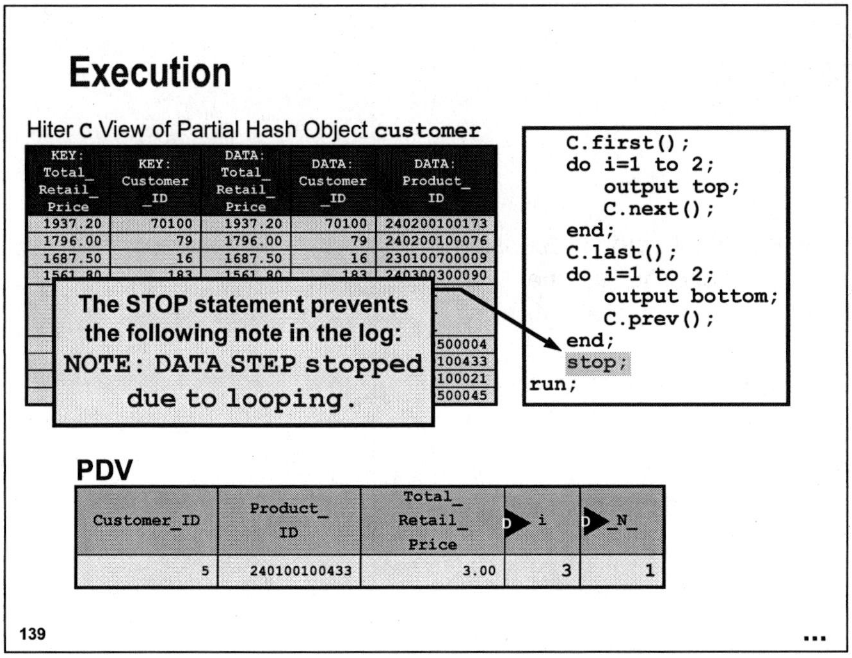

p306d04

```
proc print data=top;
   title 'Top 2 Big Spenders';
run;

proc print data=bottom;
   title 'Bottom 2 Frugal Spenders';
run;
```

Output

```
                         Top 2 Big Spenders

                                                      Total_Retail_
          Obs     Customer_ID       Product_ID          Price

            1           70100     240200100173       $1,937.20
            2              79     240200100076       $1,796.00
```

```
                       Bottom 2 Frugal Spenders

                                                      Total_Retail_
          Obs     Customer_ID       Product_ID          Price

            1              79     230100500045           $2.60
            2           11171     240200100021           $2.70
```

Using the STOP Statement

General form of the STOP statement:

```
STOP;
```

- The STOP statement causes SAS to stop processing the current DATA step immediately and resume processing statements after the end of the current DATA step.
- SAS outputs a data set for the current DATA step.
- The observation being processed when the STOP statement executes is not added.
- The STOP statement can be used alone or in an IF-THEN statement or SELECT group.

140

Exercises

Level 1

7. Using a Hiter Object

a. Use the data set **orion.shoe_sales** that contains the variables **Product_ID**, **Product_Name**, and **Total_Retail_Price** to create two data sets named **expensive** and **least_expensive**. The data set **expensive** should contain the five most expensive shoes and the data set **least_expensive** should contain the five least expensive shoes.

b. Print each of the data sets.

Listing of **expensive**

The Five Most Expensive Shoes

Obs	Product_ID	Product_Name	Total_Retail_ Price
1	240200100051	Bretagne Stabilites 2000 Goretex Shoes	$420.90
2	220200300129	Torino Men's Leather Adventure Shoes	$406.00
3	240200100227	Rubby Women's Golf Shoes w/Gore-Tex	$323.80
4	220100700024	Armadillo Road Dmx Women's Running Shoes	$313.80
5	240200100225	Rubby Men's Golf Shoes w/Goretex	$306.20

Listing of **least_expensive**

The Five Least Expensive Shoes

Obs	Product_ID	Product_Name	Total_Retail_ Price
1	240100100433	Shoelace White 150 Cm	$3.00
2	240100100434	Shoeshine Black	$16.40
3	210200400020	Kids Baby Edge Max Shoes	$38.00
4	210200400070	Tony's Children's Deschutz (Bg) Shoes	$41.60
5	220200100137	Big Guy Men's Multicourt Ii Shoes	$50.30

Level 2

8. Using a Hiter Object

a. Use the data set **orion.shoe_sales** that contains the variables **Product_ID**, **Product_Name**, and **Total_Retail_Price** to create a data set named **shoe_sales** that contains the five most expensive shoes and the five least expensive shoes. The data set should contain a new variable named **Rank** that has the value of '`Top 1`' to '`Top 5`' for the five most expensive and '`Bottom 1`' to '`Bottom 5`' for the five least expensive shoes.

b. Print the data set.

Listing of **`shoe_sales`**

Shoes

Obs	Product_ID	Product_Name	Total_Retail_ Price	Rank
1	240200100051	Bretagne Stabilites 2000 Goretex Shoes	$420.90	Top 1
2	220200300129	Torino Men's Leather Adventure Shoes	$406.00	Top 2
3	240200100227	Rubby Women's Golf Shoes w/Gore-Tex	$323.80	Top 3
4	220100700024	Armadillo Road Dmx Women's Running Shoes	$313.80	Top 4
5	240200100225	Rubby Men's Golf Shoes w/Goretex	$306.20	Top 5
6	240100100433	Shoelace White 150 Cm	$3.00	Bottom 1
7	240100100434	Shoeshine Black	$16.40	Bottom 2
8	210200400020	Kids Baby Edge Max Shoes	$38.00	Bottom 3
9	210200400070	Tony's Children's Deschutz (Bg) Shoes	$41.60	Bottom 4
10	220200100137	Big Guy Men's Multicourt Ii Shoes	$50.30	Bottom 5

Level 3

9. Using a Hiter Object

a. Use a hiter object to create a data set named **`different`** that contains unique values of **`Customer_ID`** and **`Order_Type`** from the data set named **`orion.order_fact`**. There should be 100 observations in the data set **`different`**.

b. Print the first 10 observations of the data set **`different`**.

Partial Listing of **`different`**

No Duplicates

Obs	Customer_ID	Order_ Type
1	4	1
2	4	3
3	5	1
4	5	2
5	5	3
6	9	3
7	10	1
8	10	2
9	11	3
10	12	1

6.5 Using a Hash Object for Chained Lookups (Self-Study)

Objectives

- Define a chained lookup.
- Use a hash object to perform a chained lookup.

144

Defining a Chained Lookup

A chained lookup can be one of two types of lookup operation:

1. using the value of a data variable as the key to the next FIND method
2. creating a "chain" from more than one variable

145

Business Scenario: Example 1

Because of a computer problem, some customers had to place an order more than one time. The customer IDs, along with the product IDs and the dates on which customers reordered the merchandise, are stored in a SAS data set named **orion.multiple_orders**.

Partial Listing of **orion.multiple_orders**

Customer_ID	Product_ID	Order_Date
16	220200100035	27AUG2006
16	220200100035	28AUG2006
16	220200100035	30AUG2006
49	210201000126	07APR2007
.	.	.
.	.	.
.	.	.

146

Business Scenario: Example 1

The required data set not only contains the order date, but also the next order date.

Partial Listing of **lookup**

Customer_ID	Product_ID	Order_Date	Next_Order_Date
16	220200100035	27AUG2006	28AUG2006
16	220200100035	28AUG2006	30AUG2006
16	220200100035	30AUG2006	.
49	210201000126	07APR2007	08APR2007
49	210201000126	08APR2007	10APR2007
49	210201000126	10APR2007	11APR2007
49	210201000126	11APR2007	.
.	.	.	.
.	.	.	.
.	.	.	.

147

Business Scenario: Example 1

Partial Listing of `orion.multiple_orders`

Customer_ID	Product_ID	Order_Date
16	220200100035	27AUG2006
16	220200100035	28AUG2006
16	220200100035	30AUG2006
49	210201000126	07APR2007
49	210201000126	08APR2007
49	210201000126	10APR2007
49	210201000126	11APR2007
70108	240200200071	22JUL2007
70108	240200200071	25JUL2007
70108	240200200071	26JUL2007
70108	240200200071	28JUL2007
70108	240200200071	30JUL2007
70108	240200200071	01AUG2007
70108	240200200071	02AUG2007
70108	240200200071	05AUG2007
70165	240200100050	08SEP2007
.	.	.

Partial Listing of `lookup`

Customer_ID	...	Order_Date	Next_Order_Date
16	...	27AUG2006	28AUG2006
16	...	28AUG2006	30AUG2006
16	...	30AUG2006	.
49	...	07APR2007	08APR2007
49	...	08APR2007	10APR2007
49	...	10APR2007	11APR2007
49	...	11APR2007	.
70108		22JUL2007	25JUL2007
70108		25JUL2007	26JUL2007
70108		26JUL2007	28JUL2007
70108		28JUL2007	30JUL2007
70108		30JUL2007	01AUG2007
70108		01AUG2007	02AUG2007
70108		02AUG2007	05AUG2007
70108		05AUG2007	.
.	.	.	.

148

Example 1

```
proc sort data=orion.multiple_orders
          out=multiple_orders;
   by Customer_ID;
run;

data multiple_orders;
   set multiple_orders;
   rename Order_Date=OD;
   ObsNum=_N_;
run;
```

p306d05

149 *continued...*

Example 1

```
data lookup;
   format Next_Order_Date date9.;
   keep Customer_ID Product_ID Order_Date
        Next_Order_Date;
   if _N_=1 then do;
      declare hash LU(dataset: "multiple_orders");
      LU.definekey('ObsNum');
      LU.definedata('OD');
      LU.definedone();
      call missing(OD);
   end;
   set multiple_orders(rename=(OD=Order_Date));
   by Customer_ID;
   Obs=ObsNum + 1;
   rc=LU.find(key:Obs);
   if rc=0 then Next_Order_Date=OD;
   if last.Customer_ID then Next_Order_Date=.;
run;
```

150

p306d05

6.10 Quiz

What is the purpose of the BY statement in the DATA step?

152

Execution

Partial Hash Object **LU**

ObsNum	OD
1	27AUG2006
2	28AUG2006
3	30AUG2006
4	07APR2007
5	08APR2007
.	.
.	.
.	.

```
data lookup;
   format Next_Order_Date date9.;
   keep Customer_ID Product_ID Order_Date
        Next_Order_Date;
   if _N_=1 then do;
      declare hash LU(dataset: "multiple_orders");
      LU.definekey('ObsNum');
      LU.definedata('OD');
      LU.definedone();
      call missing(OD);
   end;
   set multiple_orders(rename=(OD=Order_Date));
   by Customer_ID;
   Obs=ObsNum+1;
   rc=LU.find(key:Obs);
   if rc=0 then Next_Order_Date=OD;
   if last.Customer_ID then Next_Order_Date=.;
run;
```

PDV

Next_ Order_ Date	OD	Customer _ID	Product_ ID	Order_ Date	D ObsNum
.	.	.	.	.	.

...

D First. Customer_ID	D Last. Customer_ID	D Obs	D rc	D _N_
1	1	.	.	1

154 ...

Execution

Partial Hash Object **LU**

ObsNum	OD
1	27AUG2006
2	28AUG2006
3	30AUG2006
4	07APR2007
5	08APR2007
.	.
.	.
.	.

```
data lookup;
   format Next_Order_Date date9.;
   keep Customer_ID Product_ID Order_Date
        Next_Order_Date;
   if _N_=1 then do;
      declare hash LU(dataset: "multiple_orders");
      LU.definekey('ObsNum');
      LU.definedata('OD');
      LU.definedone();
      call missing(OD);
   end;
   set multiple_orders(rename=(OD=Order_Date));
   by Customer_ID;
   Obs=ObsNum+1;
   rc=LU.find(key:Obs);
   if rc=0 then Next_Order_Date=OD;
   if last.Customer_ID then Next_Order_Date=.;
run;
```

PDV

Next_ Order_ Date	OD	Customer _ID	Product_ ID	Order_ Date	D ObsNum
.	.	16	220200100035	27AUG2006	1

...

D First. Customer_ID	D Last. Customer_ID	D Obs	D rc	D _N_
1	0	.	.	1

155 ...

Execution

Partial Hash Object **LU**

ObsNum	OD
1	27AUG2006
2	28AUG2006
3	30AUG2006
4	07APR2007
5	08APR2007
.	.
.	.
.	.

```
data lookup;
   format Next_Order_Date date9.;
   keep Customer_ID Product_ID Order_Date
        Next_Order_Date;
   if _N_=1 then do;
      declare hash LU(dataset: "multiple_orders");
      LU.definekey('ObsNum');
      LU.definedata('OD');
      LU.definedone();
      call missing(OD);
   end;
   set multiple_orders(rename=(OD=Order_Date));
   by Customer_ID;
   Obs=ObsNum+1;
   rc=LU.find(key:Obs);
   if rc=0 then Next_Order_Date=OD;
   if last.Customer_ID then Next_Order_Date=.;
run;
```

PDV

Next_ Order_ Date	OD	Customer _ID	Product_ ID	Order_ Date	D ObsNum
.	.	16	220200100035	27AUG2006	1

...

D First. Customer_ID	D Last. Customer_ID	D Obs	D rc	D _N_
1	0	2	.	1

156 ...

Execution

Partial Hash Object **LU**

ObsNum	OD
1	27AUG2006
2	28AUG2006
3	30AUG2006
4	07APR2007
5	08APR2007
.	.
.	.
.	.

```
data lookup;
   format Next_Order_Date date9.;
   keep Customer_ID Product_ID Order_Date
        Next_Order_Date;
   if _N_=1 then do;
      declare hash LU(dataset: "multiple_orders");
      LU.definekey('ObsNum');
      LU.definedata('OD');
      LU.definedone();
      call missing(OD);
   end;
   set multiple_orders(rename=(OD=Order_Date));
   by Customer_ID;
   Obs=ObsNum+1;
   rc=LU.find(key:Obs);
   if rc=0 then Next_Order_Date=OD;
   if last.Customer_ID then Next_Order_Date=.;
run;
```

PDV

Next_ Order_ Date	OD	Customer _ID	Product_ ID	Order_ Date	D ObsNum
.	28AUG2006	16	220200100035	27AUG2006	1

...

D First. Customer_ID	D Last. Customer_ID	D Obs	D rc	D _N_
1	0	2	0	1

157 ...

Execution

Partial Hash Object **LU**

ObsNum	OD
1	27AUG2006
2	28AUG2006
3	30AUG2006
4	07APR2007
5	08APR2007
.	.
.	.
.	.

```
data lookup;
   format Next_Order_Date date9.;
   keep Customer_ID Product_ID Order_Date
        Next_Order_Date;
   if _N_=1 then do;
      declare hash LU(dataset: "multiple_orders");
      LU.definekey('ObsNum');
      LU.definedata('OD');
      LU.definedone();
      call missing(OD);
   end;
   set multiple_orders(rename=(OD=Order_Date));
   by Customer_ID;
   Obs=ObsNum+1;
   rc=LU.find(key:Obs);
   if rc=0 then Next_Order_Date=OD;
   if last.Customer_ID then Next_Order_Date=.;
run;
```

PDV

Next_ Order_ Date	OD	Customer _ID	Product_ ID	Order_ Date	D ObsNum
28AUG2006	28AUG2006	16	220200100035	27AUG2006	1

...

D First. Customer_ID	D Last. Customer_ID	D Obs	D rc	D _N_
1	0	2	0	1

158 ...

Execution

Partial Hash Object **LU**

ObsNum	OD
1	27AUG2006
2	28AUG2006
3	30AUG2006
4	07APR2007
5	08APR2007
.	.
.	.
.	.

```
data lookup;
   format Next_Order_Date date9.;
   keep Customer_ID Product_ID Order_Date
        Next_Order_Date;
   if _N_=1 then do;
      declare hash LU(dataset: "multiple_orders");
      LU.definekey('ObsNum');
      LU.definedata('OD');
      LU.definedone();
      call missing(OD);
   end;
   set multiple_orders(rename=(OD=Order_Date));
   by Customer_ID;
   Obs=ObsNum+1;
   rc=LU.find(key:Obs);
   if rc=0 then Next_Order_Date=OD;
   if last.Customer_ID then Next_Order_Date=.;
run;
```

False

PDV

Next_ Order_ Date	OD	Customer _ID	Product_ ID	Order_ Date	D ObsNum
28AUG2006	28AUG2006	16	220200100035	27AUG2006	1

...

D First. Customer_ID	D Last. Customer_ID	D Obs	D rc	D _N_
1	0	2	0	1

159 ...

Execution

Partial Hash Object **LU**

ObsNum	OD
1	27AUG2006
2	28AUG2006
3	30AUG2006
4	07APR2007
5	08APR2007
.	.
.	.
.	.

```
data lookup;
   format Next_Order_Date date9.;
   keep Customer_ID Product_ID Order_Date
        Next_Order_Date;
   if _N_=1 then do;
      declare hash LU(dataset: "multiple_orders");
      LU.definekey('ObsNum');
      LU.definedata('O
      LU.definedone();
      call missing(OD)
   end;
   set multiple_orders                    ));
   by Customer_ID;
   Obs=ObsNum+1;
   rc=LU.find(key:Obs);
   if rc=0 then Next_Order_Date=OD;
   if last.Customer_ID then Next_Order_Date=.;
run;
```

Implicit OUTPUT;
Implicit RETURN;

PDV

Next_Order_Date	OD	Customer_ID	Product_ID	Order_Date	D ObsNum
28AUG2006	28AUG2006	16	220200100035	27AUG2006	1

...

D First.Customer_ID	D Last.Customer_ID	D Obs	D rc	D _N_
1	0	2	0	1

160 ...

Execution

Partial Hash Object **LU**

ObsNum	OD
1	27AUG2006
2	28AUG2006
3	30AUG2006
4	07APR2007
5	08APR2007
.	.
.	.
.	.

```
data lookup;
   format Next_Order_Date date9.;
   keep Customer_ID Product_ID Order_Date
        Next_Order_Date;
   if _N_=1 then do;
      declare hash LU(dataset: "multiple_orders");
      LU.definekey('ObsNum');
      LU.definedata('OD');
      LU.definedone();
      call missing(OD);
   end;
   set multiple_orders(rename=(OD=Order_Date));
   by Customer_ID;
   Obs=ObsNum+1;
   rc=LU.find(key:Obs);
   if rc=0 then Next_Order_Date=OD;
   if last.Customer_ID then Next_Order_Date=.;
run;
```

PDV

Next_Order_Date	OD	Customer_ID	Product_ID	Order_Date	D ObsNum
.	.	16	220200100035	28AUG2006	2

...

D First.Customer_ID	D Last.Customer_ID	D Obs	D rc	D _N_
0	0	3	.	2

161 ...

Execution

Partial Hash Object **LU**

ObsNum	OD
1	27AUG2006
2	28AUG2006
3	30AUG2006
4	07APR2007
5	08APR2007
.	.
.	.
.	.

```
data lookup;
   format Next_Order_Date date9.;
   keep Customer_ID Product_ID Order_Date
        Next_Order_Date;
   if _N_=1 then do;
      declare hash LU(dataset: "multiple_orders");
      LU.definekey('ObsNum');
      LU.definedata('OD');
      LU.definedone();
      call missing(OD);
   end;
   set multiple_orders(rename=(OD=Order_Date));
   by Customer_ID;
   Obs=ObsNum+1;
   rc=LU.find(key:Obs);
   if rc=0 then Next_Order_Date=OD;
   if last.Customer_ID then Next_Order_Date=.;
run;
```

PDV

Next_ Order_ Date	OD	Customer _ID	Product_ ID	Order_ Date	D ObsNum
.	30AUG2006	16	220200100035	28AUG2006	2

...

D First. Customer_ID	D Last. Customer_ID	D Obs	D rc	D _N_
0	0	3	0	2

162 ...

Execution

Partial Hash Object **LU**

ObsNum	OD
1	27AUG2006
2	28AUG2006
3	30AUG2006
4	07APR2007
5	08APR2007
.	.
.	.
.	.

```
data lookup;
   format Next_Order_Date date9.;
   keep Customer_ID Product_ID Order_Date
        Next_Order_Date;
   if _N_=1 then do;
      declare hash LU(dataset: "multiple_orders");
      LU.definekey('ObsNum');
      LU.definedata('OD');
      LU.definedone();
      call missing(OD);
   end;
   set multiple_orders(rename=(OD=Order_Date));
   by Customer_ID;
   Obs=ObsNum+1;
   rc=LU.find(key:Obs);
   if rc=0 then Next_Order_Date=OD;
   if last.Customer_ID then Next_Order_Date=.;
run;
```

PDV

Next_ Order_ Date	OD	Customer _ID	Product_ ID	Order_ Date	D ObsNum
30AUG2006	30AUG2006	16	220200100035	28AUG2006	2

...

D First. Customer_ID	D Last. Customer_ID	D Obs	D rc	D _N_
0	0	3	0	2

163 ...

Execution

Partial Hash Object **LU**

ObsNum	OD
1	27AUG2006
2	28AUG2006
3	30AUG2006
4	07APR2007
5	08APR2007
.	.

```
data lookup;
   format Next_Order_Date date9.;
   keep Customer_ID Product_ID Order_Date
        Next_Order_Date;
   if _N_=1 then do;
      declare hash LU(dataset: "multiple_orders");
      LU.definekey('ObsNum');
      LU.definedata('OD');
      LU.definedone();
      call missing(OD);
   end;
   set multiple_order          (OD=Order_Date));
   by Customer_ID;
   Obs=ObsNum+1;
   rc=LU.find(key:Obs);
   if rc=0 then Next_Order_Date=OD;
   if last.Customer_ID then Next_Order_Date=.;
run;
```

False

PDV

Next_ Order_ Date	OD	Customer _ID	Product_ ID	Order_ Date	ObsNum
30AUG2006	30AUG2006	16	220200100035	28AUG2006	2

First. Customer_ID	Last. Customer_ID	Obs	rc	_N_
0	0	3	0	2

164

Execution

Partial Hash Object **LU**

ObsNum	OD
1	27AUG2006
2	28AUG2006
3	30AUG2006
4	07APR2007
5	08APR2007
.	.

```
data lookup;
   format Next_Order_Date date9.;
   keep Customer_ID Product_ID Order_Date
        Next_Order_Date;
   if _N_=1 then do;
      declare hash LU(dataset: "multiple_orders");
      LU.definekey('Obs
      LU.definedata('O
      LU.definedone();
      call missing(OD);
   end;
   set multiple_orders(rename=(OD=Order_Date));
   by Customer_ID;
   Obs=ObsNum+1;
   rc=LU.find(key:Obs);
   if rc=0 then Next_Order_Date=OD;
   if last.Customer_ID then Next_Order_Date=.;
run;
```

Implicit OUTPUT;
Implicit RETURN;

PDV

Next_ Order_ Date	OD	Customer _ID	Product_ ID	Order_ Date	ObsNum
30AUG2006	30AUG2006	16	220200100035	28AUG2006	2

First. Customer_ID	Last. Customer_ID	Obs	rc	_N_
0	0	3	0	2

165

Execution

Partial Hash Object **LU**

ObsNum	OD
1	27AUG2006
2	28AUG2006
3	30AUG2006
4	07APR2007
5	08APR2007
.	.
.	.
.	.

```
data lookup;
   format Next_Order_Date date9.;
   keep Customer_ID Product_ID Order_Date
        Next_Order_Date;
   if _N_=1 then do;
      declare hash LU(dataset: "multiple_orders");
      LU.definekey('ObsNum');
      LU.definedata('OD');
      LU.definedone();
      call missing(OD);
   end;
   set multiple_orders(rename=(OD=Order_Date));
   by Customer_ID;
   Obs=ObsNum+1;
   rc=LU.find(key:Obs);
   if rc=0 then Next_Order_Date=OD;
   if last.Customer_ID then Next_Order_Date=.;
run;
```

PDV

Next_Order_Date	OD	Customer_ID	Product_ID	Order_Date	ObsNum
.	.	16	220200100035	30AUG2006	3

...

First.Customer_ID	Last.Customer_ID	Obs	rc	_N_
0	1	4	.	3

166 ...

Execution

Partial Hash Object **LU**

ObsNum	OD
1	27AUG2006
2	28AUG2006
3	30AUG2006
4	07APR2007
5	08APR2007
.	.
.	.
.	.

```
data lookup;
   format Next_Order_Date date9.;
   keep Customer_ID Product_ID Order_Date
        Next_Order_Date;
   if _N_=1 then do;
      declare hash LU(dataset: "multiple_orders");
      LU.definekey('ObsNum');
      LU.definedata('OD');
      LU.definedone();
      call missing(OD);
   end;
   set multiple_orders(rename=(OD=Order_Date));
   by Customer_ID;
   Obs=ObsNum+1;
   rc=LU.find(key:Obs);
   if rc=0 then Next_Order_Date=OD;
   if last.Customer_ID then Next_Order_Date=.;
run;
```

PDV

Next_Order_Date	OD	Customer_ID	Product_ID	Order_Date	ObsNum
.	07APR2007	16	220200100035	30AUG2006	3

...

First.Customer_ID	Last.Customer_ID	Obs	rc	_N_
0	1	4	0	3

167 ...

Execution

Partial Hash Object **LU**

ObsNum	OD
1	27AUG2006
2	28AUG2006
3	30AUG2006
4	07APR2007
5	08APR2007
.	.
.	.
.	.

```
data lookup;
   format Next_Order_Date date9.;
   keep Customer_ID Product_ID Order_Date
        Next_Order_Date;
   if _N_=1 then do;
      declare hash LU(dataset: "multiple_orders");
      LU.definekey('ObsNum');
      LU.definedata('OD');
      LU.definedone();
      call missing(OD);
   end;
   set multiple_orders(rename=(OD=Order_Date));
   by Customer_ID;
   Obs=ObsNum+1;
   rc=LU.find(key:Obs);
   if rc=0 then Next_Order_Date=OD;
   if last.Customer_ID then Next_Order_Date=.;
run;
```

PDV

Next_ Order_ Date	OD	Customer _ID	Product_ ID	Order_ Date	D ObsNum
07APR2007	07APR2007	16	220200100035	30AUG2006	3

...

D First. Customer_ID	D Last. Customer_ID	D Obs	D rc	D _N_
0	1	4	0	3

168 ...

Execution

Partial Hash Object **LU**

ObsNum	OD
1	27AUG2006
2	28AUG2006
3	30AUG2006
4	07APR2007
5	08APR2007
.	.
.	.
.	.

```
data lookup;
   format Next_Order_Date date9.;
   keep Customer_ID Product_ID Order_Date
        Next_Order_Date;
   if _N_=1 then do;
      declare hash LU(dataset: "multiple_orders");
      LU.definekey('ObsNum');
      LU.definedata('OD');
      LU.definedone();
      call missing(OD);
   end;
   set multiple_orders(rename=(OD=Order_
   by Customer_ID;
   Obs=ObsNum+1;
   rc=LU.find(key:Obs);
   if rc=0 then Next_Order_Date=OD;
   if last.Customer_ID then Next_Order_Date=.;
run;
```

True

PDV

Next_ Order_ Date	OD	Customer _ID	Product_ ID	Order_ Date	D ObsNum
07APR2007	07APR2007	16	220200100035	30AUG2006	3

...

D First. Customer_ID	D Last. Customer_ID	D Obs	D rc	D _N_
0	1	4	0	3

169 ...

Execution

Partial Hash Object **LU**

ObsNum	OD
1	27AUG2006
2	28AUG2006
3	30AUG2006
4	07APR2007
5	08APR2007
.	.
.	.
.	.

```
data lookup;
   format Next_Order_Date date9.;
   keep Customer_ID Product_ID Order_Date
        Next_Order_Date;
   if _N_=1 then do;
      declare hash LU(dataset: "multiple_orders");
      LU.definekey('ObsNum');
      LU.definedata('OD');
      LU.definedone();
      call missing(OD);
   end;
   set multiple_orders(rename=(OD=Order_Date));
   by Customer_ID;
   Obs=ObsNum+1;
   rc=LU.find(key:Obs);
   if rc=0 then Next_Order_Date=OD;
   if last.Customer_ID then Next_Order_Date=.;
run;
```

PDV

Next_ Order_ Date	OD	Customer_ ID	Product_ ID	Order_ Date	D ObsNum
.	07APR2007	16	220200100035	30AUG2006	3

...

D First. Customer_ID	D Last. Customer_ID	D Obs	D rc	D _N_
0	1	4	0	3

170 ...

Execution

Partial Hash Object **LU**

ObsNum	OD
1	27AUG2006
2	28AUG2006
3	30AUG2006
4	07APR2007
5	08APR2007
.	.
.	.
.	.

```
data lookup;
   format Next_Order_Date date9.;
   keep Customer_ID Product_ID Order_Date
        Next_Order_Date;
   if _N_=1 then do;
      declare hash LU(dataset: "multiple_orders");
      LU.definekey('ObsNum');
      LU.definedata('OD');
      LU.definedone();
      call missing(OD);
   end;
   set multiple_orders(rename=(OD=Order_Date));
   by Customer_ID;
   Obs=ObsNum+1;
   rc=LU.find(key:Obs);
   if rc=0 then Next_Order_Date=OD;
   if last.Customer_ID then Next_Order_Date=.;
run;
```

Implicit OUTPUT;
Implicit RETURN;

PDV

Next_ Order_ Date	OD	Customer_ ID	Product_ ID	Order_ Date	D ObsNum
.	07APR2007	16	220200100035	30AUG2006	3

...

D First. Customer_ID	D Last. Customer_ID	D Obs	D rc	D _N_
0	1	4	0	3

171 ...

Execution

Partial Hash Object **LU**

ObsNum	OD
1	27AUG2006
2	28AUG2006
3	30AUG2006
4	07APR2007
5	08APR2007
.	.
.	.
.	.

```
data lookup;
   format Next_Order_Date date9.;
   keep Customer_ID Product_ID Order_Date
        Next_Order_Date;
   if _N_=1 then do;
      declare hash LU(dataset: "multiple_orders");
      LU.definekey('ObsNum');
      LU.definedata('OD');
      LU.definedone();
      ca
   end;
   set m                                rder_Date));
   by Customer_ID;
   Obs=ObsNum+1;
   rc=LU.find(key:Obs);
   if rc=0 then Next_Order_Date=OD;
   if last.Customer_ID then Next_Order_Date=.;
run;
```

Continue until EOF

PDV

Next_ Order_ Date	OD	Customer _ID	Product_ ID	Order_ Date	D ObsNum
.	.	70165	240200100050	19SEP2007	32

...

D First. Customer_ID	D Last. Customer_ID	D Obs	D rc	D _N_
0	1	33	-2147450842	32

172

Chained Lookup

```
proc print data=lookup(obs=10);
   var Customer_ID Order_Date Next_Order_Date;
   title 'Chained Lookup Example';
run;
```

PROC PRINT Output

Chained Lookup Example

Obs	Customer_ ID	Order_ Date	Next_ Order_ Date
1	16	27AUG2006	28AUG2006
2	16	28AUG2006	30AUG2006
3	16	30AUG2006	.
4	49	07APR2007	08APR2007
5	49	08APR2007	10APR2007
6	49	10APR2007	11APR2007
7	49	11APR2007	.
8	79	27SEP2007	30SEP2007
9	79	30SEP2007	01OCT2007
10	79	01OCT2007	.

173

p306d05

Business Scenario: Example 2

Suppose that you need to create a list of the **Order_Date** values, that is, the date on which a customer placed an order for a product.

Partial **orion.multiple_orders**

Customer_ID	Product_ID	Order_Date
16	220200100035	27AUG2006
16	220200100035	28AUG2006
16	220200100035	30AUG2006
49	210201000126	07APR2007
. . .	. . .	. . .

174

Business Scenario: Example 2

The new data set contains a list of all the dates on which the orders were placed.

Listing of **lookup**

All_Dates	Customer_ID	Product_ID
27AUG2006, 28AUG2006, 30AUG2006	16	220200100035
07APR2007, 08APR2007, 10APR2007, 11APR2007	49	210201000126
27SEP2007, 30SEP2007, 01OCT2007	79	240500100057
31AUG2007, 05SEP2007, 08SEP2007, 10SEP2007, 11SEP2007, 13SEP2007, 14SEP2007	171	230100500004
29JAN2007, 01FEB2007	2806	240100400058
22JUL2007, 25JUL2007, 26JUL2007, 28JUL2007, 30JUL2007, 01AUG2007, 02AUG2007, 05AUG2007	70108	240200200071
08SEP2007, 10SEP2007, 16SEP2007, 18SEP2007, 19SEP2007	70165	240200100050

175

Creating a List of Values

p306d06

```
proc sort data=orion.multiple_orders out=multiple_orders;
   by Customer_ID;
run;

data multiple_orders;
   set multiple_orders;
   rename Order_Date=OD;
   ObsNum=_N_;
run;

data lookup;
   length All_Dates $200;
   keep Customer_ID Product_ID All_Dates;
   if _N_=1 then do;
      declare hash LU(dataset: "multiple_orders");
      LU.definekey('ObsNum', 'Customer_ID');
      LU.definedata('OD');
      lu LU definedone();
      call missing(OD);
   end;
   do until (Last);
      set multiple_orders(rename=(OD=Order_Date)) end=Last;
      by Customer_ID;
      if first.Customer_ID then All_Dates=put(Order_Date, date9.);
      Obs=ObsNum + 1;
      rc=LU.find(key:Obs, key:Customer_ID);
      if rc=0 then
         All_Dates=catx(', ', All_Dates, put(OD, date9.));
      else output;
   end;
run;

proc print data=lookup;
   var Customer_ID All_Dates;
   title 'Chained Lookup Example';
run;
```

PROC PRINT Output

```
                              Chained Lookup Example

      Customer_
Obs       ID

  1       16
  2       49
  3       79
  4      171
  5     2806
  6    70108
  7    70165


Obs   All_Dates

  1   27AUG2006, 28AUG2006, 30AUG2006
  2   07APR2007, 08APR2007, 10APR2007, 11APR2007
  3   27SEP2007, 30SEP2007, 01OCT2007
  4   31AUG2007, 05SEP2007, 08SEP2007, 10SEP2007, 11SEP2007, 13SEP2007, 14SEP2007
  5   29JAN2007, 01FEB2007
  6   22JUL2007, 25JUL2007, 26JUL2007, 28JUL2007, 30JUL2007, 01AUG2007, 02AUG2007, 05AUG2007
  7   08SEP2007, 10SEP2007, 16SEP2007, 18SEP2007, 19SEP2007
```

This problem can also be solved using FIRST. and LAST. processing in the DATA step.

p306d07

```
proc sort data=orion.multiple_orders out=multiple_orders;
   by Customer_ID;
run;

data lookup;
   retain All_Dates;
   length All_Dates $200;
   keep Customer_ID Product_ID All_Dates;
   set multiple_orders;
   by Customer_ID;
   if first.Customer_ID then All_Dates=put(Order_Date, date9.);
   Next_Date=lag(Order_Date);
   if not first.Customer_ID then All_Dates=
      catx(', ', All_Dates, put(Next_Date, date9.));
   if last.Customer_ID then output;
run;

proc print data=lookup;
   title 'First. Last. Lookup Example';
run;

title;
```

Exercises

Level 1

10. Using a Hash Object to Locate the Next Value of a Variable

a. Use the data set **orion.order_fact** that contains the variables **Customer_ID**, **Product_ID**, and **Total_Retail_Price** to create a data set named **next_products**, which contains two new variables, **Next_Product_ID** and **Next_Price**. **Next_Product_ID** is the product that the customer ordered after the current product. **Next_Price** is the price of that product.

b. Print the first 10 observations of **next_products**. Format **Next_Price** with dollar signs and two digits to the right of the decimal point.

Next Product Ordered

Obs	Customer_ID	Product_ID	Total_Retail_Price	Next_Product_ID	Next_Price
1	4	240800200030	$47.70	240600100017	$53.00
2	4	240600100017	$53.00	240700200019	$16.90
3	4	240700200019	$16.90	240500100017	$214.00
4	4	240500100017	$214.00	240500100029	$58.90
5	4	240500100029	$58.90	220101400145	$16.70
6	4	220101400145	$16.70	240700100011	$80.97
7	4	240700100011	$80.97	240500200083	$201.90
8	4	240500200083	$201.90	230100100053	$92.60
9	4	230100100053	$92.60	.	.
10	5	230100500026	$247.50	240100100433	$3.00

Level 2

11. Using a Hash Object to Create a Chain of Values

a. Use the data set **orion.customer** that contains the variables **Country** and **Customer_ID** to create a data set named **customer_list** that contains a new variable, **All_Customers**, which is a list of customers for each country.

b. Open and submit the program **p306e11** that contains a PROC REPORT step.

p306e11

```
proc report data=customer_list nowd headline headskip;
   column Country All_Customers;
   define Country / width=20 order 'Customer/Country';
   define All_Customers / width=50 flow 'Customer/List';
   break after Country / skip;
run;
```

Listing of **customer_list**

```
                          Next Product Ordered

        Customer                   Customer
        Country                    List
        ____________________________________________________________

        AU                         29, 41, 53, 111, 171, 183, 195, 215

        CA                         11171, 17023, 26148, 46966, 54655, 70046, 70059,
                                   70079, 70100, 70108, 70165, 70187, 70201, 70210,
                                   70221

        DE                         9, 11, 13, 16, 19, 33, 42, 50, 61, 65

        IL                         12386, 14104, 14703, 19444, 19873

        TR                         544, 908, 928, 1033, 1100, 1684, 2788

        US                         4, 5, 10, 12, 17, 18, 20, 23, 24, 27, 31, 34, 36,
                                   39, 45, 49, 52, 56, 60, 63, 69, 71, 75, 79, 88,
                                   89, 90, 92

        ZA                         2550, 2618, 2806, 3959
```

Level 3

12. Using a Hash Object to Create a Chain of Values

a. Use the data set **orion.product_dim** to create a data set named **suppliers** that contains two variables, **All_Products** and **All_Names**. **All_Products** is a list of all the **Product_ID** values for each supplier. **All_Names** is a list of the names of all of those products. Ensure that none of the values is truncated.

b. Write a PROC REPORT step to display the data set **suppliers**. Ensure that the entire lists for **All_Products** and **All_Names** are printed.

Partial Listing of **suppliers**

```
                              Supplier Product List

                      Product                         Names of
Supplier              List                            Products
--------------------------------------------------------------------------------

3Top Sports           210201000050, 210201000067,     Kid Children's T-Shirt, Logo
                      210201000126, 210201000198,     Coord.Children's Sweatshirt,
                      210201000199, 220101400004,     Toddler Footwear Socks with
                      220101400017, 220101400018,     Knobs, South Peak Junior
                      220101400047, 220101400060,     Training Shoes, Starlite Baby
                      220101400061, 220101400088,     Shoes, Badminton Cotton,
                      220101400091, 220101400092,     Men's Cap, Men's Running Tee
                      220101400098, 220101400117,     Short Sleeves, Swimming
                      220101400130, 220101400138,     Trunks Struc, 2bwet 3 Cb
                      220101400145, 220101400148,     Swimming Trunks, 2bwet 3
                      220101400150, 220101400152,     Solid Bikini, Casual Genuine
                      220101400201, 220101400216,     Polo-Shirt, Casual Genuine
                      220101400237, 220101400238,     Tee, Casual Logo Men's
                      220101400265, 220101400269,     Sweatshirt, Casual Sport
                      220101400276, 220101400285,     Shorts, Casual.st.polo
                      220101400289, 220101400290,     Long-sleeved Polo-shirt,
                      220101400306, 220101400310,     Comp. Women's Sleeveless
                      220101400328, 2201014003        Polo, Dima 2-Layer Men's
                                                      Suit, Essence.baseball Cap,
                                                      Essence.cap Men's Bag,
                                                      Essential Suit 2 Swim Suit,
                                                      Essential Trunk 2 Swimming
                                                      Trunks, Kaitum Women's Swim
                                                      Suit, Mm Daypouch Shoulder
                                                      Bag, Mns.jacket Jacket,
                                                      Mns.long Tights, Ottis Pes
                                                      Men's Pants, Outfit Women's
                                                      Shirt, Pine Sweat with Hood,
                                                      Quali Jacket with Hood, Quali
                                                      Sweatpant, Quali Sweatshirt,
                                                      Sherpa Pes Shiny Cotton,
                                                      Short Women's Tights, Stars
                                                      Swim Suit, Tims Shorts,
                                                      Tracker Fitness Stockings,
                                                      Pytossage Bathing Sandal,
                                                      Liga Football Boot, Men's
                                                      Running Shoes Piedmmont,
                                                      Hilly Women's Crosstrainer
                                                      Shoes, Indoor Handbold
                                                      Special Shoes, Mns.raptor
                                                      Precision Sg Football, South
                                                      Peak Men's Running Shoes,
                                                      Torino Men's Leather
                                                      Adventure Shoes, T-Shirt
```

6.6 Chapter Review

Chapter Review

1. Describe a hash object.
2. When is a hash object deleted from memory?
3. What are the two types of DATA step component objects?
4. What is a key component?
5. What is the purpose of the DECLARE statement?

179

Chapter Review

6. What is the purpose of the FIND method?
7. What value does the FIND method return when it executes?
8. Are the key(s) and data item(s) variables in the PDV?

181

Chapter Review

9. Why are the DECLARE, DEFINEKEY, DEFINEDATA, and DEFINEDONE methods executed in the IF _N_=1 THEN DO group?

10. Is the DEFINEDONE method required?

183

6.7 Solutions

Solutions to Exercises

1. **Using the ADD Method to Create a Hash Object with a Single Key**

   a. Write a DATA step that creates a data set named **orders**.

   b. Use the ADD method to create a hash table containing the values of the order type as the key values and the corresponding sale type as the data values. Use the FIND method to retrieve sale type based on the variable **Order_Type** in the data set **orion.orders**.

   c. Keep only the variables **Order_ID**, **Order_Type**, and **Sale_Type**.

   d. Print the first five observations from the **orders** data set.

p306s01

```
data orders;
   length Sale_Type $40;
   keep Order_ID Order_Type Sale_Type;
   if _N_=1 then do;
      declare hash Product();
      Product.definekey('Order_Type');
      Product.definedata('Sale_Type');
      Product.definedone();
      Product.add(key:1, data:'Retail Sale');
      Product.add(key:2, data:'Catalog Sale');
      Product.add(key:3, data:'Internet Sale');
      call missing(Sale_Type);
   end;
   set orion.orders;
   rc=Product.find();
   if rc=0;
run;

proc print data=orders(obs=5);
   title;
run;
```

2. **Using the ADD Method with a Composite Key**

   a. Write a DATA step to create a data set named **emps**.

   b. Use the ADD method to add the composite key values for **State** and **Country** and the data values of **State_Name** and **Country_Name** from the table.

   c. Read from the data set **orion.employee_addresses**.

   d. Use the FIND method to perform the table lookup.

e. Print the first 10 observation of the data set **emps**.

p306s02

```
data emps;
   length State_Name $ 12 Country_Name $30;
   keep Employee_ID Country Country_Name State_Name;
   if _N_=1 then do;
      declare hash C();
      C.definekey('State', 'Country');
      C.definedata('State_Name', 'Country_Name');
      C.definedone();
      C.add(key:'FL',key:'US',data:'Florida',data:'United States');
      C.add(key:'PA',key:'US',data:'Pennsylvania',data:'United States');
      C.add(key:'CA',key:'US',data:'California',data:'United States');
      C.add(key:' ', key:'AU',data:' ',data:'Australia');
      call missing(State_Name, Country_Name);
   end;
   set orion.employee_addresses;
   rc=C.find(key:upcase(State), key:upcase(Country));
   if rc=0;
run;

proc print data=emps(obs=10);
   title;
run;
```

3. **Using the ADD Method and Creating a SAS Data Set from a Hash Object**

   a. Write a DATA step to create a hash object from the values in the table.

   b. After the hash object is created, use the OUTPUT method to create a SAS data set named **continents**.

   c. Print the **continents** data set.

p306s03

```
data _null_;
   length Continent_Name $40 Location $5 Continent_ID 8;
   if _N_=1 then do;
      declare hash C(ordered:'descending');
      C.definekey('Continent_ID');
      C.definedata('Continent_ID', 'Continent_Name', 'Location');
      C.definedone();
      C.add(key:91,data:91,data:'North America',data:'North');
      C.add(key:93,data:93,data:'Europe',data:'North');
      C.add(key:94,data:94,data:'Africa',data:'South');
      C.add(key:95,data:95,data:'Asia', data:'South');
      C.add(key:96,data:96,data:'Australia/Pacific',
                           data:'South');
      call missing(Continent_ID, Continent_Name, Location);
   end;
   C.output(dataset:"continents");
run;

proc print data=continents;
   title 'continents Data Set';
run;

title;
```

4. **Loading the Hash Object from a SAS Data Set**

   a. Write a DATA step to create a data set named **customers** that reads the variables **Customer_ID** and **Customer_Type_ID** from the data set **orion.customer**.

   b. Create a hash object and load it with the data from **orion.customer_type**. The key should be the variable **Customer_Type_ID**, and the data item should be the variable **Customer_Type**.

   c. Use the hash object to look up the **Customer_Type** description.

   d. Print the first 10 observations of the **customers** data set.

p306s04

```
data customers;
   length Customer_Type $40;
   keep Customer_ID Customer_Type_ID Customer_Type;
   if _N_=1 then do;
      declare hash Customer(dataset:'orion.customer_type');
      Customer.definekey('Customer_Type_ID');
      Customer.definedata('Customer_Type');
      Customer.definedone();
      call missing(Customer_Type);
   end;
   set orion.customer;
   if Customer.find()=0;
run;

proc print data=customers(obs=10);
   title 'customers';
run;

/* alternate solution  */
data customers;
   keep Customer_ID Customer_Type_ID Customer_Type;
   if 0 then set orion.customer_type(keep=Customer_Type_ID
                                         Customer_Type);
   if _N_=1 then do;
      declare hash Customer(dataset:'orion.customer_type');
      Customer.definekey('Customer_Type_ID');
      Customer.definedata('Customer_Type');
      Customer.definedone();
      call missing(Customer_Type);
   end;
   set orion.customer;
   if Customer.find()=0;
run;
```

5. **Loading Multiple Hash Objects from SAS Data Sets**

   a. Create a data set named **billing** that reads **Customer_ID**, **Order_Date**, **Product_ID**, **Quantity**, and **Total_Retail_Price** from **orion.order_fact**.

   b. Create a hash object from **orion.product_list** with the key **Product_ID** and the data **Product_Name**.

   c. Create a hash object from **orion.customer_dim** with the key **Customer_ID** and the data **Customer_Country** and **Customer_Name**.

   d. Create a hash object from **orion.country** with the key **Country** and the data **Country_Name**.

   e. Use the three hash objects to look up **Customer_Name**, **Country_Name**, and **Product_Name**.

f. Sort the **billing** data set by **Customer_ID** and **Product_ID** and print the first five observations.

p306s05

```
data billing;
   drop rc1 rc2 rc3 Country;
   if _N_=1 then do;
      if 0 then set orion.product_list(keep=Product_ID
                                       Product_Name);
      if 0 then set orion.customer_dim(keep=Customer_ID
                                       Customer_Country
                                       Customer_Name);
      if 0 then set orion.country(keep=Country Country_Name);

      declare hash Prod(dataset:'orion.product_list');
      Prod.definekey('Product_ID');
      Prod.definedata('Product_Name');
      Prod.definedone();

      declare hash Customer(dataset:'orion.customer_dim');
      Customer.definekey('Customer_ID');
      Customer.definedata('Customer_Country', 'Customer_Name');
      Customer.definedone();

      declare hash C(dataset:'orion.country');
      C.definekey('Country');
      C.definedata('Country_Name');
      C.definedone();
   end;
   set orion.order_fact(keep=Order_Date Quantity Product_ID
                        Total_Retail_Price Customer_ID);

   rc1=Customer.find();
   if rc1=0;
   rc2=Prod.find();
   if rc2=0;
   rc3=C.find(key:Customer_Country);
   if rc3=0;
run;

proc sort data=billing;
   by Customer_ID Product_ID;
run;

proc print data=billing(obs=5);
   var Customer_ID Customer_Name Customer_Country
       Country_Name Product_ID Product_Name Order_Date
       Quantity Total_Retail_Price;
   title1 'Billing Information';
   title2 'Using a HASH Data Step Object';
run;
```

6. Loading the Hash Object from a SAS Data Set and Retrieving Multiple Values

a. Write a DATA step to create a data set named **manager** that reads the **Employee_ID** and **Salary** variables from **orion.employee_payroll**.

b. Create hash objects from the data sets **orion.employee_addresses** and **orion.staff**.

c. Use the hash object from **orion.staff** to return the **Manager_ID** for each **Employee_ID** in **orion.employee_payroll**.

d. Use the hash object from **orion.employee_addresses** to retrieve the names for both employees and the manager for the employees.

e. Print the first five observations of the **manager** data set.

p306s06

```
data manager;
   length Employee_Name EmpName ManagerName $40;
   keep Employee_ID EmpName Manager_ID ManagerName Salary;
   if _N_=1 then do;
      declare hash M(dataset:'orion.staff');
      M.definekey('Employee_ID');
      M.definedata('Manager_ID');
      M.definedone();
      declare hash N(dataset:'orion.employee_addresses');
      N.definekey('Employee_ID');
      N.definedata('Employee_Name');
      N.definedone();
      call missing(Employee_Name);
   end;
   set orion.employee_payroll(keep=Employee_ID Salary);
   rc1=M.find(key:Employee_ID);
   rc2=N.find(key:Employee_ID);
   if rc2=0 then EmpName=Employee_Name;
   else EmpName=' ';
   rc3=N.find(key:Manager_ID);
   if rc3=0 then ManagerName=Employee_Name;
   else ManagerName=' ';
run;

proc print data=manager(obs=5);
   title "Manager Data Set";
run;
```

7. Using a Hiter Object

a. Use the data set **orion.shoe_sales** that contains the variables **Product_ID**, **Product_Name**, and **Total_Retail_Price** to create two data sets named **expensive** and **least_expensive**. The data set **expensive** should contain the five most expensive shoes and the data set **least_expensive** should contain the five least expensive shoes.

p306s07

```
data expensive least_expensive;
   drop i;
   if 0 then set orion.shoe_sales;
   if _N_=1 then do;
      declare hash Shoes(dataset:'orion.shoe_sales',
                         ordered:'descending');
      Shoes.definekey('Total_Retail_Price');
      Shoes.definedata('Total_Retail_Price',
                       'Product_ID', 'Product_Name');
      Shoes.definedone();
      declare hiter S('Shoes');
   end;

   S.first();
   do i=1 to 5;
      output expensive;
      S.next();
   end;

   S.last();
   do i=1 to 5;
     output least_expensive;
     S.prev();
   end;
   stop;
run;
```

b. Print each of the data sets.

p306s07

```
proc print data=expensive;
   title "The Five Most Expensive Shoes";
run;

proc print data=least_expensive;
   title "The Five Least Expensive Shoes";
run;
```

8. Using a Hiter Object

a. Use the data set **orion.shoe_sales** that contains the variables **Product_ID**, **Product_Name**, and **Total_Retail_Price** to create a data set named **shoe_sales** that contains the five most expensive shoes and the five least expensive shoes. The data set should contain a new variable named **Rank** that has the value of 'Top 1' to 'Top 5' for the five most expensive and 'Bottom 1' to 'Bottom 5' for the five least expensive shoes.

b. Print the data set.

p306s08

```
data shoe_sales;
   drop i;
   if 0 then set orion.shoe_sales;
   length Rank $ 8;
   if _N_=1 then do;
      declare hash Shoes(dataset:'orion.shoe_sales',
                         ordered:'descending');
      Shoes.definekey('Total_Retail_Price');
      Shoes.definedata('Total_Retail_Price',
                       'Product_ID', 'Product_Name');
      Shoes.definedone();
      declare hiter S('Shoes');
   end;

   S.first();
   do i=1 to 5;
      Rank=catx(' ', 'Top', i);
      output;
      S.next();
   end;

   S.last();
   do i=1 to 5;
      Rank=catx(' ', 'Bottom', i);
      output;
      S.prev();
   end;
   stop;
run;

proc print data=shoe_sales;
   title "Shoes";
run;
```

9. Using a Hiter Object

a. Use a hiter object to create a data set named **different** that contains unique values of **Customer_ID** and **Order_Type** from the data set named **orion.order_fact**. There should be 100 observations in the data set **different**.

b. Print the first 10 observations of the data set **different**.

p306s09

```
data different;
   drop rc;
   if _N_=1 then do;
      if 0 then set orion.order_fact(keep=Customer_ID
                                            Order_Type);
      declare hash Orders(dataset: 'orion.order_fact',
                          ordered: 'yes');
      declare hiter O_F('Orders');
      orders.defineKey('Customer_ID', 'Order_Type');
      orders.defineData('Customer_ID', 'Order_Type');
      orders.defineDone();
   end;
   rc=O_F.first();
   do while (rc=0);
      output;
      rc=O_F.next();
   end;
   stop;
run;

proc print data=different(obs=10);
   title "No Duplicates";
run;
```

10. Using a Hash Object to Locate the Next Value of a Variable

a. Use the data set **orion.order_fact** that contains the variables **Customer_ID**, **Product_ID**, and **Total_Retail_Price** to create a data set named **next_products**, which contains two new variables, **Next_Product_ID** and **Next_Price**. **Next_Product_ID** is the product that the customer ordered after the current product. **Next_Price** is the price of that product.

b. Print the first 10 observations of **next_products**.

p306s10

```
proc sort data=orion.order_fact(keep=Customer_ID Product_ID
                                      Total_Retail_Price)
          out=order_fact;
   by Customer_ID;
run;

data order_fact;
   set order_fact;
   rename Product_ID=PID Total_Retail_Price=TRP;
   ObsNum=_N_;
run;

data next_products;
   keep Customer_ID Product_ID Total_Retail_Price
        Next_Product_ID Next_Price;
   if _N_=1 then do;
      declare hash Lu(dataset: "order_fact");
      Lu.definekey('ObsNum');
      Lu.definedata('PID', 'TRP');
      Lu.definedone();
      call missing(PID, TRP);
   end;
   set order_fact(rename=(PID=Product_ID
                          TRP=Total_Retail_Price));
   by Customer_ID;
   Obs=ObsNum + 1;
   rc=Lu.find(key:Obs);
   if rc=0 then do;
      Next_Product_ID=PID;
      Next_Price=TRP;
   end;
   if last.Customer_ID then do;
      Next_Product_ID=.;
      Next_Price=.;
   end;
run;

proc print data=next_products(obs=10);
   title 'Next Product Ordered';
   format Next_Price dollar8.2;
run;
```

11. Using a Hash Object to Create a Chain of Values

a. Use the data set **orion.customer** that contains the variables **Country** and **Customer_ID** to create a data set named **customer_list** that contains a new variable, **All_Customers**, which is a list of customers for each country.

p306s11

```
proc sort data=orion.customer(keep=Country Customer_ID)
          out=customers;
   by Country;
run;

data customers;
   set customers;
   ObsNum=_N_;
run;

data customer_list;
   length All_Customers $500;
   if _N_=1 then do;
      declare hash Lu(dataset: "customers");
      Lu.definekey('ObsNum','Country');
      Lu.definedata('Country','Customer_ID');
      Lu.definedone();
   end;
   do until (Last);
      set customers end=Last;
      by Country;
      if first.Country then All_Customers=Customer_ID;
      Obs=ObsNum + 1;
      rc=Lu.find(key:Obs, key:Country);
      if rc=0 then
         All_Customers=catx(', ', All_Customers, Customer_ID);
      else output;
   end;
run;
```

b. Open and submit the program **p306e11** that contains a PROC REPORT step.

p306e11

```
proc report data=customer_list nowd headline headskip;
   column Country All_Customers;
   define Country / width=20 order 'Customer/Country';
   define All_Customers / width=50 flow 'Customer/List';
   break after Country / skip;
run;
```

12. Using a Hash Object to Create a Chain of Values

a. Use the data set **orion.product_dim** to create a data set named **suppliers** that contains two variables, **All_Products** and **All_Names**. **All_Products** is a list of all the **Product_ID** values for each supplier. **All_Names** is a list of the names of all of those products. Ensure that none of the values is truncated.

p306s12

```
proc sort data=orion.product_dim out=product_dim;
   by Supplier_ID;
run;

data product_dim;
   set product_dim;
   ObsNum=_N_;
run;

data suppliers;
   length All_Products $500 All_Names $750;
   if _N_=1 then do;
      declare hash Lu(dataset: "product_dim");
      Lu.definekey('ObsNum', 'Supplier_ID');
      Lu.definedata('Supplier_Name','Product_ID','Product_Name');
      Lu.definedone();
   end;
   do until (Last);
      set product_dim end=Last;
      by Supplier_ID;
      if first.Supplier_ID then do;
         All_Products=Product_ID;
         All_Names=Product_Name;
      end;
      Obs=ObsNum + 1;
      rc=Lu.find(key:Obs, key:Supplier_ID);
      if rc=0 then do;
         All_Products=catx(', ', All_Products, Product_ID);
         All_Names=catx(', ', All_Names, Product_Name);
      end;
      else output;
   end;
run;
```

b. Write a PROC REPORT step to display the data set **suppliers**. Ensure that the entire lists for **All_Products** and **All_Names** are printed.

```
proc report data=suppliers nowd headline headskip ls=132;
   column Supplier_Name All_Products All_Names;
   define Supplier_Name / width=30 order 'Supplier';
   define All_Products / width=30 flow 'Product/List';
   define All_Names / width=50 flow 'Names of/Products';
   break after Supplier_Name / skip;
run;
```

Solutions to Student Activities (Polls/Quizzes)

6.02 Multiple Answer Poll – Correct Answers

Which of the following could be used to assign descriptions to each of the variables `ThisYrType` and `LastYrType`?

a. Merging
(b.) Formats
(c.) IF-THEN/ELSE
d. Arrays

Merging cannot be used because the descriptions for Member Type are not stored in a SAS data set.

Arrays cannot be used because the values of the variables `ThisYrType` and `LastYrType` are not consecutive integers.

17

6.03 Multiple Answer Poll – Correct Answers

When would you **not** use quotation marks around the value for an argument to a method?

(a.) The value is numeric.
b. The value is character.
(c.) The value of a PDV variable is wanted.
d. The value is character or numeric.

32

6.04 Quiz – Correct Answer

Why were the statements and methods that instantiate and load the hash object inside of an IF-THEN/DO group?

```
data mem_type;
   length Code $2 MemberType $40;
   if _N_=1 then do;
      declare hash T();
      T.definekey('Code');
      T.definedata('MemberType');
      T.definedone();
      T.add(key:'10',data:'Orion Club members');
      T.add(key:'20',data:'Orion Club Gold members');
      T.add(key:'30',data:'Internet/Catalog Customers');
   end;
   set orion.europe_customers;
   rc1=T.find(key:ThisYrType);
   if rc1=0 then ThisYrMember=MemberType;
   rc2=T.find(key:LastYrType);
   if rc2=0 then LastYrMember=MemberType;
run;
```

The IF-THEN/DO group ensures that the statements are executed only one time. This saves memory.

41

6.05 Multiple Choice Poll – Correct Answer

What would be the value of `LastYrMember` if the value of `LastYrType` were not found in the hash object (`rc2 ne 0`)?

a. Missing (circled)
b. Orion Club members
c. Orion Club Gold members
d. Internet/Catalog

`LastYrMember` is initialized to missing at the top of the DATA step.

67

6.06 Quiz – Correct Answer

Submit the program **p306a01** and examine the SAS log.
What are the notes about **Code** and **MemberType**?

```
NOTE: Variable Code is uninitialized.
NOTE: Variable MemberType is uninitialized.
```

Why do you get those notes?

The DATA step does not provide an initial value for the variables. The descriptor portion is created by the LENGTH statement, but it does not provide initial values. The variables are not used on the left side of the equal sign (=) in an assignment statement or in a SUM statement, either of which would provide initial values.

71

6.07 Quiz – Correct Answer

As the last statement in the DO group in the program **p306a01**, add the statement:

```
call missing(Code, MemberType);
```

Do the notes disappear?

Yes

73

6.08 Multiple Choice Poll – Correct Answer

The program **p306d02** created the variable `rc` and then dropped it. How can you avoid creating the variable so that you do not have to drop it?

a. Use a WHERE statement or a WHERE= data set option.

b. Use a KEEP= or DROP= data set option in `orion.product_list`.

c. Test the result of the FIND method in the subsetting IF statement.

d. Use a KEEP or DROP statement.

97

6.09 Quiz – Correct Answer

How do you know the lengths of the character variables `Supplier_Name`, `Supplier_Address`, and `Country`?

You use PROC CONTENTS, PROC DATASETS, or the Explorer window to view the descriptor portion of `orion.supplier`.

101

6.10 Quiz – Correct Answer

What is the purpose of the BY statement in the DATA step?

The BY statement creates the variables `FIRST.Customer_ID` and `LAST.Customer_ID`. `LAST.Customer_ID` is used to reset the value of `Next_Order_Date` to missing when the value of `Customer_ID` changes.

153

Solutions to Chapter Review

Chapter Review Answers

1. Describe a hash object.

   A hash object is used in the DATA step to store data in memory and to retrieve data from memory.

2. When is a hash object deleted from memory?

   When the DATA step completes execution

3. What are the two types of DATA step component objects?

   Hash and hiter

4. What is a key component?

   The key component maps key values to data values.

5. What is the purpose of the DECLARE statement?

   To create a hash or hiter object

180

Chapter Review Answers

6. What is the purpose of the FIND method?

   The FIND method is used to retrieve data value(s) based on the value of key(s).

7. What value does the FIND method return when it executes?

   Zero when the FIND method finds the KEY value in the hash object

   Nonzero when the FIND method does not find the KEY value in the hash object

8. Are the key(s) and data item(s) variables in the PDV?

   Yes, the key(s) and data item(s) must be DATA step variables in the PDV.

182

Chapter Review Answers

9. Why are the DECLARE, DEFINEKEY, DEFINEDATA, and DEFINEDONE methods executed in the IF _N_=1 THEN DO group?

   They are executable statements. When they are in the DO group, they are only executed once per DATA step.

10. Is the DEFINEDONE method required?

    Yes

184

Chapter 7 Creating and Using Formats

7.1 Using Formats as Lookup Tables

Objectives

- Create permanent formats.
- Access permanent formats.
- Create formats from SAS data sets.
- Maintain formats.
- Use formats as lookup tables.

3

Table Lookup Using Formats

The appearance of values is controlled by formats.

- Use the FORMAT procedure to define tables that store coded values and the definitions of the codes.
- Reference these user-defined formats when a table lookup operation is needed.

4

Overview of a Format (Review)

A format is similar to stacks of buckets that are referred to by the value of a variable.

Data Value Label

- SAS puts data values and label values in the buckets when the format is used in a FORMAT statement, PUT function, or PUT statement.
- SAS uses a binary search on the **data value** bucket in order to return the value in the **label** bucket.

5

Business Scenario

The data set **orion.country** contains the country code and the country name. Create a format from this data set.

Listing of **orion.country**

Country	Country_ Name	Population	Country_ ID	Continent_ ID	Country_ FormerName
AU	Australia	20,000,000	160	96	
CA	Canada	.	260	91	
DE	Germany	80,000,000	394	93	East/West Germany
IL	Israel	5,000,000	475	95	
TR	Turkey	70,000,000	905	95	
US	United States	280,000,000	926	91	
ZA	South Africa	43,000,000	801	94	

6

Using a Control Data Set to Create a Format

p307d01

```
/* Step 1 */

/* Make a CNTLIN data set containing */
/* the variables FMTNAME, START, and */
/* LABEL.                            */

data country;
   keep Start Label FmtName;
   retain FmtName '$country';
   set orion.country(rename=(Country=Start
                             Country_Name=Label));
run;

proc print data=country noobs;
   title 'Country';
run;

/* Step 2 */
/* Use the data set COUNTRY to     */
/* make the format $country.       */


proc format library=orion.MyFmts cntlin=country fmtlib;
   select $country;
run;

/*******************************************************/
/* If there are missing country values, they can be    */
/* handled by creating the format $extra. This format  */
/* specifically sets missing values to the label       */
/* Unknown and uses the label of the $country          */
/* format for all other values. Notice that a length   */
/* of 30 is provided for the $country format.          */
/* The default would be 40.                            */
/*******************************************************/

proc format library=orion.MyFmts cntlin=country fmtlib;
   value $extra   ' '='Unknown'
             other=[$country30.];
   select $country $extra;
   title '$country format with missing';
run;

proc catalog cat=orion.MyFmts;
   contents;
run;

proc format library=orion.MyFmts fmtlib;
   select $country;
run;
```

Using a Control Data Set to Create a Format

You can create a format from a SAS data set that contains the code/value information (called a *control data set*). Use the CNTLIN= option to read the data and create the format.

General form of CNTLIN= option:

```
PROC FORMAT LIBRARY=libref.catalog
                    CNTLIN=SAS-data-set;
     <SELECT format-name format-name...;>
     <EXCLUDE format-name format-name...;>
RUN;
```

The variables **FmtName**, **Start**, and **Label** are required in order to create a format from a CNTLIN data set.

8

The CNTLIN= data set has the following features:

- must contain the variables **FmtName**, **Start**, and **Label**
- must contain the variable **Type** for character formats, unless the value for **FmtName** begins with a $
- does not require a **Type** variable for numeric formats
- assumes that the ending value of the format range is equal to the value of **Start** if no variable named **End** is found
- does not require the other variables created by the CNTLOUT= option that specify optional attributes
- can be created by a DATA step, another PROC step, or an interactive application such as the VIEWTABLE window
- can be used to create new formats, as well as re-create existing formats
- must be grouped by **FmtName** if multiple formats are specified

Setup for the Poll

The DATA step in **p307d01** creates the **country** data set.

```
data country;
   keep Start Label FmtName;
   retain FmtName '$country';
   set orion.country(rename=(Country=Start
                             Country_Name=Label));
run;
```

The DATA step in **p307d01a** creates an equivalent data set named **country**.

```
data country;
   keep Start Label FmtName;
   FmtName='$country';
   set orion.country;
   Start=Country;
   Label=Country_Name;
run;
```

10

7.01 Multiple Choice Poll

Which program should be more efficient?

a. p307d01
b. p307d01a
c. They should be equally efficient.

11

Nesting Formats

In the VALUE statement, you can specify that the format use a second format as the formatted value.

value=[*existing-format*]

Enclose the format name in square brackets:

```
proc format library=orion.MyFmts
            cntlin=country fmtlib;
   value $extra ' '='Unknown'
                other=[$country30.];
   select $country $extra;
   title '$country format with missing';
run;
```

13 p307d01

Avoid nesting formats for more than one level. The resource requirements can increase dramatically with each additional level.

How Formats Are Stored

Formats are stored as SAS catalog entries.

- SAS catalogs are special SAS files that store many different kinds of information in smaller units called *entries*.
- A single SAS catalog can contain many different catalog entries.

SAS Catalogs

work.formats

orion.formats

orion.MyFmts

Store frequently used formats in permanent catalogs.

14

Catalog entries have four-level names: *libref.catalog.entry-name.type*.

The *type* for character formats is **formatc**. The *type* for numeric formats is **format**.

Where Formats Are Stored

Without the LIBRARY= option, formats are stored in the **`work.formats`** catalog and exist for the duration of the SAS session.

```
PROC FORMAT;
```

If the LIBRARY= option specifies only a *libref*, formats are stored permanently in ***libref*.formats**.

PROC FORMAT LIBRARY=*libref*;

If the LIBRARY= option specifies *libref.catalog*, formats are stored permanently in that catalog.

PROC FORMAT LIBRARY=*libref.catalog*;

15

Documenting Formats

You can use the SAS Explorer Window to view the formats stored in a catalog.

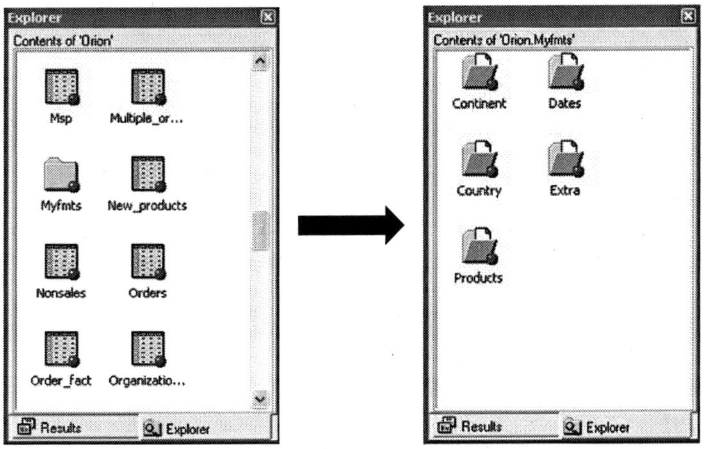

16

Documenting Formats

The CATALOG procedure manages entries in SAS catalogs.

Selected capabilities of PROC CATALOG include the following:

- creating a listing of the contents of a catalog
- copying a catalog or selected entries within a catalog
- renaming or deleting entries within a catalog
- modifying the description of a catalog entry

17

The CATALOG Procedure

```
proc catalog cat=orion.MyFmts;
   contents;
run;
```

Output

```
                    Contents of Catalog ORION.MYFMTS

# Name      Type          Create Date      Modified Date Description
--------------------------------------------------------------------
1 CONTINENT FORMAT  04Jan08:07:48:13    04Jan08:07:48:13
2 DATES     FORMAT  10Dec08:15:26:29    10Dec08:15:26:29
3 COUNTRY   FORMATC 10Dec08:16:04:50    10Dec08:16:04:50
4 EXTRA     FORMATC 10Dec08:15:55:45    10Dec08:15:55:45
5 PRODUCTS  FORMATC 09Dec07:19:11:06    09Dec07:19:11:06
```

18

p307d01

General form of the CATALOG procedure:

PROC CATALOG CATALOG=<*libref.*>*catalog* <*options*>;
  CONTENTS <OUT=*SAS-data-set*> <FILE=*fileref*>;
  COPY OUT=<*libref.*>*catalog* <*options*>;
    SELECT *entry(s)* </ *ENTRYTYPE=etype*>;
    EXCLUDE *entry(s)* </ *ENTRYTYPE=etype*>;
  DELETE *entry(s)* </ *ENTRYTYPE=etype*>;
<**RUN;**>
QUIT;

Documenting Formats

You can use the FMTLIB option in the PROC FORMAT statement to document the format.

```
proc format library=orion.MyFmts fmtlib;
   select $country;
run;
```

FORMAT NAME: $COUNTRY LENGTH: 13 NUMBER OF VALUES: 7 MIN LENGTH: 1 MAX LENGTH: 40 DEFAULT LENGTH 13 FUZZ: 0		
START	END	LABEL (VER. V7|V8 05MAY2009:12:34:42)
AU	AU	Australia
CA	CA	Canada
DE	DE	Germany
IL	IL	Israel
TR	TR	Turkey
US	US	United States
ZA	ZA	South Africa

19 p307d01

General form of the FMTLIB option:

> **PROC FORMAT** LIBRARY=*libref.catalog* **FMTLIB;**
> <**SELECT** *format-name format-name...*;>
> <**EXCLUDE** *format-name format-name...*;>
> **RUN;**

You can use either the SELECT or EXCLUDE statement to process specific formats rather than an entire catalog.

Using Formats

You can reference formats in any of the following:

- FORMAT statements
- PUT statements
- PUT functions in assignment, WHERE, or IF statements
- FORMAT= options

20

Using Formats

When a format is referenced, SAS does the following:

- loads the format from the catalog entry into memory
- performs a binary search on values in the table to execute a lookup
- returns a single result for each lookup

21

7.02 Quiz

Submit the program **p307a01**.

What error messages do you see in the SAS log?

```
data supplier_country;
   set orion.shoe_vendors;

Country_Name=put(Supplier_Country,$country.);
run;

proc freq data=orion.employee_addresses;
   tables Country;
   format Country $extra.;
run;
```

23

7.03 Quiz

1. Add the following OPTIONS statement to **p307a01** and resubmit the program. What is the result?

```
options nofmterr;
```

2. Replace the current OPTIONS statement with the following statement and resubmit the program. What is the result?

```
options fmterr fmtsearch=(orion orion.MyFmts);
```

25

Using the NOFMTERR System Option

By default, the FMTERR system option is in effect. If you use a format that SAS cannot load, SAS issues an error message and stops processing the step.

To prevent the default action, change the system option FMTERR to NOFMTERR.

OPTIONS FMTERR | NOFMTERR;

28

FMTERR	specifies that when SAS cannot find a specified variable format, it generates an error message and does not allow default substitution to occur.
NOFMTERR	replaces missing formats with the w. or $w. default format, issues a note, and continues processing.

Using the FMTSEARCH= System Option

To use permanent formats or to search multiple catalogs, use the FMTSEARCH= system option to identify the catalog(s) to be searched for the format(s).

General form of the FMTSEARCH= system option:

OPTIONS FMTSEARCH=(*item-1 item-2...item-n*);

29

Using the FMTSEARCH= System Option

```
options fmtsearch=(orion orion.MyFmts);
```

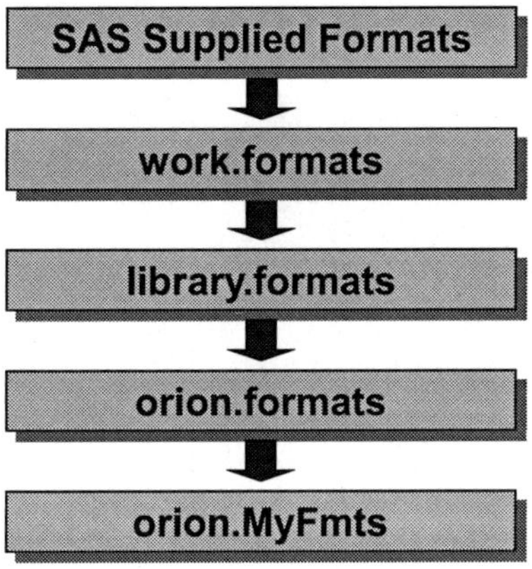

30

Because **orion** is a libref without a catalog name, **formats** is assumed to be the catalog name.

SAS supplied formats are always searched first. The **work.formats** catalog is always searched second, unless it appears in the FMTSEARCH list. If the **library** libref is assigned, the **library.formats** catalog is searched after **work.formats** and before anything else in the FMTSEARCH list, unless it appears in the list. To assign the **library** libref, use the code shown below:

```
libname library 'SAS-data-library-containing-format-catalog';
```

Maintaining Formats

To maintain formats, perform one of the following tasks:

- Edit the PROC FORMAT code that created the original format.
- Create a SAS data set from the format, edit the data set, and use the CNTLIN= option to re-create the format.

31

Maintaining Permanent Formats

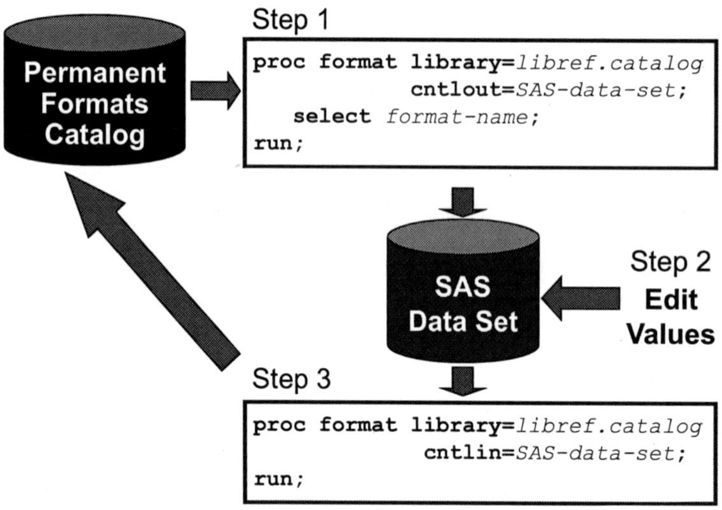

32

When the data set created by the CNTLOUT= option will be used as a CNTLIN= data set in a subsequent FORMAT procedure step, the minimum variables that must be included are **START**, **END**, **FMTNAME**, and **LABEL**.

Maintaining Permanent Formats

p307d02

```
/* Step 1 */

proc format library=orion.MyFmts cntlout=countryfmt;
   select $country;
run;

proc print data=countryfmt;
run;

/* Step 2 */

proc sql;
   insert into countryfmt(FmtName, Start, End, Label)
      values('$country', 'BR', 'BR', 'Brazil')
      values('$country', 'CH', 'CH', 'Switzerland')
      values('$country', 'MX', 'MX', 'Mexico');
quit;

/* Step 3 */

proc format library=orion.MyFmts cntlin=countryfmt fmtlib;
   select $country;
run;

/* to add Missing in the $extra Format */

proc format library=orion.MyFmts cntlin=countryfmt fmtlib;
   value $extra    ' '='Unknown'
                other=[$country30.];
   select $country $extra;
   title '$country format with missing';
run;
```

You can use either the SELECT or EXCLUDE statement to process specific formats rather than an entire catalog.

The variables in the output control data set completely describe all aspects of each format or informat, including optional settings. The output control data set contains one observation per range per format or informat in the specified catalog.

The CNTLOUT data set contains the following variables:

DEFAULT	a numeric variable that indicates the default length for format or informat
END	a character variable that gives the range's ending value
EEXCL	a character variable that indicates whether the range's ending value is excluded
FILL	for picture formats, a numeric variable whose value is the value of the FILL= option
FMTNAME	a character variable whose value is the format or informat name
FUZZ	a numeric variable whose value is the value of the FUZZ= option
HLO	a character variable that contains range information about the format or informat in the form of different letters that can appear in any combination
LABEL	a character variable whose value is the informatted or formatted value or the name of an existing informat or format
LENGTH	a numeric variable whose value is the value of the LENGTH= option
MAX	a numeric variable whose value is the value of the MAX= option
MIN	a numeric variable whose value is the value of the MIN= option
MULT	a numeric variable whose value is the value of the MULT= option
NOEDIT	for picture formats, a numeric variable whose value indicates whether the NOEDIT option is in effect
PREFIX	for picture formats, a character variable whose value is the value of the PREFIX= option
SEXCL	a character variable that indicates whether the range's starting value is excluded
START	a character variable that gives the range's starting value
TYPE	a character variable that indicates the type of format

Maintaining Permanent Formats

General form of PROC FORMAT with the CNTLOUT= option:

```
PROC FORMAT LIBRARY=libref.catalog
                    CNTLOUT=SAS-data-set;
     <SELECT format-name format-name...;>
     <EXCLUDE format-name format-name...;>
RUN;
```

34

Advantages and Disadvantages of Formats

Advantages	Disadvantages
familiarity	memory requirements to load the entire format for the binary search
no need to create additional data	use of only one variable for the table lookup
can be used with procedures	requires more disk space to store a format than to store the equivalent SAS data set
range search for both character and numeric	
binary search through lookup table	
centralized maintenance	
use of multiple PUT functions to create multiple variables	
can be stored permanently	

35

Comparing Arrays, Hash Objects, and Formats

Array	Hash Object	Format
The subscript value(s) must be numeric.	The keys can be character, numeric, or both.	Ranges can be character or numeric.
One data value can be associated with the subscript value(s).	Multiple data items can be associated with the key value.	Only one data value can be associated with a label.
An array uses less memory than a hash object.	A hash object uses more memory than an array.	A format requires more memory than a hash object.
The size of the array is determined at compilation time.	The size of the hash object is determined at execution time.	The memory requirement for the format is determined when the format is used.
Subscript values must be consecutive integers.	The keys do not have to be consecutive or sorted.	Formats support mapping a range of values or a list of discrete values to one value.
An array selects values by direct access based on the subscript value.	A hash object uses a hash function for the lookup process.	A format uses a binary search for the lookup process.
Arrays can only be used in the DATA step.	Hash objects can only be used in the DATA step.	Formats can be used in DATA and PROC steps.

36

To estimate the amount of memory used by a format, refer to Usage Note 23084 at support.sas.com/kb/23/084.html.

Exercises

Level 1

1. Creating Formats with Values from a SAS Data Set

The data set **orion.continent** contains the **Continent_ID** and the **Continent_Name** variables.

Obs	Continent_ ID	Continent_Name
1	91	North America
2	93	Europe
3	94	Africa
4	95	Asia
5	96	Australia/Pacific

a. Create a CNTLIN data set named **continent** that reads the data from **orion.continent** and contains the variables **FmtName**, **Start**, and **Label**. The name of the format should be CONTINENT.

b. Use the CNTLIN= option to create a format from the **continent** data set and store the format in the **orion.MyFmts** catalog.

c. Open the program **p306e01c** and submit it. The program should execute successfully with no errors in the SAS log.

p307e01c

```
/*******************/
/* Part C          */
/* Use continent.  */
/*******************/

data countries;
   set orion.country;
   Continent_Name=put(Continent_ID, continent.);
run;

proc print data=countries(obs=10);
   title 'Continent Names';
run;
```

d. Open the program **p307e01d**.

p307e01d

```
proc sql;
   insert into continentfmt(fmtname, Start, End, Label)
      values('continent', '90', '90', 'Antarctica')
      values('continent', '92', '92', 'South America');
quit;
```

1) Before the PROC SQL step, add a PROC FORMAT step with the CNTLOUT= option to create a control output data set named **continentfmt** from the CONTINENT format.

2) Submit the program to add new observations to the **continentfmt** data set.

3) Add another PROC FORMAT step with the CNTLIN= option to read the **continentfmt** data set and re-create the CONTINENT format. Use the FMTLIB option in this PROC FORMAT step to ensure that the new values were added to the format CONTINENT.

Level 2

2. Creating Formats with Inclusive Ranges from a SAS Data Set

The data set **orion.ages** contains three variables: **First_Age**, **Last_Age**, and **Description**.

Partial Listing of **orion.ages**

Obs	First_ Age	Last_Age	Description
1	15	30	15-30 years
2	30	45	31-45 years
3	45	60	46-60 years
4	60	75	61-75 years

a. Create a format from the **orion.ages** data set and store it permanently in the **orion.MyFmts** catalog. Use the appropriate option to view the values in the format.

b. Write a DATA step to create a data set named **sales** that reads the **Employee_ID** and **Birth_Date** variables from the **orion.sales** data set. Create a new variable named **Age** that is the employee's age as of the current date and another new variable named **Age_Cat** that is the value of the variable **Age** using the AGE format.

c. Print the first five observations of the **sales** data set to confirm that the new variables were created correctly.

PROC PRINT Output (As of May 5, 2009)

Sales Data Set

Obs	Employee_ID	Birth_ Date	Age	Age_Cat
1	120102	11AUG1969	39	31-45 years
2	120103	22JAN1949	60	46-60 years
3	120121	02AUG1944	64	61-75 years
4	120122	27JUL1954	54	46-60 years
5	120123	28SEP1964	44	31-45 years

Level 3

3. Creating Formats with Exclusive Ranges from a SAS Data Set

The data set **orion.ages_mod** contains three variables: **First_Age**, **Last_Age**, and **Description**.

Partial Listing of **orion.ages_mod**

Obs	First_ Age	Last_Age	Description
1	15	30	15-29 years
2	30	45	30-44 years
3	45	60	45-59 years
4	60	75	60-75 years

a. Create a format named **ages_mod** from the **orion.ages_mod** data set and store it permanently in the **orion.MyFmts** catalog. Use the appropriate option to view the values in the format.

> The value of the **Last_Age** variable is not to be included in the **Description** variable. Use SAS Help or SAS OnlineDoc to investigate the **EEXCL** variable that is required to get the correct results for this exercise.

b. Write a DATA step to create a data set named **sales** that reads the **Employee_ID** and **Birth_Date** variables from the **orion.sales** data set. Create a new variable named **Age** that is the employee's age as of the current date and another new variable named **Age_Cat** that is the value of the variable **Age** using the AGES_MOD format.

c. Print the first five observations of the **sales** data set to confirm that the new variables were created correctly.

PROC PRINT Output (as of May 5, 2009)

Sales Data Set

Obs	Employee_ID	Birth_ Date	Age	Age_Cat
1	120102	11AUG1969	39	30-44 years
2	120103	22JAN1949	60	45-59 years
3	120121	02AUG1944	64	60-75 years
4	120122	27JUL1954	54	45-59 years
5	120123	28SEP1964	44	30-44 years

7.2 Using a Picture Format (Self-Study)

Objectives

- Use a picture format to format numeric data.

40

Using Picture Formats

Formatting numeric data often involves inserting special characters into the numeric values.

The following illustrates the original numeric value and the required formatted value.

Original Numeric Data Value	Formatted Value
5552134567	(555)213-4567
25	25%
-25.12	25.12DR
213	**********213

41

Picture Formats

Some uses for picture formats include the following:

- displaying numbers with leading zeros (0005)
- filling numbers with special characters (***5)
- inserting *message characters* into numbers, such as parentheses (for phone numbers), percent signs, and minus signs
- customizing a date, time, or datetime display with directives
- formatting currency when there is no SAS format available

✎ Picture formats consist of placeholders for digits and special characters to be inserted into the digits.

42

Business Scenario

The data set **orion.phone** contains the phone number of the employees from the United States and Australia. The phone number is stored in a numeric variable named **Phone**. Create a data set that contains the phone number in the correct formatted form.

Partial Listing of **orion.phone**

Employee_ ID	Phone_Type	Country	Phone
120101	Home	AU	61255551849
120101	Work	AU	61255510001
120102	Home	AU	61355559700
. . .	. . .	. . .	. . .
121147	Home	US	13055510423
121148	Work	US	13055554118
121148	Home	US	13055510424

43

Using a PICTURE Format

```
proc format;
   picture us_phone
      low-high='9 (999) 999-9999';
   picture au_phone
      low-high='99 (9) 9999-9999';
run;

data phone_list;
   set orion.phone;
   if Country='AU' then
      Phone_Number=put(Phone,au_phone.);
   else if Country='US' then
      Phone_Number=put(Phone,us_phone.);
run;
```

44 p307d03

7.04 Quiz

Open and submit the program **p307d03**.

1. How are the Australian phone numbers displayed?

2. How are the United States phone numbers displayed?

46

Using a PICTURE Format

Partial Output

```
                          Phone Numbers Formatted

       Employee_    Phone_
Obs       ID         Type     Country       Phone          Phone_Number

  1     120101       Home       AU       61255551849    61 (2) 5555-1849
  2     120101       Work       AU       61255510001    61 (2) 5551-0001
  3     120102       Home       AU       61355559700    61 (3) 5555-9700
  4     120102       Work       AU       61355510002    61 (3) 5551-0002
  5     120103       Home       AU       61255553998    61 (2) 5555-3998

<observations removed>

913     121146       Work       US       12155550546    1 (215) 555-0546
914     121146       Home       US       12155510422    1 (215) 551-0422
915     121147       Work       US       13055555653    1 (305) 555-5653
916     121147       Home       US       13055510423    1 (305) 551-0423
917     121148       Work       US       13055554118    1 (305) 555-4118
918     121148       Home       US       13055510424    1 (305) 551-0424
```

49

The PICTURE Statement

The PICTURE statement in PROC FORMAT defines a pattern for data values.

```
PROC FORMAT;
     PICTURE name
     value-or-range-1 <..., value-or-range-n>='picture';
RUN;
```

50

Value Ranges in the PICTURE Statement

PICTURE *name range='picture' <options>*;

The *picture* consists of the following:

- Digit selectors that are numeric characters (0 through 9) that define positions for numeric values
  - If you use a digit selector of 0, the format suppresses leading zeros in variable values. If you use a digit selector of 1 through 9, then the format pattern displays numbers that are padded on the left with zeroes.
- Message characters that are nonnumeric characters that print as specified in the picture
  - Using the PREFIX= option, specify nonnumeric characters to be printed before the numeric digits.

51

Using a PICTURE Format

```
proc format;
   picture us_phone
      low-high='9 (999) 999-9999';
   picture au_phone
      low-high='99 (9) 9999-9999';
run;
```

Variable: Country	Variable: Phone	Variable: Phone_Number
AU	61255551849	61 (2) 5555-1849
US	12155555906	1 (215) 555-5906

52

p307d03

Using a PICTURE Format

```
proc format;
   picture us_phone
      low-high='9 (999) 999-9999';
   picture us_phone_withzeros
      low-high='0 (000) 000-9999';
run;
```

Phone	Displayed with us_phone.	Displayed with us_phone_withzeros.
12155555906	1 (215) 555-5906	1 (215) 555-5906
2155555906	0 (215) 555-5906	215) 555-5906
5555906	0 (000) 555-5906	555-5906
5906	0 (000) 000-5906	5906

53 p307d04

To insert the left parenthesis in the phone number 2155555906, use the following PROC FORMAT step:

```
proc format;
   picture us_phone_withzeros
      low-<10000000='0 (000) 000-9999'
      10000000-high='0 (000) 000-9999' (prefix='(');
run;
```

Using Digit Selectors

```
proc format;
   picture padz   low - high='999,999.99';
   picture nopad  low - high='000,000.00';
   picture mixed  low - high='000,009.99';
run;
```

Variable Value	Displayed with padz.	Displayed with nopad.	Displayed with mixed.
2381.6	002,381.60	2,381.60	2,381.60
-12.233	000,012.23	12.23	12.23
.38	000,000.38	38	0.38
12345	012,345.00	12,345.00	12,345.00
123456	123,456.00	123,456.00	123,456.00
45.987	000,045.98	45.98	45.98

All data values treated as positive values

Decimal not used with zero digit selectors

54 p307d05

7.05 Quiz

Submit the program **p307a02**. How many digits are displayed to the right of the decimal point?

```
proc format;
   picture rtfmt 0 - high='999,999.9999';
   picture wzrfmt 0 - high='000,009.0000';
run;
```

56

7.06 Quiz

Submit the program **p307a03**. How many digits are printed to the left of the decimal point?

```
proc format;
   picture small low - high='0,009.99';
   picture large low - high='000,009.99';
run;
```

58

Picture Format Examples

Data Values	Picture Format	Display As...
-12.233	`bank low-<0='009.00DR'` `0-high='009.00CR'`	12.23DR
-12.233	`sign low-<0='009.00' (prefix="-")` `0-high='009.00'`	-12.23
45.987	`numrd(round) other= '000,009.99'`	45.99
24.319	`pctrnd(round) low-high=' 009.99%'`	24.32%
24.319	`pct low-high=' 009.99%'`	24.31%

.38
1.38
	`getdec`
	`0-<1='99' (prefix='.' mult=100)`
	`1-high='00.99';`
		
		.38
		1.38

60

p307d06

Selected Options in the PICTURE Statement

To Do This...	Use This...
Specify a number to multiply the variable's value by before it is formatted	MULTIPLIER=
Specify multiple pictures for a given value or range and for overlapping ranges	MULTILABEL
Store values or ranges in the order that you define them	NOTSORTED
Round the value to the nearest display value before formatting	ROUND
Specify a character that completes the formatted value	FILL=
Specify a character prefix for the formatted value	PREFIX=

61

Inserting Characters

```
proc format;
   picture paren low - high='(999)999-9999';
   picture nospace low-high='999)999-9999'
                            (prefix= '(' );
   picture space low-high=' 999)999-9999'
                            (prefix= '(' );
run;
```

Value	Displayed with paren.	Displayed with nospace.	Displayed with space.
8005550202	800)555-0202	800)555-0202	(800)555-0202

You must ensure that the length of the format is large enough for the prefix characters and all the possible digits in your variable value. Otherwise, the formatted value might not appear properly.

62 p307d07

Date, Time, and Datetime Directives

Using special directives, it is possible to specify a picture format for extensive combinations of dates and times.

- Date, time, and datetime directives start with a percent sign (%).
- Directives are case sensitive.
- Because of the % in the directive, picture format labels that include these directives should be enclosed in single quotation marks.
- If you intend to use the date, time, or datetime directives, you must also specify the DATATYPE= option in the PICTURE statement.

PICTURE *name*
    range='*picture*' (DATATYPE=DATE | TIME | DATETIME);

63

Date Directives

Consider this date value: -3334 (November 15, 1950).

To Display	Use This Directive	Variable Display
Abbreviated weekday name	%a	Wed
Full weekday name	%A	Wednesday
Abbreviated month name	%b	NOV
Full month name	%B	November
Month value as decimal	%m	11
Day of the month (decimal)	%d	15
Year without century	%y	50
Year with century	%Y	1950

64

Date Directives

```
proc format;
   picture longdate (default=30)
     '01jan1950'd-'31dec2004'd='%A, %B %d,'
     (datatype=date);
   picture noleadz
     '01jan1950'd-'31dec2004'd='%y~%m~%d'
     (datatype=date);
   picture leadzero
     '01jan1950'd-'31dec2004'd='%0y~%0m~%0d'
     (datatype=date);
run;
```

SAS Date Value	Displayed with longdate.	Displayed with noleadz.	Displayed with leadzero.
-3334	Wednesday, November 15,	50~11~15	50~11~15
15101	Sunday, May 6,	1~5~6	01~05~06

65

p307d08

Exercises

Level 1

4. Using a PICTURE Format for Numeric Data

a. Write a PROC FORMAT step with the PICTURE statement to format the value of the variable **Order_ID** so that it appears as follows:

Variable Value	Formatted Value
1230058123	12-30-05-8123

b. Print the first five observations of the **orion.order_fact** data set to validate the formatted values of the variable.

PROC PRINT Output

```
                Formatted Values of Order_ID

                  Obs       Order_ID

                   1     12-30-05-8123
                   2     12-30-08-0101
                   3     12-30-10-6883
                   4     12-30-14-7441
                   5     12-30-31-5085
```

Level 2

5. Using a PICTURE Format for Currency Data

a. Write a PROC FORMAT step with the PICTURE statement to format the value of the variable **Total_Revenue_Price** so that it appears as follows:

Variable Value	Formatted Value
27.80	kr. 27,80 eks.moms

b. Print the first five observations of the **`orion.denmark_customers`** data set to validate the formatted values of the variable.

PROC PRINT Output

```
                    Using a PICTURE Format

               Obs     Total_Retail_Price

                1      kr. 27,80 eks.moms
                2     kr. 196,20 eks.moms
                3      kr. 97,60 eks.moms
                4      kr. 65,60 eks.moms
                5     kr. 138,20 eks.moms
```

Additional information about the Danish Kroner formatting:

Abbreviation	Meaning
`eks`	**`eksklusiv`** (exclusive)
`moms`	**`MerOMsætningsafgift`** (value added tax)

Level 3

6. Using a PICTURE Format for Date Variables

a. Write a PROC FORMAT step with the PICTURE statement to format the value of the variable **`Order_Date`** so that it appears as follows:

Variable Value	Formatted Value
15716	Saturday, 1.11.2003

b. Print the first five observations of the **`orion.order_fact`** data set to validate the formatted values of the variable.

PROC PRINT Output

```
  Obs           Order_Date

   1       Saturday, 1.11.2003
   2      Wednesday, 1.15.2003
   3         Monday, 1.20.2003
   4        Tuesday, 1.28.2003
   5       Thursday, 2.27.2003
```

7.3 Chapter Review

Chapter Review

1. What PROC FORMAT statement option is used to create a permanent format?

2. What PROC FORMAT statement option is used to create a format from a SAS data set?

3. What variables are required to create a format from a SAS data set?

68

continued...

Chapter Review

4. What PROC FORMAT option is used to view the contents of a format?

5. What PROC FORMAT option is used to create a SAS data set from a format?

6. What is the SAS system option that establishes the search path when a format is used?

70

7.4 Solutions

Solutions to Exercises

1. **Creating Formats with Values from a SAS Data Set**

   a. Create a CNTLIN data set named **continent** that reads the data from **orion.continent** and contains the variables **FmtName**, **Start**, and **Label**. The name of the format should be CONTINENT.

   p307s01

```
/*********************/
/* Part A           */
/* Make continent   */
/*********************/

data continent;
   keep Start Label FmtName;
   retain FmtName 'continent';
   set orion.continent(rename=(Continent_ID=Start
                                Continent_Name=Label));
run;

proc print data=continent(obs=10) noobs;
   title 'Continent';
run;
```

   b. Use the CNTLIN= option to create a format from the **continent** data set and store the format in the **orion.MyFmts** catalog.

   p307s01

```
/*************************************/
/* Part B                            */
/* Use continent to create format.   */
/*************************************/

proc format library=orion.MyFmts cntlin=continent fmtlib;
   select continent;
   title 'Continent format';
run;
```

   c. Open the program **p307e01c** and submit it. The program should execute successfully with no errors in the SAS log.

   d. Open the program **p307e01d**.

      1) Before the PROC SQL step, add a PROC FORMAT step with the CNTLOUT= option to create a control output data set named **continentfmt** from the CONTINENT format.

p307s01

```
/*********************/
/* Part D          */
/* Update Continent.*/
/*********************/

proc format library=orion.MyFmts cntlout=continentfmt;
   select continent;
run;
```

2) Submit the program to add new observations to the **ContinentFmt** data set.

3) Add another PROC FORMAT step with the CNTLIN= option to read the **ContinentFmt** data set and re-create the CONTINENT format. Use the FMTLIB option in this PROC FORMAT step to ensure that the new values are added to the CONTINENT format.

p307s01

```
proc format library=orion.MyFmts cntlin=continentfmt
            fmtlib;
   select continent;
run;
```

2. Creating Formats with Inclusive Ranges from a SAS Data Set

a. Create a format from the **orion.ages** data set and store it permanently in the **orion.MyFmts** catalog. Use the appropriate option to view the values in the format.

p307s02

```
data ages;
   set orion.ages (rename=(First_Age=Start Last_Age=End
                             Description=Label));
   retain FmtName 'ages';
run;

proc format library=orion.MyFmts fmtlib cntlin=ages;
   select ages;
run;
```

b. Write a DATA step to create a data set named **sales** that reads the **Employee_ID** and **Birth_Date** variables from the **orion.sales** data set. Create a new variable named **Age** that is the employee's age as of the current date and another new variable named **Age_Cat** that is the value of the variable **Age** using the AGE format.

p307s02

```
data sales;
   set orion.sales(keep=Employee_ID Birth_Date);
   Age=int(yrdif(Birth_Date, today(), 'ACT/ACT'));
   Age_Cat=put(Age, ages.);
run;
```

c. Print the first five observations of the **sales** data set to confirm that the new variables were created correctly.

p307s02

```
proc print data=sales(obs=5);
   format Birth_Date date9.;
   title 'Sales Data Set';
run;
```

3. **Creating Formats with Exclusive Ranges from a SAS Data Set**

a. Create a format named **ages_mod** from the **orion.ages_mod** data set and store it permanently in the **orion.MyFmts** catalog. Use the appropriate option to view the values in the format.

p307s03

```
data ages_mod;
   set orion.ages_mod(rename=(First_Age=Start Last_Age=End
                              Description=Label));
   retain fmtname 'ages_mod';
   EEXCL='Y';
run;

proc format library=orion.MyFmts fmtlib cntlin=ages_mod;
   select ages_mod;
run;
```

b. Write a DATA step to create a data set named **sales** that reads the **Employee_ID** and **Birth_Date** variables from the **orion.sales** data set. Create a new variable named **Age** that is the employee's age as of the current date, and another new variable named **Age_Cat** that is the value of the variable **Age** using the AGES_MOD format.

p307s03

```
options fmtsearch=(orion.MyFmts);

data sales;
   set orion.sales(keep=Employee_ID Birth_Date);
   Age=int(yrdif(Birth_Date, today(), 'ACT/ACT'));
   Age_Cat=put(Age, ages_mod.);
run;
```

c. Print the first five observations of the **sales** data set to confirm that the new variables were created correctly.

p307s03

```
proc print data=sales(obs=5);
   format birth_date date9.;
   title 'Sales Data Set';
run;
```

4. Using a PICTURE Format for Numeric Data

a. Write a PROC FORMAT step with the PICTURE statement to format the value of the variable **Order_ID** so that it appears as follows:

Variable Value	Formatted Value
1230058123	12-30-05-8123

b. Print the first five observations of the **orion.order_fact** data set to validate the formatted values of the variable.

p307s04

```
proc format;
   picture product low - high='99-99-99-9999';
run;

proc print data=orion.order_fact(obs=5);
   format Order_ID product.;
   var Order_ID;
   title "Formatted Values of Order_ID";
run;
```

5. Using a PICTURE Format for Currency Data

a. Write a PROC FORMAT step with the PICTURE statement to format the value of the variable **Total_Revenue_Price** so that it appears as follows:

Variable Value	Formatted Value
27.80	kr. 27,80 eks.moms

b. Print the first five observations of the **orion.denmark_customers** data set to validate the formatted values of the variable.

p307s05

```
proc format;
   picture kroner 0 - high='000.009,99 eks.moms' (mult=100
                                        prefix='kr. ');
run;

proc print data=orion.denmark_customers(obs=5);
   format Total_Retail_Price kroner.;
   title 'Using a PICTURE Format';
   var Total_Retail_Price;
run;
```

6. Using a PICTURE Format for Date Variables

a. Write a PROC FORMAT step with the PICTURE statement to format the value of the variable **Order_Date** so that it appears as follows:

Variable Value	Formatted Value
15716	Saturday, 1.11.2003

b. Print the first five observations of the **orion.order_fact** data set to validate the formatted values of the variable.

p307s06

```
proc format;
   picture day_of_week(default=21) low - high='%A, %m.%d.%Y'
                                          (datatype=date);
run;

proc print data=orion.order_fact(obs=5);
   title 'Day of Week Format';
   format Order_Date day_of_week.;
   var Order_Date;
run;
```

Solutions to Student Activities (Polls/Quizzes)

7.01 Multiple Choice Poll – Correct Answer

Which program should be more efficient?

a. p307d01 (circled)
b. p307d01a
c. They should be equally efficient.

12

7.02 Quiz – Correct Answer

Submit the program **p307a01**.

What error messages do you see in the SAS log?

```
24   data supplier_country;
25      set orion.shoe_vendors;
26      Country_Name=put(Supplier_Country,$country.);
                                          ---------
                                          48
ERROR 48-59: The format $COUNTRY was not found or could not be loaded.

27   run;

NOTE: The SAS System stopped processing this step because of errors.
WARNING: The data set WORK.SUPPLIER_COUNTRY may be incomplete.  When this step was stopped
         there were 0 observations and 13 variables.
WARNING: Data set WORK.SUPPLIER_COUNTRY was not replaced because this step was stopped.
NOTE: DATA statement used (Total process time):
      real time           0.00 seconds
      cpu time            0.00 seconds
28
29   proc freq data=orion.employee_addresses;
30      tables Country;
31      format Country $extra.;
ERROR: The format $EXTRA was not found or could not be loaded.
32   run;
```

24

7.03 Quiz – Correct Answer

1. Add the following OPTIONS statement to **p307a01** and resubmit the program. What is the result?

```
options nofmterr;
```

All of the procedure steps were executed with no warnings or errors in the SAS log. The user-defined formats *were not* applied.

2. Replace the current OPTIONS statement with the following statement and resubmit the program. What is the result?

```
options fmterr fmtsearch=(orion orion.MyFmts);
```

All of the procedure steps were executed with no warnings or errors in the SAS log. The user-defined formats were applied.

27

Modified p307a01s for Quiz 7.03, Step 1

```
options nofmterr;

data supplier_country;
   set orion.shoe_vendors;
   Country_Name=put(Supplier_Country,$country.);
run;

proc freq data=orion.employee_addresses;
   tables Country;
   format Country $extra.;
run;
```

Modified p307a01s for Quiz 7.03. Step 2

```
options fmtsearch=(orion orion.MyFmts);

data supplier_country;
   set orion.shoe_vendors;
   Country_Name=put(Supplier_Country,$country.);
run;

proc freq data=orion.employee_addresses;
   tables Country;
   format Country $extra.;
run;
```

7.04 Quiz – Correct Answer

Open and submit the program **p307d03**.

1. How are the Australian phone numbers displayed?

   Two digits, a blank, one digit in parentheses, a blank, four digits, a dash, four digits.

   61 (2) 5555-1849

2. How are the United States phone numbers displayed?

   The digit 1, a blank, three digits in parentheses, a blank, three digits, a dash, four digits:
   1 (215) 555-0546

7.05 Quiz – Correct Answer

Submit the program **p307a02**. How many digits are displayed to the right of the decimal point?

```
proc format;
   picture rtfmt 0 - high='999,999.9999';
   picture wzrfmt 0 - high='000,009.0000';
run;
```

Variable Value	Displayed with rtfmt.	Displayed with wzrfmt.
.5	000,000.5000	0.5000
1.5	000,001.5000	1.5000
12.55	000,012.5500	12.5500
123.555	000,123.5550	123.5550
1234.5555	001,234.5555	1,234.5555

No matter which digit selector you specify, all digits to the right of the decimal place are displayed.

7.06 Quiz – Correct Answer

Submit the program **p307a03**. How many digits are printed to the left of the decimal point?

```
proc format;
   picture small low - high='0,009.99';
   picture large low - high='000,009.99';
run;
```

Variable Value	Displayed with small.	Displayed with large.
1234.56	1,234.56	1,234.56
12345.67	2,345.67	12,345.67
123456.78	3,456.78	123,456.78
1234567.89	4,567.89	234,567.89

If the variable value is bigger than the PICTURE format, only the rightmost digits are displayed.

59

Solutions to Chapter Review

Chapter Review Answers

1. What PROC FORMAT statement option is used to create a permanent format?

   LIBRARY=

2. What PROC FORMAT statement option is used to create a format from a SAS data set?

   CNTLIN=

3. What variables are required to create a format from a SAS data set?

   FMTNAME, START, and LABEL, at a minimum. The END variable is required if the SAS data set was created using the CNTLOUT= option.

69

continued...

Chapter Review Answers

4. What PROC FORMAT option is used to view the contents of a format?

   FMTLIB

5. What PROC FORMAT option is used to create a SAS data set from a format?

   CNTLOUT=

6. What is the SAS system option that establishes the search path when a format is used?

   FMTSEARCH=(*library-1, library-2, . . . , library-n*)

71

Chapter 8 Combining Data Horizontally

8.1 DATA Step Merges and SQL Procedure Joins

Objectives

- Use the DATA step with a MERGE statement to combine more than two SAS data sets.
- Use the SQL procedure to join SAS data sets without a common variable.
- Describe the differences between the DATA step MERGE statement and PROC SQL.

3

Methods for the Match-Merge

You can perform a match-merge of two or more SAS data sets with the following techniques:

- DATA step with the MERGE statement and a BY statement
- PROC SQL join

4

The DATA Step Merge (Review)

When data sets are combined using the DATA step MERGE statement, both the matches and the nonmatches on the BY variable are included in the results.

```
data three;
   merge one two;
   by X;
run;
```

one

X	Y
1	a
1	d
4	c
5	g

two

X	Z
1	f
1	r
1	s
3	t
4	w

three

X	Y	Z
1	a	f
1	d	r
1	d	s
3		t
4	c	w
5	g	

5

8.01 Multiple Choice Poll

By default, how does the DATA step perform a merge?

a. sequentially

b. creates a Cartesian product

7

Business Scenario

The SAS data set **orion.staff** contains the employee's ID and the employee's manager's ID.

Partial Listing of **orion.staff**

Employee_ID	Start_Date	. . .	Emp_Hire_Date	Emp_Term_Date	Manager_ID
120101	01JUL2003	...	01JUL2003	.	120261
120102	01JUN1989	...	01JUN1989	.	120101
120103	01JAN1974	...	01JAN1974	.	120101
120104	01JAN1981	...	01JAN1981	.	120101
120105	01MAY1999	...	01MAY1999	.	120101
120106	01JAN1974	...	01JAN1974	.	120104
120107	01FEB1974	...	01FEB1974	.	120104
120108	01AUG2006	...	01AUG2006	.	120104
⋮	⋮	⋮	⋮	⋮	⋮

9

Business Scenario

The SAS data set **orion.employee_addresses** contains the employee's ID and name.

Partial Listing of **orion.employee_addresses**

Employee_ID	Employee_Name	. . .	State	Postal_Code	Country
121044	Abbott, Ray	. . .	FL	33135	US
120145	Aisbitt, Sandy	. . .		2001	AU
120761	Akinfolarin, Tameaka	. . .	PA	19145	US
120656	Amos, Salley	. . .	CA	92116	US
121107	Anger, Rose	. . .	PA	19142	US
121038	Anstey, David	. . .	FL	33157	US
120273	Antonini, Doris	. . .	FL	33141	US
⋮	⋮	⋮	⋮	⋮	⋮

10

Business Scenario

You need to combine these two data sets to determine the employee's name and the employee's manager's name.

Partial Listing of **names**

Employee_ID	Manager_ID	Employee_Name	Manager_Name
120102	120101	Zhou, Tom	Lu, Patrick
120103	120101	Dawes, Wilson	Lu, Patrick
120104	120101	Billington, Kareen	Lu, Patrick
120105	120101	Povey, Liz	Lu, Patrick
120121	120102	Elvish, Irenie	Zhou, Tom
120122	120102	Ngan, Christina	Zhou, Tom
120123	120102	Hotstone, Kimiko	Zhou, Tom
120124	120102	Daymond, Lucian	Zhou, Tom
⋮	⋮	⋮	⋮

11

Steps for Merging

Step 1: Sort **orion.employee_addresses** by **Employee_ID** to create the data set **addresses**.

Step 2: Merge **addresses** and **orion.staff** by **Employee_ID** to create an intermediate data set.

Step 3: Sort the intermediate data set by **Manager_ID**.

Step 4: Merge the intermediate data set and addresses. Use the RENAME= data set option to rename **Employee_ID** to **Manager_ID** and **Employee_Name** to **Manager_Name** in the **addresses** data set.

12

Using the DATA Step to Perform a Match-Merge

p308d01

```
proc sort data=orion.employee_addresses(keep=Employee_ID
                                             Employee_Name)
          out=addresses;
   by Employee_ID;
run;

data temp1;
   keep Employee_Name Employee_ID Manager_ID;
   merge orion.staff(in=S keep=Employee_ID Manager_ID)
         addresses(in=A);
   by Employee_ID;
   if S and A; /* Matches only */
run;

proc sort data=temp1;
   by Manager_ID;
run;

data names;
   merge temp1(in=T)
         addresses(rename=(Employee_ID=Manager_ID
                           Employee_Name=Manager_Name) in=A);
   by Manager_ID;
   if A and T;
run;

proc print data=names(obs= 10);
   title "Names Data Set";
run;
```

Advantages of a DATA Step Merge

Advantages of a DATA Step Merge
Multiple values can be returned.
There is no limit to the size of the tables, other than disk space.
Multiple BY variables enable lookups that depend on more than one variable.
Multiple data sets can be used.
A merge enables complex business logic to be incorporated into the new data set by using DATA step processing, such as arrays and DO loops, in addition to merging features.
The IN= data set option and subsequent IF-THEN/ELSE logic afford comprehensive control over whether to accept, reject, or process an observation depending on which data set contributed to the observation.
Observations with duplicate BY values are joined one-to-one instead of being expanded into a Cartesian product as SQL does.

14

Disadvantages of a DATA Step Merge

Disadvantages of a DATA Step Merge
Data sets must be sorted or indexed based on the BY variable(s).
An exact match on the BY variable(s) value(s) must be found.
The BY variable(s) must be present in all data sets.
When more than one data set contributes variables with the same name, the values from the variable in the rightmost data set overwrite the other like-named variables, and no warning is printed.*

* Example

```
data c;
   merge a b;
   by X;
run;
```

a

X	Y
1	2

b

X	Y
1	3

c

X	Y
1	3

15

SQL Inner Join

When PROC SQL performs an equijoin, combinations of observations from both data sets with matches on the common variable remain.

```
proc sql;
   create table three as
   select one.*, two.Z
      from one, two
      where one.X=two.X;
```

one

X	Y
1	a
1	d
4	c
5	g

two

X	Z
1	f
1	r
1	s
3	t
4	w

three

X	Y	Z
1	a	f
1	a	r
1	a	s
1	d	f
1	d	r
1	d	s
4	c	w

16

8.02 Multiple Choice Poll

By default, how does the SQL procedure perform an inner join?

a. sequentially
b. creates a Cartesian product

18

Using a PROC SQL Join to Perform a Match-Merge

p308d02

```
proc sql;
   create table namessql as
   select e.Employee_ID,
          e.Employee_Name,
          Manager_ID,
          m.Employee_Name as Manager_Name
       from orion.staff,
            orion.employee_addresses as e,
            orion.employee_addresses as m
       where e.Employee_ID=staff.Employee_ID
         and m.Employee_ID=staff.Manager_ID
       order by Manager_ID,
                Employee_ID;
quit;

proc print data=namessql(obs=10);
   title "Employee and Manager Names";
run;
```

Advantages of PROC SQL Joins

Advantages of PROC SQL Joins
Multiple data sets can be joined without having common variables in all data sets.
Data sets do not have to be sorted or indexed.
Inequality joins can be performed.
PROC SQL follows ANSI standard language definitions, so that you can use the knowledge gained from other SQL implementations.

21

Disadvantages of PROC SQL Joins

Disadvantages of PROC SQL Joins
The maximum number of tables that can be joined at one time is 256.
For simple joins, PROC SQL might require more resources than the DATA step with the MERGE statement.
Complex business logic is difficult to incorporate into the join.
Duplicate BY values are combined into a Cartesian product, which can produce an extremely large output data set.

22

Comparing Merging and SQL

Match-Merge	SQL Inner Join
There is no limit to the number of data sets nor the size of the data sets other than disk space.	The maximum number of tables that can be joined at one time is 256.
Data is processed sequentially so that observations with duplicate BY values are joined one-to-one.	Data is processed using a Cartesian product for duplicate BY values.
Multiple data sets can be created.	Only one data set can be created with one CREATE TABLE statement.
Complex business logic can be incorporated using IF-THEN or SELECT/WHEN logic.	CASE logic can be used for business logic; however, it is not as flexible as DATA step syntax.
The data sets being merged must be sorted or indexed on the BY variable(s).	The data sets being joined do not have to be sorted nor indexed.
An exact match on the BY-variable(s) value(s) must be found.	Inequality joins can be performed.
Like-named BY variables must be available in all data sets.	Common variables do not have to be in all data sets.

23

Comparison Programs

The DATA step merge and the PROC SQL inner join do not always give you the same results.

The following programs are used to generate the results for the next four result sets:

```
data three;
   merge one two;
   by X;
run;
```

```
proc sql;
   create table three as
   select one.X, one.Y, two.Z
       from one, two
       where one.X=two.X;
quit;
```

24

Merge and SQL Join Comparison

ONE-TO-ONE matches produce identical results:

one

X	Y
1	a
2	b

two

X	Z
1	f
2	g

three – DATA step and PROC SQL

X	Y	Z
1	a	f
2	b	g

25

Merge and SQL Join Comparison

ONE-TO-MANY matches produce identical results:

one

X	Y
1	a
2	b

two

X	Z
1	f
1	r
2	g

three – DATA step and PROC SQL

X	Y	Z
1	a	f
1	a	r
2	b	g

26

Merge and SQL Join Comparison

MANY-TO-MANY matches produce different results:

one

X	Y
1	a
1	c
2	b

two

X	Z
1	f
1	r
2	g

three - DATA step

X	Y	Z
1	a	f
1	c	r
2	b	g

three - PROC SQL

X	Y	Z
1	a	f
1	a	r
1	c	f
1	c	r
2	b	g

27

Reference Information

The following DATA step creates a Cartesian product:

```
data three(drop=Temp);
   set one;
   do i=1 to TotObs;
      set two(rename=(X=Temp))
              nobs=TotObs point=i;
      if X=Temp then output;
   end;
run;
```

In SAS 9.2, you can use the DATA step hash object with the MULTIDATA attribute to create a Cartesian product.

```
data three;
   drop rc;
   length X 8 Y $1;
   if _N_=1 then do;
      declare hash H(dataset:'one', multidata:'yes');
      H.definekey('X');
      H.definedata('X', 'Y');
      H.definedone();
   end;
   set two;
   rc=H.find();
   do while (rc=0);
      output;
      rc=H.find_next();
   end;
run;
```

The MULTIDATA attribute specifies whether multiple data items are allowed for each key.

For more information, consult the SAS Help facility using the path shown below:

SAS Products ⇨ **Base SAS** ⇨ **SAS 9.2 Language References: Concepts** ⇨ **DATA Step Concepts** ⇨ **Using DATA Step Component Objects** ⇨ **Using the Hash Object**

Merge and SQL Join Comparison

NONMATCHING data produces different results:

one

X	Y
1	a
2	b
3	c

two

X	Z
1	f
3	t
4	w

three - DATA step

X	Y	Z
1	a	f
2	b	
3	c	t
4		w

three - PROC SQL

X	Y	Z
1	a	f
3	c	t

28

Reference Information

The following SQL step produces results that are identical to those of the DATA step when there is nonmatching data.

```
proc sql;
   select coalesce(one.X, two.X) as X, Y, Z
      from one full join two
         on one.X=two.X;
quit;
```

The following DATA step merge produces results that are identical to those of the SQL inner join when there is nonmatching data.

```
data three;
   merge one(in=O) two(in=T);
   by X;
   if O and T;
run;
```

Exercises (Optional)

Level 1

1. Merging or Joining Three Data Sets

The data set **orion.order_fact** has details about purchases made.

Partial Listing of **orion.order_fact**

Partial orion.order_fact

Obs	Customer_ID	Employee_ID	Street_ID	Order_ Date	Delivery_ Date	Order_ID
1	63	121039	9260125492	11JAN2003	11JAN2003	1230058123
2	5	99999999	9260114570	15JAN2003	19JAN2003	1230080101
3	45	99999999	9260104847	20JAN2003	22JAN2003	1230106883
4	41	120174	1600101527	28JAN2003	28JAN2003	1230147441
5	183	120134	1600100760	27FEB2003	27FEB2003	1230315085

The data set **orion.customer_dim** has the customers' names.

Partial Listing of **orion.customer_dim**

Partial orion.customer_dim

Obs	Customer_ID	Customer_Name
1	4	James Kvarniq
2	5	Sandrina Stephano
3	9	Cornelia Krahl
4	10	Karen Ballinger
5	11	Elke Wallstab

The data set **orion.product_dim** has the product names and supplier names.

Partial Listing of **orion.product_dim**

Partial orion.product_dim

Obs	Product_ID	Product_Name	Supplier_Name
1	210200100009	Kids Sweat Round Neck,Large Logo	A Team Sports
2	210200100017	Sweatshirt Children's O-Neck	A Team Sports
3	210200200022	Sunfit Slow Swimming Trunks	Nautlius SportsWear Inc
4	210200200023	Sunfit Stockton Swimming Trunks Jr.	Nautlius SportsWear Inc
5	210200300006	Fleece Cuff Pant Kid'S	Eclipse Inc

a. Combine the three data sets to create a data set named **purchases** that contains the customer name, product name, and supplier name for the customers in the **orion.order_fact** data set.

b. Order the data by **Product_ID** and print the first five observations of the **purchases** data set.

PROC PRINT Output

Partial purchases Data Set

Obs	Customer_Name	Product_Name	Supplier_Name
1	Kyndal Hooks	Kids Sweat Round Neck,Large Logo	A Team Sports
2	Annmarie Leveille	Sweatshirt Children's O-Neck	A Team Sports
3	Najma Hicks	Sunfit Slow Swimming Trunks	Nautlius SportsWear Inc
4	Yan Kozlowski	Sunfit Stockton Swimming Trunks Jr.	Nautlius SportsWear Inc
5	Kyndal Hooks	Fleece Cuff Pant Kid'S	Eclipse Inc

Level 2

2. Merging or Joining Data to Create Multiple Data Sets

The data set **`orion.order_fact`** has details about purchases made.

Partial Listing of **`orion.order_fact`**

Partial orion.order_fact

Obs	Customer_ID	Employee_ID	Street_ID	Order_ Date	Delivery_ Date	Order_ID
1	63	121039	9260125492	11JAN2003	11JAN2003	1230058123
2	5	99999999	9260114570	15JAN2003	19JAN2003	1230080101
3	45	99999999	9260104847	20JAN2003	22JAN2003	1230106883
4	41	120174	1600101527	28JAN2003	28JAN2003	1230147441
5	183	120134	1600100760	27FEB2003	27FEB2003	1230315085

Obs	Order_ Type	Product_ID	Quantity	Total_Retail_ Price	CostPrice_ Per_Unit	Discount
1	1	220101300017	1	$16.50	$7.45	.
2	2	230100500026	1	$247.50	$109.55	.
3	2	240600100080	1	$28.30	$8.55	.
4	1	240600100010	2	$32.00	$6.50	.
5	1	240200200039	3	$63.60	$8.80	.

The data set **`orion.customer_dim`** has the customers' names.

Partial Listing of **`orion.customer_dim`**

Partial orion.customer_dim

Obs	Customer_ID	Customer_Name
1	4	James Kvarniq
2	5	Sandrina Stephano
3	9	Cornelia Krahl
4	10	Karen Ballinger
5	11	Elke Wallstab

The data set **orion.product_dim** has the product names and supplier names.

Partial Listing of **orion.product_dim**

Partial orion.product_dim

Obs	Product_ID	Product_Name	Supplier_Name
1	210200100009	Kids Sweat Round Neck,Large Logo	A Team Sports
2	210200100017	Sweatshirt Children's O-Neck	A Team Sports
3	210200200022	Sunfit Slow Swimming Trunks	Nautlius SportsWear Inc
4	210200200023	Sunfit Stockton Swimming Trunks Jr.	Nautlius SportsWear Inc
5	210200300006	Fleece Cuff Pant Kid'S	Eclipse Inc

Combine the three data sets to create the following data sets:

- a data set named **no_purchases** that contains the customers who did not make any purchases
- a data set named **purchases** that contains the customer name, product name, and supplier name for those customers in the **orion.order_fact** data set
- a data set named **no_products** that contains the product names and suppliers for products that were not purchased

Partial Listing of **no_purchases**

no_purchases Data Set

Obs	Customer_ID	Customer_Name
1	33	Rolf Robak
2	42	Thomas Leitmann

Partial Listing of **purchases**

Partial purchases Data Set

Obs	Customer_ID	Employee_ID	Street_ID	Order_ Date	Delivery_ Date	Order_ID
1	90	121028	9260111614	19NOV2007	19NOV2007	1243960910
2	49	121035	9260104510	26NOV2004	26NOV2004	1234198497
3	79	99999999	9260101874	27MAY2005	03JUN2005	1235926178
4	52	121030	9260116235	12DEC2006	12DEC2006	1240886449
5	90	121032	9260111614	03MAY2007	03MAY2007	1242149082

Obs	Order_ Type	Product_ID	Quantity	Total_Retail_ Price	CostPrice_ Per_Unit	Discount	Customer_Name
1	1	210200100009	2	$69.40	$15.50	.	Kyndal Hooks
2	1	210200100017	1	$39.00	$17.35	.	Annmarie Leveille
3	3	210200200022	2	$36.00	$7.05	.	Najma Hicks
4	1	210200200023	1	$19.80	$8.25	.	Yan Kozlowski
5	1	210200300006	1	$14.30	$7.70	.	Kyndal Hooks

Obs	Product_Name	Supplier_Name
1	Kids Sweat Round Neck,Large Logo	A Team Sports
2	Sweatshirt Children's O-Neck	A Team Sports
3	Sunfit Slow Swimming Trunks	Nautlius SportsWear Inc
4	Sunfit Stockton Swimming Trunks Jr.	Nautlius SportsWear Inc
5	Fleece Cuff Pant Kid'S	Eclipse Inc

Partial SAS Log

```
NOTE: There were 617 observations read from the data set WORK.TEMP.
NOTE: There were 481 observations read from the data set ORION.PRODUCT_DIM.
NOTE: The data set WORK.PURCHASES has 617 observations and 15 variables.
NOTE: The data set WORK.NO_PRODUCTS has 0 observations and 3 variables.
```

Level 3

3. Merging or Joining Multiple Data Sets

The data set **orion.organization_dim** has the levels of managers for each employee.

Not all **Manager_Level*n*** variables have values.

Partial Listing of **orion.organization_dim**

Partial orion.organization_dim

Obs	Employee_ID	Manager_ Level1	Manager_ Level2	Manager_ Level3	Manager_ Level4	Manager_ Level5	Manager_ Level6
1	120101	120261	120259	.	.	.	.
2	120102	120101	120261	120259	.	.	.
3	120103	120101	120261	120259	.	.	.
4	120104	120101	120261	120259	.	.	.
5	120105	120101	120261	120259	.	.	

The data set **orion.employee_addresses** contains the employee IDs and the employee names for all employees.

Partial Listing of **orion.employee_addresses**

Partial orion.employee_addresses

Obs	Employee_ ID	Employee_Name
1	121044	Abbott, Ray
2	120145	Aisbitt, Sandy
3	120761	Akinfolarin, Tameaka
4	120656	Amos, Salley
5	121107	Anger, Rose

Create a data set named **manager_names** that contains the **Employee_ID** variable, the six **Manager_ID** variables, and the six manager names.

Partial Listing of **manager_names**

```
                              Partial manager_names Data

                      Manager_  Manager_  Manager_  Manager_  Manager_  Manager_
Obs    Employee_ID     Level1    Level2    Level3    Level4    Level5    Level6       Manager1_Name

420       121144      121142    121141    120261    120259        .         .      Steiber, Reginald
421       121145      121142    121141    120261    120259        .         .      Steiber, Reginald
422       121146      121141    120261    120259         .        .         .      Bleu, Henri Le
423       121147      121142    121141    120261    120259        .         .      Steiber, Reginald
424       121148      121141    120261    120259         .        .         .      Bleu, Henri Le

                                                                   Manager5_     Manager6_
Obs    Manager2_Name         Manager3_Name         Manager4_Name         Name          Name

420   Bleu, Henri Le       Highpoint, Harry     Miller, Anthony
421   Bleu, Henri Le       Highpoint, Harry     Miller, Anthony
422   Highpoint, Harry     Miller, Anthony
423   Bleu, Henri Le       Highpoint, Harry     Miller, Anthony
424   Highpoint, Harry     Miller, Anthony
```

8.2 Using an Index to Combine Data

Objectives

- Use the SET statement with the KEY= option to combine two SAS data sets.
- Use _IORC_ to determine whether the index search was successful.

32

Business Scenario

The data set **orion.catalog** contains the order information for catalog sales and has 38 observations.

Partial Listing of **orion.catalog**

Customer_ ID	Order_ID	Quantity	Total_Retail_ Price
5	1230080101	1	247.50
15	1240080101	3	216.50
45	1230106883	1	28.30
79	1230333319	1	234.60
23	1230338566	1	35.40
. . .	. . .	. . .	. . .

33

Business Scenario

The data set **orion.customer_dim _more** contains information about customers and has 1,500 observations.

Partial Listing of **orion.customer_dim_more**

Customer_ ID	Customer_ Country	Customer _Gender	Customer_ Name	...	Customer_ Type	Customer_ Group	Customer_ Age
4	US	M	James Kvarniq	...	Orion Club members low activity	Orion Club members	33
5	US	F	Sandrina Stephano	...	Orion Club Gold members medium activity	Orion Club Gold members	28
9	DE	F	Cornelia Krahl	...	Orion Club Gold members medium activity	Orion Club Gold members	33
10	US	F	Karen Ballinger	...	Orion Club members high activity	Orion Club members	23
11	DE	F	Elke Wallstab	...	Orion Club members high activity	Orion Club members	33
. . .	. . .	. . .	. . .	. . .	. . .	. . .	. . .

34

Business Scenario

You need to combine the two data sets to create two new data sets: one with information about the customers who purchase products from the catalog for whom you have demographics and the other for customers for whom you do not have any information.

Partial PROC PRINT Output: **catalog_customers**

```
                Catalog Customers (Partial Output)

                                                        Total_Retail_
Obs      Customer_ID          Order_ID     Quantity            Price

 1                 5        1230080101         1             $247.50
 2                45        1230106883         1              $28.30
 3                79        1230333319         1             $234.60
 4                23        1230338566         1              $35.40
 5                16        1230450371         2             $128.40

       Customer_      Customer_                               Customer_
Obs     Country        Gender      Customer_Name                    Age

 1        US             F         Sandrina Stephano                 28
 2        US             F         Dianne Patchin                    28
 3        US             F         Najma Hicks                       21
 4        US             M         Tulio Devereaux                   58
 5        DE             M         Ulrich Heyde                      68
```

PROC PRINT Output: **errors**

```
No Demographic Data
     Available

Obs     Customer_ID

 1               15
 2               66
```

35

8.03 Multiple Choice Poll

If you use a DATA step MERGE to combine the data sets, how many observations are read from the larger data set, **orion.customer_dim_more**?

a. 38

b. 1,500

37

Combining a Large Data Set with a Small One

You can use multiple SET statements to combine the two data sets.

```
data catalog_customers(keep=Customer_ID Order_ID Quantity
                            Total_Retail_Price
                            Customer_Country
                            Customer_Gender
                            Customer_Name
                            Customer_Age)
     errors(keep=Customer_ID);
①  set orion.catalog(keep=Customer_ID Order_ID
                            Quantity Total_Retail_Price);
②  set orion.customer_dim_more key=Customer_ID;
   if _IORC_=0 then output catalog_customers;
   else do;
      _ERROR_=0;
      output errors;
   end;
run;
```

39 p308d03

① The data set **orion.catalog** is read sequentially.

② The data set **orion.customer_dim_more** is read by direct access.

Using the KEY= Option

An index is always used when a SET or MODIFY statement contains the KEY= option.

Specify the KEY= option in the SET statement to use an index to retrieve an observation that has key values equal to the current value of the key variable(s).

General form of the KEY= option:

SET *SAS-data-file-name* KEY=*index-name*;

40

Assign a value to the index key variable(s) before the SET statement is executed. The index is then used to retrieve an observation with the key value. WHERE processing is not allowed for a data set read with the KEY= option.

Using the _IORC_ Automatic Variable

When you use the KEY= option, SAS creates an automatic variable named _IORC_, which is an acronym for input/output return code.

You can use the value of _IORC_ to determine whether the search of the index was successful.

IORC=0	indicates that SAS found a matching observation.
IORC ne 0	indicates that the SET statement did not successfully execute. One possible cause is that SAS did **not** find a matching observation.

41

Reference Information

Monitoring I/O Error Conditions

You can use the automatic variable _IORC_ with the %SYSRC AUTOCALL macro to test for specific I/O error conditions that are created when you use the KEY= option in the SET statement.

General form for using %SYSRC with _IORC_:

> **IF** _IORC_=%SYSRC(*mnemonic*) **THEN**...

Mnemonic	Meaning
_DSENOM	No matching observation was found.
_SOK	The observation was located. _SOK has a value of 0.

The %SYSRC macro is in the AUTOCALL library. You must have the MACRO system option in effect to use this macro. Consult SAS OnlineDoc for more information. Follow the path shown below:

> **SAS OnlineDoc** ⇨ **Base SAS** ⇨ **SAS 9.2 Macro Language: Reference** ⇨ **Macro Language Dictionary** ⇨ **AutoCall Macros**

Using the IORCMSG Function

The IORCMSG function returns the formatted error message that is associated with the current value of the automatic variable _IORC_.

General form of the IORCMSG function:

> *character-variable*=IORCMSG();

Character-variable specifies a character variable with a length of 200, unless the length was previously assigned.

Example:

p308d03a

```
data catalog_customers(keep=Customer_ID Order_ID Quantity
                            Total_Retail_Price
                            Customer_Country
                            Customer_Gender
                            Customer_Name
                            Customer_Age_Group)
      errors(keep=Customer_ID);
   set orion.catalog(keep=Customer_ID Order_ID
                          Quantity Total_Retail_Price);
   set orion.customer_dim_more key=Customer_ID;
   if _IORC_=0 then output catalog_customers;
   else do;
      output errors;
      Message=iorcmsg();
      _ERROR_=0;
      putlog _N_ ' The problem is ' Message;
   end;
run;
```

✎ The PUTLOG statement writes text to the log.

Execution

orion.catalog (obs=2)

Customer_ID	Order_ID	Quantity	Total_Retail_Price
5	1230080101	1	247.50
15	1240080101	3	216.50

```
data catalog_customers(keep=Customer_ID Order_ID
                            Quantity
                            Total_Retail_Price
                            Customer_Country
                            Customer_Gender
                            Customer_Name
                            Customer_Age)
     errors(keep=Customer_ID);
   set orion.catalog(keep=Customer_ID Order_ID
                          Quantity
                          Total_Retail_Price);
   set orion.customer_dim_more key=Customer_ID;
   if _IORC_=0 then output catalog_customers;
   else do;
      _ERROR_=0;
      output errors;
   end;
run;
```

Simplified Index on orion.customer_dim_more

Customer_ID	Record Identifiers
4	RID
5	RID
9	RID
.	.
13	RID
16	RID
.	.
45	RID
.	.

Partial PDV

Customer_ID	Order_ID	Quantity	Total_Retail_Price	...	Customer_Name	...	D _IORC_	D _N_
.	.	.	.	...		...	.	1

...

Execution

orion.catalog (obs=2)

Customer_ID	Order_ID	Quantity	Total_Retail_Price
5	1230080101	1	247.50
15	1240080101	3	216.50

```
data catalog_customers(keep=Customer_ID Order_ID
                            Quantity
                            Total_Retail_Price
                            Customer_Country
                            Customer_Gender
                            Customer_Name
                            Customer_Age)
     errors(keep=Customer_ID);
   set orion.catalog(keep=Customer_ID Order_ID
                          Quantity
                          Total_Retail_Price);
   set orion.customer_dim_more key=Customer_ID;
   if _IORC_=0 then output catalog_customers;
   else do;
      _ERROR_=0;
      output errors;
   end;
run;
```

Simplified Index on orion.customer_dim_more

Customer_ID	Record Identifiers
4	RID
5	RID
9	RID
.	.
13	RID
16	RID
.	.
45	RID
.	.

Partial PDV

Customer_ID	Order_ID	Quantity	Total_Retail_Price	...	Customer_Name	...	D _IORC_	D _N_
5	1230080101	1	247.50	...		...	.	1

...

Execution

orion.catalog (obs=2)

Customer_ID	Order_ID	Quantity	Total_Retail_Price
5	1230080101	1	247.50
15	1240080101	3	216.50

```
data catalog_customers(keep=Customer_ID Order_ID
                            Quantity
                            Total_Retail_Price
                            Customer_Country
                            Customer_Gender
                            Customer_Name
                            Customer_Age)
     errors(keep=Customer_ID);
   set orion.catalog(keep=Customer_ID Order_ID
                          Quantity
                          Total_Retail_Price);
   set orion.customer_dim_more key=Customer_ID;
   if _IORC_=0 then output catalog_customers;
   else do;
      _ERROR_=0;
      output errors;
   end;
run;
```

Simplified Index on
orion.customer_dim_more

Customer_ ID	Record Identifiers
4	RID
5	RID
9	RID
.	
13	RID
16	RID
.	
45	RID
.	

Partial PDV

Customer_ ID	Order_ ID	Quantity	Total_ Retail_ Price	...	Customer_ Name	...	D _IORC_	D _N_
5	1230080101	1	247.50	...		...	.	1

44

Execution

Simplified Index on
orion.customer_dim_more

Customer_ ID	Record Identifiers
4	RID
5	RID
9	RID
.	
13	RID
16	RID
.	
45	RID
.	

Partial Listing of
orion.customer_dim_more

RID	Customer_ ID	Customer_ Country	Customer _Gender	Customer_ Name	...
1	4	US	M	James Kvarniq	...
2	5	US	F	Sandrina Stephano	
3	9	DE	F	Cornelia Krahl	...
4	10	US	F	Karen Ballinger	...
5	11	DE	F	Elke Wallstab	...
	.	.	.	.	
	45	US	F	Dianne Patchin	...
	.	.	.	.	

45

Execution

orion.catalog (obs=2)

Customer_ID	Order_ID	Quantity	Total_Retail_Price
5	1230080101	1	247.50
15	1240080101	3	216.50

```
data catalog_customers(keep=Customer_ID Order_ID
                            Quantity
                            Total_Retail_Price
                            Customer_Country
                            Customer_Gender
                            Customer_Name
                            Customer_Age)
     errors(keep=Customer_ID);
   set orion.catalog(keep=Customer_ID Order_ID
                          Quantity
                          Total_Retail_Price);
   set orion.customer_dim_more key=Customer_ID;
   if _IORC_=0 then output catalog_customers;
   else do;
      _ERROR_=0;
      output errors;
   end;
run;
```

Simplified Index on orion.customer_dim_more

Customer_ ID	Record Identifiers
4	RID
5	RID
9	RID
. . .	. . .
13	RID
16	RID
. . .	. . .
45	RID
. . .	. . .

Partial PDV

Customer_ ID	Order_ ID	Quantity	Total_ Retail_ Price	...	Customer_ Name	...	_IORC_	_N_
5	1230080101	1	247.50	...	Sandrina Stephano	...	0	1

Execution

orion.catalog (obs=2)

Customer_ID	Order_ID	Quantity	Total_Retail_Price
5	1230080101	1	247.50
15	1240080101	3	216.50

```
data catalog_customers(keep=Customer_ID Order_ID
                            Quantity
                            Total_Retail_Price
                            Customer_Country
                            Customer
                            Customer
                            Customer
     errors(keep=Customer_ID);
   set orion.catalog(keep=Customer_ID Order_ID
                          Quantity
                          Total_Retail_Price);
   set orion.customer_dim_more key=Customer_ID;
   if _IORC_=0 then output catalog_customers;
   else do;
      _ERROR_=0;
      output errors;
   end;
run;
```

True

Simplified Index on orion.customer_dim_more

Customer_ ID	Record Identifiers
4	RID
5	RID
9	RID
. . .	. . .
13	RID
16	RID
. . .	. . .
45	RID
. . .	. . .

Partial PDV

Customer_ ID	Order_ ID	Quantity	Total_ Retail_ Price	...	Customer_ Name	...	_IORC_	_N_
5	1230080101	1	247.50	...	Sandrina Stephano	...	0	1

Execution

orion.catalog (obs=2)

Customer_ID	Order_ID	Quantity	Total_Retail_Price
5	1230080101	1	247.50
15	1240080101	3	216.50

Simplified Index on orion.customer_dim_more

Customer_ ID	Record Identifiers
4	RID
5	RID
	RID
. . .	. . .
13	RID
16	RID
. . .	. . .
45	RID
. . .	. . .

```
data catalog_customers(keep=Customer_ID Order_ID
                                  Quantity

     errors(keep=Customer_ID);
   set orion.catalog(keep=Customer_ID Order_ID
                          Quantity
                          Total_Retail_Price);
   set orion.customer_dim_more key=Customer_ID;
   if _IORC_=0 then output catalog_customers;
   else do;
      _ERROR_=0;
      output errors;
   end;
run;
```

Output the current observation to `catalog_customers`

Implicit RETURN;

Partial PDV

Customer_ ID	Order_ ID	Quantity	Total_ Retail_ Price	...	Customer_ Name	...	D _IORC_	D _N_
5	1230080101	1	247.50	...	Sandrina Stephano	...	0	1

...

Execution

orion.catalog (obs=2)

Customer_ID	Order_ID	Quantity	Total_Retail_Price
5	1230080101	1	247.50
15	1240080101	3	216.50

Simplified Index on orion.customer_dim_more

Customer_ ID	Record Identifiers
4	RID
5	RID
9	RID
. . .	. . .
13	RID
16	RID
. . .	. . .
45	RID
. . .	. . .

```
data catalog_customers(keep=Customer_ID Order_ID
                                  Quantity
                                  Total_Retail_Price
                                  Customer_Country
                                  Customer_Gender
                                  Customer_Name
                                  Customer_Age)
     errors(keep=Customer_ID);
   set orion.catalog(keep=Customer_ID Order_ID
                          Quantity
                          Total_Retail_Price);
   set orion.customer_dim_more key=Customer_ID;
   if _IORC_=0 then output catalog_customers;
   else do;
      _ERROR_=0;
      output errors;
   end;
run;
```

Initialize PDV

Partial PDV

Customer_ ID	Order_ ID	Quantity	Total_ Retail_ Price	...	Customer_ Name	...	D _IORC_	D _N_
5	1230080101	1	247.50	...	Sandrina Stephano	...	0	2

...

Execution

orion.catalog (obs=2)

Customer_ID	Order_ID	Quantity	Total_Retail_Price
5	1230080101	1	247.50
15	1240080101	3	216.50

```
data catalog_customers(keep=Customer_ID Order_ID
                            Quantity
                            Total_Retail_Price
                            Customer_Country
                            Customer_Gender
                            Customer_Name
                            Customer_Age)
     errors(keep=Customer_ID);
   set orion.catalog(keep=Customer_ID Order_ID
                          Quantity
                          Total_Retail_Price);
   set orion.customer_dim_more key=Customer_ID;
   if _IORC_=0 then output catalog_customers;
   else do;
      _ERROR_=0;
      output errors;
   end;
run;
```

The 2nd iteration of the DATA step

Simplified Index on orion.customer_dim_more

Customer_ ID	Record Identifiers
4	RID
5	RID
9	RID
. . .	. . .
13	RID
16	RID
. . .	. . .
45	RID
. . .	. . .

Partial PDV

Customer_ ID	Order_ ID	Quantity	Total_ Retail_ Price	...	Customer_ Name	...	D _IORC_	D _N_
15	1240080101	3	216.50	...	Sandrina Stephano	...	0	2

...

Execution

orion.catalog (obs=2)

Customer_ID	Order_ID	Quantity	Total_Retail_Price
5	1230080101	1	247.50
15	1240080101	3	216.50

```
data catalog_customers(keep=Customer_ID Order_ID
                            Quantity
                            Total_Retail_Price
                            Customer_Country
                            Customer_Gender
                            Customer_Name
                            Customer_Age)
     errors(keep=Customer_ID);
   set orion.catalog(keep=Customer_ID Order_ID
                          Quantity
                          Total_Retail_Price);
   set orion.customer_dim_more key=Customer_ID;
   if _IORC_=0 then output catalog_customers;
   else do;
      _ERROR_=0;
      output errors;
   end;
run;
```

Simplified Index on orion.customer_dim_more

No 15 in the index

Customer_ ID	Record Identifiers
4	RID
5	RID
9	RID
. . .	. . .
13	RID
16	RID
. . .	. . .
45	RID
. . .	. . .

Partial PDV

Customer_ ID	Order_ ID	Quantity	Total_ Retail_ Price	...	Customer_ Name	...	D _IORC_	D _N_
15	1240080101	3	216.50	...	Sandrina Stephano	...	1230015	2

...

8.04 Quiz

Why do you **not** want this observation output to **catalog_customers**?

Partial PDV

Customer_ ID	Order_ ID	Quantity	Total_ Retail_ Price	...	Customer_ Name	...	_IORC_	_N_
15	1240080101	3	216.50	...	Sandrina Stephano	...	1230015	2

53

Execution

orion.catalog (obs=2)

Customer_ID	Order_ID	Quantity	Total_Retail_Price
5	1230080101	1	247.50
15	1240080101	3	216.50

```
data catalog_customers(keep=Customer_ID Order_ID
                              Quantity
                              Total_Retail_Price
                              Customer_Country
                              Customer
                              Customer
                              Customer
     errors(keep=Customer_ID);
   set orion.catalog(keep=Customer_ID Order_ID
                            Quantity
                            Total_Retail_Price);
   set orion.customer_dim_more key=Customer_ID;
   if _IORC_=0 then output catalog_customers;
   else do;
      _ERROR_=0;
      output errors;
   end;
run;
```

False

Simplified Index on orion.customer_dim_more

Customer_ ID	Record Identifiers
4	RID
5	RID
9	RID
. . .	. . .
13	RID
16	RID
. . .	. . .
45	RID
. . .	. . .

Partial PDV

Customer_ ID	Order_ ID	Quantity	Total_ Retail_ Price	...	Customer_ Name	...	_IORC_	_N_
15	1240080101	3	216.50	...	Sandrina Stephano	...	1230015	2

Execution

orion.catalog (obs=2)

Customer_ID	Order_ID	Quantity	Total_Retail_Price
5	1230080101	1	247.50
15	1240080101	3	216.50

```
data catalog_customers(keep=Customer_ID Order_ID
                            Quantity
                            Total_Retail_Price
                            Customer_Country
                            Customer_Gender
                            Customer_Name
     erro
   set ori

   set ori
   if _IORC_=0 then output catalog_customers;
   else do;
      _ERROR_=0;
      output errors;
   end;
run;
```

Output current observation to **errors**

Implicit RETURN;

Simplified Index on orion.customer_dim_more

Customer_ ID	Record Identifiers
4	RID
5	RID
9	RID
.	.
13	RID
16	RID
.	.
45	RID
.	.

Partial PDV

Customer_ ID	Order_ ID	Quantity	Total_ Retail_ Price	...	Customer_ Name	...	_IORC_	_N_
15	1240080101	3	216.50	...	Sandrina Stephano	...	1230015	2

...

Execution

orion.catalog (obs=2)

Customer_ID	Order_ID	Quantity	Total_Retail_Price
5	1230080101	1	247.50
15	1240080101	3	216.50

```
data catalog_customers(keep=Customer_ID Order_ID
                            Quantity
                            Total_Retail_Price
                            Customer_Country
                            Customer_Gender
                            Customer_Name
                            Cus
     errors(keep=Customer_ID);
   set orion.catalog(keep=Custo
                         Quant
                         Total
   set orion.customer_dim_more
   if _IORC_=0 then output catalog_customers;
   else do;
      _ERROR_=0;
      output errors;
   end;
run;
```

Continue until EOF in **orion.catalog**

Simplified Index on orion.customer_dim_more

Customer_ ID	Record Identifiers
4	RID
5	RID
9	RID
.	.
13	RID
16	RID
.	.
45	RID
.	.

Partial PDV

Customer_ ID	Order_ ID	Quantity	Total_ Retail_ Price	...	Customer_ Name	...	_IORC_	_N_
15	1240080101	3	216.50	...	Sandrina Stephano	...	1230015	2

...

8.05 Quiz

Open and submit the program **p308a01**.

1. What messages do you see in your SAS log?
2. What is the value of _ERROR_?
3. Replace the ELSE statement with the following ELSE DO group:

```
else do;
   _ERROR_=0;
   output errors;
end;
```

4. Resubmit the program and look at the log.
5. Why are there no messages now?

59

Using the _IORC_ Automatic Variable

To prevent writing the contents of the PDV to the log, perform the following tasks:

- Check the value of _IORC_.
- Set _ERROR_ to 0, if there is no match.

63

Duplicate Key Values

```
data three;
   set one;
   set two key=Variable;
run;
```

Example 1: Contiguous duplications in **one**

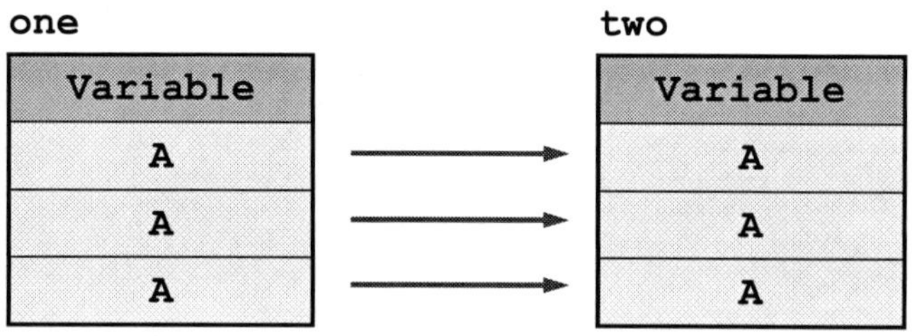

64 ...

If there are contiguous duplications in **one**, each of which has a match in **two**, then SAS performs a one-to-one read.

Duplicate Key Values

```
data three;
   set one;
   set two key=Variable;
run;
```

Example 2: Contiguous duplications in **one**

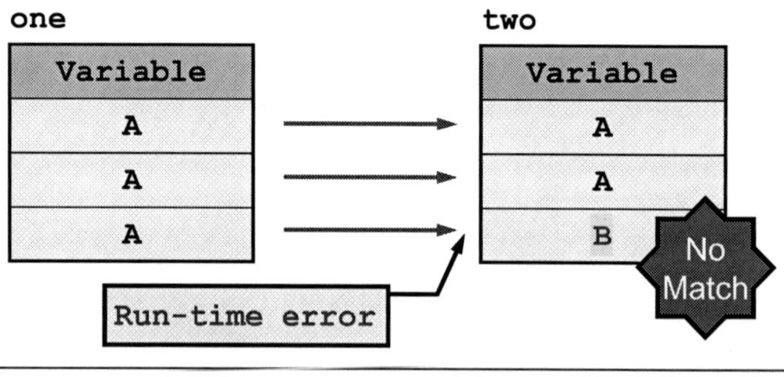

65 ...

If there are contiguous duplications in **one**, some of which do not have a match in **two**, then SAS performs a one-to-one read until it finds a non-match. At that time, SAS encounters a run-time error.

Duplicate Key Values

```
data three;
   set one;
   set two key=Variable/unique;
run;
```

Example 3: Contiguous duplications in **one** with the UNIQUE option

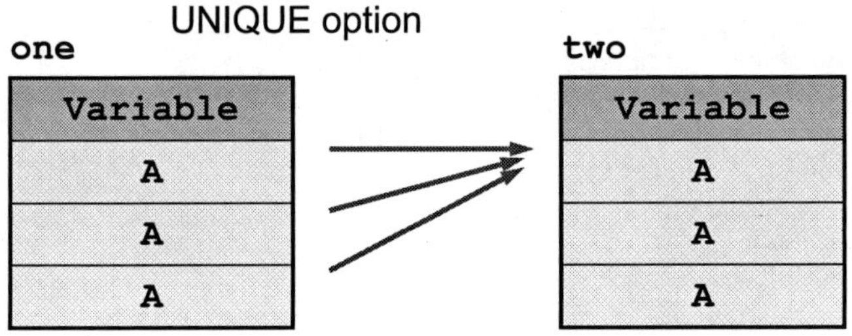

66

If there are contiguous duplications in **one** and the UNIQUE suboption in the KEY= option is used, then SAS reads the first observation in **two**.

Duplicate Key Values

```
data three;
   set one;
   set two key=Variable;
run;
```

Example 4: Noncontiguous duplications in **one**

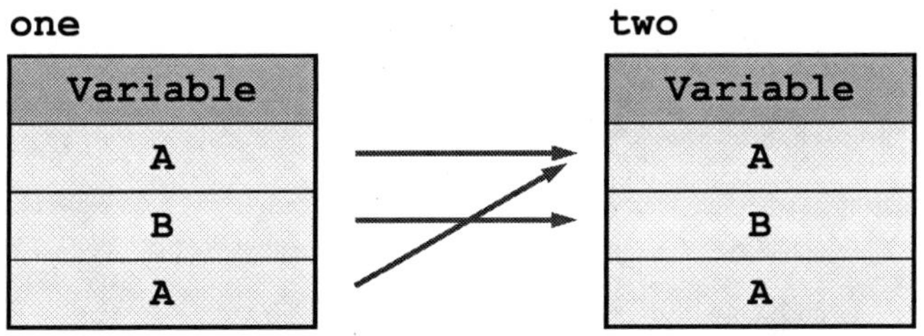

✎ Using the UNIQUE option produces the same result.

67

If there are noncontiguous duplications in **one**, then SAS reads the first observation in **two**.

Using SET/SET with the KEY= Option

Advantages	Disadvantages
Only the necessary observations are read.	An index on one data set is required.
An existing index is used.	Creating and maintaining an index uses resources.
IORC can be used to control how nonmatching data is handled.	When the indexed data set is not sorted by the key variable(s), there can be considerable increase in I/O. This increase in I/O is because of the random access of the data set and the additional I/O required to access the index.
The availability of DATA step syntax provides the full power of the DATA step.	

68

Comparing SET/SET KEY=, Merging, and SQL

Match-Merge	SQL Inner Join	SET/SET KEY=
There is no limit to the number of data sets nor the size of the data sets other than disk space.	The maximum number of tables that can be joined at one time is 256.	Two or more data sets can be combined.
Data is processed sequentially so that observations with duplicate BY values are joined one-to-one.	Data is processed using a Cartesian product for duplicate BY values.	The data set listed in the first SET statement is read sequentially; the data set in the second and subsequent SET statements is processed via the index. Observations in the first data set with duplicates are treated differently depending on whether the duplicates are contiguous or not.
Multiple data sets can be created.	Only one data set can be created with one CREATE TABLE statement.	Multiple data sets can be created.

69

continued...

Comparing SET/SET KEY=, Merging, and SQL

Match-Merge	SQL Inner Join	SET/SET KEY=
Complex business logic can be incorporated using IF-THEN or SELECT/WHEN logic.	The CASE clause can be used for business logic. However, it is not as flexible as DATA step syntax.	Complex business logic can be incorporated using IF-THEN or SELECT/WHEN logic.
The data sets being merged must be sorted or indexed on the BY variable(s).	The data sets being joined do not have to be sorted nor indexed.	The data sets on all but the first SET statement must have the index named on the KEY= option.
An exact match on the BY variable(s) value(s) must be found.	Inequality joins can be performed.	An exact match on the key value is required.
Like-named BY variables must be available in all data sets.	Common variables do not have to be in all data sets.	The indexed variable(s) must be on all data sets.

70

Using Multiple SET … KEY= Statements (Self-Study)

p308d04

You can use multiple SET statements with the KEY= option to combine several data sets. For example, create a data set that contains the customers who ordered products from the Internet and from a catalog.

```
data catalog_internet others;
   keep Customer_ID Order_ID Quantity
        Total_Retail_Price Customer_Name
        Int_OrderID Int_TotPrice Int_Quant
        In_Dim In_Int In_Cat;

   label Int_TotPrice='Total Retail Price for Internet Orders'
         Int_Quant='Quantity of Internet Orders'
         Total_Retail_Price='Total Retail Price for Catalog Orders'
         Quantity='Quantity of Catalog Orders'
         Order_ID='Catalog Order ID'
         Int_OrderID='Internet Order ID'
         In_Dim='In Customer_Dim data'
         In_Int='In Internet data'
         In_Cat='In Catalog data';

 /* orion.catalog is read sequentially. InCat is created for */
 /* educational purposes only.                               */

   set orion.catalog(keep=Customer_ID Order_ID
                     Quantity Total_Retail_Price in=InCat);

 /* orion.customer_dim is read using the index on Customer_ID */
 /* InDim is created for educational purposes only.           */

   set orion.customer_dim(in=InDim) key=Customer_ID;

 /* internet is read using the index on Customer_ID           */
 /* InInt is created for educational purposes only.           */
 /* Order_ID, Total_Retail_Price, Quantity are renamed        */
 /* so that both the values from orion.catalog data and the   */
 /* internet data are in the data set. Without the renaming,  */
 /* the values from internet would overwrite those from       */
 /* catalog.                                                  */

   set internet(in=InInt rename=(Order_ID=Int_OrderID
                                 Total_Retail_Price=Int_TotPrice
                                 Quantity=Int_Quant))
      key=Customer_ID;

 /* In_Dim, In_Int, and In_Cat are created for educational   */
 /* purposes only. They show which data set contributed      */
 /* to an observation.                                        */
```

(Continued on the next page.)

```
   In_Dim=InDim;
   In_Int=InInt;
   In_Cat=InCat;

/* The value of _IORC_=0 only when data comes from all 3 data sets */
   if _IORC_=0 then output catalog_internet;
   else do;
      _ERROR_=0;
      output others;
   end;
run;

proc print data=catalog_internet label;
   title 'Customers who order from both Catalog and Internet';
run;

proc print data=others label;
   title 'Customers who ordered from the catalog only';
   title2 'and the Customers who ordered from the catalog';
   title3 'but were not in orion.Customer_Dim';
run;
```

Exercises

Level 1

4. Combining Data Sets Using an Index to Create One Data Set

The SAS data set **orion.salesstaff** contains information about the employees who work in Sales.

Partial Listing of **orion.salesstaff**

orion.salesstaff SAS Data Set
(Partial Output)

Employee_ID	Job_Title	Salary	Gender	Birth_ Date	Emp_Hire_ Date
120121	Sales Rep. II	$26,600	F	02AUG1944	01JAN1974
120134	Sales Rep. II	$28,015	M	06JUN1949	01JAN1974
120151	Sales Rep. II	$26,520	F	21NOV1944	01JAN1974
120154	Sales Rep. III	$30,490	F	20JUL1944	01JAN1974
120166	Sales Rep. IV	$30,660	M	14JUN1944	01JAN1974

Emp_Term_ Date	Manager_ID	SSN	Employee_Name
.	120102	42-8321-982	Elvish, Irenie
30JUN2006	120102	905-76-7767	Shannan, Sian
.	120103	798-16-4924	Phaiyakounh, Julianna
.	120102	534-14-1428	Hayawardhana, Caterina
31AUG2006	120102	878-79-9390	Nowd, Fadi

The SAS data set **orion.organization_dim** contains information about all employees. There is an index on the **Employee_ID** variable.

Partial Listing of **orion.organization_dim**

```
                         orion.organization_dim SAS Data Set
                                  (Partial Output)

              Employee_
Employee_ID  Country        Company          Department          Section            Org_Group

    120101      AU      Orion Australia  Sales Management  Sales Management  Sales Management
    120102      AU      Orion Australia  Sales Management  Sales Management  Sales Management
    120103      AU      Orion Australia  Sales Management  Sales Management  Sales Management
    120104      AU      Orion Australia  Administration    Administration    Administration
    120105      AU      Orion Australia  Administration    Administration    Administration

                                                 Employee_               Employee_   Employee_
Job_Title                    Employee_Name        Gender        Salary   BirthDate   Hire_Date

Director                     Patrick Lu             M         $163,040   18AUG1976   01JUL2003
Sales Manager                Tom Zhou               M         $108,255   11AUG1969   01JUN1989
Sales Manager                Wilson Dawes           M          $87,975   22JAN1949   01JAN1974
Administration Manager       Kareen Billington      F          $46,230   11MAY1954   01JAN1981
Secretary I                  Liz Povey              F          $27,110   21DEC1974   01MAY1999

Employee_   Manager_    Manager_    Manager_    Manager_    Manager_    Manager_    Manager_
Term_Date    Levels      Level1      Level2      Level3      Level4      Level5      Level6

      .         2        120261      120259           .           .           .           .
      .         3        120101      120261      120259           .           .           .
      .         3        120101      120261      120259           .           .           .
      .         3        120101      120261      120259           .           .           .
      .         3        120101      120261      120259           .           .           .
```

a. Create a SAS data set named **sales_emps** by using an index on **Employee_ID** to combine the two data sets, **orion.salesstaff** and **orion.organization_dim**. Check the SAS log to ensure that you do not have any data errors.

b. Print the first five observations of the **sales_emps** SAS data set.

PROC PRINT Output

```
                              Sales Employee Data
                                (Partial Output)

                                                Birth_   Emp_Hire_  Emp_Term_
Obs  Employee_ID  Job_Title       Salary Gender    Date     Date       Date     Manager_ID

 1        120121 Sales Rep. II   $26,600   F    02AUG1944 01JAN1974          .      120102
 2        120134 Sales Rep. II   $28,015   M    06JUN1949 01JAN1974 30JUN2006      120102
 3        120151 Sales Rep. II   $26,520   F    21NOV1944 01JAN1974          .      120103
 4        120154 Sales Rep. III  $30,490   F    20JUL1944 01JAN1974          .      120102
 5        120166 Sales Rep. IV   $30,660   M    14JUN1944 01JAN1974 31AUG2006      120102

Obs     SSN         Employee_Name          Department    Section    Org_Group

 1 42-8321-982  Elvish, Irenie               Sales        Sales     Assorted Sports Articles
 2 905-76-7767  Shannan, Sian                Sales        Sales     Golf
 3 798-16-4924  Phaiyakounh, Julianna        Sales        Sales     Outdoors
 4 534-14-1428  Hayawardhana, Caterina       Sales        Sales     Racket Sports
 5 878-79-9390  Nowd, Fadi                   Sales        Sales     Running  Jogging
```

Level 2

5. Combining Data Sets Using an Index to Monitor Data Integrity

The data set **orion.shoe_vendors** contains information about the shoe products and their suppliers, but there are vendors in **orion.shoe_vendors** whose products are not in the Orion Star price list, which should contain all prices.

Partial Listing of **orion.shoe_vendors**

orion.shoe_vendors SAS Data Set
(Partial Output)

Product_ Line	Product_ Category	Product_ Group	Product_ID	Product_Name	Supplier_ID
21	2102	2102004	210200400002	Deschutes Boys Outdoors Training Shoes	1303
21	2102	2102004	210200400005	Kid Air Terra Grande Running Shoes	1303
21	2102	2102004	210200400007	Kid Equivalent Street Shoes	1303
21	2102	2102004	210200400009	Kid Impeccably Strong(Bg) Basket Shoes	1303
21	2102	2102004	210200400012	Kid Trainer Lite V(Bp) Street Shoes	1303

Supplier_ Name	Supplier_ Country	Group_Name	Category_Name	Line_ Name	Mfg_Suggested_ Retail_Price
Eclipse Inc	US	Eclipse, Kid's Shoes	Children Sports	Children	$69.00
Eclipse Inc	US	Eclipse, Kid's Shoes	Children Sports	Children	$73.00
Eclipse Inc	US	Eclipse, Kid's Shoes	Children Sports	Children	$79.00
Eclipse Inc	US	Eclipse, Kid's Shoes	Children Sports	Children	$114.00
Eclipse Inc	US	Eclipse, Kid's Shoes	Children Sports	Children	$54.00

The data set **orion.price_list** contains pricing information for all products.

Partial Listing of **orion.price_list**

orion.price_list SAS Data Set
(Partial Output)

Product_ID	Start_ Date	End_Date	Unit_Cost_ Price	Unit_Sales_ Price	Factor
210200100009	09JUN2007	31DEC9999	$15.50	$34.70	1.00
210200100017	24JAN2007	31DEC9999	$17.80	$40.00	1.00
210200200023	04JUL2007	31DEC9999	$8.25	$19.80	1.00
210200600067	27OCT2007	31DEC9999	$28.90	$67.00	1.00
210200600085	28AUG2007	31DEC9999	$17.85	$39.40	1.00

a. Create a simple index on the variable **Product_ID** in the data set **orion.price_list**.

b. Create a SAS data set named **shoes** and a SAS data set named **errors** by using the index on **Product_ID** to combine the two data sets, **orion.shoe_vendors** and **orion.price_list**. The **shoes** data set should have the price information for the shoe products. The **errors** data set should contain data that is in **orion.shoe_vendors,** which is not in the **price_list** data. The **errors** data set should contain only the variables **Product_ID**, **Product_Name**, and **Supplier_Name**. The **errors** data can then be used to determine why these vendors do not have observations in **price_list**.

c. Delete the **Product_ID** index on the data set **orion.price_list**.

d. Print the first five observations of the **shoes** SAS data set.

PROC PRINT Output

```
                                   shoes Data
                                (Partial Output)

Obs      Product_ID                 Product_Name                    Supplier_Name

 1      210201000198    South Peak Junior Training Shoes            3Top Sports
 2      220100400023    Ultra W802 All Terrain Women's Shoes        Ultra Sporting Goods Inc
 3      220100700002    Dmx 10 Women's Aerobic Shoes                Fuller Trading Co.
 4      220100700022    Alexis Women's Classic Shoes                Fuller Trading Co.
 5      220100700024    Armadillo Road Dmx Women's Running Shoes    Fuller Trading Co.

        Mfg_Suggested_          Unit_Cost_        Unit_Sales_
Obs      Retail_Price              Price              Price

 1          $109.00               $26.80             $60.10
 2          $168.00               $40.75             $93.60
 3          $345.00               $89.95            $188.60
 4           $93.00               $24.10             $56.90
 5          $191.00               $49.80            $104.60
```

The data set **shoes** has 27 observations.

e. Print the first five observations of the **errors** SAS data set.

PROC PRINT Output

```
                                The errors Data
                                (Partial Output)

                                                                       Supplier_
Obs      Product_ID                 Product_Name                         Name

 1      210200400002    Deschutes Boys Outdoors Training Shoes      Eclipse Inc
 2      210200400005    Kid Air Terra Grande Running Shoes          Eclipse Inc
 3      210200400007    Kid Equivalent Street Shoes                 Eclipse Inc
 4      210200400009    Kid Impeccably Strong(Bg) Basket Shoes      Eclipse Inc
 5      210200400012    Kid Trainer Lite V(Bp) Street Shoes         Eclipse Inc
```

The data set **errors** has 334 observations.

Level 3

6. Combining Data Sets Using an Index and Using the Macro Facility to Monitor Errors

The data set **orion.first_internet_order** contains the first order that a customer placed via the Internet.

Partial Listing of **orion.first_internet_order**

orion.first_internet_order SAS Data Set (Partial Output)

Customer_ID	Employee_ID	Street_ID	Order_ Date	Delivery_ Date	Order_ID
4	99999999	9260106519	02MAR2004	03MAR2004	1232410925
5	99999999	9260114570	02MAY2007	07MAY2007	1242140006
9	99999999	3940106659	15APR2004	20APR2004	1232698281
11	99999999	3940108592	29OCT2003	03NOV2003	1231653765
19	99999999	3940106547	26DEC2003	30DEC2003	1231976710

Product_ID	Quantity	Total_Retail_ Price	CostPrice_ Per_Unit	Discount
240800200030	1	$47.70	$18.80	.
240100100159	1	$31.40	$13.90	.
230100600035	1	$29.40	$14.15	.
230100200047	1	$72.70	$35.20	.
240300100020	4	$56.40	$6.05	.

The data set **orion.internet** contains multiple orders that a customer placed via the Internet. There is an index on the **Order_ID** variable.

Partial Listing of **orion.internet**

orion.internet SAS Data Set (Partial Output)

Customer_ID	Employee_ID	Street_ID	Order_ Date	Delivery_ Date	Order_ID
70046	99999999	2600100017	02APR2003	03APR2003	1230500669
36	99999999	9260128237	18APR2003	20APR2003	1230591675
171	99999999	1600101555	01MAY2003	04MAY2003	1230657844
11171	99999999	2600100032	07MAY2003	09MAY2003	1230690733
17023	99999999	2600100021	20JUN2003	25JUN2003	1230931366

Product_ID	Quantity	Total_Retail_ Price	CostPrice_ Per_Unit	Discount
240200100131	2	$148.60	$41.35	.
240500100039	1	$34.50	$15.40	.
240100100646	1	$109.90	$46.80	.
240200100043	2	$282.40	$69.40	.
240200200007	2	$166.80	$8.35	.

a. Create a data set named **`processed_orders`** that contains the variables from **`orion.first_internet_order`** and a variable named **`Comment`**. Use the index on the variable **`Order_ID`** to retrieve the matching observation from **`orion.internet`**.

b. The variable **`Comment`** has the value `Order has been processed` if the **`Order_ID`** is in both **`orion.first_internet_order`** and **`orion.internet`**. The value is `Order has not been processed` if the **`Order_ID`** is not in both data sets.

c. Use the %SYSRC AUTOCALL macro described in the reference information in this chapter. In addition, refer to SAS OnlineDoc by following the path shown below:

> **SAS OnlineDoc** ⇨ **Base SAS** ⇨ **SAS 9.2 Macro Language: Reference** ⇨ **Macro Language Dictionary** ⇨ **AutoCall Macros**

d. Print the first 10 observations of **`processed_orders`**.

PROC PRINT Output

Internet Orders
(Partial Output)

Obs	Customer_ID	Employee_ID	Street_ID	Order_ Date	Delivery_ Date	Order_ID	Product_ID
1	4	99999999	9260106519	02MAR2004	03MAR2004	1232410925	240800200030
2	5	99999999	9260114570	02MAY2007	07MAY2007	1242140006	240100100159
3	9	99999999	3940106659	15APR2004	20APR2004	1232698281	230100600035
4	11	99999999	3940108592	29OCT2003	03NOV2003	1231653765	230100200047
5	19	99999999	3940106547	26DEC2003	30DEC2003	1231976710	240300100020
6	20	99999999	9260118934	18MAY2006	24MAY2006	1239226632	220200100190
7	24	99999999	9260115784	02JAN2007	05JAN2007	1241054779	240800200021
8	25	99999999	9260114570	15JAN2007	19JAN2007	1230080101	230100500026
9	27	99999999	9260105670	28JAN2007	02FEB2007	1241286432	240800200009
10	31	99999999	9260128428	25APR2007	29APR2007	1242076538	220200200022

Obs	Quantity	Total_Retail_ Price	CostPrice_ Per_Unit	Discount	Comment
1	1	$47.70	$18.80	.	Order has been processed.
2	1	$31.40	$13.90	.	Order has been processed.
3	1	$29.40	$14.15	.	Order has been processed.
4	1	$72.70	$35.20	.	Order has been processed.
5	4	$56.40	$6.05	.	Order has been processed.
6	3	$190.50	$29.95	.	Order has been processed.
7	2	$195.60	$42.45	.	Order has been processed.
8	1	$247.50	$109.55	.	Order has not been processed.
9	2	$174.40	$34.90	.	Order has been processed.
10	1	$57.30	$33.90	.	Order has been processed.

8.3 Combining Summary and Detail Data

Objectives

- Create an output SAS data set that contains summary statistics from PROC SUMMARY.
- Combine the output SAS data set from PROC SUMMARY with a detail SAS data set.
- Use the SQL procedure to combine summary and detail data.
- Use the SQL procedure to calculate the summary statistic and combine it with every observation in the data set.
- Use the DATA step to calculate the summary statistic and combine it with every observation in the data set.

75

Business Scenario

The data set **orion.totalsalaries** has one observation for every value of **Manager_ID**.

Each observation contains the number of people who report to that manager, and **DeptSal** is the total salary for all of those employees.

Partial Listing of **orion.totalsalaries**

Manager_ID	Numemps	DeptSal
120101	4	$269,570
120102	48	$1,344,595
120103	30	$793,835
120104	15	$425,215
120259	6	$941,155
120260	3	$216,065
120261	6	$595,935
120262	10	$545,255
120270	1	$43,635
120271	9	$280,155

76

Business Scenario

You need to calculate the total salaries paid by the company. Then, divide each individual manager's **`DeptSal`** by that total to create a variable named **`Percent`**.

Partial PROC PRINT Output

Percentage of Total Salaries
for Each Manager
(Partial Output)

Obs	GrandTot	Manager_ID	Numemps	DeptSal	Percent
1	$15,695,800	120101	4	$269,570	1.72%
2	$15,695,800	120102	48	$1,344,595	8.57%
3	$15,695,800	120103	30	$793,835	5.06%
4	$15,695,800	120104	15	$425,215	2.71%
5	$15,695,800	120259	6	$941,155	6.00%
6	$15,695,800	120260	3	$216,065	1.38%
7	$15,695,800	120261	6	$595,935	3.80%
8	$15,695,800	120262	10	$545,255	3.47%
9	$15,695,800	120270	1	$43,635	0.28%
10	$15,695,800	120271	9	$280,155	1.78%

77

Combining Summary and Detail Data

The following is a common business task:

Step 1: Create a summary statistic from a data set variable.

Step 2: Combine the summary information with detail rows of the original data set.

Step 3 Calculate percentages.

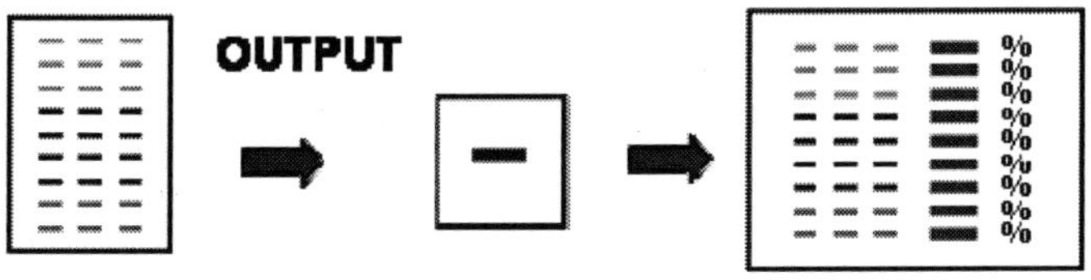

78

Creating a Summary Data Set

The following techniques can be used to create a summary data set:

- the Output Delivery System (ODS)
- ➡ the SUMMARY or MEANS procedure with an OUTPUT statement
- ➡ the DATA step
- ➡ the SQL procedure

79

Reference Information

To use the Output Delivery System to calculate the sum statistic, use the following program:

p308d05

```
ods output summary=sumdata;

proc summary data=orion.totalsalaries print sum;
   var DeptSal;
run;
```

The data set **sumdata** contains one observation with one variable, **DeptSal_Sum**, which has the value 15695800.

The SUMMARY Procedure

For numeric variables within a SAS data set, the SUMMARY procedure computes descriptive statistics such as the following:

- mean
- minimum
- maximum
- number of non-missing values
- standard deviation

80

Create the Summary Statistic

Step 1: Use the SUMMARY procedure to calculate the total of the variable **DeptSal**.

```
proc summary data=orion.totalsalaries;
   var DeptSal;
   output out=summary sum=GrandTot;
run;
```

Listing of **summary**

Obs	_TYPE_	_FREQ_	GrandTot
1	0	53	$15,695,800

81

p308d05

The output data set has variables that contain the requested statistics, plus the following variables:

TYPE	information about the class variables
FREQ	number of observations that an output level represents

PROC SUMMARY OUTPUT Statement

PROC SUMMARY can generate a report that contains the descriptive statistics. To display the report, use the PRINT option in the PROC SUMMARY statement.

The data produced by PROC SUMMARY is routed to a SAS data set using an OUTPUT statement.

General form of the SUMMARY procedure:

```
PROC SUMMARY DATA=SAS-data-set <PRINT>;
     OUTPUT OUT=SAS-data-set
                output-statistic-specification(s);
RUN;
```

82

Combining Summary and Detail Data

Step 2: Combine the summary information with the detail rows.

Step 3: Calculate the percentage.

```
data percent;
   if _N_=1 then set summary(keep=GrandTot);
   set orion.totalsalaries;
   Percent=DeptSal / GrandTot;
   format Percent percent8.2;
run;
```

83 p308d06

The _N_=1 condition causes the **summary** data set to be read only during the first iteration of the DATA step. Without it, the DATA step reaches the end of file in **summary** on the second iteration of the DATA step, and the DATA step terminates with one observation in the data set **percent**.

One observation from the data set **orion.totalsalaries** is read in each iteration of the DATA step.

Execution

summary

GrandTot
15695800

Partial **orion.totalsalaries**

Manager_ID	Numemps	DeptSal
120101	4	269570
120102	48	1344595
120103	30	793835
120104	15	425215
120259	6	941155
120260	3	216065
.	.	.
.	.	.
.	.	.

True

```
data percent;
   if _N_=1 then
      set summary(keep=GrandTot);
   set orion.totalsalaries;
   Percent=DeptSal/GrandTot;
   format Percent percent8.2;
run;
```

PDV

GrandTot	Manager_ID	Numemps	DeptSal	Percent	D _N_
.	.	.	.	.	1

84 ...

Execution

summary

GrandTot
15695800

Partial **orion.totalsalaries**

Manager_ID	Numemps	DeptSal
120101	4	269570
120102	48	1344595
120103	30	793835
120104	15	425215
120259	6	941155
120260	3	216065
.	.	.
.	.	.
.	.	.

```
data percent;
   if _N_=1 then
      set summary(keep=GrandTot);
   set orion.totalsalaries;
   Percent=DeptSal/GrandTot;
   format Percent percent8.2;
run;
```

PDV

GrandTot	Manager_ID	Numemps	DeptSal	Percent	D _N_
15695800	.	.	.	.	1

85 ...

Execution

summary

GrandTot
15695800

Partial **orion.totalsalaries**

Manager_ ID	Numemps	DeptSal
120101	4	269570
120102	48	1344595
120103	30	793835
120104	15	425215
120259	6	941155
120260	3	216065
.	.	.

```
data percent;
   if _N_=1 then
      set summary(keep=GrandTot);
   set orion.totalsalaries;
   Percent=DeptSal/GrandTot;
   format Percent percent8.2;
run;
```

PDV

GrandTot	Manager_ID	Numemps	DeptSal	Percent	D _N_
15695800	120101	4	269570	.	1

86 ...

Execution

summary

GrandTot
15695800

Partial **orion.totalsalaries**

Manager_ ID	Numemps	DeptSal
120101	4	269570
120102	48	1344595
120103	30	793835
120104	15	425215
120259	6	941155
120260	3	216065
.	.	.

```
data percent;
   if _N_=1 then
      set summary(keep=GrandTot);
   set orion.totalsalaries;
   Percent=DeptSal/GrandTot;
   format Percent percent8.2;
run;
```

PDV

GrandTot	Manager_ID	Numemps	DeptSal	Percent	D _N_
15695800	120101	4	269570	0.0172	1

87 ...

Execution

summary

GrandTot
15695800

Partial **orion.totalsalaries**

Manager_ ID	Numemps	DeptSal
120101	4	269570
120102	48	1344595
120103	30	793835
120104	15	425215
120259	6	941155
120260	3	216065
.	.	.

```
data percent;
   if _N_=1 then
      set summary(keep=GrandTot);
   set orion.totalsalaries;
   Percent=DeptSal/GrandTot;
   format Percent percent8.2;
run;
```

Implicit OUTPUT;
Implicit RETURN;

PDV

GrandTot	Manager_ID	Numemps	DeptSal	Percent	D _N_
15695800	120101	4	269570	0.0172	1

88 ...

Execution

summary

GrandTot
15695800

Partial **orion.totalsalaries**

Manager_ ID	Numemps	DeptSal
120101	4	269570
120102	48	1344595
120103	30	793835
120104	15	425215
120259	6	941155
120260	3	216065
.	.	.

```
data percent;
   if _N_=1 then
      set summary(keep=GrandTot);
   set orion.totalsalaries;
   Percent=DeptSal/GrandTot;
   format Percent percent8.2;
run;
```

Initialize PDV

PDV

GrandTot	Manager_ID	Numemps	DeptSal	Percent	D _N_
15695800	120101	4	269570	.	2

89 ...

Execution

summary

GrandTot
15695800

Partial `orion.totalsalaries`

Manager_ ID	Numemps	DeptSal
120101	4	269570
120102	48	1344595
120103	30	793835
120104	15	425215
120259	6	941155
120260	3	216065
.	.	.

False

```
data percent;
   if _N_=1 then
      set summary(keep=GrandTot);
   set orion.totalsalaries;
   Percent=DeptSal/GrandTot;
   format Percent percent8.2;
run;
```

PDV

GrandTot	Manager_ID	Numemps	DeptSal	Percent	D _N_
15695800	120101	4	269570	.	2

90 ...

Execution

summary

GrandTot
15695800

Partial `orion.totalsalaries`

Manager_ ID	Numemps	DeptSal
120101	4	269570
120102	48	1344595
120103	30	793835
120104	15	425215
120259	6	941155
120260	3	216065
.	.	.

```
data percent;
   if _N_=1 then
      set summary(keep=GrandTot);
   set orion.totalsalaries;
   Percent=DeptSal/GrandTot;
   format Percent percent8.2;
run;
```

PDV

GrandTot	Manager_ID	Numemps	DeptSal	Percent	D _N_
15695800	120102	48	1344595	.	2

91 ...

Execution

summary

GrandTot
15695800

Continue until EOF in **orion.totalsalaries**

Partial `orion.totalsalaries`

Manager_ID	Numemps	DeptSal
120101	4	269570
120102	48	1344595
120103	30	793835
120104	15	425215
120259	6	941155
120260	3	216065
.	.	.

```
data percent;
   if _N_=1 then
      set summary(keep=GrandTot);
   set orion.totalsalaries;
   Percent=DeptSal/GrandTot;
   format Percent percent8.2;
run;
```

PDV

GrandTot	Manager_ID	Numemps	DeptSal	Percent	_N_
15695800	121145	45	1216055	0.077	53

94

8.06 Quiz

Open and submit the program **p308a02**.

1. How many observations are in the resulting data set?

2. Why?

3. How did you get 53 observations in the program **p308d06**?

96

Combining Data Using the SQL Procedure

You can join a summary data set and a detail data set using the SQL procedure.

```
proc sql;
   create table percentsql as
   select Manager_ID,
          DeptSal,
          GrandTot,
          DeptSal / GrandTot as Percent
            format=percent8.2
   from orion.totalsalaries,
        summary;
quit;
```

This program takes advantage of the default Cartesian product that SQL creates with inner joins.

100 p308d07

Combining Data Using the SQL Procedure

You can also remerge overall summary results, such as grand totals, with detail data using SQL.

```
proc sql;
   create table percentsql as
   select Manager_ID,
          DeptSal,
          sum(DeptSal) as GrandTot,
          DeptSal / calculated GrandTot
                 as Percent format=8.2
   from orion.totalsalaries;
quit;
```

101 p308d08

The SUM function with one argument calculates the total for the column **DeptSal**.

Because the alias **GrandTot** is assigned to the **sum(DeptSal)** column, the SELECT statement can use the CALCULATED keyword to refer to **GrandTot** as the denominator in this calculation.

When SQL remerges summary data, it puts a note in the SAS log.

SAS Log

```
    proc sql;
2       create table percentsql as
3       select Manager_ID,
4              DeptSal,
5              sum(DeptSal) as GrandTot,
6              DeptSal/calculated GrandTot
7                     as Percent format=8.2
8       from orion.totalsalaries;
NOTE: The query requires remerging summary statistics back with the original data.
NOTE: Table WORK.PERCENTSQL created, with 53 rows and 4 columns.

9    quit;
NOTE: PROCEDURE SQL used (Total process time):
      real time           0.39 seconds
```

In addition to using the SQL procedure for calculating the percentages in one step, the REPORT procedure and the TABULATE procedure can calculate percentages in one step.

p308d08a

```
proc report data=orion.totalsalaries
            out=report_pct(drop=_break_)
            nowd;
   column Manager_ID DeptSal DeptSal=PctSal;
   define Manager_ID / display 'Manager ID';
   define DeptSal / sum 'Department Salaries';
   define PctSal / pctsum format=percent8.2
                   'Percent of Total Salaries';
run;

proc tabulate data=orion.totalsalaries
              out=tab_pct(drop=_type_ _page_ _table_);
   class Manager_ID;
   var DeptSal;
   table Manager_ID='Manager ID',
         DeptSal='Department Salaries' * (sum*f=dollar14.2 pctsum);
run;
```

Using the DATA Step

You can use the DATA step to read the data from **orion.totalsalaries**, calculate the **GrandTot** variable, and then reread the data in order to calculate the percentages.

```
data percent(drop=i);
① if _N_=1 then do i=1 to TotObs;
   ② set orion.totalsalaries(keep=DeptSal)
         nobs=TotObs;
   ③ GrandTot + DeptSal;
   end;
④ set orion.totalsalaries;
⑤ Percent=DeptSal / GrandTot;
   format Percent percent8.2;
run;
```

102 p308d09

① During the first execution of the DATA step, the DO loop executes the SET statement for each observation in the **orion.totalsalaries** data set.

② When the SET statement executes, it reads the value of **DeptSal** from **orion.totalsalaries**.

③ The SUM statement **GrandTot + DeptSal** accumulates the value of **DeptSal** into the variable **GrandTot**.

④ The DO loop completes execution when **i** is greater than **TotObs**, preventing SAS from reaching the end-of-file marker. The second SET statement reads the observations from **orion.totalsalaries** starting with observation 1.

⑤ The variable **Percent** is calculated for each of those observations.

Reference Information

In SAS 9.2 you can use the SUM method for the hash object to calculate the grand total of the variable **DeptSal**.

p308d10

```
data tot_sal / view=tot_sal;
   set orion.totalsalaries;
   Key='A';
run;

data percent;
   retain GrandTot 0;
   if _N_=1 then do;
      dcl hash H(suminc:'DeptSal');
      H.definekey('Key');
      H.definedone();
      do while(not Done);
         set tot_sal end=Done;
         H.ref();
       end;
   end;
   H.sum(sum:GrandTot);
   set orion.totalsalaries;
   Percent=DeptSal / GrandTot;
   format Percent percent8.2;
run;
```

Exercises

Level 1

7. Combining Summary Data Containing an Average with Detail Data

The data set **orion.customer_dim** contains the age for each customer.

Partial Listing of **orion.customer_dim**

orion.customer_dim SAS Data Set
(Partial Output)

Customer_ID	Customer_ Country	Customer_ Gender	Customer_Name	Customer_ FirstName	Customer_ LastName	Customer_ BirthDate	Customer_ Age_Group
4	US	M	James Kvarniq	James	Kvarniq	27JUN1974	31-45 years
5	US	F	Sandrina Stephano	Sandrina	Stephano	09JUL1979	15-30 years
9	DE	F	Cornelia Krahl	Cornelia	Krahl	27FEB1974	31-45 years
10	US	F	Karen Ballinger	Karen	Ballinger	18OCT1984	15-30 years
11	DE	F	Elke Wallstab	Elke	Wallstab	16AUG1974	31-45 years

Customer_Type	Customer_Group	Customer_ Age
Orion Club members low activity	Orion Club members	33
Orion Club Gold members medium activity	Orion Club Gold members	28
Orion Club Gold members medium activity	Orion Club Gold members	33
Orion Club members high activity	Orion Club members	23
Orion Club members high activity	Orion Club members	33

a. Calculate the average age of all customers.

b. Create a SAS data set named **age_dif**, which combines the average age of all customers with the **orion.customer_dim** data set in order to determine the difference between each customer's age and the average for all customers. (You can use any method presented in this section.)

c. Print the first five observations of the **age_dif** SAS data set.

PROC PRINT Output

The age_dif Data Set
(Partial Output)

Obs	AvgAge	Customer_ID	Customer_ Age	Age_Difference
1	41.9740	4	33	-8.9740
2	41.9740	5	28	-13.9740
3	41.9740	9	33	-8.9740
4	41.9740	10	23	-18.9740
5	41.9740	11	33	-8.9740

Level 2

8. Combining Summary Data Containing a Total with Detail Data

The data set **orion.employee_donations** contains the contributions of employees to various charities. The contributions are reported for each of four quarters.

Partial Listing of **orion.employee_donations**

```
                          orion.employee_donations SAS Data Set
                                    (Partial Output)

Employee_ID  Qtr1   Qtr2   Qtr3   Qtr4                       Recipients

    120265     .      .      .     25   Mitleid International 90%, Save the Baby Animals 10%
    120267    15     15     15     15   Disaster Assist, Inc. 80%, Cancer Cures, Inc. 20%
    120269    20     20     20     20   Cancer Cures, Inc. 10%, Cuidadores Ltd. 90%
    120270    20     10      5      .   AquaMissions International 10%, Child Survivors 90%
    120271    20     20     20     20   Cuidadores Ltd. 80%, Mitleid International 20%

    Paid_By

Cash or Check
Payroll Deduction
Payroll Deduction
Cash or Check
Payroll Deduction
```

a. Select any method to create a SAS data set named **compare** by performing the following tasks:

- Calculate the total contribution for each employee.
- Determine the average of the total contribution for all of the employees.
- Calculate the difference between the average and each individual employee's total contribution.

b. Print the first five observations of the **compare** SAS data set.

PROC PRINT Output

```
                                   The compare Data Set
                                     (Partial Output)

      Avg_
Obs Donation       Employee_ID    Qtr1     Qtr2     Qtr3     Qtr4

  1  47.2581          120265        .        .        .       25
  2  47.2581          120267       15       15       15       15
  3  47.2581          120269       20       20       20       20
  4  47.2581          120270       20       10        5        .
  5  47.2581          120271       20       20       20       20

                                                                          Total_
Obs                      Recipients                          Paid_By     Donation Difference

  1 Mitleid International 90%, Save the Baby Animals 10% Cash or Check       25     -22.2581
  2 Disaster Assist, Inc. 80%, Cancer Cures, Inc. 20%    Payroll Deduction   60      12.7419
  3 Cancer Cures, Inc. 10%, Cuidadores Ltd. 90%          Payroll Deduction   80      32.7419
  4 AquaMissions International 10%, Child Survivors 90%  Cash or Check       35     -12.2581
  5 Cuidadores Ltd. 80%, Mitleid International 20%       Payroll Deduction   80      32.7419
```

Level 3

9. Combining Summary Data Containing a Weighted Average and Detail Data

The SAS data set **orion.order_fact** contains the variables **CostPrice_Per_Unit** and **Quantity**.

Partial Listing of **orion.order_fact**

```
                              orion.order_fact SAS Data Set
                                    (Partial Output)

                                                      Order_     Delivery_
 Customer_ID       Employee_ID         Street_ID        Date       Date               Order_ID

          63            121039        9260125492   11JAN2003   11JAN2003            1230058123
           5          99999999        9260114570   15JAN2003   19JAN2003            1230080101
          45          99999999        9260104847   20JAN2003   22JAN2003            1230106883
          41            120174        1600101527   28JAN2003   28JAN2003            1230147441
         183            120134        1600100760   27FEB2003   27FEB2003            1230315085

Order_                                 Total_Retail_       CostPrice_
 Type         Product_ID     Quantity           Price         Per_Unit     Discount

   1        220101300017         1            $16.50            $7.45          .
   2        230100500026         1           $247.50          $109.55          .
   2        240600100080         1            $28.30            $8.55          .
   1        240600100010         2            $32.00            $6.50          .
   1        240200200039         3            $63.60            $8.80          .
```

The data set **orion.product_dim** contains the variables **Product_ID** and **Product_Name**.

Partial Listing of **orion.product_dim**

```
                              orion.product_dim SAS Data Set
                                    (Partial Output)

                Product_   Product_
  Product_ID    Line       Category        Product_Group              Product_Name

210200100009 Children Children Sports A-Team, Kids              Kids Sweat Round Neck,Large Logo
210200100017 Children Children Sports A-Team, Kids              Sweatshirt Children's O-Neck
210200200022 Children Children Sports Bathing Suits, Kids       Sunfit Slow Swimming Trunks
210200200023 Children Children Sports Bathing Suits, Kids       Sunfit Stockton Swimming Trunks Jr.
210200300006 Children Children Sports Eclipse, Kid's Clothes Fleece Cuff Pant Kid'S

Supplier_
 Country     Supplier_Name                  Supplier_ID

   US        A Team Sports                         3298
   US        A Team Sports                         3298
   US        Nautlius SportsWear Inc               6153
   US        Nautlius SportsWear Inc               6153
   US        Eclipse Inc                           1303
```

a. Select any method to create a SAS data set named **products** by performing the following tasks:

- Calculate the total **CostPrice_Per_Unit** weighted by **Quantity**.
- Combine the weighted total with the **orion.order_fact** data. Create a new variable **Percent** that is based on the actual total cost (**CostPrice_Per_Unit *Quantity**) and the weighted total.

b. Print the first five observations of the **products** SAS data set.

PROC PRINT Output

The products Data Set
(Partial Output)

Obs	Customer_ID	Quantity	CostPrice_ Per_Unit	Product_Name	Percent
1	90	2	$15.50	Kids Sweat Round Neck,Large Logo	0.068%
2	49	1	$17.35	Sweatshirt Children's O-Neck	0.038%
3	79	2	$7.05	Sunfit Slow Swimming Trunks	0.031%
4	52	1	$8.25	Sunfit Stockton Swimming Trunks Jr.	0.018%
5	90	1	$7.70	Fleece Cuff Pant Kid'S	0.017%

Reference Information

To create a running total for a variable, you can use either the DATA step or the SQL procedure.

p308d11

```
proc sort data=orion.order_fact out=order_fact;
   by Order_Date Order_ID;
run;

data running_totals;
   keep Order_Date Product_ID Total_Retail_Price
        Sum_Total_Retail_Price;
   set order_fact;
   Sum_Total_Retail_Price + Total_Retail_Price;
   format Sum_Total_Retail_Price dollar8.2;
run;

proc print data=running_totals(obs=10);
run;
```

Running Totals using the DATA Step

Obs	Order_ Date	Product_ID	Total_Retail_ Price	Sum_Total_ Retail_ Price
1	11JAN2003	220101300017	$16.50	$16.50
2	15JAN2003	230100500026	$247.50	$264.00
3	20JAN2003	240600100080	$28.30	$292.30
4	28JAN2003	240600100010	$32.00	$324.30
5	27FEB2003	240200200039	$63.60	$387.90
6	02MAR2003	240100400005	$234.60	$622.50
7	03MAR2003	240800200062	$35.40	$657.90
8	03MAR2003	240800200063	$73.80	$731.70
9	09MAR2003	240500100004	$127.00	$858.70
10	09MAR2003	240500200003	$23.20	$881.90

p308d11

```
proc sql;
   create table order_fact_with_obsnum as
      select monotonic() as obsnum,
             *
      from orion.order_fact;
   create table running_totals_sql as
      select o1.Order_Date,
             o1.Product_ID,
             o1.Total_Retail_Price,
             (select sum(o2.Total_Retail_Price)
             from order_fact_with_obsnum as o2
             where o2.obsnum <= o1.obsnum) as Sum_Total_Retail_Price
                                              format=dollar8.2
       from order_fact_with_obsnum as o1
       order by Order_Date, Order_ID, Sum_Total_Retail_Price;

title 'Running Totals using PROC SQL;
   select * from running_totals_sql(obs=10);
quit;
```

The *monotonic* function enables you to create row numbers in SQL that are written to the table and not only a displayed value. This Base SAS function returns 1 the first time that it is called, 2 the second time, 3 the next time, and so forth. See the SAS Usage Note 15138 for more information about the monotonic function.

Running Totals using PROC SQL

Date Order was placed by Customer	Product ID	Total Retail Price for This Product	Sum_Total_ Retail_Price
11JAN2003	220101300017	$16.50	$16.50
15JAN2003	230100500026	$247.50	$264.00
20JAN2003	240600100080	$28.30	$292.30
28JAN2003	240600100010	$32.00	$324.30
27FEB2003	240200200039	$63.60	$387.90
02MAR2003	240100400005	$234.60	$622.50
03MAR2003	240800200062	$35.40	$657.90
03MAR2003	240800200063	$73.80	$731.70
09MAR2003	240500100004	$127.00	$858.70
09MAR2003	240500200003	$23.20	$881.90

To ensure that the data sets are the same, you can use PROC COMPARE.

p308d11

```
proc compare data=running_totals compare=running_totals_sql;
   title 'Comparing the Resulting Data Sets';
run;
```

```
                    Comparing the Resulting Data Sets

                         The COMPARE Procedure
         Comparison of WORK.RUNNING_TOTALS with WORK.RUNNING_TOTALS_SQL
                            (Method=EXACT)

                           Data Set Summary

   Dataset                         Created          Modified  NVar    NObs

   WORK.RUNNING_TOTALS      28MAY08:14:40:19  28MAY08:14:40:19     4     617
   WORK.RUNNING_TOTALS_SQL  28MAY08:14:44:21  28MAY08:14:44:21     4     617

                           Variables Summary

                  Number of Variables in Common: 4.

                          Observation Summary

                   Observation      Base  Compare

                   First Obs           1        1
                   Last  Obs         617      617

      Number of Observations in Common: 617.
      Total Number of Observations Read from WORK.RUNNING_TOTALS: 617.
      Total Number of Observations Read from WORK.RUNNING_TOTALS_SQL: 617.

      Number of Observations with Some Compared Variables Unequal: 0.
      Number of Observations with All Compared Variables Equal: 617.

      NOTE: No unequal values were found. All values compared are exactly equal.
```

8.4 Combining Data Conditionally (Self-Study)

Objectives

- Combine data conditionally using multiple SET statements.
- Combine data conditionally with the SQL procedure.
- Combine data conditionally using a hash object.

106

Business Scenario

Some combinations of data are based on a condition. The data set **orion.order_fact** contains the **Total_Retail_Price** for all values of **Order_Date**.

```
orion.order_fact(where=(Order_Date between
'01SEP2007'd and '30SEP2007'd))
```

Customer_ID	Employee_ID	Street_ID	Order_Date	...	Total_Retail_Price	CostPrice_Per_Unit	Discount
928	99999999	9050100016	04SEP2007	...	$86.30	$41.40	.
27	99999999	9260105670	05SEP2007	...	$78.40	$16.45	.
31	121057	9260128428	06SEP2007	...	$50.30	$25.25	.
45	121065	9260104847	06SEP2007	...	$78.20	$39.20	.
5	121026	9260114570	09SEP2007	...	$52.50	$22.25	.
12	121051	9260103713	18SEP2007	...	$87.20	$44.95	.
69	121029	9260116402	20SEP2007	...	$23.50	$9.20	.
24	99999999	9260115784	25SEP2007	...	$46.10	$19.70	.
41	120195	1600101527	26SEP2007	...	$134.00	$28.90	.
11	99999999	3940108592	28SEP2007	...	$78.20	$19.65	.

orion.order_fact is sorted by **Order_Date**.

107

Business Scenario

The data set **orion.rates** has the average conversion rate for converting from dollars to euros for the weeks in September 2007.

orion.rates

SDate	EDate	AvgRate
01SEP2007	07SEP2007	0.73117
08SEP2007	14SEP2007	0.72184
15SEP2007	21SEP2007	0.71589
22SEP2007	30SEP2007	0.70725

✎ **orion.rates** is sorted by **SDate**.

108

Business Scenario

You need to determine the **Total_Retail_Price** in euros.

Listing of **euros**

Customer_ ID	Order_ Date	Product_ ID	Total_ Retail_ Price	SDate	EDate	AvgRate	EuroPrice
928	04SEP2007	230100600030	$86.30	01SEP2007	07SEP2007	0.73117	€ 63.10
27	05SEP2007	240500200082	$78.40	01SEP2007	07SEP2007	0.73117	€ 57.32
31	06SEP2007	220200100137	$50.30	01SEP2007	07SEP2007	0.73117	€ 36.78
45	06SEP2007	230100600015	$78.20	01SEP2007	07SEP2007	0.73117	€ 57.18
5	09SEP2007	210200500016	$52.50	08SEP2007	14SEP2007	0.72184	€ 37.90
12	18SEP2007	240200100053	$87.20	15SEP2007	21SEP2007	0.71589	€ 62.43
69	20SEP2007	210200700016	$23.50	15SEP2007	21SEP2007	0.71589	€ 16.82
24	25SEP2007	240600100102	$46.10	22SEP2007	30SEP2007	0.70725	€ 32.60
41	26SEP2007	210200600067	$134.00	22SEP2007	30SEP2007	0.70725	€ 94.77
11	30SEP2007	220200100002	$78.20	28SEP2007	30SEP2007	0.70725	€ 55.31

109

Conditionally Combining Data

What needs to be done:

Partial PDV

Order_Date	SDate	EDate	AvgRate
04SEP2007	01SEP2007	07SEP2007	0.73117

Order_Date between SDate and EDate

110 ...

Conditionally Combining Data

What needs to be done:

Partial PDV

Order_Date	SDate	EDate	AvgRate
04SEP2007	01SEP2007	07SEP2007	0.73117

Order_Date between SDate and EDate

True

Use this rate

112 ...

Conditionally Combining Data

What needs to be done:

Partial PDV

Order_Date	SDate	EDate	AvgRate
09SEP2007	01SEP2007	07SEP2007	0.73117

Order_Date between SDate and EDate

False

114 ...

Conditionally Combining Data

What needs to be done:

Partial PDV

Order_Date	SDate	EDate	AvgRate
09SEP2007	08SEP2007	14SEP2007	0.72184

Read observations from orion.rates until order_date is between SDate and EDate

115

Conditionally Combining Data

What needs to be done:

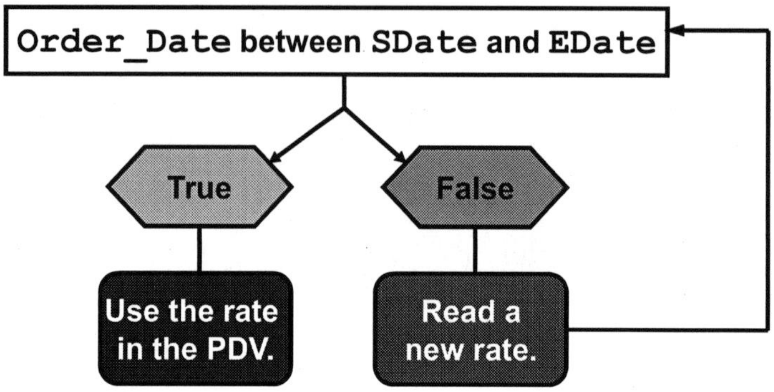

116

8.07 Poll

Can the DATA step merge be used for this task?

- ❍ Yes
- ❍ No

118

Conditionally Combining Data

The MERGE statement can be used to join data when one of the following conditions is met:

- The data can be joined by comparing values of a common BY value.

```
data three;
   merge one two;
   by X;
run;
```

- The data can be combined by observation number. In this case, there is no BY statement in the DATA step.

```
data three;
   merge one two;
run;
```

120

Multiple SET Statements (Review)

You can use multiple SET statements to combine observations from several SAS data sets.

When you use multiple SET statements, the following occurs:

- Processing stops when SAS encounters the end-of-file marker on either data set.
- The variables in the PDV are not reinitialized when a second SET statement is executed.

```
data euros;
   set orion.order_fact(where=(Order_Date
                        between '01SEP2007'd
                        and '30SEP2007'd));
   set orion.rates;
run;
```

121

Conditionally Combining Data

```
data euros;
   set orion.order_fact(where=(Order_Date between
                        '01SEP2007'd and '30SEP2007'd)
                        keep=Customer_ID Order_Date
                             Product_ID
                             Total_Retail_Price);
   do while (not (SDate le Order_Date le
                  EDate));
      set orion.rates;
   end;
   EuroPrice=Total_Retail_Price * AvgRate;
   format EuroPrice Euro10.2;
run;
```

orion.order_fact must be sorted by Order_Date.
orion.rates must be sorted by SDate.

122 p308d12

To use multiple SET statements in this fashion, both data sets must be sorted in order (ascending or descending) by the variables tested in the DO WHILE statement.

Conditionally Combining Data

```
data euros;
   set orion.order_fact(where=(Order_Da
                        '01SEP2007'd a
                        keep=Customer_I
                             Product_ID
                             Total_Retail_Price);
   do while (not (SDate le Order_Date le
                  EDate));
      set orion.rates;
   end;
   EuroPrice=Total_Retail_Price*AvgRate;
   format EuroPrice Euro10.2;
run;
```

When this is true, you do not need to read a new rate.

orion.order_fact must be sorted by Order_Date.
orion.rates must be sorted by SDate.

123 p308d12

Conditionally Combining Data

```
data euros;
   set orion.order_fact(where=(Order_Da
                        '01SEP2007'd a
                       keep=Customer_I
                           Product_ID
                           Total_Retail_Price);
   do while (not (SDate le Order_Date le
                        EDate));
      set orion.rates;
   end;
   EuroPrice=Total_Retail_Price*AvgRate;
   format EuroPrice Euro10.2;
run;
```

When this is true, you do need to read a new rate.

orion.order_fact must be sorted by **Order_Date**.

orion.rates must be sorted by **SDate**.

124

p308d12

8.08 Quiz

Why do you have to use a WHERE= data set option rather than a WHERE statement to subset by **Order_Date**?

127

Execution

Partial **orion.order_fact**

Customer_ID	...	Order_Date	...	Total_Retail_Price	...
928	...	04SEP2007	...	86.30	...
27	...	05SEP2007	...	78.40	...
31	...	06SEP2007	...	50.30	...
45	...	06SEP2007	...	78.20	...
5	...	09SEP2007	...	52.50	...
.	.	.	.	.	.

orion.rates

SDate	EDate	AvgRate
01SEP2007	07SEP2007	0.73117
08SEP2007	14SEP2007	0.72184
15SEP2007	21SEP2007	0.71589
22SEP2007	30SEP2007	0.70725

```
data euros;
   set orion.order_fact(where=(Order_Date
             between '01SEP2007'd and
                     '30SEP2007'd)
             keep=Customer_ID Order_Date
                  Product_ID
                  Total_Retail_Price);
   do while (not (SDate le Order_Date le
                  EDate));
      set orion.rates;
   end;
   EuroPrice=Total_Retail_Price*AvgRate;
   format EuroPrice Euro10.2;
run;
```

PDV

Customer_ID	Order_Date	Product_ID	Total_Retail_Price	SDate	EDate	Avg Rate	Euro Price	D _N_
928	04SEP2007	230100600030	86.30	.	.	.	.	1

129 ...

Execution

Partial **orion.order_fact**

Customer_ID	...	Order_Date	...	Total_Retail_Price	...
928	...	04SEP2007	...	86.30	...
27	...	05SEP2007	...	78.40	...
31	...	06SEP2007	...	50.30	...
45	...	06SEP2007	...	78.20	...
5	...	09SEP2007	...	52.50	...
.	.	.	.	.	.

orion.rates

SDate	EDate	AvgRate
01SEP2007	07SEP2007	0.73117
08SEP2007	14SEP2007	0.72184
15SEP2007	21SEP2007	0.715...
22SEP2007	30SEP2007	0.707...

```
data euros;
   set orion.order_fact(where=(Order_Date
             between '01SEP2007'd and
                     '30SEP2007'd)
             keep=Customer_ID Order_Date
                  Product_ID
                  Total_Retail_Price);
   do while (not (SDate le Order_Date le
                  EDate));
      set orion.rates;
   end;
   EuroPrice=Total_Retail_Price*AvgRate;
   format EuroPrice Euro10.2;
run;
```

False

PDV

Customer_ID	Order_Date	Product_ID	Total_Retail_Price	SDate	EDate	Avg Rate	Euro Price	D _N_
928	04SEP2007	230100600030	86.30	.	.	.	.	1

Is 04SEP2007 between . and .?

130 ...

Execution

Partial **orion.order_fact**

Customer_ID	...	Order_Date	...	Total_Retail_Price	...
928	...	04SEP2007	...	86.30	...
27	...	05SEP2007	...	78.40	...
31	...	06SEP2007	...	50.30	...
45	...	06SEP2007	...	78.20	...
5	...	09SEP2007	...	52.50	...
.	.	.	.	.	.

orion.rates

SDate	EDate	AvgRate
01SEP2007	07SEP2007	0.73117
08SEP2007	14SEP2007	0.72184
15SEP2007	21SEP2007	0.715..
22SEP2007	30SEP2007	0.707..

```
data euros;
   set orion.order_fact(where=(Order_Date
              between '01SEP2007'd and
                      '30SEP2007'd)
              keep=Customer_ID Order_Date
                   Product_ID
                   Total_Retail_Price);
   do while (not (SDate le Order_Date le
                               EDate));
      set orion.rates;
   end;
   EuroPrice=Total_Retail_Price*AvgRate;
   format EuroPrice Euro10.2;
run;
```

The DO WHILE condition is true, so the DO loop executes.

True

PDV

Customer_ID	Order_Date	Product_ID	Total_Retail_Price	SDate	EDate	Avg Rate	Euro Price	_N_
928	04SEP2007	230100600030	86.30	.	.	.	.	1

Is NOT (04SEP2007 between . and .)?

131 ...

Execution

Partial **orion.order_fact**

Customer_ID	...	Order_Date	...	Total_Retail_Price	...
928	...	04SEP2007	...	86.30	...
27	...	05SEP2007	...	78.40	...
31	...	06SEP2007	...	50.30	...
45	...	06SEP2007	...	78.20	...
5	...	09SEP2007	...	52.50	...
.	.	.	.	.	.

orion.rates

SDate	EDate	AvgRate
01SEP2007	07SEP2007	0.73117
08SEP2007	14SEP2007	0.72184
15SEP2007	21SEP2007	0.71589
22SEP2007	30SEP2007	0.70725

```
data euros;
   set orion.order_fact(where=(Order_Date
              between '01SEP2007'd and
                      '30SEP2007'd)
              keep=Customer_ID Order_Date
                   Product_ID
                   Total_Retail_Price);
   do while (not (SDate le Order_Date le
                               EDate));
      set orion.rates;
   end;
   EuroPrice=Total_Retail_Price*AvgRate;
   format EuroPrice Euro10.2;
run;
```

PDV

Customer_ID	Order_Date	Product_ID	Total_Retail_Price	SDate	EDate	Avg Rate	Euro Price	_N_
928	04SEP2007	230100600030	86.30	01SEP2007	07SEP2007	0.73117	.	1

132 ...

Execution

Partial **orion.order_fact**

Customer_ID	...	Order_Date	...	Total_Retail_Price	...
928	...	04SEP2007	...	86.30	...
27	...	05SEP2007	...	78.40	...
31	...	06SEP2007	...	50.30	...
45	...	06SEP2007	...	78.20	...
5	...	09SEP2007	...	52.50	...
.	.	.	.	.	.

orion.rates

SDate	EDate	AvgRate
01SEP2007	07SEP2007	0.73117
08SEP2007	14SEP2007	0.72184
15SEP2007	21SEP2007	0.71589
22SEP2007	30SEP2007	0.707

```
data euros;
   set orion.order_fact(where=(Order_Date
               between '01SEP2007'd and
                     '30SEP2007'd)
               keep=Customer_ID Order_Date
                    Product_ID
                    Total_Retail_Price);
   do while (not (SDate le Order_Date le
                            EDate));
      set orion.rates;
   end;
   EuroPrice=Total_Retail_Price*AvgRate;
   format EuroPrice Euro10.2;
run;
```

The DO WHILE condition is false, so the DO loop does not execute.

PDV

Customer_ID	Order_Date	Product_ID		SDate	EDate	Avg Rate	Euro Price	_N_
928	04SEP2007	230100600030	86.30	01SEP2007	07SEP2007	0.73117	.	1

False

Is NOT(04SEP2007 between 01SEP2007 and 07SEP2007)?

135 ...

Execution

Partial **orion.order_fact**

Customer_ID	...	Order_Date	...	Total_Retail_Price	...
928	...	04SEP2007	...	86.30	...
27	...	05SEP2007	...	78.40	...
31	...	06SEP2007	...	50.30	...
45	...	06SEP2007	...	78.20	...
5	...	09SEP2007	...	52.50	...
.	.	.	.	.	.

orion.rates

SDate	EDate	AvgRate
01SEP2007	07SEP2007	0.73117
08SEP2007	14SEP2007	0.72184
15SEP2007	21SEP2007	0.71589
22SEP2007	30SEP2007	0.70725

```
data euros;
   set orion.order_fact(where=(Order_Date
               between '01SEP2007'd and
                     '30SEP2007'd)
               keep=Customer_ID Order_Date
                    Product_ID
                    Total_Retail_Price);
   do while (not (SDate le Order_Date le
                            EDate));
      set orion.rates;
   end;
   EuroPrice=Total_Retail_Price*AvgRate;
   format EuroPrice Euro10.2;
run;
```

PDV

Customer_ID	Order_Date	Product_ID	Total_Retail_Price	SDate	EDate	Avg Rate	Euro Price	_N_
928	04SEP2007	230100600030	86.30	01SEP2007	07SEP2007	0.73117	63.10	1

136 ...

Execution

Partial **orion.order_fact**

Customer_ID	...	Order_Date	...	Total_Retail_Price	...
928	...	04SEP2007	...	86.30	...
27	...	05SEP2007	...	79.40	...
31	...	06SEP2007	...	50.30	...
45	...	06SEP2007	...	78.20	...
5	...	09SEP2007	...	52.50	...
.	.	.	.	.	.

orion.rates

SDate	EDate	AvgRate
01SEP2007		
08SEP2007		
15SEP2007		
22SEP2007	30SEP2007	0.70725

```
data euros;
   set orion.order_fact(where=(Order_Date
              between '01SEP2007'd and
                  '30SEP2007'd)
              keep=Customer_ID Order_Date
                   Product_ID
                   Total_Retail_Price);
   do while (not (SDate le Order_Date le
                            EDate));
      set orion.rates;
   end;
   EuroPrice=Total_Retail_Price*AvgRate;
   format EuroPrice Euro10.2;
run;
```

Implicit OUTPUT;
Implicit RETURN;

PDV

Customer_ID	Order_Date	Product_ID	Total_Retail_Price	SDate	EDate	AvgRate	EuroPrice	_N_
928	04SEP2007	230100600030	86.30	01SEP2007	07SEP2007	0.73117	63.10	1

137

8.09 Quiz

What variables are set to missing at the top of the DATA step?

139

Execution

Partial **orion.order_fact**

Customer_ID	...	Order_Date	...	Total_Retail_Price	...
928	...	04SEP2007	...	86.30	...
27	...	05SEP2007	...	78.40	...
31	...	06SEP2007	...	50.30	...
45	...	06SEP2007	...	78.20	...
5	...	09SEP2007	...	52.50	...
⋮	⋮	⋮	⋮	⋮	⋮

Initialize PDV

orion.rates

SDate	EDate	AvgRate
01SEP2007	07SEP2007	0.73117
08SEP2007	14SEP2007	0.72184
15SEP2007	21SEP2007	0.71589
22SEP2007	30SEP2007	0.70725

```
data euros;
   set orion.order_fact(where=(Order_Date
              between '01SEP2007'd and
                  '30SEP2007'd)
              keep=Customer_ID Order_Date
                   Product_ID
                   Total_Retail_Price);
   ... (not (SDate le Order_Date le
                        EDate));
      ...ion.rates;
   ...
   EuroPrice=Total_Retail_Price*AvgRate;
   format EuroPrice Euro10.2;
run;
```

PDV

Customer_ID	Order_Date	Product_ID	Total_Retail_Price	SDate	EDate	AvgRate	EuroPrice	_N_
928	04SEP2007	230100600030	86.30	01SEP2007	07SEP2007	0.73117	.	2

141 ...

Execution

Partial **orion.order_fact**

Customer_ID	...	Order_Date	...	Total_Retail_Price	...
928	...	04SEP2007	...	86.30	...
27	...	05SEP2007	...	78.40	...
31	...	06SEP2007	...	50.30	...
45	...	06SEP2007	...	79.20	...
5	...	09SEP2007	...	52.50	...
⋮	⋮	⋮	⋮	⋮	⋮

orion.rates

SDate	EDate	AvgRate
01SEP2007	07SEP2007	0.73117
08SEP2007	14SEP2007	0.72184
15SEP2007	21SEP2007	0.71589
22SEP2007	30SEP2007	0.70725

```
data euros;
   set orion.order_fact(where=(Order_Date
              between '01SEP2007'd and
                  '30SEP2007'd)
              keep=Customer_ID Order_Date
                   Product_ID
                   Total_Retail_Price);
   do while (not (SDate le Order_Date le
                        EDate));
      set orion.rates;
   end;
   EuroPrice=Total_Retail_Price*AvgRate;
   format EuroPrice Euro10.2;
run;
```

PDV

Customer_ID	Order_Date	Product_ID	Total_Retail_Price	SDate	EDate	AvgRate	EuroPrice	_N_
27	05SEP2007	240500200082	78.40	01SEP2007	07SEP2007	0.73117	.	2

142 ...

Execution

Partial **orion.order_fact**

Customer_ID	...	Order_Date	...	Total_Retail_Price	...
926	...	04SEP2007	...	86.30	...
27	...	05SEP2007	...	78.40	...
31	...	06SEP2007	...	50.30	...
45	...	06SEP2007	...	79.20	...
5	...	09SEP2007	...	52.50	...
.	.	.	.	.	.

orion.rates

SDate	EDate	AvgRate
01SEP2007	07SEP2007	0.73117
08SEP2007	14SEP2007	0.72184
15SEP2007	21SEP2007	0.71589
22SEP2007	30SEP2007	0.707

```
data euros;
   set orion.order_fact(where=(Order_Date
             between '01SEP2007'd and
                     '30SEP2007'd)
             keep=Customer_ID Order_Date
                  Product_ID
                  Total_Retail_Price);
   do while (not (SDate le Order_Date le
                           EDate));
      set orion.rates;
   end;
   EuroPrice=Total_Retail_Price*AvgRate;
   format EuroPrice Euro10.2;
run;
```

The DO WHILE condition is false, so the DO loop does not execute.

PDV

False

Customer_ID	Order_Date	Product_ID	[illegible]	SDate	EDate	AvgRate	EuroPrice	_N_
27	05SEP2007	240500200082	78.40	01SEP2007	07SEP2007	0.73117	.	2

Is NOT(05SEP2007 between 01SEP2007 and 07SEP2007)?

144 ...

Execution

Partial **orion.order_fact**

Customer_ID	...	Order_Date	...	Total_Retail_Price	...
926	...	04SEP2007	...	86.30	...
27	...	05SEP2007	...	78.40	...
31	...	06SEP2007	...	50.30	...
45	...	06SEP2007	...	79.20	...
5	...	09SEP2007	...	52.50	...
.	.	.	.	.	.

orion.rates

SDate	EDate	AvgRate
01SEP2007	07SEP2007	0.73117
08SEP2007	14SEP2007	0.72184
15SEP2007	21SEP2007	0.71589
22SEP2007	30SEP2007	0.70725

```
data euros;
   set orion.order_fact(where=(Order_Date
             between '01SEP2007'd and
                     '30SEP2007'd)
             keep=Customer_ID Order_Date
                  Product_ID
                  Total_Retail_Price);
   do while (not (SDate le Order_Date le
                           EDate));
      set orion.rates;
   end;
   EuroPrice=Total_Retail_Price*AvgRate;
   format EuroPrice Euro10.2;
run;
```

PDV

Customer_ID	Order_Date	Product_ID	Total_Retail_Price	SDate	EDate	AvgRate	EuroPrice	_N_
27	05SEP2007	240500200082	78.40	01SEP2007	07SEP2007	0.73117	57.32	2

145 ...

Execution

Partial **orion.order_fact**

Customer_ID	...	Order_Date	...	Total_Retail_Price	...
928	...	04SEP2007	...	86.30	...
27	...	05SEP2007	...	78.40	...
31	...	06SEP2007	...	50.30	...
45	...	06SEP2007	...	78.20	...
5	...	09SEP2007	...	52.50	...
.	.	.	.	.	.

orion.rates

SDate	EDate	AvgRate
01SEP2007	07SEP2007	0.73117
08SEP2007	14SEP2007	0.72184
15SEP2007	21SEP2007	0.71589
22SEP2007	30SEP2007	0.70725

```
data euros;
   set orion.order_fact(where=(Order_Date
               between '01SEP2007'd and
                  '30SEP2007'd)
               keep=Customer_ID Order_Date
                    Product_ID
                    Total_Retail_Price);
   do while (not (SDate le Order_Date le
                    EDate));
      set orion.rates;
   end;
   EuroPrice=Total_Retail_Price*AvgRate;
                    ro10.2;
```

Continue until Order_Date is 09SEP2007

PDV

Customer_ID	Order_Date	Product_ID	Total_Retail_Price	SDate	EDate	AvgRate	EuroPrice	_N_
5	09SEP2007	210200500016	52.50	01SEP2007	07SEP2007	0.73117	.	5

147 ...

Execution

Partial **orion.order_fact**

Customer_ID	...	Order_Date	...	Total_Retail_Price	...
928	...	04SEP2007	...	86.30	...
27	...	05SEP2007	...	78.40	...
31	...	06SEP2007	...	50.30	...
45	...	06SEP2007	...	78.20	...
5	...	09SEP2007	...	52.50	...
.	.	.	.	.	.

orion.rates

SDate	EDate	AvgRate
01SEP2007	07SEP2007	0.73117
08SEP2007	14SEP2007	0.72184
15SEP2007	21SEP2007	0.71589
22SEP2007	30SEP2007	0.707

```
data euros;
   set orion.order_fact(where=(Order_Date
               between '01SEP2007'd and
                  '30SEP2007'd)
               keep=Customer_ID Order_Date
                    Product_ID
                    Total_Retail_Price);
   do while (not (SDate le Order_Date le
                    EDate));
      set orion.rates;
   end;
   EuroPrice=Total_Retail_Price*AvgRate;
   format EuroPrice Euro10.2;
run;
```

True

PDV

Customer_ID	Order_Date	Product_ID	Total_Retail_Price	SDate	EDate	AvgRate	EuroPrice	_N_
5	09SEP2007	210200500016	52.50	01SEP2007	07SEP2007	0.73117	.	5

Is NOT(09SEP2007 between 01SEP2007 and 07SEP2007)?

149 ...

Execution

Partial **orion.order_fact**

Customer _ID	...	Order _Date	...	Total_ Retail_ Price	...
928	...	04SEP2007	...	86.30	...
27	...	05SEP2007	...	79.40	...
31	...	06SEP2007	...	50.30	...
45	...	06SEP2007	...	78.20	...
5	...	09SEP2007	...	52.50	...
.	.	.	.	.	.

orion.rates

SDate	EDate	AvgRate
01SEP2007	07SEP2007	0.73117
08SEP2007	14SEP2007	0.72184
15SEP2007	21SEP2007	0.71589
22SEP2007	30SEP2007	0.707

```
data euros;
   set orion.order_fact(where=(Order_Date
               between '01SEP2007'd and
                       '30SEP2007'd)
               keep=Customer_ID Order_Date
                    Product_ID
                    Total_Retail_Price);
   do while (not (SDate le Order_Date le
                                EDate));
      set orion.rates;
   end;
   EuroPrice=Total_Retail_Price*AvgRate;
   format EuroPrice Euro10.2;
run;
```

The DO WHILE condition is true, so the DO loop executes.

PDV

True

Customer _ID	Order_ Date	Product_ ID		SDate	EDate	Avg Rate	Euro Price	_N_
5	09SEP2007	210200500016	52.50	08SEP2007	14SEP2007	0.72184	.	5

150 ...

Execution

Partial **orion.order_fact**

Customer _ID	...	Order _Date	...	Total_ Retail_ Price	...
928	...	04SEP2007	...	86.30	...
27	...	05SEP2007	...	79.40	...
31	...	06SEP2007	...	50.30	...
45	...	06SEP2007	...	78.20	...
5	...	09SEP2007	...	52.50	...
.	.	.	.	.	.

orion.rates

SDate	EDate	AvgRate
01SEP2007	07SEP2007	0.73117
08SEP2007	14SEP2007	0.72184
15SEP2007	21SEP2007	0.71589
22SEP2007	30SEP2007	0.707

```
data euros;
   set orion.order_fact(where=(Order_Date
               between '01SEP2007'd and
                       '30SEP2007'd)
               keep=Customer_ID Order_Date
                    Product_ID
                    Total_Retail_Price);
   do while (not (SDate le Order_Date le
                                EDate));
      set orion.rates;
   end;
   EuroPrice=Total_Retail_Price*AvgRate;
   format EuroPrice Euro10.2;
run;
```

The DO WHILE condition is false, so the DO loop does not execute.

PDV

False

Customer _ID	Order_ Date	Product_ ID		SDate	EDate	Avg Rate	Euro Price	_N_
5	09SEP2007	210200500016	52.50	08SEP2007	14SEP2007	0.72184	.	5

Is NOT(09SEP2007 between 08SEP2007 and 14SEP2007)?

152 ...

Execution

Partial **orion.order_fact**

Customer_ID	...	Order_Date	...	Total_Retail_Price	...
928	...	04SEP2007	...	86.30	...
27	...	05SEP2007	...	78.40	...
31	...	06SEP2007	...	50.30	...
45	...	06SEP2007	...	78.20	...
5	...	09SEP2007	...	52.50	...
.	.	.	.	.	.

```
data euros;
   set orion.order_fact(where=(Order_Date
             between '01SEP2007'd and
                     '30SEP2007'd)
             keep=Customer_ID Order_Date
                  Product_ID
                  Total_Retail_Price);
   do while (not (SDate le Order_Date le
                          EDate));
      set orion.rates;
   end;
   EuroPrice=Total_Retail_Price*AvgRate;
   format EuroPrice Euro10.2;
run;
```

orion.rates

SDate	EDate	AvgRate
01SEP2007	07SEP2007	0.73117
08SEP2007	14SEP2007	0.72184
15SEP2007	21SEP2007	0.71589
22SEP2007	30SEP2007	0.70725

PDV

Customer_ID	Order_Date	Product_ID	Total_Retail_Price	SDate	EDate	Avg Rate	Euro Price	_N_
5	09SEP2007	210200500016	52.50	08SEP2007	14SEP2007	0.72184	37.90	5

153 ...

Execution

Partial **orion.order_fact**

Customer_ID	...	Order_Date	...	Total_Retail_Price	...
928	...	04SEP2007	...	86.30	...
27	...	05SEP2007	...	78.40	...
31	...	06SEP2007	...	50.30	...
45	...	06SEP2007	...	78.20	...
5	...	09SEP2007	...	52.50	...
.	.				

```
data euros;
   set orion.order_fact(where=(Order_Date
             between '01SEP2007'd and
                     '30SEP2007'd)
             keep=Customer_ID Order_Date
                  Product_ID
                  Total_Retail_Price);
   do while (not (SDate le Order_Date le
                          EDate));
         n.rates;

         otal_Retail_Price*AvgRate;
         Price Euro10.2;
```

Continue until EOF for **orion.order_fact**

orion.rates

SDate		
01SEP2007	07SEP2007	0.73117
08SEP2007	14SEP2007	0.72184
15SEP2007	21SEP2007	0.71589
22SEP2007	30SEP2007	0.70725

PDV

Customer_ID	Order_Date	Product_ID	Total_Retail_Price	SDate	EDate	Avg Rate	Euro Price	_N_
11	30SEP2007	220200100002	78.20	22SEP2007	30SEP2007	0.70725	55.31	10

154

The Resulting Data Set

```
proc print data=euros;
   title 'Euros';
run;
```

PROC PRINT Output

Euros

Obs	Customer_ID	Order_ Date	Product_ID	Total_Retail_ Price	SDate	EDate	AvgRate	EuroPrice
1	928	04SEP2007	230100600030	$86.30	01SEP2007	07SEP2007	0.73117	€63.10
2	27	05SEP2007	240500200082	$78.40	01SEP2007	07SEP2007	0.73117	€57.32
3	31	06SEP2007	220200100137	$50.30	01SEP2007	07SEP2007	0.73117	€36.78
4	45	06SEP2007	230100600015	$78.20	01SEP2007	07SEP2007	0.73117	€57.18
5	5	09SEP2007	210200500016	$52.50	08SEP2007	14SEP2007	0.72184	€37.90
6	12	18SEP2007	240200100053	$87.20	15SEP2007	21SEP2007	0.71589	€62.43
7	69	20SEP2007	210200700016	$23.50	15SEP2007	21SEP2007	0.71589	€16.82
8	24	25SEP2007	240600100102	$46.10	22SEP2007	30SEP2007	0.70725	€32.60
9	41	26SEP2007	210200600067	$134.00	22SEP2007	30SEP2007	0.70725	€94.77
10	11	30SEP2007	220200100002	$78.20	22SEP2007	30SEP2007	0.70725	€55.31

155

8.10 Multiple Choice Poll

Does SAS encounter the end-of-file marker (EOF) for **orion.rates**?

a. SAS encounters the EOF, but it does not stop the DATA step because there are two SET statements.

b. SAS encounters the EOF for **orion.rates**, so there are only four observations in the resulting data set **euros**.

c. The DO WHILE statement prevents the data set **orion.rates** from being read a fifth time, so the EOF is never encountered.

157

Using the SQL Procedure

You can use the SQL procedure to produce the same results.

```
proc sql;
   create table euros as
   select Customer_ID, Order_Date, Product_ID,
          Total_Retail_Price, SDate, EDate, AvgRate,
          Total_Retail_Price*AvgRate as EuroPrice
          format=Euro10.2
   from orion.order_fact, orion.rates
   where Order_Date between SDate and EDate;
title 'euros';
   select * from euros;
quit;
```

✎ Neither data set needs to be sorted.

159 p308d13

The Resulting Data Set

PROC SQL Output

euros

Customer ID	Date Order was placed by Customer	Product ID	Total Retail Price for This Product	SDate	EDate	AvgRate	EuroPrice
928	04SEP2007	230100600030	$86.30	01SEP2007	07SEP2007	0.731167	€63.10
27	05SEP2007	240500200082	$78.40	01SEP2007	07SEP2007	0.731167	€57.32
31	06SEP2007	220200100137	$50.30	01SEP2007	07SEP2007	0.731167	€36.78
45	06SEP2007	230100600015	$78.20	01SEP2007	07SEP2007	0.731167	€57.18
5	09SEP2007	210200500016	$52.50	08SEP2007	14SEP2007	0.72184	€37.90
12	18SEP2007	240200100053	$87.20	15SEP2007	21SEP2007	0.715886	€62.43
69	20SEP2007	210200700016	$23.50	15SEP2007	21SEP2007	0.715886	€16.82
24	25SEP2007	240600100102	$46.10	22SEP2007	30SEP2007	0.70725	€32.60
41	26SEP2007	210200600067	$134.00	22SEP2007	30SEP2007	0.70725	€94.77
11	28SEP2007	220200100002	$78.20	22SEP2007	30SEP2007	0.72184	€55.31

160

Using a Hash Object

p308d14

```
data euros;
   length SDate EDate AvgRate 8;
   drop rc;
   format SDate EDate Order_Date date9. EuroPrice Euro10.2;
   if _N_=1 then do;
      declare hash H(dataset: 'orion.rates', ordered: 'ascending');
      H.definekey('SDate');
      H.definedata('SDate','EDate', 'AvgRate');
      H.definedone();
      call missing(SDate, EDate, AvgRate);
      declare hiter E('H');
   end;
   set orion.order_fact(where=(Order_Date between '01SEP2007'd and
                                                  '30SEP2007'd)
                         keep=Customer_ID Order_Date Product_ID
                              Total_Retail_Price);
   E.first();
   do until (rc ne 0);
      if SDate <= Order_Date <= EDate then do;
         EuroPrice=Total_Retail_Price * AvgRate;
         output;
         leave;
      end;
      else if SDate > Order_Date then leave;
      rc=E.next();
   end;
run;
```

Which Technique Should You Use?

Two SET Statements	SQL Procedure	Hash and Hiter Objects
availability of all DATA step functionality	easy to code	availability of all DATA step functionality
fast, sequential processing of both data sets	no sorting or indexing needed	in-memory lookup table

✎ Benchmark your data to determine which is most efficient.

162

Exercises

Level 1

10. Combining Two Data Sets Conditionally Using the SQL Procedure

The data set **orion.ages_mod** contains information about age groups.

Listing of **orion.ages_mod**

orion.ages_mod SAS Data Set

Description	First_ Age	Last_Age
15-29 years	15	30
30-44 years	30	45
45-59 years	45	60
60-75 years	60	75

The data set **orion.customer** contains information about customers.

Partial Listing of **orion.customer**

orion.customer SAS Data Set
(Partial Output)

Customer_ID	Country	Gender	Personal_ ID	Customer_Name	Customer_ FirstName	Customer_ LastName
4	US	M		James Kvarniq	James	Kvarniq
5	US	F		Sandrina Stephano	Sandrina	Stephano
9	DE	F		Cornelia Krahl	Cornelia	Krahl
10	US	F		Karen Ballinger	Karen	Ballinger
11	DE	F		Elke Wallstab	Elke	Wallstab

Birth_ Date	Customer_Address	Street_ID	Street_ Number	Customer_ Type_ID
27JUN1974	4382 Gralyn Rd	9260106519	4382	1020
09JUL1979	6468 Cog Hill Ct	9260114570	6468	2020
27FEB1974	Kallstadterstr. 9	3940106659	9	2020
18OCT1984	425 Bryant Estates Dr	9260129395	425	1040
16AUG1974	Carl-Zeiss-Str. 15	3940108592	15	1040

a. Use the SQL procedure to create a data set named **age_groups** that contains the customer ID, name, age, and age group (the variable **Description** in the **orion.ages_mod** SAS data set) as of January 1, 2008. Order the data by **Customer_ID**.

Hint: The following calculates the customer age:

```
int(yrdif(Birth_Date,'01Jan2008'd, 'ACT/ACT'))
```

b. Print the first five observations of the **age_groups** data set.

PROC PRINT Output

age_groups
(Partial Output)

Obs	Customer_ID	Customer_Name	Age	Description
1	4	James Kvarniq	33	30-44 years
2	5	Sandrina Stephano	28	15-29 years
3	9	Cornelia Krahl	33	30-44 years
4	10	Karen Ballinger	23	15-29 years
5	11	Elke Wallstab	33	30-44 years

Level 2

11. Combining Two Data Sets Conditionally Using the DATA Step DO Loop

The data set **orion.ages_mod** contains information about age groups.

Listing of **orion.ages_mod**

orion.ages_mod SAS Data Set

Description	First_ Age	Last_Age
15-29 years	15	30
30-44 years	30	45
45-59 years	45	60
60-75 years	60	75

The data set **orion.customer** contains information about customers.

Partial Listing of **orion.customer**

orion.customer SAS Data Set
(Partial Output)

Customer_ID	Country	Gender	Personal_ ID	Customer_Name	Customer_ FirstName	Customer_ LastName
4	US	M		James Kvarniq	James	Kvarniq
5	US	F		Sandrina Stephano	Sandrina	Stephano
9	DE	F		Cornelia Krahl	Cornelia	Krahl
10	US	F		Karen Ballinger	Karen	Ballinger
11	DE	F		Elke Wallstab	Elke	Wallstab

Birth_ Date	Customer_Address	Street_ID	Street_ Number	Customer_ Type_ID
27JUN1974	4382 Gralyn Rd	9260106519	4382	1020
09JUL1979	6468 Cog Hill Ct	9260114570	6468	2020
27FEB1974	Kallstadterstr. 9	3940106659	9	2020
18OCT1984	425 Bryant Estates Dr	9260129395	425	1040
16AUG1974	Carl-Zeiss-Str. 15	3940108592	15	1040

a. Use the DATA step and a DO loop to create a data set named **`age_groups`** that contains the customer ID, name, age, and age group (the variable **`Description`** in the **`orion.ages_mod`** SAS data set) as of January 1, 2008.

b. Print the first five observations of the **`age_groups`** data set.

PROC PRINT Output

```
                    age_groups
                 (Partial Output)

Obs    Customer_ID    Customer_Name              Age

 1            2806    Raedene Van Den Berg        15
 2              13    Markus Sepke                15
 3            2550    Sanelisiwe Collier          15
 4           46966    Lauren Krasowski            17
 5           11171    Bill Cuddy                  17
```

Level 3

12. Combining Two Data Sets Conditionally Using the DATA Step Hash Object

The data set **`orion.ages_mod`** contains information about age groups.

Listing of **`orion.ages_mod`**

```
          orion.ages_mod SAS Data Set

                       First_
Description             Age      Last_Age

15-29 years             15          30
30-44 years             30          45
45-59 years             45          60
60-75 years             60          75
```

The data set **`orion.customer`** contains information about customers.

Partial Listing of **`orion.customer`**

```
                              orion.customer SAS Data Set
                                   (Partial Output)

                                  Personal_                             Customer_    Customer_
Customer_ID    Country    Gender     ID         Customer_Name           FirstName    LastName

          4      US         M                  James Kvarniq            James        Kvarniq
          5      US         F                  Sandrina Stephano        Sandrina     Stephano
          9      DE         F                  Cornelia Krahl           Cornelia     Krahl
         10      US         F                  Karen Ballinger          Karen        Ballinger

   Birth_                                                Street_    Customer_
    Date     Customer_Address               Street_ID    Number      Type_ID

27JUN1974    4382 Gralyn Rd                9260106519    4382          1020
09JUL1979    6468 Cog Hill Ct              9260114570    6468          2020
27FEB1974    Kallstadterstr. 9             3940106659    9             2020
18OCT1984    425 Bryant Estates Dr         9260129395    425           1040
```

a. Use the DATA step and a hash object to create a data set named **age_groups** that contains the customer ID, name, age, and age group (the variable **Description** in the **orion.ages_mod** SAS data set) as of January 1, 2008.

b. Print the first five observations of the **age_groups** data set.

PROC PRINT Output

```
                          age_groups
                       (Partial Output)

 Obs    Description     Customer_ID     Customer_Name        Age

   1    30-44 years               4    James Kvarniq          33
   2    15-29 years               5    Sandrina Stephano      28
   3    30-44 years               9    Cornelia Krahl         33
   4    15-29 years              10    Karen Ballinger        23
   5    30-44 years              11    Elke Wallstab          33
```

8.5 Chapter Review

Chapter Review

1. Given the following input data, what is one difference in data sets created by the default DATA step MERGE and the default SQL procedure **inner** join?

one

X	Y
1	a
2	b
3	c

two

X	Z
1	f
3	t
4	w

165

continued...

Chapter Review

2. When data sets are combined using the SET/SET KEY= syntax, how is the data set named in the **first** SET statement read?

3. When data sets are combined using the SET/SET KEY= syntax, how is the data set named in the **second** SET statement read?

167

continued...

Chapter Review

4. If the following program is used to combine the summary data set containing one observation with the detail data set containing fifty observations, how many observations are in the data set **combined**?

```
data combined;
   set summary;
   set detail;
run;
```

8.6 Solutions

Solutions to Exercises

1. Merging or Joining Three Data Sets

a. Combine the three data sets to create a data set named **purchases** that contains the customer name, product name, and supplier name for the customers in the **orion.order_fact** data set.

p308s01

```
/* Merge Solution */

proc sort data=orion.order_fact(keep=Customer_ID Product_ID)
          out=order_fact;
   by Customer_ID;
run;

data temp;
   merge order_fact(in=O)
         orion.customer_dim(keep=Customer_ID Customer_Name
                            in=C);
   by Customer_ID;
   if O and C;
run;

proc sort data=temp;
   by Product_ID;
run;

data purchases;
   keep Customer_Name Product_Name Supplier_Name;
   merge temp(in=T)
         orion.product_dim(keep=Product_ID Product_Name
                                Supplier_Name
                            In=P);
   by Product_ID;
   if P and T;
run;

proc print data=purchases(obs=5);
   title 'Partial purchases Data Set';
run;
```

(Continued on the next page.)

```
/* PROC SQL Solution */

proc sql;
   create table purchases as
    select Customer_Name,
           Product_Name,
           Supplier_Name
      from orion.order_fact,
           orion.product_dim,
           orion.customer_dim
      where order_fact.Customer_ID=customer_dim.Customer_ID
        and order_fact.Product_ID=product_dim.Product_ID
       order by order_fact.Product_ID;
quit;
```

b. Order the data by **`Product_ID`** and print the first five observations of the **`purchases`** data set.

p308s01

```
proc print data=purchases(obs=5);
   title 'Partial Purchases Data Set';
run;
```

2. Merging or Joining Data to Create Multiple Data Sets

Combine the three data sets to create the following data sets:

- a data set named **`no_purchases`** that contains the customers who did not make any purchases
- a data set named **`purchases`** that contains the customer name, product name, and supplier name for those customers in the **`orion.order_fact`** data set
- a data set named **`no_products`** that contains the product names and suppliers for products that were not purchased

p308s02

```
/* Merge Solution */
proc sort data=orion.order_fact out=order_fact;
   by Customer_ID;
run;

proc sort data=orion.customer_dim out=customer_dim;
   by Customer_ID;
run;

data temp no_purchases(keep=Customer_ID Customer_Name);
   merge order_fact(in=O)
         customer_dim(keep=Customer_IDCustomer_Name in=C);
   by Customer_ID;
   if O and C then output temp;
   else if C and not O then output no_purchases;
run;
```

(Continued on the next page.)

```
proc sort data=temp;
   by Product_ID;
run;
```

```
data purchases
   no_products(keep=Product_ID Product_Name
                    Supplier_Name);
   merge temp(in=T)
      orion.product_dim(keep=Product_ID Product_Name
                             Supplier_Name
                        in=P);
   by Product_ID;
   if P and T then output purchases;
   else if P and not T then output no_products;
run;

proc print data=no_purchases;
   title 'no_purchases Data Set';
run;

proc print data=purchases(obs=5);
   title 'Partial purchases Data Set';
run;

proc print data=no_products(obs=5);
   title 'Partial no_products Data Set';
run;

/* PROC SQL Solution */

proc sql;
   create table no_purchases as
      select Customer_ID,
             Customer_Name
         from orion.customer_dim
         where customer_dim.Customer_ID not in
              (select Customer_ID from orion.order_fact);

   create table no_products as
      select Product_ID, Product_Name
         from orion.product_dim
         where product_dim.Product_ID not in
              (select Product_ID from orion.order_fact);
```

(Continued on the next page.)

```
   create table purchases as
      select order_fact.*,
            Customer_Name,
            Product_Name,
            Supplier_Name
         from orion.order_fact,
             orion.product_dim,
             orion.customer_dim
         where order_fact.Customer_ID=customer_dim.Customer_ID
```

```
                and order_fact.Product_ID=product_dim.Product_ID
         order by order_fact.Product_ID;
quit;

proc print data=no_products(obs=5);
   title 'Partial no_products Data Set';
run;

proc print data=purchases(obs=5);
   title 'Partial purchases Data Set';
run;

proc print data=no_purchases;
   title 'no_purchases Data Set';
run;
```

3. **Merging or Joining Multiple Data Sets**

Create a data set named **manager_names** that contains the **Employee_ID** variable, the six **Manager_ID** variables, and the six manager names.

p308s03

```
* PROC SQL Solution */
proc sql;
create table Manager_Names as
   select e.Employee_ID,
          Manager_Level1,
          Manager_Level2,
          Manager_Level3,
          Manager_Level4,
          Manager_Level5,
          Manager_Level6,
          m1.Employee_Name as Manager1_Name,
          m2.Employee_Name as Manager2_Name,
          m3.Employee_Name as Manager3_Name,
          m4.Employee_Name as Manager4_Name,
          m5.Employee_Name as Manager5_Name,
          m6.Employee_Name as Manager6_Name
```

(Continued on the next page.)

```
   from orion.organization_dim as e
   left join orion.employee_addresses as m1
      on e.Manager_Level1=m1.Employee_ID
   left join orion.employee_addresses as m2
      on e.Manager_Level2=m2.Employee_ID
   left join orion.employee_addresses as m3
      on e.Manager_Level3=m3.Employee_ID
   left join orion.employee_addresses as m4
      on e.Manager_Level4=m4.Employee_ID
   left join orion.employee_addresses as m5
      on e.Manager_Level5=m5.Employee_ID
   left join orion.employee_addresses as m6
```

```
      on e.Manager_Level6=m6.Employee_ID
   order by e.Employee_ID;
quit;

proc print data=manager_names(firstobs=420);
   title 'Partial Manager_Names Data';
   title2 'FirstObs=420';
run;

/* Merge Solution */

proc sort data=orion.employee_addresses
   out=emp_addresses(rename=(Employee_ID=Manager_Level1
                             Employee_Name=Manager1_Name));
   by Employee_ID;
run;

proc sort data=orion.organization_dim
         out=man1(keep=Employee_ID Manager_Level1 - Manager_Level6);
   by Manager_Level1;
run;

data manager1;
   merge man1(in=M)
         emp_addresses(keep=Manager_Level1 Manager1_Name);
   by Manager_Level1;
   if M;
run;

proc sort data=manager1 out=man2;
   by Manager_Level2;
run;
```

(Continued on the next page.)

```
data manager2;
   merge man2(in=M)
         emp_addresses(rename=(Manager_Level1=Manager_Level2
                               Manager1_Name=Manger2_Name)
                       keep=Manager_Level1 Manager1_Name);
   by Manager_Level2;
   if M;
run;

proc sort data=manager2 out=man3;
   by Manager_Level3;
run;

data manager3;
   merge man3(in=M)
         emp_addresses(rename=(Manager_Level1=Manager_Level3
                               Manager1_Name=Manger3_Name)
                       keep=Manager_Level1 Manager1_Name);
```

```
   by Manager_Level3;
   if M;
run;

proc sort data=manager3 out=man4;
   by Manager_Level4;
run;

data manager4;
   merge man4(in=M)
         emp_addresses(rename=(Manager_Level1=Manager_Level4
                               Manager1_Name=Manger4_Name)
                       keep=Manager_Level1 Manager1_Name);
   by Manager_Level4;
   if M;
run;

proc sort data=manager4 out=man5;
   by Manager_Level5;
run;

data manager5;
   merge man5(in=M)
         emp_addresses(rename=(Manager_Level1=Manager_Level5
                               Manager1_Name=Manger5_Name)
                       keep=Manager_Level1 Manager1_Name);
   by Manager_Level5;
   if M;
run;

proc sort data=manager5 out=man6;
   by Manager_Level6;
run;
```

(Continued on the next page.)

```
data manager_names;
   merge man6(in=M)
         emp_addresses(rename=(Manager_Level1=Manager_Level6
                               Manager1_Name=Manger6_Name)
                       keep=Manager_Level1 Manager1_Name);
   by Manager_Level6;
   if M;
run;

proc sort data=manager_names;
   by Employee_ID;
run;

proc print data=manager_names(firstobs=420);
   title 'Partial Manager_Names Data';
   title2 'FirstObs=420';
run;
```

4. Combining Data Sets Using an Index to Create One Data Set

a. Create a SAS data set named **sales_emps** by using an index on **Employee_ID** to combine the two data sets, **orion.salesstaff** and **orion.organization_dim**. Check the SAS log to ensure that you do not have any data errors.

p308s04

```
proc datasets lib=orion nolist;
   modify organization_dim;
      index create Employee_ID;
quit;

data sales_emps;
   set orion.salesstaff;
   set orion.organization_dim(keep=Employee_ID Department
                                   Section Org_Group)
                               key=Employee_ID;
   if _IORC_=0;
run;
```

b. Print the first five observations of the **sales_emps** SAS data set.

p308s04

```
proc print data=sales_emps(obs=5);
   title 'Sales Employee Data';
   title2 '(Partial Output)';
run;
```

5. Combining Data Sets Using an Index to Monitor Data Integrity

a. Create a simple index on the variable **Product_ID** in the data set **orion.price_list**.

b. Create a SAS data set named **shoes** and a SAS data set named **errors** by using the index on **Product_ID** to combine the two data sets, **orion.shoe_vendors** and **orion.price_list**.

c. Delete the **Product_ID** index on the data set **orion.price_list**.

p308s05

```
proc datasets lib=orion nolist;
   modify price_list;
      index create Product_ID;
run;
quit;

data shoes errors(keep=Product_ID Product_Name Supplier_Name);
   set orion.shoe_vendors(keep=Product_ID Product_Name
                          Supplier_Name Mfg_Suggested_Retail_Price);
   set orion.price_list(keep=Product_ID Unit_Cost_Price
                             Unit_Sales_Price)
                        key=Product_ID;
   if _IORC_=0 then output shoes;
```

```
   else do;
      _ERROR_=0;
      output errors;
   end;
run;

proc datasets lib=orion nolist;
   modify price_list;
      index delete Product_ID;
run;
quit;
```

d. Print the first five observations of the **shoes** SAS data set.

p308s05

```
proc print data=shoes(obs=5);
   title 'Shoe Data';
   title2 '(Partial Output)';
run;
```

e. Print the first five observations of the **errors** SAS data set.

p308s05

```
proc print data=errors(obs=5);
   title 'The errors Data';
   title2 '(Partial Output)';
run;
```

6. **Combining Data Sets Using an Index and Using the Macro Facility to Monitor Errors**

   a. Create a data set named **processed_orders** that contains the variables from **orion.first_internet_order** and a variable named **Comment**. Use the index on the variable **Order_ID** to retrieve the matching observation from **orion.internet**.

   b. The variable **Comment** has the value `Order has been processed` if the **Order_ID** is in both **orion.first_internet_order** and **orion.internet**. The value is `Order has not been processed` if the **Customer_ID** is not in both data sets.

   c. Use the %SYSRC AUTOCALL macro described in the reference information in this chapter. In addition, refer to SAS OnlineDoc by following the path shown below:

      SAS OnlineDoc ⇨ Base SAS ⇨ SAS 9.2 Macro Language: Reference ⇨ Macro Language Dictionary ⇨ AutoCall Macros

p308s06

```
data processed_orders;
   set orion.first_internet_order;
   set orion.internet key=Order_ID;
   length Comment $30;
   select (_IORC_);
      when (%sysrc(_sok)) do;
         Comment='Order has been processed.';
         output;
      end;
      when (%sysrc(_dsenom)) do;
         _ERROR_=0;
         Comment='Order has not been processed.';
      output;
      end;
      otherwise;
   end;
run;
```

d. Print the first 10 observations of **processed_orders**.

p308s06

```
proc print data=processed_orders(obs=10);
   title 'Internet Orders';
   title2 '(Partial Output)';
run;
```

7. **Combining Summary Data Containing an Average with Detail Data**

   a. Calculate the average age of all customers.

   b. Create a SAS data set named **age_dif**, which combines the average age of all customers with the **orion.customer_dim** data set in order to determine the difference between each customer's age and the average for all customers. (You can use any method presented in this section.)

p308s07

```
/* Using PROC SUMMARY and the DATA step */

proc summary data=orion.customer_dim;
   var Customer_Age;
   output out=average mean=AvgAge;
run;

data age_dif;
   if _N_=1 then set average(keep=AvgAge);
   set orion.customer_dim(keep=Customer_ID Customer_Age);
   Age_Difference=Customer_Age - AvgAge;
run;

/* Using PROC SUMMARY and PROC SQL */
```

```
proc summary data=orion.customer_dim;
   var Customer_Age;
   output out=average mean=AvgAge;
run;

proc sql;
   create table age_dif as
     select AvgAge,
            Customer_ID,
            Customer_Age,
            Customer_Age - AvgAge as Age_Difference
       from orion.customer_dim,
            average;
quit;

/* Using PROC SQL only */

proc sql;
   create table age_dif as
   select mean(Customer_Age) as AvgAge,
          Customer_ID,
          Customer_Age,
          Customer_Age - calculated AvgAge as Age_Difference
   from orion.customer_dim;
quit;
```

(Continued on the next page.)

```
/* Using the DATA step only */

data age_dif;
   drop i Tot_Age;
   if _N_=1 then do i=1 to TotObs;
      set orion.customer_dim(keep=Customer_Age) nobs=TotObs;
      Tot_Age + Customer_Age;
   end;
   set orion.customer_dim(keep=Customer_ID Customer_Age);
   AvgAge=Tot_Age / TotObs;
   Age_Difference=Customer_Age - AvgAge;
run;
```

c. Print the first five observation of the **age_dif** SAS data set.

p308s07

```
proc print data=age_dif(obs=5);
   var AvgAge Customer_ID Customer_Age Age_Difference;
   title 'The age_dif Data Set';
   title2 '(Partial Output)';
run;
```

8. Combining Summary Data Containing a Total with Detail Data

a. Select any method to create a SAS data set named **compare**.

p308s08

```
/* Using PROC SUMMARY and the DATA step */

data donations;
   set orion.employee_donations;
   Total_Donation=sum(of Qtr1 - Qtr4);
run;

proc summary data=donations;
   var Total_Donation;
   output out=totals mean=Avg_Donation;
run;

data compare;
   if _N_=1 then set totals;
   set donations;
   Difference=Total_Donation - Avg_Donation;
run;
```

(Continued on the next page.)

```
/* Using PROC SUMMARY and PROC SQL*/
proc sql;
   create table donations as
   select Employee_ID,
          Qtr1,
          Qtr2,
          Qtr3,
          Qtr4,
          Recipients,
          Paid_By,
          sum(Qtr1, Qtr2, Qtr3, Qtr4) as Total_Donation
   from orion.employee_donations;

proc summary data=donations;
   var Total_Donation;
   output out=totals mean=Avg_Donation;
run;

proc sql;
   create table compare as
      select Avg_Donation,
             donations.*,
             Total_Donation - Avg_Donation as Difference
         from totals,
              donations;
quit;

/* Using PROC SQL only */
proc sql;
   create table compare as
     select mean(sum(Qtr1, Qtr2, Qtr3, Qtr4)) as Avg_Donation,
            employee_donations.*,
```

```
             sum(Qtr1, Qtr2, Qtr3, Qtr4) as Total_Donation,
             calculated Total_Donation - calculated Avg_Donation
             as Difference
          from orion.employee_donations;
quit;

/* Using the DATA step only */

data compare;
   drop i;
   if _N_=1 then do i=1 to TotObs;
      set orion.employee_donations(keep=Qtr1 - Qtr4)
                                    nobs=TotObs;
      Total + sum(of Qtr1 - Qtr4);
   end;
   set orion.employee_donations;
   Total_Donation=sum(of Qtr1 - Qtr4);
   Avg_Donation=Total / TotObs;
   Difference=Total_Donation-Avg_Donation;
run;
```

b. Print the first five observations of the **compare** SAS data set.

p308s08

```
proc print data=compare(obs=5);
   var Avg_Donation Employee_ID Qtr1 Qtr2 Qtr3 Qtr4
       Recipients Paid_By Total_Donation Difference;
   title 'The compare Data Set';
   title2 '(Partial Output)';
run;
```

9. Combining Summary Data Containing a Weighted Average and Detail Data

a. Select any method to create a SAS data set named **products** by performing the following tasks:

p308s09

```
/* Using PROC SUMMARY and the DATA STEP */

proc summary data=orion.order_fact;
   var CostPrice_Per_Unit;
   weight Quantity;
   output out=totals sum=Total_Cost;
run;

proc sort data=orion.order_fact out=order_fact;
   by Product_ID;
run;

data products(keep=Customer_ID CostPrice_Per_Unit Quantity
                   Percent Product_Name);
   if _N_=1 then set totals(keep=Total_Cost);
   merge order_fact(keep=Customer_ID Product_ID
```

```
                      CostPrice_Per_Unit Quantity in=O)
        orion.product_dim(keep=Product_ID Product_Name in=P);
   by Product_ID;
   if O and P;
   Percent=(CostPrice_Per_Unit * Quantity) / Total_Cost;
   format Percent percent9.3;
run;
```

(Continued on the next page.)

```
/* Using PROC SUMMARY and PROC SQL */

proc summary data=orion.order_fact;
   var CostPrice_Per_Unit;
   weight Quantity;
   output out=totals sum=Total_Cost;
run;

proc sql;
   create table products as
      select Customer_ID,
             CostPrice_Per_Unit,
             Quantity,
             Product_Name,
             (Quantity * CostPrice_Per_Unit) / Total_Cost as
                 Percent format=percent9.3
      from totals,
           orion.order_fact,
           orion.product_dim
      where order_fact.Product_ID=product_dim.Product_ID;
quit;

/* Using PROC SQL only */

proc sql;
   create table products as
      select Customer_ID,
             CostPrice_Per_Unit,
             Quantity,
             Product_Name,
             (Quantity * CostPrice_Per_Unit)/
              sum(Quantity * CostPrice_Per_Unit)as Percent
              format=percent9.3
      from  orion.order_fact,
            orion.product_dim
      where order_fact.Product_ID=product_dim.Product_ID;
quit;

/* Using the DATA step only */

proc sort data=orion.order_fact out=order_fact;
   by Product_ID;
```

```
run;
```

(Continued on the next page.)

```
data products(keep=Customer_ID CostPrice_Per_Unit Quantity
                   Percent Product_Name);
   if _N_=1 then do i=1 to TotObs;
      set orion.order_fact nobs=TotObs;
      Total_Cost + (Quantity * CostPrice_Per_Unit);
   end;
   merge order_fact(keep=Customer_ID Product_ID
                        CostPrice_Per_Unit Quantity
                    in=O)
         orion.product_dim(keep=Product_ID Product_Name
                           in=P);
   by Product_ID;
   if O and P;
   Percent=(CostPrice_Per_Unit * Quantity) / Total_Cost;
   format Percent percent9.3;
run;
```

b. Print the first five observations of the **products** SAS data set.

p308s09

```
proc print data=products(obs=5);
   var Customer_ID Quantity CostPrice_Per_Unit Product_Name
       Percent;
   title 'The products Data Set';
   title2 '(Partial Output)';
run;
```

10. Combining Two Data Sets Conditionally Using the SQL Procedure

a. Use the SQL procedure to create a data set named **age_groups**.

p308s10

```
proc sql;
   create table age_groups as
   select Customer_ID,
          Customer_Name,
          int(yrdif(Birth_Date, '01Jan2008'd, 'ACT/ACT')) as Age,
          Description
   from orion.customer,
        orion.ages_mod
   where calculated Age between First_Age and Last_Age
      order by Customer_ID;
quit;
```

b. Print the first five observations of the **age_groups** data set.

p308s10

```
proc print data=age_groups(obs=5);
   title 'age_groups';
```

```
   title2 '(Partial Output)';
run;
```

11. Combining Two Data Sets Conditionally Using the DATA Step DO Loop

a. Use the DATA step and a DO loop to create a data set named **age_groups.**

p308s11

```
proc sort data=orion.customer(keep=Customer_ID Birth_Date
                                   Customer_Name)
          out=customer;
   by descending Birth_Date;
run;

data age_groups;
   keep Customer_ID Customer_Name Age Description;
   set customer;
   Age=int(yrdif(Birth_Date, '01Jan2008'd, 'ACT/ACT'));
   do while (not (First_Age le Age lt Last_Age));
     set orion.ages_mod;
   end;
run;
```

b. Print the first five observations of the **age_groups** data set.

p308s11

```
proc print data=age_groups(obs=5);
   title  'age_groups';
   title2 '(Partial Output)';
run;
```

12. Combining Two Data Sets Conditionally Using the DATA Step Hash Object

a. Use the DATA step and a hash object to create a data set named **age_groups** that contains the customer ID, name, age, and age group (the variable **Description** in the **orion.ages_mod** SAS data set) as of January 1, 2008.

p308s12

```
/* Using the DATA Step Hash Object */

data age_groups;
   keep Customer_ID Customer_Name Age Description;
   if _N_=1 then do;
      if 0 then set orion.ages_mod;
      declare hash AG(dataset: 'orion.ages_mod',
                      ordered: 'ascending');
      AG.definekey('First_Age');
      AG.definedata('First_Age', 'Last_Age', 'Description');
      AG.definedone();
      declare hiter A('AG');
   end;
```

(Continued on the next page.)

```
   set orion.customer(keep=Customer_ID Birth_Date
                                 Customer_Name);
   Age=int(yrdif(Birth_Date, '01Jan2008'd, 'ACT/ACT'));
   A.first();
   do until (rc ne 0);
      if First_Age <= Age < Last_Age then do;
         output;
         leave;
      end;
      else if First_Age > Age then leave;
      rc=A.next();
   end;
run;

proc print data=age_groups(obs=5);
   title  'age_groups';
   title2 '(Partial Output)';
run;

/* alternative solution */

data age_groups(keep=Description Customer_ID Customer_Name
                     Age);
   if _N_=1 then do;
      if 0 then set orion.ages_mod;
      declare hash AG (dataset:'orion.ages_mod',
                       ordered: 'ascending');
      ag.definekey('First_Age');
      ag.definedata('Description');
      ag.definedata('First_Age', 'Last_Age');
      ag.definedone();
      declare hiter HAG('AG');
   end;
   set orion.customer(keep=Customer_ID Customer_Name
                                 Birth_Date);
   Age=int(yrdif(Birth_Date, '01JAN2008'd, 'ACT/ACT'));
   rc=HAG.first();
   do until (First_Age le Age le Last_Age);
      rc=HAG.next();
   end;
run;
```

b. Print the first five observations of the **age_groups** data set.

p308s12

```
proc print data=age_groups(obs=5);
   title  'age_groups';
   title2 '(Partial Output)';
run;
```

Solutions to Student Activities (Polls/Quizzes)

8.01 Multiple Choice Poll – Correct Answer

By default, how does the DATA step perform a merge?

a. sequentially
b. creates a Cartesian product

8

8.02 Multiple Choice Poll – Correct Answer

By default, how does the SQL procedure perform an inner join?

a. sequentially
b. creates a Cartesian product

19

8.03 Multiple Choice Poll – Correct Answer

If you use a DATA step MERGE to combine the data sets, how many observations are read from the larger data set, `orion.customer_dim_more`?

a. 38
b. 1,500

The MERGE statement reads all observations from all of the input data sets.

⚠ If there is a great disparity in size between the input data sets, merging might not be the best technique for combining them.

38

8.04 Quiz – Correct Answer

Why do you **not** want this observation output to `catalog_customers`?

Partial PDV

Customer_ ID	Order_ ID	Quantity	Total_ Retail_ Price	...	Customer_ Name	...	D _IORC_	D _N_
15	1240080101	3	216.50	...	Sandrina Stephano	...	1230015	2

Data from the previous observation is retained in the PDV. If this observation is output, the variables `Customer_Country` through `Customer_Age` would be incorrect for `Customer_ID=15`.

54

8.05 Quiz – Correct Answer

Open and submit the program **p308a01**.

1. What messages do you see in your SAS log?

The first message is as follows:

```
Customer_ID=15 Order_ID=1240080101 Quantity=3
Total_Retail_Price=$216.50 Customer_Country=US
Customer_Gender=F Customer_Name=Sandrina Stephano
Customer_FirstName=Sandrina
Customer_LastName=Stephano Customer_BirthDate=09JUL1979
Customer_Age_Group=15-30 years
Customer_Type=Orion Club Gold members medium activity
Customer_Group=Orion Club Gold members
Customer_Age=28 _ERROR_=1 _IORC_=1230015 _N_=2
```

By default, there is a maximum of 20 error messages printed in the log.

60

8.05 Quiz – Correct Answer

Open and submit the program **p308a01**.

1. What messages do you see in your SAS log?
2. What is the value of _ERROR_?

ERROR=1

When _ERROR_=1, the contents of the PDV are printed in the log.

61

8.05 Quiz – Correct Answer

Open and submit the program **p308a01**.

1. What messages do you see in your SAS log?
2. What is the value of _ERROR_?
3. Replace the ELSE statement with the following ELSE DO group:

```
else do;
   _ERROR_=0;
   output errors;
end;
```

4. Resubmit the program and look at the log.
5. Why are there no messages now?

You forced _ERROR_ to be 0 with the assignment statement _ERROR_=0. Therefore, the data error messages are not printed in the log.

62

8.06 Quiz – Correct Answer

Open and submit the program **p308a02**.

1. How many observations are in the resulting data set?
   Only one observation.
2. Why?
   When the statement `set summary(keep=GrandTot);` executes a second time, SAS encounters the end of file in the `summary` data set because that data set only has one observation in it.
3. How did you get 53 observations in the program **p308d06**?
   The statement `set summary(keep=GrandTot);` does not execute a second time because execution of the SET statement is controlled by the condition `if _N_=1`.

99

8.07 Poll – Correct Answer

Can the DATA step merge be used for this task?

- ❍ Yes
- ❍ No (circled)

119

8.08 Quiz – Correct Answer

Why do you have to use a WHERE= data set option rather than a WHERE statement to subset by `Order_Date`?

The variable `Order_Date` is only in the data set `orion.order_fact`.

128

8.09 Quiz – Correct Answer

What variables are set to missing at the top of the DATA step?

Only the variable `EuroPrice` is set to missing at the top of the DATA step because the other variable values come from an existing SAS data set.

140

8.10 Multiple Choice Poll – Correct Answer

Does SAS encounter the end-of-file marker (EOF) for `orion.rates`?

a. SAS encounters the EOF, but it does not stop the DATA step because there are two SET statements.

b. SAS encounters the EOF for `orion.rates`, so there are only four observations in the resulting data set **`euros`**.

c. The DO WHILE statement prevents the data set `orion.rates` from being read a fifth time, so the EOF is never encountered.

158

Solutions to Chapter Review

Chapter Review – Correct Answers

1. Given the following input data, what is one difference in data sets created by the default DATA step MERGE and the default SQL procedure **inner** join?

one

X	Y
1	a
2	b
3	c

two

X	Z
1	f
3	t
4	w

By default, the data created by the MERGE statement contains the matching and nonmatching rows. The data created by the PROC SQL inner join contains only the matches.

166

continued...

Chapter Review – Correct Answers

2. When data sets are combined using the SET/SET KEY= syntax, how is the data set named in the **first** SET statement read?

   sequentially

3. When data sets are combined using the SET/SET KEY= syntax, how is the data set named in the **second** SET statement read?

   direct access

168

continued...

Chapter Review – Correct Answers

4. If the following program is used to combine the summary data set containing one observation with the detail data set containing 50 observations, how many observations are in the data set **combined**?

```
data combined;
   set summary;
   set detail;
run;
```

   1

Chapter 9 Sorting SAS Data Sets

9.1 Using the SORT Procedure

Objectives

- List the reasons for sorting data.
- Define the SAS sort.
- Define threading.
- Calculate the workspace and library space required to sort a SAS data file.
- Allocate sort workspace.
- Use the EQUALS|NOEQUALS option.
- Use the SORTEDBY= option.
- Use the PRESORTED option.
- Change the collating sequence of the SORT procedure.

3

Reasons for Sorting Data

Data is sorted to accomplish the following:

- reorder the data for reporting

Create a report with employees listed in alphabetical order by last name.

- store ordered data to reduce data retrieval time

A WHERE statement executes faster if the data is sorted by the variables used in the WHERE expression.

- enable BY-group processing in both DATA and PROC steps

Create individual reports for each employee.

6

Using the SAS Sorting Utility

The SORT procedure has the following characteristics:

- supplied by SAS for all operating environments
- executes in memory up to the limit imposed by the SORTSIZE= option
- minimizes the use of external storage
- executes in parallel using multiple threads

7

Threading Terminology

In SAS®9, the SORT procedure is multi-threaded.

thread	a single, independent flow of control through a program or within a process
symmetric multiprocessing machines (SMPs)	computers with multiple CPUs that share the same memory and a thread-enabled operating system, providing the ability to spawn and process multiple threads simultaneously
parallel processing	multiple units of work scheduled for concurrent execution by the operating system

8

Parallel Processing with Four Threads

Data file partitioned into chunks

SORT

Partial results

Collate process

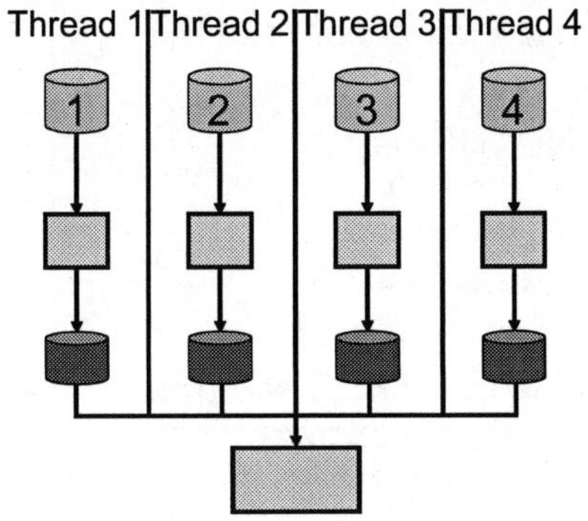

9

Multi-Threaded Processing

Threading can be enabled or disabled for the following Base SAS procedures:

- PROC MEANS/SUMMARY
- PROC REPORT
- PROC SORT
- PROC SQL (GROUP BY and ORDER BY)
- PROC TABULATE

10

When you benchmark using the threaded procedures, use the real-time statistic rather than the CPU-time statistic. The back-end collating process to re-create the single data set might result in an increase in total CPU time, while reducing wall-clock time (time from submission of code for execution to return of results).

Threaded Procedures in Base SAS

Threaded processing can be controlled using either of the following:

- SAS system option THREADS|NOTHREADS

OPTIONS THREADS | NOTHREADS;

- THREADS|NOTHREADS option in the PROC statement

PROC SORT DATA=*SAS-data-set* **THREADS | NOTHREADS;**

11

If the TAGSORT option is used with PROC SORT, threading is disabled. The TAGSORT option stores only the BY variables and the observation numbers (named *tags*) in temporary files. At the completion of the sorting process, PROC SORT uses the tags to retrieve records from the input data set in sorted order.

9.01 Quiz

Open and submit the program **p309a01**.

How many CPUs are available in your SAS session?

```
proc options option=cpucount;
run;
```

13

Threaded Procedures in Base SAS

The number of CPUs available for SAS to use can be controlled with the CPUCOUNT= SAS system option.

General form of the CPUCOUNT= SAS system option:

```
OPTIONS CPUCOUNT=ACTUAL | 1-1024;
```

ACTUAL (Default)	the number of physical processors available when the option is set
1-1024	the number of CPUs that SAS will assume are available for use by threaded-enabled applications

15

The SAS Administrator might limit the number of CPUs that are available for SAS processing, so the value **ACTUAL** might be less than the total number of CPUs in the machine that SAS is using.

9.02 Poll

Have you ever run out of space during a sort?

- ❍ Yes
- ❍ No

17

Sort Space Requirements

```
proc sort data=orion.orders;
   by Customer_ID Order_ID;
run;
```

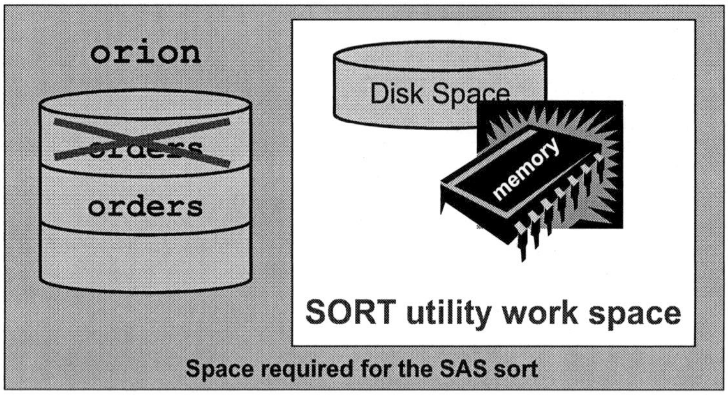

18 p309d01

Sort Space Requirements

The amount of space that the SAS sort needs depends on the following conditions:

- whether the sort can be done with threading
- the length of the observations
- the number of variables in the BY statement and their storage lengths
- the operating environment in which PROC SORT executes
- the library to which the sorted data is written

✎ A quick rule-of-thumb method for estimating the space requirements for sorting with the SAS sort is **four** times the size of the SAS data set being sorted.

19

Reference Information

The formula below calculates the **estimated** amount of space needed by a **single-threaded** PROC SORT:

bytes required=((4 * *obslen*) + (2 * *keylen*)) * *numobs*

The formula below calculates the **estimated** amount of space needed by a **multi-threaded** PROC SORT:

bytes required=3 * (*obslen* * *numobs*)

The space calculation for the **SAS 8.2** sort is as follows:

bytes required=(*keylen* + *obslen*) * *numobs* * N

obslen	length of the observation
keylen	length of the BY variables when concatenated to form a single value
numobs	number of observations in the data set

Use the CONTENTS or DATASETS procedure to gather the required information.

```
proc contents data=orion.orders;
run;
```

These space calculations assume that the SAS®9 sort can take place in memory without using utility swap files.

If you use the OVERWRITE option in the PROC SORT statement in multi-threaded environments, you need space equal to the data set size. The OVERWRITE option enables the input data set to be deleted before the replacement output data set is populated with observations. The OVERWRITE option is supported by the SAS sort and SAS multi-threaded sort only. The option has no effect if you use a host sort or the TAGSORT option.

Use the OVERWRITE option only with a data set that is backed up or with a data set that you can reconstruct. Because the input data set is deleted, data will be lost if a failure occurs while the output data set is being written.

Using the SORTSIZE= Option

Use the SORTSIZE= option in the PROC SORT statement to do the following:

- specify the amount of memory that is available to the SORT procedure
- improve the sort performance by restricting the swapping of memory to disk that is controlled by the operating system

General form of the SORTSIZE= option:

SORTSIZE=*n* | *n*K | *n*M | *n*G | MIN | MAX | *hex*X | SIZE;

20

Allocating Sort Workspace

Actual Required Workspace	Sorting	Processing Time
less than or equal to SORTSIZE= SAS system option	occurs in memory	reduced
greater than SORTSIZE= SAS system option	utility files on disk and memory	increased

⚠ The multi-threaded SAS®9 sort fails to complete a sort if the value of SORTSIZE= is too small.

21

The SORTSIZE= Option

For optimal performance, set the SORTSIZE= option to a value less than the available physical memory. This enables the programs and the operating environment to stay resident in memory.

You should investigate how resources are affected if you change the value of the SORTSIZE= option.

```
options fullstimer;
proc sort data=orion.order_fact
          sortsize=max;
   by Order_Date;
run;
```

22

p309d02

9.03 Multiple Choice Poll

Do you have a host sort utility such as SYNCSORT or DFSORT available?

- ❍ Yes
- ❍ No

24

Host Sort Utilities

A host sort utility has the following characteristics:

- is a third-party sort package
- is available for UNIX, z/OS, and Windows platforms

✎ Ask your system administrator whether a host sort utility is available at your site.

25

SAS System Options for Selecting a Host Sort

SAS System Option	What it Does	Syntax
SORTPGM=	specifies which sort utility to use	**OPTIONS** SORTPGM=*utility* | BEST | HOST | SAS;
SORTCUTP=	specifies a cut-over point in terms of the size (in bytes) of a SAS data set	**OPTIONS** SORTCUTP=*n* | *n*K | *n*M | *n*G | MAX | MIN | *hex*X;
SORTNAME=	specifies the host sort utility to be invoked if SORTPGM=BEST | HOST	**OPTIONS** SORTNAME=*host-sort-utility-name*;

26

Sorted Data

When data is sorted by SAS, the descriptor contains the following information:

1. a sort indicator that contains the variable(s) on which the data is sorted
2. whether or not the sort is validated by SAS
3. the character set used

Additional information contained in the descriptor portion includes the following:

4. the collating sequence used for ordering the data
5. collation rules, if the data set is sorted linguistically

27

Sorted Data

Partial PROC CONTENTS Output

```
                                  The CONTENTS Procedure

Data Set Name          ORION.SALESSTAFF                          Observations          163
Member Type            DATA                                      Variables             10
Engine                 V9                                        Indexes               0
Created                Monday, December 17, 2007 09:04:37 PM     Observation Length    136
Last Modified          Monday, December 17, 2007 09:04:37 PM     Deleted Observations  0
Protection                                                       Compressed            NO
Data Set Type                                                    Sorted                YES
Label
Data Representation    WINDOWS_32
Encoding               wlatin1  Western (Windows)

<lines removed >

 Sort Information

                       Sortedby        Emp_Hire_Date
                       Validated       YES
                       Character Set   ANSI
```

28 p309d03

ANSI (American National Standards Institute) is an organization in the United States that coordinates voluntary standards and conformity to those standards. ANSI works with the ISO (International Organization for Standardization) to establish global standards.

By default, the ANSI character set uses ASCII (American Standard Code for Information Interchange) for the Windows and UNIX operating environments and EBCDIC (Extended Binary Coded Decimal Interchange Code) for z/OS.

9.04 Multiple Answer Poll

If you sort a SAS data set that is in sorted order, does SAS re-sort the data?

a. No, if the sort indicator is 'YES', and the validation is 'YES'
b. No, if the sort indicator is 'YES', and the validation is 'NO'
c. Yes, regardless of the sort indicator or validation
d. Yes, if the sort indicator is 'YES', and the validation is 'NO'

30

Setting Sort Indicator and Validation

The sort indicator and validation can be set by one of the following techniques:

- sorting the data using PROC SORT or PROC SQL with an ORDER BY clause
- specifying the sort order by using the SORTEDBY= data set option
- using the PRESORTED option in the PROC SORT statement

32

Using the SORTEDBY= Option

If the input data is in sorted order, you can specify the order by using the SORTEDBY= **output** data set option.

The SORTEDBY= option has the following attributes:

- sets the sort indicator on the data set to YES
- defines the sort indicator as an asserted data order (not validated)
- requires that SAS check the order of the data as it processes it

General form of the SORTEDBY option:

data-set-name(SORTEDBY=*BY-clause* | _NULL_)

33

BY-clause	indicates the data order.
NULL	removes any existing sort information.

Using the SORTEDBY= Option

Create a SAS data set from an external file containing invoice information. The external file is in sorted order by order date.

```
filename M1 'mon1.dat';

data january(sortedby=Order_Date);
   infile M1 dlm=',';
   input Customer_ID Order_ID Order_Type
         Order_Date : date9.
         Delivery_Date : date9.;
run;
```

34 p309d04

Using the SORTEDBY= Option

Partial SAS Log

```
                              The CONTENTS Procedure

Data Set Name          WORK.JANUARY                                 Observations          4
Member Type            DATA                                         Variables             5
Engine                 V9                                           Indexes               0
Created                Sunday, January 27, 2008 05:36:23 PM         Observation Length    40
Last Modified          Sunday, January 27, 2008 05:36:23 PM         Deleted Observations  0
Protection                                                          Compressed            NO
Data Set Type                                                       Sorted                YES
Label
Data Representation    WINDOWS_32
Encoding               wlatin1  Western (Windows)

                              <lines removed>

                              Sort Information

                         Sortedby          Order_Date
                         Validated         NO
                         Character Set     ANSI
```

35 p309d04

Using the SORTEDBY= Option

Attempt to sort the data.

```
proc sort data=january;
   by Order_Date;
run;
```

Log

```
1197  proc sort data=january;
1198     by Order_Date;
1199  run;

NOTE: Input data set is already sorted, no sorting done.
NOTE: PROCEDURE SORT used (Total process time):
      real time           0.03 seconds
      cpu time            0.00 seconds
```

36 p309d05

Using the PRESORTED Option

Beginning in SAS 9.2, there is a PROC SORT statement option, PRESORTED, that checks within the input data set to determine whether the sequence of observations is in order before sorting. By specifying this option, you can avoid the cost of sorting the data set.

```
proc sort data=orion.salesstaff presorted;
   by Emp_Hire_Date;
run;
```

If the data set **orion.salesstaff** is not in sorted order by **Emp_Hire_Date**, PROC SORT with the PRESORTED option sorts the data.

37 p309d06

In SAS 9.2, the SORTVALIDATE system option specifies whether the SORT procedure verifies that a data set is sorted according to the variables in the BY statement when the sort indicator metadata designates a user-specified sort order. NOSORTVALIDATE is the default.

OPTIONS NOSORTVALIDATE | SORTVALIDATE;

Using the PRESORTED Option

Partial Log

```
1    proc sort data=orion.salesstaff  presorted;
2       by Emp_Hire_Date;
3    run;

NOTE: Input data set is already sorted, no sorting done.
NOTE: PROCEDURE SORT used (Total process time):
```

Partial PROC CONTENTS Output

```
                         Sort Information

                        Sortedby        Emp_Hire_Date
                        Validated       YES
                        Character Set   ANSI
```

38 p309d06

Sort Order

The character set determines the sort order of a particular character in relation to other characters. By default, PROC SORT uses one of the following collating sequences, depending on the environment under which the procedure is running:

- ASCII (Windows and UNIX)
- EBCDIC (z/OS)

✎ In addition, the EQUALS|NOEQUALS option in the PROC SORT statement specifies the order of the observations within a BY group in the output data set.

39

<table>
<tr><th>Collating Sequence</th><th>Default Sort Order</th></tr>
<tr><td>ASCII</td><td>blank ! " # $ % & ' ( ) * + , - . /0 1 2 3 4 5 6 7 8 9 : ; < = > ? @ A B C D E F G H I J K L M N O P Q R S T U V W X Y Z[\] ^ _ a b c d e f g h i j k l m n o p q r s t u v w x y z { } ~</td></tr>
<tr><td>EBCDIC</td><td>blank . < (+ | & ! $ *) ; ¬ - / , % _ > ?: # @ ' = " a b c d e f g h i j k l m n o p q r ~ s t u v w x y z { A B C D E F G H I } J K L M N O P Q R \S T U V W X Y Z 0 1 2 3 4 5 6 7 8 9</td></tr>
</table>

The options EBCDIC, ASCII, NATIONAL, DANISH, SWEDISH, and REVERSE can change the default collating sequence.

Using the EQUALS | NOEQUALS Option

- For observations with identical BY-variable values, EQUALS maintains the relative order of the observations within the input data set in the output data set. This is the default.
- NOEQUALS does not necessarily preserve this order in the output data set.

✎ Using NOEQUALS can save CPU and memory.

PROC SORT DATA=*SAS-data-set* **EQUALS | NOEQUALS ;**

40

9.05 Quiz

The data set **orion.salesstaff** was previously sorted in ascending order by **Employee_Hire_Date**.

Open and submit program **p309a02**.

```
proc sort data=orion.salesstaff
          out=salesstaff;
   by Employee_ID;
run;
proc print data=salesstaff;
  where Employee_ID=120134;
run;
```

For employee number=120134, which date is first?

a. The first date hired
b. The last date hired

42

EQUALS Option versus NOEQUALS Option

The EQUALS option is the default.

```
proc sort data=orion.salesstaff
          out=salesstaff equals;
   by Employee_ID;
run;
```

```
proc sort data=orion.salesstaff
          out=salesstaff noequals;
   by Employee_ID;
run;
```

⚠ When you use the NODUPKEY option to remove observations in the output data set, the choice of EQUALS or NOEQUALS can affect which observations are removed.

44 p309d07

Using the NODUPKEY and DUPOUT= Options

The SORT procedure NODUPKEY and DUPOUT= options used together create following output data sets:

- **oneemp** containing exactly one observation per **Employee_ID**
- extra containing the four duplicate **Employee_ID** observations

```
proc sort data=orion.salesstaff nodupkey
          out=oneemp
          dupout=extra;
   by Employee_ID;
run;
```

45 p309d08

Using the NODUPKEY and DUPOUT= Options

General form of the DUPOUT= and NODUPKEY options:

```
PROC SORT DATA=data-set-name
          OUT=data-set-name-2
          DUPOUT=data-set-name-3
          NODUPKEY;
    BY BY-variable(s);
RUN;
```

DUPOUT=	specifies the output data set to which duplicate observations are written.
NODUPKEY	checks for and eliminates observations with duplicate BY values.

46

Changing the Collating Sequence

You can change the collating sequence by specifying one of the these options in the PROC SORT statement.

- ASCII
- EBCDIC
- DANISH
- FINNISH
- NORWEGIAN
- POLISH
- SWEDISH
- NATIONAL
- SORTSEQ=

⚠ You can specify only one collating sequence option in a PROC SORT step.

47

✎ Refer to the "Collating Sequence" chapter of the *SAS National Language Support (NLS): User's Guide* for detailed information about the various collating sequences and when they are used.

Setup for the Poll

The data set **orion.customer** contains a variable named **Customer_Address**.

Partial listing of **orion.customer** (selected observations)

Customer_ID	Country	. . .	Customer_Address	. . .
29	AU	. . .	21 Hotham Parade	. . .
41	AU	. . .	9 Angourie Court	. . .
63	US	. . .	25 Briarforest Pl	. . .
111	AU	. . .	28 Munibung Road	. . .
171	AU	. . .	21 Parliament House c/- Senator t	. . .
183	AU	. . .	18 Fletcher Rd	. . .
195	AU	. . .	4 Burke Street Woolloongabba	. . .
215	AU	. . .	23 Benjamin Street	. . .
46966	CA	. . .	17 boul Wallberg	. . .
70221	CA	. . .	9 South Service Rd	. . .

49

9.06 Multiple Choice Poll

If the data set **orion.customer** is sorted by **Customer_Address**, which of the following is the first address listed?

a. 21 Hotham Parade

b. 9 Angourie Court

50

Using the LINGUISTIC Option

In SAS 9.2, the LINGUISTIC value for the SORTSEQ= option in the PROC SORT statement specifies that the rules and default collating sequence options are based on the language specified in the current value of the SAS system option LOCALE.

For example, the data set `orion.customer` contains customers from seven countries. The countries and associated locales are listed below:

Country	Locale
Australia	en_AU
Canada	en_CA
Germany	de_DE
Israel	he_IL
Turkey	tr_TR
United States	en_US
South Africa	en_ZA

52

Using the LINGUISTIC Suboptions

The following are selected collation rules that can be specified for the LINGUISTIC option. These rules modify the linguistic collating sequence.

Suboption	Values	Purpose
CASE_FIRST=	UPPER | LOWER	Either value can sort data so that like letters are sorted correctly irrespective of case.
NUMERIC_COLLATION=	ON | OFF	This orders integer values within the text by the numeric value instead of characters used to represent the numbers.
STRENGTH=	PRIMARY | SECONDARY | TERTIARY | QUATERNARY | IDENTICAL	The PRIMARY value supports sorting that is not case sensitive. The other values handle diacritical and punctuation differences.

53

The following table contains the values of the CASE_FIRST= suboption:

UPPER	sorts uppercase letters first, and then the lowercase letters.
LOWER	sorts lowercase letters first, and then the uppercase letters.

The following table contains the values of the STRENGTH= suboption:

Value	Type of Collation	Description
PRIMARY or 1	PRIMARY specifies differences between base characters (for example, "a" < "b").	It is the strongest difference. For example, dictionaries are divided into different sections by base character.
SECONDARY or 2	Accents in the characters are considered secondary differences (for example, "as" < "às" < "at").	A secondary difference is ignored when there is a primary difference anywhere in the strings. Other differences between letters can also be considered secondary differences, depending on the language.
TERTIARY or 3	Upper and lowercase differences in characters are distinguished at the tertiary level (for example, "ao" < "Ao" < "aò").	A tertiary difference is ignored when there is a primary or secondary difference anywhere in the strings. Another example is the difference between large and small Kana.
QUATERNARY or 4	When punctuation is ignored at level 1-3, an additional level can be used to distinguish words with and without punctuation (for example, "ab" < "a-b" < "aB").	The quaternary level should be used if ignoring punctuation is required or when processing Japanese text. This difference is ignored when there is a primary, secondary or tertiary difference.
IDENTICAL or 5	When all other levels are equal, the identical level is used as a tiebreaker. The Unicode code point values of the Normalization Form D (NFD) form of each string are compared at this level, in case there is no difference at levels 1-4.	This level should be used sparingly, as only code point values differences between two strings is an extremely rare occurrence. For example, only Hebrew cantillation marks are distinguished at this level.

proc sort data= out= ;
by ;
run;

data 1 2;
set ;
by ;
if first. ___ and last. ___ then output 1;
else output 2;
run;

Using the NUMERIC_COLLATION= Option

```
proc sort data=orion.customer
          out=customer
          sortseq=linguistic
                (numeric_collation=on);
   by Customer_Address;
run;

proc contents data=customer;
run;
```

54 p309d09

Using the NUMERIC_COLLATION= Option

Partial PROC CONTENTS Output

```
                    Sort Information

           Sortedby               Customer_Address
           Validated              YES
           Character Set          ANSI
           Collating Sequence     LINGUISTIC
           Locale                 en_US
           Strength               3
           Numeric Collation      ON
```

55 p309d09

proc sort data=
orion.salesstaff.
out= work.nodup.
by employeeid
run;

data work.nondups
work.dups;
by employee id;
if first. employeeid
and last. employeeid
then output
nondups;
else output dups;
run;

NUMERIC_COLLATION= Option

Partial Listing of **customer**

Customer_ID	Country	. . .	Customer_Address	. . .
195	AU	. . .	4 Burke Street Woolloongabba	. . .
41	AU	. . .	9 Angourie Court	. . .
70221	CA	. . .	9 South Service Rd	. . .
46966	CA	. . .	17 boul Wallberg	. . .
183	AU	. . .	18 Fletcher Rd	. . .
29	AU	. . .	21 Hotham Parade	. . .
171	AU	. . .	21 Parliament House c/- Senator t	. . .
215	AU	. . .	23 Benjamin Street	. . .
63	US	. . .	25 Briarforest Pl	. . .
111	AU	. . .	28 Munibung Road	. . .
70210	CA	. . .	40 Route 199	. . .
26148	CA	. . .	41 Main St	. . .
31	US	. . .	42 Arrowood Ln	. . .
11171	CA	. . .	69 chemin Martin	. . .

56

Exercises

Level 1

1. Using the PRESORTED Option

a. Use PROC CONTENTS to determine if the data set **orion.holidays** is sorted.

b. Write a PROC SORT step to sort the data **orion.holidays** by **Date**. Create a temporary data set named **holidays**. Use the PRESORTED option in the PROC SORT statement.

What is the resulting message in the log? ______________________________

____

____

c. Submit a PROC CONTENTS step to determine whether the data set **holidays** is sorted by **Date**.

d. Change the BY variable to **Holiday_Name** and resubmit the PROC SORT step.

What is the resulting message in the log? ______________________________

____

e. Submit a PROC CONTENTS step to determine whether the data set **holidays** is sorted by **Holiday_Name**.

Level 2

2. Creating a Sorted Data Set

a. Open the program **p309e02**.

b. Modify the program to create a data set named **profit07** and specify that it is sorted by **Company** without sorting the data set.

p309e02

```
data profit07;
   infile 'profit07.dat' dlm=',';
   input Company:$30. Sales Cost Salaries Profit;
run;
```

c. Use PROC CONTENTS to verify that **profit07** has a sort flag on the variable **Company**.

d. Use PROC PRINT to create a report grouped by the **Company** variable. Print the first 24 observations of the data.

Partial PROC PRINT Output

```
------------------------- Company=Logistics -------------------------

      Obs     Sales      Cost     Salaries     Profit

        1    124918    535949      247341     163690
        2    127416    389429      181185      80829
        3    131901    313762      145103      36757
        4    134182    642970      309099     199690
              < lines omitted >
        9    144364    241863      113212     -15713
       10    144364    339880      158696      36821
       11    150958    432257      199526      81773
       12    150958    947060      442396     353706

--------------------- Company=Orion Australia ----------------------

      Obs     Sales      Cost     Salaries     Profit

       13    119597    159404       74771     -34964
       14    123908    146004       69396     -47300
       15    132940     64236       30403     -99107
              < lines omitted >
       21    162870     79060       36898    -120708
       22    181463    163110       77705     -96057
       23    188318    186131       87454     -89641
       24    212579    257931      121060     -75708
```

e. Use the PROC SORT PRESORTED option to turn on the validated flag and use PROC CONTENTS to verify that the sort flag is set in the descriptor portion.

Level 3

3. Using the SORTSEQ=LINGUISTIC Option

The first five observations of **orion.spain_customers** are listed below:

Obs	Customer_ID	Country	Gender	Personal_ ID	Customer_Name	Customer_ FirstName
1	2	ES	F		Mercedes Martínez	Mercedes
2	7	ES	F		Julián Escorihuela Monserrate	Julián
3	21	ES	M		José Fernández de Mesa	José
4	72	ES	F		Mónica Aranda Unzurrunzaga	Mónica
5	73	ES	F		Pilar Bachs Pallarés	Pilar

Obs	Customer_LastName	Birth_ Date	Customer_Address	Street_ID	Street_ Number	Customer_ Type_ID
1	Martínez	15JAN1955	Edificio 2	8300101034	2	1010
2	Escorihuela Monserrate	07AUG1975	Co. De Los Claveles 561	8300100945	561	1040
3	Fernández de Mesa	16JUN1955	C. Santa Hortensia 2	8300100682	2	2010
4	Aranda Unzurrunzaga	04JAN1975	Apartado 64	8300100254	64	1020
5	Bachs Pallarés	04JAN1945	C. Conde de Peñalver 68	8300100485	68	1030

a. Open and submit the program **p309e03**.

What is the value of the LOCALE= option? ____________________

p309e03

```
proc options option=locale;
run;
```

b. Write a PROC SORT step to sort **orion.spain_customers** by **Customer_Name**.

c. Create an output data set named **s_customers**.

d. Use the SORTSEQ=LINGUISTIC option with the suboption LOCALE=es_ES.

e. Print the data set **s_customers** and look at the order of the variable **Customer_Name**.

9.2 BY-Group Processing (Self-Study)

Objectives

- Define BY-group processing.
- Use indexes to return the data in sorted order.
- Use indexes to combine data horizontally.
- Use a format to group data for BY-group processing.
- Use a CLASS statement.
- Specify a user-asserted sort order.

60

BY-Group Processing

BY-group processing has these characteristics:

- is a method of processing observations that are grouped or ordered by the values of the BY variables
- can be used in both DATA and PROC steps
- can be used to eliminate observations with duplicate BY values

The following techniques can be used to perform BY-group processing:

- the SORT procedure
- indexes on the data set
- the NOTSORTED option in the BY statement
- user-sort assertion
- a CLASS statement

61

9.07 Multiple Choice Poll

Which of the following would be a good use of an index for BY-group processing?

a. Your data set is sorted by the BY variable already.
b. Your data set is updated using a SET statement in the DATA step. In that case, the index would be updated after the append, and you would not have to reindex the data.
c. Your data is updated using PROC APPEND, PROC SQL, or the MODIFY statement in the DATA step. In that case, the index would be updated after the update, and you would not have to reindex the data.

63

Using an Index for BY-Group Processing

BY-group processing with an index eliminates the need to sort data.

- Having multiple indexes enables sequencing data by different variables without having to repeat the SORT procedure.
- Indexes are updated when observations are modified or added to a SAS data set.

```
options msglevel=i;
proc print data=orion.retail(obs=10);
   title 'Retail Sales';
   by Customer_ID;
   var Customer_ID Product_ID Quantity
       Total_Retail_Price;
run;
```

65 p309d10

Limitations of Using an Index for BY-Group Processing

BY-group processing with an index has the following limitations:

- less efficient than sequentially reading a sorted data set
- extra memory requirement to use the index
- extreme I/O increase

Partial SAS Log

```
608  options msglevel=i;
609  proc print data=orion.retail(obs=10);
610     title 'Retail Sales';
611     by Customer_ID;
INFO: Index Customer_ID selected for BY clause processing.
NOTE: An index was selected to execute the BY statement.
      The observations will be returned in index order rather than in physical
      order. The selected index is for the variable(s):
 Customer_ID
612     var Customer_ID Product_ID Quantity Total_Retail_Price;
613  run;
```

66 p309d10

Using an Index for BY-Group Processing

Partial PROC PRINT Output

Retail Sales

------------------------- Customer ID=4 -------------------------

Obs	Customer_ID	Product_ID	Quantity	Total_Retail_ Price
62	4	240600100017	1	$53.00
70	4	220101400145	1	$16.70
79	4	240700100011	3	$80.97
111	4	230100100053	2	$92.60

------------------------- Customer ID=5 -------------------------

Obs	Customer_ID	Product_ID	Quantity	Total_Retail_ Price
37	5	240100100433	1	$3.00
48	5	220101400276	2	$136.80
88	5	240300200018	1	$87.20
89	5	240300300071	1	$138.00
148	5	220101400265	2	$74.20
149	5	220101400387	4	$50.40

67

When a BY Statement Does Not Use an Index

A BY statement does not use an index if either of the following conditions are present:

- The BY statement includes the DESCENDING or NOTSORTED option.
- SAS is aware that the data file is physically stored in sorted order according to the BY variables.

68

Business Scenario

The data set **orion.street_code** contains the **Street_ID** and the name, city, and country for the streets.

Partial Listing of **orion.street_code**

Street_ID	Country	Street_ Name	Postal_ Code	City_Name
1600100760	AU	Fletcher Rd	4170	Colnslie
1600101527	AU	Angourie Court	5009	Kilkenny
1600101555	AU	Parliament Road	5331	Kingston-On-Murray
1600101663	AU	Burke Street Woolloongabba	217	Liverpool
1600101794	AU	Brunswick Street	8008	Melbourne

69

Business Scenario

The SAS data set **orion.order_fact** contains the information needed for the delivery of products to Orion customers. There is no index on **Street_ID** in the **orion.order_fact** data set.

Partial Listing of **orion.order_fact**

Customer_ ID	Street_ID	Delivery_Date	Order_ID	Quantity
63	9260125492	11JAN2003	1230058123	1
5	9260114570	19JAN2003	1230080101	1
45	9260104847	22JAN2003	1230106883	1
41	1600101527	28JAN2003	1230147441	2
183	1600100760	27FEB2003	1230315085	3
79	9260101874	03MAR2003	1230333319	1
23	9260126679	08MAR2003	1230338566	1
23	9260126679	08MAR2003	1230338566	2
45	9260104847	11MAR2003	1230371142	2

70

Business Scenario

Combine the two data sets to expedite delivery of customer orders.

1. Create an index on **Street_ID** in **orion.street_code**.
2. Use SET/SET with KEY=**Street_ID** to combine the data sets.

Partial Listing of **addresses**

Customer_ID	Street_ID	. . .	Street_ Name	Postal_ Code	City_ Name
63	9260125492	. . .	Briarforest Pl	62201	St. Clair
5	9260114570	. . .	Cog Hill Ct	90280	Los Angeles
45	9260104847	. . .	Angier Rd	94520	Contra Costa
41	1600101527	. . .	Angourie Court	5009	Kilkenny
183	1600100760	. . .	Fletcher Rd	4170	Colnslie
79	9260101874	. . .	Dinwiddie Ct	16648	Blair

71

Setup for the Poll

p309a03

```
proc datasets library=orion nolist;
   modify street_code;
   index create Street_ID;
quit;

data addresses;
   set orion.order_fact(keep=Customer_ID Street_ID
                 Delivery_Date Order_ID Product_ID Quantity);
   set orion.street_code(keep=Street_ID Country Street_Name
                         City_Name Postal_Code)
       key=Street_ID / unique;
run;

proc print data=addresses;
   title 'Customer Addresses';
run;
```

73

9.08 Multiple Choice Poll

How is `orion.order_fact` read?

a. Direct access via the index
b. Sequentially

74

9.09 Multiple Choice Poll

How is **orion.street_code** read?

a. Direct access via the index
b. Sequentially

76

Using Indexes

```
proc datasets library=orion nolist;
   modify street_code;
   index create Street_ID;
quit;

data addresses;
   set orion.order_fact(keep=Customer_ID
                             Street_ID
                             Delivery_Date
                             Order_ID
                             Product_ID
                             Quantity) ;
   set orion.street_code(keep=Street_ID
                              Country
                              Street_Name
                              Ci
                              Po
      key=Street_ID / unique;
run;
```

orion.order_fact is read sequentially.

orion.street_code is read by accessing the index and directly accessing the appropriate observation.

78 p309a03

The UNIQUE option causes a KEY= search to use the first matching observation from the indexed data set, if there are duplicates.

The UNIQUE Option

Option	Processing	Results
none	Begins searching at the top of the index **only** when the KEY= value changes (sequential matching operation on consecutive duplicate key values).	Run-time error if there are fewer duplicates in the indexed data. The PDV contains values from the last match.
UNIQUE	**Always** begins searching at the top of the index.	Duplicate values in the first data set are always matched with the first matching key value in the indexed data set.

⚠ UNIQUE does **not** indicate that the keys are unique in the indexed data set.

79

Duplicate Key Values (Review)

```
data three;
   set one;
   set two key=Variable;
run;
```

Example 2: Contiguous duplications in **one**

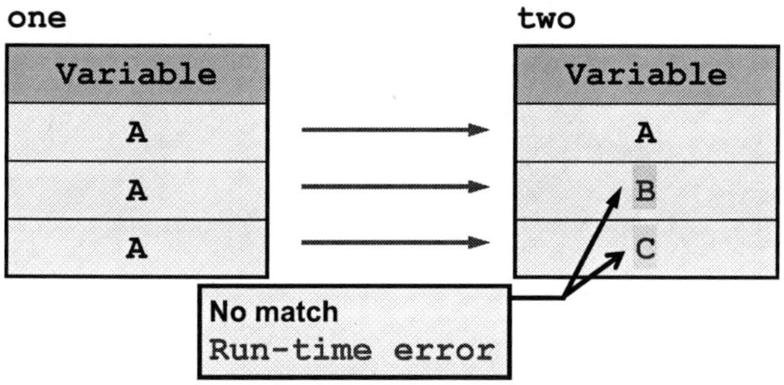

80

Duplicate Key Values (Review)

```
data three;
   set one;
   set two key=Variable / unique;
run;
```

Example 3: Contiguous duplications in **one** with the UNIQUE option

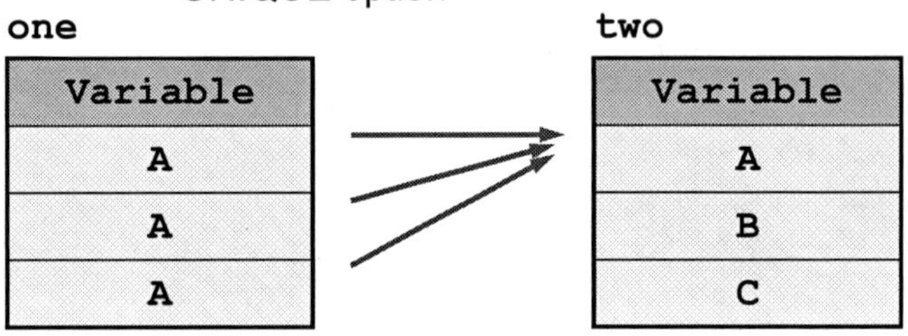

81

9.10 Quiz

Open and submit the program **p309a03**.

Are there any data errors in the log?

```
data addresses;
   set orion.order_fact(keep=Customer_ID Street_ID
             Delivery_Date Order_ID Product_ID Quantity);
   set orion.street_code(keep=Street_ID Country
             Street_Name City_Name Postal_Code)
             key=Street_ID / unique;
run;
```

83

9.11 Quiz

Open and submit the program **p309a04**.

1. What does the SAS log show for this DATA step?
2. Why do you get those error messages?

```
data addresses2;
   set orion.order_fact(keep=Customer_ID Street_ID
             Delivery_Date Order_ID Product_ID Quantity);
   set orion.street_code(keep=Street_ID Country
             Street_Name City_Name Postal_Code)
             key=Street_ID;
run;
```

85

Comparing the Data Sets

```
proc compare data=addresses
             compare=addresses2;
run;
```

The data values in the **addresses** data set and the data values in the **addresses2** data sets are equal.

```
                    Observation Summary

Observation      Base  Compare

First Obs           1        1
Last  Obs         617      617

Number of Observations in Common: 617.
Total Number of Observations Read from WORK.ADDRESSES: 617.
Total Number of Observations Read from WORK.ADDRESSES2: 617.

Number of Observations with Some Compared Variables Unequal: 0.
Number of Observations with All Compared Variables Equal: 617.

NOTE: No unequal values were found. All values compared are exactly equal.
```

88 **p309a04**

Business Scenario

You must print the data set **orion.shoe_vendors** by **Group_Name** for the vendors where the variable **Mfg_Suggested_Retail_Price** is greater than $100.

Mfg_Suggested_Retail_Price>100

Obs	Group_Name	Supplier_Name	Category_Name	Mfg_Suggested_ Retail_Price
4	Eclipse, Kid's Shoes	Eclipse Inc	Children Sports	$114.00
13	Eclipse, Kid's Shoes	Eclipse Inc	Children Sports	$130.00
29	Eclipse, Kid's Shoes	Eclipse Inc	Children Sports	$114.00
30	Eclipse, Kid's Shoes	Eclipse Inc	Children Sports	$117.00
43	Tracker Kid's Clothes	3Top Sports	Children Sports	$106.00
55	Tracker Kid's Clothes	3Top Sports	Children Sports	$113.00
59	Tracker Kid's Clothes	3Top Sports	Children Sports	$109.00
68	LSF	Eclipse Inc	Clothes	$141.00
69	LSF	Petterson AB	Clothes	$130.00
70	LSF	Petterson AB	Clothes	$140.00
71	LSF	3Top Sports	Clothes	$144.00
72	LSF	Petterson AB	Clothes	$125.00
73	LSF	Triple Sportswear Inc	Clothes	$162.00

89

Setup for the Poll

Partial Listing

Mfg_Suggested_Retail_Price>100

Obs	Group_Name	Supplier_Name	Category_Name	Mfg_Suggested_ Retail_Price
4	Eclipse, Kid's Shoes	Eclipse Inc	Children Sports	$114.00
13	Eclipse, Kid's Shoes	Eclipse Inc	Children Sports	$130.00
29	Eclipse, Kid's Shoes	Eclipse Inc	Children Sports	$114.00
30	Eclipse, Kid's Shoes	Eclipse Inc	Children Sports	$117.00
43	Tracker Kid's Clothes	3Top Sports	Children Sports	$106.00
55	Tracker Kid's Clothes	3Top Sports	Children Sports	$113.00
59	Tracker Kid's Clothes	3Top Sports	Children Sports	$109.00
68	LSF	Eclipse Inc	Clothes	$141.00
69	LSF	Petterson AB	Clothes	$130.00
70	LSF	Petterson AB	Clothes	$140.00
71	LSF	3Top Sports	Clothes	$144.00
72	LSF	Petterson AB	Clothes	$125.00
73	LSF	Triple Sportswear Inc	Clothes	$162.00

```
proc print data=orion.shoe_vendors;
   title 'Mfg_Suggested_Retail_Price>100';
   where Mfg_Suggested_Retail_Price>100;
   var Group_Name Supplier_Name Category_Name
       Mfg_Suggested_Retail_Price;
run;
```

91 p309a05

9.12 Multiple Choice Poll

Which of the following is true of the data set **orion.shoe_vendors**?

a. The data set is sorted by the variable **Group_Name**.
b. The data set is not sorted by the variable **Group_Name**. However, it is grouped by **Group_Name**.
c. The data set is neither sorted nor grouped by the variable **Group_Name**.

92

Using the NOTSORTED Option

```
proc print data=orion.shoe_vendors n;
   title 'shoe_vendors BY Group_Name Notsorted';
   by Group_Name notsorted;
   where Mfg_Suggested_Retail_Price>100;
   var Supplier_Name Category_Name
       Mfg_Suggested_Retail_Price;
run;
```

⚠ The NOTSORTED option turns off sequence checking. If your data is not grouped, it can produce a very large amount of output.

94 p309d11

Using the NOTSORTED Option

Partial PROC PRINT Output

```
                    shoe_vendors BY Group_Name Notsorted

--------------- Group Name=Eclipse, Kid's Shoes ---------------

          Supplier_                            Mfg_Suggested_
   Obs      Name         Category_Name          Retail_Price

     4   Eclipse Inc   Children Sports             $114.00
    13   Eclipse Inc   Children Sports             $130.00
    29   Eclipse Inc   Children Sports             $114.00
    30   Eclipse Inc   Children Sports             $117.00

                           N = 4

-------------- Group Name=Tracker Kid's Clothes --------------

          Supplier_                            Mfg_Suggested_
   Obs      Name         Category_Name          Retail_Price

    43   3Top Sports   Children Sports             $106.00
    55   3Top Sports   Children Sports             $113.00
    59   3Top Sports   Children Sports             $109.00

                           N = 3

----------------------- Group Name=LSF -----------------------

                                                Mfg_Suggested_
Obs   Supplier_Name              Category_Name   Retail_Price

 68   Eclipse Inc                   Clothes           $141.00
```

95

Features of the NOTSORTED Option

The NOTSORTED option has the following features:

- can appear anywhere in the BY statement
- is useful if you have data that falls into other logical groupings, such as chronological order or categories
- can be used to access **`First.`*`variable`*** or **`Last.`*`variable`*** in the DATA step
- cannot be used with the MERGE and UPDATE statements

General form of the NOTSORTED option:

```
BY variable-name NOTSORTED;
```

96

The BYSORTED SAS system option can be used to affect how SAS treats all SAS data sets. The BYSORTED SAS system option has the following characteristics:

- specifies that observations in a data set or data sets are sorted in alphabetic or numeric order
- should be used if the data set is ordered by the BY variable

```
OPTIONS BYSORTED;
```

If observations with the same BY value are grouped together but are not necessarily sorted in alphabetic or numeric order, use the NOBYSORTED option.

```
OPTIONS NOBYSORTED;
```

The default is BYSORTED.

When the NOBYSORTED option is specified, you do **not** have to specify the NOTSORTED option in a BY statement to access grouped data.

9.13 Quiz

Open and submit the program **p309a06**.

```
proc print data=orion.order_fact(obs=10);
   title 'Using the NOTSORTED Option with Ungrouped Data';
   by Customer_ID notsorted;
   var Order_ID Order_Date Delivery_Date Quantity --
       CostPrice_Per_Unit;
run;
```

1. Was the data grouped?

2. What do you notice about the output?

98

Business Scenario

Create a SAS data set that contains the total quantity of items sold each year.

The values of **`Order_Date`** and **`Quantity`** are in the data set **`orion.order_fact`**.

Partial Listing of **`orion.order_fact`**

Order_Date	Quantity
11JAN2003	1
15JAN2003	1
20JAN2003	1
28JAN2003	2
27FEB2003	3
02MAR2003	1
03MAR2003	1
03MAR2003	2
09MAR2003	2
09MAR2003	1
15MAR2003	2

101

Using the GROUPFORMAT Option

```
data yr_totals;
   keep Order_Date YrTot;
   set orion.order_fact(keep=Order_Date
                              Quantity);
   format Order_Date year4.;
   by groupformat Order_Date;
   if first.Order_Date then YrTot=0;
   YrTot + Quantity;
   if last.Order_Date;
run;
```

102 p309d12

The GROUPFORMAT option enables the BY statement to use the YEAR4. format to create **FIRST.Order_Date** and **LAST.Order_Date**.

The NOTSORTED option can be used with the GROUPFORMAT option if the data is grouped, but not sorted.

9.14 Quiz

Open and submit the program **p309a07**.

```
data yr_totals;
   keep Order_Date YrTot;
   set orion.order_fact(keep=Order_Date
                              Quantity);
   format Order_Date year4.;
   by groupformat Order_Date;
   if first.Order_Date then YrTot=0;
   YrTot + Quantity;
   if last.Order_Date;
run;
proc print data=yr_totals;
   title 'Total Quantity Sold each Year';
run;
```

How many observations are in the data set **yr_total**?

104

The GROUPFORMAT Option

General form of the GROUPFORMAT option:

BY GROUPFORMAT *variable-name* <NOTSORTED>;

Advantages	Disadvantages
can be used to create ordered/grouped reports without sorting the data	requires that the data set be sorted by the GROUPFORMAT variable or grouped by the formatted values of the GROUPFORMAT variable
causes the DATA step to process formatted BY values in the same way that SAS procedures do	available only in the DATA step
frequently eliminates the need for another step	

107

Using the CLASS Statement in a Procedure

Instead of using a BY statement to group data, you can use the CLASS statement to specify the variables whose values define the subgroup combinations for analysis by a SAS procedure.

General form of the CLASS statement:

CLASS *variable(s) </ options>*;

You can use the CLASS statement with the following Base SAS procedures:

- PROC MEANS
- PROC TABULATE
- PROC SUMMARY
- PROC UNIVARIATE

108

Reference Information

Selected options for the CLASS statement are as follows:

ORDER=	specifies the order in which to group the levels of the class variables in the output. The values for ORDER= can be any of the following:	
	INTERNAL	orders values by ascending **unformatted** values. The INTERNAL order yields the same order as the SORT procedure. The order depends on your operating environment. This sort sequence is particularly useful for displaying dates chronologically. The term UNFORMATTED is an alias for INTERNAL. INTERNAL is the default order.
	DATA	orders values according to their order in the input data set.
	FORMATTED	orders values by the ascending **formatted** values. This order depends on your operating environment.
	FREQ	orders values by descending frequency count.
DESCENDING	specifies to sort the class variable values in descending order.	
GROUPINTERNAL	specifies not to apply formats to the class variables when the MEANS, SUMMARY, or TABULATE procedures group the values to create combinations of class variables.	
MISSING	considers missing values as valid class variable levels. Special missing values that represent numeric values (the letters A through Z and the underscore (_) character) are each considered as a separate value.	

Using the CLASS Statement

What are the differences between using a BY statement and using a CLASS statement in a procedure?

BY Statement	CLASS Statement
The data set must be sorted or indexed on the BY variables.	The data does not need to be sorted or indexed on the CLASS variables.
BY-group processing holds only one BY group in memory at a time.	The CLASS statement accumulates aggregates for all CLASS groups simultaneously in memory.
A percentage for the entire report **cannot** be calculated with procedures such as PROC REPORT or PROC TABULATE.	A percentage for the entire report can be calculated with procedures such as PROC REPORT or PROC TABULATE.

109

9.15 Quiz

1. Open and submit the program **p309a08**.
2. Change the BY statement to a CLASS statement and resubmit the program.
3. Are the statistics created with a CLASS statement equal to those created with a BY statement?

```
proc means data=orion.order_fact mean median
           maxdec=2;
   format Order_Date year4.;
   class Order_Date;
   var Quantity -- CostPrice_Per_Unit;
run;
```

111

Using the SUMSIZE= Memory Option

The SUMSIZE= option specifies a limit on the amount of memory that is available for data summarization procedures when there are class variables.

```
SUMSIZE=n | nK | nM | nG | nT | hexX | MIN | MAX
```

The SUMSIZE= system option affects the Base SAS procedures such as the MEANS, REPORT, SUMMARY, and TABULATE procedures.

Proper specification of SUMSIZE= can improve procedure performance by restricting the swapping of memory that is controlled by the operating environment.

113

The SUMSIZE= option is available as both a SAS system option and as a PROC statement option.

Exercises

Level 1

4. Using the GROUPFORMAT Option

a. Open the program **p309e04** that creates a format named **`salaryfmt`**.

p309e04

```
proc format;
   value salaryfmt
                  .='Missing'
         low - 50000='Up to $50,000'
     50000 <- 100000='$50,000+ to $100,000'
      100000 <- high='More than $100,000';
run;
```

b. Write a DATA step to do the following:

- Create a data set named **`payroll`**.
- Read only the **`Salary`** variable from the **`orion.employee_payroll`** data set.
- Group the data by **`Salary`** using the SALARYFMT format. (Hint: Sort the data by **`Salary`** before the DATA step.)
- Create a variable named **`TotalSal`** that accumulates the value of **`Salary`**.
- Create a variable named **`Count`** that accumulates number of observations for each group.
- Create a variable named **`AvgSalary`** that is the average of **`Salary`** for each group.
- Format **`TotalSal`** and **`AvgSalary`** with dollar signs and two digits to the right of the decimal point.

c. Print the data set.

Obs	Salary	AvgSalary	TotalSal	Count
1	Up to $50,000	$30,565.77	$11,309,335.00	370
2	$50,000+ to $100,000	$64,075.56	$2,883,400.00	45
3	More than $100,000	$215,207.22	$1,936,865.00	9

Level 2

5. Creating BY Groups with PROC TABULATE

a. Open the **p309e05** program that contains the PROC TABULATE step below.

p309e05

```
options ls=80;

proc tabulate data=purchased_products format=comma12.2;
   where Supplier_Name contains 'Sports';
   by descending Order_Type;
   class Customer_Age_Group Supplier_Name;
   var Quantity Total_Retail_Price;
   table Supplier_Name,
         Customer_Age_Group * Total_Retail_Price=' '*sum=' '
          / printmiss misstext='$0' box='Total Retail Price';
   title 'Products by Sales Supplier and Customer Age Group';
run;
```

b. Add a PROC SORT step to sort the data set **orion.purchased_products** by **Order_Type** and create a temporary SAS data set named **purchased_products** so that the PROC TABULATE step creates the desired output shown below.

PROC TABULATE Output

Page 1

```
                Products by Sales Supplier and Customer Age Groups

-------------------------------- Order Type=3 --------------------------------
```

Total Retail Price	Customer Age Group		
	15-30 years	31-45 years	46-60 years
Supplier Name			
3Top Sports	8,923.17	8,728.44	4,631.40
Greenline Sports Ltd	1,232.00	1,767.18	1,474.08
Pro Sportswear Inc	5,684.60	2,863.30	2,623.10
Top Sports	$0	355.20	$0
Triple Sportswear Inc	$0	18.20	18.20

Page 2

```
                Products by Sales Supplier and Customer Age Group

  ------------------------------- Order Type=2 -------------------------------
```

Total Retail Price	Customer Age Group			
	15-30 years	31-45 years	46-60 years	61-75 years
Supplier Name				
3Top Sports	8,211.90	7,512.20	6,225.16	4,445.20
Greenline Sports Ltd	1,255.80	998.30	875.58	1,423.90
Pro Sportswear Inc	5,797.40	2,115.50	2,148.30	2,446.60
Top Sports	$0	88.80	$0	$0
Triple Sportswear Inc	161.80	1,001.00	254.50	53.80

c. Modify the program so that the PROC SORT step is not necessary and the PROC TABULATE step reads from the data set **orion.purchased_products**. Resubmit the program.

> If necessary, consult SAS OnlineDoc or the SAS Help facility about PROC TABULATE in order to determine what changes must be made to the program.

PROC TABULATE Output

```
                Products by Sales Supplier and Customer Age Group

 Order Type 3
```

Total Retail Price	Customer Age Group			
	15-30 years	31-45 years	46-60 years	61-75 years
Supplier Name				
3Top Sports	8,923.17	8,728.44	4,631.40	$0
Greenline Sports Ltd	1,232.00	1,767.18	1,474.08	$0
Pro Sportswear Inc	5,684.60	2,863.30	2,623.10	$0
Top Sports	$0	355.20	$0	$0
Triple Sportswear Inc	$0	18.20	18.20	$0

Page 2

```
                  Products by Sales Supplier and Customer Age Group

   Order Type 2
```

Total Retail Price	Customer Age Group			
	15-30 years	31-45 years	46-60 years	61-75 years
Supplier Name				
3Top Sports	8,211.90	7,512.20	6,225.16	4,445.20
Greenline Sports Ltd	1,255.80	998.30	875.58	1,423.90
Pro Sportswear Inc	5,797.40	2,115.50	2,148.30	2,446.60
Top Sports	$0	88.80	$0	$0
Triple Sportswear Inc	161.80	1,001.00	254.50	53.80

Level 3

6. Sorting Data Multiple Ways

There are two additional techniques that you can use to sort data:

- using a DATA step hash object and the OUTPUT method
- using the SQL procedure ORDER BY clause

a. Starting a new SAS session between each of these tasks, benchmark the results of sorting the data set named **temp**. Turn on the appropriate option to record the resources used.

The program **p309e06** creates a temporary data set named **temp** with three variables and four million observations.

p309e06

```
data temp;
   do I=1 to 1000;
      do J=1 to 1000;
         do Name='Mary','Sue','Bob','Ted';
            output;
         end;
      end;
   end;
run;
```

b. Open the program **p309e06**, add a PROC SORT step to create a data set named **`sorted_sort`** that is sorted by **`Name`**, and submit the program. Record the usage statistics.

CPU ______________________________

Memory ______________________________

I/O ______________________________

I/O statistics are not available in the Windows operating system.

c. Open the program **p309e06**, add a PROC SQL step to create a new table in sorted order for **`Name`** from **`temp`**, and submit the program. Record the usage statistics.

CPU ______________________________

Memory ______________________________

I/O ______________________________

I/O statistics are not available in the Windows operating system.

d. Open the program **p309e06**, write a DATA step using a hash object to sort the data, and submit the program. Record the usage statistics.

CPU ______________________________

Memory ______________________________

I/O ______________________________

I/O statistics are not available in the Windows operating system.

9.3 Chapter Review

Chapter Review

1. Define a threaded sort.

2. What is the NOEQUALS option in the PROC SORT statement?

3. What is the purpose of the DUPOUT= option?

116

9.4 Solutions

Solutions to Exercises

1. **Using the PRESORTED Option**

   a. Use PROC CONTENTS to determine whether the data set **orion.holidays** is sorted.

   p309s01

```
proc contents data=orion.holidays;
run;
```

   b. Write a PROC SORT step to sort the data **orion.holidays** by **Date**. Create a temporary data set named **holidays**. Use the PRESORTED option in the PROC SORT statement.

   What is the resulting message in the log?

   p309s01

```
proc sort data=orion.holidays out=holidays presorted;
   by Date;
run;
```

```
294  proc sort data=orion.holidays out=holidays presorted;
295     by Date;
296  run;

NOTE: Sort order of input data set has been verified.
NOTE: Input data set is already sorted; it has been copied to the output data set.
NOTE: There were 364 observations read from the data set ORION.HOLIDAYS.
NOTE: The data set WORK.HOLIDAYS has 364 observations and 2 variables.
NOTE: PROCEDURE SORT used (Total process time):
      real time           0.01 seconds
      cpu time            0.01 seconds
```

   c. Submit a PROC CONTENTS step to determine whether the data set **holidays** is sorted by **Date**.

   p309s01

```
proc contents data=holidays;
run;
```

d. Change the BY variable to **Holiday_Name** and resubmit the PROC SORT step.

What is the resulting message in the log?

p309s01

```
proc sort data=orion.holidays out=holidays presorted;
   by Holiday_Name;
run;
```

```
297  proc sort data=orion.holidays out=holidays presorted;
298     by Holiday_Name;
299  run;

NOTE: Input data set is not in sorted order.
NOTE: There were 364 observations read from the data set ORION.HOLIDAYS.
NOTE: The data set WORK.HOLIDAYS has 364 observations and 2 variables.
NOTE: PROCEDURE SORT used (Total process time):
      real time           0.01 seconds
      cpu time            0.01 seconds
```

e. Submit a PROC CONTENTS step to determine if the data set **holidays** is sorted by **Holiday_Name**.

p309s01

```
proc contents data=holidays;
run;
```

2. Creating a Sorted Data Set

a. Open the program **p309e02**.

b. Modify the program to create a data set named **profit07** and specify that it is sorted by **Company** without sorting the data set.

p309s02

```
data profit07(sortedby=Company);
   infile 'profit07.dat' dlm=',';
   input Company : $30. Sales Cost Salaries Profit;
run;
```

c. Use PROC CONTENTS to verify that **profit07** has a sort flag on the variable **Company**.

p309s02

```
proc contents data=profit07;
run;
```

d. Use PROC PRINT to create a report grouped by the variable **Company**.

p309s02

```
proc print data=profit07(obs=24);
   by Company;
run;
```

e. Use the PROC SORT PRESORTED option to turn on the validated flag, and use PROC CONTENTS to verify that the sort flag is set in the descriptor portion.

p309s02

```
proc sort data=profit07 presorted;
   by Company;
run;

proc contents data=profit07;
run;
```

3. Using the SORTSEQ=LINGUISTIC Option

a. Open and submit the program **p309e03**.

What is the value of the LOCALE option? **The answer is dependent on your site.**

p309e03

```
proc options option=locale;
run;
```

b. Write a PROC SORT step to sort **orion.spain_customers** by **Customer_Name**.

c. Create an output data set named **s_customers**.

d. Use the SORTSEQ=LINGUISTIC option with the suboption LOCALE=es_ES.

e. Print the data set **s_customers** and look at the order of the variable **Customer_Name**.

p309s03

```
proc sort data=orion.spain_customers out=s_customers
          sortseq=linguistic(locale=es_ES);
   by Customer_Name;
run;

proc print data=s_customers;
   var Customer_Name;
run;
```

4. Using the GROUPFORMAT Option

a. Open the program **p309e04** that creates a format named **salaryfmt**.

b. Write a DATA step to do the following:

- Create a data set named **Payroll**.
- Read only the **Salary** variable from the **orion.employee_payroll** data set.

- Group the data by **Salary** using the **salaryfmt** format. (Hint: Sort the data by **Salary** before the DATA step.)
- Create a variable named **TotalSal** that accumulates the value of **Salary**.
- Create a variable named **Count** that accumulates number of observations for each group.
- Create a variable named **AvgSalary** that is the average of **Salary** for each group.
- Format **TotalSal** and **AvgSalary** with dollar signs and two digits to the right of the decimal point.

c. Print the data set.

p309s04

```
proc sort data=orion.employee_payroll out=employee_payroll;
   by Salary;
run;

data payroll;
   set employee_payroll(keep=Salary);
   by Salary groupformat;
   format Salary salaryfmt. AvgSalary TotalSal dollar15.2;
   if first.Salary then do;
      TotalSal=0;
      Count=0;
   end;
   TotalSal+Salary;
   Count+1;
   if last.Salary then do;
      AvgSalary=TotalSal/Count;
      output;
   end;
run;

proc print data=payroll;
run;
```

5. Creating BY Groups with PROC TABULATE

a. Open the **p309e05** program that contains the PROC TABULATE step.

b. Add a PROC SORT step to sort the data set **orion.purchased_products** by **Order_Type** and create a temporary SAS data set named **purchased_products** so that the PROC TABULATE step creates the desired output.

p309s05

```
options ls=80;
proc sort data=orion.purchased_products
          out=purchased_products;
   by descending Order_Type;
run;

proc tabulate data=purchased_products format=comma12.2;
   where Supplier_Name contains 'Sports';
   by descending Order_Type;
   class Customer_Age_Group Supplier_Name;
   var Quantity Total_Retail_Price;
   table Supplier_Name,
         Customer_Age_Group * Total_Retail_Price=' '*sum=' '
          / printmiss misstext='$0' box='Total Retail Price';
   title 'Products by Sales Supplier and Customer Age Group';
run;
```

c. Modify the program so that the PROC SORT step is not necessary and the PROC TABULATE step reads from the data set **orion.purchased_products**. Resubmit the program.

p309s05

```
proc tabulate data=orion.purchased_products format=comma12.2;
   where Supplier_Name contains 'Sports';
   class Supplier_Name Customer_Age_Group ;
   class Order_Type / descending;
   var Quantity Total_Retail_Price;
   table Order_Type,
         Supplier_Name,
         Customer_Age_Group * Total_Retail_Price=' '*sum=' '
         / printmiss misstext='$0' box='Total Retail Price';
   title 'Products by Sales Supplier and Customer Age Group';
run;
```

6. Sorting Data Multiple Ways

a. Starting a new SAS session between each of these tasks, benchmark the results of sorting the data set named **`temp`**. Turn on the appropriate option to record the resources used.

The program **p309e06** creates a temporary data set named **`temp`** with three variables and four million observations.

b. Open the program **p309e06**, add a PROC SORT step to create a data set named **`sorted_sort`** that is sorted by **`Name`**, and submit the program. Record the usage statistics.

p309s06

```
proc sort data=temp out=sorted_sort;
   by Name;
run;
```

CPU Answers vary according to operating environment.

Memory Answers vary according to operating environment.

I/O Answers vary according to operating environment.

I/O statistics are not available in the Windows operating system.

c. Open the program **p309e03**, add a PROC SQL step to create a new table in sorted order for **`Name`** from **`temp`**, and submit the program. Record the usage statistics.

p309s06

```
proc sql;
   create table sorted_sql as
   select *
      from temp
         order by Name;
quit;
```

CPU Answers vary according to operating environment.

Memory Answers vary according to operating environment.

I/O Answers vary according to operating environment.

I/O statistics are not available on the Windows operating system.

d. Open the program **p309e06**, write a DATA step using a hash object to sort the data, and submit the program. Record the usage statistics.

p309s06

```
data _null_;
   length Name $4 I J 8;
   if _N_=1 then do;
      declare hash S(dataset:'temp', ordered:'Ascending');
      S.definekey('Name', 'I', 'J');
      S.definedata('Name', 'I', 'J');
      S.definedone();
      call missing(Name, I, J);
   end;
   S.output(dataset:'sorted_hash');
run;
```

CPU Answers vary according to operating environment.

Memory Answers vary according to operating environment.

I/O Answers vary according to operating environment.

I/O statistics are not available on the Windows operating system.

Solutions to Student Activities (Polls/Quizzes)

9.01 Quiz – Correct Answer

Open and submit the program **p309a01**.

How many CPUs are available in your SAS session?

```
proc options option=cpucount;
run;
```

The answer varies based on the operating environment.

14

9.04 Multiple Answer Poll – Correct Answer

If you sort a SAS data set that is in sorted order, does SAS re-sort the data?

a. No, if the sort indicator is 'YES', and the validation is 'YES'
b. No, if the sort indicator is 'YES', and the validation is 'NO'
c. Yes, regardless of the sort indicator or validation
d. Yes, if the sort indicator is 'YES', and the validation is 'NO'

31

9.05 Quiz – Correct Answer

The data set **orion.salesstaff** was previously sorted in ascending order by **Employee_Hire_Date**.

Open and submit program **p309a02**.

```
proc sort data=orion.salesstaff
          out=salesstaff;
   by Employee_ID;
run;
proc print data=salesstaff;
  where Employee_ID=120134;
run;
```

For employee number=120134, which date is first?

a. The first date hired

b. The last date hired

The original order of the data is maintained within the new sort order because of the default EQUALS option.

43

9.06 Multiple Choice Poll – Correct Answer

If the data set **orion.customer** is sorted by **Customer_Address**, which of the following is the first address listed?

a. 21 Hotham Parade

b. 9 Angourie Court

Because 2 is less than 9, the 21 Hotham Parade would be the first in the sorted data set.

51

9.07 Multiple Choice Poll – Correct Answer

Which of the following would be a good use of an index for BY-group processing?

a. Your data set is sorted by the BY variable already.
b. Your data set is updated using a SET statement in the DATA step. In that case, the index would be updated after the append, and you would not have to reindex the data.
c. Your data is updated using PROC APPEND, PROC SQL, or the MODIFY statement in the DATA step. In that case, the index would be updated after the update, and you would not have to reindex the data.

64

9.08 Multiple Choice Poll – Correct Answer

How is `orion.order_fact` read?

a. Direct access via the index
b. Sequentially

75

9.09 Multiple Choice Poll – Correct Answer

How is **orion.street_code** read?

a. Direct access via the index
b. Sequentially

77

9.10 Quiz – Correct Answer

Open and submit the program **p309a03**.

Are there any data errors in the log?

No

```
data addresses;
   set orion.order_fact(keep=Customer_ID Street_ID
             Delivery_Date Order_ID Product_ID Quantity);
   set orion.street_code(keep=Street_ID Country
             Street_Name City_Name Postal_Code)
             key=Street_ID / unique;
run;
```

84

9.11 Quiz – Correct Answer

Open and submit the program **p309a04**.

1. What does the SAS log show for this DATA step?

Partial SAS Log

```
940  data addresses2;
941     set orion.order_fact(keep=Customer_ID Street_ID Delivery_Date Order_ID Product_ID
941! Quantity) ;
942     set orion.street_code(keep=Street_ID Country Street_Name City_Name Postal_Code)
943         key=Street_ID;
944  run;

Customer_ID=23 Street_ID=9260126679 Delivery_Date=08MAR2003 Order_ID=1230338566
Product_ID=240800200063 Quantity=2 Country=US Street_Name=Ferdilah Ln Postal_Code=76092
City_Name=Tarrant _ERROR_=1 _IORC_=1230015 _N_=8
Customer_ID=45 Street_ID=9260104847 Delivery_Date=11MAR2003 Order_ID=1230371142
Product_ID=240500200003 Quantity=1 Country=US Street_Name=Angier Rd Postal_Code=94520
City_Name=Contra Costa _ERROR_=1 _IORC_=1230015 _N_=10
<lines omitted>
Customer_ID=2806 Street_ID=8010100089 Delivery_Date=01SEP2003 Order_ID=1231316727
Product_ID=240100400143 Quantity=2 Country=ZA Street_Name=Quinn Street Postal_Code=2001
City_Name=Newtown _ERROR_=1 _IORC_=1230015 _N_=82
ERROR: Limit set by ERRORS= option reached.  Further errors of this type will not be printed.
Customer_ID=36 Street_ID=9260128237 Delivery_Date=17SEP2003 Order_ID=1231414059
Product_ID=240800200008 Quantity=1 Country=US Street_Name=Halstead Cir Postal_Code=55033
City_Name=Washington _ERROR_=1 _IORC_=1230015 _N_=86
```

86

9.11 Quiz – Correct Answer

Open and submit the program **p309a04**.

1. What does the SAS log show for this DATA step?
2. Why do you get those error messages?

Without the UNIQUE option, the following conditions exist:

- **The value of _IORC_ ne 0.**
- **The value of _ERROR_ =1.**
- **The log contains data error messages.**

87

9.12 Multiple Choice Poll – Correct Answer

Which of the following is true of the data set **orion.shoe_vendors**?

a. The data set is sorted by the variable **Group_Name**.

b. The data set is not sorted by the variable **Group_Name**. However, it is grouped by **Group_Name**.

c. The data set is neither sorted nor grouped by the variable **Group_Name**.

93

9.13 Quiz – Correct Answer

Open and submit the program **p309a06**.

```
proc print data=orion.order_fact(obs=10);
   title 'Using the NOTSORTED Option with Ungrouped Data';
   by Customer_ID notsorted;
   var Order_ID Order_Date Delivery_Date Quantity --
       CostPrice_Per_Unit;
run;
```

1. Was the data grouped?

   No

2. What do you notice about the output?

   Some of the values of Customer_ID are repeated. Because the NOTSORTED option turns off sequence checking, every time that the value of Customer_ID changes, a new BY group is created.

100

9.14 Quiz – Correct Answer

Open and submit the program **p309a07**.

```
data yr_totals;
   keep Order_Date YrTot;
   set orion.order_fact(keep=Order_Date
                              Quantity);
   format Order_Date year4.;
   by groupformat Order_Date;
   if first.Order_Date then YrTot=0;
   YrTot + Quantity;
   if last.Order_Date;
run;
proc print data=yr_totals;
   title 'Total Quantity Sold each Year';
run;
```

How many observations are in the data set `yr_total`? **5**

105

9.14 Quiz – Correct Answer

```
proc print data=yr_totals;
   title 'Total Quantity Sold each Year';
run;
```

PROC PRINT Output

```
Total Quantity Sold each Year

         Order_     Yr
  Obs     Date      Tot

   1      2003      233
   2      2004      182
   3      2005      153
   4      2006      225
   5      2007      285
```

106

9.15 Quiz – Correct Answer

1. Open and submit the program **p309a08**.
2. Change the BY statement to a CLASS statement and resubmit the program.
3. Are the statistics created with a CLASS statement equal to those created with a BY statement?

   Yes

```
proc means data=orion.order_fact mean median
           maxdec=2;
   format Order_Date year4.;
   class Order_Date;
   var Quantity -- CostPrice_Per_Unit;
run;
```

112

Solutions to Chapter Review

Chapter Review Answers

1. Define a threaded sort.

   On multiprocessor systems, the threaded sort uses multiple processors to execute the sort processing through simultaneous execution.

2. What is the NOEQUALS option in the PROC SORT statement?

   The NOEQUALS option does not necessarily preserve the original order of the input data set in the output data set.

3. What is the purpose of the DUPOUT= option?

   The DUPOUT= option specifies the output data set to which duplicate observations are written when used in conjunction with the NODUPKEY option.

117

Chapter 10 Programmer Efficiency

10.1 Introduction

Objectives

- List various programming techniques for improving programmer efficiency.
- Provide examples of using the macro facility.
- Use functions.
- Substitute a procedure for a DATA step.

3

Techniques for Programmer Efficiency

- Use the macro facility for repetitive coding tasks.
- Select appropriate functions for processing data.
- Use procedures instead of the DATA step where possible.
- Combine multiple steps into one step, where possible.
- Write flexible programs.
- Create SAS views instead of SAS files.
- Use FILE and PUT statements to write programs that are data-dependent.

4

10.01 Multiple Answer Poll

Do you use any of the following features of the macro facility?

a. Macro variables
b. Macro definitions
c. Neither of these

6

Using the Macro Facility

The macro facility is available to make your programs more flexible, dynamic, and easy to maintain.

The macro facility is comprised of two components:

- macro variables
- macro definitions

⚠ The macro facility is a powerful tool. However, a detailed discussion of using macro variables and macro definitions is beyond the scope of this course.

7

Using the Macro Facility

Example of using a macro variable:

```
%let list=5, 9, 18, 31, 56;

proc print data=orion.customer;
   where Customer_ID in (&list);
   title "Customer ID Values of &list";
run;
```

8

p310d01

Using the Macro Facility

Using a macro definition is a two-step process.

1. Create the macro definition.

```
%macro PrintSubset(dsname, var, list);

proc print data=&dsname;
   where &var in (&list);
   title "&var Values of &list";
run;

%mend PrintSubset;
```

2. Call the macro definition.

```
%PrintSubset(orion.customer, Customer_ID,
             %str(5, 9, 18, 31, 56))
```

9 p310d02

The %STR function masks (that is, removes the normal meaning of) these special tokens:

+ - * / , < > = ; ' "

LT EQ GT LE GE NE AND OR NOT

blank

General form of the %STR function:

%STR(*argument*)

argument can be any combination of text and macro triggers.

10.02 Quiz

In addition to saving programmer time, does creating a macro variable or a macro definition always save computer resources?

Why or why not?

11

Selecting Appropriate Functions for Data Processing

Example of selecting appropriate functions for data processing:

Use one of the CAT functions…

```
data description;
   set orion.organization_dim;
   Employment_Description=catx(' - ', of Company -- Job_Title);
run;
```

…instead of the concatenation operator and the TRIM function.

```
data description;
   set orion.organization_dim;
   Employment_Description=trim(Company)||' - '||
                          trim(Department)||' - '||
                          trim(Section)||' - '||
                          trim(Org_Group)||' - '||
                          trim(Job_Title);
run;
```

14 p310d03

The concatenation operator can be !! or ||.

The SAS®9 CAT functions are listed in the table below:

Function	Use	Example
CAT	concatenates character strings without removing leading or trailing blanks.	`newvar=cat(var1,var);`
CATQ	concatenates character or numeric values by using a delimiter to separate items and by adding quotation marks to strings that contain the delimiter.	`newvar=catq('N','var1','var')`
CATS	concatenates character strings and removes leading and trailing blanks.	`newvar=cats(var1,var);`
CATT	concatenates character strings and removes trailing blanks only.	`newvar=catt(var1,var);`
CATX	concatenates character strings, removes leading and trailing blanks, and inserts separators.	`newvar=catx(' ',var1,var);`

If you do not specify the length of the new variable, the value of the new variable returned by any of the CAT functions has a length of 200.

CATQ is new in SAS 9.2.

If the receiving variable is numeric, the CAT functions remove leading and trailing blanks from numeric arguments after they format the numeric values with the BEST. format. No note is written to the log when the BEST. format is used.

Using Procedures

Example of selecting appropriate procedures for data processing:

Use the SUMMARY procedure…

```
proc summary data=orion.shoe_vendors nway;
   var Mfg_Suggested_Retail_Price;
   class Line_Name;
   output out=summary(keep=Line_Name Avg_MSP)
          mean=Avg_MSP;
run;
```

15

p310d04

continued...

Using Procedures

…instead of the DATA step.

```
proc sort data=orion.shoe_vendors
          out=shoe_vendors;
   by Line_Name;
run;
data sum;
   keep Line_Name Avg_MSP;
   set shoe_vendors;
   by Line_Name;
   if first.Line_Name then do;
      Tot_MSP=0;
      Count=0;
   end;
   Tot_MSP + Mfg_Suggested_Retail_Price;
   Count + 1;
   if last.Line_Name then do;
      Avg_MSP=Tot_MSP/Count;
      output;
   end;
run;
```

16

p310d04

10.2 Writing Flexible Programs: Combining Raw Data Files Vertically

Objectives

- Develop a program that is flexible.
- Using the FILENAME statement, create a SAS data set from multiple raw data files.
- Using the FILEVAR= option, create a SAS data set from multiple raw data files.

18

Flexible Programming

Programs that run in a production environment should be as flexible as possible so that there is little, if any, editing of the program code when the program is submitted.

These programs are often developed using the following steps:

1. Write an initial version of the program quickly, even if it requires editing on subsequent submissions.
2. Add syntax, such as the DATE and TIME functions, that can extract current information.
3. Make the program as efficient as possible.

19

Business Scenario

You need to use 12 raw data files to create a SAS data set that contains the data for the current month and the two previous months.

The raw data files have the same file structure and similar names: **mon1.dat**, **mon2.dat**, and so forth. They are all comma-separated files with these fields in the same order: **Customer_ID**, **Order_ID**, **Order_Type**, **Order_Date**, and **Delivery_Date**.

Partial Listing of **mon1.dat**

```
         1    1    2    2    3    3    4    4    5    5    6
1---5----0----5----0----5----0----5----0----5----0----5----0
53,1232087464,1,13JAN2007,13JAN2007
49,1232092527,1,13JAN2007,13JAN2007
34,1232161564,1,23JAN2007,23JAN2007
2618,1232173841,3,25JAN2007,30JAN2007
```

20

Business Scenario

Every month you need to provide reports that contain three months of data to Orion executives. The three months are the current month and the previous two months (*rolling quarter*).

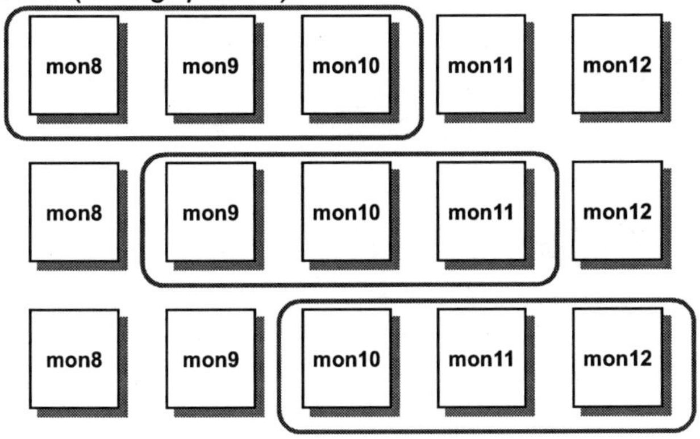

21

Vertical Combination Methods

Raw data can be combined vertically using several methods:

- concatenating files using multiple INFILE statements
- concatenating files using a FILENAME statement
- using the FILEVAR= option to read a list of files
- using operating system techniques

22

Use multiple INFILE statements to solve these programming tasks:

- Reading a record from one raw data file, a record from the second raw data file, a record from the third raw data file, and so on (similar to an interleave)
- Concatenating raw data files that have different file layouts

Operating system techniques are outside the scope of this course.

Reading Multiple Raw Data Files

To read multiple raw data files, you can use the FILENAME statement.

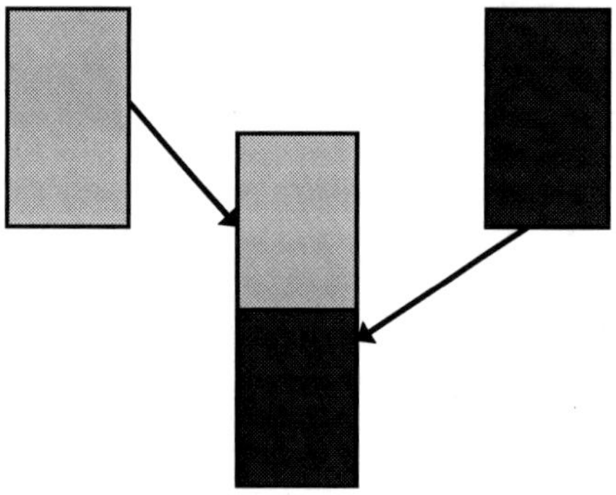

23

Using the FILENAME Statement

```
filename MON ('mon3.dat' 'mon2.dat' 'mon1.dat');
*filename MON ('.workshop.rawdata(mon3)'
               '.workshop.rawdata(mon2)'
               '.workshop.rawdata(mon1)'); * z/OS;

data quarter;
   infile MON dlm=',';
   input Customer_ID Order_ID Order_Type
         Order_Date : date9. Delivery_Date : date9.;
run;
```

Partial Listing of **mon1.dat**

```
         1    1    2    2    3    3    4    4    5    5    6
1---5----0----5----0----5----0----5----0----5----0----5----0
53,1232087464,1,13JAN2007,13JAN2007
49,1232092527,1,13JAN2007,13JAN2007
34,1232161564,1,23JAN2007,23JAN2007
2618,1232173841,3,25JAN2007,30JAN2007
```

24 p310d05

In Windows and UNIX, you can use the * wildcard to specify that all 12 monthly raw data files are to be read.

```
filename MON ('mon*.dat');
```

SAS Log

```
764  filename MON ('mon3.dat' 'mon2.dat' 'mon1.dat'); * PC and Unix;
765  *filename MON ('.workshop.rawdata(mon3)'
766                 '.workshop.rawdata(mon2)'
767                 '.workshop.rawdata(mon1)'); * z/OS;
768
769  data quarter;
770     infile MON dlm=',';
771     input Customer_ID Order_ID Order_Type
772           Order_Date : date9. Delivery_Date : Date9.;
773  run;

NOTE: The infile MON is:

      File Name='S:\Workshop\mon3.dat,

      File List=('S:\Workshop\mon3.dat' 'S:\Workshop\mon2.dat' 'S:\Workshop\mon1.dat'),
      RECFM=V,LRECL=256

NOTE: The infile MON is:

      File Name= S:\Workshop\mon2.dat,

      File List=('S:\Workshop\mon3.dat' 'S:\Workshop\mon2.dat' 'S:\Workshop\mon1.dat'),
      RECFM=V,LRECL=256

NOTE: The infile MON is:
```

(Continued on the next page.)

```
      File Name=S:\Workshop\mon1.dat,

      File List=('S:\Workshop\mon3.dat' 'S:\Workshop\mon2.dat' 'S:\Workshop\mon1.dat'),
      RECFM=V,LRECL=256

NOTE: 9 records were read from the infile MON.
      The minimum record length was 34.
      The maximum record length was 38.
NOTE: 7 records were read from the infile MON.
      The minimum record length was 35.
      The maximum record length was 38.
NOTE: 4 records were read from the infile MON.
      The minimum record length was 35.
      The maximum record length was 37.
NOTE: The data set WORK.QUARTER has 20 observations and 5 variables.
NOTE: DATA statement used (Total process time):
      real time           2.71 seconds
      cpu time            0.03 seconds

774
775  proc print data=quarter;
776     title 'quarter ';
777  run;

NOTE: There were 20 observations read from the data set WORK.QUARTER.
NOTE: PROCEDURE PRINT used (Total process time):
      real time           1.34 seconds
      cpu time            0.00 seconds
```

FILENAME Statement Syntax

General form of the FILENAME statement:

> **FILENAME** *fileref* ('*external-file1*'
> '*external-file2*' ...
> '*external-filen*');

fileref	any valid SAS name that is eight characters or fewer
'external-file'	the physical name of an external file; the physical name is the name that is recognized by the operating environment

25

A FILENAME statement can associate a fileref with multiple physical external files.

10.03 Quiz

1. Open and submit the program **p310a01**.
2. How many observations are in the data set `quarter`?
3. Change the files referenced by **MON** to the current month and the two previous months. How many observations are in the data set `quarter`?

27

INFILE Statement with FILEVAR= Option

To make the program more flexible, use the FILEVAR= option in the INFILE statement to provide the name of the raw data file instead of using the FILENAME statement, which would need to be edited every month.

```
infile ORD filevar=NextFile;
```

ORD	an arbitrarily named placeholder, not an actual filename or a fileref that was assigned to a file previously; SAS uses this placeholder for reporting processing information to the SAS log.
NextFile	a variable whose value contains the name of the raw data file to be read (`mon9.dat`, `mon10.dat`, `mon11.dat`, and so on).

29

INFILE Statement with FILEVAR= Option

- The FILEVAR= option names a variable whose change in value causes the INFILE statement to close the current input file and open a new one.
- When the next INPUT statement executes, it reads from the new file that the FILEVAR= variable specifies.

General form of the FILEVAR= variable option:

INFILE *file-specification* FILEVAR=*variable*;

variable a temporary character variable that contains the physical filename of the raw data file to be read

30

Similar to automatic variables, the FILEVAR= variable is not written to the data set. The FILEVAR= variable can read raw data files conditionally.

Creating the Filename

The names of the raw data files can be constructed programmatically.

In this example, the raw data files are named in a consistent form.

mon + 9 + .dat
mon + 10 + .dat
mon + 11 + .dat

There are multiple techniques for creating the names of the raw data files.

31

10.04 Quiz

If the value of the variable **i** is the number of the month, which of the following could be used to create the name of the raw data file?

a.
```
NextFile=cats("mon",i,".dat");
```

b.
```
NextFile="mon"||put(i,2.)||".dat";
NextFile=compress(NextFile);
```

c.
```
NextFile=compress("mon"||put(i,2.)||".dat");
```

33

Creating the Filename

After the value of **NextFile** is created, the FILEVAR= option identifies the raw data file to be read.

```
do i=11,10,9;
   NextFile=cats("mon",i,"dat");
   infile ORD filevar=NextFile dlm=',';
end;
```

When i=11

NextFile=mon11.dat

When i=10

NextFile=mon10.dat

When i=9

NextFile=mon9.dat

35

Reading Raw Data

```
data movingq;
   drop i;
   do i=11, 10, 9;
 ①    NextFile=cats("mon",i,".dat");
 ②    infile ORD filevar=NextFile dlm=',';
 ③    input Customer_ID
             Order_ID
             Order_Type
             Order_Date : date9.
             Delivery_Date : date9.;
 ④     output;
   end;
 ⑤ stop;
run;
```

36 p310d06

The first four of the following statements are within the DO loop:

① The assignment statement creates the name of the raw data file.

② The INFILE statement with the FILEVAR= option names the raw data file. In addition, the FILEVAR= option closes the current file and opens a new file if the value of the FILEVAR= variable changes.

③ The INPUT statement copies a record of the raw data file, converts it to SAS format, and writes it to the PDV.

④ The OUTPUT statement outputs the observation that is created by the INPUT statement.

⑤ The STOP statement outside the DO loop stops the DATA step after all of the observations are written.

In this example, the DATA step does not encounter the end of file. If the STOP statement were not included, the program would continue to execute the DO loop repetitively. Therefore, the STOP statement is needed to prevent an infinite loop of the DATA step.

SAS Log

```
807
808  data movingq;
809     drop i;
810     do i=11,10,9;
811        NextFile=cats("mon",put(i,2.),".dat"); * PC and UNIX;
812        *NextFile=cats(".lwprg3.rawdata(mon",put(i,2.),")"); * mainframe ;
813        infile ORD filevar=NextFile dlm=',';
814        input Customer_ID Order_ID Order_Type
815              Order_Date:date9. Delivery_Date:Date9.;
816        output;
817     end;
818     stop;
819  run;

NOTE: The infile ORD is:

      File Name=S:\Workshop\mon11.dat,
      RECFM=V,LRECL=256

NOTE: The infile ORD is:

      File Name=S:\Workshop\mon10.dat,
      RECFM=V,LRECL=256

NOTE: The infile ORD is:

      File Name=S:\Workshop\mon9.dat,
      RECFM=V,LRECL=256

NOTE: 1 record was read from the infile ORD.
      The minimum record length was 35.
      The maximum record length was 35.
NOTE: 1 record was read from the infile ORD.
      The minimum record length was 36.
      The maximum record length was 36.
NOTE: 1 record was read from the infile ORD.
      The minimum record length was 34.
      The maximum record length was 34.
NOTE: The data set WORK.MOVINGQ has 3 observations and 5 variables.
NOTE: DATA statement used (Total process time):
      real time           0.18 seconds
      cpu time            0.01 seconds


820
821  proc print data=movingq;
822    title 'Moving Quarter Data';
823  run;

NOTE: There were 3 observations read from the data set WORK.MOVINGQ.
NOTE: PROCEDURE PRINT used (Total process time):
      real time           0.00 seconds
      cpu time            0.00 seconds
```

Setup for the Poll

Refer to the following program for the next two polls:

```
data movingq;
   drop i;
   do i=11, 10, 9;
      NextFile=cats("mon", i, ".dat");
      infile ORD filevar=NextFile dlm=',';
      input Customer_ID Order_ID Order_Type
            Order_Date : date9. Delivery_Date : date9.;
      output;
   end;
   stop;
run;
```

38

10.05 Poll

Is the STOP statement necessary?

- ❍ Yes
- ❍ No

39

10.06 Multiple Choice Poll

How many observations are in **movingq**?

a. One observation per record in all of the raw data files
b. 0
c. 1
d. 3

41

Reading Raw Data

```
data movingq;
   drop i;
   do i=11, 10, 9;
      NextFile=cats("mon", i, ".dat");
      infile ORD filevar=NextFile dlm=','
             end=LastObs;
      do while (not LastObs);
         input Customer_ID
               Order_ID
               Order_Type
               Order_Date : date9.
               Delivery_Date : date9.;
         output;
      end;
   end;
   stop;
run;
```

43 p310d07

The DO WHILE statement continues to execute the INFILE statement for every record of the raw data file until the value of **LastObs=1**. The DO WHILE statement checks the condition at the top of the loop.

The END= option creates the variable **LastObs** that can be used to determine the end of the raw data file. The END= option names a variable whose value is one of the following:

0	when the current input data record is **not** the last in the current input file
1	when the current input record is the last in the current input file

Partial SAS Log

```
data movingq;
   drop i;
   do i=11, 10, 9;
      NextFile=cats("mon", i, ".dat");
      infile ORD filevar=NextFile dlm=','
             end=LastObs;
      do while (not LastObs);
         input Customer_ID
               Order_ID
               Order_Type
               Order_Date : date9.
               Delivery_Date : date9.;
         output;
      end;
   end;
   stop;
run;

NOTE: The infile ORD is:
      Filename=S:\workshop\mon11.dat,
      RECFM=V,LRECL=256,File Size (bytes)=297,
      Last Modified=27Jan2008:20:33:40,
      Create Time=27Jan2008:20:33:40

NOTE: The infile ORD is:
      Filename= S:\workshop\mon10.dat,
      RECFM=V,LRECL=256,File Size (bytes)=265,
      Last Modified=27Jan2008:20:33:28,
      Create Time=27Jan2008:20:33:28

NOTE: The infile ORD is:
      Filename= S:\workshop\mon9.dat,
      RECFM=V,LRECL=256,File Size (bytes)=109,
      Last Modified=27Jan2008:20:33:16,
      Create Time=27Jan2008:20:33:16

NOTE: 8 records were read from the infile ORD.
      The minimum record length was 35.
      The maximum record length was 36.
NOTE: 7 records were read from the infile ORD.
      The minimum record length was 35.
      The maximum record length was 38.
NOTE: 3 records were read from the infile ORD.
      The minimum record length was 34.
      The maximum record length was 35.
NOTE: The data set WORK.MOVINGQ has 18 observations and 5 variables.
NOTE: DATA statement used (Total process time):
      real time           0.01 seconds
      cpu time            0.01 seconds
```

Reading the Current Month

```
data movingq;
   drop MonNum MidMon LastMon i;
   MonNum=month(today());
   MidMon=MonNum - 1;
   LastMon=MidMon - 1;
   do i=MonNum, Midmon, LastMon;
      NextFile=cats("mon", i, ".dat");
      infile ORD filevar=NextFile dlm=','
             end=LastObs;
      do while (not LastObs);
         input Customer_ID
               Order_ID
               Order_Type
               Order_Date : date9.
               Delivery_Date : date9.;
         output;
      end;
   end;
   stop;
run;
```

44 p310d08

The MONTH function is used to obtain the month number of today's date to begin the rolling month range. The month numbers of the two months prior to today's month number are then calculated.

Setup for the Poll

The following program is submitted:

```
data movingq;
   drop MonNum MidMon LastMon i;
   MonNum=month(today());
   MidMon=MonNum - 1;
   LastMon=MidMon - 1;
   do i=MonNum, Midmon, LastMon;
      NextFile=cats("mon", i, ".dat");
      infile ORD filevar=NextFile dlm=','
             end=LastObs;
      do while (not LastObs);
         input Customer_ID
               Order_ID
               Order_Type
               Order_Date : date9.
               Delivery_Date : date9.;
         output;
      end;
   end;
   stop;
run;
```

46 p310d08

10.07 Poll

Will the SAS code in **p310d08** produce the correct results if the current month is January or February?

- ❍ Yes
- ❍ No

47

INTNX Function

The INTNX function increments a date value by a given interval or intervals, and returns a date value.

```
EDate=intnx('interval', BDate, increment)
```

Formatted Value of **BDate**	Using the INTNX Function	Formatted Value of **EDate**
04JUL2008	`intnx('year', BDate, -1)`	01JAN2007
04JUL2008	`intnx('year', BDate, 0)`	01JAN2008
04JUL2008	`intnx('year', BDate, 1)`	01JAN2009
04JUL2008	`intnx('month', BDate, -2)`	01MAY2008
04JUL2008	`intnx('month', BDate, -1)`	01JUN2008
04JUL2008	`intnx('month', BDate, 0)`	01JUL2008
04JUL2008	`intnx('month', BDate, 1)`	01AUG2008
04JUL2008	`intnx('month', BDate, 2)`	01SEP2008

49

The INTNX function can increment date, time, or datetime values by a given interval or intervals, and returns a date, time, or datetime value.

The program **p310d08a** contains the SAS DATA step code to replicate these results.

```
data dates;
   BDate='04JUL2008'd;
   PreviousYear=intnx('year', BDate, -1);
   ThisYear=intnx('year', BDate, 0);
   NextYear=intnx('year', BDate, 1);
   TwoYearsFromNow=intnx('month', BDate, -2);
   PreviousMonth=intnx('month', BDate, -1);
   ThisMonth=intnx('month', BDate, 0);
   NextMonth=intnx('month', BDate, 1);
   TwoMonthsFromNow=intnx('month', BDate, 2);
   format BDate PreviousYear ThisYear NextYear TwoYearsFromNow
          PreviousMonth ThisMonth NextMonth TwoMonthsFromNow date9.;
run;

proc print data=dates;
   title 'INTNX Function Results';
run;
```

INTNX Function

General form of the INTNX function:

INTNX(*'interval'*, *start-from*, *increment*<, *alignment*>)

'interval'	specifies a character constant or a variable containing a date, datetime, or time interval.
start-from	specifies a SAS expression that represents a SAS date, datetime, or time value identifying a starting point.
increment	specifies a negative or positive integer that represents the specific number of intervals.
alignment	controls the position of SAS dates within the interval.

50

The INTNX function also supports multiples of an interval and shifted intervals.

General form of the INTNX function with multiples and shift indexes:

INTNX(*interval<multiple><.shift-index>*, *start-from*, *increment* <,*alignment*>)

interval specifies a character constant, a variable, or an expression that contains a datetime interval such as WEEK, SEMIYEAR, QTR, or HOUR. The type of interval (date, datetime, or time) must match the type of the value in start-from and increment.

multiple specifies a multiple of the interval. It sets the interval equal to a multiple of the interval type. For example, YEAR2 consists of two-year, or biennial, periods.

shift-index specifies the starting point of the interval. By default, the starting point is 1. A value that is greater than 1 shifts the start to a later point within the interval. The unit for shifting depends on the interval. For example, YEAR.3 specifies yearly periods that are shifted to start on the first of March of each calendar year and to end in February of the following year. The shift index cannot be greater than the number of periods in the entire interval. For example, YEAR2.24 has a valid shift index, but YEAR2.25 is invalid because there is no twenty-fifth month in a two-year interval. If the default shift period is the same as the interval type, then you can shift only multi-period intervals with the shift index. For example, because MONTH type intervals shift by MONTH sub-periods by default, you cannot shift monthly intervals with the shift index. However, you can shift bimonthly intervals with the shift index, because two MONTH intervals exist in each MONTH2 interval. The interval name MONTH2.2, for example, specifies bimonthly periods starting on the first day of even-numbered months.

start-from specifies a SAS expression that represents a SAS date, time, or datetime value that identifies a starting point.

increment specifies a negative, positive, or zero integer that represents the number of date, time, or datetime intervals. *Increment* is the number of intervals to shift the value of start-from.

alignment controls the position of SAS dates within the interval. *Alignment* can be one of these values:

The values of *alignment* can be as follows:

BEGINNING | B	specifies that the returned date is aligned to the beginning of the interval (DEFAULT).
MIDDLE | M	specifies that the returned date is aligned to the midpoint of the interval.
END | E	specifies that the returned date is aligned to the end of the interval.
SAMEDAY | S | SAME	specifies that the date that is returned is aligned to the same calendar date with the corresponding interval increment.

Alignment is new in SAS®9.

Using the INTNX Function

```
data movingq;
   drop MonNum MidMon LastMon i;
   MonNum=month(today());
   MidMon=month(intnx('month', today(), -1));
   LastMon=month(intnx('month', today(), -2));
   do i=MonNum, Midmon, LastMon;
      NextFile=cats("mon", i, ".dat");
      infile ORD filevar=NextFile dlm=','
             end=LastObs;
      do while (not LastObs);
         input Customer_ID
               Order_ID
               Order_Type
               Order_Date : date9.
               Delivery_Date : date9.;
         output;
      end;
   end;
   stop;
run;
```

51

p310d09

For z/OS (OS/390):

```
NextFile='.prog3.rawdata(mon'||put(i,2.)||')';
```

SAS Log

```
data movingq;
   drop MonNum MidMon LastMon i;
   MonNum=month(today());
   MidMon=month(intnx('month', today(), -1));
   LastMon=month(intnx('month', today(), -2));
   do i=MonNum, Midmon, LastMon;
      NextFile=cats("mon", i, ".dat");
      infile ORD filevar=NextFile dlm=','
             end=LastObs;
      do while (not LastObs);
         input Customer_ID
               Order_ID
               Order_Type
               Order_Date : date9.
               Delivery_Date : date9.;
         output;
      end;
   end;
   stop;
run;

NOTE: The infile ORD is:
      Filename=S:\workshop\mon5.dat,
      RECFM=V,LRECL=256,File Size (bytes)=411,
      Last Modified=27Jan2008:20:32:30,
      Create Time=27Jan2008:20:32:30
```

(Continued on the next page.)

```
NOTE: The infile ORD is:
      Filename= S:\workshop\mon4.dat,
      RECFM=V,LRECL=256,File Size (bytes)=522,
      Last Modified=27Jan2008:20:32:18,
      Create Time=27Jan2008:20:32:18

NOTE: The infile ORD is:
      Filename= S:\workshop\mon3.dat,
      RECFM=V,LRECL=256,File Size (bytes)=334,
      Last Modified=27Jan2008:20:32:04,
      Create Time=27Jan2008:20:32:04

NOTE: 11 records were read from the infile ORD.
      The minimum record length was 34.
      The maximum record length was 36.
NOTE: 14 records were read from the infile ORD.
      The minimum record length was 34.
      The maximum record length was 38.
NOTE: 9 records were read from the infile ORD.
      The minimum record length was 34.
      The maximum record length was 38.
NOTE: The data set WORK.MOVINGQ has 34 observations and 5 variables.
NOTE: DATA statement used (Total process time):
      real time           0.03 seconds
      cpu time            0.03 seconds
```

✎ This program was run in May.

10.08 Quiz

Which of the following would make the program more efficient?

a.
```
Today=today();
MonNum=month(Today);
MidMon=month(intnx('month', Today, -1));
LastMon=month(intnx('month', Today, -2));
```

b.
```
Today=today();
MonNum=month(today());
MidMon=month(intnx('month', today(), -1));
LastMon=month(intnx('month', today(), -2));
```

c.
```
retain Today MonNum MidMon LastMon;
if _N_=1 then do;
   Today=today();
   MonNum=month(Today);
   MidMon=month(intnx('month', Today, -1));
   LastMon=month(intnx('month', Today, -2));
end;
```

53

Using the INTNX Function

```
data movingq;
   drop Today MonNum MidMon LastMon i;
   retain Today MonNum MidMon LastMon;
   if _N_=1 then do;
      Today=today();
      MonNum=month(Today);
      MidMon=month(intnx('month', Today, -1));
      LastMon=month(intnx('month', Today, -2));
   end;
   do i=MonNum, MidMon, LastMon;
      NextFile=cats("mon", i, ".dat");
      infile ORD filevar=NextFile dlm=',' end=LastObs;
      do while (not LastObs);
         input Customer_ID Order_ID Order_Type
               Order_Date : date9. Delivery_Date : date9.;
         output;
      end;
   end;
   stop;
run;
```

55 p310d10

How Does FILEVAR= Work? (Self-Study)

Suppose you had three simple raw data files.

a

```
         1
1---5----0
1,   4
1,   5
```

b

```
         1
1---5----0
2,   5
```

c

```
         1
1---5----0
3,   8
3,   9
```

56

Execution (Self-Study)

a

```
         1
1---5----0
1,  4
1,  5
```

b

```
         1
1---5----0
2,  5
```

c

```
         1
1---5----0
3,  8
3,  9
```

```
data one;
   do i='a', 'b', 'c';
      NextFile=cats(i,".dat");
      infile ORD filevar=NextFile dlm=','
                end=LastObs;
      do while(not LastObs);
         input Num1 Num2;
         output;
      end;
   end;
   stop;
run;
```

Input Buffer

1	2	3	4	5	6

PDV

i	D NextFile	D LastObs	Num1	Num2	D _ERROR_	D _N_
		0	.	.	0	1

57

Execution (Self-Study)

a

```
         1
1---5----0
1,  4
1,  5
```

b

```
         1
1---5----0
2,  5
```

c

```
         1
1---5----0
3,  8
3,  9
```

```
data one;
   do i='a', 'b', 'c';
      NextFile=cats(i,".dat");
      infile ORD filevar=NextFile dlm=','
                end=LastObs;
      do while(not LastObs);
         input Num1 Num2;
         output;
      end;
   end;
   stop;
run;
```

i is initialized to 'a'

Input Buffer

1	2	3	4	5	6

PDV

i	D NextFile	D LastObs	Num1	Num2	D _ERROR_	D _N_
a		0	.	.	0	1

58

Execution (Self-Study)

a

```
         1
1---5----0
1,   4
1,   5
```

b

```
         1
1---5----0
2,   5
```

c

```
         1
1---5----0
3,   8
3,   9
```

```
data one;
   do i='a', 'b', 'c';
      NextFile=cats(i,".dat");
      infile ORD filevar=NextFile dlm=','
                end=LastObs;
      do while(not LastObs);
         input Num1 Num2;
         output;
      end;
   end;
   stop;
run;
```

Input Buffer

1	2	3	4	5	6

PDV

i	D NextFile	D LastObs	Num1	Num2	D _ERROR_	D _N_
a	a.dat	0	.	.	0	1

59

Execution (Self-Study)

a

```
         1
1---5----0
1,   4
1,   5
```

b

```
         1
1---5----0
2,   5
```

c

```
         1
1---5----0
3,   8
3,   9
```

```
data one;
   do i='a', 'b', 'c';
      NextFile=cats(i,".dat");
      infile ORD filevar=NextFile dlm=','
                end=LastObs;
      do while(not LastObs);
         input Num1 Num2;
         output;
      end;
   end;
   stop;
run;
```

LastObs=0

Input Buffer

1	2	3	4	5	6

PDV

i	D NextFile	D LastObs	Num1	Num2	D _ERROR_	D _N_
a	a.dat	0	.	.	0	1

60

`LastObs` is reset to 0 because the value of FILEVAR= changed and a new file is opened.

Execution (Self-Study)

a

```
         1
1---5----0
1,   4
1,   5
```

b

```
         1
1---5----0
2,   5
```

c

```
         1
1---5----0
3,   8
3,   9
```

```
data one;
   do i='a', 'b', 'c';
      NextFile=cats(i,".dat");
      infile ORD filevar=NextFile dlm=','
                end=LastObs;
      do while(not LastObs);
         input Num1 Num2;
         output;
      end;
   end;
   stop;
run;
```

Input Buffer

1	2	3	4	5	6

The DO WHILE evaluates the condition at the top of the loop.

PDV

i	D NextFile	D LastObs	Num1	Num2	D _ERROR_	D _N_
a	a.dat	0	.	.	0	1

61 ...

Execution (Self-Study)

a

```
         1
1---5----0
1,   4
1,   5
```

b

```
         1
1---5----0
2,   5
```

c

```
         1
1---5----0
3,   8
3,   9
```

```
data one;
   do i='a', 'b', 'c';
      NextFile=cats(i,".dat");
      infile ORD filevar=NextFile dlm=','
                end=LastObs;
      do while(not LastObs);
         input Num1 Num2;
         output;
      end;
   end;
   stop;
run;
```

Input Buffer

1	2	3	4	5	6
1	,				4

LastObs=0

PDV

i	D NextFile	D LastObs	Num1	Num2	D _ERROR_	D _N_
a	a.dat	0	1	4	0	1

62 ...

Execution (Self-Study)

a

```
         1
1---5----0
1,   4
1,   5
```

b

```
         1
1---5----0
2,   5
```

c

```
         1
1---5----0
3,   8
3,   9
```

```
data one;
   do i='a', 'b', 'c';
      NextFile=c
      infile ORD
                 end=LastObs;
      do while(not LastObs);
         input Num1 Num2;
         output;
      end;
   end;
   stop;
run;
```

Output current observation

Input Buffer

1	2	3	4	5	6
1	,				4

one

Num1	Num2
1	4

PDV

i	D NextFile	D LastObs	Num1	Num2	D _ERROR_	D _N_
a	a.dat	0	1	4	0	1

63

...

Execution (Self-Study)

a

```
         1
1---5----0
1,   4
1,   5
```

b

```
         1
1---5----0
2,   5
```

c

```
         1
1---5----0
3,   8
3,   9
```

```
data one;
   do i='a', 'b', 'c';
      NextFile=cats(i,".dat");
      infile ORD filevar=NextFile dlm=','
                 end=LastObs;
      do while(not LastObs);
         input Num1 Num2;
         output;
      end;
   end;
   stop;
run;
```

The DO WHILE loop executes.

Input Buffer

1	2	3	4	5	6
1	,				4

one

Num1	Num2
1	4

PDV

i	D NextFile	D LastObs	Num1	Num2	D _ERROR_	D _N_
a	a.dat	0	1	4	0	1

64

...

Execution (Self-Study)

a

```
         1
1---5----0
1,  4
1,  5
```

b

```
         1
1---5----0
2,  5
```

c

```
         1
1---5----0
3,  8
3,  9
```

```
data one;
   do i='a', 'b', 'c';
      NextFile=cats(i,".dat");
      infile ORD filevar=NextFile dlm=','
             end=LastObs;
      do while(not LastObs);
         input Num1 Num2;
         output;
      end;
   end;
   stop;
run;
```

LastObs=1

Input Buffer

1	2	3	4	5	6
1	,				5

one

Num1	Num2
1	4

PDV

i	NextFile	LastObs	Num1	Num2	_ERROR_	_N_
a	a.dat	1	1	5	0	1

65

Execution (Self-Study)

a

```
         1
1---5----0
1,  4
1,  5
```

b

```
         1
1---5----0
2,  5
```

c

```
         1
1---5----0
3,  8
3,  9
```

```
data one;
   do i='a', 'b', 'c';
      NextFile=c
      infile ORD
             end=LastObs;
      do while(not LastObs);
         input Num1 Num2;
         output;
      end;
   end;
   stop;
run;
```

Output current observation

Input Buffer

1	2	3	4	5	6
1	,				5

one

Num1	Num2
1	4
1	5

PDV

i	NextFile	LastObs	Num1	Num2	_ERROR_	_N_
a	a.dat	1	1	5	0	1

66

Execution (Self-Study)

a

	1
1---5----0	
1, 4	
1, 5	

b

	1
1---5----0	
2, 5	

c

	1
1---5----0	
3, 8	
3, 9	

```
data one;
   do i='a', 'b', 'c';
      NextFile=cats(i,".dat");
      infile ORD filevar=NextFile dlm=','
                end=LastObs;
      do while(not LastObs);
         input Num1 Num2;
         output;
      end;
   end;
   stop;
run;
```

The DO WHILE loop does not execute.

Input Buffer

1	2	3	4	5	6
1	,				5

one

Num1	Num2
1	4
1	5

PDV

i	D NextFile	D LastObs	Num1	Num2	D _ERROR_	D _N_
a	a.dat	1	1	5	0	1

67

Execution (Self-Study)

a

	1
1---5----0	
1, 4	
1, 5	

b

	1
1---5----0	
2, 5	

c

	1
1---5----0	
3, 8	
3, 9	

```
data one;
   do i='a', 'b', 'c';
      NextFile=cats(i,".dat");
      infile ORD filevar=NextFile dlm=','
                end=LastObs;
      do while(not LastObs);
         input Num1 Num2;
         output;
      end;
   end;
   stop;
run;
```

i increments to 'b'.

Input Buffer

1	2	3	4	5	6
1	,				5

one

Num1	Num2
1	4
1	5

PDV

i	D NextFile	D LastObs	Num1	Num2	D _ERROR_	D _N_
b	a.dat	1	1	5	0	1

68

Execution (Self-Study)

a

```
         1
1---5----0
1,  4
1,  5
```

b

```
         1
1---5----0
2,  5
```

c

```
         1
1---5----0
3,  8
3,  9
```

```
data one;
   do i='a', 'b', 'c';
      NextFile=cats(i,".dat");
      infile ORD filevar=NextFile dlm=','
                end=LastObs;
      do while(not LastObs);
         input Num1 Num2;
         output;
      end;
   end;
   stop;
run;
```

Input Buffer

1	2	3	4	5	6
1	,				5

one

Num1	Num2
1	4
1	5

PDV

i	D NextFile	D LastObs	Num1	Num2	D _ERROR_	D _N_
b	b.dat	1	1	5	0	1

69

...

Execution (Self-Study)

a

```
         1
1---5----0
1,  4
1,  5
```

b

```
         1
1---5----0
2,  5
```

c

```
         1
1---5----0
3,  8
3,  9
```

```
data one;
   do i='a', 'b', 'c';
      NextFile=cats(i,".dat");
      infile ORD filevar=NextFile dlm=','
                end=LastObs;
      do while(not LastObs);
         input Num1 Num2;
         output;
      end;
   end;
   stop;
run;
```

LastObs=0

Input Buffer

1	2	3	4	5	6
1	,				5

one

Num1	Num2
1	4
1	5

PDV

i	D NextFile	D LastObs	Num1	Num2	D _ERROR_	D _N_
b	b.dat	0	1	5	0	1

70

...

Execution (Self-Study)

a

```
         1
1---5----0
1,   4
1,   5
```

b

```
         1
1---5----0
2,   5
```

c

```
         1
1---5----0
3,   8
3,   9
```

```
data one;
   do i='a', 'b', 'c';
      NextFile=cats(i,".dat");
      infile ORD filevar=NextFile dlm=','
                end=LastObs;
      do while(not LastObs);
         input Num1 Num2;
         output;
      end;
   end;
   stop;
run;
```

The DO WHILE loop executes.

Input Buffer

1	2	3	4	5	6
1	,				5

one

Num1	Num2
1	4
1	5

PDV

i	D NextFile	D LastObs	Num1	Num2	D _ERROR_	D _N_
b	b.dat	0	1	5	0	1

71

Execution (Self-Study)

a

```
         1
1---5----0
1,   4
1,   5
```

b

```
         1
1---5----0
2,   5
```

c

```
         1
1---5----0
3,   8
3,   9
```

```
data one;
   do i='a', 'b', 'c';
      NextFile=cats(i,".dat");
      infile ORD filevar=NextFile dlm=','
                end=LastObs;
      do while(not LastObs);
         input Num1 Num2;
         output;
      end;
   end;
   stop;
run;
```

LastObs=1

Input Buffer

1	2	3	4	5	6
2	,				5

one

Num1	Num2
1	4
1	5

PDV

i	D NextFile	D LastObs	Num1	Num2	D _ERROR_	D _N_
b	b.dat	1	2	5	0	1

72

Execution (Self-Study)

a
```
         1
1---5----0
1,   4
1,   5
```

b
```
         1
1---5----0
2,   5
```

c
```
         1
1---5----0
3,   8
3,   9
```

```
data one;
   do i='a', 'b', 'c';
      NextFile=c
      infile ORD
                end=LastObs;
      do while(not LastObs);
         input Num1 Num2;
         output;
      end;
   end;
   stop;
run;
```

Output current observation

Input Buffer

1	2	3	4	5	6
2	,				5

one

Num1	Num2
1	4
1	5
2	5

PDV

i	D NextFile	D LastObs	Num1	Num2	D _ERROR_	D _N_
b	b.dat	1	2	5	0	1

73

...

Execution (Self-Study)

a
```
         1
1---5----0
1,   4
1,   5
```

b
```
         1
1---5----0
2,   5
```

c
```
         1
1---5----0
3,   8
3,   9
```

```
data one;
   do i='a', 'b', 'c';
      NextFile=cats(i,".dat");
      infile ORD filevar=NextFile dlm=','
                end=LastObs;
      do while(not LastObs);
         input Num1 Num2;
         output;
      end;
   end;
   stop;
run;
```

The DO WHILE loop does not execute.

Input Buffer

1	2	3	4	5	6
2	,				5

one

Num1	Num2
1	4
1	5
2	5

PDV

i	D NextFile	D LastObs	Num1	Num2	D _ERROR_	D _N_
b	b.dat	1	2	5	0	1

74

...

Execution (Self-Study)

a

```
         1
1---5----0
1,  4
1,  5
```

b

```
         1
1---5----0
2,  5
```

c

```
         1
1---5----0
3,  8
3,  9
```

```
data one;
   do i='a', 'b', 'c';
      NextFile=cats(i,".dat");
      infile ORD filevar=NextFile dlm=','
                end=LastObs;
      do while(not LastObs);
         input Num1 Num2;
         output;
      end;
   end;
   stop;
run;
```

i increments to 'c'.

Input Buffer

1	2	3	4	5	6
2	,				5

one

Num1	Num2
1	4
1	5
2	5

PDV

i	D NextFile	D LastObs	Num1	Num2	D _ERROR_	D _N_
c	b.dat	1	2	5	0	1

75 ...

Execution (Self-Study)

a

```
         1
1---5----0
1,  4
1,  5
```

b

```
         1
1---5----0
2,  5
```

c

```
         1
1---5----0
3,  8
3,  9
```

```
data one;
   do i='a', 'b', 'c';
      NextFile=cats(i,".dat");
      infile ORD filevar=NextFile dlm=','
                end=LastObs;
      do while(not LastObs);
         input Num1 Num2;
         output;
      end;
   end;
   stop;
run;
```

Input Buffer

1	2	3	4	5	6
2	,				5

one

Num1	Num2
1	4
1	5
2	5

PDV

i	D NextFile	D LastObs	Num1	Num2	D _ERROR_	D _N_
c	c.dat	1	2	5	0	1

76 ...

Execution (Self-Study)

a

```
         1
1---5----0
1,   4
1,   5
```

b

```
         1
1---5----0
2,   5
```

c

```
         1
1---5----0
3,   8
3,   9
```

```
data one;
   do i='a', 'b', 'c';
      NextFile=cats(i,".dat");
      infile ORD filevar=NextFile dlm=','
                end=LastObs;
      do while(not LastObs);
         input Num1 Num2;
         output;
      end;
   end;
   stop;
run;
```

LastObs=0

Input Buffer

1	2	3	4	5	6
2	,				5

one

Num1	Num2
1	4
1	5
2	5

PDV

i	NextFile	LastObs	Num1	Num2	_ERROR_	_N_
c	c.dat	0	2	5	0	1

77 ...

Execution (Self-Study)

a

```
         1
1---5----0
1,   4
1,   5
```

b

```
         1
1---5----0
2,   5
```

c

```
         1
1---5----0
3,   8
3,   9
```

```
data one;
   do i='a', 'b', 'c';
      NextFile=cats(i,".dat");
      infile ORD filevar=NextFile dlm=','
                end=LastObs;
      do while(not LastObs);
         input Num1 Num2;
         output;
      end;
   end;
   stop;
run;
```

The DO WHILE loop executes.

Input Buffer

1	2	3	4	5	6
2	,				5

one

Num1	Num2
1	4
1	5
2	5

PDV

i	NextFile	LastObs	Num1	Num2	_ERROR_	_N_
c	c.dat	0	2	5	0	1

78 ...

Execution (Self-Study)

a

```
         1
1---5----0
1,  4
1,  5
```

b

```
         1
1---5----0
2,  5
```

c

```
         1
1---5----0
3,  8
3,  9
```

```
data one;
   do i='a', 'b', 'c';
      NextFile=cats(i,".dat");
      infile ORD filevar=NextFile dlm=','
                end=LastObs;
      do while(not LastObs);
         input Num1 Num2;
         output;
      end;
   end;
   stop;
run;
```

LastObs=0

Input Buffer

1	2	3	4	5	6
3	,				8

one

Num1	Num2
1	4
1	5
2	5

PDV

i	D NextFile	D LastObs	Num1	Num2	D _ERROR_	D _N_
c	c.dat	0	3	8	0	1

79

Execution (Self-Study)

a

```
         1
1---5----0
1,  4
1,  5
```

b

```
         1
1---5----0
2,  5
```

c

```
         1
1---5----0
3,  8
3,  9
```

```
data one;
   do i='a', 'b', 'c';
      NextFile=c
      infile ORD
                end=LastObs;
      do while(not LastObs);
         input Num1 Num2;
         output;
      end;
   end;
   stop;
run;
```

Output current observation

Input Buffer

1	2	3	4	5	6
3	,				8

one

Num1	Num2
1	4
1	5
2	5
3	8

PDV

i	D NextFile	D LastObs	Num1	Num2	D _ERROR_	D _N_
c	c.dat	0	3	8	0	1

80

Execution (Self-Study)

a

```
         1
1---5----0
1,   4
1,   5
```

b

```
         1
1---5----0
2,   5
```

c

```
         1
1---5----0
3,   8
3,   9
```

```
data one;
   do i='a', 'b', 'c';
      NextFile=cats(i,".dat");
      infile ORD filevar=NextFile dlm=','
                 end=LastObs;
      do while(not LastObs);
         input Num1 Num2;
         output;
      end;
   end;
   stop;
run;
```

The DO WHILE loop executes.

Input Buffer

1	2	3	4	5	6
3	,				8

one

Num1	Num2
1	4
1	5
2	5
3	8

PDV

i	D NextFile	D LastObs	Num1	Num2	D _ERROR_	D _N_
c	c.dat	0	3	8	0	1

81 ...

Execution (Self-Study)

a

```
         1
1---5----0
1,   4
1,   5
```

b

```
         1
1---5----0
2,   5
```

c

```
         1
1---5----0
3,   8
3,   9
```

```
data one;
   do i='a', 'b', 'c';
      NextFile=cats(i,".dat");
      infile ORD filevar=NextFile dlm=','
                 end=LastObs;
      do while(not LastObs);
         input Num1 Num2;
         output;
      end;
   end;
   stop;
run;
```

LastObs=1

Input Buffer

1	2	3	4	5	6
3	,				9

one

Num1	Num2
1	4
1	5
2	5
3	8

PDV

i	D NextFile	D LastObs	Num1	Num2	D _ERROR_	D _N_
c	c.dat	1	3	9	0	1

82 ...

Execution (Self-Study)

a

```
         1
1---5----0
1,  4
1,  5
```

b

```
         1
1---5----0
2,  5
```

c

```
         1
1---5----0
3,  8
3,  9
```

```
data one;
   do i='a', 'b', 'c';
      NextFile=c
      infile ORD
                 end=LastObs;
      do while(not LastObs);
         input Num1 Num2;
         output;
      end;
   end;
   stop;
run;
```

Output current observation

Input Buffer

1	2	3	4	5	6
3	,				9

one

Num1	Num2
1	4
1	5
2	5
3	8
3	9

PDV

i	D NextFile	D LastObs	Num1	Num2	D _ERROR_	D _N_
c	c.dat	1	3	9	0	1

83

...

Execution (Self-Study)

a

```
         1
1---5----0
1,  4
1,  5
```

b

```
         1
1---5----0
2,  5
```

c

```
         1
1---5----0
3,  8
3,  9
```

```
data one;
   do i='a', 'b', 'c';
      NextFile=cats(i,".dat");
      infile ORD filevar=NextFile dlm=','
                 end=LastObs;
      do while(not LastObs);
         input Num1 Num2;
         output;
      end;
   end;
   stop;
run;
```

The DO WHILE loop does not execute.

Input Buffer

1	2	3	4	5	6
3	,				9

one

Num1	Num2
1	4
1	5
2	5
3	8
3	9

PDV

i	D NextFile	D LastObs	Num1	Num2	D _ERROR_	D _N_
c	c.dat	1	3	9	0	1

84

...

Execution (Self-Study)

a

```
         1
1---5----0
1,  4
1,  5
```

b

```
         1
1---5----0
2,  5
```

c

```
         1
1---5----0
3,  8
3,  9
```

```
data one;
   do i='a', 'b', 'c';
      NextFile=cats(i,".dat");
      infile ORD filevar=NextFile dlm=','
                end=LastObs;
      do while(not LastObs);
         input Num1 Num2;
         output;
      end;
   end;
   stop;
run;
```

The values of i are all assigned.

Input Buffer

1	2	3	4	5	6
3	,				9

one

Num1	Num2
1	4
1	5
2	5
3	8
3	9

PDV

i	NextFile	LastObs	Num1	Num2	_ERROR_	_N_
c	c.dat	1	3	9	0	1

85

Execution (Self-Study)

a

```
         1
1---5----0
1,  4
1,  5
```

b

```
         1
1---5----0
2,  5
```

c

```
         1
1---5----0
3,  8
3,  9
```

```
data one;
   do i='a', 'b', 'c';
      NextFile=cats
      infile ORD fi                  =','
                end
      do while(not LastObs);
         input Num1 Num2;
         output;
      end;
   end;
   stop;
run;
```

The DATA step stops execution.

Input Buffer

1	2	3	4	5	6
3	,				9

one

Num1	Num2
1	4
1	5
2	5
3	8
3	9

PDV

i	NextFile	LastObs	Num1	Num2	_ERROR_	_N_
c	c.dat	1	3	9	0	1

86

Exercises

Level 1

1. Using the FILENAME Statement

The raw data files **level_1**, **level_2**, and **level_3** contain customer information for the three types of customers: Orion Club Gold members, Orion Club members, and Internet/Catalog customers. The fields in each file are delimited with commas.

The raw data files use the naming convention **level_#**. For example:

- For directory based: **level_1.dat**
- For z/OS (OS/390): **'.prog3.rawdata(level_1)'**

a. Open the program **p310e01**, which contains the following statements:

p310e01

```
data all_levels;
   length Customer_Name $ 40 Customer_Age_Group $ 12
          Customer_Type $ 40 Customer_Group $ 40;
   input Customer_Name $ Customer_Age_Group $ Customer_Type $
         Customer_Group $;
run;

proc print data=all_levels;
run;
```

b. Use the FILENAME statement to concatenate the three raw data files.

c. Modify the DATA step to use the fileref created in part **b** to create the SAS data set **all_levels**.

d. Print the **`all_levels`** data set.

Partial PROC PRINT Output

```
                                     Customer_
 Obs     Customer_Name               Age_Group                 Customer_Type

   1     Sandrina Stephano          15-30 years     Orion Club Gold members medium activity
   2     Cornelia Krahl             31-45 years     Orion Club Gold members medium activity
   3     Markus Sepke               15-30 years     Orion Club Gold members low activity
   4     Oliver S. Füßling          31-45 years     Orion Club Gold members high activity
   5     Cynthia Martinez           46-60 years     Orion Club Gold members medium activity

 Obs         Customer_Group

   1     Orion Club Gold members
   2     Orion Club Gold members
   3     Orion Club Gold members
   4     Orion Club Gold members
   5     Orion Club Gold members

         < lines removed >

                                         Customer_
   Obs     Customer_Name                 Age_Group                Customer_Type

    67     Soberina Berent              15-30 years     Orion  Club members medium activity
    68     Alex Santinello              15-30 years     Orion  Club members medium activity
    69     Kenan Talarr                 31-45 years     Orion  Club members high activity
    70     Ulrich Heyde                 61-75 years     Internet/Catalog Customers
    71     Tulio Devereaux              46-60 years     Internet/Catalog Customers
    72     Robyn Klem                   46-60 years     Internet/Catalog Customers
    73     Cynthia Mccluney             31-45 years     Internet/Catalog Customers
    74     Candy Kinsey                 61-75 years     Internet/Catalog Customers
    75     Phenix Hill                  31-45 years     Internet/Catalog Customers
    76     Avinoam Zweig                46-60 years     Internet/Catalog Customers
    77     Lauren Marx                  31-45 years     Internet/Catalog Customers

   Obs           Customer_Group

    67     Orion Club members
    68     Orion Club members
    69     Orion Club members
    70     Internet/Catalog Customers
    71     Internet/Catalog Customers
    72     Internet/Catalog Customers
    73     Internet/Catalog Customers
    74     Internet/Catalog Customers
    75     Internet/Catalog Customers
    76     Internet/Catalog Customers
    77     Internet/Catalog Customers
```

Level 2

2. Using the FILEVAR= Option to Read from Raw Data

The raw data files **level_1**, **level_2**, and **level_3** contain customer information for the three types of customers: Orion Club Gold members, Orion Club members, and Internet/Catalog customers.

The raw data files use the naming convention **level_#**. For example:

- For directory based: **level_1.dat**
- For z/OS (OS/390): **'.prog3.rawdata(level_1)'**

a. Open the program **p310e02**, which contains the following statements:

p310e02

```
data all_levels;
   length Customer_Name $ 40 Customer_Age_Group $ 12
          Customer_Type $ 40 Customer_Group $ 40;

   input Customer_Name $ Customer_Age_Group $ Customer_Type $
         Customer_Group $;
run;

proc print data=all_levels;
run;
```

b. Use the FILEVAR= option to concatenate the three raw data files and create the SAS data set **all_levels**.

c. Print the **`all_levels`** data set.

Partial Listing of **`all_levels`**

```
                                Customer_
Obs     Customer_Name           Age_Group                  Customer_Type

  1     Sandrina Stephano      15-30 years    Orion Club Gold members medium activity
  2     Cornelia Krahl         31-45 years    Orion Club Gold members medium activity
  3     Markus Sepke           15-30 years    Orion Club Gold members low activity
  4     Oliver S. Füßling      31-45 years    Orion Club Gold members high activity
  5     Cynthia Martinez       46-60 years    Orion Club Gold members medium activity

Obs         Customer_Group

  1     Orion Club Gold members
  2     Orion Club Gold members
  3     Orion Club Gold members
  4     Orion Club Gold members
  5     Orion Club Gold members

      < lines removed >

                                Customer_
Obs     Customer_Name           Age_Group                 Customer_Type

 67     Soberina Berent        15-30 years    Orion  Club members medium activity
 68     Alex Santinello        15-30 years    Orion  Club members medium activity
 69     Kenan Talarr           31-45 years    Orion  Club members high activity
 70     Ulrich Heyde           61-75 years    Internet/Catalog Customers
 71     Tulio Devereaux        46-60 years    Internet/Catalog Customers
 72     Robyn Klem             46-60 years    Internet/Catalog Customers
 73     Cynthia Mccluney       31-45 years    Internet/Catalog Customers
 74     Candy Kinsey           61-75 years    Internet/Catalog Customers
 75     Phenix Hill            31-45 years    Internet/Catalog Customers
 76     Avinoam Zweig          46-60 years    Internet/Catalog Customers
 77     Lauren Marx            31-45 years    Internet/Catalog Customers

Obs         Customer_Group

 67     Orion Club members
 68     Orion Club members
 69     Orion Club members
 70     Internet/Catalog Customers
 71     Internet/Catalog Customers
 72     Internet/Catalog Customers
 73     Internet/Catalog Customers
 74     Internet/Catalog Customers
 75     Internet/Catalog Customers
 76     Internet/Catalog Customers
 77     Internet/Catalog Customers
```

Level 3

3. Using the FILEVAR= Option to Read Filenames from a SAS Data Set

The SAS data set **orion.month_file** contains the names of the raw data files that need to be concatenated.

Listing of **orion.month_file**

Obs	File_Name
1	mon1.dat
2	mon2.dat
3	mon3.dat
4	mon4.dat
5	mon5.dat
6	mon6.dat
7	mon7.dat
8	mon8.dat
9	mon9.dat
10	mon10.dat
11	mon11.dat
12	mon12.dat

The starter file **p310e03** contains the following DATA step program:

p310e03

```
data all_months;
   format Order_Date Delivery_Date date9.;
   input Customer_ID Order_ID Order_Type
         Order_Date : date9. Delivery_Date : Date9.;
run;

proc print data=all_months;
run;
```

a. Use the FILEVAR= option to create a SAS data set named **All_Months** from the raw data files named in **orion.month_file**.

b. Print the first 10 observations of the **All_Months** SAS data set.

Partial Listing of **All_Months**

Obs	Order_ Date	Delivery_ Date	Customer_ ID	Order_ID	Order_ Type
1	13JAN2007	13JAN2007	53	1232087464	1
2	13JAN2007	13JAN2007	49	1232092527	1
3	23JAN2007	23JAN2007	34	1232161564	1
4	25JAN2007	30JAN2007	2618	1232173841	3
5	01FEB2007	04FEB2007	89	1232217725	2
6	05FEB2007	05FEB2007	195	1232240447	1
7	05FEB2007	06FEB2007	70046	1232241009	3
8	15FEB2007	15FEB2007	171	1232307056	1
9	15FEB2007	15FEB2007	20	1232311932	1
10	18FEB2007	22FEB2007	23	1232331499	2

10.3 Creating Views

Objectives

- List the types of SAS data sets.
- Create and use DATA step views.
- List the advantages of DATA step views.
- List guidelines for using DATA step views.

90

SAS Data Sets

Instead of creating a SAS data file that contains three months of raw data, as discussed previously, you can create a DATA step view.

✎ SAS views are physically smaller than the corresponding file would be.

91

A SAS data file…	A DATA step view…
is a SAS file with a member type of DATA.	is a SAS file with a member type of VIEW.
enables read or write capabilities.	is read-only.
contains data and a descriptor portion that are stored on disk.	contains no data.
	contains a partially compiled DATA step.

A SAS Data File

```
filename fileref 'ext-file';
data orion.newdata;
   infile fileref;
   <additional SAS statements>
run;
```

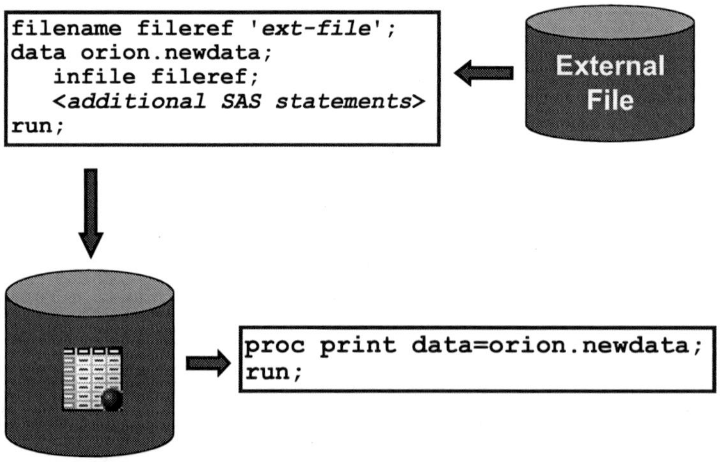


```
proc print data=orion.newdata;
run;
```

92 ...

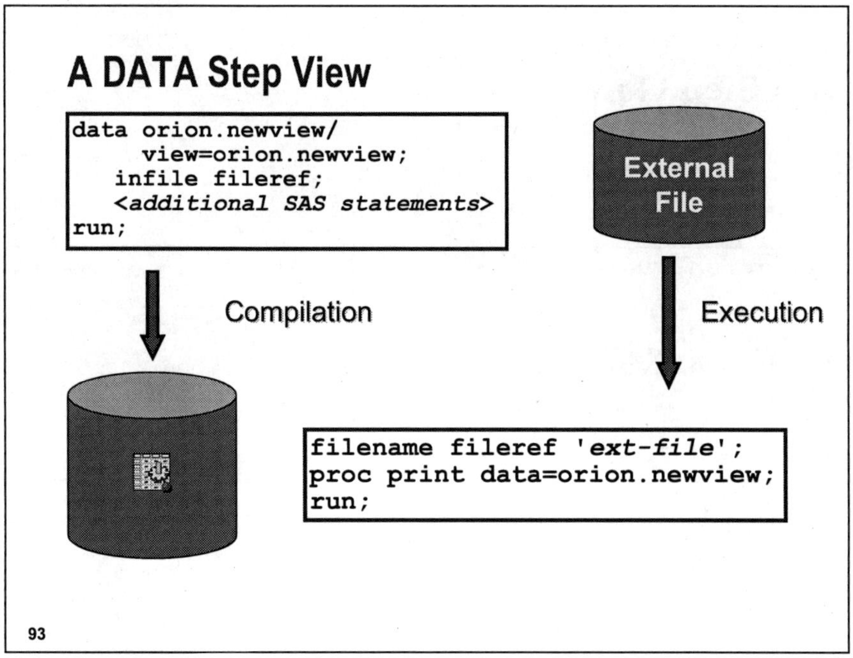

The name of a DATA view must be different from the name of any existing SAS data file or view in the same SAS library.

Creating a DATA Step View

p310d11, p310d12

p310d11

```
data orion.quarter / view=orion.quarter;
   infile MON dlm=',';
   input Customer_ID Order_ID Order_Type
         Order_Date : date9. Delivery_Date : date9.;
run;
```

SAS Log

```
1005
1006  data orion.quarter / view=orion.quarter;
1007     infile MON dlm=',';
1008     input Customer_ID Order_ID Order_Type
1009           Order_Date : date9. Delivery_Date : Date9.;
1010  run;

NOTE: DATA STEP view saved on file ORION.QUARTER.
NOTE: A stored DATA STEP view cannot run under a different operating system.
NOTE: DATA statement used (Total process time):
      real time           0.17 seconds
      cpu time            0.00 seconds
```

p310d11

```
filename MON ('mon3.dat' 'mon2.dat' 'mon1.dat'); * PC and UNIX;
*filename MON ('.workshop.rawdata(mon3)'
               '.workshop.rawdata(mon2)'
               '.workshop.rawdata(mon1)'); * z/OS;

proc print data=orion.quarter;
   title 'quarter';
run;
```

Partial PROC PRINT Output

quarter

Obs	Customer_ ID	Order_ID	Order_ Type	Order_ Date	Delivery_ Date
1	53	1232087464	1	17179	17179
2	49	1232092527	1	17179	17179
3	34	1232161564	1	17189	17189
4	2618	1232173841	3	17191	17196
5	89	1232217725	2	17198	17201
6	195	1232240447	1	17202	17202
7	70046	1232241009	3	17202	17203
8	171	1232307056	1	17212	17212
9	20	1232311932	1	17212	17212
10	23	1232331499	2	17215	17219
11	13	1232373481	2	17222	17225
12	4	1232410925	3	17227	17228
13	4	1232455720	1	17234	17234
14	19	1232478868	1	17238	17238
15	70201	1232517885	3	17244	17249
16	4	1232530384	3	17245	17246
17	49	1232530393	1	17245	17245
18	92	1232554759	1	17249	17249
19	195	1232590052	1	17255	17255
20	89	1232601472	2	17256	17259

SAS Log

```
1011  filename MON ('mon3.dat' 'mon2.dat' 'mon1.dat'); * PC and Unix;
1012  *filename MON ('.workshop.rawdata(mon3)'
1013                 '.workshop.rawdata(mon2)'
1014                 '.workshop.rawdata(mon1)'); * z/OS;
1015
1016  proc print data=orion.quarter;
1017     title ' quarter';
1018  run;

NOTE: The infile MON is:

      File Name=S:\Workshop\mon3.dat,

      File List=('S:\Workshop\mon3.dat' 'S:\Workshop\mon2.dat' S:\Workshop\mon1.dat'),
      RECFM=V,LRECL=256

NOTE: The infile MON is:

      File Name= S:\Workshop\mon2.dat,

      File List=('S:\Workshop\mon3.dat' 'S:\Workshop\mon2.dat' 'S:\Workshop\mon1.dat'),
      RECFM=V,LRECL=256
```

(Continued on the next page.)

```
NOTE: The infile MON is:

      File Name=S:\Workshop\mon1.dat,

      File List=('S:\Workshop\mon3.dat' 'S:\Workshop\mon2.dat' 'S:\Workshop\mon1.dat'),
      RECFM=V,LRECL=256

NOTE: 9 records were read from the infile MON.
      The minimum record length was 34.
      The maximum record length was 38.
NOTE: 7 records were read from the infile MON.
      The minimum record length was 35.
      The maximum record length was 38.
NOTE: 4 records were read from the infile MON.
      The minimum record length was 35.
      The maximum record length was 37.

NOTE: View ORION.QUARTER.VIEW used (Total process time):
      real time           0.25 seconds
      cpu time            0.00 seconds

NOTE: There were 20 observations read from the data set ORION.QUARTER_MON.
NOTE: PROCEDURE PRINT used (Total process time):
      real time           0.81 seconds
      cpu time            0.00 seconds
```

p310d12

```
data orion.movingq / view=orion.movingq;
   drop Today MonNum MidMon LastMon i;
   retain Today MonNum MidMon LastMon;
   if _N_=1 then do;
      Today=today();
      MonNum=month(Today);
      MidMon=month(intnx('month', Today, -1));
      LastMon=month(intnx('month', Today, -2));
   end;
   do i=MonNum, MidMon, LastMon;
      NextFile=cats("mon", i, ".dat"); * Windows and UNIX;
      *NextFile=cats(".workshop.rawdata(mon", i, ")"); * z/OS ;
      infile ORD filevar=NextFile dlm=',' end=LastObs;
      do while (not LastObs);
         input Customer_ID Order_ID Order_Type
               Order_Date : date9. Delivery_Date : date9.;
         output;
      end;
   end;
   stop;
run;
```

SAS Log

```
data orion.movingq / view=orion.movingq;
   drop MonNum MidMon LastMon i;
   retain Today MonNum MidMon LastMon;
   if _N_=1 then do;
      Today=today();
      MonNum=month(Today);
      MidMon=month(intnx('month', Today, -1));
      LastMon=month(intnx('month', Today, -2));
   end;
   do i=MonNum, MidMon, LastMon;
      NextFile=cats("mon", i, ".dat"); * Windows and UNIX;
      *NextFile=cats(".workshop.rawdata(mon", i, ")"); * z/OS ;
      infile ORD filevar=NextFile dlm=',' end=LastObs;
      do while (not LastObs);
         input Customer_ID Order_ID Order_Type
               Order_Date : date9. Delivery_Date : date9.;
         output;
      end;
   end;
   stop;
run;

NOTE: DATA STEP view saved on file ORION.MOVINGQ.
NOTE: A stored DATA STEP view cannot run under a different operating system.
NOTE: DATA statement used (Total process time):
      real time           0.18 seconds
      cpu time            0.00 seconds
```

p310d12

```
proc print data=orion.movingq;
   title 'movingq';
   format Order_Date date9.
          Delivery_Date date9.;
run;
```

Partial PROC PRINT Output (created in May)

MovingQ

Obs	Customer_ ID	Order_ID	Order_ Type	Order_ Date	Delivery_ Date
1	19	1232805509	1	01MAY2007	03MAY2007
2	45	1232857157	2	08MAY2007	12MAY2007
3	908	1232889267	2	13MAY2007	17MAY2007
4	34	1232897220	1	14MAY2007	14MAY2007
5	544	1232936635	2	20MAY2007	21MAY2007
6	111	1232946301	2	22MAY2007	24MAY2007
7	52	1232956741	3	23MAY2007	24MAY2007
8	171	1232972274	1	26MAY2007	26MAY2007
9	183	1232985693	1	28MAY2007	28MAY2007
10	4	1232998740	1	29MAY2007	29MAY2007

SAS Log

```
192  proc print data=orion.movingq;
193     title 'movingq';
194     format Order_Date date9.
195            Delivery_Date date9.;
196  run;

NOTE: The infile ORD is:
      Filename=S:\workshop\mon5.dat,
      RECFM=V,LRECL=256,File Size (bytes)=411,
      Last Modified=27Jan2008:20:32:30,
      Create Time=27Jan2008:20:32:30

NOTE: The infile ORD is:
      Filename= S:\workshop\\mon4.dat,
      RECFM=V,LRECL=256,File Size (bytes)=522,
      Last Modified=27Jan2008:20:32:18,
      Create Time=27Jan2008:20:32:18

NOTE: The infile ORD is:
      Filename= S:\workshop\mon3.dat,
      RECFM=V,LRECL=256,File Size (bytes)=334,
      Last Modified=27Jan2008:20:32:04,
      Create Time=27Jan2008:20:32:04

NOTE: 11 records were read from the infile ORD.
      The minimum record length was 34.
      The maximum record length was 36.
NOTE: 14 records were read from the infile ORD.
      The minimum record length was 34.
      The maximum record length was 38.
NOTE: 9 records were read from the infile ORD.
      The minimum record length was 34.
      The maximum record length was 38.
NOTE: View ORION.MOVINGQ.VIEW used (Total process time):
      real time           0.06 seconds
      cpu time            0.03 seconds

NOTE: There were 34 observations read from the data set ORION.MOVINGQ.
NOTE: PROCEDURE PRINT used (Total process time):
      real time           0.06 seconds
      cpu time            0.03 seconds
```

DATA Statement with VIEW= Option Syntax

General form of the DATA statement with VIEW= option:

```
DATA data-set-name(s) /VIEW=view-name;
      <INFILE fileref;>
      <INPUT variable(s);>
     <SET/MERGE>
RUN;
```

view-name specifies a name that the DATA step uses to store the partially compiled DATA step.

⚠ The *view-name* must match one of the data set names.

95

You can also create SAS data files in the DATA step that creates the view, but you can only create one view per DATA step.

✎ The SAS data file is not created until the view is accessed.

10.09 Quiz

Open and submit the program **p310a02**.

What does the log report?

```
data view=orion.movingq;
   describe;
run;
```

97

The DESCRIBE Statement

You can use the DESCRIBE statement to retrieve program source code from a DATA step view.

SAS writes the source statements to the SAS log.

General form of the DESCRIBE statement:

```
DATA VIEW =view-name;
    DESCRIBE;
RUN;
```

99

Creating Views with the SQL Procedure

You can create views with the SQL procedure by using the CREATE VIEW statement.

```
proc sql;
   create view orion.names_view as
   select e.Employee_ID, e.Employee_Name,
          Manager_ID,
          m.Employee_Name as Manager_Name
      from orion.staff,
           orion.employee_addresses as e,
           orion.employee_addresses as m
      where e.Employee_ID=staff.Employee_ID
        and m.Employee_ID=staff.Manager_ID;
quit;
```

100 p310d13

The SQL procedure DESCRIBE statement retrieves the SQL view code and reports it in the log.

PROC SQL;
 DESCRIBE VIEW view-*name*;
QUIT;

SAS Log

```
1213  proc sql;
1214     describe view orion.names_view;
NOTE: SQL view ORION.NAMES_VIEW is defined as:

select e.Employee_ID, e.Employee_Name, Manager_ID, m.Employee_Name as Manager_Name
from ORION.STAFF, ORION.EMPLOYEE_ADDRESSES e, ORION.EMPLOYEE_ADDRESSES m
where (e.Employee_ID=staff.Employee_ID) and (m.Employee_ID=staff.Manager_ID);

1215  quit;
NOTE: PROCEDURE SQL used (Total process time):
real time           0.00 seconds
cpu time            0.00 seconds
```

Creating Views with the SQL Procedure

You can also embed a SAS LIBNAME statement in a PROC SQL view with the USING clause. This enables you to store SAS libref information in the view. The scope of the libref is local to the view, and it will not conflict with an identically named libref in the SAS session.

```
proc sql;
   create view orion.names_view as
   select e.Employee_ID, e.Employee_Name,
          Manager_ID,
          m.Employee_Name as Manager_Name
       from orion.staff,
            orion.employee_addresses as e,
            orion.employee_addresses as m
       where e.Employee_ID=staff.Employee_ID
         and m.Employee_ID=staff.Manager_ID
       using libname orion 's:\workshop';
quit;
```

101 p310d14

For more information about the USING clause in PROC SQL, consult SAS OnlineDoc:

SAS OnlineDoc ⇨ **Base SAS** ⇨ **SAS 9.2 SQL Procedure User's Guide** ⇨ **Creating and Updating Tables and Views**

Advantages of Views

Advantages of Using Views
Data from multiple sources can be combined.
Complex code can be stored for reuse.
Errors and programming time can be reduced.
You can access the most current data in changing files
A SAS copy of a large data file does not have to be stored.
You can avoid creating intermediate copies of data.

102

10.10 Quiz

What is the advantage of the following program?

```
data bonus_view(keep=Manager_ID YrEndBonus)
      / view=bonus_view;
   set orion.staff;
   YrEndBonus=Salary * 0.05;
   where Job_Title contains 'Manager';
run;

proc means data=bonus_view mean sum;
   class Manager_ID;
   var YrEndBonus;
run;
```

104 p310d15

Using Views to Avoid Intermediate Data

Views can be used to avoid the I/O associated when you create a data set to be used in a subsequent step.

Using views to avoid intermediate data has the following characteristics:

- does not reduce the CPU resources required to complete the task. A view might *increase* the total CPU time.
- eliminates writing and reading temporary data sets.
- reduces the *real time* required to complete a job by eliminating one or more I/O bound segments.

106

Using Views to Avoid Intermediate Data

Example of avoiding the I/O needed to create intermediate data.

```
data four;
   set one two three;
run;
proc sort data=four;
   by X;
run;
```

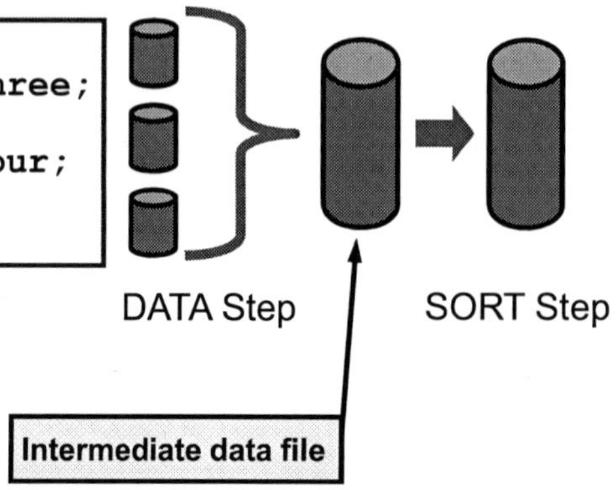

107

continued...

Using Views to Avoid Intermediate Data

Example of avoiding the I/O needed to create intermediate data.

```
data four / view=four;
   set one two three;
run;
proc sort data=four;
   by X;
run;
```

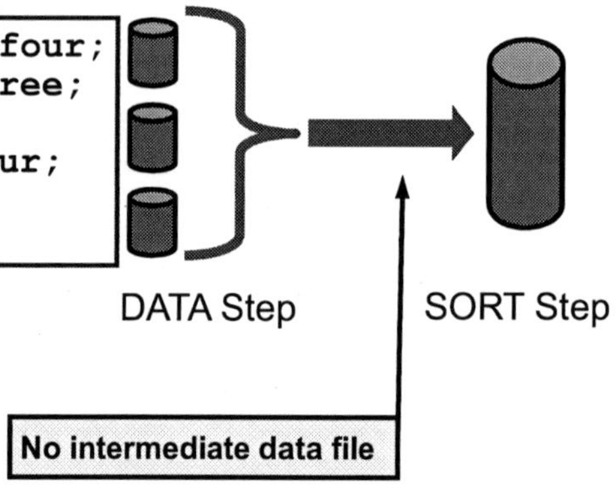

108

Using the PRESORTED Option with Views

The following example creates the data view **profit_07**. The SORT step then reads the data from **profit.dat**, validates the sort flag, and creates the data file **profit07**.

```
data profit07_view /
             view=profit07_view;
   infile 'profit07.dat' dlm=',';
   input Company : $30. Sales Cost
         Salaries Profit;
run;

proc sort data=profit07_view
          out=profit07 presorted;
   by Company;
run;
```

109 p310d16

PRESORTED is a SAS 9.2 option.

Disadvantages of Views

Disadvantages of Using Views
The code executes each time that you use a view.
System resources are increased.
You run the risk of having your data change between consecutive executions of the same program.
Depending on how many reads or passes of the data are required, processing overhead increases.

110

Guidelines for Creating and Using Views

If data is used many times in one program, it is more efficient to create and reference a SAS data file than to create and reference a view.

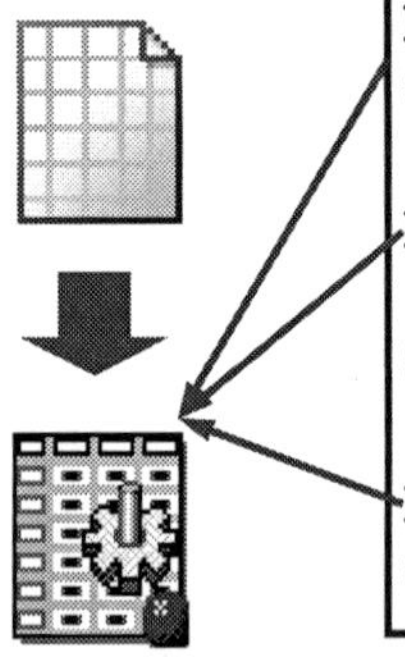

```
proc print data=orion.sview;
run;

proc freq data=orion.sview;
   tables Order_Type;
run;

proc means data=orion.sview;
run;
```

111

Setup for the Poll

The following program is executed:

```
data orion.sview / view=orion.sview;
  infile 'rawdata.dat';
  input variable-list;
  <additional statements>
run;
proc print data=orion.sview;
run;
proc freq data=orion.sview;
   tables Order_Type;
run;
proc means data=orion.sview;
run;
```

113

10.11 Multiple Choice Poll

How many times is the **rawdata** file read?

a. 4
b. 3
c. 2
d. 1
e. 0

114

Guidelines for Creating and Using Views

If data is used many times in one program, it is more efficient to create and reference a SAS data file than to create and reference a view.

```
data order;
   set orion.sview;
run;

proc print data=order;
run;

proc freq data=order;
   tables Order_Type;
run;

proc means data=order;
run;
```

116

Guidelines for Creating and Using Views

You might experience a degradation in performance when you use a SAS data view with a procedure that requires multiple passes through the data.

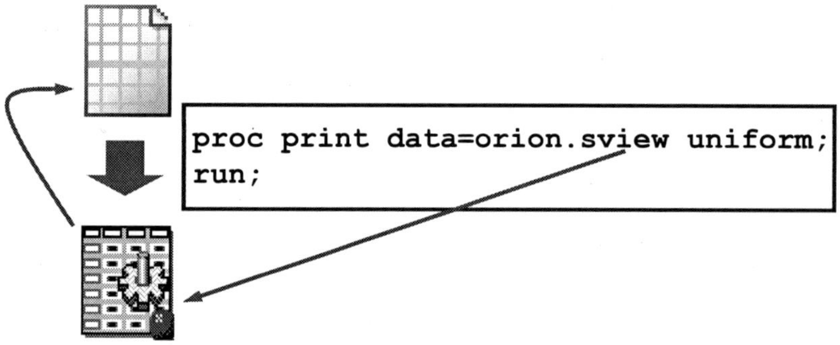

```
proc print data=orion.sview uniform;
run;
```

117

The PRINT procedure with the UNIFORM option, the CLASS statement in the MEANS/SUMMARY, TABULATE, and UNIVARIATE procedures, and many SAS/STAT procedures require multiple passes through the data.

In the case of multiple passes in a step, the view creates a temporary spill file so that SAS does not have to read the data from disk multiple times.

Guidelines for Creating and Using Views

In the PRINT procedure, the WIDTH= option along with a FORMAT statement on variables can reduce execution time.

```
proc print data=orion.sview
           width=full;
   <FORMAT statement to format any
    variable that does not have a
    permanent format assigned to it>
run;
```

118

WIDTH=*column-width*   determines the column width for each variable.

value of *column-width*	Use	Alias
FULL	uses a variable's formatted width as the column width.	
MINIMUM	uses, for each variable, the minimum column width that accommodates all values of the variable.	MIN
UNIFORM	uses each variable's formatted width as its column width on all pages. If the variable does not have a format that explicitly specifies a field width, PROC PRINT uses the widest data value as the column width.	U
UNIFORMBY	formats all columns uniformly within a BY group, using each variable's formatted width as its column width. If the variable does not have a format that explicitly specifies a field width, PROC PRINT uses the widest data value as the column width.	UBY

Guidelines for Creating and Using Views

Avoid creating views on files whose structures often change.

File1

```
         1    1    2
1---5----0----5----0
John Smith     21
```

File2

```
         1    1    2
1---5----0----5----0
John Smith Ted Jones
```

File3

```
         1    1    2
1---5----0----5----0
21 John Smith
```

```
filename rawdata 'file1';
proc print data=orion.sview;
run;
filename rawdata 'file2'
proc freq data=orion.sview;
   tables JobCode;
run;
filename rawdata 'file3'
proc means data=orion.sview;
run;
```

119

Which to Use: DATA Step View or SQL View?

DATA Step View	SQL View
DATA step views are versatile because they use DATA step processing, including DO loops and IF-THEN/ELSE statements.	PROC SQL views do not use DATA step programming; it is not as easy to perform conditional processing.
DATA step views do not have write capability; that is, they cannot directly change the data that they access.	PROC SQL views can both read and update the data that they reference. The update can take place **only** if there is only one table underlying the view. If there are joins, you cannot update through an SQL view.
The DATA step can read data from many different file formats; for example, text files.	PROC SQL can only read data that is a SAS data set or coming from a relational database.

120

continued...

Which to Use: DATA Step View or SQL View?

DATA Step View	SQL View
There is no way to subset the underlying data used by a DATA step view prior to using the view. Even if only part of the data is needed, the entire underlying data must be loaded into memory when the view is used.	You can also use the power of the SQL language to subset your data prior to processing it. This saves memory when you have a large view, but need to select only a small portion of the data contained in the view.
The DATA step does not have an equivalent to the USING clause in SQL.	The USING clause in PROC SQL can assign the libref in the view itself.
The DATA step does not support a subquery in a WHERE statement.	PROC SQL supports subqueries in WHERE clauses.
The DATA step can read data from a DBMS only if a LIBNAME statement is assigned using the appropriate engine.	PROC SQL has a CONNECT TO component that sends SQL statements to a DBMS using the SQL Pass-Through Facility.

121

Reference Information

Creating a View and a File

Only one view can be created in a DATA step.

In addition to the view name, you can specify other data set names in the DATA statement. The data sets are not created until the view is processed.

p310d17

```
data orion.movingq errors / view=orion.movingq;
   drop MonNum MidMon LastMon i;
   retain Today;
   if _N_=1 then Today=today();
   MonNum=month(Today);
   MidMon=month(intnx('month', Today, -1));
   LastMon=month(intnx('month', Today, -2));
   do i=MonNum, Midmon, LastMon;
      NextFile=cats("mon", i, ".dat");
      infile ORD filevar=NextFile dlm=','
             end=LastObs;
      do while (not LastObs);
         input Customer_ID
               Order_ID
               Order_Type
               Order_Date : date9.
               Delivery_Date : date9.;
         if _ERROR_=0 then output orion.movingq;
         else output errors;
      end;
   end;
   stop;
run;

proc print data=orion.movingq;
   title 'movingq';
   format Order_Date date9.
          Delivery_Date date9.;
run;

proc print data=errors;
   title 'Errors';
run;
```

Using Macro Variables

Because SAS macro variables are resolved during compilation, any macro variables used in a DATA step view are resolved when the view is created.

You can use the SYMGET function to postpone macro resolution until the view is executed.

p310d18

```
%let OrderType=2;

data orion.movingq / view= orion.movingq;
   drop MonNum MidMon LastMon i Today;
   retain Today;
   if _N_=1 then Today=today();
   MonNum=month(Today);
   MidMon=month(intnx('month', Today, -1));
   LastMon=month(intnx('month', Today, -2));
   do i=MonNum, Midmon, LastMon;
      NextFile=cats("mon", i, ".dat");
      infile ORD filevar=NextFile dlm=','
             end=LastObs;
      do while (not LastObs);
         input Customer_ID
               Order_ID
               Order_Type
               Order_Date : date9.
               Delivery_Date : date9.;
         if Order_Type=input(symget('OrderType'), 2.) then
               output orion.movingq;
      end;
   end;
   stop;
run;

proc print data=orion.movingq;
   title 'Using a Macro Variable';
   format Order_Date date9.
          Delivery_Date date9.;
run;
```

PROC PRINT Output (from May)

Using a Macro Variable

Obs	Customer_ ID	Order_ID	Order_ Type	Order_ Date	Delivery_ Date
1	45	1232857157	2	08MAY2007	12MAY2007
2	908	1232889267	2	13MAY2007	17MAY2007
3	544	1232936635	2	20MAY2007	21MAY2007
4	111	1232946301	2	22MAY2007	24MAY2007
5	54655	1232618023	2	03APR2007	06APR2007
6	5	1232728634	2	19APR2007	23APR2007
7	89	1232601472	2	31MAR2007	03APR2007

Exercises

Level 1

4. Creating a DATA Step View

a. Create a view named **cc_donations**.

1) Read only the observations from the data set **orion.employee_donations** where the value of the variable **Paid_By** is `Credit Card`.

2) Create a variable named **Total_Donations** as the total of the variable values for **Qtr1**, **Qtr2**, **Qtr3**, and **Qtr4**.

3) Create a new variable **Donation_Category** with the following values:

Value of Total_Donations	Donation_Category
Less than 100	Less than $100
Greater than or equal 100	$100 or more

b. Open and submit the program **p310e04** to create a report from the view **cc_donations**. Use the variable **Donation_Category** as a class variable and the variable **Total_Donations** as an analysis variable. Verify that the view was created correctly.

p310e04

```
proc means data=cc_donations sum n nonobs maxdec=2;
   class Donation_Category;
   var Total_Donations;
run;
```

Preferred PROC MEANS Output

```
                    The MEANS Procedure

           Analysis Variable : Total_Donations

        Donation_
        Category                    Sum           N
        ------------------------------------------
        $100 or more             200.00           2

        Less than $100          1475.00          32
        ------------------------------------------
```

Level 2

5. Creating a View and a File in One DATA Step

a. In one DATA step, create a view named **younger60** and a file named **older60**.

b. Read from the data set **orion.employee_payroll**.

Partial Listing of **orion.employee_payroll**

Obs	Employee_ID	Employee_ Gender	Salary	Birth_ Date	Employee_ Hire_Date	Employee_ Term_Date	Marital_ Status	Dependents
1	120101	M	163040	18AUG1976	01JUL2003	.	S	0
2	120102	M	108255	11AUG1969	01JUN1989	.	O	2
3	120103	M	87975	22JAN1949	01JAN1974	.	M	1
4	120104	F	46230	11MAY1954	01JAN1981	.	M	1
5	120105	F	27110	21DEC1974	01MAY1999	.	S	0

c. Use the variable **Birth_Date** to calculate each employee's age as of today.

- The view should contain the employees who are younger than 60.
- The file should contain the employees who are 60 or older.

d. Attempt to print the file **older60** unsuccessfully.

SAS Log

```
22    proc print data=older60;
ERROR: File WORK.OLDER60.DATA does not exist.
23    title 'Older60 Data Set';
24    run;

NOTE: The SAS System stopped processing this step because of errors.
NOTE: PROCEDURE PRINT used (Total process time):
      real time           0.06 seconds
      cpu time            0.01 seconds
```

e. Print the view **younger60**.

Partial PROC PRINT Output

Younger60 Data Set

Obs	Employee_ID	Employee_ Gender	Salary	Birth_ Date	Employee_ Hire_Date
1	120101	M	163040	18AUG1976	01JUL2003
2	120102	M	108255	11AUG1969	01JUN1989
3	120104	F	46230	11MAY1954	01JAN1981
4	120105	F	27110	21DEC1974	01MAY1999
5	120108	F	27660	23FEB1984	01AUG2006

Obs	Employee_ Term_Date	Marital_ Status	Dependents	Age
1	.	S	0	32
2	.	O	2	39
3	.	M	1	55

```
          4      .          S          0        34
          5      .          S          0        25
```

✎ The PROC PRINT output was generated on June 23, 2009. Your results might vary due to the value of **`Age`**.

f. Print the file **`older60`** successfully.

Partial PROC PRINT Output

```
                          Older60 Data Set

                           Employee_                        Birth_     Employee_
 Obs       Employee_ID      Gender         Salary            Date     Hire_Date

   1            120103        M            87975        22JAN1949     01JAN1974
   2            120106        M            26960        23DEC1944     01JAN1974
   3            120107        F            30475        21JAN1949     01FEB1974
   4            120113        F            26870        10MAY1944     01JAN1974
   5            120114        F            31285        08FEB1944     01JAN1974

      Employee_     Marital_
 Obs  Term_Date      Status      Dependents      Age

   1      .            M              1           60
   2      .            M              2           64
   3      .            M              2           60
   4      .            S              0           65
   5      .            M              3           65
```

✎ The PROC PRINT output was generated on June 23, 2009. Your results might vary due to the value of **`Age`**.

g. Why could you not print **`older60`** in step **d**?

____

____

Level 3

6. Creating a View with the SQL Procedure and the USING Clause

You can embed a SAS LIBNAME statement in a view with the USING clause. This enables you to store SAS libref information in the view. The scope of the libref is local to the view, and it will not conflict with an identically named libref in the SAS session.

The starter program **p310e06** contains a PROC SQL step that creates a view.

p310e06

```
proc sql;
   create view orion.payroll_donations as
```

```
        select Employee_ID, Qtr1, Qtr2, Qtr3, Qtr4,
               sum(Qtr1, Qtr2, Qtr3, Qtr4) as Total_Donations
        from orion.employee_donations
        where Paid_By='Payroll Deduction';
quit;

proc print data=orion.payroll_donations;
run;
```

a. Open the program **p310e06**, and edit it to assign the libref with the USING clause. The appropriate library definition is listed below.

Windows	s:\workshop
UNIX	.
z/OS	.prg3.sasdata

b. Submit a LIBNAME statement to assign a libref of **sasdata** to the library specified in the table above.

c. Submit a PROC PRINT step to print the view **sasdata.payroll_donations**.

Partial PROC PRINT Output

orion.payroll_donations View

Obs	Employee_ID	Qtr1	Qtr2	Qtr3	Qtr4	Total_ Donations
1	120267	15	15	15	15	60
2	120269	20	20	20	20	80
3	120271	20	20	20	20	80
4	120272	10	10	10	10	40
5	120669	15	15	15	15	60

d. Submit a LIBNAME statement to clear the **sasdata** libref.

10.4 Using FILE and PUT Statements to Create a SAS Program File

Objectives

- Use a DATA step to write SAS program code.
- Include the code and submit it.

125

Using the DATA Step to Create a Program

The DATA step provides the complete control necessary to write flexible programs.

Selected features when you use the DATA step for writing SAS code are as follows:

- FILE statement options
- line and column pointer controls in a PUT statement
- IF/THEN logic
- DATA step functions
- DO loop processing

126

Example of Using the DATA Step

```
proc sql;
   create table jobs as
      select distinct Job_Title
         from orion.salesstaff;
quit;

data _null_;
   set jobs;
   file 'jobs.sas';
   put 'proc print data=orion.salesstaff;';
   put 'title "Listing for Job Title '
        Job_Title '";';
   put 'where Job_Title="' Job_Title
        '";' / 'run;' /;
run;
```

jobs

Job_Title
Sales Rep. I
Sales Rep. II
Sales Rep. III
Sales Rep. IV

128 p310d19

jobs

Job_Title
Sales Rep. I
Sales Rep. II
Sales Rep. III
Sales Rep. IV

```
data _null_;
   set jobs;
   file 'jobs.sas';
   put 'proc print data=orion.salesstaff;';
   put 'title "Listing for Job Title '
        Job_Title '";';
   put 'where Job_Title="' Job_Title
        '";' / 'run;' /;
run;
```

PDV

Job_Title	_N_
Sales Rep. I	1

129 ...

jobs

Job_Title
Sales Rep. I
Sales Rep. II
Sales Rep. III
Sales Rep. IV

```
data _null_;
   set jobs;
   file 'jobs.sas';
   put 'proc print data=orion.salesstaff;';
   put 'title "Listing for Job Title '
        Job_Title '";';
   put 'where Job_Title="' Job_Title
        '";' / 'run;' /;
run;
```

PDV

Job_Title	D _N_
Sales Rep. I	1

jobs.sas

```
         1    1    2    2    3    3    4    4    5    5    6    6    7    7
1---5----0----5----0----5----0----5----0----5----0----5----0----5----0----5
```

130 ...

jobs

Job_Title
Sales Rep. I
Sales Rep. II
Sales Rep. III
Sales Rep. IV

```
data _null_;
   set jobs;
   file 'jobs.sas';
   put 'proc print data=orion.salesstaff;';
   put 'title "Listing for Job Title '
        Job_Title '";';
   put 'where Job_Title="' Job_Title
        '";' / 'run;' /;
run;
```

PDV

Job_Title	D _N_
Sales Rep. I	1

jobs.sas

```
         1    1    2    2    3    3    4    4    5    5    6    6    7    7
1---5----0----5----0----5----0----5----0----5----0----5----0----5----0----5
proc print data=orion.salesstaff;
```

131 ...

jobs

Job_Title
Sales Rep. I
Sales Rep. II
Sales Rep. III
Sales Rep. IV

```
data _null_;
   set jobs;
   file 'jobs.sas';
   put 'proc print data=orion.salesstaff;';
   put 'title "Listing for Job Title '
        Job_Title '";';
   put 'where Job_Title="' Job_Title
        '";' / 'run;' /;
run;
```

PDV

Job_Title	_N_
Sales Rep. I	1

jobs.sas

```
         1    1    2    2    3    3    4    4    5    5    6    6    7    7
1---5----0----5----0----5----0----5----0----5----0----5----0----5----0----5
proc print data=orion.salesstaff;
title "Listing for Job Title Sales Rep. I";
```

132 ...

jobs

Job_Title
Sales Rep. I
Sales Rep. II
Sales Rep. III
Sales Rep. IV

```
data _null_;
   set jobs;
   file 'jobs.sas';
   put 'proc print data=orion.salesstaff;';
   put 'title "Listing for Job Title '
        Job_Title '";';
   put 'where Job_Title="' Job_Title
        '";' / 'run;' /;
run;
```

PDV

Job_Title	_N_
Sales Rep. I	1

jobs.sas

```
         1    1    2    2    3    3    4    4    5    5    6    6    7    7
1---5----0----5----0----5----0----5----0----5----0----5----0----5----0----5
proc print data=orion.salesstaff;
title "Listing for Job Title Sales Rep. I";
where Job_Title="Sales Rep. I";
```

133 ...

jobs

Job_Title
Sales Rep. I
Sales Rep. II
Sales Rep. III
Sales Rep. IV

```
data _null_;
   set jobs;
   file 'jobs.sas';
   put 'proc print data=orion.salesstaff;';
   put 'title "Listing for Job Title '
        Job_Title '";';
   put 'where Job_Title="' Job_Title
        '";' / 'run;' /;
run;
```

PDV

Job_Title	D _N_
Sales Rep. I	1

jobs.sas

```
         1    1    2    2    3    3    4    4    5    5    6    6    7    7
1---5----0----5----0----5----0----5----0----5----0----5----0----5----0----5
proc print data=orion.salesstaff;
title "Listing for Job Title Sales Rep. I";
where Job_Title="Sales Rep. I";
run;
```

134 ...

jobs

Job_Title
Sales Rep. I
Sales Rep. II
Sales Rep. III
Sales Rep. IV

```
data _null_;
   set jobs;
   file 'jobs.sas';
   put 'proc print data=orion.salesstaff;';
   put 'title "Listing for Job Title '
        Job_Title '";';
   put 'where Job_Title="' Job_Title
        '";' / 'run;' /;
run;
```

Implicit RETURN;

PDV

Job_Title	D _N_
Sales Rep. I	1

jobs.sas

```
         1    1    2    2    3    3    4    4    5    5    6    6    7    7
1---5----0----5----0----5----0----5----0----5----0----5----0----5----0----5
proc print data=orion.salesstaff;
title "Listing for Job Title Sales Rep. I";
where Job_Title="Sales Rep. I";
run;
```

135 ...

jobs

Job_Title
Sales Rep. I
Sales Rep. II
Sales Rep. III
Sales Rep. IV

```
data _null_;
   set jobs;
   file 'jobs.sas';
   put 'proc print data=orion.salesstaff;';
   put 'title "Listing for Job Title '
        Job_Title '";';
   put 'where Job_Title="' Job_Title
        '";' / 'run;' /;
run;
```

PDV

Job_Title	_N_
Sales Rep. IV	4

Processing continues until the end of file in `work.jobs`.

jobs.sas

```
         1    1    2    2    3    3    4    4    5    5    6    6    7    7
1---5----0----5----0----5----0----5----0----5----0----5----0----5----0----5
proc print data=orion.salesstaff;
title "Listing for Job Title Sales Rep. IV";
where Job_Title="Sales Rep. IV";
run;
```

136

Using the DATA Step

General form of the DATA step to create a report or raw data file:

> **DATA** _NULL_;
>   *...DATA step statements...*
>   **FILE** *file-specification*;
>   **PUT** *@n variable1 format ... @n variable-n format*;
>   *...DATA step statements...*
> **RUN;**

⚠ Using the _NULL_ option in the DATA statement does not create a data set when the DATA step executes.

137

10.12 Multiple Answer Poll

Which resources can you conserve by using the _NULL_ keyword in the DATA statement?

a. I/O
b. CPU
c. Memory
d. Programmer time

139

Using the FILE Statement

Use the FILE statement to specify the external file in which to write the SAS code generated by the PUT statements in the current DATA step.

General form of the FILE statement:

FILE *file-specification <options>*;

The file specification in the FILE statement can be any one of the following:

- PRINT to write the PUT statements to the current output destination
- the name of an external file
- a file reference to an external file

Omitting the FILE statement directs the results of the PUT statement to the Log window.

141

Using the PUT Statement

The PUT statement writes values to an external location that is specified in the most recently executed FILE statement.

PUT *pointer-controls variables formats 'literals'*;

Some PUT statement specifications are listed below:

- constant text

```
put 'title "Listing for Job Title ' Job_Title '";';
```

- variable values

```
put 'title "Listing for Job Title ' Job_Title '";';
```

142

The %INCLUDE Statement

The %INCLUDE statement retrieves SAS source code from an external file and compiles and executes the code.

```
%include 'jobs.sas' / source2;
```

General form of the %INCLUDE statement:

%INCLUDE *file-specification* < / SOURCE2 >;

file-specification	provides the physical name or fileref of the file to be retrieved and placed on the input stack.
SOURCE2	requests that inserted SAS statements appear in the SAS log.

143

Viewing the Source in the Log

```
77   %include 'jobs.sas' / source2;
NOTE: %INCLUDE (level 1) file jobs.sas is file jobs.sas.
78   +proc print data=orion.salesstaff;
79   +title "Listing for Job Title Sales Rep. I ";
80   +where Job_Title="Sales Rep. I ";
81   +run;

NOTE: There were 63 observations read from the data set ORION.SALESSTAFF.
      WHERE Job_Title='Sales Rep. I ';
NOTE: PROCEDURE PRINT used (Total process time):
      real time           0.00 seconds
      cpu time            0.00 seconds

82   +
83   +proc print data=orion.salesstaff;
84   +title "Listing for Job Title Sales Rep. II ";
85   +where Job_Title="Sales Rep. II ";
86   +run;

NOTE: There were 50 observations read from the data set ORION.SALESSTAFF.
      WHERE Job_Title='Sales Rep. II ';
NOTE: PROCEDURE PRINT used (Total process time):
      real time           0.00 seconds
      cpu time            0.00 seconds
```

144

continued...

Viewing the Source in the Log

```
88   +proc print data=orion.salesstaff;
89   +title "Listing for Job Title Sales Rep. III ";
90   +where Job_Title="Sales Rep. III ";
91   +run;

NOTE: There were 34 observations read from the data set ORION.SALESSTAFF.
      WHERE Job_Title='Sales Rep. III ';
NOTE: PROCEDURE PRINT used (Total process time):
      real time           0.00 seconds
      cpu time            0.00 seconds

92   +
93   +proc print data=orion.salesstaff;
94   +title "Listing for Job Title Sales Rep. IV ";
95   +where Job_Title="Sales Rep. IV ";
96   +run;

NOTE: There were 16 observations read from the data set ORION.SALESSTAFF.
      WHERE Job_Title='Sales Rep. IV ';
NOTE: PROCEDURE PRINT used (Total process time):
      real time           0.00 seconds
      cpu time            0.00 seconds

97   +
NOTE: %INCLUDE (level 1) ending.
```

145

Using the DATA Step to Send e-Mail

p310d20

You need to send an e-mail that provides the delivery date of a customer's order. The customer names are in the data set **`orion.customer_dim`**. The delivery date is in the data set **`orion.order_fact`**.

In the DATA _NULL_ step perform the following steps:

1. Merge **`orion.customer_dim`** and the sorted copy of **`orion.order_fact`**.
2. Use the FILE statement to route the text file to a SAS program file.
3. Create a variable named **`Address`** that contains the customer's e-mail address.
4. Use a PUT statement to create a FILENAME statement with the EMAIL option and the value of **`Address`**, along with a subject for the e-mail.
5. Use PUT statements to write a DATA step that writes the message.
6. Use the %INCLUDE statement to execute the program.

Do **not** submit the %INCLUDE statement that is commented out below. There are no mail servers attached to the classroom machines and the generated e-mail addresses are not valid e-mail addresses.

p310d20

```
proc sort data=orion.order_fact(keep=Customer_ID Order_ID
                                         Delivery_Date)
           out=order_fact(obs=50);
   by Customer_ID;
run;

data _null_;
   merge orion.customer_dim(keep=Customer_FirstName
                                  Customer_LastName Customer_ID)
         order_fact;
   by Customer_ID;
   file 'email.sas';
   if first.Customer_ID then do;
      Address=catt(Customer_FirstName,'.',
                   Customer_LastName,'@something.com');
      FullName=catx(' ', Customer_FirstName, Customer_LastName);
      put "filename mail email '" Address "' subject='Purchases';";
      put 'data _null_;';
      put 'file mail;';
      put "put '" FullName +(-1) ",';";
      put "put 'Thank you for your orders.';";
      put "put 'They will be delivered as follows:'//;";
      put "put @10 'Your order number'
               @30 'Expected Delivery Date'/;";
   end;
```

(Continued on the next page.)

```
   DT=put(Delivery_Date,mmddyy10.);
   put "put @15 '" Order_ID"' @35 '" DT "';";
   if last.Customer_ID then do;
      put "put /'Your friends at Orion Star';";
      put "run;";
   end;
run;

/*
%include 'email.sas';
*/
```

Partial Listing of **email.sas**

```
filename mail email 'James.Kvarniq@something.com ' subject='Purchases';
data _null_;
file mail;
put 'James Kvarniq,';
put 'Thank you for your orders.';
put 'They will be delivered as follows:'//;
put @10 'Your order number' @30 'Expected Delivery Date'/;
put @15 '1232410925 ' @35 '03/03/2004 ';
put @15 '1232455720 ' @35 '03/09/2004 ';
put @15 '1232530384 ' @35 '03/21/2004 ';
put @15 '1232654929 ' @35 '04/09/2004 ';
put @15 '1232654929 ' @35 '04/09/2004 ';
put @15 '1232709099 ' @35 '04/16/2004 ';
put @15 '1232998740 ' @35 '05/29/2004 ';
put @15 '1233543560 ' @35 '08/20/2004 ';
put @15 '1234348668 ' @35 '12/18/2004 ';
put /'Your friends at Orion Star';
run;
```

Advantages of Using FILE/PUT to Write Code

The advantanges of using FILE/PUT statements to write code are as follows:

- There is more flexibility for generating code than when using the macro facility.
- The source code can be kept for future use.
- You can look at the code before executing it.
- You can write to several files at the same time that will make up the complete program.
- The code can be used to write macro code (dynamic macro names).

147

Exercises

Level 1

7. Creating Two SAS Programs with One DATA Step

The data set **orion.customer_type** contains the variables **Customer_Type_ID**, **Customer_Type**, **Customer_Group_ID**, and **Customer_Group**.

Partial Listing of **orion.Customer_Type**

Obs	Customer_ Type_ID	Customer_Type	Customer_ Group_ID	Customer_Group
1	1010	Orion Club members inactive	10	Orion Club members
2	1020	Orion Club members low activity	10	Orion Club members
3	1030	Orion Club members medium activity	10	Orion Club members
4	1040	Orion Club members high activity	10	Orion Club members
5	2010	Orion Club Gold members low activity	20	Orion Club Gold members
6	2020	Orion Club Gold members medium activity	20	Orion Club Gold members
7	2030	Orion Club Gold members high activity	20	Orion Club Gold members
8	3010	Internet/Catalog Customers	30	Internet/Catalog Customers

a. Write a DATA step to build the following two PROC FORMAT steps. Under Windows and UNIX, name the files **customer_type.sas** and **customer_group.sas**. Under z/OS, name the files **.workshop.sascode(customer_type)** and **.workshop.sascode(customer_group)**.

Preferred Output from the DATA Step for **customer_group**

```
proc format fmtlib;
   value GrpLevl
      10="Orion Club members"
      20="Orion Club Gold members"
      30="Internet/Catalog Customers";
run;
```

Preferred Output from the DATA Step for **customer_type**

```
proc format fmtlib;
   value TypeLevl
      1010="Orion Club members inactive"
      1020="Orion Club members low activity"
      1030="Orion Club members medium activity"
      1040="Orion Club members high activity"
      2010="Orion Club Gold members low activity"
      2020="Orion Club Gold members medium activity"
      2030="Orion Club Gold members high activity"
      3010="Internet/Catalog Customers";
run;
```

Hint: To create the value for the label, use the $QUOTE format that writes data values that are enclosed in double quotation marks. Investigate the descriptor portion of the data set to determine the appropriate width.

b. Use the %INCLUDE statement to execute the code.

Partial SAS Log

```
95   %include 'Customer_Type.sas'/source2;
NOTE: %INCLUDE (level 1) file Customer_Type.sas is file S:\workshop\Customer_Type.sas.
96  +proc format fmtlib;
97  +value TypLevl
98  +1010="Orion Club members inactive"
99  +1020="Orion Club members low activity"
100 +1030="Orion Club members medium activity"
101 +1040="Orion Club members high activity"
102 +2010="Orion Club Gold members low activity"
103 +2020="Orion Club Gold members medium activity"
104 +2030="Orion Club Gold members high activity"
105 +3010=Internet/Catalog Customers"
106 +;
NOTE: Format TYPLEVL has been output.
106!+ run;

NOTE: PROCEDURE FORMAT used (Total process time):
      real time           0.23 seconds
      cpu time            0.04 seconds
```

Level 2

8. Sending e-Mail Using the DATA Step

The data set **orion.employee_donations** contains the variables **Employee_ID**, **Qtr1**, **Qtr2**, **Qtr3**, **Qtr4**, and **Recipients**.

Partial Listing of **orion.Employee_Donations**

```
Employee
    _ID     Qtr1    Qtr2    Qtr3    Qtr4                   Recipients

120265        .       .       .      25     Mitleid International 90%,
                                            Save the Baby Animals 10%
120267       15      15      15      15     Disaster Assist, Inc. 80%,
                                            Cancer Cures, Inc. 20%
120269       20      20      20      20     Cancer Cures, Inc. 10%,
                                            Cuidadores Ltd. 90%
120270       20      10       5       .     AquaMissions International 10%,
                                            Child Survivors 90%
120271       20      20      20      20     Cuidadores Ltd. 80%,
                                            Mitleid International 20%
```

The data set **orion.employee_addresses** contains the names of the employees.

Open the program **p310e08**, which contains a DATA step with a MERGE statement, and edit the program to generate an e-mail for each employee to inform him that the total contribution was mailed. Under Windows and UNIX, name the file **donations.sas**. Under z/OS, name the file **.workshop.sascode(donations)**. Do not include the program file. However, open the program file to verify that it is correct.

p310e08

```
proc sort data=orion.employee_addresses out=employee_addresses;
   by Employee_ID;
run;

data _null_;
   merge orion.employee_donations(in=d) employee_addresses;
   by Employee_ID;
   if d;
run;
```

Partial Contents of **donations**

```
filename mail email 'Wanda.Branly@orion.com ' subject='Your Donation';
data _null_;
file mail;
   put 'Your donation of $25 has been sent to Mitleid International
      90%, Save the Baby Animals 10% ';
run;
filename mail email 'Belanda.Rink@orion.com ' subject='Your Donation';
data _null_;
file mail;
   put 'Your donation of $60 has been sent to Disaster Assist, Inc.
      80%, Cancer Cures, Inc. 20% ';
run;
```

Level 3

9. Writing PROC PRINT Steps Using SQL DICTIONARY Table Views

You can use the SQL procedure to obtain information about your SAS session. This information is stored in special tables called DICTIONARY tables that are only available in an SQL step. However, there are PROC SQL views, stored in the SASHELP library, that reference the DICTIONARY tables and that can be used in other SAS procedures and in the DATA step.

One of those views, **Sashelp.VCOLUMN**, contains information such as name, type, length, and format about all columns in all tables contained in currently assigned librefs.

a. Use the DATA step to read from **Sashelp.VCOLUMN** and create a program containing PROC PRINT steps that create reports for every data set in the **orion** library that contains the variable **Product_ID**. PROC PRINT should only print five observations from each of the data sets.

Hint: The variables in **Sashelp.VCOLUMN** that you need to use are as follows:

Name of Variable	Value of Variable	Use in the Program
LIBNAME	ORION	In a WHERE statement
COLUMN	Product_ID	In a WHERE statement
MEMNAME	The value you need to retrieve from **Sashelp.VCOLUMN**	In the DATA= option in the PROC PRINT statement and in the TITLE statement

The variable values in **Sashelp.VCOLUMN** are case sensitive.

The starter program **p310e09** can be used as a starting point for this exercise.

p310e09

```
data _null_;
   set sashelp.vcolumn;
   where Libname='ORION' and Name='Product_ID';
   file 'print_products.sas';
run;
```

b. Store the program in a file named **Print_Products.sas** under Windows and UNIX and **.workshop.sascode(Print_Products)** under z/OS.

Partial Contents of **Print_Products**

```
proc print data=ORION.CATALOG(obs=5);run;
title 'First Five Observations of ORION.CATALOG ';
run;
proc print data=ORION.DENMARK_CUSTOMERS(obs=5);run;
title 'First Five Observations of ORION.DENMARK_CUSTOMERS ';
run;
proc print data=ORION.FIRST_INTERNET_ORDER(obs=5);run;
title 'First Five Observations of ORION.FIRST_INTERNET_ORDER ';
run;
proc print data=ORION.INTERNET(obs=5);run;
title 'First Five Observations of ORION.INTERNET ';
run;
proc print data=ORION.MULTIPLE_ORDERS(obs=5);run;
title 'First Five Observations of ORION.MULTIPLE_ORDERS ';
run;
proc print data=ORION.NEW_PRODUCTS(obs=5);run;
title 'First Five Observations of ORION.NEW_PRODUCTS ';
run;
proc print data=ORION.ORDER_FACT(obs=5);run;
title 'First Five Observations of ORION.ORDER_FACT ';
run;
proc print data=ORION.PRICE_LIST(obs=5);run;
title 'First Five Observations of ORION.PRICE_LIST ';
run;
proc print data=ORION.PRICE_NEW(obs=5);run;
title 'First Five Observations of ORION.PRICE_NEW ';
run;
proc print data=ORION.PRODUCT_DIM(obs=5);run;
title 'First Five Observations of ORION.PRODUCT_DIM ';
run;
proc print data=ORION.PRODUCT_LIST(obs=5);run;
title 'First Five Observations of ORION.PRODUCT_LIST ';
run;
```

c. Use the %INCLUDE statement to execute the code or open the program to verify that it is correct. (You can use the SAS Editor window, PROC FSLIST, or Notepad to verify the contents of the program file.)

10.5 Using the FCMP Procedure (Self-Study)

Objectives

- List reasons to use the FCMP procedure.
- Examine the syntax for the FCMP procedure.
- Create functions using the FCMP procedure.
- Use the user-written functions.
- Create subroutines using the FCMP procedure.

151

The FCMP procedure is new for use in the DATA step in SAS 9.2.

Using PROC FCMP

PROC FCMP is a method of simplifying the repetitive use of business rules. PROC FCMP provides the following functionality:

- ability to write functions and CALL routines using DATA step syntax
- storage of these functions in a package within a SAS data set
- use of functions and subroutines previously defined in the current FCMP procedure step, as well as most DATA step functions, within the routines

✎ In SAS 9.2, these functions can be called from a DATA step.

152

Why Create a Function with PROC FCMP?

PROC FCMP creates programs that have the following attributes:

- **simpler** programs that are easier to read, write, and modify
- **independent** routines because any program that calls a routine is not affected by the routine's implementation
- **reusable** routines that can be called by any program that can read the data set where the routine is stored

153

Business Scenario

The marketing department at Orion needs to have a report created daily. The requirements are that the report must include a column that is the customer ID concatenated with a comment.

Partial Listing

Using the FCMP Procedure

Obs	Customer_ID	Delivery_ Date	Order_ Type	Marketing_Comment
1	63	11JAN2003	1	000000000063 - Mail In-Store Coupon
2	5	19JAN2003	2	000000000005 - Send New Catalog
3	45	22JAN2003	2	000000000045 - Send New Catalog
4	41	28JAN2003	1	000000000041 - Mail In-Store Coupon
5	183	27FEB2003	1	000000000183 - Mail In-Store Coupon

154

Example of PROC FCMP

```
proc fcmp outlib=orion.functions.Marketing;
   function MKT(ID, Date, Type) $ 40;
      if '01Jan2008'd - Date>90 then do;
         if Type=1 then return(catx(' - ',
            put(ID, z12.), 'Mail In-Store Coupon'));
         else if Type=2 then return(catx(' - ',
            put(ID, z12.), 'Send New Catalog'));
          else return(catx(' - ',
            put(ID, z12.),'Send Email'));
      end;
      else return(catx(' - ', put(ID, z12.),
        'Wait to Contact'));
   endsub;
run;
quit;
```

155 p310d21

The PROC FCMP Statement

```
proc fcmp outlib=orion.functions.Marketing;
```

General form of the PROC FCMP statement:

PROC FCMP OUTLIB= | OUTCAT=*libname.data-set.package*;

OUTLIB= | OUTCAT= *libname.data-set.package*	specifies the three-level name of an output package to which the compiled subroutines and functions are written when the PROC FCMP step ends.

⚠ The OUTLIB= | OUTCAT= argument is required.

156

The FUNCTION Statement

```
proc fcmp outlib=orion.functions.Marketing;
   function MKT(ID, Date, Type) $ 40;
```

- This code creates a function named **MKT** in a package named **Marketing**.
- The package is stored in the data set **orion.functions**.

A *package* is a collection of routines that have unique names.

157

The Function Definition

Within one PROC FCMP step, you can define multiple functions.

Each function definition consists of this block of code:

FUNCTION *name* (*parameter-1*, ...,
parameter-N);
program-statements;
RETURN (*expression*);
ENDSUB;

158

The FUNCTION Statement

```
function MKT(ID, Date, Type) $ 40;
```

General form of the FUNCTION statement:

FUNCTION *function-name*(*argument-1* <$>,
argument-2 <$>, ...,
argument-n <$>) <$> <*length*>;

function-name	specifies the name of the function.
argument	specifies one or more arguments in the function.
$	specifies a character value.
length	specifies the length of a character value.

159

The RETURN Statement

```
if '01Jan2008'd - Date > 90 then do;
   if Type=1 then return(catx(' - ',
      put(ID, z12.), 'Mail In-Store Coupon'));
      else if Type=2 then return(catx(' - ',
         put(ID, z12.), 'Send New Catalog'));
      else return(catx(' - ',
         put(ID, z12.), 'Send Email'));
   end;
   else return(catx(' - ', put(ID, z12.),
      'Wait to Contact'));
```

General form of the RETURN statement:

RETURN (*expression*);

expression	specifies the value that is returned from the function.

All functions **must** return a value.

160

The ENDSUB Statement

```
endsub;
```

General form of the ENDSUB statement:

```
ENDSUB;
```

The ENDSUB statement ends the function definition.

161

Using the Function

The functions created by PROC FCMP can be called within the following:

- the DATA step
- the COMPUTE block within a REPORT procedure step
- the SQL procedure
- selected SAS/STAT procedures
- selected SAS/ETS procedures
- SAS/OR procedures, such as the NLIN, MODEL, and NLP procedures

162

Support for PROC FCMP functions used in WHERE statements and PROC COMPUTAB was added in the platform for SAS Business Analytics 9.2 release.

Using a Function

```
options cmplib=orion.functions;

data temp;
   set orion.order_fact;
   Marketing_Comment=
      MKT(Customer_ID,Delivery_Date,Order_Type);
run;

proc print data=temp(obs=5);
   title 'Using the FCMP Procedure';
   var Customer_ID Delivery_Date
       Order_Type Marketing_Comment;
run;
```

163

p310d22

Using the FCMP Function

Partial Listing

Using the FCMP Procedure

Obs	Customer_ID	Delivery_ Date	Order_ Type	Marketing_Comment
1	63	11JAN2003	1	000000000063 - Mail In-Store Coupon
2	5	19JAN2003	2	000000000005 - Send New Catalog
3	45	22JAN2003	2	000000000045 - Send New Catalog
4	41	28JAN2003	1	000000000041 - Mail In-Store Coupon
5	183	27FEB2003	1	000000000183 - Mail In-Store Coupon

164

Using the Function

In order to use the function in a DATA step or supported PROC step, use the CMPLIB= SAS system option.

```
options cmplib=orion.functions;
```

General form of the CMPLIB= SAS system option:

CMPLIB=*libref.data-set* | (*libref. data-set-1* ... *libref. data-set-n*);

libref. data-set specifies the libref and data set name of the compiled subroutines that are to be included during the program compilation.

165

The order of the *libref.data-set* names in the list (*libref. data-set-1* ... *libref. data-set-n*) determines the order in which the data sets are searched.

Setup for the Quiz

```
proc fcmp outlib=orion.functions.Marketing;
   function MKT(ID, Date, Type) $ 40;
      if '01Jan2008'd - Date > 90 then do;
         if Type=1 then return(catx(' - ',
            put(ID, z12.), 'Mail In-Store Coupon'));
         else if Type=2 then return(catx(' - ',
            put(ID, z12.), 'Send New Catalog'));
         else return(catx(' - ',
            put(ID, z12.), 'Send Email'));
      end;
      else return(catx(' - ', put(ID, z12.),
        'Wait to Contact'));
   endsub;
run;
quit;
```

167

10.13 Quiz

Specify the argument of the MKT function that corresponds to the each of following variables:

Variable	Argument
Customer_ID	
Delivery_Date	
Order_Type	

```
options cmplib=orion.functions;
data temp;
   set orion.order_fact;
   Marketing_Comment =
     MKT(Customer_ID,Delivery_Date,Order_Type);
run;
```

168

Business Scenario

You need to create two functions.

Function Name	Use of Function
MONDAY	takes a SAS date as the argument and creates a SAS date for the Monday of that week.
FRIDAY	takes a SAS date as the argument and creates a SAS date for the Friday of that week.

```
proc fcmp outlib=orion.functions.DateType;
   function MONDAY(Date);
      return(intnx('week.2', Date, 0));
   endsub;
   function FRIDAY(Date);
      return(intnx('week.7', Date, 1)- 1);
   endsub;
run;
quit;
```

170 p310d23

Using the INTNX Function

You can create multiples of intervals and shift their starting points to construct more complex interval specifications by using multipliers and shift indexes in the INTNX function.

General form of the INTNX function:

INTNX(*interval<multiple><.shift-index>*, *start-from*, *increment<,alignment>*)

interval<multiple><.shift-index>

171

Using the INTNX Function

```
date='01jan2008'd;
```

Tuesday, January 1, 2008

Function	Result
`INTNX('week',Date,0)`	Sunday, December 30, 2007
`INTNX('week.2',Date,0)`	Monday, December 31, 2007
`INTNX('week2',Date,0)`	Sunday, December 23, 2007
`INTNX('week2.2',Date,0)`	Monday, December 24, 2007
`INTNX('week.6',Date,1)`	Friday, January 4, 2008
`INTNX('week.7',Date,1)`	Saturday, January 5, 2008
`INTNX('week.7',Date,1)-1`	Friday, January 4, 2008

172

Business Scenario

The data set **`orion.Order_Fact`** contains the delivery date and order number for customer orders. If the delivery date is on Saturday or Sunday, the order will be delivered on Saturday. However, if the delivery date is a weekday, then the order will be delivered on some day between Monday and Friday in that week.

Partial Listing

Delivery Information

Customer	Order Number	When you can expect your delivery
4	1232410925	Between Monday, March 1, 2004 and Friday, March 5, 2004
	1232455720	Between Monday, March 8, 2004 and Friday, March 12, 2004
	1232530384	Saturday, March 20, 2004
	1232654929	Between Monday, April 5, 2004 and Friday, April 9, 2004
	1232709099	Between Monday, April 12, 2004 and Friday, April 16, 2004
	1232998740	Saturday, May 29, 2004
	1233543560	Between Monday, August 16, 2004 and Friday, August 20, 2004
	1234348668	Saturday, December 18, 2004
5	1230080101	Saturday, January 18, 2003

173

Creating and Using Functions

p310d23

```
proc fcmp outlib=orion.functions.DateType;
   function MONDAY(Date);
   return(intnx('week.2', Date, 0));
endsub;
   function FRIDAY(Date);
   return(intnx('week.7', Date, 1)-1);
endsub;
run;
quit;

option cmplib=orion.functions;

proc report data=orion.Order_Fact ls=120
            headline headskip nowd;
   title 'Delivery Information';
   column Customer_ID Order_ID Delivery_Date
          Expect_Delivery;
   define Customer_ID / group width =10 'Customer';
   define Delivery_Date / group  noprint;
   define Order_ID / group 'Order Number' width=12;
   define Expect_Delivery / computed
                            'When you can expect your delivery'
                             width=70 center;
   compute Expect_Delivery / char length=70;
      First_Of_Week=MONDAY(Delivery_Date);
      End_Of_Week=FRIDAY(Delivery_Date);
      if weekday(Delivery_Date) not in (1, 7) then
         Expect_Delivery=catx(' ', 'Between',
                                 put(First_Of_Week, weekdate.),
                                'and', put(End_Of_Week, weekdate.));
      else if weekday(Delivery_Date)=1 then
         Expect_Delivery=put(Delivery_Date - 1, weekdate.);
      else Expect_Delivery=put(Delivery_Date, weekdate.);
   endcomp;
   break after Customer_ID / skip;
run;
```

Partial Listing

Delivery Information

Customer	Order Number	When you can expect your delivery
4	1232410925	Between Monday, March 1, 2004 and Friday, March 5, 2004
	1232455720	Between Monday, March 8, 2004 and Friday, March 12, 2004
	1232530384	Saturday, March 20, 2004
	1232654929	Between Monday, April 5, 2004 and Friday, April 9, 2004
	1232709099	Between Monday, April 12, 2004 and Friday, April 16, 2004
	1232998740	Saturday, May 29, 2004
	1233543560	Between Monday, August 16, 2004 and Friday, August 20, 2004
	1234348668	Saturday, December 18, 2004
5	1230080101	Saturday, January 18, 2003
	1231663230	Between Monday, October 27, 2003 and Friday, October 31, 2003
	1231842118	Between Monday, December 1, 2003 and Friday, December 5, 2003
	1231950921	Between Monday, December 22, 2003 and Friday, December 26, 2003
	1231956902	Between Monday, December 22, 2003 and Friday, December 26, 2003
	1232007693	Saturday, January 3, 2004
	1232728634	Between Monday, April 19, 2004 and Friday, April 23, 2004
	1233315988	Between Monday, July 12, 2004 and Friday, July 16, 2004
	1233682051	Between Monday, September 13, 2004 and Friday, September 17, 2004
	1237890730	Between Monday, December 5, 2005 and Friday, December 9, 2005
	1242140006	Between Monday, May 7, 2007 and Friday, May 11, 2007
	1242159212	Between Monday, May 7, 2007 and Friday, May 11, 2007
	1242493791	Saturday, June 9, 2007
	1243315613	Saturday, September 8, 2007
	1244296274	Between Monday, December 24, 2007 and Friday, December 28, 2007
9	1232698281	Between Monday, April 19, 2004 and Friday, April 23, 2004
	1236028541	Saturday, June 11, 2005
	1236673732	Between Monday, August 15, 2005 and Friday, August 19, 2005
	1237825036	Between Monday, December 5, 2005 and Friday, December 9, 2005
	1238053337	Between Monday, December 26, 2005 and Friday, December 30, 2005

Advantages of PROC FCMP

Advantages of Using the FCMP Procedure
A library of reusable routines can be built using DATA step syntax.
Complex programs can be simplified by abstracting common computations into named program units.
FCMP routines are independent from their use and can be reused in any DATA step program that has access to their storage locations.
FCMP routines enable programmers to read, write, and maintain complex code easily.

175

Disadvantages of PROC FCMP

Disadvantages of Using the FCMP Procedure
User-written functions and routines can only be used in the DATA step, COMPUTE blocks in PROC REPORT, PROC SQL, and selected procedures in SAS/STAT, SAS/ETS, and SAS/OR.
Knowledge of the FCMP syntax is needed.

176

Creating Subroutines Using PROC FCMP

To create a subroutine using the FCMP procedure, use the following syntax:

```
SUBROUTINE subroutine-name (argument-1,..., argument-n);
    OUTARGS out-argument-1, ..., out-argument-n;
    ... more-program-statements ...
ENDSUB;
```

subroutine-name	specifies the name of a subroutine.
argument	specifies one or more arguments in the subroutine.
out-argument	specifies arguments from the argument list that you want the subroutine to update.

177

Support for PROC FCMP subroutines used in %SYSFUNC and %SYSCALL macro functions, ODS tagsets, and the Graph Template Language was added in the platform for SAS Business Analytics 9.2 release.

Difference between Functions and CALL Routines

Functions	Call Routines
Can require arguments and must return a value.	Do not return a value and can modify their parameters.
All parameters are passed by value. This means that the value of the actual parameter, the variable, or the value passed to the function from the calling environment is copied before being used by the function. This ensures that any modification of the formal parameter by the function does not change the original value.	The formal parameters listed in the OUTARGS statement are passed by reference instead of by value. This means that any modification of the formal parameter by the CALL routine modifies the original variable that was passed.

178

Creating Subroutines Using PROC FCMP

p310d24

```
proc fcmp outlib=orion.functions.Directory;
function DIROPEN(DIR$);
   length DIR$ 256 FREF $ 8;
   rc=filename(FREF, DIR);
   if rc=0 then do;
      DID=dopen(FREF);
      rc=filename(FREF);
   end;
   else do;
      MSG=sysMSG();
      put MSG '(DIROPEN(' DIR= ')';
      DID=.;
   end;
   return(DID);
endsub;

subroutine DIRCLOSE(DID);
   outargs DID;
   rc=dCLOSE(DID);
   DID=.;
endsub;

subroutine DIR_entries(DIR$, FILES[*] $, N, TRUNC);
   outargs FILES, N, TRUNC;
   length DIRentry $ 256;
   if TRUNC then return;
   DID=DIROPEN(DIR);
   if DID <= 0 then return;
   dnum=dnum(DID);
   do i=1 to DNUM;
      ENTRY=dread(DID, i);
```

(Continued on the next page.)

```
/* If this entry is a file, then add to array */
/* Else ENTRY is a directory, recurse.        */
      FID=mopen(DID, ENTRY);
      ENTRY=trim(DIR) || '\' || ENTRY;
      if FID > 0 then do;
         rc=fCLOSE(FID);
         if n < dim(FILES) then do;
            TRUNC=0;
            N=N + 1;
            FILES{N}=ENTRY;
         end;
         else do;
            DIR=1;
            call DIRCLOSE(DID);
            return;
         end;
      end;
      else
         call DIR_entries(ENTRY, FILES, N, TRUNC);
   end;
   call DIRCLOSE(DID);
   return;
endsub;
run;

options cmplib=orion.functions;

data _null_;
   array FILES[1000] $ 256 _temporary_;
   DNUM=0;
   TRUNC=0;
   call DIR_entries(".", FILES, DNUM, TRUNC);
   if TRUNC then put 'ERROR: Not enough result array entries.

increase array size.';
   do i=1 to DNUM;
      put FILES{i};
   end;
run;
```

Partial SAS Log

```
options cmplib=orion.functions;
data _null_;
   array files[1000] $ 256 _temporary_;
   DNUM=0;
   TRUNC=0;
   call dir_entries("S:\Workshop\", FILES, DNUM,
trunc);
   if trunc then put 'ERROR: Not enough result array entries.
Increase array size.';
   do i=1 to DNUM;
      put files[i];
   end;
run;

S:\Workshop\city.sas7bdat
S:\Workshop\continent.sas7bdat
S:\Workshop\country.sas7bdat
S:\Workshop\county.sas7bdat
S:\Workshop\customer.sas7bdat
S:\Workshop\customer_dim.sas7bdat
S:\Workshop\customer_type.sas7bdat
S:\Workshop\discount.sas7bdat
S:\Workshop\employee_addresses.sas7bdat
S:\Workshop\employee_organization.sas7bdat
S:\Workshop\employee_payroll.sas7bdat
S:\Workshop\employee_phones.sas7bdat
S:\Workshop\funcs.sas7bdat
S:\Workshop\funcs.sas7bndx
S:\Workshop\functions.sas7bdat
S:\Workshop\functions.sas7bndx
S:\Workshop\geography_dim.sas7bdat
S:\Workshop\geo_type.sas7bdat
S:\Workshop\lookup_agegroup.sas7bdat
S:\Workshop\lookup_country.sas7bdat
S:\Workshop\lookup_custgrp.sas7bdat
S:\Workshop\lookup_euday.sas7bdat
S:\Workshop\lookup_order_type.sas7bdat
S:\Workshop\lookup_product.sas7bdat
S:\Workshop\lookup_usday.sas7bdat
S:\Workshop\orders.sas7bdat
S:\Workshop\order_fact.sas7bdat
S:\Workshop\order_item.sas7bdat
S:\Workshop\organization.sas7bdat
S:\Workshop\organization_dim.sas7bdat
S:\Workshop\org_level.sas7bdat
S:\Workshop\postal_code.sas7bdat
S:\Workshop\price_list.sas7bdat
S:\Workshop\product_dim.sas7bdat
S:\Workshop\product_level.sas7bdat
S:\Workshop\product_list.sas7bdat
S:\Workshop\staff.sas7bdat
S:\Workshop\state.sas7bdat
S:\Workshop\street_code.sas7bdat
S:\Workshop\supplier.sas7bdat
S:\Workshop\time_dim.sas7bdat
```

Your results might show a different path.

DATA Step Functions Used in the Demonstration

filename	assigns or de-assigns a fileref to an external file, directory, or output device.
dopen	opens a directory using a previously assigned fileref and returns a directory identifier value.
sysmsg	returns the text of error messages or warning messages from the last data set or external file function executed.
dclose	closes a directory that was opened by the DOPEN function.
dnum	returns the number of members in a directory.
dread	returns the name of a directory member.
mopen	opens a file by directory ID and member name, and returns the file identifier or a 0.
fclose	closes an external file, directory, or directory member.

180

Using Arrays in PROC FCMP

You can use arrays in PROC FCMP.

- The ARRAY statement in PROC FCMP is similar to the ARRAY statement that is used in the DATA step.
- In FCMP routines, arrays can be resized. This is done by calling the built-in CALL routine DYNAMIC_ARRAY.

When you reference an array, square braces [ ] or curly braces { } **must** be used.

181

The Scope of Argument Variables in User-Defined Functions

The scope of argument variables in user-defined functions is as follows:

- A variable's *scope* is the section of code where a variable's value can be used.
- Variables declared outside of routines created by PROC FCMP are not accessible inside a routine.
- Variables declared inside a routine are not accessible outside of the routine. Variables declared within a routine are called *local variables* because their scope is “local” to the routine.

Local variables store intermediate results of a computation and cannot be accessed after a routine returns.

182

Exercises

Level 1

10. Using the FCMP Procedure to Store a Formula in a Function

a. Open the program **p310e10** and submit it.

p310e10

```
data test;
   set orion.order_fact(keep=Employee_ID Quantity
                             Total_Retail_Price);
   if Quantity > 2 then
      Kick_Back_Amt=Quantity * Total_Retail_Price / 5;
   else Kick_Back_Amt=Quantity * Total_Retail_Price / 10;
run;

proc print data=test(obs=5);
run;
```

b. Use PROC FCMP to encapsulate the IF/THEN logic into a function named **KB**. Store the function in **work.functions.Marketing**.

c. Write a DATA step to create a data set named **kick_backs** that uses the KB function to create a variable named **Kick_Back_Amt**. Set the appropriate system option so that the new function can be utilized. The DATA step should **not** contain any IF/THEN logic.

d. Print the first five observations of the SAS data set **kick_backs**.

PROC PRINT Output

Obs	Employee_ID	Quantity	Total_Retail_ Price	Kick_ Back_Amt
1	121039	1	$16.50	1.65
2	99999999	1	$247.50	24.75
3	99999999	1	$28.30	2.83
4	120174	2	$32.00	6.40
5	120134	3	$63.60	38.16

Level 2

11. Using the FCMP Procedure to Store a Date Calculation in a Function

The INTCK function can be used to calculate the differences between two dates, but it does not take into consideration whether either of the dates is a leap year date (February 29). If that is important to your date calculations, the following formula can be used. (An explanation of the formula is at the end of the exercise description.)

```
intck('year',BirthDate,ActualDate)
      -(put(BirthDate,mmddyy4.) gt put(ActualDate,mmddyy4.))
      +(put(BirthDate,mmddyy4.)||put(ActualDate,mmddyy4.)||
        put(ActualDate+1,mmddyy4.)='022902280301')
```

a. Open the program **p310e11** that contains the formula and a DATA step that generates test data.

p310e11

```
data real_ages;
   do Birth_Date='28feb1960'd to '01mar1960'd;
      do Actual_Date='28feb2004'd to '01mar2004'd,
                     '28feb2005'd to '01mar2005'd;

         /* Calculate Real Age */

         Age=intck('year', Birth_Date, Actual_Date);
         output;
      end;
   end;
   format Birth_Date Actual_Date worddate.;
run;

proc print data=real_ages;
   var Birth_Date Actual_Date Age;
   title1 'Age Calculations based using INTCK';
run;
```

b. Write a PROC FCMP step that creates a function named AGE that contains the formula. Store the function in `work.functions.Marketing`.

c. Add an assignment statement to the DATA step in **p310e11** that creates a variable named `Real_Age` using the AGE function and a variable named `Age` using the INTCK function.

d. Print the data to ensure that the function is correctly calculating **`Real_Age`**.

PROC PRINT Output

Age Calculations based using INTCK

Obs	Birth_Date	Actual_Date	Real_Age	Age
1	February 28, 1960	February 28, 2004	44	44
2	February 28, 1960	February 29, 2004	44	44
3	February 28, 1960	March 1, 2004	44	44
4	February 28, 1960	February 28, 2005	45	45
5	February 28, 1960	March 1, 2005	45	45
6	February 29, 1960	February 28, 2004	43	44
7	February 29, 1960	February 29, 2004	44	44
8	February 29, 1960	March 1, 2004	44	44
9	February 29, 1960	February 28, 2005	45	45
10	February 29, 1960	March 1, 2005	45	45
11	March 1, 1960	February 28, 2004	43	44
12	March 1, 1960	February 29, 2004	43	44
13	March 1, 1960	March 1, 2004	44	44
14	March 1, 1960	February 28, 2005	44	45
15	March 1, 1960	March 1, 2005	45	45

e. Create a data set named **`customer_ages`** from the **`orion.customer_dim`** data set. The new data set should contain a new variable named **`Real_Age`** using the AGE function with **`Customer_BirthDate`** as the **`Birth_Date`** variable and `01JAN2008` as the value of **`Actual_Date`**. The new data set should also contain a new variable named **`Age`** calculated using the INTCK function. Print the first five observations of **`customer_ages`**.

✎ There is a variable, **`Customer_Age`**, in the data set **`orion.customer_dim`**. Do **not** use this variable.

PROC PRINT Output

Age Calculations based on Calendar-Based Algorithm

Obs	Customer_ID	Customer_Name	Customer_ BirthDate
1	4	James Kvarniq	June 27, 1974
2	5	Sandrina Stephano	July 9, 1979
3	9	Cornelia Krahl	February 27, 1974
4	10	Karen Ballinger	October 18, 1984
5	11	Elke Wallstab	August 16, 1974

Obs	Customer_Group	Real_Age	Age
1	Orion Club members	33	34
2	Orion Club Gold members	28	29
3	Orion Club Gold members	33	34
4	Orion Club members	23	24
5	Orion Club members	33	34

Explanation of the Formula Used in This Exercise

The following describes the syntax when `BirthDate='29FEB2008'D` and `ActualDate='28FEB2009'd`:

- `intck('year', BirthDate, ActualDate)` returns the number of January firsts (1st) between the two dates. In this example, there is one January 1st between the two dates.
- `put(BirthDate, mmddyy4.) gt put(ActualDate, mmddyy4.)` determines if the birthday is later than the actual day. If the expression is true, it returns a 1; if false, a 0. Because 0229 > 0203, the expression returns a 1. In this example, `0229 gt 0228` is true, so 1 is subtracted from the number of years returned from the INTCK formula.
- `put(BirthDate,mmddyy4.)||put(ActualDate,mmddyy4.)|| put(ActualDate+1,mmddyy4.)='022902280301'` compares the text value `022902280301` to `022902280301`. If the expression is true, it returns a 1; if false, a 0. In this case, the expression is true, so 1 is added to the number of years returned from the INTCK formula.

Level 3

12. Creating a Function Using DATA SAS File I/O Functions

a. Use PROC FCMP to create a function named NUMS that takes one argument, which is the name of a SAS data set, and returns the number of logical observations in the data set. Refer to SAS OnlineDoc or the SAS Help facility to determine which SAS file I/O functions are required.

b. Open the program **p310e12** and submit it. Look in the log to ensure that the function is working correctly.

p310e12

```
data _null_;
   X=NUMS('orion.internet');
   put X=;
run;
```

Partial SAS Log

```
218  data _null_;
219     X=NUMS('orion.Internet');
220     put X=;
221  run;
X=123
```

10.6 Chapter Review

Chapter Review

1. What are two parts of the macro facility?

2. What is the purpose of the FILEVAR= option in the INFILE statement?

3. What does the INTNX function do?

185

Chapter Review

4. What is the difference between a SAS data file and a SAS data view?

187

continued...

Chapter Review

5. Why would you use the FILE statement?

6. What is the purpose of the PUT statement?

189

10.7 Solutions

Solutions to Exercises

1. **Using the FILENAME Statement**

   a. Open the program **p310e01**.

   b. Use the FILENAME statement to concatenate the three raw data files.

   c. Modify the DATA step to use the fileref created in part **b** to create the SAS data set **all_levels**.

   d. Print the **all_levels** data set.

   p310s01

```
filename levels ('level_1.dat' 'level_2.dat' 'level_3.dat');

data all_levels;
   length Customer_Name $ 40 Customer_Age_Group $ 12
      Customer_Type $ 40 Customer_Group $ 40;
   infile levels dlm=',';
   input Customer_Name $ Customer_Age_Group $ Customer_Type $
         Customer_Group $;
run;

proc print data=all_levels;
run;
```

2. **Using the FILEVAR= Option to Read from Raw Data**

   a. Open the program **p310e02**.

   b. Use the FILEVAR= option to concatenate the three raw data files and create the SAS data set **all_levels**.

c. Print the `all_levels` data set.

p310s02

```
data all_levels;
   drop i;
   length Customer_Name $ 40 Customer_Age_Group $ 12
          Customer_Type $ 40 Customer_Group $ 40;
   do i=1 to 3;
      NextFile=cats('level_', i, '.dat');  *  Windows and UNIX;
      infile levels filevar=NextFile dlm=','
                      end=Last;
      do while (Last=0);
         input Customer_Name $ Customer_Age_Group $
               Customer_Type $
               Customer_Group $;
         output;
      end;
   end;
   stop;
run;

proc print data=all_levels;
run;
```

3. Using the FILEVAR= Option to Read Filenames from a SAS Data Set

a. Use the FILEVAR= option to create a SAS data set named `All_Months` from the raw data files named in `orion.month_file`.

b. Print the first 10 observations of the `All_Months` SAS data set.

p310s03

```
data all_months;
   set orion.month_file;
   format Order_Date Delivery_Date date9.;
   infile ORD filevar=File_Name dlm=','
              end=LastObs;
   do while (not LastObs);
      input Customer_ID Order_ID Order_Type
            Order_Date : date9. Delivery_Date : Date9.;
      output;
   end;
run;

proc print data=all_months;
run;
```

4. Creating a DATA Step View

a. Create a view named **cc_donations**.

1) Read only the observations from the data set **orion.employee_donations** where the value of the variable **Paid_By** is Credit Card.

2) Create a variable named **Total_Donations** as the total of the variables **Qtr1**, **Qtr2**, **Qtr3**, and **Qtr4**.

3) Create a new variable **Donation_Category** with the following values:

Value of Total_Donations	Donation_Category
Less than 100	Less than $100
Greater than or equal 100	$100 or more

b. Open and submit the program **p310e04** to create a report from the view **cc_donations**. Use the variable **Donation_Category** as a class variable and the variable **Total_Donations** as an analysis variable. Verify that the view was created correctly.

p310s04

```
data cc_donations / view=cc_donations;
   set orion.employee_donations;
   length Donation_Category $15;
   where Paid_By='Credit Card';
   Total_Donations=sum(of Qtr1-Qtr4);
   if Total_Donations >= 100 then
      Donation_Category='$100 or more';
   else Donation_Category='Less than $100';
run;

proc means data=cc_donations sum n nonobs maxdec=2;
   class Donation_Category;
   var Total_Donations;
run;
```

5. Creating a View and a File in One DATA Step

a. In one DATA step, create a view named **younger60** and a file named **older60**.

b. Read from the data set **orion.employee_payroll**.

c. Use the variable **Birth_Date** to calculate each employee's age as of today.

- The view should contain the employees who are younger than 60.
- The file should contain the employees who are 60 or older.

p310s05

```
data older60 younger60 / view=younger60;
   set orion.employee_payroll;
   Age=int(yrdif(Birth_Date, today(),'act/act'));
   if Age >= 60 then output older60;
   else output younger60;
   format Birth_Date Employee_Hire_Date Employee_Term_Date
          date9.;
run;
```

d. Attempt to print the file **older60** unsuccessfully.

p310s05

```
proc print data=older60;
   title 'Older60 Data Set';
run;
```

SAS Log

```
22    proc print data=older60;
ERROR: File WORK.OLDER60.DATA does not exist.
23    title 'Older60 Data Set';
24    run;

NOTE: The SAS System stopped processing this step because of errors.
NOTE: PROCEDURE PRINT used (Total process time):
      real time           0.06 seconds
      cpu time            0.01 seconds
```

e. Print the view **younger60**.

p310s05

```
proc print data=younger60;
   title 'Younger60 Data Set';
run;
```

f. Print the file **older60** successfully.

p310s05

```
proc print data=older60;
   title 'Older60 Data Set';
run;
```

g. Why could you not print **older60** in step **d**?

The file is not created until the view is executed. When you printed the view in part **e**, the file was generated.

6. Creating a View with the SQL Procedure and the USING Clause

a. Open the program **p310e06** and edit it to assign the libref with the USING clause.

p310s06

```
proc sql;
   create view orion.payroll_donations as
      select Employee_ID, Qtr1, Qtr2, Qtr3, Qtr4,
             sum(Qtr1, Qtr2, Qtr3, Qtr4) as Total_Donations
      from orion.employee_donations
      where Paid_By='Payroll Deduction'
      using libname orion 's:\Workshop';
quit;
```

b. Submit a LIBNAME statement to assign a libref of `sasdata` to the library specified in the table above.

p310s06

```
libname sasdata '.'; *Windows/UNIX;
*libname sasdata '.prg3.sasdata'; *z/OS;
*libname sasdata 's:\workshop'; *Windows;
```

c. Submit a PROC PRINT step to print the view `sasdata.payroll_donations`.

p310s06

```
proc print data=sasdata.payroll_donations;
run;
```

d. Submit a LIBNAME statement to clear the `sasdata` libref.

p310s06

```
libname sasdata clear;
```

7. Creating Two SAS Programs with One DATA Step

a. Write a DATA step to build the two PROC FORMAT steps. Under Windows and UNIX, name the files **Customer_Type.sas** and **Customer_Group.sas**. Under z/OS, name the files **.workshop.sascode(Customer_Type)** and **.workshop.sascode(Customer_Group)**.

p310s07

```
data _null_;
   set orion.customer_type end=LastObs;
   by Customer_Group_ID;
   file 'customer_type.sas';  *  Windows and UNIX;
*  file '.workshop.sascode(custtype)';  *  z/OS;
   if _N_=1 then put 'proc format fmtlib; value TypLevl ';
   Value=put(Customer_Type_ID, 12.);
   Label=put(Customer_Type, $quote50.);
   put Value '=' Label ;
   if LastObs then put ';run;';
   file 'customer_group.sas';  *  Windows and UNIX;
*  file '.workshop.sascode(cusgroup)';  *  z/OS;
   if _N_=1 then put 'proc format fmtlib; value GrpLevl ';
   Value=put(Customer_Group_ID, 4.);
   Label=put(Customer_Group, $quote40.);
   if first.Customer_Group_ID then put Value '=' Label ;
   if LastObs then put ';run;';
run;
```

b. Use the %INCLUDE statement to execute the code.

p310s07

```
/* Windows and UNIX */
%include 'Customer_Type.sas'/source2;
%include 'Customer_Group.sas'/source2;

/* z/OS */
%include '.workshop.sascode(Customer_Type)'/source2;
%include '.workshop.sascode(Customer_Group)'/source2;
```

SAS Log

```
95   %include 'Customer_Type.sas'/source2;
NOTE: %INCLUDE (level 1) file Customer_Type.sas is file S:\workshop\Customer_Type.sas.
96  +proc format fmtlib;
97  +value TypLevl
98  +1010 ="Orion Club members inactive"
99  +1020 ="Orion Club members low activity"
100  +1030 ="Orion  Club members medium activity"
101 +1040 ="Orion  Club members high activity"
102 +2010 ="Orion Club Gold members low activity"
103 +2020 ="Orion Club Gold members medium activity"
104 +2030 ="Orion Club Gold members high activity"
105 +3010 ="Internet/Catalog Customers"
106 +;
NOTE: Format TYPLEVL has been output.
106!+ run;

NOTE: PROCEDURE FORMAT used (Total process time):
      real time           0.23 seconds
      cpu time            0.04 seconds

NOTE: %INCLUDE (level 1) ending.
106
107  %include 'Customer_Group.sas'/source2;
NOTE: %INCLUDE (level 1) file Customer_Group.sas is file S:\workshop\Customer_Group.sas.
108 +proc format fmtlib;
109 +value GrpLevl
110 +10 ="Orion Club members"
111 +20 ="Orion Club Gold members"
112 +30 ="Internet/Catalog Customers"
113 +;
NOTE: Format GRPLEVL has been output.
113!+ run;

NOTE: PROCEDURE FORMAT used (Total process time):
      real time           0.00 seconds
      cpu time            0.00 seconds

NOTE: %INCLUDE (level 1) ending.
```

PROC FORMAT Output

```
      FORMAT NAME: GRPLEVL LENGTH:   26   NUMBER OF VALUES:    3
   MIN LENGTH:   1  MAX LENGTH:  40  DEFAULT LENGTH  26  FUZZ:        0
```

START	END	LABEL (VER. V7|V8 18FEB2008:18:08:41)
10	10	Orion Club members
20	20	Orion Club Gold members
30	30	Internet/Catalog Customers

```
      FORMAT NAME: TYPLEVL LENGTH:   39   NUMBER OF VALUES:    8
   MIN LENGTH:   1  MAX LENGTH:  40  DEFAULT LENGTH  39  FUZZ:        0
```

START	END	LABEL (VER. V7|V8 18FEB2008:18:08:41)
1010	1010	Orion Club members inactive
1020	1020	Orion Club members low activity
1030	1030	Orion Club members medium activity
1040	1040	Orion Club members high activity
2010	2010	Orion Club Gold members low activity
2020	2020	Orion Club Gold members medium activity
2030	2030	Orion Club Gold members high activity
3010	3010	Internet/Catalog Customers

8. Sending e-Mail Using the DATA Step

Open the program **p310e08**, which contains a DATA step with a MERGE statement, and edit the program to generate e-mails for each employee informing him that the total contribution was mailed. Under Windows and UNIX, name the file **donations.sas**. Under z/OS, name the files **.workshop.sascode(donations)**. Do not include the program file. However, open the program file to verify that it is correct.

p310s08

```
proc sort data=orion.employee_addresses out=employee_addresses;
   by Employee_ID;
run;

data _null_;
   merge orion.employee_donations(in=D) employee_addresses;
   by Employee_ID;
   if D;
   Total_Donation=sum(of Qtr1-Qtr4);
   Email=compress(scan(Employee_Name,2,',')||'.'
                  ||scan(Employee_Name,1,',')||'@orion.com');
   file 'donations.sas';
   put "filename mail email '" Email "' subject='Your Donation';";
   put 'data _null_;';
   put 'file mail;';
   put "put 'Your donation of " Total_Donation dollar3.
       " has been sent to " Recipients "';";
   put 'run;';
run;
```

Open the program file, **donations.sas**, to verify that it is correct.

Partial Contents of **donation.sas**

```
filename mail email 'Wanda.Branly@orion.com ' subject='Your Donation';
data _null_;
file mail;
   put 'Your donation of $25 has been sent to Mitleid International
      90%, Save the Baby Animals 10% ';
run;
filename mail email 'Belanda.Rink@orion.com ' subject='Your Donation';
data _null_;
file mail;
   put 'Your donation of $60 has been sent to Disaster Assist, Inc.
      80%, Cancer Cures, Inc. 20% ';
run;
```

9. Writing PROC PRINT Steps Using SQL Dictionary Table Views

a. Use the DATA step to read from **Sashelp.VCOLUMN** and create a program containing PROC PRINT steps that create reports for every data set in the **orion** library that contains the variable **Product_ID**. PROC PRINT should only print five observations from each of the data sets.

b. Store the program in a file named **Print_Products.sas** under Windows and UNIX and **.workshop.sascode(Print_Products)** under z/OS.

p310s09

```
data _null_;
   set sashelp.vcolumn;
   where Libname='ORION' and Name='Product_ID';
   file 'print_products.sas';  *  Windows and UNIX;
/* file '.workshop.sascode(prinprod)';  *  z/OS;  */
   Prt=cats(Libname, '.', Memname);
   Pgm_Line=catt('proc print data=', Prt, '(obs=5);');
   Title=catx(' ', "title 'First Five Observations of", Prt,
              "';");
   put Pgm_Line;
   put Title;
   put 'run;';
run;
```

c. Use the %INCLUDE statement to execute the code or open the program to verify that it is correct.

p310s09

```
/* Windows and UNIX */
%include 'Print_Products.sas'/source2;

/* z/OS */
%include '.workshop.sascode(Print_Products)'/source2;
```

10. Using the FCMP Procedure to Store a Formula in a Function

a. Open the program **p310e10** and submit it.

b. Use PROC FCMP to encapsulate the IF/THEN logic into a function named **KB**. Store the function in **work.functions.Marketing**.

p310s10

```
proc fcmp outlib=work.functions.Marketing;
   function KB(Quantity, Price);
   if Quantity > 2 then return(Quantity * Price / 5);
   else return(Quantity * Price / 10);
endsub;
run;
quit;
```

c. Write a DATA step to create a data set named **kick_backs** that uses the KB function to create a variable named **Kick_Back_Amt**. The DATA step should **not** contain any IF/THEN logic.

p310s10

```
options cmplib=work.functions;

data kick_backs;
   set orion.order_fact(keep=Employee_ID Quantity
                               Total_Retail_Price);
   Kick_Back_Amt=KB(Quantity, Total_Retail_Price);
run;
```

d. Print the first five observations of the SAS data set **kick_backs**.

p310s10

```
proc print data=kick_backs (obs=5);
run;
```

11. Using the FCMP Procedure to Store a Date Calculation in a Function

a. Open the program **p310e11** that contains the formula and a DATA step that generates test data.

b. Write a PROC FCMP step that creates a function named AGE that contains the formula. Store the function in **work.functions.Marketing**.

p310s11

```
proc fcmp outlib=work.functions.Marketing;
  function AGE(BirthDate, ActualDate);
  return(intck('year', BirthDate, ActualDate)
       -(put(BirthDate, mmddyy4.) gt put(ActualDate, mmddyy4.))
       +(put(BirthDate, mmddyy4.)||put(ActualDate, mmddyy4.)||
       put(ActualDate + 1, mmddyy4.)='022902280301')
        );
  endsub;
run;
quit;
```

c. Add an assignment statement to the DATA step in **p310e11** that creates a variable named **Real_Age** using the AGE function and a variable named **Age** by using the INTCK function.

p310s11

```
options cmplib=work.functions;

data real_ages;
   do Birth_Date='28feb1960'd to '01mar1960'd;
      do Actual_Date='28feb2004'd to '01mar2004'd,
                     '28feb2005'd to '01mar2005'd;
         Real_Age=AGE (Birth_Date, Actual_Date);
         Age=intck('year', Birth_Date, Actual_Date);
         output;
      end;
   end;
   format Birth_Date Actual_Date worddate.;
run;
```

d. Print the data to ensure that the function is correctly calculating **Real_Age**.

p310s11

```
proc print data=real_ages;
   var Birth_Date Actual_Date Real_Age Age;
   title1 'Age Calculations using INTCK';
run;
```

e. Create a data set named **customer_ages** from the **orion.customer_dim** data set. The new data set should contain a new variable named **Real_Age** using the AGE function with **Customer_BirthDate** as the **Birth_Date** variable and **01JAN2008** as the value of **Actual_Date**. The new data set should also contain a new variable named **Age** calculated using the INTCK function. Print the first five observations of **customer_ages**.

p310s11

```
data customer_ages;
   set orion.customer_dim(keep=Customer_ID Customer_Name
                           Customer_Group Customer_BirthDate);
   Real_Age=AGE(Customer_BirthDate,'01jan2008'd);
   Age=intck('year',Customer_BirthDate,'01jan2008'd);
   format Customer_BirthDate worddate.;
run;

proc print data=customer_ages(obs=5);
   title1 'Age Calculations using INTCK;
run;
```

12. Creating a Function Using DATA SAS File I/O Functions

a. Use PROC FCMP to create a function named NUMS that takes one argument, which is the name of a SAS data set, and returns the number of logical observations in the data set. Refer to SAS OnlineDoc or the SAS Help facility to determine which SAS file I/O functions are required.

SAS OnlineDoc ⇨ **Base SAS** ⇨ **SAS 9.2 Language Reference Dictionary** ⇨ **Dictionary of Language Elements** ⇨ **Functions and CALL Routines by Category**

b. Open the program **p310e12** and submit it. Look in the log to ensure that the function is working correctly.

p310s12

```
proc fcmp outlib=work.functions.Marketing;
   function NUMS(DSN $);
      length DSN $41;
      DSID=open(DSN);
      return(attrn(DSID, "NLOBSF"));
      DSID=close(DSID);
   endsub;
   run;
quit;

options cmplib=work.functions;

data _null_;
   X=NUMS('orion.internet');
   put X=;
run;
```

Solutions to Student Activities (Polls/Quizzes)

10.02 Quiz – Correct Answer

In addition to saving programmer time, does creating a macro variable or a macro definition always save computer resources?

No

Why or why not?

An inefficient program is not made more efficient if you use macro variables or change the program into a macro definition.

13

10.03 Quiz – Correct Answer

1. Open and submit the program **p310a01**.
2. How many observations are in the data set `quarter`? **20**
3. Change the files referenced by **MON** to the current month and the two previous months. How many observations are in the data set `quarter`?

   The answer depends on the current month.

You want the program to reference the current month and the two months without editing the program every time that it is submitted.

28

10.04 Quiz – Correct Answers

If the value of the variable **i** is the number of the month, which of the following could be used to create the name of the raw data file?

(a.)
```
NextFile=cats("mon",i,".dat");
```

(b.)
```
NextFile="mon"||put(i,2.)||".dat";
NextFile=compress(NextFile);
```

(c.)
```
NextFile=compress("mon"||put(i,2.)||".dat");
```

34

10.05 Poll – Correct Answer

Is the STOP statement necessary?

- (❍) Yes
- ❍ No

40

10.06 Multiple Choice Poll – Correct Answer

How many observations are in **`movingq`**?

a. One observation per record in all of the raw data files
b. 0
c. 1
d. 3

42

10.07 Poll – Correct Answer

Will the SAS code in **p310d08** produce the correct results if the current month is January or February?

❍ Yes
❍ No

48

10.08 Quiz – Correct Answer

Which of the following would make the program more efficient?

(a.)
```
Today=today();
MonNum=month(Today);
MidMon=month(intnx('month', Today, -1));
LastMon=month(intnx('month', Today, -2));
```

b.
```
Today=today();
MonNum=month(today());
MidMon=month(intnx('month', today(), -1));
LastMon=month(intnx('month', today(), -2));
```

★ (c.)
```
retain Today MonNum MidMon LastMon;
if _N_=1 then do;
   Today=today();
   MonNum=month(Today);
   MidMon=month(intnx('month', Today, -1));
   LastMon=month(intnx('month', Today, -2));
end;
```

★ Most efficient

54

10.09 Quiz – Correct Answer

Open and submit the program **p310a02**.

What does the log report? **The code that is stored in the view**

```
NOTE: DATA step view ORION.MOVINGQ is defined as:

data orion.movingq / view=orion.movingq;
   drop MonNum MidMon LastMon I;
   retain Today MonNum MidMon LastMon;
   if _N_=1 then
      do;
         Today=today();
         MonNum=month(Today);
         MidMon=month(intnx('month', Today, -1));
         LastMon=month(intnx('month', Today, -2));
      end;
   do I=MonNum, MidMon, LastMon;
      NextFile=cats("mon", i, ".dat");
      infile ORD filevar=NextFile dlm=',' end=LastObs;
      do while (not LastObs);
         input Customer_ID Order_ID Order_Type Order_Date : date9. Delivery_Date : date9.;
         output;
      end;
   end;
   stop;
run;
```

98

10.10 Quiz – Correct Answer

What is the advantage of the following program?

```
data bonus_view(keep=Manager_ID YrEndBonus)
       / view=bonus_view;
   set orion.staff;
   YrEndBonus=Salary * 0.05;
   where Job_Title contains 'Manager';
run;

proc means data=bonus_view mean sum;
   class Manager_ID;
   var YrEndBonus;
run;
```

The program avoids the output associated with the DATA step.

105 p310d15

10.11 Multiple Choice Poll – Correct Answer

How many times is the **`rawdata`** file read?

a. 4
b. 3
c. 2
d. 1
e. 0

115

10.12 Multiple Answer Poll – Correct Answers

Which resources can you conserve by using the _NULL_ keyword in the DATA statement?

a. I/O
b. CPU
c. Memory
d. Programmer time

140

10.13 Quiz – Correct Answer

Specify the argument of the MKT function that corresponds to the each of following variables:

Variable	Argument
Customer_ID	ID
Delivery_Date	Date
Order_Type	Type

```
options cmplib=orion.functions;
data temp;
   set orion.order_fact;
   Marketing_Comment =
      MKT(Customer_ID,Delivery_Date,Order_Type);
run;
```

169

Solutions to Chapter Review

Chapter Review – Correct Answers

1. What are two parts of the macro facility?

   Macro variables and macro definitions

2. What is the purpose of the FILEVAR= option in the INFILE statement?

   The FILEVAR= option names a variable whose change in value causes the INFILE statement to close the current input file and open a new one.

3. What does the INTNX function do?

   The INTNX function increments a SAS date value by a given interval or intervals, and returns a SAS date value.

186

continued...

Chapter Review – Correct Answers

4. What is the difference between a SAS data file and a SAS data view?

   A SAS data file stores the data on disk, whereas a SAS data view stores the instructions for data manipulation on disc. For a view, the DATA step or PROC SQL step is not executed until the view is referenced.

188

continued...

Chapter Review – Correct Answers

5. Why would you use the FILE statement?

   Use the FILE statement to specify the external file in which to write the text generated by the PUT statements in the current DATA step.

6. What is the purpose of the PUT statement?

   The PUT statement writes text to an external location.

190

Chapter 11 Customizing Your SAS Session (Self-Study)

11.1 Introduction

Objectives

- Review the OPTIONS procedure.
- List reasons for customizing a SAS session.
- Describe the methods that are used to customize a SAS session.

3

Using the OPTIONS Procedure (Review)

The OPTIONS procedure lists the current settings of SAS system options in the SAS log.

General form of the OPTIONS procedure:

PROC OPTIONS *<option(s)>*;

Option	Tasks
DEFINE	displays the option's description, type, and group.
VALUE	displays the option's value and scope.
LISTGROUPS	displays groups and group descriptions (SAS 9.2).
GROUP=	displays options belonging to one or more groups.
OPTION=	displays a single option.

4

11.01 Quiz

Open and submit the program **p311a01**.

```
proc options listgroups;
run;
```

1. What group would you use to display options used for procedure output?
2. Change the LISTGROUPS option in the PROC OPTIONS statement to the GROUP= option to display the options used for the procedure output that you identified in part 1.
3. What is the value of the LINESIZE= option?

6

In SAS 9.2 you can view multiple groups using the following syntax:

PROC OPTIONS GROUP=(*group1 group2*);
RUN;

p311a2.sas

```
proc options group=(sort memory);
run;
```

Reasons for Customizing a SAS Session

You can customize actions taken by SAS when SAS starts. Aspects of your SAS session that you might want to control when the session starts include the following:

- specifying system options in effect when the session starts
- executing SAS statements such as LIBNAME statements automatically
- changing the working and default folders for Open and Save As actions when you use the SAS windowing environment

8

Techniques for Customizing a SAS Session

These three techniques can be used to customize a SAS session:

- SAS configuration file
- autoexec file
- SAS Registry

9

Defining the Three Techniques

The three techniques are defined in the table below.

configuration file	an external file that contains SAS system options used to establish the SAS session
autoexec file	a file that contains SAS statements that are executed immediately after SAS initializes and before any user input is accepted
SAS Registry	a type of SAS file called an *item store* that contains configuration data for one or more SAS software products

10

Comparing the Three Techniques

Configuration File	Autoexec File	SAS Registry
Easy to change	Easiest to change	**Change with caution**
a text file named `sasv9.cfg` in Windows and UNIX	a SAS program with a `.sas` extension in Windows and UNIX	a SAS file named `regstry.sas7bitm`
processed before SAS initializes	processed after SAS initializes	processed during initialization
can be edited with a SAS text editor or an ASCII text editor	can be edited with any text editor	can be changed with PROC REGISTRY code or by using the REGISTRY window
contains only system options and the location of SAS components	contains SAS code such as OPTIONS statements or LIBNAME statements	consists of keys and sub-keys that refer to particular aspects of SAS

11

z/OS users can create a user configuration file using any text editor to write SAS system options into a physical file. The physical file can then be specified in the CONFIG= invocation system option interactively or in batch mode.

11.02 Multiple Answer Poll

Which of the following have you investigated?

a. SAS configuration file
b. autoexec.sas file
c. SAS Registry
d. None of the above

13

11.2 Editing the Configuration File

Objectives

- Define the purpose of the configuration file.
- List the two parts of the configuration file.
- Create a custom configuration file.
- Use the custom configuration file.

16

Defining the Configuration File

The SAS configuration file is a text file that contains SAS system options and SAS installation locations used to establish the SAS session.

- In Windows and UNIX, the configuration file has an extension of `.cfg`.
- You can view the configuration file using any text editor, including the SAS Program Editor window.

17

Purpose of the Configuration File

Three types of system options are in the configuration file:

- initialization options (for example, –SGIO)
- options that can be specified in an OPTIONS statement (for example, FULLSTIMER)
- the –SET option that creates operating system environment variables that indicate the location of the following files:
  - SAS Help and Documentation files
  - message files
  - pathnames to the SAS executable files

18

Importance of the Configuration File

- You must have at least one configuration file in order for SAS to initialize.
- You can have multiple configuration files that are all processed when your SAS session begins.

⚠ The SAS configuration file is particularly important because it specifies the folders that are searched for the various components of SAS products.

19

Viewing the Configuration File

The configuration file is divided into two sections separated by a warning note.

- The first section specifies SAS system options that are not updated by the SAS setup applications. **Put system options in this section.**
- The second section is used by the SAS setup applications for updating information about where SAS software is installed. **Do not edit below this line.**

20

The Top of the Configuration File

```
/* set default locations                                              */
-fontsloc "!sasroot\core\resource"
-TRAINLOC ""
/* set the default fileref for the PARMCARDS= option                 */
-SET FT15F001  'FT15F001.DAT'
/*-------------------------------------------------------------------\
| SAS System FORMCHARS, used by pressing ALT then the decimal         |
| number for the Extended ASCII character.                            |
\-------------------------------------------------------------------*/
/* This is the OEM character set                                     */
/* -FORMCHAR "³ÄÚÂ¿ÃÅ´ÀÁÙ+=|-/\<>*" */
/* This is the ANSI character set (for SAS Monospace font and
ANSI Sasfont) */
-FORMCHAR "│─┌┬┐├┼┤└┴┘+=|-/\<>*"
/* This is the ANSI character set                                    */
/* -FORMCHAR "|----|+|---+=|-/\<>*" */
```

This is the section that you can edit.
Only system options can be added here.
Those system options are in effect when SAS initializes.

21

System Option	Purpose
-FONTSLOC	specifies the location that contains the SAS fonts that are loaded by some Universal Printer drivers.
-TRAINLOC	specifies the base location of SAS online training courses.
-SET	defines a SAS (internal) environment variable. In this case, the variable, **`FT15F001`**, specifies the file reference of a file that SAS opens when it encounters a PARMCARDS (or PARMCARDS4) statement in a procedure. The PARMCARDS statement is used in the BMDP and EXPLODE procedures.
-FORMCHAR	specifies formatting characters used to construct tabular output outlines and dividers for various procedures, such as the FREQ and TABULATE procedures. If you omit formatting characters as an option in the procedure, the default specifications given in the FORMCHAR= system option are used. Notice that you can also specify a hexadecimal character constant as a formatting character. When you use a hex constant with this option, SAS interprets the value of the hexadecimal constant as appropriate for your operating system.

The Warning Message in the Configuration File

```
/*-------------------------------------------------------------\
| WARNING:  INSTALL Application edits below this line.  User    |
|           options should be added above this box comment.     |
|           INSTALL Application maintains and modifies the      |
|           following options; -SASAUTOS, -SASHELP, -SASMSG,     |
|           -PATH, and -MAPS.  It also maintains and modifies   |
|           the following CONFIG variables with the -SET option; |
|           INSTALL, USAGE, LIBRARY, SAMPSIO, SAMPSRC, SASCBT,   |
|           and SASEXT01-SASEXT50.  It preserves all lines above |
|           the line containing 'DO NOT EDIT BELOW THIS LINE'.   |
\-------------------------------------------------------------*/
/* DO NOT EDIT BELOW THIS LINE - INSTALL Application edits below this line */
/* * * * * * * * * * * * * * * * * * * * * * * * * * * * * * * * * * * * */
```

22

Partial Configuration File Setup Information

```
-SET sasext0 "C:\Program Files\SAS\SASFoundation\9.2"
-SET sasroot "C:\Program Files\SAS\SASFoundation\9.2"
-SET sasext1 "C:\Program Files\SAS\SASFoundation\9.2\nls"
/* Setup the MYSASFILES system variable                       */
-SET MYSASFILES "?CSIDL_PERSONAL\My SAS Files\9.2"
/* Setup the default SAS System user profile folder           */
-SASUSER "?CSIDL_PERSONAL\My SAS Files\9.2"
/* Setup the default SAS System user work folder              */
-WORK "!TEMP\SAS Temporary Files"
/* Setup the SAS System configuration folder                  */
-SET SASCFG "C:\Program Files\SAS\SASFoundation\9.2\nls\en"
/* location of help    in OS help format */
-HELPLOC ("!MYSASFILES\classdoc" "!sasroot\nls\en\help"
"!sasroot\core\help")
<lines removed>
```

This is the section that you should **not** edit. This provides the information about where SAS is installed.

23

The following are SAS librefs, which are established in the configuration file:

SAS System Libref	What the Option Does
SASUSER	points to the location of the Sasuser library.
WORK	points to the high-level location of the Work library.
HELPLOC	points to and concatenates the locations of the SAS Help facility files.

The following are SAS internal environment variables, which are set in the configuration file:

Environment Variable	What the Variable Does
sasroot	sets the location where SAS software was installed, often referred to as the current or working location or only as sasroot.
sasext0	sets the location for additional SAS software modules.
sasext1	sets the location for the National Language Support modules.
MYSASFILES	sets the location for the Sasuser libref as an environment variable.
sascfg	sets the location for the .sasv9 configuration file.

Configuration Files in Windows and UNIX

The following information applies to Windows and UNIX:

- The configuration file typically resides in the directory where SAS was installed. By default, this directory is the !SASROOT directory.
- The systems administrator can edit this configuration file so that it contains appropriate options for your site.
- You can create a customized configuration file.

⚠ In UNIX, there can be a restricted configuration file containing options that you cannot change.

24

Reference Information

Location of the Configuration File in the Windows Operating Environment

In previous releases of SAS, the default configuration file was stored in the !SASROOT folder. The !SASROOT folder is the folder in which you install SAS.

Starting with SAS®9, SAS creates two default configuration files during installation. Both configuration files are named SASV9.CFG.

SAS stores one of these files in the !SASROOT folder and the other in the !sasroot\nls*language-code* folder. The *language-code* is a two-letter language code that indicates the SAS default language.

The SASV9.CFG file that is located in the !SASROOT folder contains a CONFIG system option that specifies the location of the configuration file for the SAS default language. The default system options that are used to start SAS are specified in the !sasroot\nls*language-code*\SASV9.CFG file. For example, if SAS is installed in the default folder and the default language is English, the SASV9.CFG file in the !SASROOT folder contains this line:

```
-config "c:\program files\SAS\SASFoundation\9.2\nls\en\sasv9.cfg"
```

Use the RESTRICT option in the PROC OPTIONS statement to view the restricted options.

```
PROC OPTIONS RESTRICT;
RUN;
```

Configuration Files in z/OS

In z/OS, SAS uses two types of configuration files:

- the system configuration file, which is used by all users at your site by default. Your on-site SAS support personnel maintain the system configuration file for your site.
- a user configuration file, which is generally used by an individual user or department.

25

Creating a Custom Configuration File

These steps enable creating a custom configuration file:

1. Use a text editor to write SAS system options into a file.
2. Specify one or more system options, and apply the syntax that you use when you type those options at an operating system command prompt.
3. Save the file.

✎ Specifics for each operating environment are noted on subsequent slides.

26

UNIX Specifics: Creating a Configuration File

Example:

```
-nocenter
-nodate
-msglevel i
-linesize 64
-pagesize 56
-work /users/myuserid/tmp
```

Save the file to either a **sasv9.cfg** or **.sasv9.cfg** file.

27

UNIX Specifics: –WORK System Option

The –WORK SAS system option specifies the location of the Work library.

-WORK *pathname*

pathname specifies the directory (not a filename) where your Work SAS library can be created or found. SAS will create the directory if it does not exist. You must have Write permission to the location specified in *pathname*.

28

Windows Specifics: Creating a Configuration File

To ensure that all of the required system options are defined in the custom configuration file, copy the default file and modify the copy.

- Name the file **`sasv9.cfg`** or **`.sasv9.cfg`**.
- Store the file in the Windows user-profile folder or use the –CONFIG option when you invoke SAS.

✎ In Windows NT, the path for the Windows user-profile folder is
`c:\Documents and Settings\`*`user-id`*`\`
`My Documents\My SAS Files\9.2`

29

continued...

Windows Specifics: Creating a Configuration File

Example

```
-nocenter
-nodate
-msglevel i
-linesize 64
-pagesize 56
-work "c:\temp"
-sasinitialfolder s:\workshop

/* set default locations                                     */
-fontsloc "!sasroot\core\resource"
-TRAINLOC ""
/* set the default fileref for the PARMCARDS= option         */
-SET FT15F001  'FT15F001.DAT'
/*-----------------------------------------------------------\
| SAS System FORMCHARS, used by pressing ALT then the decimal |
| number for the Extended ASCII character.                    |
\-----------------------------------------------------------*/
/* This is the OEM character set                             */
/* -FORMCHAR "³ÃÚÂ¿ÃÅ´ÀÁÙ+=|-/\<>*" */
/* This is the ANSI character set (for SAS Monospace font and ANSI Sasfont) */
-FORMCHAR "|─┌┬┐├┼┤└┴┘+=|-/\<>*"
/* This is the ANSI character set                            */
/* -FORMCHAR "|----|+|---+=|-/\<>*" */
```

30

Windows Specifics: –WORK System Option

The –WORK SAS system option specifies the location of the Work library.

```
-WORK "library-specification"
```

"library-specification"	specifies an environment variable or a Windows pathname. The value of ***library-specification*** must resolve to a valid Windows directory or subdirectory pathname. The ***library-specification*** must be enclosed in double quotation marks.

31

Windows Specifics: –SASINITIALFOLDER

In the Windows operating environment, the -SASINITIALFOLDER SAS system option changes the working folder and the default folders for the Open and Save As dialog boxes to the specified folder after SAS initialization is complete.

```
-SASINITIALFOLDER newfolder
```

newfolder	specifies the path to the current working folder and the default folders for the Open and Save As dialog boxes. If *newfolder* contains spaces, it must be enclosed in quotation marks.

32

z/OS Specifics: Creating a Configuration File

Use any text editor to write SAS system options into a physical file.

- The configuration file can be either a sequential data set or a member of a partitioned data set and can have either fixed length or variable length records.
- Each line of a configuration file can contain one or more system options. If you specify more than one system option on a line, use either a blank space or a comma to separate the options.

33

continued...

z/OS Specifics: Creating a Configuration File

Example

```
nocenter
nodate
msglevel=i
linesize=64
pagesize=56
-work userid.myfile.mywork
```

⚠ When you specify SAS system options in a configuration file, blank spaces are not permitted before or after an equal sign.

34

z/OS Specifics: –WORK System Option

The –WORK SAS system option specifies the location of the Work library.

```
-WORK library-specification
```

library-specification	can be a DDNAME that was previously associated with a SAS library using JCL or TSO commands or the name of a physical file that comprises a SAS data library.

35

11.03 Quiz

In the Windows operating environment, navigate to

`C:\Program Files\SAS\SASFoundation\9.2\nls\en\sasv9.cfg`

Which option is set to open the SAS windowing environment and the Explorer window?

Should you edit that option?

37

UNIX: Specifying a Configuration File

One way to specify a configuration file is to use the -CONFIG system option in the SAS command.

```
sas -config name-of-configuration-file
```

⚠ When you specify the –CONFIG option, SAS still processes restricted configuration files and uses the restricted settings instead of those specified in the custom configuration file.

39

For more information, consult the SAS Help facility by following the path described below:

Using SAS Software in Your Operating Environment ⇨ **SAS 9.2 Companion for UNIX Environments** ⇨ **Running SAS Software Under UNIX** ⇨ **Getting Started with SAS in UNIX Environments** ⇨ **Customizing Your SAS Session by Using Configuration and Autoexec Files**

UNIX: Specifying a Configuration File

If you do not use the -CONFIG option, SAS processes the configuration files in the following order:

1. sasv9.cfg in the !SASROOT directory
2. sasv9_local.cfg in the !SASROOT directory
3. .sasv9.cfg in your home directory
4. sasv9.cfg in your home directory
5. sasv9.cfg in your current directory
6. any restricted configuration files

40

Windows: Specifying a Configuration File

When you use a file that is located in a different folder or that has a different name from your default configuration file, use the –CONFIG system option to specify the location of the configuration file.

For example, the `Target` field of the SAS Properties dialog box for the SAS icon shortcut might contain the following:

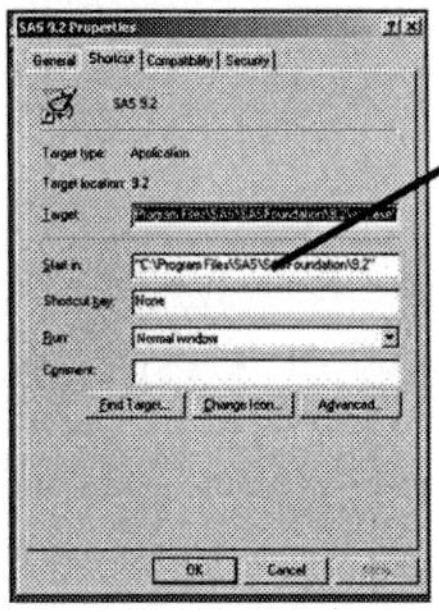

"c:\program files\SAS\SASFoundation\9.2\sas.exe -config c:\mysas\mysasconfig.CFG"

41

For more information, consult the SAS Help facility by following the path described below:

Using SAS Software in Your Operating Environment ⇨ **SAS 9.2 Companion for Windows** ⇨ **Running SAS under Windows** ⇨ **Getting Started** ⇨ **Files Used by SAS**

z/OS: Specifying a Configuration File

To tell SAS where to find your user configuration file, do the following:

- If you use the SAS cataloged procedure to invoke SAS in batch mode, use the CONFIG= parameter; for example:

```
//S1 EXEC SAS,CONFIG='MY.CONFIG.FILE'
```

- If you use the SAS CLIST or SASRX exec to invoke SAS under TSO, use the CONFIG operand; for example:

```
sas config('''my.config.file''') or
sasrx -config 'my.config.file'
```

42

For more information, consult the SAS Help facility by following the path described below:

Using SAS Software in Your Operating Environment ⇨ **SAS 9.2 Companion for z/OS** ⇨ **Running SAS Software under z/OS** ⇨ **Initializing and Configuring SAS Software** ⇨ **Customizing Your SAS Session**

11.3 Creating an Autoexec.sas File

Objectives

- Define an autoexec file.
- Create an autoexec file.
- Execute the autoexec file.

45

Defining an Autoexec File

An autoexec file has the following characteristics:

- It is a SAS program file with a file extension of `.sas` in Windows and UNIX.
- It contains SAS statements that are executed immediately after SAS initializes and before any user input is accepted. These SAS statements can be used to invoke SAS programs automatically, set up librefs and/or filerefs for use during your SAS session, or set system options.
- It is not required in order to run SAS.

46

11.04 Poll

Have you ever created an autoexec file?

- ❍ Yes
- ❍ No

48

Example of an Autoexec File

UNIX:

```
libname orion '/user/workshop';
options fmtsearch=(orion.myfmts orion)
        nodate nonumber ls=80;
%include 'p303d01.sas';
```

Windows:

```
libname orion 's:\workshop';
options fmtsearch=(orion.myfmts orion)
        nodate nonumber ls=80;
%include 'p303d01.sas';
```

z/OS:

```
libname orion '.prg3.sasdata';
options fmtsearch=(orion.myfmts orion)
        nodate nonumber ls=80;
%include '.prg3.sascode(p303d01)';
```

p311d01

49

Using an Autoexec File

- There is no autoexec file by default.
- To create one, use a text editor to create a program and save the program in the appropriate location.
- If you do have an autoexec file, the default name is autoexec.sas.

⚠ The appropriate location is dependent on your operating environment.

50

UNIX: Location for the Autoexec.sas File

In the UNIX operating environment, you can save the autoexec file in any folder. SAS uses the following search order to find the autoexec.sas file:

1. your current directory
2. your home directory
3. the !SASROOT directory

51

Windows: Location for the Autoexec.sas File

In the Windows operating environment, you can save the autoexec file in any folder. SAS uses the following search order to find the autoexec.sas file:

1. the current folder
2. the paths that are specified by the Windows PATH environment variable
3. the root folder of the current drive
4. the folder that contains the sas.exe file

52

z/OS: Location for the Autoexec File

- Under z/OS, an autoexec file can be either a sequential data set or a member of a partitioned data set.
- You must specify the location of the autoexec file when you invoke SAS.

Method of Invoking SAS	Syntax for Using the AUTOEXEC File
Command line invocation	`sas autoexec('''my.auto.exec''')`
Batch	`//MYJOB EXEC SAS` `//SASEXEC DD DSN=MY.AUTO.EXEC,DISP=SHR`

53

11.05 Poll

Is the code from the autoexec file included as part of your log?

- ❍ Yes
- ❍ No

55

Using the ECHOAUTO System Option

The configuration option, ECHOAUTO, determines whether the code in the autoexec file is written to the log.

```
NOECHOAUTO | ECHOAUTO
```

NOECHOAUTO	specifies that SAS source lines that are read from the autoexec file are not printed in the SAS log, even though they are executed (DEFAULT).
ECHOAUTO	specifies that SAS source lines that are read from the autoexec file be printed in the SAS log.

⚠ Regardless of the setting of this option, messages that result from errors in the autoexec files are printed in the SAS log.

57

Disabling the Autoexec File

You can use the NOAUTOEXEC SAS system option at invocation to specify that SAS is **not** to process any autoexec files.

Windows/UNIX

```
sas -noautoexec
```

z/OS

```
sas autoexec(noautoexec)
```

58

11.4 Using the SAS Registry

Objectives

- Define the SAS Registry.
- Investigate techniques for modifying the SAS Registry.

61

Defining the SAS Registry

The *SAS Registry* is the central storage area for configuration data for SAS. Customizations to the SAS Registry remain in effect for more than one SAS session.

Examples of what the registry stores are listed below:

- the libraries and file shortcuts that SAS assigns at startup
- the menu definitions for Explorer pop-up menus
- the printers that are defined for use
- configuration data for various SAS products

62

Storage Location for the SAS Registry

The registry consists of two parts:

- One part is stored in the Sashelp library.
- The other part is stored in the Sasuser library.

⚠ The SAS Registry is not displayed in the SAS Explorer window.

63

Techniques for Modifying the Configuration

Changes to configuration are saved in the SAS Registry when you make changes using tools such as the following:

- the New Library window
- the Universal Print windows
- the Explorer Options window

64

Using the New Library Window

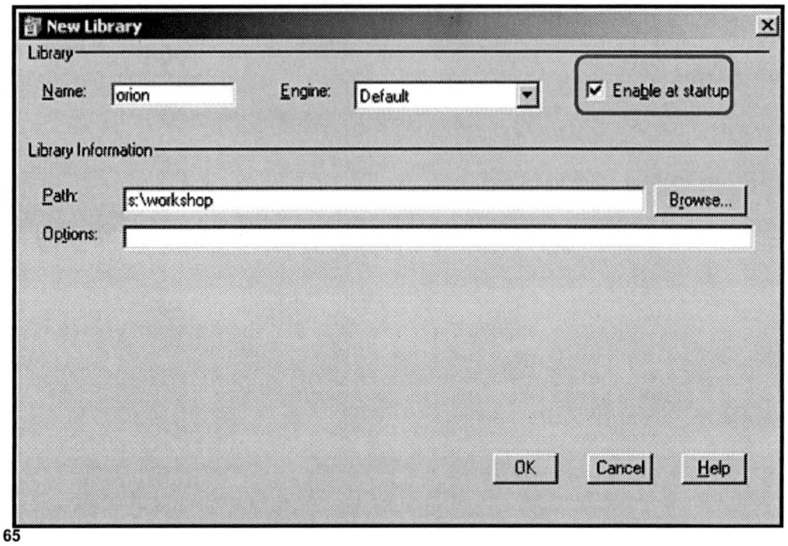

65

Using the Print Setup Window

Universal printers should be configured by using either the PRTDEF procedure or the Print Setup window.

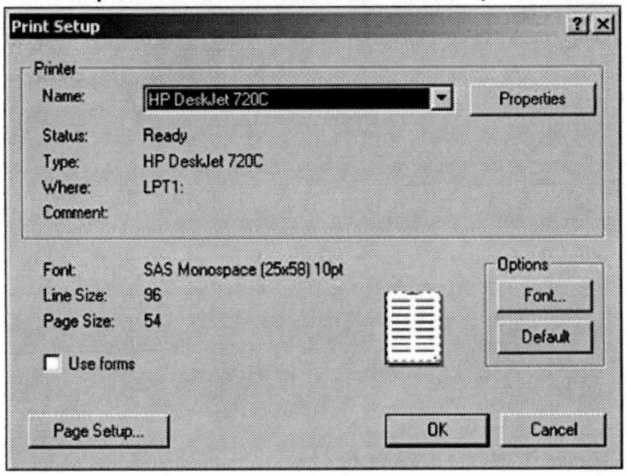

✎ To open the Print Setup window, select **File** ⇨ **Print Setup**.

66

The PRTDEF procedure creates printer definitions in batch mode either for an individual user or for all SAS users at your site. Your system administrator can create printer definitions in the SAS Registry and make these printers available to all SAS users at your site by using PROC PRTDEF with the USESASHELP option. An individual user can create personal printer definitions in the SAS Registry by using PROC PRTDEF.

PROC PRTDEF *<option(s)>*;

Option	Task
DATA=	specifies the input data set that contains the printer attributes.
DELETE	specifies that the default operation is to delete the printer definitions from the registry.
FOREIGN	specifies that the registry entries are created for export to a different host.
LIST	specifies that a list of printers that are created or replaced will be written to the log.
REPLACE	specifies that any printer name that already exists will be modified by using the information in the printer attributes data set.
USESASHELP	specifies whether the printer definitions are available to all users or only the users running PROC PRTDEF.

Customizing the SAS Explorer

Use the Explorer Options window to configure Explorer settings.

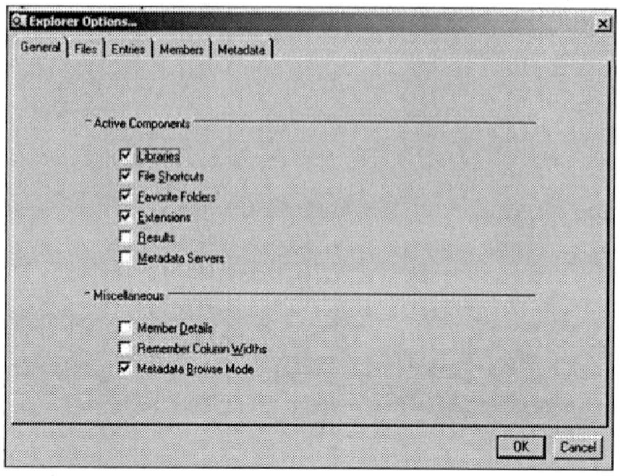

✎ To open the Explorer Options window, with the Explorer window active, select **Tools** ⇨ **Options** ⇨ **Explorer**.

67

Techniques for Modifying the Configuration

You can also make changes to configuration by using one of the following techniques:

- the interactive SAS Registry Editor
- the REGISTRY procedure

The SAS Registry is designed for use by system administrators and experienced SAS users.

⚠ Do not make a mistake when you edit the registry. Your SAS system might become unstable or unusable. This can negatively affect any SAS session.

68

11.06 Quiz

Open the Registry Editor by selecting

Solutions ⇨ **Accessories** ⇨ **Registry Editor**

or use the REGEDIT command on the command line.

Which key would contain settings from the LIBNAME window?

70

Using the Registry Editor

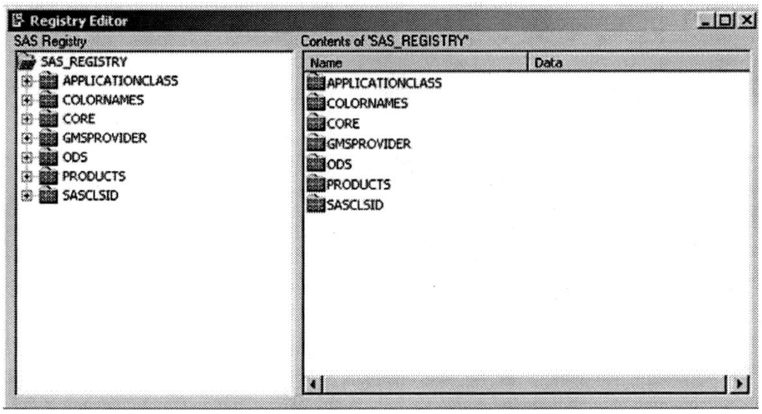

✎ To open the Registry Editor window, select **Solutions** ⇨ **Accessories** ⇨ **Registry Editor** or use the REGEDIT command on the command line.

72

Viewing the LIBNAME Keys

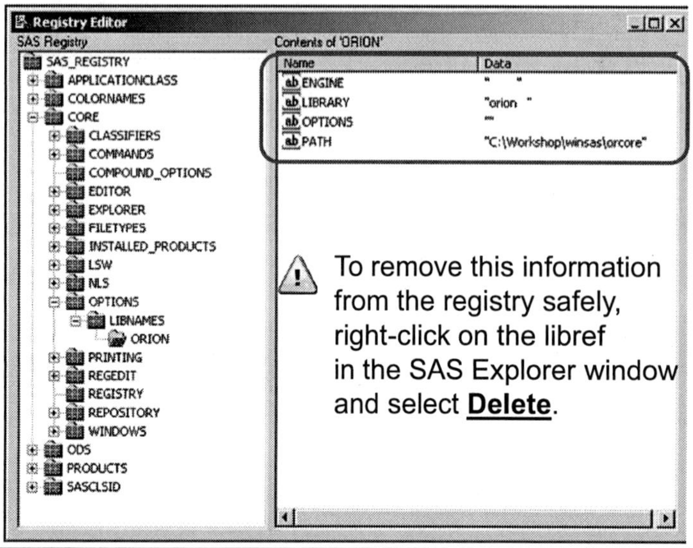

To remove this information from the registry safely, right-click on the libref in the SAS Explorer window and select **Delete**.

73

Viewing Printer Keys

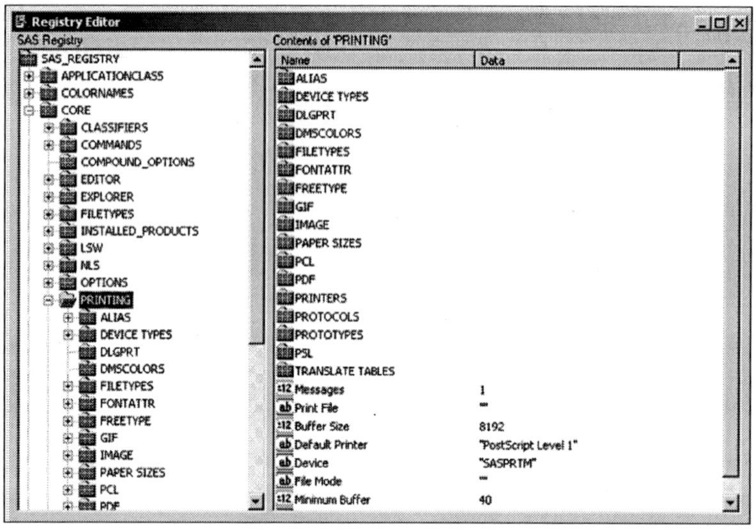

74

Viewing the SAS Explorer Keys

Use the Registry Editor to view the current Explorer settings in the SAS Registry.

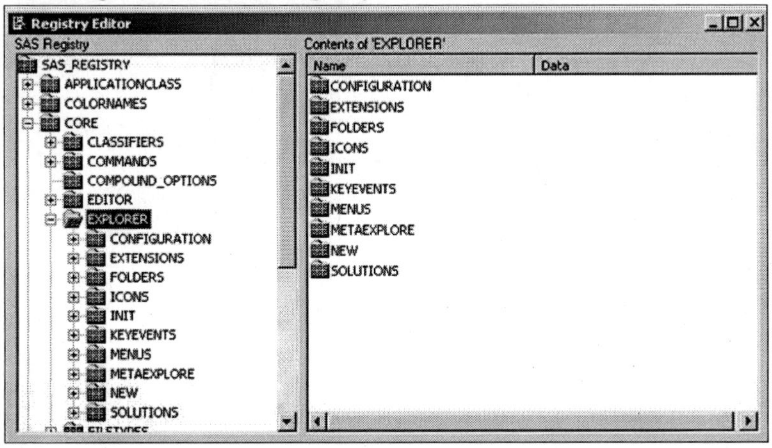

75

Registry Key	What Portion of the Explorer It Configures
CORE\EXPLORER\CONFIGURATION	The portions of the Explorer that are initialized at startup.
CORE\EXPLORER\MENUS	The context menus that are displayed in the Explorer.
CORE\EXPLORER\KEYEVENTS	The valid key events for the 3270 interface. This key is used only on the mainframe platforms.
CORE\EXPLORER\ICONS	The icons displayed in the Explorer. If the icon value is -1, this causes the icon to be hidden in the Explorer.
CORE\EXPLORER\NEW	What types of objects are available from the **File** ⇨ **New** menu in Explorer.

Using the Registry Procedure

The REGISTRY procedure enables you to maintain the SAS Registry.

You can create registry files with the SAS Registry Editor or with any text editor.

A registry file must have a particular structure:

- Each entry in the registry file consists of a key name, followed on the next line by one or more values.
- The key name identifies the key or subkey that you are defining.
- Any values that follow specify the names or data to associate with the key.

76

The REGISTRY procedure enables you to do the following:

- import registry files to populate the Sashelp and Sasuser registries
- export all or part of the registry to another file
- list the contents of the registry in the SAS log
- compare the contents of the registry to a file
- uninstall a registry file
- deliver detailed status information about when a key or value will be overwritten or uninstalled
- delete entries in the Sasuser registry
- validate that the registry exists
- list diagnostic information

Using the REGISTRY Procedure

General form of the REGISTRY procedure:

```
PROC REGISTRY <option(s)>;
RUN;
```

Selected Options	Use
COMPAREREG1= and COMPAREREG2=	compare two registry files.
COMPARETO=	compares the contents of a registry to a file.
EXPORT=	writes the contents of a registry to the specified file.
LISTHELP	writes the contents of the Sashelp portion of the registry to the SAS log.

77

Using the REGISTRY Procedure

Partial Log

Example

```
proc registry listuser;
run;
```

✎ The LISTUSER option reports the contents of the Sasuser portion of the SAS Registry in the log.

```
201  proc registry listuser;
NOTE: Contents of SASUSER REGISTRY.
[  HKEY_USER_ROOT]
[    CORE]
[      EXPLORER]
[        CONFIGURATION]
[          CUSTOM LISTVIEWS]
[            LV_XEXPLIN]
[              COLUMN1]
              Column Name="Name"
[              COLUMN2]
              Column Name="Engine"
[              COLUMN3]
              Column Name="Type"
[              COLUMN4]
              Column Name="Host Pathname"
[              COLUMN5]
              Column Name="Modified"
[              DMSEXP]
[                COLUMN1]
                Column Width=int:108
[                COLUMN2]
                Column Width=int:72
[                COLUMN3]
                Column Width=int:108
[                COLUMN4]
                Column Width=int:315
[                COLUMN5]
                Column Width=int:158
```

78 p311d02 *continued...*

Using the REGISTRY Procedure

```
[        OPTIONS]
[          LIBNAMES]
[            ORION]
             ENGINE="          "
             LIBRARY="orion    "
             OPTIONS=""
             PATH="S:\Workshop"
[        PRINTING]
       Print File=""
[        REGEDIT]
[          INIT]
           colwidth=int:180
           treewidth=int:230
[      PRODUCTS]
[        BASE]
[          Enhanced Editor]
[            Use_As_Default]
[          Viewtable]
           Height=int:102
           HorizontalPosition=int:0
           VerticalPosition=int:36
           Width=int:100
NOTE: PROCEDURE REGISTRY used (Total process time):
      real time           0.00 seconds
      cpu time            0.00 seconds
```

Key for the library definition that was enabled at startup

79 p311d02

Using the REGISTRY Procedure

```
proc registry list
     startat='core\printing\paper sizes';
run;
```

LIST	writes the contents of the entire SAS registry to the SAS log.
STARTAT=key	starts exporting or writing or comparing the contents of a registry at the specified key.

✎ The LIST option generates a great deal of output without the STARTAT= option.

80 p311d03

Using the REGISTRY Procedure

Partial Log

```
00  proc registry list startat='core\printing\paper sizes';
401  run;

NOTE: Contents of SASHELP REGISTRY starting at subkey [core\printing\paper sizes]
core\printing\paper sizes]
[    13x18]
    Height=double:18
    Units="IN"
    Width=double:13
[    16K]
    Height=double:10.75
    Units="IN"
    Width=double:7.75
[    24x108]
    Height=double:108
    Units="IN"
    Width=double:24
[    24x48]
    Height=double:48
    Units="IN"
    Width=double:24
```

81

11.07 Quiz

Open and submit **p311a03**.

p311a03

```
proc registry list startat='core\options\libnames';
run;
```

Are there any libraries listed?

83

11.5 Solutions

Solutions to Student Activities (Polls/Quizzes)

11.01 Quiz – Correct Answer

Open and submit the program **p311a01**.

```
proc options listgroups;
run;
```

1. What group would you use to display options used for procedure output?

   LISTCONTROL

2. Change the LISTGROUPS option in the PROC OPTIONS statement to the GROUP= option to display the options used for the procedure output that you identified in part 1.
3. What is the value of the LINESIZE= option?

   The value is operating-environment-specific.

7

```
proc options group=listcontrol;
run;
```

11.03 Quiz – Correct Answer

In the Windows operating environment, navigate to

`C:\Program Files\SAS\SASFoundation\9.2\nls\en\sasv9.cfg`

Which option is set to open the SAS windowing environment and the Explorer window?

`-dmsexp`

Should you edit that option?

No

38

11.05 Poll – Correct Answer

Is the code from the autoexec file included as part of your log?

❍ Yes

❍ No (circled)

56

11.06 Quiz – Correct Answer

Open the Registry Editor by selecting

Solutions ⇨ **Accessories** ⇨ **Registry Editor**

or use the REGEDIT command on the command line.

Which key would contain settings from the LIBNAME window?

Core

71

11.07 Quiz – Correct Answer

Open and submit **p311a03**.

p311a03

```
proc registry list startat='core\options\libnames';
run;
```

Are there any libraries listed?

No, if you used a LIBNAME statement to assign the libref `orion`

Yes, if you used the Enable at Startup check box in the New Libraries window to assign the libref `orion`

84

Chapter 12 Learning More

12.1 Conclusions

Objectives

- Review techniques for conserving computer resources.

3

Techniques for Reducing I/O Operations

The techniques for reducing I/O operations include the following:

- Minimize the number of variables and observations.
- Reduce the number of times that the data is processed.
- Use a SAS data file to process the same raw data file repeatedly.
- Use the SASFILE statement to process a small SAS data set repeatedly.
- Minimize the size of the SAS data set.
- Use appropriate BUFSIZE= and/or BUFNO= options for random or sequential access.

4

continued...

Techniques for Reducing I/O Operations

- Bypass system file caching in Windows and UNIX.
- Create views in programs that require intermediate temporary SAS data files.
- Create indexes on variables used for WHERE processing.

5

Techniques for Reducing Data Set Size

The techniques for reducing data set size include the following:

- Store integers as reduced-length numerics.
- Compress the data set.

Reducing the size of a SAS data set reduces the I/O required to process it.

6

Reducing Memory Usage

The techniques for reducing memory usage include the following:

- Use small data set page sizes when you create data sets that will be accessed in a sparse, random pattern.
- Use a single read buffer when the data is accessed randomly instead of sequentially.
- Use BY-group processing instead of CLASS statements in those procedures that support both, especially where you have pre-sorted data or can use an existing index.

7

Selected Additional Resources for Specific Topics

Permanently Store and Use Formats

- http://support.sas.com/faq/018/FAQ01816.html

Functions by Category

- http://support.sas.com/onlinedoc/913/getDoc/en/lrdict.hlp/a000245860.htm

Creating Custom Date and Number Formats

- http://support.sas.com/techsup/unotes/SN/008/008510.html
- http://support.sas.com/onlinedoc/913/getDoc/en/proc.hlp/a002473467.htm

Using the DATA Step Merge or the SQL Procedure

- http://support.sas.com/techsup/technote/ts644.pdf
- http://support.sas.com/techsup/technote/ts705.pdf
- http://support.sas.com/techsup/technote/ts553.html
- http://support.sas.com/techsup/technote/ts320.html
- http://support.sas.com/resources/papers/sgf09/336-2009.pdf
- http://support.sas.com/resources/papers/proceedings09/037-2009.pdf

Pipes and Threads: Performance Testing

- http://www2.sas.com/proceedings/forum2007/196-2007.pdf

SAS Efficiency

- http://www2.sas.com/proceedings/forum2007/042-2007.pdf
- http://www2.sas.com/proceedings/forum2007/209-2007.pdf

Hash Tables

- http://www2.sas.com/proceedings/forum2007/039-2007.pdf
- http://www2.sas.com/proceedings/sugi31/244-31.pdf
- http://support.sas.com/resources/papers/sgf2008/hashing92.pdf
- http://support.sas.com/rnd/base/datastep/dot/hash-getting-started.pdf
- http://support.sas.com/rnd/base/datastep/dot/iterator-getting-started.pdf

Arrays

- http://support.sas.com/rnd/papers/sgf07/arrays1780.pdf

Numeric Precision

- http://support.sas.com/techsup/technote/ts654.pdf

What's New in SAS 9.2

- http://support.sas.com/software/index.html

The FCMP Procedure

- http://www2.sas.com/proceedings/forum2007/008-2007.pdf

Solving SAS Performance Problems: Employing Host-Based Tools

- http://support.sas.com/rnd/papers/sugi31/practicalperf.pdf
- http://support.sas.com/techsup/technote/ts684/ts684.html

Configuring SAS I/O Subsystem

- http://support.sas.com/rnd/papers/sgf07/sgf2007-iosubsystem.pdf
- http://www.sas.com/partners/directory/hp/sasapp.pdf
- http://www2.sas.com/proceedings/forum2007/203-2007.pdf
- www.nesug.info/Proceedings/nesug07/as/as04.pdf
- http://support.sas.com/resources/papers/proceedings09/310-2009.pdf

Threading

- http://www2.sas.com/proceedings/sugi29/217-29.pdf
- http://www2.sas.com/proceedings/sugi28/282-28.pdf

Scalability and Performance Papers

- http://support.sas.com/rnd/scalability/papers/index.html

12.2 SAS Resources

Objectives

- Identify areas of support that SAS offers.
- List additional resources.

9

Education

Comprehensive training to deliver greater value to your organization

- More than 200 course offerings
- World-class instructors
- Multiple delivery methods: instructor-led and self-paced
- Training centers around the world

http://support.sas.com/training/

10

SAS Publishing

SAS offers a complete selection of publications to help customers use SAS software to its fullest potential:

- Multiple delivery methods: e-books, CD-ROM, and hard-copy books
- Wide spectrum of topics
- Partnerships with outside authors, other publishers, and distributors

http://support.sas.com/publishing/

11

SAS Global Certification Program

SAS offers several globally recognized certifications.

- Computer-based certification exams – typically 60-70 questions and 2-3 hours in length
- Preparation materials and practice exams available
- Worldwide directory of SAS Certified Professionals

http://support.sas.com/certify/

12

Support

SAS provides a variety of self-help and assisted-help resources.

- SAS Knowledge Base
- Downloads and hot fixes
- License assistance
- SAS discussion forums
- SAS Technical Support

http://support.sas.com/techsup/

13

User Groups

SAS supports many local, regional, international, and special-interest SAS user groups.

- SAS Global Forum
- Online SAS Community: www.sasCommunity.org

http://support.sas.com/usergroups/

14

Selected Additional Resources

Search Papers Presented at SAS Global Forum (previously known as SUGI)

- http://support.sas.com/events/sasglobalforum/previous/online.html

SAS Code Samples on support.sas.com

- http://support.sas.com/ctx/samples/index.jsp

SAS Code Samples from Specific Books

- http://support.sas.com/documentation/onlinedoc/code.samples.html

List of all SAS Products and Solutions

- http://www.sas.com/products/index.html

List of Papers

- http://support.sas.com/resources/papers/

12.3 Beyond This Course

Objectives

- Identify the next set of courses that follow this course.

16

Next Steps

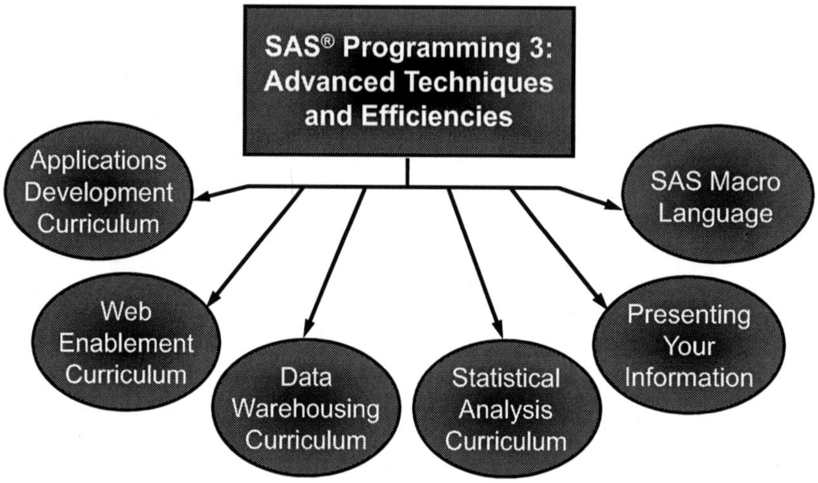

17

Next Steps

To learn more about this:	Enroll in the following:
Using the Macro Facility	SAS Macro Language 1: Essentials SAS Macro Language 2: Advanced Techniques
Creating tabular and summary reports	SAS Report Writing 1: Using Procedures and ODS
Creating graphic reports with SAS/GRAPH software	SAS Color Graphics
Processing data with Structured Query Language (SQL)	SAS SQL 1: Essentials

18

Next Steps

In addition, there are prerecorded short technical discussions and demonstrations called e-lectures.

http://support.sas.com/training/

19

Appendix A Index

Total = sum (of Qtr1 - Qtr4)

QTR1	QTR2	VAR1	QTR3	QTR4

VAR1 not included

Total = sum (of Qtr1 - Fourth);

QTR1	2ND	Q3	FOURTH	VAR2

VAR2 not included

Prefix

Proc contents data = ___ varnum;

Total = sum(of Tot:) - sum everything starts w/ Tot

Special

Total = sum (of _numeric_)